activebook™ EXPERIENCE 2.0 USER GUIDE

> What Is the activebook Experience?

The activebook experience is a new kind of textbook that combines the best elements of print and electronic media. In addition to a traditional printed text, you have access to an online version of the book that not only exactly mirrors the printed text, but also is enhanced by a variety of multimedia examples and interactive exercises. The new features in version 2.0 are the direct result of suggestions from students and faculty. For example, activebook version 2.0 allows you to highlight important topics and create margin notes. Both features can be used to create a personalized study guide that helps you focus on exactly what you need to know to do well in your course.

> The Registration Process

Accessing your activebook is a quick and easy, one-time process. Simply go to http://www.prenhall.com/myactivebook and scroll down the page until you see the listing for your activebook. Click on **Register**.

To register your activebook, click on **Register**.

Follow the onscreen directions to complete the four-step registration wizard. In the last step you will be asked to input your access code. Your access code is found in the tear-out card in the front of your print activebook. After your access code has been verified, you'll be taken to your new activebook homepage. From this point on, log onto this book-specific homepage.

If you have already registered for Prentice Hall's My Companion Website or a previous `activebook`, there is no need to register again. Simply login using your existing username and password and use the **Add Book** link to register your new `activebook` and add it to your existing homepage.

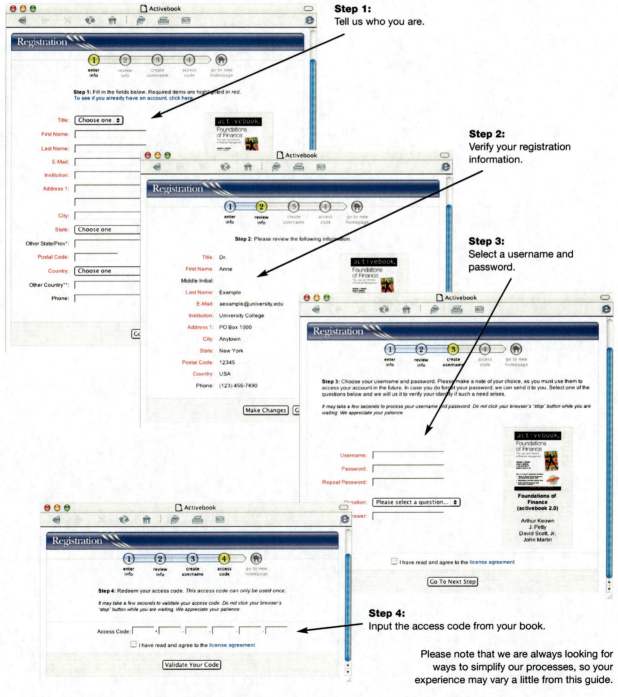

Step 1:
Tell us who you are.

Step 2:
Verify your registration information.

Step 3:
Select a username and password.

Step 4:
Input the access code from your book.

Please note that we are always looking for ways to simplify our processes, so your experience may vary a little from this guide.

Now you have successfully completed the registration process. The next time you want to access your activebook, simply go to http://www.prenhall.com/myactivebook (bookmark this page) and click on **Login** after you have scrolled to the section for your activebook. Remember to store your username and password in a safe place. If you do forget your username or password, click on **Login** and then click on **Forgot Your Password?**.

> The activebook Experience Homepage

You have a variety of tools at your disposal from your activebook homepage. You can quickly go anywhere in your book and read your notes and highlighted material. If you are linked to your professor, you can view the course syllabus and communicate with your professor. In short, you've got all the resources you need in one place.

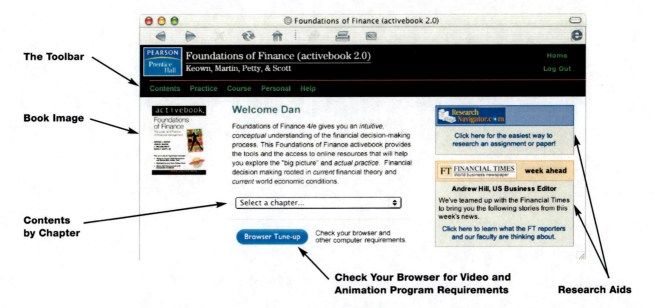

The Toolbar

Book Image

Contents by Chapter

Check Your Browser for Video and Animation Program Requirements

Research Aids

> The activebook Toolbar

The version 2.0 navigation and resources have been organized to help you quickly find what you need. Be sure to take a moment to familiarize yourself with each menu option.

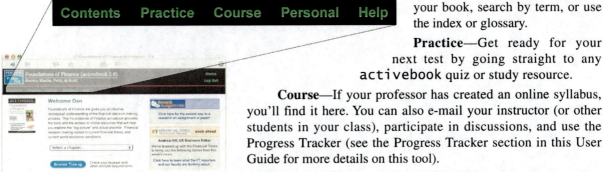

Contents—Go to any chapter in your book, search by term, or use the index or glossary.

Practice—Get ready for your next test by going straight to any activebook quiz or study resource.

Course—If your professor has created an online syllabus, you'll find it here. You can also e-mail your instructor (or other students in your class), participate in discussions, and use the Progress Tracker (see the Progress Tracker section in this User Guide for more details on this tool).

Personal—If you've used the highlighting or margin notes features of activebook 2.0, you can go straight to them from here or print them out for study purposes.

Help—You'll find answers to frequently asked questions, information on how to set up your computer to work well with the activebook, and e-mail addresses and telephone numbers for personal assistance.

> The Table of Contents Page

You can go to the table of contents from your homepage by selecting **Table of Contents** from the **Contents** menu on the toolbar or by clicking on the image of your text. You can search for a specific section or topic by selecting **Search** from the **Contents** menu.

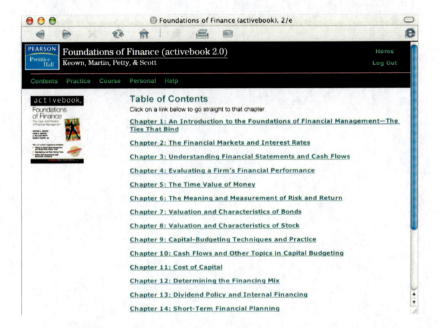

> The Chapter Outline Page

Clicking on any chapter link from your activebook homepage or the table of contents will take you to the chapter outline page. From here, you can jump to any topic or section in the chapter by clicking on the heading. You can use the toolbar links to review your highlights and margin notes for the chapter or go straight to the chapter quizzes or exercises.

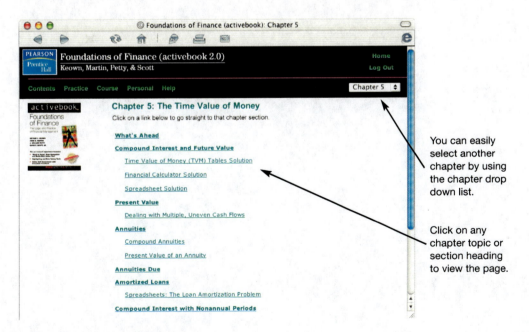

You can easily select another chapter by using the chapter drop down list.

Click on any chapter topic or section heading to view the page.

The activebook version 2.0 includes several features that allow you to personalize your text, create study guides with the material you need to study, and access notes and additional materials your professor may make available to you.

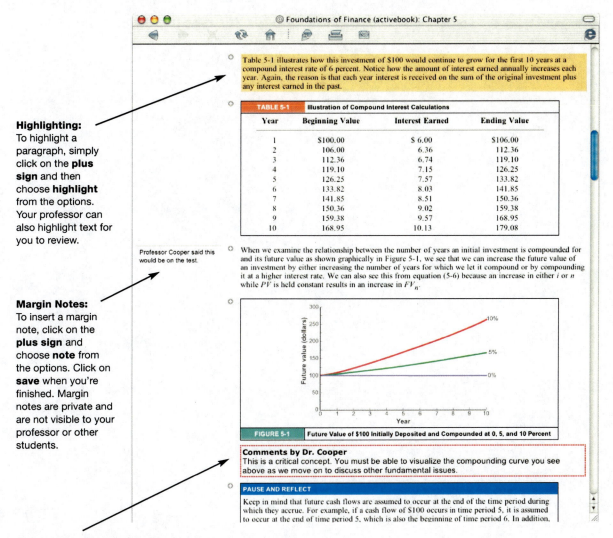

Highlighting: To highlight a paragraph, simply click on the **plus sign** and then choose **highlight** from the options. Your professor can also highlight text for you to review.

Margin Notes: To insert a margin note, click on the **plus sign** and choose **note** from the options. Click on **save** when you're finished. Margin notes are private and are not visible to your professor or other students.

Professor Comments: Your professor can insert comments. Professor comments appear within the chapter text but are easily identified with your professor's name and are surrounded by a red border.

Within the browser window:

Table 5-1 illustrates how this investment of $100 would continue to grow for the first 10 years at a compound interest rate of 6 percent. Notice how the amount of interest earned annually increases each year. Again, the reason is that each year interest is received on the sum of the original investment plus any interest earned in the past.

TABLE 5-1	Illustration of Compound Interest Calculations		
Year	Beginning Value	Interest Earned	Ending Value
1	$100.00	$ 6.00	$106.00
2	106.00	6.36	112.36
3	112.36	6.74	119.10
4	119.10	7.15	126.25
5	126.25	7.57	133.82
6	133.82	8.03	141.85
7	141.85	8.51	150.36
8	150.36	9.02	159.38
9	159.38	9.57	168.95
10	168.95	10.13	179.08

Professor Cooper said this would be on the test.

When we examine the relationship between the number of years an initial investment is compounded for and its future value as shown graphically in Figure 5-1, we see that we can increase the future value of an investment by either increasing the number of years for which we let it compound or by compounding it at a higher interest rate. We can also see this from equation (5-6) because an increase in either i or n while PV is held constant results in an increase in FV_n.

| FIGURE 5-1 | Future Value of $100 Initially Deposited and Compounded at 0, 5, and 10 Percent |

Comments by Dr. Cooper
This is a critical concept. You must be able to visualize the compounding curve you see above as we move on to discuss other fundamental issues.

PAUSE AND REFLECT
Keep in mind that future cash flows are assumed to occur at the end of the time period during which they accrue. For example, if a cash flow of $100 occurs in time period 5, it is assumed to occur at the end of time period 5, which is also the beginning of time period 6. In addition,

There are a number of ways to move from page to page and from chapter to chapter as you read your activebook.

To go to a different chapter, click on **Contents** on the toolbar and select the chapter from the table of contents list.

If you'd like to skip to a different page in the chapter, simply select it from the drop-down list.

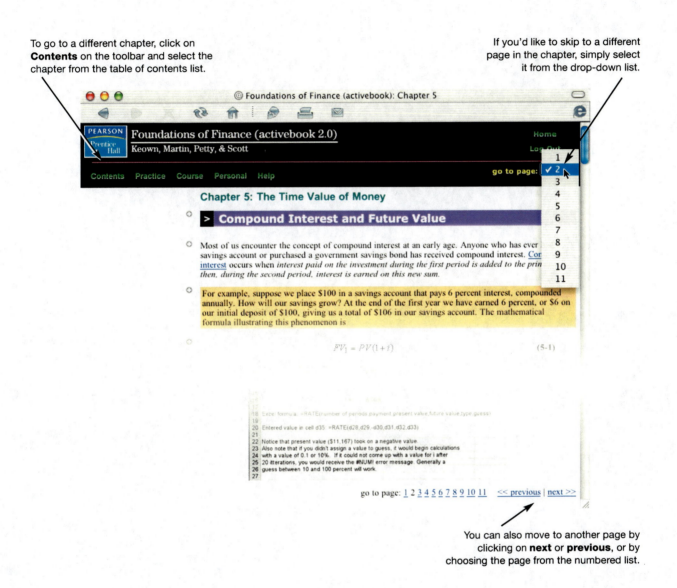

You can also move to another page by clicking on **next** or **previous**, or by choosing the page from the numbered list.

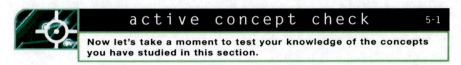
Throughout your `activebook`, you'll encounter rectangular boxes (see the following example). You'll find boxes labeled "active exercise," "active example," "video exercise," "active concept check," and "active poll." When you click on one of these boxes, a pop-up window will appear on your screen, giving you an opportunity to further explore the ideas you're learning about in the text. For easy reference, each of these boxes is numbered consecutively throughout the chapter. The following example describes what you'll find behind a concept check heading.

> ### active concept check 5-1
> Now let's take a moment to test your knowledge of the concepts you have studied in this section.

After you click on a concept check heading, a short quiz appears. Click on the button next to your answer for each question, and then click on **How did I do?** at the bottom of the pop-up page.

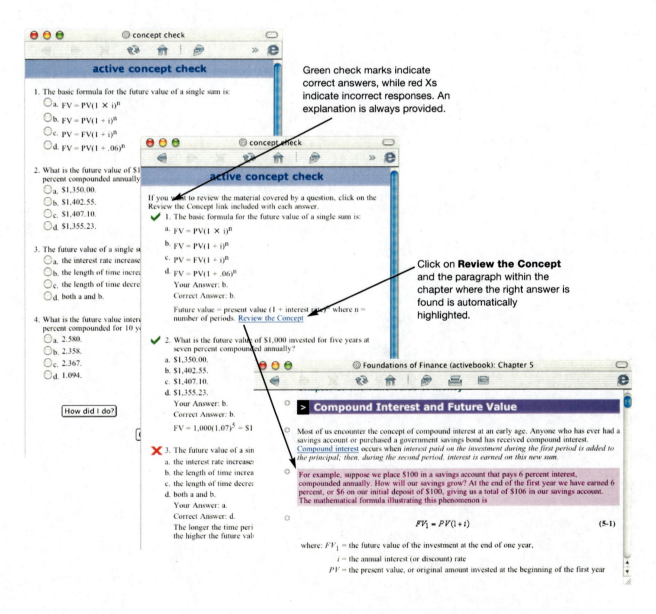

Green check marks indicate correct answers, while red Xs indicate incorrect responses. An explanation is always provided.

Click on **Review the Concept** and the paragraph within the chapter where the right answer is found is automatically highlighted.

You may also want to try out video exercises. Click on the **video exercise** heading to get started…

…then click on the video box in the pop-up window to play the video clip.

IMPORTANT NOTE:
You'll need the free QuickTime video player and the free Flash player to view the video and animation activities in your activebook. To see if your computer has these free programs installed, click on the **Browser Tuneup** link on your activebook homepage.

Ever wonder what other students are thinking about the topics discussed in your course? The **active poll** feature allows you to share your opinion and see what other students from around the world have to say about a specific topic. Click on the **active poll** heading to view the poll question. After you respond, you'll see the results compiled from all other students who have responded to the question.

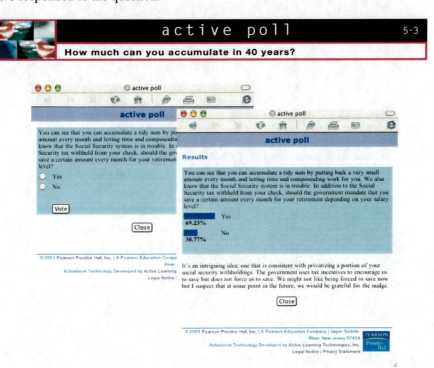

The results of every Active Concept Check and Practice Test (short tests found at the end of every chapter) are recorded in the **Progress Tracker** so you can quickly see what areas of the chapter you may need to review. Your professor can also see these results. To access your Progress Tracker, click on the **Course** menu from the toolbar and then select **Progress Tracker**.

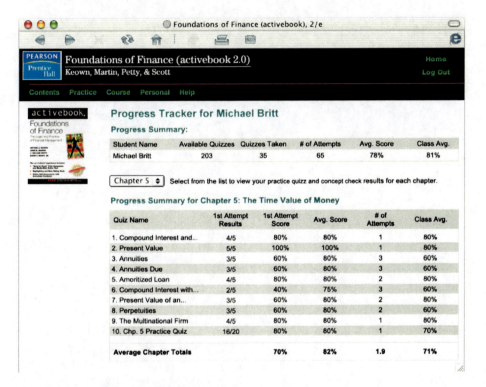

The **Progress Tracker** displays both course summary information and chapter-specific results.

As you've seen, the activebook experience has a host of tools to help you do well in class. Here are a few ideas on how to take advantage of them.

1. **Use the Active Concept Checks.** These powerful tools help you identify what you know and what you don't know. When you answer a question incorrectly, use the **Review the Concept** link. It will automatically highlight the paragraph you need to review.

2. **Print out your highlights and margin notes.** After you've read a chapter and made highlights and notes, use the **Personal** link on the toolbar to examine your highlights and notes and then print out the page (**file**, then **print** in most browsers) to make a very focused, personal study guide.

3. **Use the Progress Tracker.** To get a quick glance at how you've done over one or several chapters, go to **Course** and click on the **Progress Tracker**. You'll see how well you did on active concept checks in each chapter. Find the ones you did poorly on and then check your highlights. Take the concept check again, or use the active exercises in that section to help strengthen your knowledge.

4. **Watch for notes from your professor.** Your professor may put notes right in the flow of the text. These notes will point out material you should pay special attention to.

5. **Make notes in the print activebook.** When you are reading from the print text, make notes to remind yourself to go online and check out an active exercise or other activity that could be helpful.

6. **Use the communication features under Course.** E-mail your professor to ask about concepts you don't understand. This will also tell your professor about topics that need to be discussed again during class.

You are now ready to begin learning the activebook way! Be sure and let us know what you think of this new version of the most powerful interactive textbook available. Send your suggestions and comments to activebooks@prenhall.com. Good luck with your course!

Principles of Marketing

ACTIVEBOOK VERSION 1.0

Philip Kotler
NORTHWESTERN UNIVERSITY

Gary Armstrong
UNIVERSITY OF NORTH CAROLINA

Prentice
Hall

Upper Saddle River, New Jersey 07458

Executive Editor: Whitney Blake
Editor-in-Chief: Jeff Shelstad
Assistant Editor: Anthony Palmiotto
Editorial Assistant: Melissa Pellerano
Marketing Manager: Shannon Moore
Managing Editor (Production): John Roberts
Permissions Coordinator: Suzanne Grappi
Associate Director, Manufacturing: Vincent Scelta
Design Manager: Patricia Smythe
Interior Design: Cheryl Asherman
Cover Design: Cheryl Asherman
Associate Director, Multimedia Production: Karen Goldsmith
Composition: GGS
Full-Service Project Management: GGS
Printer/Binder: Quebecor World/Taunton

Credits and acknowledgments borrowed from other sources and reproduced, with permission, in this textbook appear on the appropriate pages within the book.

Prentice Hall

10 9 8 7 6 5 4 3 2 1
ISBN 0-13-064853-1

C O N T E N T S

> What Is an Activebook?

The activebook is a new kind of textbook that combines the best elements of print and electronic media. In addition to this print version, you'll have access to an online version of your book that is enhanced by a variety of multimedia elements. These include active exercises, interactive quizzes, and poll questions. These elements give you a chance to explore the text's issues in more depth.

> How to Redeem Your Access Code

Redeeming your access code is fast and easy. To complete this one-time registration process, go to **www.pren-hall.com/myactivebook**. Follow the new user link to register and redeem your access code. Enter the access code bound inside your book, and complete the simple registration form. When you are done, click **submit**. It will take a few minutes to redeem your access code, and then you will be taken to your activebook homepage.

> The Activebook Homepage

In this section you'll become acquainted with the features of an activebook. Once you're familiar with the features and their functions, you'll be on your way to getting the most from your activebook.

1. The Toolbar

Let's begin with the commands in the tool bar near the top of the activebook homepage. This bar features eight commands: **add book, view favorites, add notes, view notes, profile, password, help,** and **log out.**

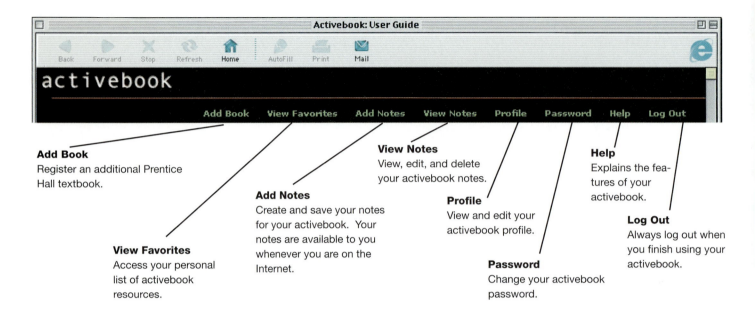

Add Book
Register an additional Prentice Hall textbook.

View Favorites
Access your personal list of activebook resources.

Add Notes
Create and save your notes for your activebook. Your notes are available to you whenever you are on the Internet.

View Notes
View, edit, and delete your activebook notes.

Profile
View and edit your activebook profile.

Password
Change your activebook password.

Help
Explains the features of your activebook.

Log Out
Always log out when you finish using your activebook.

Now let's take a look at the features presented in the navigation bar on the left side of the screen.

2. The Smart Calendar and Other Resources

The Smart Calendar
Instantly view all the activities for the month for your activebook by clicking on a date.

Research Links
Provides a selection of annotated links to additional resources and search sites.

Student Success
Links to Prentice Hall's Student Success Web site. You will find numerous features designed to help you through your educational journey (for example, career paths, money matters, and employment opportunities).

Contact Us
Contact Prentice Hall either via telephone or e-mail to share your ideas about your activebook or to ask questions.

FAQ
Find answers to commonly asked questions about your activebook.

3. Additional Resources

After redeeming your access code, you can make use of the following resources.

What's New
Shows the resources that have been recently added to your activebook.

Chapter Pop Up Menu
Selects a chapter in your activebook.

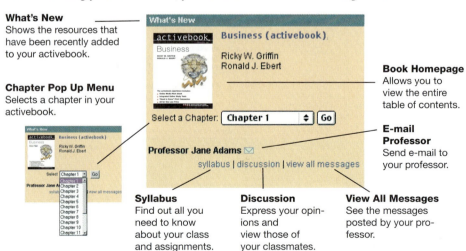

Book Homepage
Allows you to view the entire table of contents.

E-mail Professor
Send e-mail to your professor.

Syllabus
Find out all you need to know about your class and assignments.

Discussion
Express your opinions and view those of your classmates.

View All Messages
See the messages posted by your professor.

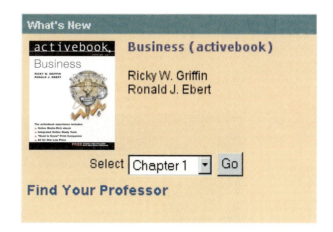

> Finding Your Professor

If your professor has posted course material, you can create a link to him or her on your activebook home-page. Once connected to your professor, you can access the **syllabus, view messages** from him or her, and **e-mail** him or her.

To Find Your Professor

- Click on **find your professor**.
- Search for your professor's name (using his or her last name or your school's name). Then select it.
- Click **submit** and you will return to your activebook homepage.

> Viewing Your Professor's Syllabus

If your professor is using the **syllabus** feature, click the **syllabus** link to check assignments and course announcements.

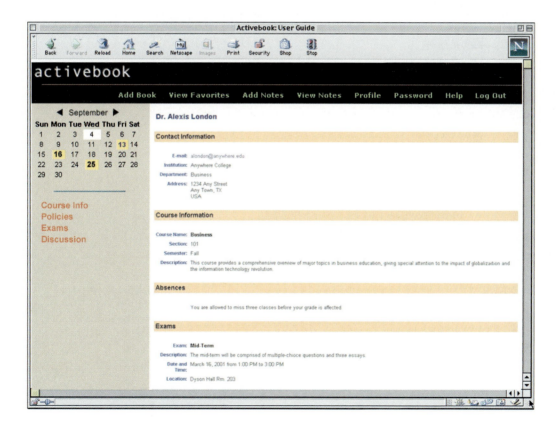

> Exploring Your Activebook

When you're ready to begin, select a chapter. You will find active elements throughout the chapter. They are the key components that make an activebook *active*. In every chapter you will find: the **what's ahead** section, **objectives**, **active concept checks**, **key terms**, and a **chapter wrap-up**. Each chapter may also include a **gearing-up quiz**, **video examples or exercises**, **audio examples or exercises**, **active polls**, and **active figures, maps,** and **graphs**.

Let's take a look at these elements.

Every chapter begins with **what's ahead**. This section tells you what material the chapter will cover.

Clicking on any link in the chapter outline takes you to the core text.

The **Book Home** to the table of contents for the entire book, where the full chapter titles are provided.

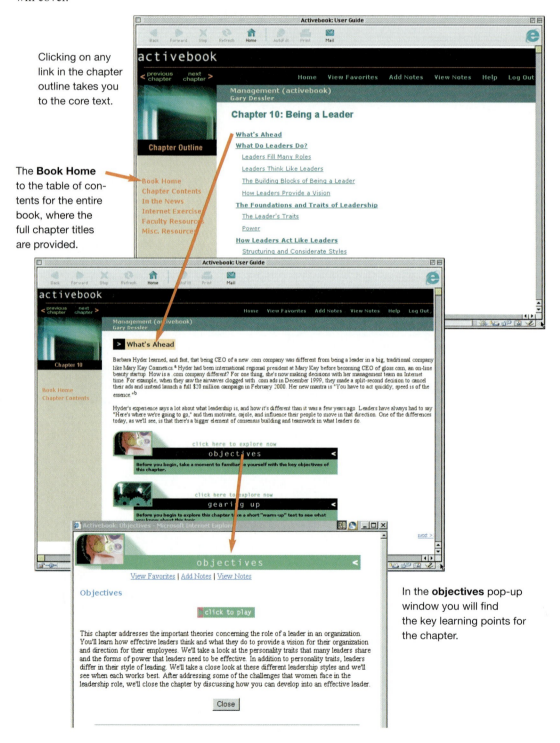

In the **objectives** pop-up window you will find the key learning points for the chapter.

Another element that can appear in the **what's ahead** section is the **gearing up quiz**. This quiz is designed to get you thinking about important topics in the chapter.

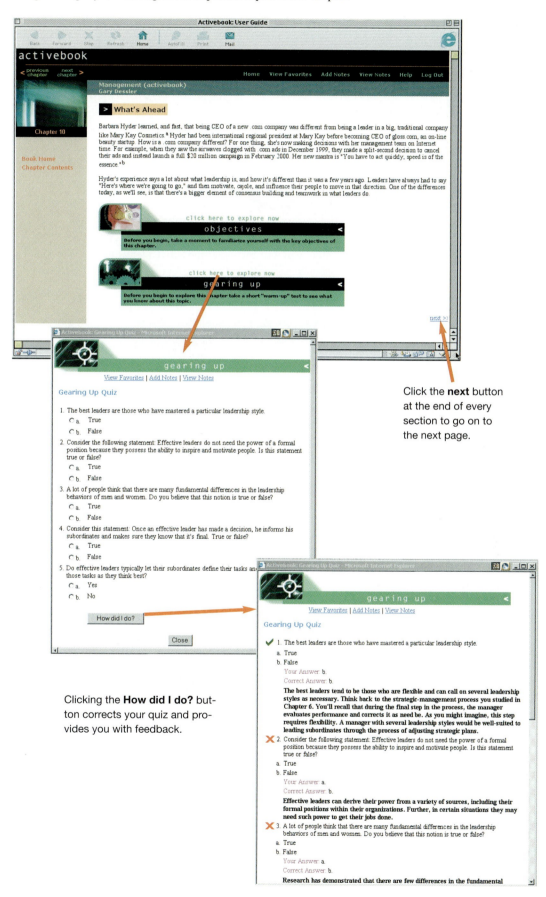

Click the **next** button at the end of every section to go on to the next page.

Clicking the **How did I do?** button corrects your quiz and provides you with feedback.

After gearing up, you're ready to start reading the chapter. Activebook chapters are divided into major sections.

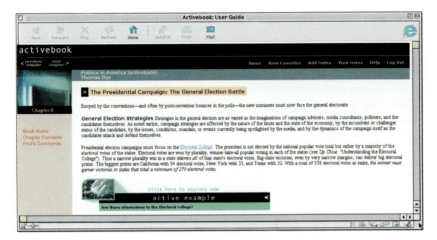

As you read each section, you will encounter the active elements. Let's become acquainted with some of these active elements.

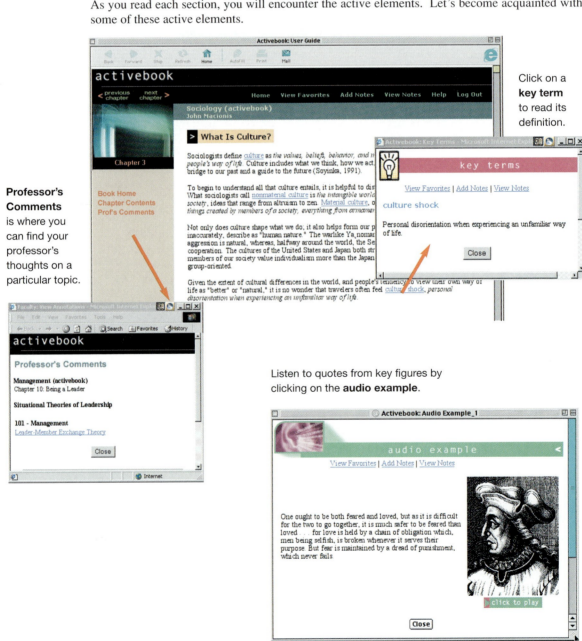

Click on a **key term** to read its definition.

Professor's Comments is where you can find your professor's thoughts on a particular topic.

Listen to quotes from key figures by clicking on the **audio example**.

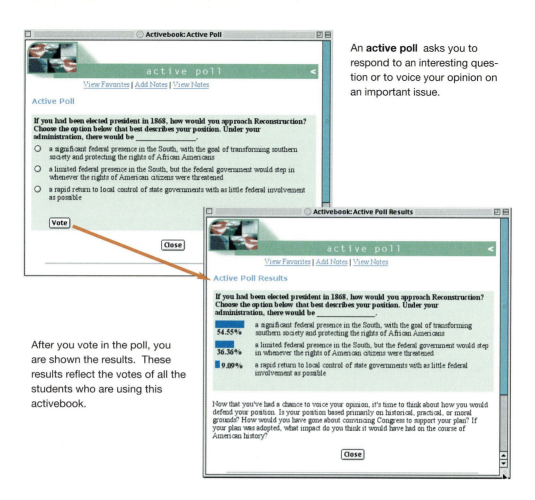

An **active poll** asks you to respond to an interesting question or to voice your opinion on an important issue.

After you vote in the poll, you are shown the results. These results reflect the votes of all the students who are using this activebook.

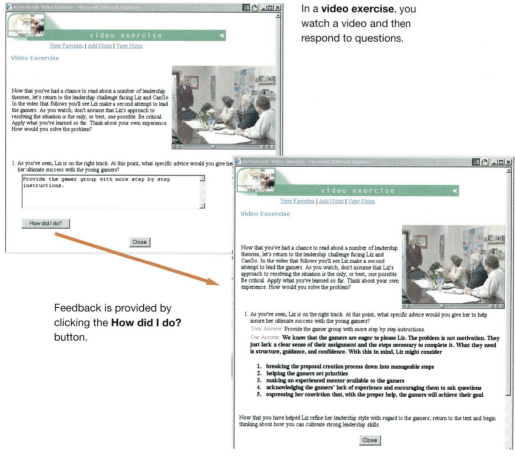

In a **video exercise**, you watch a video and then respond to questions.

Feedback is provided by clicking the **How did I do?** button.

In addition to **video exercises** you might also find an **active exercise** or an **active example**.

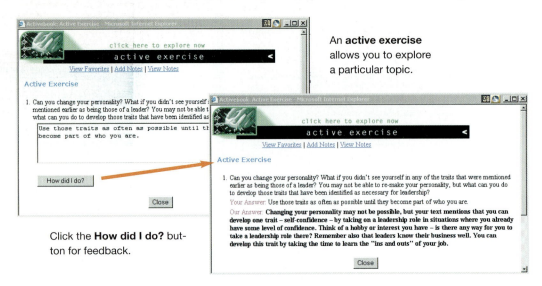

An **active exercise** allows you to explore a particular topic.

Click the **How did I do?** button for feedback.

Active concept checks occur at the end of every major section in your activebook.

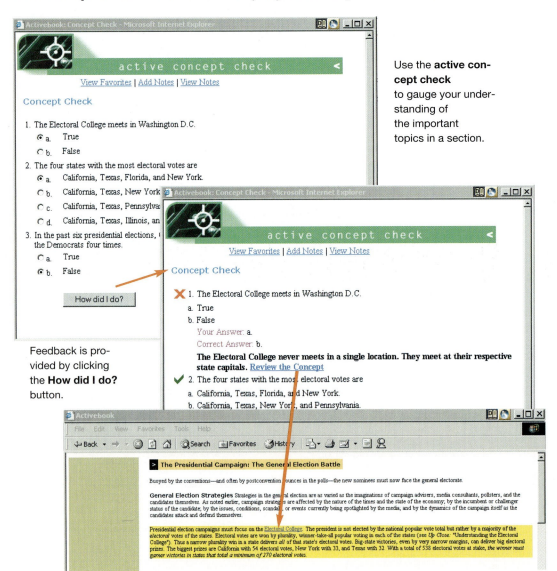

Use the **active concept check** to gauge your understanding of the important topics in a section.

Feedback is provided by clicking the **How did I do?** button.

Click **review the concept** to jump to where the material was discussed in the chapter.

All of your end-of-chapter resources and a practice quiz can be found in the **chapter wrap-up** section.

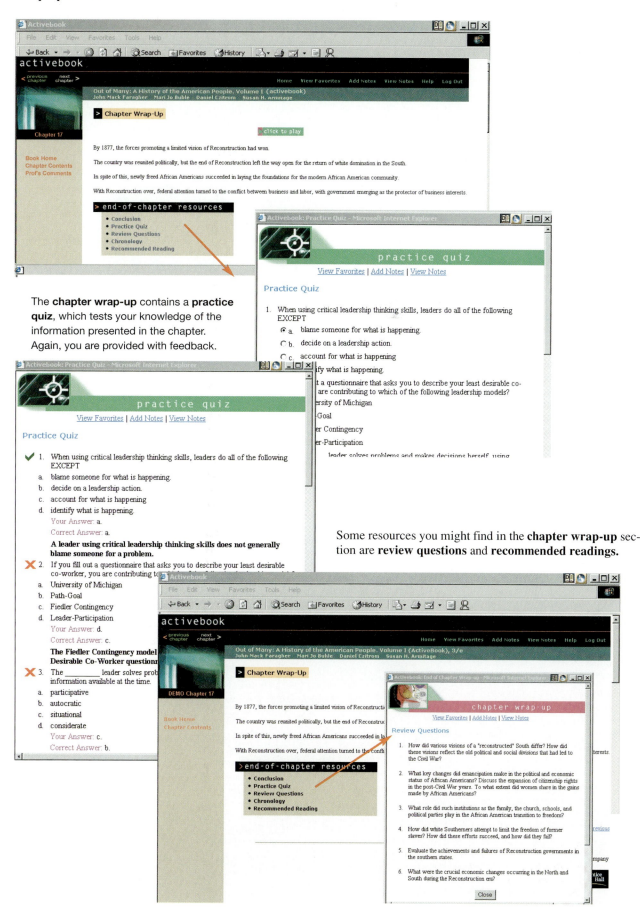

The **chapter wrap-up** contains a **practice quiz**, which tests your knowledge of the information presented in the chapter. Again, you are provided with feedback.

Some resources you might find in the **chapter wrap-up** section are **review questions** and **recommended readings**.

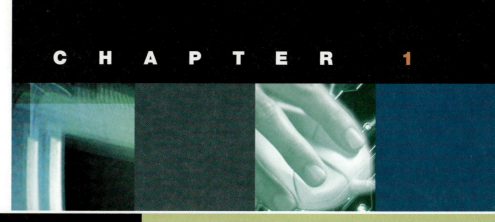

C H A P T E R 1

Marketing in a Changing World: Creating Customer Value and Satisfaction

 What's Ahead

The "swoosh"—it's everywhere! Just for fun, try counting the swooshes whenever you pick up the sports pages or watch a pickup basketball game or tune into a televised golf match. Nike has built the ubiquitous swoosh (which represents the wing of Nike, the Greek goddess of victory) into one of the best-known brand symbols on the planet.

The power of its brand and logo speaks loudly of Nike's superb marketing skills. The company's strategy of building superior products around popular athletes and its classic "Just do it!" ad campaign have forever changed the face of sports marketing. Nike spends hundreds of millions of dollars each year on big-name endorsements, splashy promotional events, and lots of attention-getting ads. Over the years, Nike has associated itself with some of the biggest names in sports. No matter what your sport, chances are good that one of your favorite athletes wears the Nike swoosh.

Nike knows, however, that good marketing is more than promotional hype and promises—it means consistently delivering real value to customers. Nike's initial success resulted from the technical superiority of its running and basketball shoes, pitched to serious athletes who were frustrated by the lack of innovation in athletic equipment. To this day, Nike leads the industry in product development and innovation.

Nike gives its customers more than just good athletic gear. As the company notes on its Web page (_www.nike.com_), "Nike has always known the truth—it's not so much the shoes but where they take you." Beyond shoes, apparel, and equipment, Nike markets a way of life, a sports culture, a "just do it" attitude. Phil Knight, Nike's founder and chief executive, says, "Basically, our culture and our style is to be a rebel." The company was built on a genuine passion for sports, a maverick disregard for convention, hard work, and serious sports performance. Ask anyone at Nike and that person will tell you: Nike is athletes, athletes are sports, _Nike is sports._

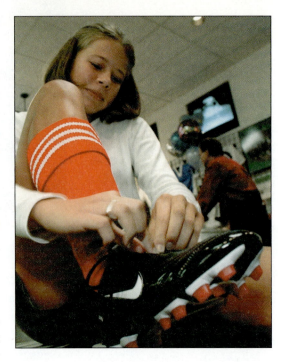

Nike seems to care as much about its customers' lives as their bodies. It doesn't just promote sales, it promotes _sports_ for the benefit of all. For example, a recent series of "Nike: Just do it" ads provided strong support to women's sports and the many benefits of sports participation for girls and young women. Nike also invests in a wide range of lesser known sports, even though they provide less lucrative marketing opportunities. Such actions establish Nike as not just a producer of good athletic gear but also as a good and caring company.

Taking care of customers has paid off handsomely for Nike. Over the decade ending in 1997, Nike's revenues grew at an incredible annual rate of 21 percent; annual return to investors averaged 47 percent. Nike flat-out dominates the world's athletic footwear market. It currently captures an eye-popping 47 percent share of the U.S. market—twice that of its nearest competitor, Reebok—and a 27 percent share internationally. Nike moved aggressively into new product categories, sports, and regions of the world. In only a few years, Nike's sports apparel business grew explosively to account for nearly a quarter of Nike's $9.5 billion in yearly sales. And Nike slapped its familiar swoosh logo on everything from sunglasses and soccer balls to batting gloves and hockey sticks. It invaded a dozen new sports, including baseball, golf, ice and street hockey, in-line skating, wall climbing, and hiking.

In 1998, however, Nike stumbled and its sales slipped. Many factors contributed to the company's sales woes. The "brown shoe" craze for hiking and outdoor styles such as Timberland's ate into the athletic sneaker business. Competition improved: A revitalized Adidas saw its U.S. sales surge as Nike's sales declined. To make matters worse, college students on many campuses protested against Nike for its alleged exploitation of child labor in Asia and its commercialization of sports.

But Nike's biggest obstacle may be its own incredible success—it may have over-swooshed America. The brand now appears to be suffering from big-brand backlash, and the swoosh is becoming too common to be cool. According to one analyst, "When Tiger Woods made his debut in Nike gear, there were so many logos on him that he looked as if he'd got caught in an embroidering machine." A Nike executive admits, "There has been a little bit of backlash about the number of swooshes that are out there." Moreover, with sales of more than $9 billion, Nike has moved from maverick to mainstream. Today, rooting for Nike is like rooting for Microsoft.

To address these problems, Nike returned to the basics—focusing on innovation, developing new product lines, creating subbrands (such as the Michael Jordan line with its "jumping man" logo), and deemphasizing the swoosh. For example, recent advertising focuses once again on product performance and concludes with the Nike script logo name—not a swoosh in sight. The sports giant is also trimming its costs, including substantial cuts in its formerly lavish advertising budget. These moves appear to be working, and Nike's profits and stock price are once again on the rise.

Nike is also entering new markets aggressively, especially overseas markets. Nike sales outside the United States now represent about 38 percent of total sales. However, to dominate globally as it does in the United States, Nike must dominate in soccer, the world's most popular sport. The multibillion-dollar world soccer market currently accounts for only 3 percent of its sales. Now, soccer is Nike's top priority. In typical fashion, Nike has set World Cup 2002 as its deadline for becoming the world's number-one supplier of soccer footwear, apparel, and equipment.

Elbowing its way to the top by 2002 won't be easy. World soccer has long been dominated by Adidas, which claims an 80 percent global market share in soccer gear. Nike will have to build in just a few years what Adidas has built over the past 50. Employing classic in-your-face marketing tactics, Nike is spending hundreds of millions of dollars in an all-out assault on competitors. Nike's open-wallet spending has dazzled the soccer world, and its vast resources are rapidly changing the economics of the game. For example, it paid a record-setting $200 million over 10 years to snatch sponsorship of the World Cup champion Brazil national team from Umbro. Similarly, it paid $130 million for sponsorship of the U.S. soccer team.

Competitors can hope that Nike's slump will continue, but few are counting on it. Most can only sit back and marvel at Nike's marketing prowess. One market analyst comments, "Nike remains one of the great American brands, as well known around the world as Coke or McDonald's." Says Fila's advertising vice president, "They are so formidable, no matter how well we may execute something, our voice will never be as loud as theirs." As for soccer, the president of Puma North America sees Nike's tactics as heavy-handed but has little doubt that Nike's superb marketing will prevail. He states flatly, "Nike will control the soccer world."

Still, winning in worldwide soccer, or in anything else Nike does, will take more than just writing fat checks. To stay on top, Nike will have to deliver worldwide the same kind of quality, innovation, and value that built the brand so powerfully in the United States. It will have to earn respect on a country-by-country basis and become a part of the cultural fabric of each new market. No longer the rebellious, anti-establishment upstart, huge Nike must continually reassess its relationships with customers. Says Knight, "Now that we've [grown so large], there's a fine line between being a rebel and being a bully. [To our customers,] we have to be beautiful as well as big."[1]

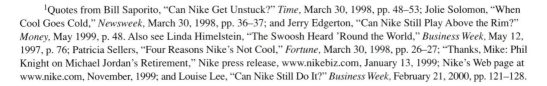

> **objectives**

Before you begin, take a moment to familiarize yourself with the key objectives of this chapter.

[1]Quotes from Bill Saporito, "Can Nike Get Unstuck?" *Time,* March 30, 1998, pp. 48–53; Jolie Solomon, "When Cool Goes Cold," *Newsweek,* March 30, 1998, pp. 36–37; and Jerry Edgerton, "Can Nike Still Play Above the Rim?" *Money,* May 1999, p. 48. Also see Linda Himelstein, "The Swoosh Heard 'Round the World," *Business Week,* May 12, 1997, p. 76; Patricia Sellers, "Four Reasons Nike's Not Cool," *Fortune,* March 30, 1998, pp. 26–27; "Thanks, Mike: Phil Knight on Michael Jordan's Retirement," Nike press release, www.nikebiz.com, January 13, 1999; Nike's Web page at www.nike.com, November, 1999; and Louise Lee, "Can Nike Still Do It?" *Business Week,* February 21, 2000, pp. 121–128.

Today's successful companies at all levels have one thing in common: Like Nike they are strongly customer focused and heavily committed to marketing. These companies share an absolute dedication to understanding and satisfying the needs of customers in well-defined target markets. They motivate everyone in the organization to produce superior value for their customers, leading to high levels of customer satisfaction. As Bernie Marcus of Home Depot asserts, "All of our people understand what the Holy Grail is. It's not the bottom line. It's an almost blind, passionate commitment to taking care of customers."

› What Is Marketing?

Marketing, more than any other business function, deals with customers. Understanding, creating, communicating, and delivering customer value and satisfaction are at the very heart of modern marketing thinking and practice. Although we will explore more detailed definitions of marketing later in this chapter, perhaps the simplest definition is this one: *Marketing is the delivery of customer satisfaction at a profit.* The twofold goal of marketing is to attract new customers by promising superior value and to keep current customers by delivering satisfaction.

Wal-Mart has become the world's largest retailer by delivering on its promise, "Always low prices—always." FedEx dominates the U.S. small-package freight industry by consistently making good on its promise of fast, reliable small-package delivery. Ritz-Carlton promises and delivers truly "memorable experiences" for its hotel guests. Coca-Cola, long the world's leading soft drink, delivers on the simple but enduring promise, "Always Coca-Cola"—always thirst-quenching, always good with food, always cool, always a part of your life. These and other highly successful companies know that if they take care of their customers, market share and profits will follow.

Sound marketing is critical to the success of every organization—large or small, for-profit or not-for-profit, domestic or global. Large for-profit firms such as Microsoft, Sony, FedEx, Wal-Mart, IBM, and Marriott use marketing. But so do not-for-profit organizations such as colleges, hospitals, museums, symphony orchestras, and even churches. Moreover, marketing is practiced not only in the United States but also in the rest of the world. Most countries in North and South America, Western Europe, and Asia have well-developed marketing systems. Even in Eastern Europe and other parts of the world where marketing has long had a bad name, dramatic political and social changes have created new opportunities for marketing. Business and government leaders in most of these nations are eager to learn everything they can about modern marketing practices.

You already know a lot about marketing—it's all around you. You see the results of marketing in the abundance of products in your nearby shopping mall. You see marketing in the advertisements that fill your TV, spice up your magazines, stuff your mailbox, or enliven your Internet pages. At home, at school, where you work, and where you play, you are exposed to marketing in almost everything you do. Yet, there is much more to marketing than meets the consumer's casual eye. Behind it all is a massive network of people and activities competing for your attention and purchasing dollars.

This book will give you a more complete and formal introduction to the basic concepts and practices of today's marketing. In this chapter, we begin by defining marketing and its core concepts, describing the major philosophies of marketing thinking and practice, and discussing some of the major new challenges that marketers face as we whirl into the new millennium.

MARKETING DEFINED

What does the term *marketing* mean? Many people think of marketing only as selling and advertising. It is no wonder—every day we are bombarded with television commercials, newspaper ads, direct-mail campaigns, Internet pitches, and sales calls. However, selling and advertising are only the tip of the marketing iceberg. Although they are important, they are only two of many marketing functions and are often not the most important ones.

Today, marketing must be understood not in the old sense of making a sale—"telling and selling"—but in the new sense of *satisfying customer needs.* Selling occurs only after a product is produced. By contrast, marketing starts long before a company has a product. Marketing is the homework that managers undertake to assess needs, measure their extent and intensity, and determine

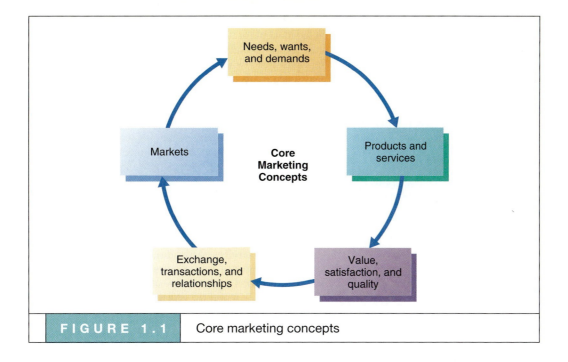

FIGURE 1.1 Core marketing concepts

whether a profitable opportunity exists. Marketing continues throughout the product's life, trying to find new customers and keep current customers by improving product appeal and performance, learning from product sales results, and managing repeat performance. If the marketer does a good job of understanding consumer needs, develops products that provide superior value, and prices, distributes, and promotes them effectively, these products will sell very easily. Thus, selling and advertising are only part of a larger "marketing mix"—a set of marketing tools that work together to affect the marketplace.

We define **marketing** as a social and managerial process whereby individuals and groups obtain what they need and want through creating and exchanging products and value with others.[2] To explain this definition, we will examine the following important terms: *needs, wants,* and *demands; products* and *services; value, satisfaction,* and *quality; exchange, transactions,* and *relationships;* and *markets.* Figure 1.1 shows that these core marketing concepts are linked, with each concept building on the one before it.

NEEDS, WANTS, AND DEMANDS

The most basic concept underlying marketing is that of human needs. Human **needs** are states of felt deprivation. They include basic *physical* needs for food, clothing, warmth, and safety; *social* needs for belonging and affection; and *individual* needs for knowledge and self-expression. These needs were not invented by marketers; they are a basic part of the human makeup.

Wants are the form human needs take as they are shaped by culture and individual personality. An American *needs* food but *wants* a hamburger, French fries, and a soft drink. A person in Mauritius *needs* food but *wants* a mango, rice, lentils, and beans. Wants are shaped by one's society and are described in terms of objects that will satisfy needs.

People have almost unlimited wants but limited resources. Thus, they want to choose products that provide the most value and satisfaction for their money. When backed by buying power, wants become **demands.** Consumers view products as bundles of benefits and choose products that give them the best bundle for their money. A Honda Civic means basic transportation, affordable price, and fuel economy; a Lexus means comfort, luxury, and status. Given their wants and resources, people demand products with the benefits that add up to the most satisfaction.

Outstanding marketing companies go to great lengths to learn about and understand their customers' needs, wants, and demands. They conduct consumer research about consumer likes and dislikes. They

---

[2]Here are some other definitions: "*Marketing* is the performance of business activities that direct the flow goods and services from producer to consumer or user." "*Marketing* is getting the right goods to the right people at the right place at the right time at the right price with the right communication and promotion." "*Marketing* is the creation of a standard of living." The American Marketing Association offers this definition: "*Marketing* is the process of planning and executing the conception, pricing, promotion, and distributing of ideas, goods, and services to create exchanges that satisfy individual and organizational objectives."

analyze customer inquiry, warranty, and service data. They observe customers using their own and competing products and train salespeople to be on the lookout for unfulfilled customer needs.

In these outstanding companies, people at all levels—including top management—stay close to customers. For example, top executives from Wal-Mart spend two days each week visiting stores and mingling with customers. At Disney World, at least once in his or her career, each manager spends a day touring the park in a Mickey, Minnie, Goofy, or other character costume. Moreover, all Disney World managers spend a week each year on the front line—taking tickets, selling popcorn, or loading and unloading rides. At AT&T, CEO C. Michael Armstrong often visits one of the company's customer service centers, dons a headset, and fields orders to get a better sense of the problems and frustrations that AT&T business customers face.[3] At Marriott, to stay in touch with customers, Chairman of the Board and President Bill Marriott personally reads some 10 percent of the 8,000 letters and 2 percent of the 750,000 guest comment cards submitted by customers each year. Understanding customer needs, wants, and demands in detail provides important input for designing marketing strategies.

PRODUCTS AND SERVICES

People satisfy their needs and wants with products and services. A **product** is anything that can be offered to a market to satisfy a need or want. The concept of *product* is not limited to physical objects—anything capable of satisfying a need can be called a product. In addition to tangible goods, products include **services,** which are activities or benefits offered for sale that are essentially intangible and do not result in the ownership of anything. Examples include banking, airline, hotel, tax preparation, and home repair services.

More broadly defined, products also include other entities such as *experiences, persons, places, organizations, information,* and *ideas.* For example, by orchestrating several services and goods, companies can create, stage, and market experiences. Disneyland is an experience; so is a visit to Nikeworld or Barnes & Noble. In fact, as products and services increasingly become commodities, experiences have emerged for many firms as the next step in differentiating the company's offer. In recent years, for example, a rash of theme stores and restaurants have burst onto the scene offering much more than just merchandise or food:

> Stores such as Niketown, Cabella's, and Recreational Equipment Incorporated draw consumers in by offering fun activities, fascinating displays, and promotional events (sometimes labeled "shoppertainment" or "entertailing"). At theme restaurants such as the Hard Rock Cafe, Planet Hollywood, or the House of Blues, the food is just a prop for what's known as "eatertainment." [One] entrepreneur in Israel has entered the experience economy with the opening of Cafe Ke'ilu, which roughly translates as "Cafe Make Believe." Manager Nir Caspi told a reporter that people come to cafes to be seen and to meet people, not for the food; Cafe Ke'ilu pursues that observation to its logical conclusion. The establishment serves its customers empty plates and mugs and charges guests $3 during the week and $6 on weekends for the social experience.[4]

Thus, the term *product* includes much more than just physical goods or services. Consumers decide which events to experience, which entertainers to watch on television, which places to visit on vacation, which organizations to support through contributions, and which ideas to adopt. To the consumer, these are all products. If at times the term *product* does not seem to fit, we could substitute other terms such as *satisfier, resource,* or *marketing offer.*

Many sellers make the mistake of paying more attention to the specific products they offer than to the benefits produced by these products. They see themselves as selling a product rather than providing a solution to a need. A manufacturer of drill bits may think that the customer needs a drill bit, but what the customer *really* needs is a hole. These sellers may suffer from "marketing myopia"—they are so taken with their products that they focus only on existing wants and lose sight of underlying customer needs.[5] They forget that a product is only a tool to solve a consumer problem. These sellers

[3] Andrew Kupfer, "AT&T Gets Lucky," *Fortune,* November 9, 1998, pp. 108–10.

[4] See B. Joseph Pine II and James Gilmore, "Welcome to the Experience Economy," *Harvard Business Review,* July–August 1998, p. 99. Also see Philip Kotler, *Marketing Management: Analysis, Planning, Implementation, and Control,* 10th ed. (Upper Saddle River, NJ: Prentice Hall, 2000), pp. 3–5.

[5] See Theodore Levitt's classic article, "Marketing Myopia," *Harvard Business Review,* July–August 1960, pp. 45–56. For more recent discussions, see Dhananjayan Kashyap, "Marketing Myopia Revisited A Look Through the 'Colored Glass of a Client,'" *Marketing and Research Today,* August 1996, pp. 197–201; Colin Grant, "Theodore Levitt's Marketing Myopia," *Journal of Business Ethics,* February 1999, pp. 397–406; and Jeffrey M. O'Brien, "Drums in the Jungle," *MC Technology Marketing Intelligence,* March 1999, pp. 22–30.

will have trouble if a new product comes along that serves the customer's need better or less expensively. The customer with the same *need* will *want* the new product.

> **active exercise**

Take a moment to consider how two firms approach the challenge of service marketing.

VALUE, SATISFACTION, AND QUALITY

Consumers usually face a broad array of products and services that might satisfy a given need. How do they choose among these many products and services? Consumers make buying choices based on their perceptions of the value that various products and services deliver.

Customer value is the difference between the values the customer gains from owning and using a product and the costs of obtaining the product. For example, FedEx customers gain a number of benefits. The most obvious are fast and reliable package delivery. However, when using FedEx, customers also may receive some status and image values. Using FedEx usually makes both the package sender and the receiver feel more important. When deciding whether to send a package via FedEx, customers will weigh these and other values against the money, effort, and psychic costs of using the service. Moreover, they will compare the value of using FedEx against the value of using other shippers—UPS, Airborne, the U.S. Postal Service—and select the one that gives them the greatest delivered value.

Customers often do not judge product values and costs accurately or objectively. They act on *perceived* value. For example, does FedEx really provide faster, more reliable delivery? If so, is this better service worth the higher prices FedEx charges? The U.S. Postal Service argues that its express service is comparable, and its prices are much lower. However, judging by market share, most consumers perceive otherwise. FedEx dominates with more than a 45 percent share of the U.S. express-delivery market, compared with the U.S. Postal Service's 8 percent. The Postal Service's challenge is to change these customer value perceptions.[6]

Customer satisfaction depends on a product's perceived performance in delivering value relative to a buyer's expectations. If the product's performance falls short of the customer's expectations, the buyer is dissatisfied. If performance matches expectations, the buyer is satisfied. If performance exceeds expectations, the buyer is delighted. Outstanding marketing companies go out of their way to keep their customers satisfied. Satisfied customers make repeat purchases, and they tell others about their good experiences with the product. The key is to match customer expectations with company performance. Smart companies aim to *delight* customers by promising only what they can deliver, then delivering *more* than they promise.[7]

Customer satisfaction is closely linked to quality. In recent years, many companies have adopted **total quality management (TQM)** programs, designed to constantly improve the quality of their products, services, and marketing processes. Quality has a direct impact on product performance and hence on customer satisfaction.

In the narrowest sense, quality can be defined as "freedom from defects." But most customer-centered companies go beyond this narrow definition of quality. Instead, they define quality in

[6]See Andy Cohen, "Federal Express," *Sales & Marketing Management,* November 1996, p. 50. For good discussions of defining and measuring customer value, see Howard E. Butz Jr. and Leonard D. Goodstein, "Measuring Customer Value: Gaining Strategic Advantage," *Organizational Dynamics,* Winter 1996, pp. 63–77; Robert B. Woodruff, "Customer Value: The Next Source of Competitive Advantage," *Journal of the Academy of Marketing Science,* Spring 1997, pp. 139–53; James C. Anderson and James A. Narus, "Business Marketing: Understand What Customers Value," *Harvard Business Review,* November–December 1998, pp. 53–61; and W. Chan Kim and Renee Mauborgne, "Creating New Market Space," *Harvard Business Review,* January–February 1999, pp. 83–93.

[7]For more on customer satisfaction, see Jaclyn Fierman, "Americans Can't Get No Satisfaction," *Fortune,* December 11, 1995, p. 186; Richard A. Spreng, Scott B. MacKenzie, and Richard W. Olshavsky, "A Reexamination of the Determinants of Customer Satisfaction," *Journal of Marketing,* July 1996, pp. 15–32; Thomas A. Stewart, "A Satisfied Customer Isn't Enough," *Fortune,* July 21, 1997, pp. 112–13; and Subhash Sharma, Ronald W. Niedrich, and Greg Dobbins, "A Framework for Monitoring Customer Satisfaction," *Industrial Marketing Management,* May 1999, pp. 231–43.

terms of customer satisfaction. For example, the vice president of quality at Motorola, a company that pioneered total quality efforts in the United States, says that "Quality has to do something for the customer. . . . Our definition of a defect is 'if the customer doesn't like it, it's a defect.'"[8] Similarly, the American Society for Quality defines *quality* as the totality of features and characteristics of a product or service that bear on its ability to *satisfy customer needs*. These customer-focused definitions suggest that a company has achieved total quality only when its products or services meet or exceed customer expectations. Thus, the fundamental aim of today's *total quality* movement has become *total customer satisfaction*. Quality begins with customer needs and ends with customer satisfaction. We will examine customer satisfaction, value, and quality more fully in chapter 18.

[8]Lois Therrien, "Motorola and NEC: Going for Glory," *Business Week,* special issue on quality, 1991, pp. 60–61. For more on quality, see Roland T. Rust, Anthony J. Zahorik, and Timothy L. Keiningham, "Return on Quality (ROQ): Making Service Quality Financially Accountable," *Journal of Marketing,* April 1995, pp. 58–70; Iris Mohr-Jackson, "Managing a Total Quality Orientation: Factors Affecting Customer Satisfaction," *Industrial Marketing Management,* March 1998, pp. 109–25; Melissa Larson, "Whatever Happened to TQM?" *Quality,* June 1999, pp. 32–35; and Zhu Zhiwei and Larry Scheuermann, "A Comparison of Quality Programs: Total Quality Management and ISO 9000," *Total Quality Management,* March 1999, pp. 291–95.

We're about to reveal a Saturn trade secret. But first, raise your right hand and repeat after us, "I promise that what I'm about to hear will stay with me for the rest of my life." Promise? Okay, here goes: Treat people the same way you would like to be treated.

Which got us to thinking one day, what would a service area be without pinups?

Not *those* pinups, but rather pictures of Saturn owners. That way, when people brought their cars in for an oil change or something, we'd be able to place a name with a face.

Think about it. *Hey you* is not exactly the most endearing greeting, especially to someone who took the time to shop at your place and who spent their hard-earned money on one of your cars. *Hi, Yvonne* or *Hi, Steve* doesn't seem like it would be asking too much. It's certainly how we would like to be greeted if we were bringing in our car. Of course, it would go even further if our name were Steve, but hopefully you get the point.

A DIFFERENT KIND OF COMPANY A DIFFERENT KIND OF CAR

Relationship marketing: Saturn builds lasting relationships with customers. Many dealers post "pinups" of customers in their service areas to help employees place customer faces with cars. "Hey you is not exactly the most endearing greeting, especially to someone who took the time to shop at your place and who spent hard-earned money on one of your cars."

> **active example**

Take a moment to explore one company's success in delivering value and satisfaction.

EXCHANGE, TRANSACTIONS, AND RELATIONSHIPS

Marketing occurs when people decide to satisfy needs and wants through exchange. **Exchange** is the act of obtaining a desired object from someone by offering something in return. Exchange is only one of many ways that people can obtain a desired object. For example, hungry people could find food by hunting, fishing, or gathering fruit. They could beg for food or take food from someone else. Or they could offer money, another good, or a service in return for food.

As a means of satisfying needs, exchange has much in its favor. People do not have to prey on others or depend on donations, nor must they possess the skills to produce every necessity for themselves. They can concentrate on making things that they are good at making and trade them for needed items made by others. Thus, exchange allows a society to produce much more than it would with any alternative system.

Whereas exchange is the core concept of marketing, a transaction, in turn, is marketing's unit of measurement. A **transaction** consists of a trade of values between two parties: One party gives X to another party and gets Y in return. For example, you pay Sears $350 for a television set. This is a classic *monetary transaction,* but not all transactions involve money. In a *barter transaction,* you might trade your old refrigerator in return for a neighbor's secondhand television set.

In the broadest sense, the marketer tries to bring about a response to some offer. The response may be more than simply buying or trading goods and services. A political candidate, for instance, wants votes, a church wants membership, and a social action group wants idea acceptance. Marketing consists of actions taken to obtain a desired response from a target audience toward some product, service, idea, or other object.

Transaction marketing is part of the larger idea of **relationship marketing.** Beyond creating short-term transactions, marketers need to build long-term relationships with valued customers, distributors, dealers, and suppliers. They want to build strong economic and social connections by promising and consistently delivering high-quality products, good service, and fair prices. Increasingly, marketing is shifting from trying to maximize the profit on each individual transaction to building mutually beneficial relationships with consumers and other parties. In fact, ultimately, a company wants to build a unique company asset called a *marketing network.* A marketing network consists of the company and all its supporting stakeholders: customers, employees, suppliers, distributors, retailers, ad agencies, and others with whom it has built mutually profitable business relationships. Increasingly, competition is not between companies but rather between whole networks, with the prize going to the company that has built the better network. The operating principle is simple: Build a good network of relationships with key stakeholders and profits will follow.[9]

MARKETS

The concepts of exchange and relationships lead to the concept of a market. A **market** is the set of actual and potential buyers of a product. These buyers share a particular need or want that can be satisfied through exchanges and relationships. Thus, the size of a market depends on the number of people who exhibit the need, have resources to engage in exchange, and are willing to offer these resources in exchange for what they want.

Originally the term *market* stood for the place where buyers and sellers gathered to exchange their goods, such as a village square. Economists use the term *market* to refer to a collection of buyers and sellers who transact in a particular product class, as in the housing market or the grain market. Marketers, however, see the sellers as constituting an industry and the buyers as constituting a market. The relationship between the *industry* and the *market* is shown in Figure 1.2. Sellers and the buyers are connected by four flows. The sellers send products, services, and communications to the market; in return, they receive money and information. The inner loop shows an exchange of money for goods; the outer loop shows an exchange of information.

Modern economies operate on the principle of division of labor, whereby each person specializes in producing something, receives payment, and buys needed things with this money. Thus, modern economies abound in markets. Producers go to resource markets (raw material markets, labor markets, money markets), buy resources, turn them into goods and services, and sell them to intermediaries, who sell them to consumers. The consumers sell their labor, for which they receive income to pay for the goods and services that they buy. The government is another market that plays several roles. It buys goods from resource, producer, and intermediary markets; it pays them; it taxes these markets (including consumer markets); and it returns needed public services. Thus, each nation's economy and the whole world economy consist of complex, interacting sets of markets that are linked through exchange processes.

Marketers are keenly interested in markets. Their goal is to understand the needs and wants of specific markets and to select the markets that they can serve best. In turn, they can develop products and services that will create value and satisfaction for customers in these markets, resulting in sales and profits for the company.

MARKETING

The concept of markets finally brings us full circle to the concept of marketing. Marketing means managing markets to bring about exchanges and relationships for the purpose of creating value and satisfying needs and wants. Thus, we return to our definition of marketing as a process by which individuals and groups obtain what they need and want by creating and exchanging products and value with others.

Exchange processes involve work. Sellers must search for buyers, identify their needs, design good products and services, set prices for them, promote them, and store and deliver them. Activities

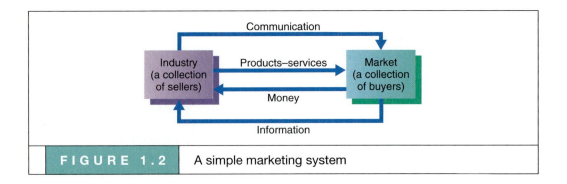

| FIGURE 1.2 | A simple marketing system |

[9]See James C. Anderson, Hakan Hakansson, and Jan Johanson, "Dyadic Business Relationships Within a Business Network Context," *Journal of Marketing,* October 15, 1994, pp. 1–15. For more discussion of relationship marketing, see Thomas W. Gruen, "Relationship Marketing: The Route to Marketing Efficiency and Effectiveness," *Business Horizons,* November–December 1997, pp. 32–38; and John V. Petrof, "Relationship Marketing: The Emperor in Used Clothes," *Business Horizons,* March–April 1998, pp. 79–82.

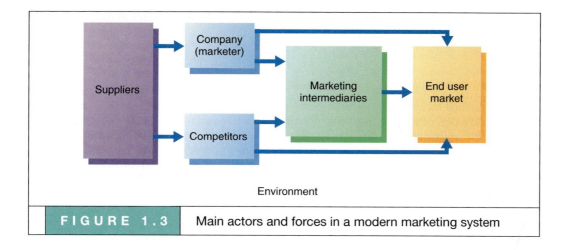

| FIGURE 1.3 | Main actors and forces in a modern marketing system |

such as product development, research, communication, distribution, pricing, and service are core marketing activities. Although we normally think of marketing as being carried on by sellers, buyers also carry on marketing activities. Consumers do marketing when they search for the goods they need at prices they can afford. Company purchasing agents do marketing when they track down sellers and bargain for good terms.

Figure 1.3 shows the main elements in a modern marketing system. In the usual situation, marketing involves serving a market of end users in the face of competitors. The company and the competitors send their respective products and messages to consumers either directly or through marketing intermediaries to the end users. All of the actors in the system are affected by major environmental forces (demographic, economic, physical, technological, political–legal, social–cultural).

Each party in the system adds value for the next level. Thus, a company's success depends not only on its own actions but also on how well the entire system serves the needs of final consumers. Wal-Mart cannot fulfill its promise of low prices unless its suppliers provide merchandise at low costs. Ford cannot deliver high quality to car buyers unless its dealers provide outstanding service.

> active concept check

Now let's take a moment to test your knowledge of what you've just read.

> Marketing Management

We define **marketing management** as the analysis, planning, implementation, and control of programs designed to create, build, and maintain beneficial exchanges with target buyers for the purpose of achieving organizational objectives. Thus, marketing management involves managing demand, which in turn involves managing customer relationships.

DEMAND MANAGEMENT

Some people think of marketing management as finding enough customers for the company's current output but this view is too limited. The organization has a desired level of demand for its products. At any point in time, there may be no demand, adequate demand, irregular demand, or too much demand, and marketing management must find ways to deal with these different demand states. Marketing management is concerned not only with finding and increasing demand but also with changing or even reducing it.

For example, the Golden Gate Bridge sometimes carries an unsafe level of traffic, and Yosemite National Park is badly overcrowded in the summer. Power companies sometimes have trouble meeting demand during peak usage periods. In these and other cases of excess demand, **demarketing** may be required to reduce demand temporarily or permanently. The aim of demarketing is not to destroy demand but only to reduce or shift it.[10] Thus, marketing management seeks to affect the level, timing, and nature of demand in a way that helps the organization achieve its objectives. Simply put, marketing management is *demand management*.

BUILDING PROFITABLE CUSTOMER RELATIONSHIPS

Managing demand means managing customers. A company's demand comes from two groups: new customers and repeat customers. Traditionally, marketers have focused on *attracting* new customers and creating *transactions* with them. In today's marketing environment, however, changing demographic, economic, and competitive factors mean that there are fewer new customers to go around. The costs of attracting new customers are rising. Thus, although finding new customers remains very important, the emphasis is shifting toward *retaining* profitable customers and building lasting *relationships* with them.

Companies have also discovered that losing a customer means losing not just a single sale but also a lifetime's worth of purchases and referrals. For example, the *customer lifetime value* of a Taco Bell customer exceeds $12,000. For Lexus, one satisfied customer is worth $600,000 in lifetime purchases. Thus, working to keep profitable customers makes good economic sense.[11] The key to customer retention is superior customer value and satisfaction. With this in mind, many companies are going to extremes to keep their customers satisfied.

MARKETING MANAGEMENT PRACTICE

All kinds of organizations use marketing, and they practice it in widely varying ways. Many large firms apply standard marketing practices in a formalized way. However, other companies use marketing in a less formal and orderly fashion. A recent book, *Radical Marketing,* praises companies such as Harley-Davidson, Virgin Atlantic Airways, and Boston Beer for succeeding by breaking many of the rules of marketing.[12] Instead of commissioning expensive marketing research, spending huge sums on mass advertising, and operating large marketing departments, these companies stretched their limited resources, lived close to their customers, and created more satisfying solutions to customer needs. They formed buyer's clubs, used creative public relations, and focused on delivering high product quality and winning long-term customer loyalty. It seems that not all marketing must follow in the footsteps of marketing giants such as Procter & Gamble.

In fact, marketing practice often passes through three stages: entrepreneurial marketing, formulated marketing, and intrepreneurial marketing.

- *Entrepreneurial marketing:* Most companies are started by individuals who live by their wits. They visualize an opportunity and knock on every door to gain attention. Jim Koch, founder of Boston Beer Company, whose Samuel Adams beer has become a top-selling "craft" beer, started out in 1984 carrying bottles of Samuel Adams beer from bar to bar to persuade bartenders to carry it. He would coax them into adding Samuel Adams beer to their menus. For 10 years, he couldn't afford advertising; he sold his beer through direct selling and grassroots public relations. Today, however, his business pulls in $210 million, making it the leader in the craft beer market.

- *Formulated marketing:* As small companies achieve success, they inevitably move toward more formulated marketing. Boston Beer recently opted to spend more than $15 million on television advertising in selected markets. The company now employs more than 175 salespeople and has a marketing department that carries out market research. Although Boston Beer is far less sophisticated than its arch-competitor, Anheuser-Busch, it has adopted some of the tools used in professionally run marketing companies.

- *Intrepreneurial marketing:* Many large and mature companies get stuck in formulated marketing, poring over the latest Nielsen numbers, scanning market research reports, and trying to fine-tune dealer relations and advertising messages. These companies sometimes lose the marketing creativity and passion that they had at the start. They now need to reestablish within their companies the

---

[10]For more discussion on demand states, see Kotler, *Marketing Management: Analysis, Planning, Implementation, and Control,* chap. 1.

[11]For more on assessing customer value, see Gordon A. Wyner, "Customer Valuation: Linking Behavior and Economics," *Marketing Research,* Summer 1996, pp. 36–38; Gordon A. Wyner, "Which Customers Will Be Valuable in the Future?" *Marketing Research,* Fall 1996, pp. 44–46; Bill Stoneman, "Banking on Customers," *American Demographics,* February 1997, pp. 37–41; Paul D. Berger, "Customer Lifetime Value: Marketing Models and Applications," *Journal of Interactive Marketing,* Winter 1998, pp. 17–30; and Libby Estell, "This Call Center Accelerates Sales," *Sales & Marketing Management,* February 1999, p. 72.

[12]Sam Hill and Glenn Rifkin, *Radical Marketing* (New York: HarperBusiness, 1999).

entrepreneurial spirit and actions that made them successful in the first place. They need to encourage more initiative and "intrepreneurship" at the local level. Their brand and product managers need to get out of the office, start living with their customers, and visualize new and creative ways to add value to their customers' lives.

The bottom line is that effective marketing can take many forms. There will be a constant tension between the formulated side of marketing and the creative side. It is easier to learn the formulated side of marketing, which will occupy most of our attention in this book. But we will also see how real marketing creativity and passion operate in many companies—whether small or large, new or mature—to build and retain success in the marketplace.

> ## active concept check

Now let's take a moment to test your knowledge of what you've just read.

> ## Marketing Management Philosophies

We describe marketing management as carrying out tasks to achieve desired exchanges with target markets. What *philosophy* should guide these marketing efforts? What weight should be given to the interests of the organization, customers, and society? Very often these interests conflict.

There are five alternative concepts under which organizations conduct their marketing activities: the *production, product, selling, marketing,* and *societal marketing* concepts.

THE PRODUCTION CONCEPT

The **production concept** holds that consumers will favor products that are available and highly affordable. Therefore, management should focus on improving production and distribution efficiency. This concept is one of the oldest philosophies that guides sellers.

The production concept is still a useful philosophy in two types of situations. The first occurs when the demand for a product exceeds the supply. Here, management should look for ways to increase production. The second situation occurs when the product's cost is too high and improved productivity is needed to bring it down. For example, Henry Ford's whole philosophy was to perfect the production of the Model T so that its cost could be reduced and more people could afford it. He joked about offering people a car of any color as long as it was black.

For many years, Texas Instruments (TI) followed a philosophy of increased production and lower costs in order to bring down prices. It won a major share of the American handheld calculator market using this approach. However, companies operating under a production philosophy run a major risk of focusing too narrowly on their own operations. For example, when TI used this strategy in the digital watch market, it failed. Although TI's watches were priced low, customers did not find them very attractive. In its drive to bring down prices, TI lost sight of something else that its customers wanted—namely, affordable, *attractive* digital watches.

THE PRODUCT CONCEPT

Another major concept guiding sellers, the **product concept,** holds that consumers will favor products that offer the most in quality, performance, and innovative features. Thus, an organization should devote energy to making continuous product improvements. Some manufacturers believe that if they can build a better mousetrap, the world will beat a path to their door.[13] But they are often rudely shocked. Buyers may well be looking for a better solution to a mouse problem but not necessarily for a better mousetrap. The solution might be a chemical spray, an exterminating

---

[13]Ralph Waldo Emerson offered this advice: "If a man . . . makes a better mousetrap . . . the world will beat a path to his door." Several companies, however, have built better mousetraps yet failed. One was a laser mousetrap costing $1,500. Contrary to popular assumptions, people do not automatically learn about new products, believe product claims, or willingly pay higher prices.

service, or something that works better than a mousetrap. Furthermore, a better mousetrap will not sell unless the manufacturer designs, packages, and prices it attractively; places it in convenient distribution channels; brings it to the attention of people who need it; and convinces buyers that it is a better product.

The product concept also can lead to marketing myopia. For instance, railroad management once thought that users wanted *trains* rather than *transportation* and overlooked the growing challenge of airlines, buses, trucks, and automobiles. Many colleges have assumed that high school graduates want a liberal arts education and thus have overlooked the increasing challenge of vocational schools.

THE SELLING CONCEPT

Many organizations follow the **selling concept,** which holds that consumers will not buy enough of the organization's products unless it undertakes a large-scale selling and promotion effort. The concept is typically practiced with unsought goods—those that buyers do not normally think of buying, such as encyclopedias or insurance. These industries must be good at tracking down prospects and selling them on product benefits.

Most firms practice the selling concept when they have overcapacity. Their aim is to sell what they make rather than make what the market wants. Such marketing carries high risks. It focuses on creating sales transactions rather than on building long-term, profitable relationships with customers. It assumes that customers who are coaxed into buying the product will like it. Or, if they don't like it, they will possibly forget their disappointment and buy it again later. These are usually poor assumptions to make about buyers. Most studies show that dissatisfied customers do not buy again. Worse yet, whereas the average satisfied customer tells three others about good experiences, the average dissatisfied customer tells ten others about his or her bad experiences.[14]

THE MARKETING CONCEPT

The **marketing concept** holds that achieving organizational goals depends on determining the needs and wants of target markets and delivering the desired satisfactions more effectively and efficiently than competitors do. The marketing concept has been stated in colorful ways, such as "We make it happen for you" (Marriott); "To fly, to serve" (British Airways); "We're not satisfied until you are" (GE); and "Let us exceed your expectations" (Celebrity Cruise Lines).

The selling concept and the marketing concept are sometimes confused. Figure 1.4 compares the two concepts. The selling concept takes an *inside-out* perspective. It starts with the factory, focuses on the company's existing products, and calls for heavy selling and promotion to obtain profitable sales. It focuses primarily on customer conquest—getting short-term sales with little concern about who buys or why.

In contrast, the marketing concept takes an *outside-in* perspective. As Herb Kelleher, Southwest Airlines's colorful CEO, puts it, "We don't have a Marketing Department; we have a Customer Department." The marketing concept starts with a well-defined market, focuses on customer needs,

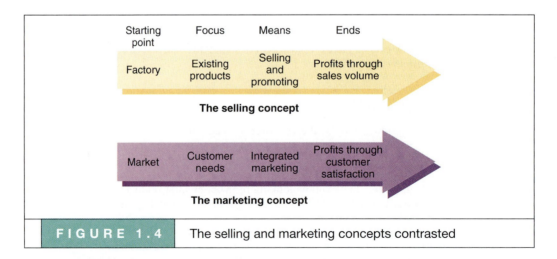

Starting point	Focus	Means	Ends
Factory	Existing products	Selling and promoting	Profits through sales volume

The selling concept

| Market | Customer needs | Integrated marketing | Profits through customer satisfaction |

The marketing concept

FIGURE 1.4   The selling and marketing concepts contrasted

[14]Barry Farber and Joyce Wycoff, "Customer Service: Evolution and Revolution," *Sales & Marketing Management,* May 1991, p. 47. Also see Jaclyn Fierman, "Americans Can't Get No Satisfaction," *Fortune,* December 11, 1995, pp. 186–94.

The marketing concept: L.L. Bean and its reps dedicate themselves to delivering the promise first spelled out in a 1916 L.L. Bean circular and still practiced today.

coordinates all the marketing activities affecting customers, and makes profits by creating long-term customer relationships based on customer value and satisfaction. Thus, under the marketing concept, customer focus and value are the *paths* to sales and profits. In the words of one Ford executive, "If we're not customer driven, our cars won't be either."

Many successful and well-known companies have adopted the marketing concept. Procter & Gamble, Disney, Wal-Mart, Marriott, Nordstrom, Dell Computer, and Southwest Airlines follow it faithfully. The goal is to build customer satisfaction into the very fabric of the firm. L.L. Bean, the highly successful catalog retailer, was founded on the marketing concept. In 1912, in his first circulars, L.L. Bean included the following notice: "I do not consider a sale complete until goods are worn out and the customer still is satisfied. We will thank anyone to return goods that are not perfectly satisfactory. . . . Above all things we wish to avoid having a dissatisfied customer."

Today, L.L. Bean dedicates itself to giving "perfect satisfaction in every way." To inspire its employees to practice the marketing concept, L.L. Bean has for decades displayed posters around its offices that proclaim the following:

> What is a customer? A customer is the most important person ever in this company—in person or by mail. A customer is not dependent on us, we are dependent on him. A customer is not an interruption of our work, he is the purpose of it. We are not doing a favor by serving him, he is doing us a favor by giving us the opportunity to do so. A customer is not someone to argue or match wits with—nobody ever won an argument with a customer. A customer is a person who brings us his wants—it is our job to handle them profitably to him and to ourselves.

In contrast, many companies claim to practice the marketing concept but do not. They have the *forms* of marketing, such as a marketing vice president, product managers, marketing plans, and marketing research, but this does not mean that they are market-focused and customer-driven companies. The question is whether they are finely tuned to changing customer needs and competitor strategies. Formerly great companies—General Motors, Sears, Zenith—all lost substantial market share because they failed to adjust their marketing strategies to the changing marketplace.

Implementing the marketing concept often means more than simply responding to customers' stated desires and obvious needs. *Customer-driven* companies research current customers to learn about their desires, gather new product and service ideas, and test proposed product improvements. Such customer-driven marketing usually works well when a clear need exists and when customers know what they want. In many cases, however, customers *don't* know what they want or even what is possible. Such situations call for *customer-driving* marketing—understanding customer needs even better than customers themselves do, and creating products and services that will meet existing and latent needs now and in the future.

> Customers are notoriously lacking in foresight. Ten or 15 years ago, how many of us were asking for cellular telephones, fax machines, and copiers at home, 24-hour discount brokerage accounts, multivalve automobile engines, compact disk players, cars with onboard navigation systems, handheld global satellite positioning receivers, MTV, or the Home Shopping Network? As Akio Morita, Sony's visionary leader puts it: "Our plan is to lead the public with new products rather than ask them what kinds of products they want. The public does not know

what is possible, but we do. So instead of doing a lot of market research, we refine our thinking on a product and its use and try to create a market for it by educating and communicating with the public."[15]

Several years of hard work are needed to turn a sales-oriented company into a marketing-oriented company. Customer satisfaction is no longer a fad. As one marketing analyst notes, "It's becoming a way of life in corporate America . . . as embedded into corporate cultures as information technology and strategic planning."[16]

active exercise <

Take a moment to consider how these marketing concepts apply to the work of an actual company.

THE SOCIETAL MARKETING CONCEPT

The **societal marketing concept** holds that the organization should determine the needs, wants, and interests of target markets. It should then deliver superior value to customers in a way that maintains or improves the consumer's *and the society's* well being. The societal marketing concept is the newest of the five marketing management philosophies.

The societal marketing concept questions whether the pure marketing concept is adequate in an age of environmental problems, resource shortages, rapid population growth, worldwide economic problems, and neglected social services. It asks if the firm that senses, serves, and satisfies individual wants is always doing what's best for consumers and society in the long run. According to the societal marketing concept, the pure marketing concept overlooks possible conflicts between consumer *short-run wants* and consumer *long-run welfare.*

Consider the fast-food industry. Most people see today's giant fast-food chains as offering tasty and convenient food at reasonable prices. Yet many consumer and environmental groups have voiced concerns. Critics point out that hamburgers, fried chicken, French fries, and most other foods sold by fast-food restaurants are high in fat and salt. The products are wrapped in convenient packaging, but this leads to waste and pollution. Thus, in satisfying consumer wants, the highly successful fast-food chains may be harming consumer health and causing environmental problems.

Such concerns and conflicts led to the societal marketing concept. As Figure 1.5 shows, the societal marketing concept calls on marketers to balance three considerations in setting their marketing policies: company profits, consumer wants, *and* society's interests. Originally, most companies based their marketing decisions largely on short-run company profit. Eventually, they began to recognize the long-run importance of satisfying consumer wants, and the marketing concept emerged. Now many companies are beginning to think of society's interests when making their marketing decisions.

One such company is Johnson & Johnson, rated each year in a *Fortune* magazine poll as one of America's most admired companies, especially for its community and environmental responsibility. Johnson & Johnson's concern for societal interests is summarized in a company document called "Our Credo," which stresses honesty, integrity, and putting people before profits. Under this credo, Johnson & Johnson would rather take a big loss than ship a bad batch of one of its products. The company supports many community and employee programs that benefit its consumers and workers and the environment. Johnson & Johnson's chief executive puts it this way: "If we keep trying to do what's right, at the end of the day we believe the marketplace will reward us."[17]

The company backs these words with actions. Consider the tragic tampering case in which eight people died from swallowing cyanide-laced capsules of Tylenol, a Johnson & Johnson brand.

[15]Gary Hamel and C. K. Prahalad, "Seeing the Future First," *Fortune,* September 5, 1994, pp. 64–70. Also see Philip Kotler, *Kotler on Marketing* (New York: Free Press, 1999), pp. 20–24.

[16]Howard Schlossberg, "Customer Satisfaction: Not a Fad, but a Way of Life," *Marketing News,* June 10, 1991, p. 18. Also see Bernard J. Jaworski and Ajay K. Kohli, "Market Orientation: Antecedents and Consequences," *Journal of Marketing,* July 1993, pp. 53–70; and E. K. Valentin, "The Marketing Concept and the Conceptualization of Market Strategy," *Journal of Marketing Theory and Practice,* Fall 1996, pp. 16–27.

[17]See "Leaders of the Most Admired," *Fortune,* January 29, 1990, pp. 40–54; and Thomas A. Stewart, "America's Most Admired Companies," *Fortune,* March 2, 1998, pp. 70–82.

Our Credo

We believe our first responsibility is to the doctors, nurses and patients,
to mothers and fathers and all others who use our products and services.
In meeting their needs everything we do must be of high quality.
We must constantly strive to reduce our costs
in order to maintain reasonable prices.
Customers' orders must be serviced promptly and accurately.
Our suppliers and distributors must have an opportunity
to make a fair profit.

We are responsible to our employees,
the men and women who work with us throughout the world.
Everyone must be considered as an individual.
We must respect their dignity and recognize their merit.
They must have a sense of security in their jobs.
Compensation must be fair and adequate,
and working conditions clean, orderly and safe.
We must be mindful of ways to help our employees fulfill
their family responsibilities.
Employees must feel free to make suggestions and complaints.
There must be equal opportunity for employment, development
and advancement for those qualified.
We must provide competent management,
and their actions must be just and ethical.

We are responsible to the communities in which we live and work
and to the world community as well.
We must be good citizens — support good works and charities
and bear our fair share of taxes.
We must encourage civic improvements and better health and education.
We must maintain in good order
the property we are privileged to use,
protecting the environment and natural resources.

Our final responsibility is to our stockholders.
Business must make a sound profit.
We must experiment with new ideas.
Research must be carried on, innovative programs developed
and mistakes paid for.
New equipment must be purchased, new facilities provided
and new products launched.
Reserves must be created to provide for adverse times.
When we operate according to these principles,
the stockholders should realize a fair return.

Johnson & Johnson

Johnson & Johnson's concern for society is summarized in its credo and in the company's actions over the years. Says one executive, "It's just plain good business."

Although Johnson & Johnson believed that the pills had been altered in only a few stores, not in the factory, it quickly recalled all of its product. The recall cost the company $240 million in earnings. In the long run, however, the company's swift recall of Tylenol strengthened consumer confidence and loyalty, and Tylenol remains the nation's leading brand of pain reliever. In this and other cases, Johnson & Johnson management has found that doing what's right benefits both consumers and the company. Says the chief executive, "The Credo should not be viewed as some kind of social welfare program . . . it's just plain good business."[18] Thus, over the years, Johnson & Johnson's dedication to consumers and community service has made it one of America's most admired companies *and* one of the most profitable.

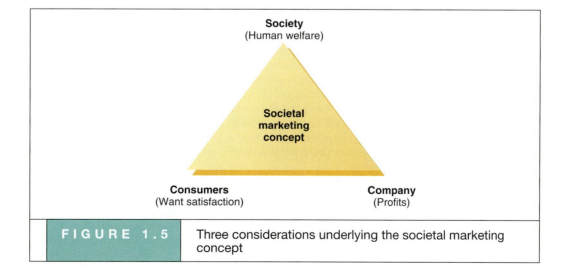

Society
(Human welfare)

Societal marketing concept

Consumers
(Want satisfaction)

Company
(Profits)

| FIGURE 1.5 | Three considerations underlying the societal marketing concept |

---

[18]"Leaders of the Most Admired," p. 54.

active example   <

Take a moment to consider how one prominent firm approaches societal marketing.

active concept check   <

Now let's take a moment to test your knowledge of what you've just read.

> Marketing Challenges in the New "Connected" Millennium

As the world spins into the first decade of the twenty-first century, dramatic changes are occurring in the marketing arena. Richard Love of Hewlett-Packard observes, "The pace of change is so rapid that the ability to change has now become a competitive advantage." Yogi Berra, the legendary New York Yankees catcher, summed it up more simply when he said, "The future ain't what it used to be." Technological advances, rapid globalization, and continuing social and economic shifts—all are causing profound changes in the marketplace. As the marketplace changes, so must those who serve it.

The major marketing developments today can be summed up in a single theme: *connectedness*. Now, more than ever before, we are all connected to each other and to things near and far in the world around us. Moreover, we are connecting in new and different ways. Where it once took weeks or months to travel across the United States, we can now travel around the globe in only hours or days. Where it once took days or even weeks to receive news about important world events, we now see them as they are occurring through live satellite broadcasts. Where it once took days or weeks to correspond with others in distant places, they are now only moments away by phone or the Internet.

In this section, we examine the major trends and forces that are changing the marketing landscape and challenging marketing strategy in this new, connected millennium. As shown in Figure 1.6 and discussed in the following pages, sweeping changes in connecting technologies are causing marketers to redefine how they connect with the marketplace—with their customers, with marketing partners inside and outside the company, and with the world around them. We first look at the dramatic changes that are occurring in the connecting technologies. Then, we examine how these changes are affecting marketing connections.

TECHNOLOGIES FOR CONNECTING

The major force behind the new connectedness is technology. Explosive advances in computer, telecommunications, information, transportation, and other connecting technologies has had a major impact on the way companies bring value to their customers. The technology boom has created exciting new ways to learn about and track customers, create products and services tailored to meet customer needs, distribute products more efficiently and effectively, and communicate with customers in large groups or one-to-one. For example, through videoconferencing, marketing researchers at a company's headquarters in New York can look in on focus groups in Chicago or Paris without ever stepping onto a plane. With only a few clicks of a mouse button, a direct marketer can tap into online data services to learn anything from what car you drive to what you read to what flavor of ice cream you prefer.

Using today's vastly more powerful computers, marketers create detailed databases and use them to target individual customers with offers designed to meet their specific needs and buying patterns. With a new wave of communication and advertising tools—ranging from cell phones, fax machines, and CD-ROM to interactive TV and video kiosks at airports and shopping malls—marketers can zero in on selected customers with carefully targeted messages. Through electronic commerce, customers can design, order, and pay for products and services without ever leaving home. Then, through the marvels of express delivery, they can receive their purchases in less than 24 hours.

From virtual reality displays that test new products to online virtual stores that sell them, the boom in computer, information, telecommunication, and transportation technology is affecting every aspect

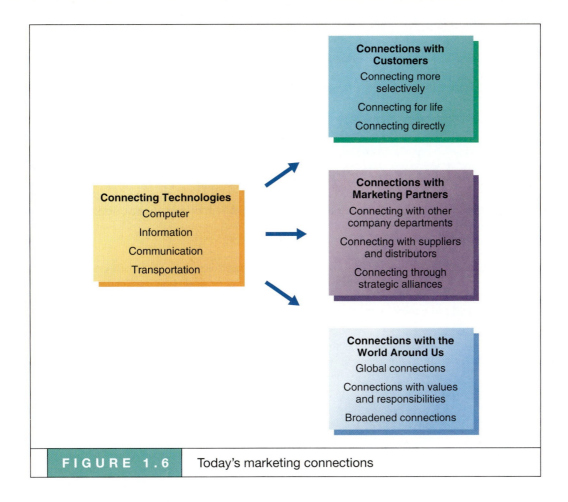

Connecting Technologies
Computer
Information
Communication
Transportation

Connections with Customers
Connecting more selectively
Connecting for life
Connecting directly

Connections with Marketing Partners
Connecting with other company departments
Connecting with suppliers and distributors
Connecting through strategic alliances

Connections with the World Around Us
Global connections
Connections with values and responsibilities
Broadened connections

FIGURE 1.6	Today's marketing connections

of marketing. Consider the rapidly changing face of personal selling. Many companies now equip their salespeople with the latest sales automation tools, including the capacity to develop individualized multimedia presentations and to develop customized market offerings and contracts. Many buyers now prefer to meet salespeople on their computer screens rather than in the office. An increasing amount of personal selling is occurring through videoconferences or live Internet presentations, where buyers and sellers can interact across great distances without the time, costs, or delays of travel.

The Internet

Perhaps the most dramatic new technology driving the connected age is the **Internet.** The Internet is a vast and burgeoning global web of computer networks with no central management or ownership. It was created during the late 1960s by the U.S. Department of Defense, initially to link government labs, contractors, and military installations. Today, the Internet links computer users of all types around the world. Anyone with a PC, a modem, and the right software—or a TV with a set-top "Web box"—can browse the Internet to obtain or share information on almost any subject and to interact with other users.

The Internet has been hailed as the technology behind a new model for doing business. It allows anytime, anywhere connections to information, entertainment, and communication. Companies are using the Internet to build closer relationships with customers and marketing partners and to sell and distribute their products more efficiently and effectively. They are rapidly converting from "snail mail" and the telephone to the *Internet* (connecting with customers), *intranets* (connecting with others in the company), and *extranets* (connecting with strategic marketing partners, suppliers, and dealers). Beyond competing in traditional *marketplaces,* they now have access to exciting new *marketspaces.*

Internet usage surged in the early 1990s with the development of the user-friendly World Wide Web. The U.S. Internet population grew from only 6 million households in 1994 to more than 40 million today; it will grow to a projected 60 million households by the year 2003. The Internet is truly a worldwide phenomenon. Forrester Research projects that U.S. Internet purchasing will grow from only about $21.5 billion in 1995 to more than $1.4 trillion in 2003.[19] Notes one analyst, "In just [a few

[19]Internet usage and buying statistics provided by Forrester Research, August 1999.

short years], the Net has gone from a playground for nerds into a vast communications and trading center where . . . people swap information and do deals around the world. . . . More than 400,000 companies have hung www.single.com atop their digital doorways with the notion that being anywhere on the Net means selling virtually everywhere."[20]

Companies of all types are now attempting to snare new customers on the Web. Many traditional "brick-and-mortar" companies have now ventured online in an effort to snare new customers and build stronger customer relationships. For example

Car makers such as Toyota (www.Toyota.com) use the Internet to develop relationships with owners as well as to sell cars. Its site offers product information, dealer services and locations, leasing information, and much more. For example, visitors to the site can view any of seven lifestyle magazines—*alt.Terrain, A Man's Life, Women's Web Weekly, Sportzine, Living Arts, Living Home,* and *Car Culture*—designed to appeal to Toyota's well-educated, above-average-income target audience.

Sports fans can cozy up with Nike by logging onto www.nike.com, where they can check out the latest Nike products, explore the company's history, or download their favorite athlete's stats. Through its Web page, in addition to its mass-media presence, Nike relates with customers in a more personal, one-to-one way.

The Internet has also spawned an entirely new breed of companies—the so-called "dot coms"—which operate *only* online. For example

Fast-growing eToys is quickly becoming an indispensable ally to time-starved parents looking for a fast and convenient way to buy toys for their children. The three-year-old Web-only retailer pioneered in selling everything from teddy bears to Barbies online. Now the site offers more than 100,000 toys, books, software, videos, and other kid items. Twenty-four hours a day, seven days a week, shoppers can click onto eToys (www.eToys.com), search for a specific item or browse one of several categories, drop their selections into a virtual shopping cart, pay for them with a credit card, and have them delivered within a day or two by express shipping. The eToys Web site also offers recommendations by age groups, a gift registry, a bestsellers list, and features on the latest

Companies of all types are now snaring new customers on the Web, including an entirely new breed of companies—the so-called "dot coms," such as eToys—which operate only online.

[20]Robert D. Hof, "The 'Click Here' Economy," *Business Week,* June 22, 1998, pp. 122–28.

[21]Patricia Sellers, "Inside the First E-Christmas," *Fortune,* February 1, 1999, pp. 70–73; Nanette Byrnes and Paul C. Judge, "Internet Anxiety," *Business Week,* June 28, 1999, pp. 79–88; Heather Green, "The Great Yuletide Shakeout," *Business Week,* November 1, 1999, p. Eb22.

children's products. Is the site successful? After only three years, eToys has won some 600,000 customers and almost $30 million of their purchases. "There is tremendous competition," says eToys CEO Toby Lenk. "The difference is we are just kids and we are just the Web."[21]

It seems that almost every business—from garage-based start-ups to established giants such as IBM, GE, Marriott Hotels, JCPenney, and American Airlines—is setting up shop on the Internet. All are racing to explore and exploit the Web's marketing possibilities. However, for all its potential, the Internet does have drawbacks. Despite growing use of the Web for shopping, in a recent survey 54 percent of Web users said that they were not likely to use the Internet for online purchases ever in the future. Although the value of a Web site is difficult to measure, the actuality is that few companies have made much money from their Internet efforts.[22]

Thus, changes in connecting technologies are providing exciting new opportunities for marketers. We now look at the ways these changes are affecting how companies connect with their customers, marketing partners, and the world around us (see Figure 1.6).

CONNECTIONS WITH CUSTOMERS

The most profound new developments in marketing involve the ways in which today's companies are connecting with their customers. Yesterday's companies focused on mass marketing to all comers at arm's length. Today's companies are selecting their customers more carefully and building more lasting and direct relationships with these carefully targeted customers.

Connecting with More Carefully Selected Customers

Few firms today still practice true mass marketing—selling in a standardized way to any customer who comes along. Today, most marketers are realizing that they don't want to connect with just *any* customers. Instead, most are targeting fewer, potentially more profitable customers.

The United States—in fact, the world—has become more of a "salad bowl" of diverse ethnic, cultural, social, and locational groups. Although these diverse groups have mixed together, they maintain diversity by keeping and valuing important differences. Moreover, customers themselves are connecting in new ways to form specific "consumer communities," in which buyers connect with each other by common interests, situations, and activities.

Greater diversity and these new consumer connections have meant greater market fragmentation. In response, most firms have moved from mass marketing to segmented marketing, in which they target carefully chosen submarkets or even individual buyers. "One-to-one marketing" has become the order of the day for some marketers. They build extensive customer databases containing rich information on individual customer preferences and purchases. Then, they mine these databases to gain segment and customer insights by which they can "mass-customize" their offerings to deliver greater value to individual buyers.

At the same time that companies are finding imaginative new ways to deliver more value *to* customers, they are also beginning to assess carefully the value *of* customers to the firm. They want to connect only with customers that they can serve *profitably.* Once they identify profitable customers, firms can create attractive offers and special handling to capture these customers and earn their loyalty. The banking industry has led the way in assessing customer profitability. After decades of casting a wide net to lure as many customers as possible, many banks are now mining their vast databases to identify winning customers and weed out losing ones. Take First Union as an example:

> Fielding phone calls at First Union's huge customer service center [in Charlotte, NC], Amy Hathcock is surrounded by reminders to deliver the personal touch. Televisions hang from the ceiling so she can glance at the Weather Channel to see if her latest caller just came in from the rain; a bumper sticker in her cubicle encourages, "Practice random kindness and senseless acts of beauty." But when it comes to answering yes or no to a customer who wants a lower credit-card interest rate or to escape the bank's $28 bounced-check fee, there is nothing random about it. The service all depends on the color of a tiny square—green, yellow, or red—that pops up on Ms. Hathcock's computer screen next to the customer's name. For customers who get a red pop-up, Ms. Hathcock rarely budges; these are the ones whose accounts lose money for the bank. Green means the customers generate hefty profits for First Union and should be granted waivers. Yellow is for in-between customers: There's a chance to negotiate. The bank's computer system, called "Einstein," takes just 15 seconds to pull up the ranking on a customer,

---

[22]Wallys W. Conhaim, "E-Commerce," *Link-Up,* March–April 1998, pp. 8–10.

using a formula that calculates [customer value based on the account's] minimum balances, account activity, branch visits, and other variables. "Everyone isn't all the same anymore," says Steven G. Boehm, general manager of First Union's customer-information center.[23]

Connecting for a Customer's Lifetime

At the same time that companies are being more selective about which customers they choose to serve, they are serving those they choose in a deeper, more lasting way. In the past, many companies have focused on finding *new customers* for their products and closing *sales* with them. In recent years, this focus has shifted toward keeping *current customers* and building lasting *relationships* based on superior customer satisfaction and value. Increasingly, the goal is shifting from making a profit on each sale to making long-term profits by managing the lifetime value of a customer.

In turn, as businesses do a better and better job of keeping old customers, competitors find it increasingly difficult to acquire new customers. As a result, marketers now spend less time figuring out how to increase "share of market" and more time trying to grow "share of customer." They offer greater variety to current customers and train employees to cross-sell and up-sell in order to market more products and services to existing customers. For example, Amazon.com began as an online bookseller, but now offers music, videos, gifts, toys, consumer electronics, home improvement items, and even an online auction as well, increasing per-customer sales. In addition, based on each customer's purchase history, the company recommends related books, CDs, or videos that might be of interest. In this way, Amazon.com captures a greater share of each customer's leisure and entertainment budget.

Connecting Directly

Today, beyond connecting more deeply, many companies are also taking advantage of new technologies that let them connect more *directly* with their customers. In fact, direct marketing is booming. Virtually all products are now available without going to a store—by telephone, mail-order catalogs, kiosks, and electronic commerce. For example, customers surfing the Internet can view pictures of almost any product, read the specs, shop among online vendors for the best prices and terms, speak with online vendors' shopping consultants, and even place and pay for their orders—all with only a few mouse clicks. Business-to-business purchasing over the Internet has increased even faster than online consumer buying. Business purchasing agents routinely shop on the Web for items ranging from standard office supplies to high-priced, high-tech computer equipment.

Some companies sell *only* via direct channels—firms such as Dell Computer, Lands' End, 1-800-Flowers, and Amazon.com, to name only a few. Other companies use direct connections as a supplement to their other communications and distribution channels. For example, Procter & Gamble sells

Share of customer: To capture a greater share of customers' leisure and entertainment budget, Amazon.com recommends books, CDs, videos, gifts, and home improvement items based on customers' purchase histories.

[23]Rick Brooks, "Unequal Treatment: Alienating Customers Isn't Always a Bad Idea, Many Firms Discover," *Wall Street Journal,* January 7, 1999, p. A1. Also see Erika Rasmusson, "Wanted: Profitable Customers," *Sales & Marketing Management,* May 1999, pp. 28–34.

Pampers disposable diapers through retailers, supported by millions of dollars of mass-media advertising. However, P&G uses its www.Pampers.com Web site to build relationships with young parents by providing information and advice on everything from diapering to baby care and child development. Similarly, you can't buy crayons from the Crayola Web site (www.crayola.com). However, you can find out how to remove crayon marks from your prize carpeting or freshly painted walls.

Direct marketing is redefining the buyer's role in connecting with sellers. Instead of being the targets of a company's one-way marketing efforts, customers have now become active participants in shaping the marketing offer and process. Many companies now let customers design their own desired products online. For example, shoppers at the Lands' End site (www.LandsEnd.com) can build a "personal model" with their own hair color, height, and shape. They then visit an online dressing room, where they can try clothes on the model to see how they would look in them. The site also gives buyers tips on how best to dress given their individual body styles.

Some marketers have hailed direct marketing as the "marketing model of the next millennium." They envision a day when all buying and selling will involve direct connections between companies and their customers. Others, although agreeing that direct marketing will play a growing and important role, see it as just one more way to approach the marketplace. We will examine the exploding world of direct marketing in more detail in chapter 8.

> active exercise

Take a moment to explore how a few companies have responded to the challenge of connecting with customers in our technological age.

CONNECTIONS WITH MARKETING PARTNERS

In these ever more connected times, major changes are occurring in how marketers connect with others inside and outside the company to jointly bring greater value to customers.

Connecting Inside the Company

Traditionally, marketers have played the role of intermediary, charged with understanding customer needs and representing the customer to different company departments, which then acted upon these needs. The old thinking was that marketing is done only by marketing, sales, and customer support people. However, in today's connected world, every functional area can interact with customers, especially electronically. Marketing no longer has sole ownership of customer interactions. The new thinking is that every employee must be customer focused. David Packard, cofounder of Hewlett-Packard, wisely said: "Marketing is far too important to be left only to the marketing department."[24]

Today's forward-looking companies are reorganizing their operations to align them better with customer needs. Rather than letting each department pursue its own objectives, firms are linking all departments in the cause of creating customer value. Rather than assigning only sales and marketing people to customers, they are forming cross-functional customer teams. For example, Procter & Gamble assigns "customer development teams" to each of its major retailer accounts. These teams—consisting of sales and marketing people, operations and logistics specialists, market and financial analysts, and others—coordinate the efforts of many P&G departments toward serving the retailer and helping it to be more successful.

Connecting with Outside Partners

Rapid changes are also occurring in how marketers connect with their suppliers, channel partners, and even competitors. Most companies today are networked companies, relying heavily on partnerships with other firms.

Supply Chain Management. Marketing channels consist of distributors, retailers, and others who connect the company to its buyers. The *supply chain* describes a longer channel, stretching from raw

---

[24]Philip Kotler, *Kotler on Marketing* (New York: Free Press, 1999), p. 20.

materials to components to final products that are carried to final buyers. For example, the supply chain for personal computers consists of suppliers of computer chips and other components, the computer manufacturer, and the distributors, retailers, and others who sell the computers to businesses and final customers. Each member of the supply chain creates and captures only a portion of the total value generated by the supply chain.

Through *supply chain management,* many companies today are strengthening their connections with partners all along the supply chain. They know that their fortunes rest not only on how well they perform but also on how well their entire supply chain performs against competitors' supply chains. Rather than treating suppliers as vendors and distributors as customers, it treats both as partners in delivering value to consumers. For example, Wal-Mart works with suppliers like Procter & Gamble, Rubbermaid, and Black & Decker to streamline logistics and reduce joint distribution costs, resulting in lower prices to consumers. Saturn, on the one hand, works closely with carefully selected suppliers to improve quality and operations efficiency. On the other hand, it works with its franchise dealers to provide top-grade sales and service support that will bring customers in the door and keep them coming back.

Strategic Alliances.   Beyond managing the supply chain, today's companies are also discovering that they need *strategic* partners if they hope to be effective. In the new global environment, with greater competition from more and more products and choices, going it alone is going out of style. *Strategic alliances* are booming across the entire spectrum of industries and services. A recent study found that one in every four dollars earned by the top 1,000 U.S. companies flows from alliances, double the rate in the early 1990s.[25] As Jim Kelly, CEO at UPS puts it, "the old adage 'If you can't beat 'em, join 'em,' is being replaced by 'Join 'em and you can't be beat.'" Notes another analyst

> [Think about] how Home Depot and other large retailers operate behind the scenes. They might sell do-it-yourself to consumers, but their own business proposition is do-it-together. Increasingly, enlightened companies are forming strategic alliances with customers, suppliers, and other venture partners. . . . They are replacing go-it-alone strategies with reliance on partnering. . . . Do-it-together means leveraging the strengths of a business partner to create more value and build more sales than either company could do alone. . . . Large companies often count on technological breakthroughs from tiny focused partners who, in turn, need large partners to reach international markets and build credibility. Every search for ways to build sales should include a search for partners who can help reach that goal faster.[26]

Many strategic alliances take the form of *marketing alliances.* These may be *product* or *service alliances* in which one company licenses another to produce its product, or two companies jointly market their complementary products. For instance, Apple Computer joined with Digital Vax to codesign, comanufacture, and comarket a new product. Through *promotional alliances,* one company agrees to join in a promotion for another company's product or service. For example, McDonald's teamed up with Ty to offer an incredibly successful Beanie Babies promotion for its value meals. Companies may form *logistics alliances* in which one company offers distribution services for another company's product. Abbott Laboratories warehouses and delivers all of 3M's medical and surgical products to hospitals across the United States. Finally, one or more companies may join in special *pricing alliances,* as when hotel and rental car companies join forces to offer mutual price discounts.

Companies need to give careful thought to finding partners who might complement their strengths and offset their weaknesses. Well-managed alliances can have a huge impact on sales and profits. Corning, the $5-billion-a-year glass and ceramics maker, is renowned for making partnerships. It has derived half of its profits from joint ventures that apply its glass technology to various products in many countries, and even defines itself as a "network of organizations." That network includes German and Korean electronics giants, Siemens and Samsung, and Mexico's biggest glassmaker, Vitro. Another good example is AT&T and Sovintel, a Russian telephone company. The two joined forces to offer high-speed ISDN services for digitized voice, data, and video communication between the two countries. By joining together, the two telecommunications companies can offer new services for more business customers than either could do alone.[27]

---

[25]Thor Valdmanis, "Alliances Gain Favor over Risky Mergers," *USA Today,* February 4, 1999, p. 3B.

[26]Rosabeth Moss Kanter, "Why Collaborate?" *Executive Excellence,* April 1999, p. 8.

[27]Ibid.; and Kotler, *Marketing Management: Analysis, Planning, Implementation, and Control,* p. 82. For more on strategic alliances, see Peter Lorange and Johan Roos, *Strategic Alliances: Formation, Implementation and Evolution* (Cambridge, MA: Blackwell, 1992); Jordan D. Lewis, *Partnerships for Profit: Structuring and Managing Strategic Alliances* (New York: Free Press, 1990); and Gabor Gari, "Leveraging the Rewards of Strategic Alliances," *The Journal of Business Strategy,* April 1999, pp. 40–43.

CONNECTIONS WITH THE WORLD AROUND US

Beyond redefining their relationships with customers and partners, marketers are taking a fresh look at the ways in which they connect with the broader world around them. Here we look at trends toward increasing globalization, more concern for social environmental responsibility, and greater use of marketing by nonprofit and public-sector organizations.

Global Connections

In an increasingly smaller world, many marketers are now connected *globally* with their customers and marketing partners. The world economy has undergone radical change during the past two decades. Geographical and cultural distances have shrunk with the advent of jet planes, fax machines, global computer and telephone hookups, world television satellite broadcasts, and other technical advances. This has allowed companies to greatly expand their geographical market coverage, purchasing, and manufacturing. The result is a vastly more complex marketing environment for both companies and consumers.

Today, almost every company, large or small, is touched in some way by global competition—from the neighborhood florist that buys its flowers from Mexican nurseries to the U.S. electronics manufacturer that competes in its home markets with giant Japanese rivals; from the fledgling Internet retailer that finds itself receiving orders from all over the world to the large American consumer goods producer that introduces new products into emerging markets abroad.

American firms have been challenged at home by the skillful marketing of European and Asian multinationals. Companies such as Toyota, Siemens, Nestlé, Sony, and Samsung have often outperformed their U.S. competitors in American markets. Similarly, U.S. companies in a wide range of industries have found new opportunities abroad. Coca-Cola, General Motors, Exxon, IBM, General Electric, DuPont, Motorola, and dozens of other American companies have developed truly global operations, making and selling their products worldwide.

Today, companies are not only trying to sell more of their locally produced goods in international markets, they also are buying more components and supplies abroad. For example, Bill Blass, one of America's top fashion designers, may choose cloth woven from Australian wool with designs printed in Italy. He will design a dress and fax the drawing to a Hong Kong agent, who will place the order with a Chinese factory. Finished dresses will be air-freighted to New York, where they will be redistributed to department and specialty stores around the country.

Thus, managers in countries around the world are increasingly taking a global, not just local, view of the company's industry, competitors, and opportunities. They are asking: What is global marketing? How does it differ from domestic marketing? How do global competitors and forces affect our business? To what extent should we "go global"? Many companies are forming strategic alliances with foreign companies, even competitors, who serve as suppliers or marketing partners. Winning companies in the future may well be those that have built the best global networks.

Connections with Our Values and Social Responsibilities

Marketers are reexamining their connections with social values and responsibilities and with the very Earth that sustains us. As the worldwide consumerism and environmentalism movements mature, today's marketers are being called upon to take greater responsibility for the social and environmental impact of their actions. Corporate ethics and social responsibility have become hot topics in almost every business arena, from the corporate boardroom to the business school classroom. And few companies can ignore the renewed and very demanding environmental movement.

The social responsibility and environmental movements will place even stricter demands on companies in the future. Some companies resist these movements, budging only when forced by legislation or consumer outcries. More forward-looking companies, however, readily accept their responsibilities to the world around them. They view socially responsible actions as an opportunity to do well by doing good—to profit by serving the best long-run interests of their customers and communities. Some companies—such as Ben & Jerry's, Saturn, The Body Shop, and others—are practicing "caring capitalism" and distinguishing themselves by being more civic-minded and caring. They are building social responsibility and action into their company value and mission statements. For example, Ben & Jerry's mission statement challenges all employees, from top management to ice cream scoopers in each store, to include concern for individual and community welfare in their day-to-day decisions.[28]

[28]See Ben & Jerry's full mission statement online at www.benjerry.com. For more reading on environmentalism, see William S. Stavropoulos, "Environmentalism's Third Wave," *Executive Speeches,* August–September 1996, pp. 28–30; Stuart L. Hart, "Beyond Greening: Strategies for a Sustainable World," *Harvard Business Review,* January–February 1997, pp. 67–76; and Michael Lounsbury, "From Heresy to Dogma: An Institutional History of Corporate Environmentalism," *Administrative Science Quarterly,* March 1999, pp. 193–95. For more on marketing and social responsibility, see Daniel Kadlec, "The New World of Giving," *Time,* May 5, 1997, pp. 62–64; Heather Salerno, "From Selling Cars to Building Playgrounds," *Washington Post,* June 9, 1997, p. F11; and "Can Doing Good Be Good for Business?" *Fortune,* February 2, 1998, pp. 148G–48J.

Broadening Connections

More and more different kinds of organizations are using marketing to connect with customers and other important constituencies. In the past, marketing has been most widely applied in the for-profit business sector. In recent years, however, marketing also has become a major component in the strategies of many nonprofit organizations, such as colleges, hospitals, museums, symphony orchestras, and even churches. Consider the following examples:

Siskin Hospital, a rehabilitation facility in the southeastern United States, has developed a marketing Web site—**www.siskinrehab.org**. The purpose of the site is to position the hospital as a leader in the rehabilitation field. It provides information and education to the hospital's 14 distinct target audiences, ranging from current and potential patients to health care professionals, hospital staff, job seekers, and the general public. Visitors to the Web site can browse through an online newsletter to learn more about physical rehabilitation and Suskin's programs; review case histories of past patients and their successes; ask questions of the hospital's doctors, nurses, and therapists; and link to other information sources on the Web or in the hospital's "Patient's Library." Siskin regularly markets the Web site through events, specialty advertising items with the imprinted Web site address, and high-impact, direct-mail pieces sent to key prospective users. How has the effort paid off? The site receives more than 400 hits per day and averages 10 to 15 inquiries weekly from potential employees or individuals seeking information on specific rehabilitation-related conditions or treatment programs.[29]

At the Sausalito Presbyterian Church, an affluent congregation just across the Golden Gate Bridge from San Francisco, worshipers who'd rather watch football or go to the beach on Sunday morning do church on Saturday evening, at a rock and gospel music service called "Saturday Night Alive." What's particularly revealing about this gathering is the way it's advertised on the church's Web site, **www.SausalitoPresbyterian.com**. Saturday night worship, it seems, is very user-friendly. "Following the service," the Web page reads, "there is plenty of time to go to dinner, the movies, attend a party or other activities." It's a small but significant disclaimer, revealing how worship must now be marketed as just another diversion in the busy lives of folks in northern California. Church leaders across the nation are using computerized demographic studies and other sophisticated marketing techniques to fill their pews. "Mainline churches don't have to die," says church marketing consultant Richard Southern. "Anyone can learn these marketing and

Siskin Hospital's marketing Web site provides information and education to the 14 distinct target audiences, positioning the hospital as a leader in the rehabilitation field.

[29]Thomas G. Widmer and C. David Shepherd, "Developing a Hospital Web Site as a Marketing Tool: A Case Study," *Marketing Health Services,* Spring 1999, pp. 32–33.

outreach techniques. You don't have to change your theology or your political stance." Southern encourages "an essential . . . shift in the way church is done," putting the needs of potential "customers" before the needs of the institutional church. "Baby boomers think of churches like they think of supermarkets," Southern observes. "They want options, choices, and convenience. Imagine if Safeway was only open one hour a week, had only one product, and didn't explain it in English."[30]

Similarly, many private colleges, facing declining enrollments and rising costs, are using marketing to compete for students and funds. They are defining target markets, improving their communication and promotion, and responding better to student needs and wants. Many performing arts groups—even the Lyric Opera Company of Chicago, which has seasonal sellouts—face huge operating deficits that they must cover by more aggressive donor marketing. Finally, many long-standing nonprofit organizations—the YMCA, the Salvation Army, the Girl Scouts—have lost members and are now modernizing their missions and "products" to attract more members and donors.[31]

Even government agencies have shown an increased interest in marketing. For example, the U.S. Army has a marketing plan to attract recruits, and various government agencies are now designing *social marketing campaigns* to encourage energy conservation and concern for the environment or to discourage smoking, excessive drinking, and drug use. Even the once-stodgy U.S. Postal Service has developed innovative marketing to sell commemorative stamps, promote its priority mail services against those of its competitors, and lift its image. It has invested heavily in its "Fly Like an Eagle" image advertising campaign. Roxanne Symko, the USPS's manager of advertising and promotion, comments, "We want to position ourselves in a new light, as innovative and looking forward."[32]

Thus, it seems that every type of organization can connect through marketing. The continued growth of nonprofit and public-sector marketing presents new and exciting challenges for marketing managers.

> ## active example

Take a moment to consider what some American Internet firms have accomplished abroad.

THE NEW CONNECTED WORLD OF MARKETING

So, today, smart marketers of all kinds are taking advantage of new opportunities for connecting with their customers, their marketing partners, and the world around them. Table 1.1 compares the old marketing thinking to the new. The old marketing thinking saw marketing as little more than selling or advertising. It viewed marketing as customer acquisition rather than customer care. It emphasized trying to make a profit on each sale rather than trying to profit by managing customer lifetime value. It also concerned itself with trying to sell products rather than to understand, create, communicate, and deliver real value to customers.

Fortunately, this old marketing thinking is now giving way to newer ways of thinking. Today's smart marketing companies are improving their customer knowledge and customer connections. They are targeting profitable customers, then finding innovative ways to capture and keep these customers. They are forming more direct connections with customers and building lasting customer relationships. They are using more targeted media and integrating their marketing communications to deliver meaningful and consistent messages through every customer contact. They are employing more technologies such as videoconferencing, sales automation software, and the Internet, intranets, and

[30]Richard Cimino and Don Lattin, "Choosing My Religion," *American Demographics,* April 1999, pp. 60–65.

[31]For other examples, and for a good review of nonprofit marketing, see Philip Kotler and Alan R. Andreasen, *Strategic Marketing for Nonprofit Organizations,* 5th ed. (Upper Saddle River, NJ: Prentice Hall, 1996); Philip Kotler and Karen Fox, *Strategic Marketing for Educational Institutions* (Upper Saddle River, NJ: Prentice Hall, 1995); Norman Shawchuck, Philip Kotler, Bruce Wren, and Gustave Rath, *Marketing for Congregations: Choosing to Serve People More Effectively* (Nashville, TN: Abingdon Press, 1993); William P. Ryan, "The New Landscape for Nonprofits," *Harvard Business Review,* January–February 1999, pp. 127–36; Denise Nitterhouse, "Nonprofit and Social Marketing," *Nonprofit Management and Leadership,* Spring 1999, pp. 323–28; and Diane Bradley, "Uncle Sam Wants You . . . to Have Fun," *Business Week,* February 21, 2000, pp. 98–101.

[32]Ira Teinowitz, "Postal Service Tries Image of Innovation," *Advertising Age,* October 1998, p. 6.

TABLE 1.1	Marketing Connections in Transition
The Old Marketing Thinking	**The New Marketing Thinking**
Connections with Customers	
Be sales and product centered	Be market and customer centered
Practice mass marketing	Target selected market segments or individuals
Focus on products and sales	Focus on customer satisfaction and value
Make sales to customers	Develop customer relationships
Get new customers	Keep old customers
Grow share of market	Grow share of customer
Serve any customer	Serve profitable customers, "fire" losing ones
Communicate through mass media	Connect with customers directly
Make standardized products	Develop customized products
Connections with Marketing Partners	
Leave customer satisfaction and value to sales and marketing	Enlist all departments in the cause of customer satisfaction and value
Go it alone	Partner with other firms
Connections with the World Around Us	
Market locally	Market locally *and* globally
Assume profit responsibility	Assume social and environmental responsibility
Market for profits	Market for nonprofits
Conduct commerce in market*places*	Conduct e-commerce in market*spaces*

extranets. They see their suppliers and distributors as partners, not adversaries. In sum, they are forming new kinds of connections for delivering superior value to their customers.

We will explore all of these developments in more detail in future pages. For now, we must recognize that marketing will continue to change dramatically as we move into the twenty-first century. The new millennium offers many exciting opportunities for forward-thinking marketers.

active concept check <

Now let's take a moment to test your knowledge of what you've just read.

 Chapter Wrap-Up

Now that you've reached the end of the chapter, you may wish to explore the concepts you've been reading about in greater detail, or test yourself to see how well you've comprehended the material. In the box below you'll find a number of links. Click on any one of these links to find additional chapter resources.

> end-of-chapter resources

- **Review of Concept Connections**
- **Practice Quiz**
- **Issues for Discussion**
- **Key Terms**
- **Marketing Applications**
- **Internet Connections**
- **Company Case**

CHAPTER 2

Strategic Planning and the Marketing Process

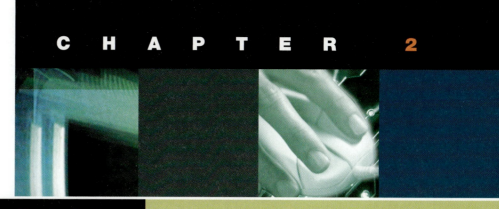

> What's Ahead

For more than 25 years, Intel has dominated the microprocessor market for personal computers. Its sales and profits have soared accordingly. In the little more than a dozen years since IBM introduced its first PCs based on Intel's 8088 microprocessor, the chip giant's sales have jumped more than twentyfold to over $25 billion. Its share of the microprocessor market now tops 90 percent, turning competitors such as Advanced Micro Devices (AMD) and Cyrix into little more than also-rans. During the past 10 years, with gross margins hovering at around 60 percent, Intel's average annual return has been an astounding 36 percent.

Intel's stunning success results from strong strategic planning and its relentless dedication to a simple marketing strategy: Provide the most value and satisfaction to customers through product leadership. Some companies deliver superior value through convenience and low prices; others by coddling their customers and tailoring products to meet the special needs of precisely defined market niches. In contrast, Intel's strong connection with consumers rests on delivering superior value by creating a continuous stream of leading-edge products. Then, it communicates its superior value directly to final buyers. The result is intense customer loyalty and preference, both from the computer and software producers who add ever more features that require increasingly brawny microprocessors and from final PC buyers who want their PCs to do ever more cool things.

Intel's microprocessors are true wonders of modern technology. Intel invests heavily to develop state-of-the-art products and bring them quickly to marketlast year alone it spent a whopping $5 billion on R&D and capital spending. The result is a rapid succession of ever better

Don't just get onto the Internet, get into it.

chips that no competitor can match. For example, less than a decade ago, we marveled at Intel's i386 microprocessors, which contained one-quarter-million transistors and ran at clock speeds approaching 20 megahertz. However, Intel's next generation Pentium series microprocessors contained more than 5 million transistors and ran at speeds exceeding 450 megahertz. Its current Pentium III processor will soon break the 1 gigahertz (1,000 megahertz) mark. Incredibly, the Intel microprocessors of 2011 will pack a cool *billion* transistors and will blaze along at clock speeds of 10 gigahertz (or 10,000 megahertz).

In fact, Intel has innovated at such a torrid pace that its microprocessors have at times outpaced market needs and capabilities. For example, in the early 1990s, the industry's existing bus systemthe internal network that directs the flow of electrons within a computer—served up data at a far slower rate than Intel's new Pentium could handle. Why should producers buy the faster chips if existing PC architecture couldn't take advantage of them? Instead of waiting for PC makers to act, Intel quickly designed a new bus called PCI and shared it with computer makers. The PCI became the standard bus on PCs, paving the way for Intel's faster chips.

Intel's growth depends on increasing the demand for microprocessors, which in turn depends on growth in PC applications and sales. Thus, moving into the new millennium, Intel has taken its marketing strategy a step further. Rather than sitting back and relying on others to create new market applications requiring its increasingly powerful microprocessors, it now develops such applications itself. According to one account, to ensure continued growth in the demand for its microprocessors, Intel has set out "to make the PC the central appliance in our lives. In [Intel's] vision, we will use PCs to watch TV, to play complex games on the Internet, to store and edit family photos, to manage the appliances in our homes, and to stay in regular video contact with our family, friends, and co-workers." Of course, at the heart of all of these applications will be the latest Intel-powered PC.

To realize this vision, Intel has invested heavily in market development. For example, it set up the Intel Architecture Labs (IAL), where 600 employees work to expand the market for all PC-related products, not just Intel products. One IAL project involves finding ways to help popularize Internet telephony, through which PC owners can make long-distance voice phone calls over the Internet. IAL helped develop better technology for making such calls, worked with the Internet industry to develop telephony standards, and gave away Intel software supporting the standard. Next, Intel will promote technologies and software for Internet videophones. It expects that PC makers will soon build these telephony functions into their products. The result: More people will buy new PCs containing powerful Intel microprocessors.

In recent years, Intel has also invested in dozens of small companies working on projects that might spark demand for the processing power that only Intel can supply. The company's widely varied investments include the Palace, which creates virtual Web communities; Citrix

Systems, which makes software to link Internet users; biztravel.com, an online travel service; and CyberCash, which is developing an online payment system. Another Intel acquisition, OnLive! Technologies, is an Internet chat room program that offers online interactions through 3-D characters. "The next killer app," says the former head of Intel's Internet and Communications Group, "is use of the Internet for online [socializing]." He sees the day when individuals can use computers in their own homes to watch a ball game or movie as a group, making comments through their online 3-D characters as they watch. Again, such connections will require far more computing power than today's PCs afford, and new Intel chips will provide the needed power.

Intel's marketing strategy goes far beyond superior products and market development. In mid-1991, Intel began strengthening its direct connections with consumers by launching the "Intel Inside" advertising campaign. Traditionally, chip companies like Intel had marketed only to the manufacturers who buy chips directly. But as long as microprocessors remained anonymous little lumps hidden inside a user's computer, Intel remained at the mercy of the clone makers and other competitors. The groundbreaking "Intel Inside" campaign appeals directly to final computer buyersIntel's customers' customers. Brand-awareness ads—such as those in the current "Bunny People" campaign—create brand personality and convince PC buyers that Intel microprocessors really are superior. Intel also subsidizes ads by PC manufacturers that include the "Intel Inside" logo. Over the years, the hundreds of millions of dollars invested in the "Intel Inside" campaign have created strong brand preference for Intel chips among final buyers. This, in turn, has made Intel's chips more attractive to computer manufacturers.

Looking ahead, Intel must plan its strategy carefully. Its continued torrid growth and industry dominance will depend on its ability to produce a steady flow of state-of-the-art chips for markets ranging from inexpensive home computers to high-end servers. It will have to create irresistible new applications that will lure new consumers into PC ownership and encourage current owners to trade up their machines. Intel's top executives don't foresee any slowing of the pace. Says Intel President Craig Barrett, "We picture ourselves going down the road at 120 miles an hour. Somewhere there's going to be a brick wall, . . . but our view is that it's better to run into the wall than to anticipate it and fall short."[1]

> objectives

Before you begin, take a moment to familiarize yourself with the key objectives of this chapter.

> gearing up

Before we begin our exploration this chapter, take a short warm-up test to see what you know about this topic.

[1]Quotes from David Kirkpatrick, "Intel's Amazing Profit Machine,"*Fortune,* February 17, 1997, pp. 60–72; and Damon Darlin, "Intel's Palace," *Forbes,* September 9, 1996, pp. 42–43. Also see Andy Reinhardt, "Pentium: The Next Generation," *Business Week,* May 12, 1997, pp. 42–43; "The Fortune 500 Largest Firms," *Fortune,* April 22, 1998, pp. F1–F2; Brent Schlender, "The New Man Inside Intel," *Fortune,* May 11, 1998, pp. 161–62; Lawrence M. Fisher, "Sales of High-End Chips Help Intel Beat Estimates," *New York Times,* January 13, 1999; and "Intel Breaks 1 GHz, Presents Pentium III," *Semiconductor International,* April 1999, p. 22.

All companies must look ahead and develop long-term strategies to meet the changing conditions in their industries. Each company must find the game plan that makes the most sense given its specific situation, opportunities, objectives, and resources. The hard task of selecting an overall company strategy for long-run survival and growth is called *strategic planning.*

In this chapter, we look first at the organization's overall strategic planning. Next, we discuss marketing's role in the organization as it is defined by the overall strategic plan. Finally, we explain the marketing management process—the process that marketers undertake to carry out their role in the organization.

> Strategic Planning

Many companies operate without formal plans. In new companies, managers are sometimes so busy they have no time for planning. In small companies, managers sometimes think that only large corporations need formal planning. In mature companies, many managers argue that they have done well without formal planning and that therefore it cannot be too important. They may resist taking the time to prepare a written plan. They may argue that the marketplace changes too quickly for a plan to be useful, that it would end up collecting dust.

Granted, planning is not much fun, and it takes time away from doing. Yet companies must plan. As someone said, "If you fail to plan, you are planning to fail."[2] Formal planning can yield many benefits for all types of companies, large and small, new and mature.

The process of planning may be as important as the plans that emerge. Planning encourages management to think systematically about what has happened, what is happening, and what might happen. It forces the company to sharpen its objectives and policies, leads to better coordination of company efforts, and provides clearer performance standards for control. The argument that planning is less useful in a fast-changing environment makes little sense. In fact, the opposite is true: Sound planning helps the company to anticipate and respond quickly to changes, and to prepare better for sudden developments. Thus planning turns out to be an essential part of good management.

Companies usually prepare annual plans, long-range plans, and strategic plans. The annual and long-range plans deal with the company's current businesses and how to keep them going. In contrast, the strategic plan involves adapting the firm to take advantage of opportunities in its constantly changing environment. We define **strategic planning** as the process of developing and maintaining a strategic fit between the organization's goals and capabilities and its changing marketing opportunities.

Strategic planning sets the stage for the rest of the planning in the firm. It relies on defining a clear company mission, setting supporting company objectives, designing a sound business portfolio, and coordinating functional strategies (see Figure 2.1). At the corporate level, the company first defines its overall purpose and mission. This mission then is turned into detailed supporting objectives that guide the whole company. Next, headquarters decides what portfolio of businesses and products is best for the company and how much support to give each one. In turn, each business and product unit must develop detailed marketing and other departmental plans that support the companywide plan. Thus, marketing planning occurs at the business unit, product, and market levels. It supports company strategic planning with more detailed planning for specific marketing opportunities.[3]

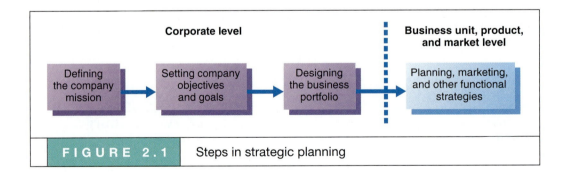

| FIGURE 2.1 | Steps in strategic planning |

[2]See Philip Kotler, *Kotler on Marketing* (New York: Free Press, 1999), pp. 165–66.

[3]For a more detailed discussion of corporate- and business-level strategic planning as they apply to marketing, see Philip Kotler, *Marketing Management: Analysis, Planning, Implementation, and Control,* 10th ed. (Upper Saddle River, NJ: Prentice Hall, 2000), chap. 3.

1 We've been on a roll for 67 years.

2 Now we've popped up with another big idea. It's an ingenious dispensing system that pops up strips of tape – pre-cut, one at a time, right into your hand. New Scotch™ Pop-up Tape Strips make gift wrapping easier, especially when you've got your hands full. We're making tape even more handy, because we make the leap *from need to...*

3M *Innovation*

© 3M 1997 78-6900-8329-6(1171)ii   For more information, call 1-800-3M-HELPS, or Internet: http://www.3M.com

> Company mission: 3M does more than just make adhesives, scientific equipment, health care, and communications products. It solves people's problems by putting innovation to work for them.

DEFINING THE COMPANY'S BUSINESS AND MISSION

An organization exists to accomplish something. At first, it has a clear purpose or mission, but over time its mission may become unclear as the organization grows, adds new products and markets, or faces new conditions in the environment. When management senses that the organization is drifting, it must renew its search for purpose. It is time to ask: What is our business? Who is the customer? What do consumers value? What should our business be? These simple-sounding questions are among the most difficult the company will ever have to answer. Successful companies continuously raise these questions and answer them carefully and completely.

Many organizations develop formal mission statements that answer these questions. A **mission statement** is a statement of the organization's purpose—what it wants to accomplish in the larger environment. A clear mission statement acts as an "invisible hand" that guides people in the organization.

> **video example**
>
> **Before you can develop a mission, you need a vision. Consider the challenge of articulating one.**

Traditionally companies have defined their businesses in product terms ("We manufacture furniture") or in technological terms ("We are a chemical-processing firm"). But mission statements should be *market oriented*. Products and technologies eventually become outdated, but basic market needs may last forever. A market-oriented mission statement defines the business in terms of satisfying basic customer needs. For example, AT&T is in the communications business, not the telephone business. 3M does more than just make adhesives, scientific equipment, and health care products. It solves people's problems by putting innovation to work for them. Southwest Airlines sees itself as providing not just air travel but total customer service. Its mission: "The mission of Southwest Airlines is dedication to the highest quality of customer service delivered with a sense of warmth, friendliness, individual pride, and company spirit." Likewise, Amazon.com's mission isn't simply to sell books, CDs, videos, toys, and consumer electronics. Instead, it wants to "transform Internet buy-

TABLE 2.1	Market-Oriented Business Definitions	
Company	**Product-Oriented Definition**	**Market-Oriented Definition**
Revlon	We make cosmetics.	We sell lifestyle and self-expression; success and status; memories, hopes, and dreams.
Disney	We run theme parks.	We create fantasies—a place where America still works the way it's supposed to.
Wal-Mart	We run discount stores.	We deliver value through low prices to Middle Americans.
Xerox	We make copying, fax, and other office machines.	We make businesses more productive by helping them scan, store, retrieve, revise, distribute, print, and publish documents.
O. M. Scott	We sell grass seed and fertilizer.	We deliver green, healthy-looking yards.
Home Depot	We sell tools and home repair and improvement items.	We provide advice and solutions that transform ham-handed homeowners into Mr. and Mrs. Fixits.
Amazon.com	We sell books, videos, CDs, toys, consumer electronics, home improvement items, and other products.	We make the Internet buying consumer experience fast, easy, and enjoyable— we're the place where you can find and discover anything you want to buy online.
Ritz-Carlton Hotels	We rent rooms.	We create the Ritz-Carlton experience—one which enlivens the senses, instills well-being, and fulfills even the unexpressed wishes and needs of our guests.

ing into the fastest, easiest, and most enjoyable shopping experience possible—to be the place where you can find and discover anything you want to buy online."[4] Table 2.1 provides several other examples of product-oriented versus market-oriented business definitions.

Management should avoid making its mission too narrow or too broad. A pencil manufacturer that says it is in the communication equipment business is stating its mission too broadly. Missions should be *realistic*. Singapore Airlines would be deluding itself if it adopted the mission to become the world's largest airline. Missions should also be *specific*. Many mission statements are written for public relations purposes and lack specific, workable guidelines. The statement "We want to become the leading company in this industry by producing the highest-quality products with the best service at the lowest prices" sounds good, but it is full of generalities and contradictions. Celestial Seasonings' mission statement is very specific: "Our mission is to grow and dominate the U.S. specialty tea market by exceeding consumer expectations with: The best tasting, 100 percent natural hot and iced teas, packaged with Celestial art and philosophy, creating the most valued tea experience. . . ."[5]

Missions should fit the *market environment*. The Girl Scouts of America would not recruit successfully in today's environment with their former mission: "to prepare young girls for motherhood and wifely duties." The organization should base its mission on its *distinctive competencies*. McDonald's could probably enter the solar energy business, but that would not take advantage of its core competence—providing low-cost food and fast service to large groups of customers.

Finally, mission statements should be *motivating*. A company's mission should not be stated as making more sales or profits—profits are only a reward for undertaking a useful activity. A company's employees need to feel that their work is significant and that it contributes to people's lives. Contrast the missions of IBM and Microsoft. When IBM sales were $50 billion, then-President John Akers said that IBM's mission was to become a $100 billion company by the end of the century. Meanwhile,

---

[4]The preceding examples are from Romauld A. Stone, "Mission Statements Revisited," *SAM Advanced Management Journal,* Winter 1996, pp. 31–37; Rhymer Rigby, "Mission Statements," *Management Today,* March 1998, pp. 56–58; and "About Amazon.com," accessed online at www.amazon.com, September 1999.

[5]Stone, "Mission Statements Revisited," p. 33.

Microsoft's long-term mission has been IAYF—"information at your fingertips"—to put information at the fingertips of every person. Microsoft's mission is much more motivating than is IBM's.[6]

One study found that "visionary companies" set a purpose beyond making money. For example, Walt Disney Company's aim is "making people happy." But even though profits may not be part of these companies' mission statements, they are the inevitable result. The study showed that 18 visionary companies outperformed other companies in the stock market by more than 6 to 1 over the period from 1926 to 1990.[7]

> active example

Consider the mission statement of one of today's most notable companies.

SETTING COMPANY OBJECTIVES AND GOALS

The company's mission needs to be turned into detailed supporting objectives for each level of management. Each manager should have objectives and be responsible for reaching them. For example, Monsanto operates in many businesses, including agriculture, pharmaceuticals, and food products. The company defines its mission as one of helping to feed the world's exploding population while at the same time sustaining the environment. This mission leads to a hierarchy of objectives, including business objectives and marketing objectives. Monsanto's overall objective is to create environmentally better products and get them to market faster at lower costs. For its part, the agricultural division's objective is to increase agricultural productivity and reduce chemical pollution by researching new pest-and disease-resistant crops that produce higher yields without chemical spraying. But research is expensive and requires improved profits to plow back into research programs. So improving profits becomes another major business objective. Profits can be improved by increasing sales or reducing costs. Sales can be increased by improving the company's share of the U.S. market, by

Monsanto defines its mission as one of "food, health, hope"—of helping to feed the world's exploding population while at the same time sustaining the environment. This mission leads to specific business and marketing objectives.

---

[6]See Bradley Johnson, "Bill Gates' Vision of Microsoft in Every Home," *Advertising Age,* December 19, 1994, pp. 14–15. For more on mission statements, see J. W. Graham and W. C. Havlick, *Mission Statements: A Guide to the Corporate and Nonprofit Sectors* (New York: Garland Publishing, 1994); P. Jones and L. Kahaner, *Say It and Live It: The 50 Corporate Mission Statements That Hit the Mark* (New York: Doubleday, 1995); Thomas A. Stewart, "A Refreshing Change: Vision Statements That Make Sense," *Fortune,* September 30, 1996, pp. 195–96; and Christopher K. Bart, "Making Mission Statements Count," *CA Magazine,* March 1999, pp. 37–38.

[7]Gilbert Fuchsberg, " 'Visioning' Mission Becomes Its Own Mission," *Wall Street Journal,* January 7, 1994, pp. B1, 3. Also see Sal Marino, "Where There Is No Visionary, Companies Falter," *Industry Week,* March 15, 1999, p. 20.

entering new foreign markets, or both. These goals then become the company's current marketing objectives.[8]

Marketing strategies must be developed to support these marketing objectives. To increase its U.S. market share, Monsanto might increase its product's availability and promotion. To enter new foreign markets, the company may cut prices and target large farms abroad. These are its broad marketing strategies. Each broad marketing strategy must then be defined in greater detail. For example, increasing the product's promotion may require more salespeople and more advertising; if so, both requirements will have to be spelled out. In this way, the firm's mission is translated into a set of objectives for the current period. The objectives should be as specific as possible. The objective to "increase our market share" is not as useful as the objective to "increase our market share to 15 percent by the end of the second year."

active concept check   <

Now let's take a moment to test your knowledge of what you've just read.

> Designing the Business Portfolio

Guided by the company's mission statement and objectives, management now must plan its **business portfolio**—the collection of businesses and products that make up the company. The best business portfolio is the one that best fits the company's strengths and weaknesses to opportunities in the environment. The company must (1) analyze its *current* business portfolio and decide which businesses should receive more, less, or no investment; and (2) develop growth strategies for adding *new* products or businesses to the portfolio.[9]

ANALYZING THE CURRENT BUSINESS PORTFOLIO

The major activity in strategic planning is business **portfolio analysis,** whereby management evaluates the businesses making up the company. The company will want to put strong resources into its more profitable businesses and phase down or drop its weaker ones. For example, in recent years, Dial Corporation has strengthened its portfolio by selling off its less attractive businesses: bus line (Greyhound), knitting supplies, meatpacking, and computer leasing businesses. At the same time, it invested more heavily in its consumer products (Dial soap, Armour Star meats, Purex laundry products, and others) and services (Premier Cruise Lines, Dobbs airport services).

Management's first step is to identify the key businesses making up the company. These can be called the strategic business units. A **strategic business unit (SBU)** is a unit of the company that has a separate mission and objectives and that can be planned independently from other company businesses. An SBU can be a company division, a product line within a division, or sometimes a single product or brand.

The next step in business portfolio analysis calls for management to assess the attractiveness of its various SBUs and decide how much support each deserves. In some companies, this is done informally. Management looks at the company's collection of businesses or products and uses judgment to decide how much each SBU should contribute and receive. Other companies use formal portfolio-planning methods.

The purpose of strategic planning is to find ways in which the company can best use its strengths to take advantage of attractive opportunities in the environment. So most standard portfolio-analysis methods evaluate SBUs on two important dimensions—the attractiveness of the SBU's market or industry and the strength of the SBU's position in that market or industry. The best-known portfolio-planning method was developed by the Boston Consulting Group, a leading management consulting firm.

The Boston Consulting Group Approach

Using the Boston Consulting Group (BCG) approach, a company classifies all its SBUs according to the **growth-share matrix** shown in Figure 2.2. On the vertical axis, *market growth rate* provides a

---

[8]See Linda Grant, "Monsanto's Bet: There's Gold in Going Green," *Fortune,* April 14, 1997, pp. 116–18; Richard A. Melcher and Amy Barrett, "Fields of Genes," *Business Week,* April 12, 1999, p. 62; and David Stipp, "Is Monsanto's Biotech Worth Less Than a Hill of Beans?" *Fortune,* February 21, 2000, pp. 157–60.

[9]For an interesting discussion of assessing the business portfolio, see John O. Whitney, "Strategic Renewal of Business Units," *Harvard Business Review,* July–August 1996, pp. 84–98.

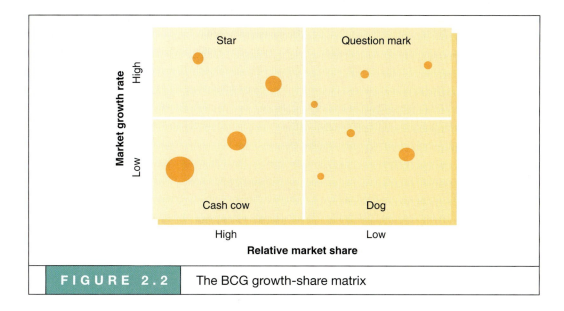

Star	**Question mark**
Cash cow	**Dog**

Market growth rate: High / Low

Relative market share: High / Low

FIGURE 2.2	The BCG growth-share matrix

measure of market attractiveness. On the horizontal axis, *relative market share* serves as a measure of company strength in the market. By dividing the growth-share matrix as indicated, four types of SBUs can be distinguished:

Stars: Stars are high-growth, high-share businesses or products. They often need heavy investment to finance their rapid growth. Eventually their growth will slow down, and they will turn into cash cows.

Cash cows: Cash cows are low-growth, high-share businesses or products. These established and successful SBUs need less investment to hold their market share. Thus, they produce a lot of cash that the company uses to pay its bills and to support other SBUs that need investment.

Question marks: Question marks are low-share business units in high-growth markets. They require a lot of cash to hold their share, let alone increase it. Management has to think hard about which question marks it should try to build into stars and which should be phased out.

Dogs: Dogs are low-growth, low-share businesses and products. They may generate enough cash to maintain themselves but do not promise to be large sources of cash.

The ten circles in the growth-share matrix represent a company's ten current SBUs. The company has two stars, two cash cows, three question marks, and three dogs. The areas of the circles are proportional to the SBU's dollar sales. This company is in fair shape, although not in good shape. It wants to invest in the more promising question marks to make them stars and to maintain the stars so that they will become cash cows as their markets mature. Fortunately, it has two good-sized cash cows whose income helps finance the company's question marks, stars, and dogs. The company should take some decisive action concerning its dogs and its question marks. The picture would be worse if the company had no stars, if it had too many dogs, or if it had only one weak cash cow.

Once it has classified its SBUs, the company must determine what role each will play in the future. One of four strategies can be pursued for each SBU. The company can invest more in the business unit in order to *build* its share. Or it can invest just enough to *hold* the SBU's share at the current level. It can *harvest* the SBU, milking its short-term cash flow regardless of the long-term effect. Finally, the company can *divest* the SBU by selling it or phasing it out and using the resources elsewhere.

As time passes, SBUs change their positions in the growth-share matrix. Each SBU has a life cycle. Many SBUs start out as question marks and move into the star category if they succeed. They later become cash cows as market growth falls, then finally die off or turn into dogs toward the end of their life cycle. The company needs to add new products and units continuously so that some of them will become stars and, eventually, cash cows that will help finance other SBUs.

The General Electric Approach

General Electric introduced a comprehensive portfolio planning tool called a *strategic business-planning grid* (see Figure 2.3). Like the BCG approach, it uses a matrix with two dimensions—one representing industry attractiveness (the vertical axis) and one representing company strength in the industry (the horizontal axis). The best businesses are those located in highly attractive industries where the company has high business strength.

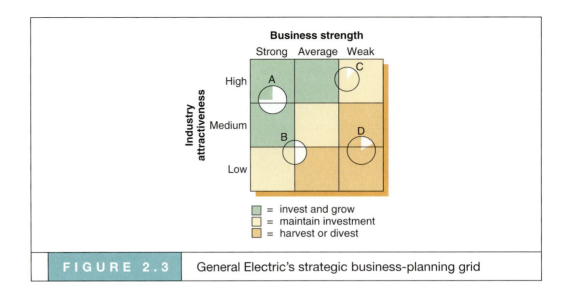

| FIGURE 2.3 | General Electric's strategic business-planning grid |

The GE approach considers many factors besides market growth rate as part of industry attractiveness. It uses an industry attractiveness index made up of market size, market growth rate, industry profit margin, amount of competition, seasonality and cyclicity of demand, and industry cost structure. Each of these factors is rated and combined in an index of industry attractiveness. For our purposes, an industry's attractiveness will be described as high, medium, or low. As an example, Kraft has identified numerous highly attractive industries—natural foods, specialty frozen foods, physical fitness products, and others. It has withdrawn from less attractive industries such as bulk oils and cardboard packaging.

For *business strength,* the GE approach again uses an index rather than a simple measure of relative market share. The business strength index includes factors such as the company's relative market share, price competitiveness, product quality, customer and market knowledge, sales effectiveness, and geographic advantages. These factors are rated and combined in an index of business strength, which can be described as strong, average, or weak. Thus, Kraft has substantial business strength in food and related industries but is relatively weak in the home appliances industry.

The grid is divided into three zones. The green cells at the upper left include the strong SBUs in which the company should invest and grow. The yellow diagonal cells contain SBUs that are medium in overall attractiveness. The company should maintain its level of investment in these SBUs. The three orange cells at the lower right indicate SBUs that are low in overall attractiveness. The company should give serious thought to harvesting or divesting these SBUs.

The circles represent four company SBUs; the areas of the circles are proportional to the relative sizes of the industries in which these SBUs compete. The pie slices within the circles represent each SBU's market share. Thus, circle A represents a company SBU with a 75 percent market share in a good-size, highly attractive industry in which the company has strong business strength. Circle B represents an SBU that has a 50 percent market share, but the industry is not very attractive. Circles C and D represent two other company SBUs in industries where the company has small market shares and not much business strength. Altogether, the company should build A, maintain B, and make some hard decisions about what to do with C and D.

Management would also plot the projected positions of the SBUs with and without changes in strategies. By comparing current and projected business grids, management can identify the major strategic issues and opportunities it faces.

Problems with Matrix Approaches

The BCG and other formal methods revolutionized strategic planning. However, such approaches have limitations. They can be difficult, time-consuming, and costly to implement. Management may find it difficult to define SBUs and measure market share and growth. In addition, these approaches focus on classifying *current* businesses but provide little advice for *future* planning. Management must still rely on its own judgment to set the business objectives for each SBU, to determine what resources each will be given, and to figure out which new businesses should be added.

Formal planning approaches can also lead the company to place too much emphasis on market-share growth or growth through entry into attractive new markets. Using these approaches, many companies plunged into unrelated and new high-growth businesses that they did not know how to manage—with very bad results. At the same time, these companies were often too quick to abandon, sell, or milk to death their healthy mature businesses. As a result, many companies that diversified too broadly in the past now are narrowing their focus and getting back to the basics of serving one or a few industries that they know best.

Despite such problems, and although many companies have dropped formal matrix methods in favor of more customized approaches that are better suited to their situations, most companies remain firmly committed to strategic planning. During the 1970s, many companies embraced high-level corporate strategy planning as a kind of magical path to growth and profits. By the 1980s, however, such strategic planning took a backseat to cost and efficiency concerns, as companies struggled to become more competitive through improved quality, restructuring, downsizing, and reengineering. Recently, strategic planning has made a strong comeback. However, unlike former strategic-planning efforts, which rested mostly in the hands of senior managers, today's strategic planning has been decentralized. Increasingly, companies are moving responsibility for strategic planning out of company headquarters and placing it in the hands of cross-functional teams of line and staff managers who are close to their markets. Some teams even include customers and suppliers in their strategic-planning processes.[10]

Such analysis is no cure-all for finding the best strategy. But it can help management to understand the company's overall situation, to see how each business or product contributes, to assign resources to its businesses, and to orient the company for future success. When used properly, strategic planning is just one important aspect of overall strategic management, a way of thinking about how to manage a business.

DEVELOPING GROWTH STRATEGIES IN THE AGE OF CONNECTEDNESS

Beyond evaluating current businesses, designing the business portfolio involves finding businesses and products the company should consider in the future. Companies need growth if they are to compete more effectively, satisfy their stakeholders, and attract top talent. "Growth is pure oxygen," states one executive. "It creates a vital, enthusiastic corporation where people see genuine opportunity. . . . In that way, growth is more than our single most important financial driver; it's an essential part of our corporate culture." At the same time, a firm must be careful not to make growth itself an objective. The company's objective must be "profitable growth."

Marketing has the main responsibility for achieving profitable growth for the company. Marketing must identify, evaluate, and select market opportunities and lay down strategies for capturing them. One useful device for identifying growth opportunities is the **product–market expansion grid,** shown in Figure 2.4.[11] We apply it here to Starbucks.

First, Starbucks management might consider whether the company can achieve deeper **market penetration**—making more sales to current customers without changing its products. It might add new stores in current market areas to make it easier for more customers to visit. Improvements in advertising, prices, service, menu selection, or store design might encourage customers to stop by more often or to buy more during each visit. For example, Starbucks recently began adapting its menu to local tastes around the country.

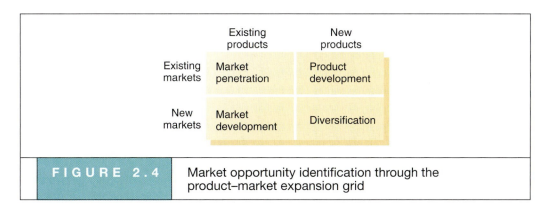

	Existing products	New products
Existing markets	Market penetration	Product development
New markets	Market development	Diversification

FIGURE 2.4   Market opportunity identification through the product–market expansion grid

[10]See John A. Byrne, "Strategic Planning," *Business Week,* August 26, 1996, pp. 46–51; Pete Bogda, "Fifteen Years Later, the Return of 'Strategy,'" *Brandweek,* February 1997, p. 18; and Diane Sanchez, "Now That's Customer Focus," *Sales & Marketing Management,* April 1998, p. 24. Also see Nryan W. Barry, "A Beginner's Guide to Strategic Planning," *The Futurist,* April 1998, pp. 33–36; and Ian Wilson, "Strategic Planning for the Millennium: Resolving the Dilemma," *Long Range Planning,* August 1998, pp. 507–13.

[11]H. Igor Ansoff, "Strategies for Diversification," *Harvard Business Review,* September–October 1957, pp. 113–24. Also see Kotler, *Kotler on Marketing,* pp. 46–48.

> In the South, where customers tend to come later in the day and linger for a bit, [such tailoring] meant adding more appealing dessert offerings, as well as designing larger, more comfortable locations. [In Atlanta, Starbucks] opened bigger stores with such amenities as couches and outdoor tables, so that people would feel comfortable hanging out, especially in the evening. . . . "Building on its Atlanta experience, Starbucks is tailoring its stores to local tastes around the country. That's why you find café au lait as well as toasted items in New Orleans, neither of which is available elsewhere in the country. (Bagel sales in New Orleans tripled once Starbucks began toasting them.) Or why coffee cake is featured in the Northeast, where it's more popular.[12]

Basically, Starbucks would like to increase patronage by current customers and attract competitors' customers to Starbucks shops.

Second, Starbucks management might consider possibilities for **market development**—identifying and developing new markets for its current products. For instance, managers could review new *demographic markets*—such as senior consumers or ethnic groups—to see if new groups could be encouraged to visit Starbucks coffee shops for the first time or to buy more from them. Managers also could review new *geographical markets*. Starbucks is now expanding swiftly into new U.S. markets, especially in the Southeast and Southwest. It is also developing its international markets, with stores popping up rapidly in Asia, Europe, and Australia.

Third, management could consider **product development**—offering modified or new products to current markets. For example, Starbucks is increasing its food offerings in an effort to bring customers into its stores during the lunch and dinner hours and to increase the amount of the average customer's sales ticket. The company is also partnering with other firms to sell coffee in supermarkets and to extend its brand to new products, such as coffee ice cream (with Breyer's) and bottled Frappuccino drinks (with PepsiCo).

Fourth, Starbucks might consider **diversification.** It could start up or buy businesses outside of its current products and markets. For example, Starbucks is testing two new restaurant concepts—Café Starbucks and Circadia—in an effort to offer new formats to related but new markets. In a more extreme diversification, Starbucks might consider leveraging its strong brand name by making and marketing a line of branded casual clothing consistent with the "Starbucks experience." However, this would probably be unwise. Companies that diversify too broadly into unfamiliar products or industries can lose their market focus, something that some critics are already concerned about with Starbucks.

active exercise

Consider how one prominent company is using technology to grow its customer base.

PLANNING CROSS-FUNCTIONAL STRATEGIES

The company's strategic plan establishes what kinds of businesses the company will be in and its objectives for each. Then, within each business unit more detailed planning must take place. The major functional departments in each unit—marketing, finance, accounting, purchasing, manufacturing, information systems, human resources, and others—must work together to accomplish strategic objectives.

Marketing's Role in Strategic Planning

There is much overlap between overall company strategy and marketing strategy. Marketing looks at consumer needs and the company's ability to satisfy them; these same factors guide the company's overall mission and objectives.

Marketing plays a key role in the company's strategic planning in several ways. First, marketing provides a guiding *philosophy*—the marketing concept—that suggests company strategy should revolve around serving the needs of important consumer groups. Second, marketing provides *inputs* to strategic planners by helping to identify attractive market opportunities and by assessing the firm's potential to take advantage of them. Finally, within individual business units, marketing designs *strategies* for reaching the unit's objectives. Once the unit's objectives are set, marketing's task is to carry them out profitably.

---

[12]Nelson D. Schwartz, "Still Perking After All These Years," *Fortune,* May 24, 1999, pp. 203–10.

Marketing and the Other Business Functions

Marketers play an important role in delivering customer value and satisfaction. However, as we noted in chapter 1, marketing cannot do this alone. Because customer value and satisfaction are affected by the performance of other functions, *all* departments must work together to deliver superior value and satisfaction. Marketing plays an integrative role to help ensure that all departments work together toward this goal.

Cross-Functional Conflict

Each business function has a different view of which publics and activities are most important. Operations focuses on suppliers and production; finance is concerned with stockholders and sound investment; marketing emphasizes consumers and products, pricing, promotion, and distribution. Ideally, the different functions should work in harmony to produce value for consumers. But in practice, departmental relations are full of conflicts and misunderstandings. The marketing department takes the consumer's point of view. But when marketing tries to develop customer satisfaction, it often causes other departments to do a poorer job *in their terms.* Marketing department actions can increase purchasing costs, disrupt production schedules, increase inventories, and create budget headaches. Thus, the other departments may resist bending their efforts to the will of the marketing department.

Yet marketers must get all departments to "think consumer" and to put the consumer at the center of company activity. Customer satisfaction requires a total company, cross-functional effort to deliver superior value to target customers.

> Creating value for buyers is much more than a "marketing function"; rather, [it's] analogous to a symphony orchestra in which the contribution of each subgroup is tailored and integrated by a conductor—with a synergistic effect. A seller must draw upon and integrate effectively . . . its entire human and other capital resources. . . . [Creating superior value for buyers] is the proper focus of the entire business and not merely of a single department in it.[13]

The DuPont "Adopt a Customer" program recognizes the importance of having people in all of its functions who are "close to the customer." For example, operators from DuPont's nylon spinning mills visit customer factories where DuPont nylon is transformed into swimsuits and other garments, talking to the customer's operators about quality and other problems they encounter with the nylon. Then, the DuPont operators represent their customers on the factory floor. If quality or delivery problems arise, the operators are more likely to see their adopted customers' point of view and to make decisions that will keep this customer happy.[14]

Jack Welch, General Electric's highly regarded CEO, tells his employees: "Companies can't give job security. Only customers can!" He emphasizes that all General Electric people, regardless of their department, have an impact on customer satisfaction and retention. His message: "If you are not thinking customer, you are not thinking."[15]

> active concept check

Now let's take a moment to test your knowledge of what you've just read.

> Strategic Planning and Small Businesses

Many discussions of strategic planning focus on large corporations with many divisions and products. However, small businesses can also benefit from sound strategic planning. Whereas most small ven-

---

[13]John C. Narver and Stanley F. Slater, "The Effect of a Market Orientation on Business Profitability," *Journal of Marketing,* October 1990, pp. 20–35.

[14]See Brian Dumaine, "Creating a New Company Culture," *Fortune,* January 15, 1990, p. 128; and Howard E. Butz Jr. and Leonard D. Goodstein, "Measuring Customer Value: Gaining Strategic Advantage," *Organizational Dynamics,* Winter 1996, pp. 63–77.

[15]Kotler, *Kotler on Marketing,* pp. 20–22.

tures start out with extensive business and marketing plans used to attract potential investors, strategic planning often falls by the wayside once the business gets going. Entrepreneurs and presidents of small companies are more likely to spend their time "putting out fires" than planning. But what does a small firm do when it finds that it has taken on too much debt, when its growth is exceeding production capacity, or when it's losing market share to a competitor with lower prices? Strategic planning can help small business managers to anticipate such situations and determine how to prevent or handle them.

King's Medical Company of Hudson, Ohio, provides an example of how one small company uses very simple strategic-planning tools to chart its course every three years. King's Medical owns and manages magnetic-resonance-imaging (MRI) equipment—million-dollar-plus machines that produce X-ray-type pictures. Several years ago, Dr. William Patton, Ph.D., then a consultant and the company's "planning guru," pointed to strategic planning as the key to his small company's very rapid growth and high profit margins. Patton claimed, "A lot of literature says there are three critical issues to a small company: cash flow, cash flow, cash flow. I agree those issues are critical, but so are three more: planning, planning, planning." King's Medical's planning process, which hinges on an assessment of the company, its place in the market, and its goals, includes the following steps.[16]

Small business strategic planning: King's Medical Company uses very simple strategic planning tools to chart its course.

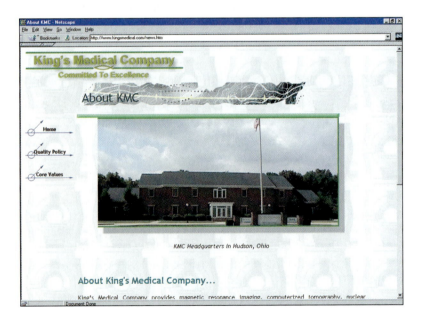

[16]Leslie Brokaw, "The Secrets of Great Planning," *Inc.*, October 1992, p. 152; and Kotler, *Marketing Management: Analysis, Planning, Implementation, and Control*, chap. 3.

1. Identify the major elements of the business environment in which the organization has operated over the past few years.

2. Describe the mission of the organization in terms of its nature and function for the next two years.

3. Explain the internal and external forces that will impact the mission of the organization.

4. Identify the basic driving force that will direct the organization in the future.

5. Develop a set of long-term objectives that will identify what the organization will become in the future.

6. Outline a general plan of action that defines the logistical, financial, and personnel factors needed to integrate the long-term objectives into the total organization.

Clearly, strategic planning is crucial to a small company's future. Thom Wellington, president of Wellington Environmental Consulting and Construction, Inc., says that it's important to do strategic planning at a site away from the office. An off-site location offers psychologically neutral ground where employees can be "much more candid," and it takes entrepreneurs away from the scene of the fires they spend so much time stamping out.[17]

> ## active exercise
Take a moment to consider how a small company can compete against a corporate giant.

> ## active poll
Take a moment to give your opinion about the marketing environment.

> ## active concept check
Now let's take a moment to test your knowledge of what you've just read.

> ## The Marketing Process

The strategic plan defines the company's overall mission and objectives. Within each business unit, marketing plays a role in helping to accomplish the overall strategic objectives. Marketing's role and activities in the organization are shown in Figure 2.5, which summarizes the entire **marketing process** and the forces influencing company marketing strategy.

Target consumers stand in the center. The goal is to build strong and profitable connections with these consumers. The company first identifies the total market, then divides it into smaller segments, selects the most promising segments, and focuses on serving and satisfying these segments. It designs a marketing mix made up of factors under its control—product, price, place, and promotion. To find the best marketing mix and put it into action, the company engages in marketing analysis, planning, implementation, and control. Through these activities, the company watches and adapts to the mar-

---

[17]Bradford McKee, "Think Ahead, Set Goals, and Get Out of the Office," *Nation's Business,* May 1993, p. 10. For more on small business strategic planning, see Nancy Drozdow, "Tools for Strategy Development in Family Firms," *Sloan Management Review,* Fall 1997, pp. 75–88; and Wendy M. Beech, "In It for the Long Haul," *Black Enterprise,* March 1998, p. 25.

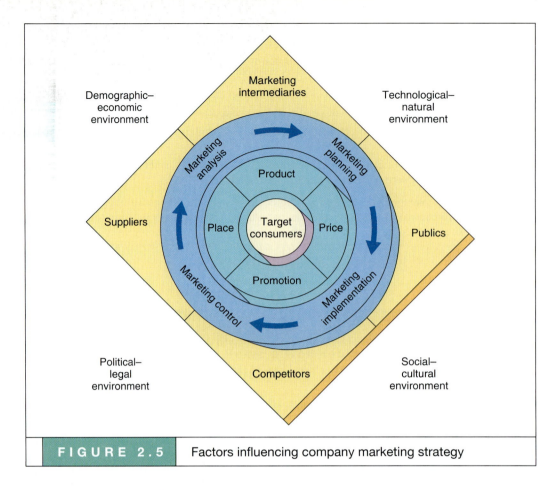

Demographic–
economic
environment

Marketing
intermediaries

Technological–
natural
environment

Marketing
analysis

Marketing
planning

Product

Suppliers

Place

Target
consumers

Price

Publics

Promotion

Marketing
control

Marketing
implementation

Political–
legal
environment

Competitors

Social–
cultural
environment

FIGURE 2.5 | Factors influencing company marketing strategy

keting environment. We will now look briefly at each element in the marketing process. In later chapters, we will discuss each element in more depth.

CONNECTING WITH CONSUMERS

To succeed in today's competitive marketplace, companies must be customer centered, winning customers from competitors, then keeping and growing them by delivering greater value. But before it can satisfy consumers, a company must first understand their needs and wants. Thus, sound marketing requires a careful analysis of consumers. Companies know that they cannot connect profitably all consumers in a given market—at least not all consumers in the same way. There are too many different kinds of consumers with too many different kinds of needs. And some companies are in a better position to serve certain segments of the market. Thus, each company must divide up the total market, choose the best segments, and design strategies for profitably serving chosen segments better than its competitors do. This process involves three steps: *market segmentation, market targeting*, and *market positioning*.

Market Segmentation

The market consists of many types of customers, products, and needs, and the marketer has to determine which segments offer the best opportunity for achieving company objectives. Consumers can be grouped and served in various ways based on geographic, demographic, psychographic, and behavioral factors. The process of dividing a market into distinct groups of buyers with different needs, characteristics, or behavior who might require separate products or marketing mixes is called **market segmentation.**

Every market has segments, but not all ways of segmenting a market are equally useful. For example, Tylenol would gain little by distinguishing between male and female users of pain relievers if both respond the same way to marketing efforts. A **market segment** consists of consumers who respond in a similar way to a given set of marketing efforts. In the car market, for example, consumers who choose the biggest, most comfortable car regardless of price make up one market segment. Another segment would be customers who care mainly about price and operating economy. It would be difficult to make one model of car that was the first choice of every consumer. Companies are wise to focus their efforts on meeting the distinct needs of one or more market segments.

Market Targeting

After a company has defined market segments, it can enter one or many segments of a given market. **Market targeting** involves evaluating each market segment's attractiveness and selecting one or more segments to enter. A company should target segments in which it can profitably generate the greatest customer value and sustain it over time. A company with limited resources might decide to serve only one or a few special segments or "market niches." This strategy limits sales but can be very profitable. Or a company might choose to serve several related segments—perhaps those with different kinds of customers but with the same basic wants. Or a large company might decide to offer a complete range of products to serve all market segments.

Most companies enter a new market by serving a single segment, and if this proves successful, they add segments. Large companies eventually seek full market coverage. They want to be the General Motors of their industry. GM says that it makes a car for every "person, purse, and personality." The leading company normally has different products designed to meet the special needs of each segment.

Market Positioning

After a company has decided which market segments to enter, it must decide what positions it wants to occupy in those segments. A product's *position* is the place the product occupies relative to competitors in consumers' minds. If a product is perceived to be exactly like another product on the market, consumers would have no reason to buy it.

Market positioning is arranging for a product to occupy a clear, distinctive, and desirable place relative to competing products in the minds of target consumers. Thus, marketers plan positions that distinguish their products from competing brands and give them the greatest strategic advantage in their target markets. For example, the Ford Taurus is "built to last"; Chevy Blazer is "like a rock." Saturn is "a different kind of company, different kind of car," and you can just "Imagine Yourself in a Mercury." Lexus avows "the relentless pursuit of excellence," Jaguar is positioned as "a blending of art and machine," and Mercedes is "engineered like no other car in the world." The luxurious Bentley promises "18 handcrafted feet of shameless luxury." Such deceptively simple statements form the backbone of a product's marketing strategy.

In positioning its product, the company first identifies possible competitive advantages on which to build the position. To gain competitive advantage, the company must offer greater value to chosen target segments, either by charging lower prices than competitors do or by offering more benefits to justify higher prices. But if the company positions the product as *offering* greater value, it must then *deliver* that greater value. Thus, effective positioning begins with actually *differentiating* the company's marketing offer so that it gives consumers more value than they are offered by the competition. Once the company has chosen a desired position, it must take strong steps to deliver and communicate that position to target consumers. The company's entire marketing program should support the chosen positioning strategy.

Positioning: Bentley promises "18 hand-crafted feet of shameless luxury." Such deceptively simple statements form the backbone of a product's marketing strategy.

Take a moment to consider how companies today try to meet the needs of individual consumers.

MARKETING STRATEGIES FOR COMPETITIVE ADVANTAGE

To be successful, the company must do a better job than its competitors of satisfying target consumers. Thus, marketing strategies must be geared to the needs of consumers and also to the strategies of competitors.

Designing competitive marketing strategies begins with thorough competitor analysis. The company constantly compares the value and customer satisfaction delivered by its products, prices, channels, and promotion with those of its close competitors. In this way it can discern areas of potential advantage and disadvantage. The company asks: Who are our competitors? What are their objectives and strategies? What are their strengths and weaknesses? How will they react to different competitive strategies we might use?

The competitive marketing strategy a company adopts depends on its industry position. A firm that dominates a market can adopt one or more of several *market leader* strategies. Well-known leaders include Coca-Cola (soft drinks), Microsoft (computer software), Caterpillar (large construction equipment), IBM (computers and information technology services), Wal-Mart (retailing), Boeing (aircraft), and America Online (Internet and online services). *Market challengers* are runner-up companies that aggressively attack competitors to get more market share. For example, Pepsi challenges Coke, Komatsu challenges Caterpillar, and MSN challenges America Online. The challenger might attack the market leader, other firms its own size, or smaller local and regional competitors.

Some runner-up firms will choose to follow rather than challenge the market leader. Firms using *market follower* strategies seek stable market shares and profits by following competitors' product offers, prices, and marketing programs. Smaller firms in a market, or even larger firms that lack established positions, often adopt *market nicher* strategies. They specialize in serving market niches that major competitors overlook or ignore. For example, Arm & Hammer has a lock on the baking soda corner of most consumer goods categories, including toothpaste, deodorizers, and others. Oshkosh Truck has found its niche as the world's largest producer of airport rescue trucks and front-loading concrete mixers. "Nichers" avoid direct confrontations with the majors by specializing along market, customer, product, or marketing mix lines. Through smart niching, smaller firms in an industry can be as profitable as their larger competitors. We will discuss competitive marketing strategies more fully in chapter 18.

Nichers specialize along market, customer, product, or marketing-mix lines. For example, Arm & Hammer has a lock on the baking soda corner of most consumer goods categories.

> # video example

Take a moment to watch a group of managers discuss competitive advantage.

DEVELOPING THE MARKETING MIX

Once the company has decided on its overall competitive marketing strategy, it is ready to begin planning the details of the marketing mix, one of the major concepts in modern marketing. We define **marketing mix** as the set of controllable, tactical marketing tools that the firm blends to produce the response it wants in the target market. The marketing mix consists of everything the firm can do to influence the demand for its product. The many possibilities can be collected into four groups of variables known as the "four Ps": *product, price, place,* and *promotion.*[18] Figure 2.6 shows the particular marketing tools under each *P.*

Product means the goods-and-services combination the company offers to the target market. Thus, a Ford Taurus product consists of nuts and bolts, spark plugs, pistons, headlights, and thousands of other parts. Ford offers several Taurus styles and dozens of optional features. The car comes fully serviced and with a comprehensive warranty that is as much a part of the product as the tailpipe.

Price is the amount of money customers have to pay to obtain the product. Ford calculates suggested retail prices that its dealers might charge for each Taurus. But Ford dealers rarely charge the full sticker price. Instead, they negotiate the price with each customer, offering discounts, trade-in allowances, and credit terms to adjust for the current competitive situation and to bring the price into line with the buyer's perception of the car's value.

Place includes company activities that make the product available to target consumers. Ford maintains a large body of independently owned dealerships that sell the company's many different models. Ford selects its dealers carefully and supports them strongly. The dealers keep an inventory of Ford automobiles, demonstrate them to potential buyers, negotiate prices, close sales, and service the cars after the sale.

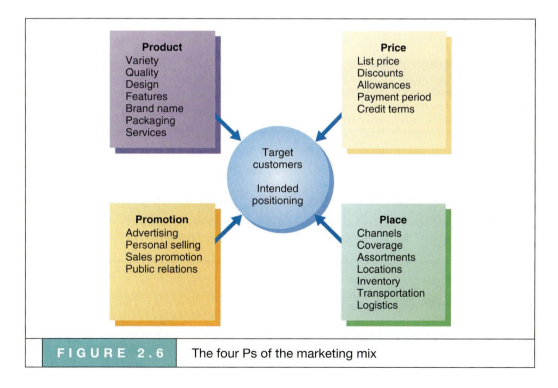

| FIGURE 2.6 | The four Ps of the marketing mix |

[18]The four Ps classification was first suggested by E. Jerome McCarthy, *Basic Marketing: A Managerial Approach* (Homewood, IL: Irwin, 1960). For more discussion of this classification scheme, see Walter van Waterschoot and Christophe Van den Bulte, "The 4P Classification of the Marketing Mix Revisited," *Journal of Marketing,* October 1992, pp. 83–93; and Michael G. Harvey, Robert F. Lusch, and Branko Cavarkapo, "A Marketing Mix for the 21st Century," *Journal of Marketing Theory and Practice,* Fall 1996, pp. 1–15.

Promotion means activities that communicate the merits of the product and persuade target customers to buy it. Ford spends more than $1.2 billion each year on advertising to tell consumers about the company and its products. Dealership salespeople assist potential buyers and persuade them that Ford is the best car for them. Ford and its dealers offer special promotions—sales, cash rebates, low financing rates—as added purchase incentives.

An effective marketing program blends all of the marketing mix elements into a coordinated program designed to achieve the company's marketing objectives by delivering value to consumers. The marketing mix constitutes the company's tactical tool kit for establishing strong positioning in target markets.

Some critics feel that the four Ps may omit or underemphasize certain important activities. For example, they ask, "Where are services?" Just because they don't start with a P doesn't justify omitting them. The answer is that services, such as banking, airline, and retailing services, are products too. We might call them *service products.* "Where is packaging?" the critics might ask. Marketers would answer that they include packaging as just one of many product decisions. All said, as Figure 2.6 suggests, many marketing activities that might appear to be left out of the marketing mix are subsumed under one of the four Ps. The issue is not whether there should be four, six, or ten Ps so much as what framework is most helpful in designing marketing programs.

There is another concern, however, that is valid. It holds that the four Ps concept takes the seller's view of the market, not the buyer's view. From the buyer's viewpoint, in this age of connectedness, the four Ps might be better described as the four Cs:[19]

4Ps	4Cs
Product	Customer solution
Price	Customer cost
Place	Convenience
Promotion	Communication

Thus while marketers see themselves as selling a product, customers see themselves as buying value or a solution to their problem. Customers are interested in more than the price; they are interested in the total costs of obtaining, using, and disposing of a product. Customers want the product and service to be as conveniently available as possible. Finally, they want two-way communication. Marketers would do well to first think through the four Cs and then build the four Ps on that platform.

active example <

Take a moment to consider how one industry deals with government controls on promotion.

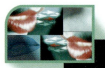

active poll <

Take a moment to give your opinion about the marketing environment.

> ## Managing the Marketing Effort

The company wants to design and put into action the marketing mix that will best achieve its objectives in its target markets. Figure 2.7 shows the relationship between the four marketing management functions—*analysis, planning, implementation,* and *control.* The company first develops overall strategic plans, then translates these companywide strategic plans into marketing and other plans for each division, product, and brand. Through implementation, the company turns the plans into actions.

[19]Robert Lauterborn, "New Marketing Litany: 4P's Passé; C-Words Take Over," *Advertising Age,* October 1, 1990, p. 26. Also see Kotler, *Marketing Management: Analysis, Planning, Implementation, and Control,* chap. 1, p. 16.

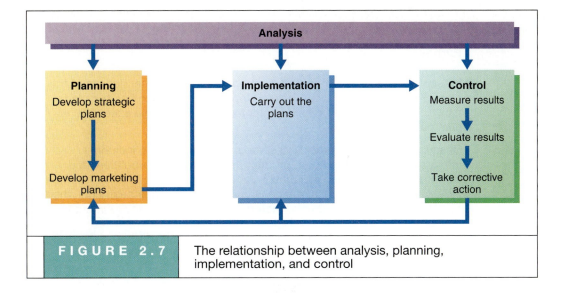

| FIGURE 2.7 | The relationship between analysis, planning, implementation, and control |

Control consists of measuring and evaluating the results of marketing activities and taking corrective action where needed. Finally, marketing analysis provides information and evaluations needed for all of the other marketing activities.

MARKETING ANALYSIS

Managing the marketing function begins with a complete analysis of the company's situation. The company must analyze its markets and marketing environment to find attractive opportunities and to avoid environmental threats. It must analyze company strengths and weaknesses as well as current and possible marketing actions to determine which opportunities it can best pursue. Marketing provides input to each of the other marketing management functions. We discuss marketing analysis more fully in chapter 4.

> video example

Take a moment to watch a manager discuss an opportunity in her company's marketing environment.

MARKETING PLANNING

Through strategic planning, the company decides what it wants to do with each business unit. Marketing planning involves deciding on marketing strategies that will help the company attain its overall strategic objectives. A detailed marketing plan is needed for each business, product, or brand. What does a marketing plan look like? Our discussion focuses on product or brand plans.

Table 2.2 outlines the major sections of a typical product or brand plan. The plan begins with an executive summary, which quickly overviews major assessments, goals, and recommendations. The main section of the plan presents a detailed analysis of the current marketing situation as well as potential threats and opportunities. It next states major objectives for the brand and outlines the specifics of a marketing strategy for achieving them.

A **marketing strategy** is the marketing logic whereby the company hopes to achieve its marketing objectives. It consists of specific strategies for target markets, positioning, the marketing mix, and marketing expenditure levels. In this section, the planner explains how each strategy responds to the threats, opportunities, and critical issues spelled out earlier in the plan. Additional sections of the marketing plan lay out an action program for implementing the marketing strategy along with the details of a supporting *marketing budget*. The last section outlines the controls that will be used to monitor progress and take corrective action.[20]

[20]For more on marketing plans, see Jay Winchester, "What's the Plan?" *Sales & Marketing Management,* October 1997, pp. 73–78.

TABLE 2.2	Contents of a Marketing Plan
Section	**Purpose**
Executive summary	Presents a brief summary of the main goals and recommendations of the plan for management review, helping top management to find the plan's major points quickly. A table of contents should follow the executive summary.
Current marketing situation	Describes the target market and company's position in it, including information about the market, product performance, competition, and distribution. This section includes: • A *market description* that defines the market and major segments, then reviews customer needs and factors in the marketing environment that may affect customer purchasing. • A *product review* that shows sales, prices, and gross margins of the major products in the product line. • A review of *competition,* which identifies major competitors and assesses their market positions and strategies for product quality, pricing, distribution, and promotion. • A review of *distribution,* which evaluates recent sales trends and other developments in major distribution channels.
Threats and opportunity analysis	Assesses major threats and opportunities that the product might face, helping management to anticipate important positive or negative developments that might have an impact on the firm and its strategies.
Objectives and issues	States the marketing objectives that the company would like to attain during the plan's term and discusses key issues that will affect their attainment. For example, if the goal is to achieve a 15 percent market share, this section looks at how this goal might be achieved.
Marketing strategy	Outlines the broad marketing logic by which the business unit hopes to achieve its marketing objectives and the specifics of target markets, positioning, and marketing expenditure levels. It outlines specific strategies for each marketing mix element and explains how each responds to the threats, opportunities, and critical issues spelled out earlier in the plan.
Action programs	Spells out how marketing strategies will be turned into specific action programs that answer the following questions: *What* will be done? *When* will it be done? *Who* is responsible for doing it? *How* much will it cost?
Budgets	Details a supporting marketing budget that is essentially a projected profit-and-loss statement. It shows expected revenues (forecasted number of units sold and the average net price) and expected costs (of production, distribution, and marketing). The difference is the projected profit. Once approved by higher management, the budget becomes the basis for materials buying, production scheduling, personnel planning, and marketing operations.
Controls	Outlines the control that will be used to monitor progress and allow higher management to review implementation results and spot products that are not meeting their goals.

MARKETING IMPLEMENTATION

Planning good strategies is only a start toward successful marketing. A brilliant marketing strategy counts for little if the company fails to implement it properly. **Marketing implementation** is the process that turns marketing *plans* into marketing *actions* in order to accomplish strategic marketing objectives. Implementation involves day-to-day, month-to-month activities that effectively put the marketing plan to work. Whereas marketing planning addresses the *what* and *why* of marketing activities, implementation addresses the *who, where, when*, and *how.*

Many managers think that "doing things right" (implementation) is as important, or even more important, than "doing the right things" (strategy). The fact is that both are critical to success.[21] However, companies can gain competitive advantages through effective implementation. One firm can have essentially the same strategy as another yet win in the marketplace through faster or better execution. Still, implementation is difficult—it is often easier to think up good marketing strategies than it is to carry them out.

In an increasingly connected world, people at all levels of the marketing system must work together to implement marketing plans and strategies. At Black & Decker, for example, marketing implementation for the company's power tool products requires day-to-day decisions and actions by thousands of people both inside and outside the organization. Marketing managers make decisions about target segments, branding, packaging, pricing, promoting, and distributing. They connect with people elsewhere in the company to get support for their products and programs. They talk with engineering about product design, with manufacturing about production and inventory levels, and with finance about funding and cash flows. They also connect with outside people, such as advertising agencies to plan ad campaigns and the media to obtain publicity support. The sales force urges Home Depot, Wal-Mart, and other retailers to advertise Black & Decker products, provide ample shelf space, and use company displays.

Successful marketing implementation depends on how well the company blends its people, organizational structure, decision and reward systems, and company culture into a cohesive action program that supports its strategies. At all levels, the company must be staffed by people who have the needed skills, motivation, and personal characteristics. The company's formal organization structure plays an important role in implementing marketing strategy; so do its decision and reward systems. For example, if a company's compensation system rewards managers for short-run profit results, they will have little incentive to work toward long-run market-building objectives.

Finally, to be successfully implemented, the firm's marketing strategies must fit with its company culture, the system of values and beliefs shared by people in the organization. A study of America's most successful companies found that these companies have almost cultlike cultures built around strong, market-oriented missions. At companies such as Wal-Mart, Microsoft, Nordstrom, Citicorp, Procter & Gamble, Walt Disney, and Hewlett-Packard, "employees share such a strong vision that they know in their hearts what's right for their company."[22]

MARKETING DEPARTMENT ORGANIZATION

The company must design a marketing department that can carry out marketing strategies and plans. If the company is very small, one person might do all of the marketing work—research, selling, advertising, customer service, and other activities. As the company expands, a marketing department organization emerges to plan and carry out marketing activities. In large companies, this department contains many specialists. Thus, Black & Decker has product and market managers, sales managers and salespeople, market researchers, advertising experts, and other specialists.

Modern marketing departments can be arranged in several ways. The most common form of marketing organization is the *functional organization* in which different marketing activities are headed by a functional specialist—a sales manager, advertising manager, marketing research manager, customer service manager, new-product manager. A company that sells across the country or internationally often uses a *geographic organization* in which its sales and marketing people are assigned to specific countries, regions, and districts. Geographic organization allows salespeople to settle into a territory, get to know their customers, and work with a minimum of travel time and cost.

Companies with many, very different products or brands often create a *product management organization*. Using this approach, a product manager develops and implements a complete strategy and marketing program for a specific product or brand. Product management first appeared at Procter & Gamble in 1929. A new company soap, Camay, was not doing well, and a young P&G executive was assigned to give his exclusive attention to developing and promoting this product. He was suc-

---

[21]For a good discussion of gaining advantage through implementation effectiveness versus strategic differentiation, see Michael E. Porter, "What Is Strategy," *Harvard Business Review,* November–December 1996, pp. 61–78. Also see Charles H. Noble and Michael P. Mokwa, "Implementing Marketing Strategies: Developing and Testing a Managerial Theory," *Journal of Marketing,* October 1999, pp. 57–73.

[22]Brian Dumaine, "Why Great Companies Last," *Business Week,* January 16, 1995, p. 129. See James C. Collins and Jerry I. Porras, *Built to Last: Successful Habits of Visionary Companies* (New York: HarperBusiness, 1995); Geoffrey Brewer, "Firing Line: What Separates Visionary Companies from All the Rest?" *Performance,* June 1995, pp. 12–17; and Rob Goffee and Gareth Jones, *The Character of a Corporation: How Your Company's Culture Can Make or Break Your Business* (New York: HarperBusiness, 1998).

cessful, and the company soon added other product managers.[23] Since then, many firms, especially consumer products companies, have set up product management organizations. However, recent dramatic changes in the marketing environment have caused many companies to rethink the role of the product manager.

For companies that sell one product line to many different types of markets that have different needs and preferences, a *market management organization* might be best. A market management organization is similar to the product management organization. Market managers are responsible for developing marketing strategies and plans for their specific markets. This system's main advantage is that the company is organized around the needs of specific customer segments.

Large companies that produce many different products flowing into many different geographic and customer markets usually employ some *combination* of the functional, geographic, product, and market organization forms. This ensures that each function, product, and market receives its share of management attention. However, it can also add costly layers of management and reduce organizational flexibility. Still, the benefits of organizational specialization usually outweigh the drawbacks.[24]

MARKETING CONTROL

Because many surprises occur during the implementation of marketing plans, the marketing department must practice constant marketing control. **Marketing control** involves evaluating the results of marketing strategies and plans and taking corrective action to ensure that objectives are attained. Figure 2.8 shows that implementation involves four steps. Management first sets specific marketing goals. It then measures its performance in the marketplace and evaluates the causes of any differences between expected and actual performance. Finally, management takes corrective action to close the gaps between its goals and its performance. This may require changing the action programs or even changing the goals.

Operating control involves checking ongoing performance against the annual plan and taking corrective action when necessary. Its purpose is to ensure that the company achieves the sales, profits, and other goals set out in its annual plan. It also involves determining the profitability of different products, territories, markets, and channels.

Strategic control involves looking at whether the company's basic strategies are well matched to its opportunities. Marketing strategies and programs can quickly become outdated, and each company should periodically reassess its overall approach to the marketplace. A major tool for such strategic control is a **marketing audit.** The marketing audit is a comprehensive, systematic, independent, and periodic examination of a company's environment, objectives, strategies, and activities to determine problem areas and opportunities. The audit provides good input for a plan of action to improve the company's marketing performance.[25]

The marketing audit covers *all* major marketing areas of a business, not just a few trouble spots. It assesses the marketing environment, marketing strategy, marketing organization, marketing systems, marketing mix, and marketing productivity and profitability. The audit is normally conducted by an

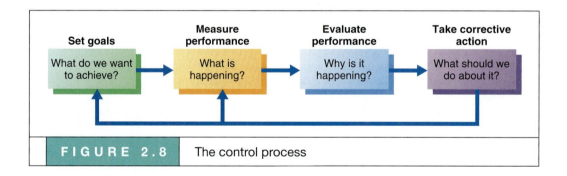

Set goals	Measure performance	Evaluate performance	Take corrective action
What do we want to achieve?	What is happening?	Why is it happening?	What should we do about it?

FIGURE 2.8 The control process

[23]Joseph Winski, "One Brand, One Manager," *Advertising Age,* August 20, 1987, p. 86. Also see Jack Neff, "P&G Redefines the Brand Manager," *Advertising Age,* October 13, 1997, pp. 1, 18; Alan J. Bergstrom, "Brand Management Poised for Change," *Marketing News,* July 7, 1997, p. 5; James Bell, "Brand Management for the Next Millennium," *The Journal of Business Strategy,* March–April 1998, p. 7; and Jack Neff, "The New Brand Management," *Advertising Age,* November 8, 1999, pp. S2, S18.

[24]For more complete discussions of marketing organization approaches and issues, see Robert W. Ruekert, Orville C. Walker Jr., and Kenneth J. Roering, "The Organization of Marketing Activities: A Contingency Theory of Structure and Performance," *Journal of Marketing,* Winter 1985, pp. 13–25; Ravi S. Achrol, "Evolution of the Marketing Organization: New Forms for Turbulent Environments," *Journal of Marketing,* October 1991, pp. 77–93; and Geoffrey Brewer, "Love the Ones You're With," *Sales & Marketing Management,* February 1997, pp. 38–45.

[25]For details, see Kotler, *Marketing Management: Analysis, Planning, Implementation, and Control,* chap. 20.

TABLE 2.3	Marketing Audit Questions

Marketing Environment Audit

1. The *macroenvironment:* What major *demographic, economic, natural, technological, political,* and *cultural* trends pose threats and opportunities for this company?
2. The *task environment:*
   - *Markets and customers:* What is happening to marketing size, growth, geographic distribution, and profits? What are the major market segments? How do customers make their buying decisions? How do they rate the company on product quality, value, and service?
   - *Other factors* in the marketing system: Who are the company's major *competitors* and what are their strategies, strengths, and weaknesses? How are the company's *channels* performing? What trends are affecting *suppliers?* What key *publics* provide problems or opportunities?

Marketing Strategy Audit

1. *Business mission and marketing objectives:* Is the mission clearly defined and market oriented? Has the company set clear objectives to guide marketing planning and performance?
2. *Marketing strategy:* Does the company have a strong marketing strategy for achieving its objectives?
3. *Budgets:* Has the company budgeted sufficient resources to segments, products, territories, and marketing mix elements?

Marketing Organization Audit

1. *Formal structure:* Are marketing activities optimally structured along functional, product, market, and territory lines?
2. *Functional efficiency:* Do marketing and sales communicate effectively? Is marketing staff well trained, supervised, motivated, and evaluated?
3. *Cross-functional efficiency:* Do marketing people work well with people in operations, R&D, purchasing, human resources, information technology, and other nonmarketing areas?

Marketing Systems Audit

1. *Marketing information system:* Is the marketing intelligence system providing accurate and timely information? Is the company using marketing research effectively?
2. *Marketing planning system:* Does the company prepare annual, long-term, and strategic plans? Are they used?
3. *Marketing control system:* Are annual plan objectives being achieved? Does management periodically analyze product, market, and channel sales and profitability?
4. *New-product development:* Does the company have an effective new-product development process? Has the company succeeded with new products?

Marketing Productivity Audit

1. *Profitability analysis:* How profitable are the company's different products, markets, territories, and channels? Should the company enter, expand, or withdraw from any business segments?
2. *Cost-effectiveness analysis:* Do any marketing activities have excessive costs? How can costs be reduced?

Marketing Function Audit

1. *Products:* What are the company's product line objectives? Should some current products be phased out or new products be added? Would some products benefit from changes in quality, features, or style?
2. *Price:* Are the company's pricing policies and procedures appropriate? Are prices in line with customers' perceived value?
3. *Distribution:* What are the company's distribution objectives and strategies? Should existing channels be changed or new ones added?
4. *Promotion:* Does the company have well-developed *advertising, sales promotion,* and *public relations* programs? Is the *sales force* large enough and well trained, supervised, and motivated?

objective and experienced outside party. Table 2.3 shows the kinds of questions the marketing auditor might ask. The findings may come as a surprise—and sometimes as a shock—to management. Management then decides which actions make sense and how and when to implement them.

THE MARKETING ENVIRONMENT

Managing the marketing function would be hard enough if the marketer had to deal only with the controllable marketing mix variables. But the company operates in a complex marketing environment, consisting of uncontrollable forces to which the company must adapt. The environment produces both threats and opportunities. The company must carefully analyze its environment so that it can avoid the threats and take advantage of the opportunities.

The company's marketing environment includes forces close to the company that affect its ability to serve consumers, such as other company departments, channel members, suppliers, competitors, and publics. It also includes broader demographic and economic forces, political and legal forces, technological and ecological forces, and social and cultural forces. In order to connect effectively with consumers, others in the company, external partners, and the world around them, marketers need to consider all of these forces when developing and positioning its offer to the target market. The marketing environment is discussed more fully in chapter 3.

active concept check <

Now let's take a moment to test your knowledge of what you've just read.

> **Chapter Wrap-Up**

Now that you've reached the end of the chapter, you may wish to explore the concepts you've been reading about in greater detail, or test yourself to see how well you've comprehended the material. In the box below you'll find a number of links. Click on any one of these links to find additional chapter resources.

> end-of-chapter resources

- **Review of Concept Connections**
- **Practice Quiz**
- **Issues for Discussion**
- **Key Terms**
- **Marketing Applications**
- **Internet Connections**
- **Company Case**

CHAPTER 3

The Marketing Environment

> What's Ahead

As we hurtle into the new millennium, social experts are busier than ever assessing the impact of a host of environmental forces on consumers and the marketers who serve them. "An old year turns into a new one," observes one such expert, "and the world itself, at least for a moment, seems to turn also. Images of death and rebirth, things ending and beginning, populate . . . and haunt the mind. Multiply this a thousand-fold, and you get 'millennial fever' . . . driving consumer behavior in all sorts of interesting ways."

Such millennial fever has hit the nation's baby boomers, the most commercially influential demographic group in history, especially hard. The oldest boomers, now in their fifties, are resisting the aging process with the vigor they once reserved for antiwar protests. Other factors are also at work. Today, people of all ages seem to feel a bit overworked, overstimulated, and overloaded. "Americans are overwhelmed . . . by the breathtaking onrush of the Information Age, with its high-speed modems, cell phones, and pagers," suggests the expert. "While we hail the benefits of the wired '90s, at the same time we are buffeted by the rapid pace of change."

The result of this "millennial fever" is a yearning to turn back the clock, to return to simpler times. This yearning has in turn produced a massive nostalgia wave. "We are creating a new culture, and we don't know what's going to happen," explains a noted futurist. "So we need some warm fuzzies from our past." Marketers of all kinds have responded to these nostalgia pangs by recreating products and images that help take consumers back to "the good old days." Examples are plentiful: Kellogg has revived old Corn Flakes packaging and car makers have created retro roadsters such as the Porsche Boxter. A Pepsi commercial rocks to the Rolling Stones's "Brown Sugar," James Brown's "I Feel Good" helps sell Senokot laxatives, and

Janis Joplin's raspy voice crows, "Oh Lord, won't you buy me a Mercedes-Benz?" Disney developed an entire town—Celebration, Florida—to recreate the look and feel of 1940s neighborhoods. Heinz reintroduced its classic glass ketchup bottle, supported by nostalgic "Heinz was there" ads showing two 1950s-era boys eating hot dogs at a ballpark. Master marketer Coca-Cola resurrected the old red button logo and its heritage contour bottle. The current ad theme, "Always Coca-Cola," encapsulates both the past and the future. According to a Coca-Cola marketing executive, when the company introduced a plastic version of its famous contour bottle in 1994, sales grew by double digits in some markets.

Lemon.

Lime.

Drivers wanted

Perhaps no company has more riding on the nostalgia wave than Volkswagen. The original Volkswagen Beetle first sputtered into America in 1949. With its simple, buglike design, no-frills engineering, and economical operation, the Beetle was the antithesis of Detroit's chrome-laden gas guzzlers. Although most owners would readily admit that their Beetles were underpowered, noisy, cramped, and freezing in the winter, they saw these as endearing qualities. Overriding these minor inconveniences, the Beetle was cheap to buy and own, dependable, easy to fix, fun to drive, and anything but flashy.

During the 1960s, as young baby boomers by the thousands were buying their first cars, demand exploded and the Beetle blossomed into an unlikely icon. Bursting with personality, the understated Bug came to personify an era of rebellion against conventions. It became the most popular car in American history, with sales peaking at 423,000 in 1968. By the late 1970s, however, the boomers had moved on, Bug mania had faded, and Volkswagen had dropped Beetle production for the United States. Still, more than 20 years later, the mere mention of these chugging oddities evokes smiles and strong emotions. Almost everyone over the age of 25, it seems, has a "feel-good" Beetle story to tell.

Now, in an attempt to surf the nostalgia wave, Volkswagen has introduced a New Beetle. Outwardly, the reborn Beetle resembles the original, tapping the strong emotions and memories of times gone by. Beneath the skin, however, the New Beetle is packed with modern features. According to an industry expert, "The Beetle comeback is . . . based on a combination of romance and reason—wrapping up modern conveniences in an old-style package. Built into the dashboard is a bud vase perfect for a daisy plucked straight from the 1960s. But right next to it is a high-tech, multispeaker stereo—and options like power windows, cruise control, and a power sunroof make it a very different car than the rattly old Bug. The new version . . . comes with all the modern features car buyers demand, such as four air bags and power outlets for cell phones. But that's not why VW expects folks to buy it. With a familiar bubble shape that still makes people smile as it skitters by, the new Beetle offers a pull that is purely emotional."

Advertising for the New Beetle plays strongly on the nostalgia theme, while at the same time refreshing the old Beetle heritage. "If you sold your soul in the '80s," tweaks one ad, "here's your chance to buy it back." Other ads read, "Less flower, more power," and "Comes with wonderful new features. Like heat." Still another ad declares "0 to 60? Yes." The car's Web page (*www3.vw.com/cars/newbeetle/main.html*) summarizes: "The New Beetle has what any Beetle always had. Originality. Honesty. A point of view. It's an exhaustive and zealous rejection of banality. Isn't the world ready for that kind of car again?"

Volkswagen invested $560 million to bring the New Beetle to market. However, this investment appears to be paying big dividends. Demand quickly outstripped supply. Even before the first cars reached VW showrooms, dealers across the country had long waiting lists of people who'd paid for the car without ever seeing it, let alone driving it. One California dealer claimed that the New Beetle was such a traffic magnet that he had to remove it from his showroom floor every afternoon at 2 P.M. to discourage gawkers and let his salespeople work with serious prospects. The dealer encountered similar problems when he took to the streets in the new car. "You can't change lanes," said the dealer. "People drive up beside you to look."

Volkswagen's initial first-year sales projections of 50,000 New Beetles in North America proved pessimistic. After only nine months, the company had sold more than 64,000 of the new Bugs in the United States and Canada. The smart little car also garnered numerous distinguished awards, including *Motor Trend*'s 1999 Import Car of the Year, *Time* magazine's The Best of 1998 Design, *Business Week*'s Best New Products, and 1999 North American Car of the Year, awarded by an independent panel of top journalists who cover the auto industry.

The New Beetle appears to be a cross-generational hit, appealing to more than the stereotyped core demographic target of Woodstock-recovered baby boomers. Even kids too young to remember the original Bug appear to love this new one. "It's like you have a rock star here and everybody wants an autograph," states a VW sales manager. "I've never seen a car that had such a wide range of interest, from 16-year-olds to 65-year-olds." One wait-listed customer confirms the car's broad appeal. "In 1967, my Dad got me a VW. I loved it. I'm sure the new one will take me back," says the customer. "I'm getting the New Beetle as a surprise for my daughter, but I'm sure I'm going to be stealing it from her all the time."

"Millennial fever" results from the convergence of a wide range of forces in the marketing environment—from technological, economic, and demographic forces to cultural, social, and political ones. Most trend analysts believe that the nostalgia craze will only grow as the baby boomers continue to age. If so, the New Beetle, so full of the past, has a very bright future. "The Beetle is not just empty nostalgia," says Gerald Celente, publisher of *Trend Journal.* "It is a practical car that is also tied closely to the emotions of a generation." Says another trend analyst, the New Beetle "is our romantic past, reinvented for our hectic here-and-now. Different, yet deeply familiar—a car for the times."[1]

> **objectives**

Before you begin, take a moment to familiarize yourself with the key objectives of this chapter.

[1]Quotes from James R. Rosenfield, "Millennial Fever," *American Demographics,* December 1997, pp. 47–51; Keith Naughton and Bill Vlasic, "The Nostalgia Boom: Why the Old Is New Again," *Business Week,* March 23, 1998, pp. 58–64; and "New Beetles: Drivers Wanted," accessed online at www.vw.com/cars/newbeetle/main.html, August 11, 1998. Also see Greg Farrell, "Getting the Bugs Out," *Brandweek,* April 6, 1998, pp. 30–40; "Beetle Mania," *Adweek,* July 13, 1998, p. 24; "Volkswagen's New Beetle Selected 1999 North American Car of the Year," press release accessed online at www.vw.com, January 4, 1999; remarks by Jens Neumann at the 1999 North American International Auto Show, accessed online at www.vw.com, January 4, 1999; and Judann Pollack, "Heinz Waxes Nostalgic over Revived Glass Bottle," *Advertising Age,* May 3, 1999, p. 17.

As noted in chapter 1, marketers operate in an increasingly connected world. Today's marketers must connect effectively with customers, others in the company, and external partners in the face of major environmental forces that buffet all of these actors. A company's **marketing environment** consists of the actors and forces outside marketing that affect marketing management's ability to develop and maintain successful relationships with its target customers. The marketing environment offers both opportunities and threats. Successful companies know the vital importance of constantly watching and adapting to the changing environment.

As we enter the new millennium, both consumers and marketers wonder what the future will bring. The environment continues to change at a rapid pace. For example, think about how you buy groceries today. How will your grocery buying change during the next few decades? What challenges will these changes present for marketers? Here's what two leading futurists envision for the year 2025.[2]

We won't be shopping in 21-aisle supermarkets in 2025, predicts Gary Wright, corporate demographer for Procter & Gamble in Cincinnati. The growth of e-commerce and the rapid speed of the Internet will lead to online ordering of lower priced, nonperishable products—everything from peanut butter to coffee filters. Retailers will become "bundlers," combining these orders into large packages of goods for each household and delivering them efficiently to their doorsteps. As a result, we'll see mergers between retailing and home-delivery giants—think Wal-MartExpress, a powerful combo of Wal-Mart and Federal Express. Consumers won't waste precious time searching for the best-priced bundle. Online information agents will do it for them, comparing prices among competitors.

Smart information agents also play a role in the world imagined by Ryan Mathews, futurist at First Matter LLC in Detroit. By 2025, computers will essentially be as smart as humans, he contends, and consumers will use them to exchange information with on-screen electronic agents that ferret out the best deals online. Thanks to embedded-chip technology in the pantry, products on a CHR (continuous household replenishment) list—like paper towels and pet food—will sense when they're running low and reorder themselves automatically. If the information agent finds a comparable but cheaper substitute for a CHR product, the item will be switched instantly.

Such pictures of the future give marketers plenty to think about. A company's marketers take the major responsibility for identifying and predicting significant changes in the environment. More than any other group in the company, marketers must be the trend trackers and opportunity seekers. Although every manager in an organization needs to observe the outside environment, marketers have two special aptitudes. They have disciplined methods—marketing intelligence and marketing research—for collecting information about the marketing environment. They also spend more time in the customer and competitor environment. By conducting systematic environmental scanning, marketers are able to revise and adapt marketing strategies to meet new challenges and opportunities in the marketplace.

The marketing environment is made up of a *microenvironment* and a *macroenvironment*. The **microenvironment** consists of the forces close to the company that affect its ability to serve its customers—the company, suppliers, marketing channel firms, customer markets, competitors, and publics. The **macroenvironment** consists of the larger societal forces that affect the microenvironment—demographic, economic, natural, technological, political, and cultural forces. We look first at the company's microenvironment.

[2]Jennifer Lach, "Dateline America: May 1, 2025," *American Demographics,* May 1999, pp. 19–20.

Marketing management's job is to attract and build relationships with customers by creating customer value and satisfaction. However, marketing managers cannot accomplish this task alone. Their success will depend on other actors in the company's microenvironment—other company departments, suppliers, marketing intermediaries, customers, competitors, and various publics, which combine to make up the company's value delivery system.

THE COMPANY

In designing marketing plans, marketing management takes other company groups into account—groups such as top management, finance, research and development (R&D), purchasing, manufacturing, and accounting. All these interrelated groups form the internal environment (see Figure 3.1). Top management sets the company's mission, objectives, broad strategies, and policies. Marketing managers make decisions within the plans made by top management, and marketing plans must be approved by top management before they can be implemented.

Marketing managers must also work closely with other company departments. Finance is concerned with finding and using funds to carry out the marketing plan. The R&D department focuses on designing safe and attractive products. Purchasing worries about getting supplies and materials, whereas manufacturing is responsible for producing the desired quality and quantity of products. Accounting has to measure revenues and costs to help marketing know how well it is achieving its objectives. Together, all of these departments have an impact on the marketing department's plans and actions. Under the marketing concept, all of these functions must "think consumer," and they should work in harmony to provide superior customer value and satisfaction.

SUPPLIERS

Suppliers are an important link in the company's overall customer value delivery system. They provide the resources needed by the company to produce its goods and services. Supplier problems can seriously affect marketing. Marketing managers must watch supply availability—supply shortages or delays, labor strikes, and other events can cost sales in the short run and damage customer satisfaction in the long run. Marketing managers also monitor the price trends of their key inputs. Rising supply costs may force price increases that can harm the company's sales volume.

MARKETING INTERMEDIARIES

Marketing intermediaries help the company to promote, sell, and distribute its goods to final buyers. They include *resellers, physical distribution firms, marketing services agencies,* and *financial intermediaries. Resellers* are distribution channel firms that help the company find customers or make sales to them. These include wholesalers and retailers, who buy and resell merchandise. Selecting and working with resellers is not easy. No longer do manufacturers have many small, independent resellers from which to choose. They now face large and growing reseller organizations. These organizations frequently have enough power to dictate terms or even shut the manufacturer out of large markets.

Physical distribution firms help the company to stock and move goods from their points of origin to their destinations. Working with warehouse and transportation firms, a company must determine

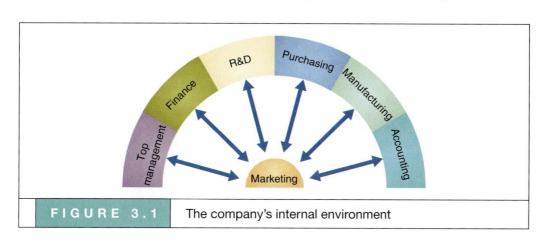

| FIGURE 3.1 | The company's internal environment |

the best ways to store and ship goods, balancing factors such as cost, delivery, speed, and safety. *Marketing services agencies* are the marketing research firms, advertising agencies, media firms, and marketing consulting firms that help the company target and promote its products to the right markets. When the company decides to use one of these agencies, it must choose carefully because these firms vary in creativity, quality, service, and price. *Financial intermediaries* include banks, credit companies, insurance companies, and other businesses that help finance transactions or insure against the risks associated with the buying and selling of goods. Most firms and customers depend on financial intermediaries to finance their transactions.

Like suppliers, marketing intermediaries form an important component of the company's overall value delivery system. In its quest to create satisfying customer relationships, the company must do more than just optimize its own performance. It must partner effectively with marketing intermediaries to optimize the performance of the entire system.

Thus, today's marketers recognize the importance of working with their intermediaries as partners rather than simply as channels through which they sell their products. For example, Coca-Cola recently signed a 10-year deal with Wendy's that will make Coke the exclusive soft drink provider to the fast-food chain, picking up more than 700 Wendy's franchises that were previously served by Pepsi. In the deal, Coca-Cola promised Wendy's much more that just its soft drinks. It pledged the powerful marketing support that comes along with an exclusive partnership with Coke.

> [Along with the soft drinks,] Wendy's gets a cross-functional team of 50 Coke employees in various regions of the country who are now dedicated to "understanding the nuances of Wendy's business," says [a Wendy's executive]. Wendy's also will benefit from Coke dollars in joint marketing campaigns. "There are significant, big-time marketing sponsorships that they can bring to Wendy's, as they have to other chains," [adds the executive]. "That's huge." Bigger still is the staggering amount of consumer research that Coca-Cola provides its partners. [Coke] provides both analysis of syndicated information and access to Coke's own internal research aimed at "trying to understand consumers as they eat out." Coke goes to great lengths to understand beverage drinkers—and to make sure their partners can use those insights. . . . The company also has analyzed the demographics of every zip code in the country and used the information to create a software program called Solver. By answering questions about their target audience, franchise owners can determine which Coke brands are preferred by the clientele in their area. [Coca-Cola] also has been studying the design of drive-through menu boards to better understand which layouts, fonts, letter sizes, colors, and visuals induce consumers to order more food and drink. Coke even aids its partners with research on issues that are not related to soft drink sales, such as hiring and retaining workers while unemployment is low.[3]

CUSTOMERS

The company needs to study its customer markets closely. Figure 3.2 shows five types of customer markets. *Consumer markets* consist of individuals and households that buy goods and services for personal consumption. *Business markets* buy goods and services for further processing or for use in their production process, whereas *reseller markets* buy goods and services to resell at a profit. *Government markets* are made up of government agencies that buy goods and services to produce public services or transfer the goods and services to others who need them. Finally, *international markets* consist of these buyers in other countries, including consumers, producers, resellers, and governments. Each market type has special characteristics that call for careful study by the seller.

COMPETITORS

The marketing concept states that to be successful, a company must provide greater customer value and satisfaction than its competitors do. Thus, marketers must do more than simply adapt to the needs of target consumers. They also must gain strategic advantage by positioning their offerings strongly against competitors' offerings in the minds of consumers.

No single competitive marketing strategy is best for all companies. Each firm should consider its own size and industry position compared to those of its competitors. Large firms with dominant positions in an industry can use certain strategies that smaller firms cannot afford. But being large is not enough. There are winning strategies for large firms, but there are also losing ones. Small firms can develop strategies that give them better rates of return than large firms enjoy.

---

[3]Sarah Lorge, "The Coke Advantage," *Sales & Marketing Management,* December 1998, p. 17.

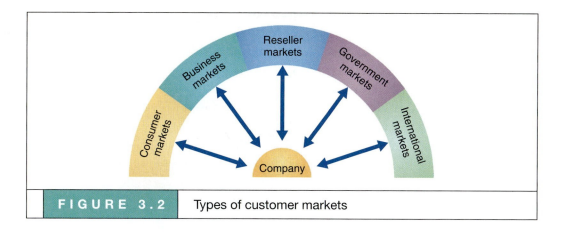

FIGURE 3.2 Types of customer markets

PUBLICS

The company's marketing environment also includes various publics. A **public** is any group that has an actual or potential interest in or impact on an organization's ability to achieve its objectives. Figure 3.3 shows seven types of publics.

- *Financial publics* influence the company's ability to obtain funds. Banks, investment houses, and stockholders are the major financial publics.

- *Media publics* carry news, features, and editorial opinion. They include newspapers, magazines, and radio and television stations.

- *Government publics:* Management must take government developments into account. Marketers must often consult the company's lawyers on issues of product safety, truth in advertising, and other matters.

- *Citizen action publics:* A company's marketing decisions may be questioned by consumer organizations, environmental groups, minority groups, and others. Its public relations department can help it stay in touch with consumer and citizen groups.

- *Local publics* include neighborhood residents and community organizations. Large companies usually appoint a community relations officer to deal with the community, attend meetings, answer questions, and contribute to worthwhile causes.

- *General public:* A company needs to be concerned about the general public's attitude toward its products and activities. The public's image of the company affects its buying.

- *Internal publics* include workers, managers, volunteers, and the board of directors. Large companies use newsletters and other means to inform and motivate their internal publics. When employees feel good about their company, this positive attitude spills over to external publics.

A company can prepare marketing plans for these major publics as well as for its customer markets. Suppose the company wants a specific response from a particular public, such as goodwill, favorable word of mouth, or donations of time or money. The company would have to design an offer to this public that is attractive enough to produce the desired response.

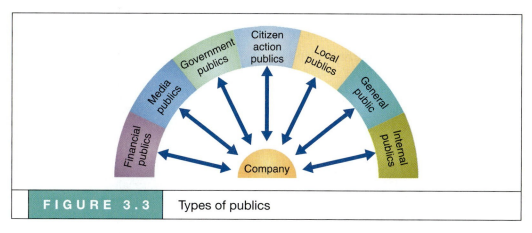

FIGURE 3.3   Types of publics

Publics: In this ad, Wal-Mart recognizes the importance of both its local and employee publics. Its Competitive Edge scholarship program "is just one of the reasons Wal-Mart associates (such as Maxine) in Mississippi, and all over the country, are proud to get involved in the communities they serve."

active exercise <

Explore some aspects of one firm's microenvironment.

active concept check <

Now let's take a moment to test your knowledge of what you've just read.

> ### The Company's Macroenvironment

The company and all of the other actors operate in a larger macroenvironment of forces that shape opportunities and pose threats to the company. Figure 3.4 shows the six major forces in the company's macroenvironment. In the remaining sections of this chapter, we examine these forces and show how they affect marketing plans.

DEMOGRAPHIC ENVIRONMENT

Demography is the study of human populations in terms of size, density, location, age, gender, race, occupation, and other statistics. The demographic environment is of major interest to marketers because it involves people, and people make up markets.

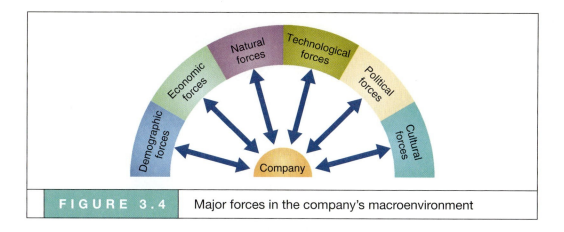

| FIGURE 3.4 | Major forces in the company's macroenvironment |

The world population is growing at an explosive rate. It now totals more than 6 billion and will exceed 7.9 billion by the year 2025.[4] The explosive world population growth has major implications for business. A growing population means growing human needs to satisfy. Depending on purchasing power, it may also mean growing market opportunities. For example, to curb its skyrocketing population, the Chinese government has passed regulations limiting families to one child each. As a result, Chinese children are spoiled and fussed over as never before. Known in China as "little emperors," Chinese children are being showered with everything from candy to computers as a result of what's known as the "six-pocket syndrome." As many as six adults—including parents and two sets of doting grandparents—may be indulging the whims of each child. Parents in the average Beijing household now spend about 40 percent of their income on their cherished only child. This trend has encouraged toy companies such as Japan's Bandai Company (known for its Mighty Morphin Power Rangers), Denmark's Lego Group, and Mattel to enter the Chinese market.[5]

The world's large and highly diverse population poses both opportunities and challenges. Thus, marketers keep close track of demographic trends and developments in their markets, both at home and abroad. They track changing age and family structures, geographic population shifts, educational characteristics, and population diversity. Here, we discuss the most important demographic trends in the United States.

Changing Age Structure of the Population

The U.S. population stood at more than 273 million in 1999 and may reach 300 million by the year 2020.[6] The single most important demographic trend in the United States is the changing age structure of the population. As shown in Figure 3.5, the age distribution of the U.S. population is rapidly assuming an "hourglass" shape. Two very large age groups, the baby boomer generation and the baby boomlet generation, surround the smaller Generation Xers.

> **video example**

Pause here to see how CanGo deals with its demographic environment.

The Baby Boomers. The post–World War II **baby boom** produced 78 million baby boomers born between 1946 and 1964. Since then, the baby boomers have become one of the most powerful forces shaping the marketing environment. The boomers have presented a moving target, creating new markets as they grew from infancy to their preadolescent, teenage, young adult, and now middle-age to mature years. Today's baby boomers account for about 30 percent of the population but earn more than half of all personal income.

[4]World POPClock, U.S. Census Bureau, www.census.gov, September 1999. This Web site provides continuously updated projections of the world population.

[5]Sally D. Goll, "Marketing: China's (Only) Children Get the Royal Treatment," *Wall Street Journal,* February 8, 1995, pp. B1, B3; and Lorien Holland, "Baby Boom," *Far Eastern Economic Review,* June 24, 1999, p. 61.

[6]See Diane Crispell, "Generations to 2025," *American Demographics,* January 1995, p. 4; and POPClock Projection, U.S. Census Bureau, www.census.gov, September 1999.

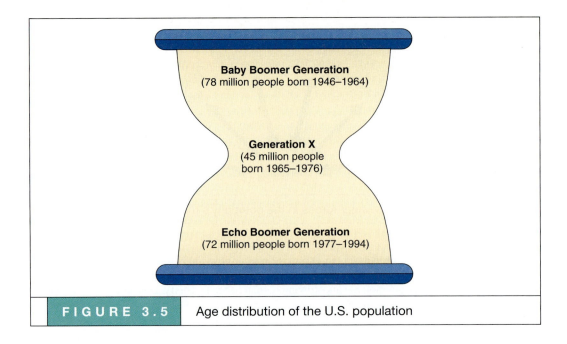

Baby boomers cut across all walks of life. But marketers typically have paid the most attention to the smaller upper crust of the boomer generation—its more educated, mobile, and wealthy segments. These segments have gone by many names. In the 1980s, they were called "yuppies" (young urban professionals), "bumpies" (black upwardly mobile professionals) "yummies" (young upwardly mobile mommies), and "DINKs" (dual-income, no-kids couples). In the 1990s, however, yuppies and DINKs gave way to a new breed, with names such as "DEWKs" (dual earners with kids) and "MOBYs" (mother older, baby younger). Now, to the chagrin of many in this generation, they are acquiring such titles as "WOOFs" (well-off older folks) or even "GRUMPIES" (just what the name suggests).

The oldest boomers are now in their fifties; the youngest are in their mid-to-late thirties. Thus, the boomers have evolved from the "youthquake generation" to the "backache generation." They are also reaching their peak earning and spending years. Thus, they constitute a lucrative market for housing, furniture and appliances, healthful foods and beverages, physical fitness products, high-priced cars, convenience products, and travel and financial services.

The maturing boomers are experiencing the pangs of midlife and rethinking the purpose and value of their work, responsibilities, and relationships. They are approaching life with a new stability and reasonableness in the way they live, think, eat, and spend. As they continue to age, they will create a large and important seniors market. By 2025, there will be 64 million baby boomers aged 61 to 79, a 90 percent increase in the size of this population from today.[7]

Generation X. The baby boom was followed by a "birth dearth," creating another generation of 45 million people born between 1965 and 1976. Author Douglas Coupland calls them "Generation X," because they lie in the shadow of the boomers and lack obvious distinguishing characteristics. Others call them the "baby busters," "shadow generation," "twentysomethings," or "yiffies"—young, individualistic, freedom-minded few.

The GenXers are defined as much by their shared experiences as by their age. Increasing divorce rates and higher employment for their mothers made them the first generation of latchkey kids. Whereas the boomers created a sexual revolution, the GenXers have lived in the age of AIDS. Having grown up during times of recession and corporate downsizing, they have developed a more cautious economic outlook. As a result, the GenXers are a more skeptical bunch, cynical of frivolous marketing pitches that promise easy success. They buy lots of products, such as sweaters, boots, cosmetics, electronics, cars, fast food, beer, computers, and mountain bikes. However, their cynicism makes them more savvy shoppers, and their financial pressures make them more value conscious. They like lower prices and a more functional look. The GenXers respond to honesty in advertising, and they like irreverence and sass and ads that mock the traditional advertising approach. For example, recent Miller Brewing Company ads appealing to this group advised "It's time to embrace your inner idiot" and one features images of a frenetic, sloppy hot-dog-eating contest.

[7]Lach, "Dateline America: May 1, 2025," p. 19.

GenXers share new cultural concerns. They care about the environment and respond favorably to socially responsible companies. Although they seek success, they are less materialistic; they prize experience, not acquisition. They are cautious romantics who want a better quality of life and are more interested in job satisfaction than in sacrificing personal happiness and growth for promotion.

Once labeled as "The MTV generation: Net surfing, nihilistic [body-piercing slackers] whining about McJobs," the GenXers are now growing up and beginning to take over. They do surf the Internet more than other groups, but with serious intent. The GenXers are poised to displace the lifestyles, culture, and materialistic values of the baby boomers. They represent $125 billion in annual purchasing power. By the year 2010, they will have overtaken the baby boomers as a primary market for almost every product category. According to one analyst, "They are flocking to technology start-ups, founding small businesses, and even taking up causes—all in their own way. There are the next big thing. Boomers, beware!"[8]

The Echo Boomers.   Both the baby boomers and GenXers will one day be passing the reins to the latest demographic group, the **echo boomers** (or baby boomlet generation). Born between 1977 and 1994, these children of the baby boomers now number 72 million, dwarfing the GenXers and almost equal in size to the baby boomer segment. Ranging from preteens to twenties, the echo boomer generation is still forming its buying preferences and behaviors.

The baby boomlet has created large and growing kid and teens markets. Teens and preteens under 20 years of age spend $130 billion on their own and influence upward of $500 billion of their parents' spending.[9] After years of bust, markets for children's toys and games, clothes, furniture, and food are enjoying a boom. For instance, Sony and other electronics firms are now offering products designed especially for children. In recent years, designers and retailers have created new lines, new products, and even new stores devoted to children and teens—Tommy Hilfiger, DKNY, Gap, Toys "R" Us, Guess, Talbots, Pottery Barn, and Eddie Bauer, to name just a few. A number of new media have appeared that cater specifically to this market: *Time, Sports Illustrated,* and *People* have all started new editions for kids and teens. Banks offer banking and investment services for kids, including investment camps. Major advertising agencies have even opened new divisions—such as Saatchi & Saatchi Advertising's Kid Connection division and Grey Advertising's 18 & Under division—that specialize in helping their clients shape their appeals for young audiences.[10]

Like the trailing edge of the Generation Xers ahead of them, one distinguishing characteristic of the echo boomers is their utter fluency and comfort with computer, digital, and Internet technology. For this reason, one analyst has christened them the Net-Gens (or N-Gens). He observes:

> What makes this generation different . . . is not just its demographic muscle, but it is the first to grow up surrounded by digital media. Computers and other digital technologies, such as digital cameras, are commonplace to N-Gen members. They work with them at home, in school, and they use them for entertainment. Increasingly these technologies are connected to the Internet. . . . Constantly surrounded by technology, today's kids are accustomed to its strong presence in their lives. [They] are so bathed in bits that they are no more intimidated by digital technology than a VCR or a toaster. And it is through their use of the digital media that N-Gen will develop and superimpose its culture on the rest of society. Boomers stand back. Already these kids are learning, playing, communicating, working, and creating communities very differently than did their parents. They are a force for social transformation.[11]

Generational Marketing.   Do marketers have to create separate products and marketing programs for each generation? Some experts caution that each generation spans decades of time and many socioeconomic levels. "These segments are so large they're meaningless as marketing targets," notes one such expert. "'Matures' range in age from 54 to 90; that isn't a target, it's a happening." Similarly, . . . "boomers span almost twenty years." He suggests that marketers should form more precise age-specific segments within each group.

Others warn that marketers have to be careful about turning off one generation each time they craft a product or message that appeals effectively to another. "The idea is to try to be broadly inclusive and

[8]Margot Hornblower, "Great X," *Time,* June 9, 1997, pp. 58–69. Also see Janus Dietz, "When Gen X Meets Aging Baby Boomers," *Marketing News,* May 10, 1999, p. 17.

[9]See Philip Kotler, *Marketing Management: Analysis, Planning, Implementation, and Control,* 10th ed. (Upper Saddle River, NJ: Prentice Hall, 2000), p. 141.

[10]See James U. McNeal, "Tapping the Three Kids' Markets," *American Demographics,* April 1998, pp. 37–40; Carolyn M. Edy, "Babies Mean Business," *American Demographics,* May 1999, pp. 46–47; and Jennifer Gilbert, "New Teen Obsession," *Advertising Age,* February 14, 2000, p. 38.

[11]Accessed online from www.growingupdigital.com/ FLecho.html, October 1999. Also see Douglas Tapscott, *Growing Up Digital: The Rise of the Net Generation* (New York: McGraw-Hill, 1999).

at the same time offer each generation something specifically designed for it. Tommy Hilfiger has big brand logos on his clothes for teenagers and little pocket polo logos on his shirts for baby boomers. It's a brand that has a more inclusive than exclusive strategy."[12]

video exercise <

Before we proceed further, let's revisit the question of how CanGo can make the most of the demographic environment.

The Changing American Family

The "traditional household" consists of a husband, wife, and children (and sometimes grandparents). Yet, the once American ideal of the two-child, two-car suburban family has lately been losing some of its luster. In fact, couples with children under 18 now make up only about 35 percent of all U.S. families.[13] In the United States today, one in eight households is "diverse" or "nontraditional" and includes single live-alones, adult live-togethers of one or both sexes, single-parent families, childless married couples, or empty nesters. More people are divorcing or separating, choosing not to marry, marrying later, or marrying without the intention to have children. Marketers must increasingly consider the special needs of nontraditional households, because they are now growing more rapidly than traditional households. Each group has a distinctive set of needs and buying habits. For example, people in the SSWD group (single, separated, widowed, divorced) need smaller apartments; inexpensive and smaller appliances, furniture, and furnishings; and food packaged in smaller sizes.

The number of working women has also increased greatly. This trend has spawned the child day care business and increased consumption of convenience foods and services, career-oriented women's clothing, financial services, and many other business opportunities. Here are two examples:

> More and more workplaces and child care centers are installing monitoring setups such as "I See You" equipment from Simplex Knowledge in White Plains, New York. This system allows parents to see their children at different points throughout the day. Via still photos taken by a camera in the child care center and posted on a secure Web site on the Internet, working parents who long to spend more time with their young ones get reassuring glimpses throughout the day.[14]

> Whereas shopping malls are in decline, there's been a boom in niche malls that cater to the needs of working women. Shops at Somerset Square in Glastonbury, Connecticut, is one such open-air shopping center. It features a customized retail mix of specialty shops, targeted promotions, and phone-in shopping in which shoppers phone ahead with sizes and color preferences while store employees perform a "wardrobing" service. Many of the stores also informally extend hours for working women who find time to shop only before or after work.[15]

active example <

Consider in greater depth the marketing implications of the changing American family.

[12]See J. Walker Smith and Ann Clurman, *Rocking the Ages* (New York: HarperBusiness, 1998); and Mercedes M. Cardona, "Hilfiger's New Apparel Lines Getting Individual Efforts," *Advertising Age,* February 8, 1999, p. 24.

[13]See Diane Crispell, "Married Couples Endure," *American Demographics,* January 1998, p. 39; and www.census .gov/population/projections/nation/hh-fam/table5n.txt, accessed online, June 1999.

[14]Sue Shellenbarger, " 'Child-Care Cams': Are They Good News for Working Parents?" *Wall Street Journal,* August 19, 1998, p. B11.

[15]Kelly Shermach, "Niche Malls: Innovation for an Industry in Decline," *Marketing News,* February 26, 1996, p. 1.

Geographic Shifts in Population

This is a period of great migratory movements between and within countries. Americans, for example, are a mobile people with about 12 million U.S. households (more than one out of every ten) moving each year.[16] Over the past two decades, the U.S. population has shifted toward the Sunbelt states. The West and South have grown while the Midwest and Northeast states have lost population. Such population shifts interest marketers because people in different regions buy differently. For example, research shows that people in Seattle buy more toothbrushes per capita than people in any other U.S. city; people in Salt Lake City eat more candy bars; people from New Orleans use more ketchup; and people in Miami drink more prune juice.

Also, for more than a century, Americans have been moving from rural to metropolitan areas. In the 1950s, they made a massive exit from the cities to the suburbs. Today, the migration to the suburbs continues, and demographers are noting another shift that they call "the rural rebound." Nonmetropolitan counties that lost population to cities for most of this century are now attracting large numbers of urban refugees. More and more Americans are moving to "micropolitan areas," small cities located beyond congested metropolitan areas. These smaller micros offer many of the advantages of metro areas—jobs, restaurants, diversions, community organizations—but without the population crush, traffic jams, high crime rates, and high property taxes often associated with heavily urbanized areas.[17]

The shift in where people live has also caused a shift in where they work. For example, the migration toward micropolitan and rural areas has resulted in a rapid increase in the number of people who "telecommute"—work at home or in a remote office and conduct their business by phone, fax, modem, or the Internet. This trend, in turn, has created a booming SOHO (small office/home office) market. Nearly 40 million Americans are now working out of their homes with the help of electronic conveniences like personal computers, cell phones, fax machines, and handheld organizers. Many marketers are actively courting the home office segment of this lucrative SOHO market. One example is Kinko's Copy Centers:

> Founded in the 1970s as a campus photocopying business, Kinko's is now reinventing itself as the well-appointed office outside the home. Where once there were copy machines, Kinko's 902 stores in this country and abroad now feature a uniform mixture of fax machines, ultrafast color printers, and networks of computers equipped with popular software programs and high-speed Internet connections. People can come to a Kinko's store to do all their office jobs: they can copy, send and receive faxes, use various pro-

Geographic shifts: The shift in where people live has also caused a shift in where they work, creating a booming SOHO (small office/home office) market.

[16] Dan Fost, "Americans on the Move," *American Demographics*, Tools Supplement, January–February 1997, pp. 10–13.

[17] See Kevin Heubusch, "Small Is Beautiful," *American Demographics*, January 1998, pp. 43–49; Brad Edmondson, "A New Era for Rural Americans," *American Demographics*, September 1997, pp. 30–31; and Kenneth M. Johnson and Calvin L. Beale, "The Rural Rebound," *The Wilson Quarterly*, Spring 1998, pp. 16–27.

grams on the computer, go on the Internet, order stationery and other printed supplies, and even teleconference. As more and more people join the work-at-home trend, Kinko's offers an escape from the isolation of the home office. The office-support chain is hoping to increase its share of industry revenue by getting people to spend more time—and hence, more money—at its stores. Besides adding state-of-the-art equipment, the company is talking to Starbucks about opening up coffee shops adjacent to some Kinko's. The lettering on the Kinko's door sums up the $1 billion company's new business model: "Your branch office/Open 24 hours."[18]

A Better-Educated and More White-Collar Population

The U.S. population is becoming better educated. For example, in 1996, 82 percent of the U.S. population over age 25 had completed high school and 24 percent had completed college, compared with 69 percent and 17 percent in 1980. The rising number of educated people will increase the demand for quality products, books, magazines, travel, personal computers, and Internet services. It suggests a decline in television viewing because college-educated consumers watch less TV than the population at large. The workforce also is becoming more white collar. Between 1950 and 1985, the proportion of white-collar workers rose from 41 percent to 54 percent, that of blue-collar workers declined from 47 percent to 33 percent, and that of service workers increased from 12 percent to 14 percent. These trends have continued into the new millennium.[19]

Increasing Diversity

Countries vary in their ethnic and racial makeup. At one extreme is Japan, where almost everyone is Japanese. At the other extreme is the United States, with people from virtually all nations. The United States has often been called a melting pot in which diverse groups from many nations and cultures have melted into a single, more homogenous whole. Instead, the United States seems to have become more of a "salad bowl" in which various groups have mixed together but have maintained their diversity by retaining and valuing important ethnic and cultural differences.

Marketers are facing increasingly diverse markets, both at home and abroad as their operations become more international in scope. In the United States alone, ethnic population growth is six times greater than the Caucasian growth rate, and ethnic consumers buy more than $600 billion of goods and services each year. The U.S. population is 72 percent white, with African Americans making up another 13 percent. The Hispanic population has grown rapidly and now stands at about 11 percent of the U.S. population. The U.S. Asian population also has grown rapidly in recent years and now totals about 3 percent of the population. The remaining 1 percent of the population is made up of Native Americans, Eskimos, and Aleuts. During the next half century, the proportions of both Hispanics and Asians will more than double. Moreover, there are nearly 25 million people living in the United States—over 9 percent of the population—who were born in another country.[20]

Many large companies, ranging from large retailers such as Sears and Wal-Mart to consumer products companies such as Levi-Strauss and Procter & Gamble, now target specially designed products and promotions to one or more of these groups. Miller beer, for example, created television ads for the Hispanic market shown exclusively on Spanish-speaking channels. Even within the Hispanic market, however, different consumers have diverse interests and beliefs depending on country of origin, length of time in the United States, geographic placement, and other factors. Thus, although Miller employs the same visual elements across the country, it alters background music and voice-overs to reflect differences between, for example, Cubans in New York City and Mexican Americans in Los Angeles.

[18]Lauri J. Flynn, "Not Just a Copy Shop Any Longer, Kinko's Pushes Its Computer Services," *New York Times,* July 6, 1998, p. D12. Also see Carol Leonetti Dannhauser, "Who's in the Home Office," *American Demographics,* June 1999, pp. 50–56.

[19]See Fabian Linden, "In the Rearview Mirror," *American Demographics,* April 1984, pp. 4–5; Peter Francese, "America at Mid-Decade," *American Demographics,* February 1995, pp. 23–29; Rebecca Piirto Heath, "The New Working Class," *American Demographics,* January 1998, pp. 51–55; and *Digest of Education Statistics 1997,* National Center for Education Statistics, January 1998, at http://nces01.ed.gov/pubs/digest97.

[20]See "A True Melting Pot," *Advertising Age,* February 17, 1997, p. S2; "Foreign-Born Diversity," *American Demographics,* July 1997, p. 33; Nancy Coltun Webster, "Multicultural," *Advertising Age,* November 17, 1997, pp. S1–S2; and "Diversity," *Advertising Age,* February 16, 1998, pp. S1, S14.

Diversity goes beyond ethnic heritage. For example, there are more than 52 million disabled people in the United States—a market larger than African Americans or Hispanics—representing almost $800 million in annual spending power. People with mobility challenges are an ideal target market for companies such as Peapod (**www.peapod.com**), which teams up with large supermarket chains in many heavily populated areas to offer online grocery shopping and home delivery. They also represent a growing market for travel, sports, and other leisure-oriented products and services.[21]

ECONOMIC ENVIRONMENT

Markets require buying power as well as people. The **economic environment** consists of factors that affect consumer purchasing power and spending patterns. Nations vary greatly in their levels and distribution of income. Some countries have *subsistence economies*—they consume most of their own agricultural and industrial output. These countries offer few market opportunities. At the other extreme are *industrial economies,* which constitute rich markets for many different kinds of goods. Marketers must pay close attention to major trends and consumer spending patterns both across and within their world markets. Following are some of the major economic trends in the United States.

Changes in Income

During the 1980s—tabbed the "roaring eighties" by some—American consumers fell into a consumption frenzy, fueled by income growth, federal tax reductions, rapid increases in housing values, and a boom in borrowing. They bought and bought, seemingly without caution, amassing record levels of debt. "It was fashionable to describe yourself as 'born to shop.' When the going gets tough, it was said, the tough go shopping."[22]

During the 1990s, the baby boom generation moved into its prime wage-earning years, and the number of small families headed by dual-career couples continued to increase. Thus, many consumers continued to demand quality products and better service, and they were able to pay for them. However, the free spending and high expectations of the 1980s were dashed by the recession in the early 1990s. In fact, the 1990s became the decade of the "squeezed consumer." Along with rising incomes in some segments came increased financial burdens—repaying debts acquired during earlier spending splurges, facing increased household and family expenses, and saving for college tuition payments and retirement. These financially squeezed consumers sobered up, pulled back, and adjusted to their changing financial situations. They spent more carefully and sought greater value in the products and services they bought. *Value marketing* became the watchword for many marketers.

As we move into the 2000s, despite several years of strong economic performance, consumers continue to spend carefully. Hence, the trend toward value marketing continues. Rather than offering high quality at a high price, or lesser quality at very low prices, marketers are looking for ways to offer today's more financially cautious buyers greater value—just the right combination of product quality and good service at a fair price.

Marketers should pay attention to *income distribution* as well as average income. Income distribution in the United States is still very skewed. At the top are *upper-class* consumers, whose spending patterns are not affected by current economic events and who are a major market for luxury goods. There is a comfortable *middle class* that is somewhat careful about its spending but can still afford the good life some of the time. The *working class* must stick close to the basics of food, clothing, and shelter and must try hard to save. Finally, the *underclass* (persons on welfare and many retirees) must count their pennies when making even the most basic purchases.

Over the past three decades, the rich have grown richer, the middle class has shrunk, and the poor have remained poor. In 1994, the top 5 percent of income-earning households in the United States captured over 21 percent of aggregate income, up from 16.6 percent in 1970. Meanwhile, the share of income captured by the bottom 20 percent of income-earning households decreased from 4.1 percent to 3.6 percent.[23] This distribution of income has created a two-tiered market. Many companies are aggressively targeting the affluent:

---

[21]Dan Frost, "The Fun Factor: Marketing Recreation to the Disabled," *American Demographics,* February 1998, pp. 54–58; and Michelle Wirth Fellman, "Selling IT Goods to Disabled End-Users," *Marketing News,* March 15, 1999, pp. 1, 17.

[22]James W. Hughes, "Understanding the Squeezed Consumer," *American Demographics,* July 1991, pp. 44–50. For more on consumer spending trends, see Cheryl Russell, "The New Consumer Paradigm," *American Demographics,* April 1999, pp. 50–58.

[23]See U.S. Census Bureau, Income Inequity—Table 2, February 25, 1997, at www.census.gov/hes/income/incineq/p60tb2. html; John McManus, "Gap Analysis," *American Demographics,* July 1999, p. 6; and Frank Levy, "Rhetoric and Reality," *Harvard Business Review,* September–October 1999, pp. 163–71.

Driven by the heavenward ascent of the Dow, low unemployment and inflation, and vast numbers of duel-income boomers in their prime earning years, . . . marketers have responded with a ceaseless array of pricey, upscale products aimed at satisfying wealthy Americans' appetite for "the very best": leather-lined SUVs as big as tanks, $1,300 sheets, restaurant-quality appliances, and vast cruise ships offering every form of luxurious coddling. . . . Huge increases in wealth among the very rich have fueled the sales of $17,500 Patek Philippe watches that are sold as family heirlooms (thus justifying the price tag), created the clamor for a $48,000 Lexus (options extra), and resulted in a two-year waiting list for $14,000 Hermes Kelly bags.[24]

Other companies are now tailoring their marketing offers to two different markets—the affluent and the less affluent. For example, Walt Disney Company markets two distinct Winnie-the-Pooh bears:

The original line-drawn figure appears on fine china, pewter spoons, and pricey kids' stationery found in upscale specialty and department stores such as Nordstrom and Bloomingdale's. The plump, cartoonlike Pooh, clad in a red shirt and a goofy smile, adorns plastic key chains, polyester bed sheets, and animated videos. It sells in Wal-Mart stores and five-and-dime shops. Except at Disney's own stores, the two Poohs do not share the same retail shelf. [Thus, Disney offers both] upstairs and downstairs Poohs, hoping to land customers on both sides of the [income] divide.[25]

Changing Consumer Spending Patterns

Table 3.1 shows the proportion of total expenditures made by U.S. households at different income levels for major categories of goods and services. Food, housing, and transportation use up most household income. However, consumers at different income levels have different spending patterns. Some of these differences were noted over a century ago by Ernst Engel, who studied how people shifted their spending as their income rose. He found that as family income rises, the percentage spent on food declines, the percentage spent on housing remains about constant (except for such utilities as gas, electricity, and public services, which decrease), and both the percentage spent on most other categories and that devoted to savings increase. **Engel's laws** generally have been supported by later studies.

Changes in major economic variables such as income, cost of living, interest rates, and savings and borrowing patterns have a large impact on the marketplace. Companies watch these variables by using economic forecasting. Businesses do not have to be wiped out by an economic downturn or

TABLE 3.1	Consumer Spending at Different Income Levels		
	% of Spending at Different Income Levels		
Expenditure	**$10,000–15,000**	**$20,000–30,000**	**$70,000 and Over**
Food	16.4	15.6	11.6
Housing	35.9	31.3	29.5
Utilities	9.4	7.9	4.7
Clothing	5.4	5.5	5.2
Transportation	15.6	17.8	17.0
Health care	6.5	6.8	5.9
Entertainment	4.9	4.7	5.7
Tobacco	1.3	1.3	0.37
Contributions	2.1	3.2	4.7
Insurance	3.4	7.6	15.6

Source: Consumer Expenditure Survey, U.S. Department of Labor, Bureau of Labor Statistics, Bulletin 2462, September 1995, pp. 15–17. Also see Paula Mergenhagan, "What Can Minimum Wage Buy," *American Demographics,* January 1996, pp. 18–21.

[24]Debra Goldman, "Paradox of Pleasure," *American Demographics,* May 1999, pp. 50–53.

[25]David Leonhardt, "Two-Tier Marketing," *Business Week,* March 17, 1997, pp. 82–90.

caught short in a boom. With adequate warning, they can take advantage of changes in the economic environment.

NATURAL ENVIRONMENT

The **natural environment** involves the natural resources that are needed as inputs by marketers or that are affected by marketing activities. Environmental concerns have grown steadily during the past three decades. Some trend analysts labeled the 1990s as the "Earth Decade," claiming that the natural environment is the major worldwide issue facing business and the public. The Earth Day movement turned 30 in the year 2000. In many cities around the world, air and water pollution have reached dangerous levels. World concern continues to mount about the depletion of the earth's ozone layer and the resulting "greenhouse effect," a dangerous warming of the Earth. And many environmentalists fear that we soon will be buried in our own trash.

Marketers should be aware of several trends in the natural environment. The first involves growing *shortages of raw materials*. Air and water may seem to be infinite resources, but some groups see long-run dangers. Air pollution chokes many of the world's large cities and water shortages are already a big problem in some parts of the United States and the world. Renewable resources, such as forests and food, also have to be used wisely. Nonrenewable resources, such as oil, coal, and various minerals, pose a serious problem. Firms making products that require these scarce resources face large cost increases, even if the materials do remain available.

A second environmental trend is *increased pollution*. Industry will almost always damage the quality of the natural environment. Consider the disposal of chemical and nuclear wastes; the dangerous mercury levels in the ocean; the quantity of chemical pollutants in the soil and food supply; and the littering of the environment with nonbiodegradable bottles, plastics, and other packaging materials.

A third trend is *increased government intervention* in natural resource management. The governments of different countries vary in their concern and efforts to promote a clean environment. Some, like the German government, vigorously pursue environmental quality. Others, especially many poorer nations, do little about pollution, largely because they lack the needed funds or political will. Even the richer nations lack the vast funds and political accord needed to mount a worldwide environmental effort. The general hope is that companies around the world will accept more social responsibility, and that less expensive devices can be found to control and reduce pollution.

In the United States, the Environmental Protection Agency (EPA) was created in 1970 to set and enforce pollution standards and to conduct pollution research. In the future, companies doing business in the United States can expect strong controls from government and pressure groups. Instead of opposing regulation, marketers should help develop solutions to the material and energy problems facing the world.

Concern for the natural environment has spawned the so-called green movement. Today, enlightened companies go beyond what government regulations dictate. They are developing *environmentally sustainable* strategies and practices in an effort to create a world economy that the planet can support indefinitely. They are responding to consumer demands with ecologically safer products, recyclable or biodegradable packaging, better pollution controls, and more energy-efficient operations. 3M runs a Pollution Prevention Pays program that has led to a substantial reduction in pollution and costs. AT&T uses a special software package to choose the least harmful materials, cut hazardous waste, reduce energy use, and improve product recycling in its operations. McDonald's eliminated polystyrene cartons and now uses smaller, recyclable paper wrappings and napkins. IBM's AS/400e series of midrange business computers is more energy efficient, contains recycled content, and is designed to be disassembled for recycling. Dixon-Ticonderoga, the folks who developed the first pencil made in the United States, developed Prang crayons made from soybeans rather than paraffin wax, a by-product of oil drilling. Soybeans are a renewable resource and produce brighter, richer colors and a smoother texture. More and more, companies are recognizing the link between a healthy economy and a healthy ecology.[26]

TECHNOLOGICAL ENVIRONMENT

The **technological environment** is perhaps the most dramatic force now shaping our destiny. Technology has released such wonders as antibiotics, organ transplants, notebook computers, and the

[26]For more discussion, see the "Environmentalism" section in chap. 20. Also see Michael E. Porter and Claas van der Linde, "Green *and* Competitive: Ending the Stalemate," *Harvard Business Review,* September–October 1995, pp. 120–34; Stuart L. Hart, "Beyond Greening: Strategies for a Sustainable World," *Harvard Business Review,* January–February 1997, pp. 67–76; Jacquelyn Ottman, "Environment Winners Show Sustainable Strategies," *Marketing News,* April 27, 1998, p. 6; Lisa E. Phillips, "Green Attitude," *American Demographics,* April 1999, pp. 46–47; and Forest L. Reinhardt, "Bringing the Environment down to Earth," *Harvard Business Review,* July–August 1999, pp. 149–57.

Internet. It also has released such horrors as nuclear missiles, chemical weapons, and assault rifles. It has released such mixed blessings as the automobile, television, and credit cards. Our attitude toward technology depends on whether we are more impressed with its wonders or its blunders.

The technological environment changes rapidly. Think of all of today's common products that were not available 100 years ago, or even 30 years ago. Abraham Lincoln did not know about automobiles, airplanes, radios, or the electric light. Woodrow Wilson did not know about television, aerosol cans, automatic dishwashers, room air conditioners, antibiotics, or computers. Franklin Delano Roosevelt did not know about xerography, synthetic detergents, tape recorders, birth control pills, or earth satellites. John F. Kennedy did not know about personal computers, compact disk players, VCRs, or the World Wide Web.

New technologies create new markets and opportunities. However, every new technology replaces an older technology. Transistors hurt the vacuum-tube industry, xerography hurt the carbon-paper business, the auto hurt the railroads, and compact disks hurt phonograph records. When old industries fought or ignored new technologies, their businesses declined. Thus, marketers should watch the technological environment closely. Companies that do not keep up with technological change soon will find their products outdated. They will miss new product and market opportunities.

The United States leads the world in research and development spending.[27] Scientists today are researching a wide range of promising new products and services, ranging from practical solar energy, electric cars, and cancer cures to voice-controlled computers and genetically engineered food crops. Today's research usually is carried out by research teams rather than by lone inventors like Thomas Edison, Samuel Morse, or Alexander Graham Bell. Many companies are adding marketing people to R&D teams to try to obtain a stronger marketing orientation. Scientists also speculate on fantasy products, such as flying cars, three-dimensional televisions, and space colonies. The challenge in each case is not only technical but also commercial—to make *practical, affordable* versions of these products.

As products and technology become more complex, the public needs to know that these are safe. Thus, government agencies investigate and ban potentially unsafe products. In the United States, the Federal Food and Drug Administration has set up complex regulations for testing new drugs. The Consumer Product Safety Commission sets safety standards for consumer products and penalizes companies that fail to meet them. Such regulations have resulted in much higher research costs and in longer times between new-product ideas and their introduction. Marketers should be aware of these regulations when applying new technologies and developing new products.

active example <

Click here to consider how one organization has dealt with changes in the technological environment.

POLITICAL ENVIRONMENT

Marketing decisions are strongly affected by developments in the political environment. The **political environment** consists of laws, government agencies, and pressure groups that influence and limit various organizations and individuals in a given society.

Legislation Regulating Business

Even the most liberal advocates of free-market economies agree that the system works best with at least some regulation. Well-conceived regulation can encourage competition and ensure fair markets for goods and services. Thus, governments develop *public policy* to guide commerce—sets of laws and regulations that limit business for the good of society as a whole. Almost every marketing activity is subject to a wide range of laws and regulations.

Increasing Legislation. Legislation affecting business around the world has increased steadily over the years. The United States has many laws covering issues such as competition, fair trade practices, environmental protection, product safety, truth in advertising, packaging and labeling, pricing, and other important areas (see Table 3.2). The European Commission has been active in establishing a new framework of laws covering competitive behavior, product standards, product liability, and commercial transactions for the nations of the European Union. Several countries have gone farther

[27]See M. F. Wolff, "Real R&D Spending Increase Forecast for 1998," *Research Technology Management,* March–April, 1998, p. 6.

TABLE 3.2

TABLE 3.2	Major U.S. Legislation Affecting Marketing

Legislation	Purpose
Sherman Antitrust Act (1890)	Prohibits monopolies and activities (price-fixing, predatory pricing) that restrain trade or competition in interstate commerce.
Federal Food and Drug Act (1906)	Forbids the manufacture or sale of adulterated or fraudulently labeled foods and drugs. Created the Food and Drug Administration.
Clayton Act (1914)	Supplements the Sherman Act by prohibiting certain types of price discrimination, exclusive dealing, and tying clauses (which require a dealer to take additional products in a seller's line).
Federal Trade Commission Act (1914)	Establishes a commission to monitor and remedy unfair trade methods.
Robinson–Patman Act (1936)	Amends Clayton Act to define price discrimination as unlawful. Empowers FTC to establish limits on quantity discounts, forbid some brokerage allowances, and prohibit promotional allowances except when made available on proportionately equal terms.
Wheeler–Lea Act (1938)	Makes deceptive, misleading, and unfair practices illegal regardless of injury to competition. Places advertising of food and drugs under FTC jurisdiction.
Lanham Trademark Act (1946)	Protects and regulates distinctive brand names and trademarks.
National Traffic and Safety Act (1958)	Provides for the creation of compulsory safety standards for automobiles and tires.
Fair Packaging and Labeling Act (1966)	Provides for the regulation of packaging and labeling of consumer goods. Requires that manufacturers state what the package contains, who made it, and how much it contains.
Child Protection Act (1966)	Bans sale of hazardous toys and articles. Sets standards for child-resistant packaging.
Federal Cigarette Labeling and Advertising Act (1967)	Requires that cigarette packages contain the following statement: "Warning: The Surgeon General Has Determined That Cigarette Smoking Is Dangerous to Your Health."
National Environmental Policy Act (1969)	Establishes a national policy on the environment. The 1970 Reorganization Plan establishes the Environmental Protection Agency.
Consumer Product Safety Act (1972)	Establishes the Consumer Product Safety Commission and authorizes it to set safety standards for consumer products as well as exact penalties for failure to uphold those standards.
Magnuson–Moss Warranty Act (1975)	Authorizes FTC to determine rules and regulations for consumer warranties and provides consumer access to redress, such as the "class-action" suit.
Children's Television Act (1990)	Limits number of commercials aired during children's programs.
Nutrition Labeling and Education Act (1990)	Requires that food product labels provide detailed nutritional information.
Telephone Consumer Protection Act (1991)	Establishes procedures to avoid unwanted telephone solicitations. Limits marketers' use of automatic telephone-dialing systems and artificial or prerecorded voices.

than the United States in passing strong consumerism legislation. For example, Norway bans several forms of sales promotion—trading stamps, contests, premiums—as being inappropriate or unfair ways of promoting products. Thailand requires food processors selling national brands to market low-price brands also, so that low-income consumers can find economy brands on the shelves. In India, food companies must obtain special approval to launch brands that duplicate those already existing on the market, such as additional cola drinks or new brands of rice.

Understanding the public policy implications of a particular marketing activity is not a simple matter. For example, in the United States, there are many laws created at the national, state, and local levels, and these regulations often overlap. Aspirins sold in Dallas are governed both by federal labeling laws and by Texas state advertising laws. Moreover, regulations are constantly changing—what was allowed last year may now be prohibited, and what was prohibited may now be allowed. For example, with the demise of the Soviet bloc, ex-Soviet nations are rapidly passing laws to both regulate and promote an open-market economy. Marketers must work hard to keep up with changes in regulations and their interpretations.

Business legislation has been enacted for a number of reasons. The first is to *protect companies* from each other. Although business executives may praise competition, they sometimes try to neutralize it when it threatens them. So laws are passed to define and prevent unfair competition. In the United States, such laws are enforced by the Federal Trade Commission and the Antitrust Division of the Attorney General's office.

The second purpose of government regulation is to *protect consumers* from unfair business practices. Some firms, if left alone, would make shoddy products, tell lies in their advertising, and deceive consumers through their packaging and pricing. Unfair business practices have been defined and are enforced by various agencies.

The third purpose of government regulation is to *protect the interests of society* against unrestrained business behavior. Profitable business activity does not always create a better quality of life. Regulation arises to ensure that firms take responsibility for the social costs of their production or products.

Changing Government Agency Enforcement. International marketers will encounter dozens, or even hundreds, of agencies set up to enforce trade policies and regulations. In the United States, Congress has established federal regulatory agencies such as the Federal Trade Commission, the Food and Drug Administration, the Interstate Commerce Commission, the Federal Communications Commission, the Federal Power Commission, the Civil Aeronautics Board, the Consumer Products Safety Commission, the Environmental Protection Agency, and the Office of Consumer Affairs. Because such government agencies have some discretion in enforcing the laws, they can have a major impact on a company's marketing performance. At times, the staffs of these agencies have appeared to be overly eager and unpredictable. Some of the agencies sometimes have been dominated by lawyers and economists who lacked a practical sense of how business and marketing work. In recent years, the Federal Trade Commission has added staff marketing experts, who can better understand complex business issues.

New laws and their enforcement will continue or increase. Business executives must watch these developments when planning their products and marketing programs. Marketers need to know about the major laws protecting competition, consumers, and society. They need to understand these laws at the local, state, national, and international levels.[28]

Increased Emphasis on Ethics and Socially Responsible Actions

Written regulations cannot possibly cover all potential marketing abuses, and existing laws are often difficult to enforce. However, beyond written laws and regulations, business is also governed by social codes and rules of professional ethics. Enlightened companies encourage their managers to look beyond what the regulatory system allows and simply "do the right thing." These socially responsible firms actively seek out ways to protect the long-run interests of their consumers and the environment.

The recent rash of business scandals and increased concerns about the environment have created fresh interest in the issues of ethics and social responsibility. Almost every aspect of marketing involves such issues. Unfortunately, because these issues usually involve conflicting interests, well-meaning people can honestly disagree about the right course of action in a given situation. Thus, many industrial and professional trade associations have suggested codes of ethics, and many companies now are developing policies and guidelines to deal with complex social responsibility issues.

---

[28]For a summary of U.S. legal developments in marketing, see Louis W. Stern and Thomas L. Eovaldi, *Legal Aspects of Marketing Strategy: Antitrust and Consumer Protection Issues* (Upper Saddle River, NJ: Prentice Hall, 1984); Robert J. Posch Jr., *The Complete Guide to Marketing and the Law* (Upper Saddle River, NJ: Prentice Hall, 1988); Robert J. Posch Jr., *The Complete Guide to Marketing and the Law, 1990 Cumulative Supplement* (Upper Saddle River, NJ: Prentice Hall, 1990); Dorothy Cohen, *Legal Issues in Marketing Decision Making* (Southwestern Publishing, 1994); and Theodore L. Banks, *Distribution Law: Antitrust Principles and Practice* (Aspen Publishers, 1998).

The boom in e-commerce and Internet marketing has created a new set of social and ethical issues. Privacy issues are the primary concern. For example, Web site visitors often provide extensive personal information that might leave them open to abuse by unscrupulous marketers. Moreover, both Intel and Microsoft have been accused of covert, high-tech computer chip and software invasions of customers' personal computers to obtain information for marketing purposes.

Another cyberspace concern is that of access by vulnerable or unauthorized groups. For example, marketers of adult-oriented materials have found it difficult to restrict access by minors. In a more specific example, sellers using eBay.com, the online auction Web site, recently found themselves the victims of a 13-year-old boy who'd bid on and purchased more than $3 million worth of high-priced antiques and rare art works on the site. eBay has a strict policy against bidding by anyone under 18 but works largely on the honor system. Unfortunately, this honor system did little to prevent the teenager from taking a cyberspace joyride.[29]

Of course, cyberspace also has its own examples of more typical consumer abuses. For example, although America Online has been hugely successful and is the country's most popular online service provider, it has lost millions of dollars due to consumer complaints regarding unethical marketing tactics:

> In 1998, America Online agreed to pay a $2.6 million penalty and revamp some of its business practices to settle deceptive-marketing complaints brought by 44 state attorneys general. In this instance, AOL failed to clearly notify consumers that the "50 free hours" in its online service's much-touted trial memberships must be used within a one-month period and that users would incur subscription fees after the first month. This was AOL's third settlement with state regulators in less than two years. Previous settlements dealt with the company's data network congestion in early 1997 (due to a move to flat rate pricing that gave the company more subscriptions than it had equipment to handle) and efforts in late 1996 to switch customers to a higher priced subscription plan. The three agreements not only cost the company $34 million in total, but created a barrage of negative publicity that AOL had to work hard to counter.[30]

In chapter 20, we discuss a broad range of societal marketing issues in greater depth.

> ## active poll

Some industries feel the weight of the political environment more than others. Take a moment to give your opinion on one instance.

CULTURAL ENVIRONMENT

The **cultural environment** is made up of institutions and other forces that affect a society's basic values, perceptions, preferences, and behaviors. People grow up in a particular society that shapes their basic beliefs and values. They absorb a world view that defines their relationships with others. The following cultural characteristics can affect marketing decision making.

Persistence of Cultural Values

People in a given society hold many beliefs and values. Their core beliefs and values have a high degree of persistence. For example, most Americans believe in working, getting married, giving to charity, and being honest. These beliefs shape more specific attitudes and behaviors found in everyday life. *Core* beliefs and values are passed on from parents to children and are reinforced by schools, churches, business, and government.

Secondary beliefs and values are more open to change. Believing in marriage is a core belief; believing that people should get married early in life is a secondary belief. Marketers have some chance of changing secondary values, but little chance of changing core values. For example, family-planning marketers could argue more effectively that people should get married later than that they should not get married at all.

---

[29]"13-Year-Old Bids over $3M for Items in eBay Auctions," *USA Today,* April 30, 1999, p. 10B.

[30]Rajiv Chandrasekaran, "AOL Settles Marketing Complaints," *Washington Post,* May 29, 1998, p. F1.

Shifts in Secondary Cultural Values

Although core values are fairly persistent, cultural swings do take place. Consider the impact of popular music groups, movie personalities, and other celebrities on young people's hairstyling, clothing, and sexual norms. Marketers want to predict cultural shifts in order to spot new opportunities or threats. Several firms offer "futures" forecasts in this connection, such as the Yankelovich Monitor, Market Facts' BrainWaves Group, and the Trends Research Institute. The Yankelovich Monitor tracks 41 U.S. cultural values, such as "antibigness," "mysticism," "living for today," "away from possessions," and "sensuousness." Monitor describes the percentage of the population that shares the attitude as well as the percentage that goes against the trend.[31] For instance, the percentage of people who value physical fitness and well-being has risen steadily over the years. Such information helps marketers cater to trends with appropriate products and communication appeals.

The major cultural values of a society are expressed in people's views of themselves and others, as well as in their views of organizations, society, nature, and the universe.

People's Views of Themselves. People vary in their emphasis on serving themselves versus serving others. Some people seek personal pleasure, wanting fun, change, and escape. Others seek self-realization through religion, recreation, or the avid pursuit of careers or other life goals. People use products, brands, and services as a means of self-expression, and they buy products and services that match their views of themselves.

In the 1980s, personal ambition and materialism increased dramatically, with significant marketing implications. In a "me society," people buy their "dream cars" and take their "dream vacations." They tended to spend to the limit on self-indulgent goods and services. Today, in contrast, people are adopting more conservative behaviors and ambitions. They are more cautious in their spending patterns and more value driven in their purchases. Moving into the new millennium, materialism, flashy spending, and self-indulgence have been replaced by more sensible spending, saving, family concerns, and helping others. The aging baby boomers are limiting their spending to products and services that improve their lives instead of boosting their images. This suggests a bright future for products and services that serve basic needs and provide real value rather than those relying on glitz and hype.

People's Views of Others. Recently, observers have noted a shift from a me society to a "we society" in which more people want to be with and serve others. Notes one trend tracker, "People want to get out, especially those 48 million people working out of their home and feeling a little cooped-up [and] all those shut-ins who feel unfulfilled by the cyberstuff that was supposed to make them feel like never leaving home."[32] This trend suggests a greater demand for "social support" products and services that improve direct communication between people, such as health clubs and family vacations.

People's Views of Organizations. People vary in their attitudes toward corporations, government agencies, trade unions, universities, and other organizations. By and large, people are willing to work for major organizations and expect them, in turn, to carry out society's work. The late 1980s saw a sharp decrease in confidence in and loyalty toward America's business and political organizations and institutions. In the workplace, there has been an overall decline in organizational loyalty. During the 1990s, waves of company downsizings bred cynicism and distrust. Many people today see work not as a source of satisfaction but as a required chore to earn money to enjoy their nonwork hours.

This trend suggests that organizations need to find new ways to win consumer and employee confidence. They need to review their advertising communications to make sure their messages are honest. Also, they need to review their various activities to make sure that they are being good corporate citizens. More companies are linking themselves to worthwhile causes, measuring their images with important publics, and using public relations to build more positive images.[33]

People's Views of Society. People vary in their attitudes toward their society; patriots defend it, reformers want to change it, malcontents want to leave it. People's orientation to their society influences their consumption patterns, levels of savings, and attitudes toward the marketplace.

The past two decades have seen an increase in consumer patriotism. For example, one study showed that over 80 percent of those surveyed say, "Americans should always try to buy American"—up from 72 percent in 1972.[34] Many U.S. companies have responded with "made in

---

[31]For more on today's shifting values, see Chip Walker and Elissa Moses, "The Age of Self-Navigation," *American Demographics,* September 1996, pp. 36–42; and Paul H. Ray, "The Emerging Culture," *American Demographics,* February 1997, pp. 29–34.

[32]See Cyndee Miller, "Trendspotters: 'Dark Ages' Ending; So Is Cocooning," *Marketing News,* February 3, 1997, pp. 1, 16.

[33]Also see V. Kasturi Rangan, Sohel Karim, and Sheryl K. Sandberg, "Do Better at Doing Good," *Harvard Business Review,* May–June 1996, pp. 42–54; Julie Garrett and Lisa Rochlin, "Cause Marketers Must Learn to Play by Rules," *Marketing News,* May 12, 1997, p. 4; and Sarah Lorge, "Is Cause-Related Marketing Worth It?" *Sales & Marketing Management,* June 1998, p. 72.

America" themes and flag-waving promotions. For example, Black & Decker added a flaglike symbol to its tools. For the past several years, the American textile industry has blitzed consumers with its "Crafted with Pride in the USA" advertising campaign, insisting that "made in the USA" matters. In 1991, many companies used patriotic appeals and promotions to express their support of American troops in the Gulf War and to ride the wave of national pride and patriotism that followed.

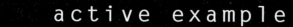

> ## active example

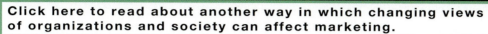

Click here to read about another way in which changing views of organizations and society can affect marketing.

People's Views of Nature.   People vary in their attitudes toward the natural world. Some feel ruled by it, others feel in harmony with it, and still others seek to master it. A long-term trend has been people's growing mastery over nature through technology and the belief that nature is bountiful. More recently, however, people have recognized that nature is finite and fragile, that it can be destroyed or spoiled by human activities.

Love of nature is leading to more camping, hiking, boating, fishing, and other outdoor activities. Business has responded by offering more products and services catering to these interests. Tour operators are offering more wilderness adventures, and retailers are offering more fitness gear and apparel. Food producers have found growing markets for "natural" products such as natural cereal, natural ice cream, and health foods. Marketing communicators are using appealing natural backgrounds in advertising their products.

People's Views of the Universe.   Finally, people vary in their beliefs about the origin of the universe and their place in it. Although most Americans practice religion, religious conviction and practice have been dropping off gradually through the years. Some futurists, however, have noted a renewed interest in spirituality, perhaps as a part of a broader search for a new inner purpose. People have been moving away from materialism and dog-eat-dog ambition to seek more permanent values—family, community, earth, faith—and a more certain grasp of right and wrong.

"Americans are on a spiritual journey," observes one expert, "increasingly concerned with the meaning of life and issues of the soul and spirit. The journey can encompass religion, but it is much more likely to take the form of . . . 'spiritual individualism.'" This new spiritualism affects consumers in everything from the television shows they watch and the books they read to the products and services they buy. "Since consumers don't park their beliefs and values on the bench outside the marketplace," adds the expert, "they are bringing this awareness to the brands they buy. Tapping into this heightened sensitivity presents a unique marketing opportunity for brands."[35]

> ## active concept check

Now let's take a moment to test your knowledge of what you've just read.

> ## Responding to the Marketing Environment

Someone once observed, "There are three kinds of companies: those who make things happen; those who watch things happen; and those who wonder what's happened."[36] Many companies view the marketing environment as an uncontrollable element to which they must adapt. They passively accept the marketing environment and do not try to change it. They analyze the environmental forces and

[34]Bill McDowell, "New DDB Needham Report: Consumers Want It All," *Advertising Age,* November 1996, pp. 32–33.

[35]Myra Stark, "Celestial Season," *Brandweek,* November 16, 1998, pp. 25–26. Also see Jennifer Harrison, "Advertising Joins the Journal of the Soul," *American Demographics,* June 1997, pp. 22–28; David B. Wolfe, "The Psychological Center of Gravity," *American Demographics,* April 1998, pp. 16–19; and Richard Cimino and Don Lattin, "Choosing My Religion," *American Demographics,* April 1999, pp. 60–65.

[36]Philip Kotler, *Kotler on Marketing* (New York: Free Press, 1999), p. 3.

design strategies that will help the company avoid the threats and take advantage of the opportunities the environment provides.

Other companies take an **environmental management perspective**.[37] Rather than simply watching and reacting, these firms take aggressive actions to affect the publics and forces in their marketing environment. Such companies hire lobbyists to influence legislation affecting their industries and stage media events to gain favorable press coverage. They run advertorials (ads expressing editorial points of view) to shape public opinion. They press lawsuits and file complaints with regulators to keep competitors in line, and they form contractual agreements to better control their distribution channels.

Often, companies can find positive ways to overcome seemingly uncontrollable environmental constraints. For example

Cathay Pacific Airlines . . . determined that many travelers were avoiding Hong Kong because of lengthy delays at immigration. Rather than assuming that this was a problem they could not solve, Cathay's senior staff asked the Hong Kong government how to avoid these immigration delays. After lengthy discussions, the airline agreed to make an annual grant-in-aid to the government to hire more immigration inspectors—but these reinforcements would service primarily the Cathay Pacific gates. The reduced waiting period increased customer value and thus strengthened [Cathay's competitive advantage].[38]

video example   <

Responding to the marketing environment also involves identifying and capturing new markets. Consider one example.

Marketing management cannot always control environmental forces. In many cases, it must settle for simply watching and reacting to the environment. For example, a company would have little success trying to influence geographic population shifts, the economic environment, or major cultural values. But whenever possible, smart marketing managers will take a *proactive* rather than *reactive* approach to the marketing environment.

active concept check   <

Now let's take a moment to test your knowledge of what you've just read.

> **Chapter Wrap-Up**

Now that you've reached the end of the chapter, you may wish to explore the concepts you've been reading about in greater detail, or test yourself to see how well you've comprehended the material. In the box below you'll find a number of links. Click on any one of these links to find additional chapter resources.

[37]See Carl P. Zeithaml and Valerie A. Zeithaml, "Environmental Management: Revising the Marketing Perspective," *Journal of Marketing*, Spring 1984, pp. 46–53.

[38]Howard E. Butz Jr. and Leonard D. Goodstein, "Measuring Customer Value: Gaining the Strategic Advantage," *Organizational Dynamics*, Winter 1996, pp. 66–67.

> end-of-chapter resources

- Review of Concept Connections
- Practice Quiz
- Issues for Discussion
- Key Terms
- Marketing Applications
- Internet Connections
- Company Case

Marketing Research and Information Systems

> What's Ahead

In 1985, in what has now become an all-time classic marketing tale, the Coca-Cola Company made a major marketing blunder. After 99 successful years, it set aside its long-standing rule—"Don't mess with Mother Coke"—and dropped its original formula Coke! In its place came *New* Coke with a sweeter, smoother taste.

At first, amid the introductory flurry of advertising and publicity, New Coke sold well. But sales soon went flat, as a stunned public reacted. Coke began receiving sacks of mail and more than 1,500 phone calls each day from angry consumers. A group called "Old Cola Drinkers" staged protests, handed out T-shirts, and threatened a class-action suit unless Coca-Cola brought back the old formula. After only three months, the Coca-Cola Company brought old Coke back. Now called "Coke Classic," it sold side-by-side with New Coke on supermarket shelves. The company said that New Coke would remain its flagship brand, but consumers had a different idea. By the end of that year, Classic was outselling New Coke in supermarkets by two to one.

Quick reaction saved the company from potential disaster. It stepped up efforts for Coke Classic and slotted New Coke into a supporting role. Coke Classic again became the company's main brand, and the country's leading soft drink. New Coke became the company's "attack brand"—its Pepsi stopper—and ads boldly compared New Coke's taste with Pepsi's. Still, New Coke managed only a 2 percent market share. In the spring of 1990, the company repackaged New Coke and relaunched it as a brand extension with a new name, Coke II. Today, Coke Classic captures more than 20 percent of the U.S. soft drink market; Coke II holds a miniscule 0.1 percent.

Why was New Coke introduced in the first place? What went wrong? Many analysts blame the blunder on poor marketing research.

In the early 1980s, although Coke was still the leading soft drink, it was slowly losing market share to Pepsi. For years, Pepsi had successfully mounted the "Pepsi Challenge," a series of televised taste tests showing that consumers preferred the sweeter taste of Pepsi. By early 1985, although Coke led in the overall market,

Pepsi led in share of supermarket sales by 2 percent. (That doesn't sound like much, but 2 percent of the huge U.S. soft drink market amounts to more than $1 billion in retail sales!) Coca-Cola had to do something to stop the loss of its market share, and the solution appeared to be a change in Coke's taste.

Coca-Cola began the largest new-product research project in the company's history. It spent more than two years and $4 million on research before settling on a new formula. It conducted some 200,000 taste tests—30,000 on the final formula alone. In blind tests, 60 percent of consumers chose the new Coke over the old, and 52 percent chose it over Pepsi. Research showed that New Coke would be a winner, and the company introduced it with confidence. So what happened?

Looking back, we can see that Coke defined its marketing research problem too narrowly. The research looked only at taste; it did not explore consumers' feelings about dropping the old Coke and replacing it with a new version. It took no account of the *intangibles*—Coke's name, history, packaging, cultural heritage, and image. However, to many people, Coke stands alongside baseball, hot dogs, and apple pie as an American institution; it represents the very fabric of America. Coke's symbolic meaning turned out to be more important to many consumers than its taste. Research addressing a broader set of issues would have detected these strong emotions.

Coke's managers may also have used poor judgment in interpreting the research and planning strategies around it. For example, they took the finding that 60 percent of consumers preferred New Coke's taste to mean that the new product would win in the marketplace, as when a political candidate wins with 60 percent of the vote. But it also meant that 40 percent still liked the original formula. By dropping the old Coke, the company trampled the taste buds of the large core of loyal Coke drinkers who didn't want a change. The company might have been wiser to leave the old Coke alone and introduce New Coke as a brand extension, as it later did successfully with Cherry Coke.

The Coca-Cola Company has one of the largest, best-managed, and most advanced marketing research operations in America. Good marketing research has kept the company atop the rough-and-tumble soft drink market for decades. But marketing research is far from an exact science. Consumers are full of surprises and figuring them out can be awfully tough. If Coca-Cola can make a large marketing research mistake, any company can.[1]

[1]See "Coke 'Family' Sales Fly as New Coke Stumbles," *Advertising Age,* January 17, 1986, p. 1; Jack Honomichl, "Missing Ingredients in 'New' Coke's Research," *Advertising Age,* July 22, 1985, p. 1; Leah Rickard, "Remembering New Coke," *Advertising Age,* April 17, 1995, p. 6; Debra Goldman, "Power to the People," *Adweek,* October 6, 1997, p. 74; Kent Steinreide and Sarah Theodore, "1997 Soft Drink Wrap-Up," *Beverage Industry,* March 1998, pp. 36–42; and Rick Wise, "Why Things Go Better with Coke," *The Journal of Business Strategy,* January–February 1999, pp. 15–19.

> **objectives**

Before you begin, take a moment to familiarize yourself with the key objectives of this chapter.

> **gearing up**

Before we begin our exploration this chapter, take a short warm-up test to see what you know about this topic.

In order to produce superior value and satisfaction for customers, companies need information at almost every turn. As the New Coke story highlights, good products and marketing programs begin with a thorough understanding of consumer needs and wants. Companies also need an abundance of information on competitors, resellers, and other actors and forces in the marketplace.

Increasingly, marketers are viewing information not just as an input for making better decisions but also as an important strategic asset and marketing tool. In today's marketing, a company's information may prove to be its chief competitive advantage. Competitors can copy each other's equipment, products, and procedures, but they cannot duplicate the company's information and intellectual capital. Several companies have recently recognized this by appointing vice presidents of knowledge, learning, or intellectual capital.[2]

A century ago, most companies were small and knew their customers firsthand. Managers picked up marketing information by being around people, observing them, and asking questions. In more recent times, however, many factors have increased the need for more, better, and faster information. As companies become national or international in scope, they need more information on larger, more distant markets. As incomes increase and buyers become more selective, sellers need better information about how buyers respond to different products and appeals. As sellers use more complex marketing approaches and face more competition, they need information on the effectiveness of their marketing tools. Finally, in today's more rapidly changing environments, managers need more up-to-date information to make timely decisions.

Fortunately, increasing information requirements have been met by an explosion of information technologies. The past 30 years have witnessed the emergence of small but powerful computers, fax machines, CD-ROM drives, videoconferencing, the Internet, and a host of other advances that have revolutionized information handling. Using improved information systems, companies can now generate information in great quantities.

In fact, today's managers often receive too much information. For example, one study found that with all the companies offering data, and with all the information now available through supermarket scanners, a packaged-goods brand manager is bombarded with 1 million to 1 *billion* new numbers each week. Another study found that, on average, American office workers spend 60 percent of their time processing documents; a typical manager reads about a million words a week. The typical business Internet user receives 25 e-mails a day; 15 percent of users receive between 50 and 100 e-mails per day. Thus, the running out of information is not a problem but seeing through the "data smog" is.[3]

Despite this data glut, marketers frequently complain that they lack enough information of the *right* kind. For example, a recent survey of managers found that although half the respondents said they couldn't cope with the volume of information coming at them, two-thirds wanted even more. The researcher concluded that, "despite the volume, they're still not getting what they want."[4] Thus, most marketing managers don't need *more* information, they need *better* information. Companies have

---

[2]See Philip Kotler, *Kotler on Marketing* (New York: Free Press, 1999), p. 73.

[3]Joseph M. Winski, "Gentle Rain Turns into Torrent," *Advertising Age,* June 3, 1991, p. 34; David Shenk, *Data Smog: Surviving the Information Glut* (San Francisco: HarperSanFrancisco, 1997); Nancy Doucette, "Relieving Information Overload," *Rough Notes,* February 1998, pp. 26–27; and Diane Trommer, "Information Overload—Study Finds Intranet Users Overwhelmed with Data," *Electronic Buyers' News,* April 20, 1998, p. 98.

[4]Alice LaPlante, "Still Drowning!" *Computer World,* March 10, 1997, pp. 69–70.

greater capacity to provide managers with good information, but often have not made good use of it. Many companies are now studying their managers' information needs and designing information systems to meet those needs.

> The Marketing Information System

A **marketing information system (MIS)** consists of people, equipment, and procedures to gather, sort, analyze, evaluate, and distribute needed, timely, and accurate information to marketing decision makers. Figure 4.1 shows that the MIS begins and ends with marketing managers. First, it interacts with these managers to *assess information needs*. Next, it *develops needed information* from internal company data, marketing intelligence activities, marketing research, and information analysis. Finally, the MIS *distributes information* to managers in the right form at the right time to help them make better marketing decisions.

video example <

Take a moment to listen to how one prominent company uses marketing research.

ASSESSING INFORMATION NEEDS

A good marketing information system balances the information managers would *like* to have against what they really *need* and what is *feasible* to offer. The company begins by interviewing managers to find out what information they would like. Some managers will ask for whatever information they can get without thinking carefully about what they really need. Too much information can be as harmful as too little. Other managers may omit things they ought to know or may not know to ask for some types of information they should have. For example, managers might need to know that a competitor plans to introduce a new product during the coming year. Because they do not know about the new

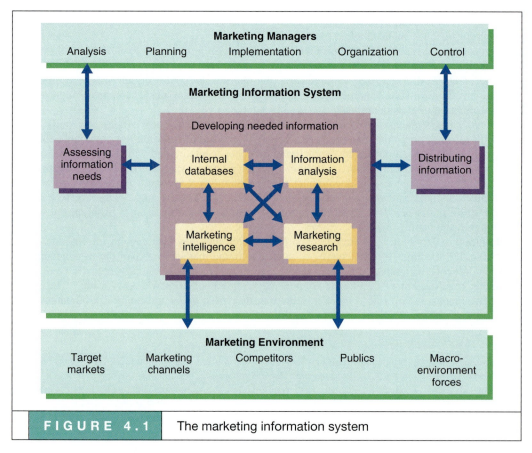

| FIGURE 4.1 | The marketing information system |

product, they do not think to ask about it. The MIS must watch the marketing environment in order to provide decision makers with information they should have to make key marketing decisions.

Sometimes the company cannot provide the needed information, either because it is not available or because of MIS limitations. For example, a brand manager might want to know how competitors will change their advertising budgets next year and how these changes will affect industry market shares. The information on planned budgets probably is not available. Even if it is, the company's MIS may not be advanced enough to forecast resulting changes in market shares.

Finally, the costs of obtaining, processing, storing, and delivering information can mount quickly. The company must decide whether the benefits of having additional information are worth the costs of providing it, and both value and cost are often hard to assess. By itself, information has no worth; its value comes from its *use*. In many cases, additional information will do little to change or improve a manager's decision, or the costs of the information may exceed the returns from the improved decision. Marketers should not assume that additional information will always be worth obtaining. Rather, they should weigh carefully the costs of additional information against the benefits resulting from it.

DEVELOPING INFORMATION

The information needed by marketing managers can be obtained from *internal data, marketing intelligence,* and *marketing research.* The information analysis system then processes this information to make it more useful for managers.

Internal Data

Many companies build extensive **internal databases,** computerized collections of information obtained from data sources within the company. Marketing managers can readily access and work with information in the database to identify marketing opportunities and problems, plan programs, and evaluate performance.

Information in the database can come from many sources. The accounting department prepares financial statements and keeps detailed records of sales, costs, and cash flows. Manufacturing reports on production schedules, shipments, and inventories. The sales force reports on reseller reactions and competitor activities. The marketing department furnishes information on customer demographics, psychographics, and buying behavior, and the customer service department keeps records of customer satisfaction or service problems. Research studies done for one department may provide useful information for several others.

Here is an example of how one company uses internal databases to make better marketing decisions:[5]

USAA, which provides financial services to U.S. military personnel and their families, maintains a customer database built from customer purchasing histories and from information collected directly from customers. To keep the database fresh, the organization regularly surveys its 3 million customers worldwide to learn such things as whether they have children (and if so, how old they are), if they have moved recently, and when they plan to retire. USAA uses the database to tailor marketing offers to the specific needs of individual customers. For example, if the family has college-age children, the USAA sends those children information on how to manage their credit cards. If the family has younger children, it sends booklets on things like financing a child's education. Or, for customers looking toward retirement, it sends information on estate planning. Through skillful use of its database, USAA serves each customer uniquely, resulting in high levels of customer loyalty—the roughly $7 billion company retains 97 percent of its customers. Says USAA's chief marketing executive, "We make it a point, in all of our materials, to let [customers] know that we're there for them as they make transactions."

Internal databases usually can be accessed more quickly and cheaply than other information sources, but they also present some problems. Because internal information was collected for other purposes, it may be incomplete or in the wrong form for making marketing decisions. For example, sales and cost data used by the accounting department for preparing financial statements must be adapted for use in evaluating product, sales force, or channel performance. Data ages quickly; keeping the database current requires a major effort. In addition, a large company produces mountains of information, and keeping track of it all is difficult. The database information must be well integrated

---

[5] See Geoffrey Brewer, "The Customer Stops Here," *Sales & Marketing Management,* March 1998, pp. 31–36.

and readily accessible through user-friendly interfaces so that managers can find it easily and use it effectively.

Every company contains more information than any manager can possibly know or analyze. The information is scattered in countless databases, plans, and records, and in heads of many longtime managers. The company must somehow bring order to its information gold mine so that its managers can more easily find answers to questions and make informed decisions. Increasingly, companies are creating *data warehouses* to house their customer data in a single, more accessible location. Then, using powerful *data mining* techniques, they search for meaningful patterns in the data and communicate them to managers.

active example ⟨

Take a moment to consider how the Internet can facilitate the marketing research process.

Marketing Intelligence

Marketing intelligence is the systematic collection and analysis of publicly available information about competitors and developments in the marketing environment. A marketing intelligence system gathers, analyzes, and distributes information about the company's competitive, technological, customer, economic, social, and political and regulatory environments. Its goal is to improve strategic decision making, assess and track competitors' actions, and provide early warning of opportunities and threats. The marketing intelligence system determines what intelligence is needed, collects it by searching the environment, and delivers it to marketing managers.

Competitive intelligence gathering has grown dramatically as more and more companies are now busily snooping on their competitors. Techniques range from quizzing the company's own employees and benchmarking competitors' products to researching the Internet, lurking around industry trade shows, and rooting through rivals' trash bins.

Much intelligence can be collected from the company's own personnel—executives, engineers and scientists, purchasing agents, and the sales force. For example, a few years back, Xerox learned that listening to its own salespeople could pay off handsomely.

> While talking with a Kodak copier salesperson, a Xerox technician learned that the salesperson was being trained to service Xerox products. The Xerox employee reported back to his boss, who in turn passed the news to Xerox's intelligence unit. Using such clues as a classified ad Kodak placed seeking new people with Xerox product experience, Xerox verified Kodak's plan—code-named Ulysses—to service Xerox copiers. To protect its profitable service business, Xerox designed a Total Satisfaction Guarantee, which allowed copier returns for any reason as long as *Xerox* did the servicing. By the time Kodak launched Ulysses, Xerox had been promoting its new program for three months.[6]

However, company people are often busy and fail to pass on important information. The company must sell its people on their importance as intelligence gatherers, train them to spot new developments, interact with them on an ongoing basis, and urge them to report intelligence back to the company.

The company can also get suppliers, resellers, and key customers to pass along important intelligence about competitors and their products. For example, prior to introducing its Good News disposable razor in the United States, Gillette told a large Canadian account about the planned U.S. introduction date. The Canadian distributor promptly called Bic and told it about the impending product launch. By putting on a crash program, Bic was able to start selling its razor shortly after Gillette did.

The company can obtain good information by observing competitors or analyzing physical evidence. It can buy and analyze competitors' products, monitor their sales, and check for new patents. For example, to design the first Taurus models, Ford compiled a list of more than 400 features its customers said they liked best about competing cars. Then it matched or topped the best of the competition. The result: Taurus soon became America's best-selling car.

---

[6]Stan Crock, "They Snoop to Conquer," *Business Week,* October 28, 1996, p. 172.

Companies can also examine other types of physical evidence. For example, to gauge competitor shipping volumes, some companies have measured the rust on rails of railroad sidings to their competitors' plants or watched competitors' loading docks at the end of a quarter to see how much merchandise was being moved at the last minute. Other firms regularly check out competitors' parking lots—full lots might indicate plenty of work and prosperity; half-full lots might suggest hard times.[7]

Some companies even rifle their competitors' garbage, which is legally considered abandoned property once it leaves the premises. Although most companies now shred technical documents, they may overlook the almost-as-revealing refuse from the marketing or public relations departments. In one example of garbage snatching, Avon admitted that it had hired private detectives to paw through the dumpster of rival Mary Kay Cosmetics. An outraged Mary Kay sued to get its garbage back, but Avon claimed that it had done nothing illegal. The dumpster had been located in a public parking lot, and Avon had videotapes to prove it.[8]

Government agencies are another good intelligence source. For example, a company can't legally photograph a competitor's plant from the air. However, publicly available aerial photos are often on file with the U.S. Geological Survey or Environmental Protection Agency. In another instance, a company attempting to assess the capacity of a competitor's plant struck gold when it found that a publicly available Uniform Commercial Code filing the competitor had submitted to the state contained a detailed list of all the equipment in the competitor's plant.

Competitors themselves may reveal information through their annual reports, business publications, trade show exhibits, press releases, advertisements, and Web pages. The Internet is proving to be a vast new source of competitor-supplied information. Most companies now place volumes of information on their Web sites, providing details to attract customers, partners, suppliers, or franchisees, and that same information is available to competitors at the click of a mouse button. Press releases that never made it into the press are posted on Web sites, letting firms keep abreast of competitors' new products and organizational changes. Help wanted ads posted on the Web quickly reveal competitors' expansion priorities. For example, check Allied Signal's Web site and you'll find that it provides revenue goals and reveals the company's production-defect rate along with its plans to improve it. Mail Boxes Etc., a chain of mailing services, provides data on its average franchise, including square footage, number of employees, operating hours, and more—all valuable insights for a competitor.

It's not only company-sponsored Web sites that hold rich competitor intelligence booty. Researchers can also glean valuable nuggets of information from trade association Web sites. For example, when he was controller of Stone Container's specialty-packaging division, Gary Owen visited a trade association Web site and noticed that a rival had won an award for a new process using ultraviolet-resistant lacquers. The site revealed the machines' configuration and run rate, which Stone's engineers used to figure out how to replicate the process.[9]

Using Internet search engines such as Yahoo! or Infoseek, marketers can search specific competitor names, events, or trends and see what turns up. Intelligence seekers also pore through any of thousands of online databases. Some are free. For example, the U.S. Security and Exchange Commission's Edgar database (www.sec.gov) provides access to a huge stockpile of financial and other information on public companies. For a fee, companies can subscribe to any of more than 3,000 *online databases* and information search services such as Dialog, DataStar, LEXIS-NEXIS, Dow Jones News Retrieval, UMI ProQuest, and Dun & Bradstreet's Online Access. We discuss these and other online data services in more detail later in the chapter. Using such databases, companies can conduct complex information searches in a flash from the comfort of their keyboards.

One Internet site (www.fuld.com) provides a Competitive Intelligence Guide offering sleuthing tips. Another Web service—Company Sleuth (www.company sleuth.com)—provides users with a steady stream of intelligence data gleaned from the Internet. It searches the Web and gives users daily e-mail reports detailing the business activities, financial moves, and Internet dealings of competitors, prospects, and clients, often before the information is officially reported. "In today's information age, companies are leaving a paper trail of information online," says Joshua Kopelman, executive vice president of Infonautics, the company that offers the service. "Company Sleuth uncovers hard-to-find and seemingly hidden business news and information for users so they don't have to simply rely on old news or intuition when making investment and business decisions."[10]

Some companies set up an office to collect and circulate marketing intelligence. The staff scans major publications, searches the Internet, summarizes important news, and sends bulletins to marketing managers. It develops a file of intelligence information and helps managers evaluate new information. These services greatly improve the quality of information available to marketing managers.

---

[7]See Suzie Amer, "Masters of Intelligence," *Forbes,* April 5, 1999, p. 18.

[8]Bruce Hager, "Dumpster Raids? That's Not Very Ladylike, Avon," *Business Week,* April 1, 1991, p. 32.

[9]"Spy/Counterspy," *Context,* Summer 1998, pp. 20–21.

[10]"Company Sleuth Uncovers Business Info for Free," *Link-Up,* January–February 1999, pp. 1, 8.

The growing use of marketing intelligence raises a number of ethical issues. Although most of the preceding techniques are legal, and some are considered to be shrewdly competitive, many involve questionable ethics. Clearly, companies should take advantage of publicly available information. However, they should not stoop to snoop. With all the legitimate intelligence sources now available, a company does not have to break the law or accepted codes of ethics to get good intelligence.[11]

Marketing Research

In addition to information about competitors and environmental happenings, marketers often need formal studies of specific situations. For example, Toshiba wants to know how many and what kinds of people or companies will buy its new superfast notebook computer. Or Barat College in Lake Forest, Illinois, needs to know what percentage of its target market has heard of Barat, how they heard, what they know, and how they feel about Barat. In such situations, the marketing intelligence system will not provide the detailed information needed. Managers will need marketing research.

We define **marketing research** as the systematic design, collection, analysis, and reporting of data relevant to a specific marketing situation facing an organization. Every marketer needs research. Marketing researchers engage in a wide variety of activities, ranging from market potential and market share studies, to assessments of customer satisfaction and purchase behavior, to studies of pricing, product, distribution, and promotion activities.

active exercise   <

Take a moment to consider one valuable data collection technique.

A company can conduct marketing research in its own research department or have some or all of it done outside, depending on its own research skills and resources. Although most large companies have their own marketing research departments, they often use outside firms to do special research tasks or special studies. A company with no research department has to buy the services of research firms.

Information Analysis

Information gathered by the company's marketing intelligence and marketing research systems often requires more analysis, and sometimes managers may need more help to apply the information to their marketing problems and decisions. This help may include advanced statistical analysis to learn more about both the relationships within a set of data and their statistical reliability. Such analysis allows managers to go beyond means and standard deviations in the data and to answer questions about markets, marketing activities, and outcomes.

Information analysis might also involve a collection of analytical models that will help marketers make better decisions. Each model represents some real system, process, or outcome. These models can help answer the questions of *what if* and *which is best*. During the past 20 years, marketing scientists have developed numerous models to help marketing managers make better marketing mix decisions, design sales territories and sales call plans, select sites for retail outlets, develop optimal advertising mixes, and forecast new-product sales.[12]

DISTRIBUTING INFORMATION

Marketing information has no value until managers use it to make better marketing decisions. The information gathered through marketing intelligence and marketing research must be distributed to the right marketing managers at the right time. Most companies have centralized marketing information systems that provide managers with regular performance reports, intelligence updates, and

[11]For more on marketing and competitive intelligence, see David B. Montgomery and Charles Weinberg, "Toward Strategic Intelligence Systems," *Marketing Management,* Winter 1998, pp. 44–52; Morris C. Attaway Sr., "A Review of Issues Related to Gathering and Assessing Competitive Intelligence," *American Business Review,* January 1998, pp. 25–35; and Larry Kanaher, *Competitive Intelligence: How to Gather, Analyze, and Use Information to Move Your Business to the Top* (Touchstone Books, 1998).

[12]For a review of marketing models, see Gary Lilien, Philip Kotler, and Sridhar Moorthy, *Marketing Models* (Upper Saddle River, NJ: Prentice Hall, 1992); and Gary Lilien and Arvind Rangaswamy, *Marketing Engineering: Marketing Analysis and Planning in an Information Age* (Addison Wesley Longman, 1998).

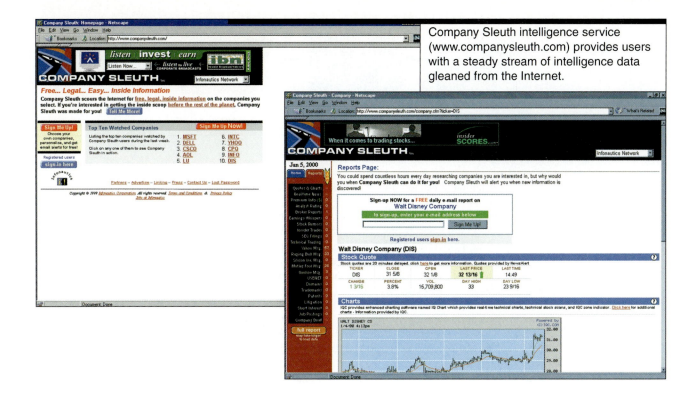

Company Sleuth intelligence service (www.companysleuth.com) provides users with a steady stream of intelligence data gleaned from the Internet.

reports on the results of studies. Managers need these routine reports for making regular planning, implementation, and control decisions. But marketing managers may also need nonroutine information for special situations and on-the-spot decisions. For example, a sales manager having trouble with a large customer may want a summary of the account's sales and profitability over the past year. Or a retail store manager who has run out of a best-selling product may want to know the current inventory levels in the chain's other stores.

Developments in information technology have caused a revolution in information distribution. With recent advances in computers, software, and telecommunication, most companies have decentralized their marketing information systems. In most companies today, marketing managers have direct access to the information network, at any time and from virtually any location.

While working at a home office, in a hotel room, on an airplane—any place where they can turn on a laptop computer and phone in—today's managers can obtain information from company databases or outside information services, analyze the information using statistical packages and models, prepare reports using word processing and presentation software, and communicate with others in the network through electronic communications. Such systems offer exciting prospects. They allow managers to get the information they need directly and quickly and to tailor it to their own needs.

> active concept check

Now let's take a moment to test your knowledge of what you've just read.

> The Marketing Research Process

The marketing research process (see Figure 4.2) has four steps: *defining the problem and research objectives, developing the research plan, implementing the research plan,* and *interpreting and reporting the findings.*

DEFINING THE PROBLEM AND RESEARCH OBJECTIVES

The marketing manager and the researcher must work closely together to define the problem carefully, and they must agree on the research objectives. The manager best understands the decision for

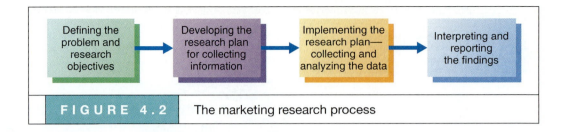

| Defining the problem and research objectives | → | Developing the research plan for collecting information | → | Implementing the research plan— collecting and analyzing the data | → | Interpreting and reporting the findings |

FIGURE 4.2   The marketing research process

which information is needed; the researcher best understands marketing research and how to obtain the information.

Managers should know enough about marketing research to help in the planning and the interpretation of research results. If they know little about marketing research, they may obtain the wrong information, accept wrong conclusions, or ask for information that costs too much. Experienced marketing researchers who understand the manager's problem should also be involved at this stage. The researcher must be able to help the manager define the problem and suggest ways that research can help the manager make better decisions.

Defining the problem and research objectives is often the hardest step in the research process. The manager may know that something is wrong, without knowing the specific causes. For example, managers of a large discount retail store chain hastily decided that falling sales were caused by poor advertising, and they ordered research to test the company's advertising. When this research showed that current advertising was reaching the right people with the right message, the managers were puzzled. It turned out that the real problem was that the chain was not delivering the prices, products, and service promised in the advertising. Careful problem definition would have avoided the cost and delay of doing advertising research. In the classic New Coke case, Coca-Cola defined its research problem too narrowly, with disastrous results.

After the problem has been defined carefully, the manager and researcher must set the research objectives. A marketing research project might have one of three types of objectives. The objective of **exploratory research** is to gather preliminary information that will help define the problem and suggest hypotheses. The objective of **descriptive research** is to describe things such as the market potential for a product or the demographics and attitudes of consumers who buy the product. The objective of **causal research** is to test hypotheses about cause-and-effect relationships. For example, would a 10 percent decrease in tuition at a private college result in an enrollment increase sufficient to offset the reduced tuition? Managers often start with exploratory research and later follow with descriptive or causal research.

The statement of the problem and research objectives guides the entire research process. The manager and researcher should put the statement in writing to be certain that they agree on the purpose and expected results of the research.

DEVELOPING THE RESEARCH PLAN

The second step of the marketing research process calls for determining the information needed, developing a plan for gathering it efficiently, and presenting the plan to marketing management. The plan outlines sources of existing data and spells out the specific research approaches, contact methods, sampling plans, and instruments that researchers will use to gather new data.

Determining Specific Information Needs

Research objectives must be translated into specific information needs. For example, suppose Campbell decides to conduct research on how consumers would react to the company replacing its familiar red-and-white condensed soup can with a container more relevant to today's consumer lifestyles.[13] It's considering the introduction of new bowl-shaped plastic containers that it has used successfully for a number of its other products. The containers would cost more but would allow consumers to heat the soup in a microwave oven without adding water or milk and to eat it without using dishes. This research might call for the following specific information:

---

[13]See Judann Pollack, "Campbell Loses Its Appetite for Condensed Soup," *Advertising Age,* February 15, 1999, pp. 1, 42.

- The demographic, economic, and lifestyle characteristics of current soup users. (Busy working couples might find the convenience of the new packaging worth the price; families with children might want to pay less and wash the pan and bowls.)

- Consumer-usage patterns for soup: how much soup they eat, where, and when. (The new packaging might be ideal for adults eating lunch on the go, but less convenient for parents feeding lunch to several children.)

- Retailer reactions to the new packaging. (Failure to get retailer support could hurt sales of the new package.)

- Consumer attitudes toward the new packaging. (The red-and-white Campbell can has become an American institution—will consumers accept the new packaging?)

- Forecasts of sales of both new and current packages. (Will the new packaging increase Campbell's profits?)

Campbell managers will need these and many other types of information to decide whether to introduce the new packaging.

Gathering Secondary Information

To meet the manager's information needs, the researcher can gather secondary data, primary data, or both. **Secondary data** consist of information that already exists somewhere, having been collected for another purpose. **Primary data** consist of information collected for the specific purpose at hand.

Researchers usually start by gathering secondary data. The company's internal database provides a good starting point. However, the company can also tap a wide assortment of external information sources, ranging from company, public, and university libraries to government and business publications. Table 4.1 describes a number of other important sources of secondary data, including commercial data services, online database services, and Internet data sources.

Commercial Data Sources. Companies can buy secondary data reports from outside suppliers. For example, Nielsen Marketing Research sells data on brand shares, retail prices, and percentages of stores stocking different brands. Information Resources, Inc. sells supermarket scanner purchase data from a panel of 60,000 households nationally, with measures of trial and repeat purchasing, brand loyalty, and buyer demographics. The *Monitor* service by Yankelovich and Partners sells information on important social and lifestyle trends.[14] These and other firms supply high-quality data to suit a wide variety of marketing information needs.

Online Databases and Internet Data Sources. Using commercial **online databases,** marketing researchers can conduct their own searches of secondary data sources. A recent survey of marketing researchers found that 81 percent use such online services for conducting research.[15] A readily available online database exists to fill almost any marketing information need. General database services such as CompuServe, Dialog, and LEXIS-NEXIS put an incredible wealth of information at the keyboards of marketing decision makers. For example, a company doing business in Germany can check out CompuServe's German Company Library of financial and product information on over 48,000 German-owned firms. A U.S. auto parts manufacturer can punch up Dun & Bradstreet Financial Profiles and Company Reports to develop biographical sketches of key General Motors, Ford, and DaimlerChrysler executives. Just about any information a marketer might need—demographic data, today's Associated Press news wire reports, a list of active U.S. trademarks in the United States—is available from online databases.[16]

The Internet offers a mind-boggling array of databases and other secondary information sources, many free to the user. Beyond commercial Web sites offering information for a fee, almost every industry association, government agency, business publication, and news medium offers free information to those tenacious enough to find their Web sites. In fact, there are so many Web sites offering data that finding the right ones can become an almost overwhelming task.

---

[14]For more on research firms that supply marketing information, see Jack Honomichl, "Honomichl 50," special section, *Marketing News,* June 7, 1999, pp. H1–H39; and Honomichl, "Honomichl Global 25," special section, *Marketing News,* August 16, 1999, pp. H1–H23.

[15]"Researching Researchers," *Marketing Tools,* September 1996, pp. 35–36.

[16]See Marydee Ojala, "The Daze of Future Business Research," *Online,* January–February 1998, pp. 78–80; and Guy Kawasaki, "Get Your Facts Here," *Forbes,* March 23, 1998, p. 156.

| **TABLE 4.1** | Commercial, Online Database, and Internet Data Sources |

Commercial Data Services

Here are just a few of the dozens of commercial research houses selling data to subscribers:

AC Nielsen Corporation provides supermarket scanner data on sales, market share, and retail prices (ScanTrack), data on household purchasing (ScanTrack National Electronic Household Panel), data on television audiences (Nielsen National Television Index), and others.

Information Resources, Inc. provides supermarket scanner data for tracking grocery product movement (InfoScan) and single-source data collection (BehaviorScan).

The Arbitron Company provides local-market radio audience and advertising expenditure information, along with a wealth of other media and ad spending data.

PMSI/Source Infomatics provides reports on the movement of pharmaceuticals, hospital laboratory supplies, animal health products, and personal care products.

MMRI (Simmons Market Research Bureau) provides reports covering television markets, sporting goods, and proprietary drugs, giving lifestyle and geodemographic data by sex, income, age, and brand preferences (selective markets and media reaching them).

Dun & Bradstreet provides a database containing information on more than 50 million individual companies around the globe—who they are, where they are, and what they do.

Online Database Services

Here are only a few of the many online database services:

Dialog offers several services, including ABI/INFORM, which provides information on business management and administration from over 800 publications. The site also provides access to full-text reports and newsletters from 50 industries and a collection of U.S. public opinion surveys. In addition, subscribers can view Dun & Bradstreet data, such as census statistics and business directories, by searching through Donnelly Demographics and Dun's Electronic Business Directory.

LEXIS-NEXIS, in addition to providing access to articles from a wide range of business magazines and journals, features in-depth research reports from research firms, SEC filings, Standard & Poor's, and worldwide investment banks. Users can also access information from consumer goods and marketing trade publications. The service also includes PROMT/ PLUS, which tracks competitors and industries, identifies trends, and evaluates advertising and promotion techniques.

CompuServe provides a variety of online database services. For example, its *Business Demographics* files summarize statistics on state employees by industry codes and categorize retail trade businesses by employee counts. By mining the *Neighborhood Report,* a user can access summaries of the demographics of any zip code in the United States. Other CompuServe databases offer full-text articles, news releases, and market and industry research report indices. The service also provides access to an additional 850 databases, ranging from newspapers and newsletters to government reports and patent records.

Dow Jones News Retrieval specializes in providing in-depth financial, historical, and operational information on public and private companies. The site offers Standard & Poor's profiles as well as Dun & Bradstreet profiles and company reports. In addition, the service compares stock price, volume, and data on companies and industries and summarizes same-day business and financial stories from both the United States and Japan.

Internet Data Sources

Most of the above online information services also provide Web-based versions. Literally thousands of other Web sites also offer data, often at little or no cost. The best way to locate such sources is by using Internet search engines to search specific topics. Here is just a tiny sampling of sites offering specialized information on a variety of business related topics.

The **U.S. Securities and Exchange Commission** Edgar database (www.sec.gov) provides financial information on public companies. The **Small Business Administration** (www.sbaonline.gov) site provides a rich variety of information for small business managers, along with links to dozens of other relevant sites. **Avenue Technologies** (www.com .avetech/avenue) presents summaries and full reports on over 25,000 public, private, and international companies. Similarly, **Dun & Bradstreet's Online Access** (www.dbisna.com/dbis/product/secure.html) offers short financial reports on 10 million U.S. companies. In addition to garnering financial information on companies and industries, Internet users can do real-time research. **Ecola's 24-Hour Newsstand** (www.ecola.com/news) links users to the Web sites of over 2,000 newspapers, journals, and computer publications. Researchers can view recent new articles online through *CNN Interactive* (www.cnn.com). Market researchers can visit the **American Demographics** site (www.demographics.com) and browse a directory of marketing experts.

Sources: See Christel Beard and Betsey Wiesendanger, "The Marketer's Guide to Online Databases," *Sales & Marketing Management,* January 1993, pp. 37–41; Susan Greco, "The Online Sleuth," *Inc.,* October 1996, pp. 88–89; Marydee Ojala, "The Daze of Future Business Research," *Online,* January–February 1998, pp. 78–80; Guy Kawasaki, "Get Your Facts Here," *Forbes,* March 23, 1998, p. 156; and Larry Kanaher, *Competitive Intelligence: How to Gather, Analyze, and Use Information to Move Your Business to the Top* (Touchstone Books, 1998).

Online database services such as Compuserve, Dialog, and LEXIS-NEXIS put an incredible wealth of information at the keyboards of marketing decision makers.

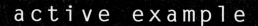

> active example

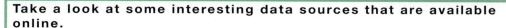

Take a look at some interesting data sources that are available online.

Advantages and Disadvantages of Secondary Data. Secondary data can usually be obtained more quickly and at a lower cost than primary data. For example, an Internet or online database search might provide all the information Campbell needs on soup usage, quickly and at almost no cost. A study to collect primary information might take weeks or months and cost thousands of dollars. Also, secondary sources sometimes can provide data an individual company cannot collect on its own— information that either is not directly available or would be too expensive to collect. For example, it would be too expensive for Campbell to conduct a continuing retail store audit to find out about the market shares, prices, and displays of competitors' brands. But it can buy the InfoScan service from Information Resources, Inc., which provides this information from thousands of scanner-equipped supermarkets in dozens of U.S. markets.

Secondary data can also present problems. The needed information may not exist—researchers can rarely obtain all the data they need from secondary sources. For example, Campbell will not find existing information about consumer reactions to new packaging that it has not yet placed on the market. Even when data can be found, they might not be very usable. The researcher must evaluate secondary information carefully to make certain it is *relevant* (fits research project needs), *accurate* (reliably collected and reported), *current* (up-to-date enough for current decisions), and *impartial* (objectively collected and reported).

Secondary data provide a good starting point for research and often help to define problems and research objectives. In most cases, however, the company must also collect primary data.

Planning Primary Data Collection

Good decisions require good data. Just as researchers must carefully evaluate the quality of secondary information, they also must take great care when collecting primary data to make sure that it will be relevant, accurate, current, and unbiased. Table 4.2 shows that designing a plan for primary data collection calls for a number of decisions on *research approaches, contact methods, sampling plan,* and *research instruments.*

Research Approaches. **Observational research** is the gathering of primary data by observing relevant people, actions, and situations. For example, a maker of personal care products might pretest its ads by showing them to people and measuring eye movements, pulse rates, and other physical reactions. Consumer packaged-goods marketers might visit supermarkets and observe shoppers as they browse the store, pick up products and examine packages, and make actual buying decisions. Or

TABLE 4.2	Planning Primary Data Collection		
Research Approaches	**Contact Methods**	**Sampling Plan**	**Research Instruments**
Observation	Mail	Sampling unit	Questionnaire
Survey	Telephone	Sample size	Mechanical instruments
Experiment	Personal	Sampling procedure	
	Online		

a bank might evaluate possible new branch locations by checking traffic patterns, neighborhood conditions, and the location of competing branches. Steelcase used observation to help design new office furniture for use by work teams.

> To learn firsthand how teams actually operate, it set up video cameras at various companies and studied the tapes, looking for motions and behavior patterns that customers themselves might not even notice. It found that teams work best when they can do some work together and some privately. So Steelcase designed highly successful modular office units called Personal Harbor. These units are "rather like telephone booths in size and shape." They can be arranged around a common space where a team works, letting people work together but also alone when necessary. Says a Steelcase executive, "Market data wouldn't necessarily have pointed us that way. It was more important to know how people actually work."[17]

Urban Outfitters, the fast-growing specialty clothing chain, prefers observation to other types of market research. "We're not after people's statements," notes the chain's president, "we're after their actions." The company develops customer profiles by videotaping and taking photographs of customers in its stores. This helps managers determine what people are actually wearing and allows them to make quick decisions on merchandise.[18]

active exercise

Consider the most direct approach to gathering marketing data.

Several companies sell information collected through *mechanical* observation. For example, Nielsen Media Research attaches *people meters* to television sets in selected homes to record who watches which programs. It then rates the size and demographic makeup of audiences for different television programs. The television networks use these ratings to judge program popularity and to set charges for advertising time. Advertisers use the ratings when selecting programs for their commercials. *Checkout scanners* in retail stores record consumer purchases in detail. Consumer products companies and retailers use scanner information to assess and improve product sales and store performance. Some marketing research firms now offer **single-source data systems** that electronically monitor both consumers' purchases and consumers' exposure to various marketing activities in an effort to better evaluate the link between the two.

Observational research can be used to obtain information that people are unwilling or unable to provide. In some cases, observation may be the only way to obtain the needed information. In contrast, some things simply cannot be observed, such as feelings, attitudes and motives, or private

[17]Justin Martin, "Ignore Your Customer," *Fortune,* May 1, 1995, pp. 121–26; and "Even Executives Are Losing Their Offices," *HR Magazine,* March 1998, p. 77. Also see William B. Helmreich, "Louder Than Words: On-Site Observational Research," *Marketing News,* March 1, 1999, p. 16; Kenneth Labich, "Attention Shoppers: This Man Is Watching You," *Fortune,* July 19, 1999, pp. 131–34; and Kendra Parker, "How do You Like Your Beef?" *American Demographics,* January 2000, pp. 35–37.

[18]Martin, "Ignore Your Customers," p. 126.

behavior. Long-term or infrequent behavior is also difficult to observe. Because of these limitations, researchers often use observation along with other data collection methods.

Survey research is the approach best suited for gathering *descriptive* information. A company that wants to know about people's knowledge, attitudes, preferences, or buying behavior can often find out by asking individuals directly.

Survey research is the most widely used method for primary data collection, and it is often the only method used in a research study. Researchers interview tens of millions of Americans each year in surveys. The major advantage of survey research is its flexibility. It can be used to obtain many different kinds of information in many different situations. Depending on the survey design, it also may provide information more quickly and at lower cost than observational or experimental research.

However, survey research also presents some problems. Sometimes people are unable to answer survey questions because they cannot remember or have never thought about what they do and why. Or people may be unwilling to respond to unknown interviewers or about things they consider private. Respondents may answer survey questions even when they do not know the answer in order to appear smarter or more informed. Or they may try to help the interviewer by giving pleasing answers. Finally, busy people may not take the time, or they might resent the intrusion into their privacy.

Whereas observation is best suited for exploratory research and surveys for descriptive research, **experimental research** is best suited for gathering *causal* information. Experiments involve selecting matched groups of subjects, giving them different treatments, controlling unrelated factors, and checking for differences in group responses. Thus, experimental research tries to explain cause-and-effect relationships. Observation and surveys may be used to collect information in experimental research.

Before adding a new sandwich to the menu, researchers at McDonald's might use experiments to answer questions such as the following:

■ How much will the new sandwich increase McDonald's sales?

■ How will the new sandwich affect the sales of other menu items?

■ Which advertising approach would have the greatest effect on sales of the sandwich?

■ How would different prices affect the sales of the product?

■ Should the new item be targeted toward adults, children, or both?

To test the effects of two different prices, McDonald's could set up a simple experiment: It could introduce the new sandwich at one price in its restaurants in one city and at another price in restaurants in another city. If the cities are similar, and if all other marketing efforts for the sandwich are the same, then differences in sales in the two cities could be related to the price charged. More complex experiments could be designed to include other variables and other locations.

Contact Methods.   Information can be collected by mail, telephone, personal interview, or online. Table 4.3 shows the strengths and weaknesses of each of these contact methods.

Mail questionnaires can be used to collect large amounts of information at a low cost per respondent. Respondents may give more honest answers to more personal questions on a mail questionnaire

TABLE 4.3	Strengths and Weaknesses of Contact Methods			
	Mail	**Telephone**	**Personal**	**Online**
Flexibility	Poor	Good	Excellent	Good
Quantity of data that can be collected	Good	Fair	Excellent	Good
Control of interviewer effects	Excellent	Fair	Poor	Fair
Control of Sample	Fair	Excellent	Fair	Poor
Speed of data collection	Poor	Excellent	Good	Excellent
Response rate	Fair	Good	Good	Good
Cost	Good	Fair	Poor	Excellent

Source: Adapted with permission from *Marketing Research: Measurement and Method,* 7th ed., by Donald S. Tull and Del I. Hawkins. Copyright 1993 by Macmillan Publishing Company.

than to an unknown interviewer in person or over the phone. Also, no interviewer is involved to bias the respondent's answers. However, mail questionnaires are not very flexible—all respondents answer the same questions in a fixed order, and the researcher cannot adapt the questionnaire based on earlier answers. Mail surveys usually take longer to complete, and the response rate—the number of people returning completed questionnaires—is often very low. Finally, the researcher often has little control over the mail questionnaire sample. Even with a good mailing list, it is hard to control *who* at the mailing address fills out the questionnaire.

Telephone interviewing is one of the best methods for gathering information quickly, and it provides greater flexibility than mail questionnaires. Interviewers can explain difficult questions, and they can skip some questions or probe on others depending on the answers they receive. Response rates tend to be higher than with mail questionnaires, and telephone interviewing also allows greater sample control. Interviewers can ask to speak to respondents with the desired characteristics, or even by name.

However, with telephone interviewing, the cost per respondent is higher than with mail questionnaires. Also, people may not want to discuss personal questions with an interviewer. Using an interviewer also introduces interviewer bias—the way interviewers talk, how they ask questions, and other differences may affect respondents' answers. Finally, different interviewers may interpret and record responses differently, and under time pressures some interviewers might even cheat by recording answers without asking questions.

Personal interviewing takes two forms—individual and group interviewing. *Individual interviewing* involves talking with people in their homes or offices, on the street, or in shopping malls. Such interviewing is flexible. Trained interviewers can hold a respondent's attention for a long time and can explain difficult questions. They can guide interviews, explore issues, and probe as the situation requires. They can show subjects actual products, advertisements, or packages and observe reactions and behavior. In most cases, personal interviews can be conducted fairly quickly. However, individual personal interviews may cost three to four times as much as telephone interviews.

Group interviewing consists of inviting six to ten people to gather for a few hours with a trained moderator to talk about a product, service, or organization. The participants normally are paid a small sum for attending. The meeting is held in a pleasant place and refreshments are served to foster an informal setting. The moderator encourages free and easy discussion, hoping that group interactions will bring out actual feelings and thoughts. At the same time, the moderator "focuses" the discussion—hence the name **focus group interviewing.** The comments are recorded through written notes or on videotapes that are studied later.

Focus group interviewing has become one of the major marketing research tools for gaining insight into consumer thoughts and feelings. However, focus group studies usually employ small sample sizes to keep time and costs down, and it may be hard to generalize from the results. Because interviewers have more freedom in personal interviews, the problem of interviewer bias is greater.

Today, modern communications technology is changing the way that focus groups are conducted:

In the old days, advertisers and agencies flew their staff to Atlanta or Little Rock to watch focus groups from behind one-way mirrors. The staff usually spent more time in hotels and taxis than they did doing research. Today, they are staying home. Videoconferencing links, television monitors, remote-control cameras, and digital transmission are boosting the amount of focus group research done over long-distance lines. [In a typical videoconferencing system], two cameras focused on the group are controlled by clients who hold a remote keypad. Executives in a far-off boardroom can zoom in on faces and pan the focus group at will. . . . A two-way sound system connects remote viewers to the backroom, focus group room, and directly to the monitor's earpiece. [Recently], while testing new product names in one focus group, the [client's] creative director . . . had an idea and contacted the moderator, who tested the new name on the spot.[19]

In addition, with the development of the Internet, many companies are now conducting online focus groups:

Janice Gjersten, director of marketing for WP-Studio, an online entertainment company, wanted to conduct traditional focus groups to gauge reaction to a new Web site. However, she found that an online focus group netted more honest answers. Gjersten contacted Cyber Dialogue, which provided focus group respondents drawn from its 10,000-person database. The focus group was held in an online chat room, which Gjersten "looked in on" from her office computer. Gjersten could interrupt the moderator at any time with flash e-mails unseen by the respondents. Although the online focus group lacked voice and body cues, Gjersten says she will never conduct a tradi-

[19]Rebecca Piirto Heather, "Future Focus Groups," *American Demographics,* January 1994, p. 6. For more on focus groups, see Thomas L. Greenbaum, "Focus Group by Video Next Trend of the '90s," *Marketing News,* July 29, 1996, p. 4; Howard Furmansky, "Debunking the Myths About Focus Groups," *Marketing News,* June 23, 1997, p. 2; and Judith Langer, "15 Myths of Qualitative Research: It's Conventional, but Is It Wisdom?" *Marketing News,* March 1, 1999, p. 13.

tional focus group again. Not only were respondents more honest, but the cost for the online group was one-third that of a traditional focus group and a full report came to her in one day, compared to four weeks.[20]

As this example suggests, the latest technology to hit marketing research is the fast-growing Internet. Increasingly, marketing researchers are collecting primary data through **online (Internet) marketing research**—*Internet surveys* and *online focus groups*. Although online research offers much promise, and some analysts predict that the Internet will soon be the primary marketing research tool, others are more cautious.

Advances in computers and communications technology have also had a large impact on methods of obtaining information. For example, most research firms now do Computer Assisted Telephone Interviewing (CATI). Professional interviewers call respondents around the country, often using phone numbers drawn at random. When the respondent answers, the interviewer reads a set of questions from a video screen and types the respondent's answers directly into the computer.

Other firms use *computer interviewing* in which respondents sit down at a computer, read questions from a screen, and type their own answers into the computer. The computers might be located at a research center, trade show, shopping mall, or retail location. For example, Boston Market uses touch-screen computers in its restaurants to obtain instant feedback from customers. Other researchers are conducting interactive focus groups using computers. Some researchers are even using Completely Automated Telephone Surveys (CATS), which employ voice response technology to conduct interviews. The recorded voice of an interviewer asks the questions, and respondents answer by pressing numbers on their push-button phones.[21]

Sampling Plan. Marketing researchers usually draw conclusions about large groups of consumers by studying a small sample of the total consumer population. A **sample** is a segment of the population selected to represent the population as a whole. Ideally, the sample should be representative so that the researcher can make accurate estimates of the thoughts and behaviors of the larger population.

Designing the sample requires three decisions. First, *who* is to be surveyed (what *sampling unit*)? The answer to this question is not always obvious. For example, to study the decision-making process for a family automobile purchase, should the researcher interview the husband, wife, other family members, dealership salespeople, or all of these? The researcher must determine what information is needed and who is most likely to have it.

Second, *how many* people should be surveyed (what *sample size*)? Large samples give more reliable results than small samples. It is not necessary to sample the entire target market or even a large portion to get reliable results, however. If well chosen, samples of less than 1 percent of a population can often give good reliability.

Third, *how* should the people in the sample be *chosen* (what *sampling procedure*)? Table 4.4 describes different kinds of samples. Using *probability samples,* each population member has a known chance of being included in the sample, and researchers can calculate confidence limits for sampling error. But when probability sampling costs too much or takes too much time, marketing researchers often take *nonprobability samples,* even though their sampling error cannot be measured. These varied ways of drawing samples have different costs and time limitations as well as different accuracy and statistical properties. Which method is best depends on the needs of the research project.

Research Instruments. In collecting primary data, marketing researchers have a choice of two main research instruments—the *questionnaire* and *mechanical devices*. The *questionnaire* is by far the most common instrument, whether administered in person, by phone, or online. Questionnaires are very flexible—there are many ways to ask questions. However, they must be developed carefully and tested before they can be used on a large scale. A carelessly prepared questionnaire usually contains several errors (see Table 4.5).

In preparing a questionnaire, the marketing researcher must first decide what questions to ask. Questionnaires frequently leave out questions that should be answered and include questions that cannot be answered, will not be answered, or need not be answered. Each question should be checked to see that it contributes to the research objectives.

[20]Sarah Schafer, "Communications: Getting a Line on Customers," *Inc. Technology,* 1996, p. 102. Also see "Online or Off Target?" *American Demographics,* November 1998, pp. 20–21; Langer, "15 Myths of Qualitative Research: It's Conventional, but Is It Wisdom?" pp. 13–14; and James Heckman, "Turning the Focus Online," *Marketing News,* February 28, 2000, p. 15.

[21]Peter J. DePaulo and Rick Weitzer, "Interactive Phones Technology Delivers Survey Data Quickly," *Marketing News,* June 6, 1994, pp. 33–34; Peter Francese, "Managing Marketing Information," *American Demographics,* September 1995, pp. 56–62; Emil E. Becker, "Automated Interviewing Has Advantages," *Marketing News,* January 2, 1995, p. 9; and Thomas Kiely, "Wired Focus Groups," *Harvard Business Review,* January–February 1998, pp. 12–16.

TABLE 4.4	Types of Samples
Probability Sample	
Simple random sample	Every member of the population has a known and equal chance of selection.
Stratified random sample	The population is divided into mutually exclusive groups (such as age groups), and random samples are drawn from each group.
Cluster (area) sample	The population is divided into mutually exclusive groups (such as blocks), and the researcher draws a sample of the groups to interview.
Nonprobability Sample	
Convenience sample	The researcher selects the easiest population members from which to obtain information.
	The researcher uses his or her judgment to select population members who are good prospects for accurate information.
Judgment sample	The researcher finds and interviews a prescribed number of people in each of several categories.

The *form* of each question can influence the response. Marketing researchers distinguish between closed-end questions and open-end questions. *Closed-end questions* include all the possible answers, and subjects make choices among them. Examples include multiple-choice questions and scale questions. *Open-end questions* allow respondents to answer in their own words. In a survey of airline users, Delta might simply ask, "What is your opinion of Delta Airlines?" Or it might ask people to complete a sentence: "When I choose an airline, the most important consideration is. . . ." These and other kinds of open-end questions often reveal more than closed-end questions because respondents are not limited in their answers. Open-end questions are especially useful in exploratory research, when the researcher is trying to find out *what* people think but not measuring *how many* people think in a certain way. Closed-end questions, on the other hand, provide answers that are easier to interpret and tabulate.

Researchers should also use care in the *wording* and *ordering* of questions. They should use simple, direct, unbiased wording. Questions should be arranged in a logical order. The first question should create interest if possible, and difficult or personal questions should be asked last so that respondents do not become defensive.

Although questionnaires are the most common research instrument, *mechanical instruments* also are used. We discussed two mechanical instruments, people meters and supermarket scanners, earlier in the chapter. Another group of mechanical devices measures subjects' physical responses. For example, a galvanometer measures the strength of interest or emotions aroused by a subject's exposure to different stimuli, such as an ad or picture. The galvanometer detects the minute degree of sweating that accompanies emotional arousal. The tachistoscope flashes an ad to a subject at an exposure range from less than one-hundredth of a second to several seconds. After each exposure, respondents describe everything they recall. Eye cameras are used to study respondents' eye movements to determine at what points their eyes focus first and how long they linger on a given item.

Presenting the Research Plan

At this stage, the marketing researcher should summarize the plan in a *written proposal*. A written proposal is especially important when the research project is large and complex or when an outside firm carries it out. The proposal should cover the management problems addressed and the research objectives, the information to be obtained, the sources of secondary information or methods for collecting primary data, and the way the results will help management decision making. The proposal also should include research costs. A written research plan or proposal ensures that the marketing manager and researchers have considered all the important aspects of the research, and that they agree on why and how the research will be done.

TABLE 4.5	Types of Questions

A. Closed-End Questions

Name	Description	Example
Dichotomous	A question offering two answer choices.	"In arranging this trip, did you personally phone Delta?" Yes ❑ No ❑
Multiple choice	A question offering three or more answer choices.	"With whom are you traveling on this flight?" No one ❑ Children only ❑ Spouse ❑ Business associates/friends/relatives ❑ Spouse and children ❑ An organized tour group ❑
Likert scale	A statement with which the respondent shows the amount of agreement or disagreement.	"Small airlines generally give better service than large ones." Strongly disagree — Disagree — Neither agree nor disagree — Agree — Strongly Agree 1 ❑ 2 ❑ 3 ❑ 4 ❑ 5 ❑
Semantic differential	A scale is inscribed between two bipolar words, and the respondent selects the point that represents the direction and intensity of his or her feelings.	Delta Airlines Large X __ __ __ __ __ Small Experienced __ __ __ __ X __ Inexperienced Modern __ __ __ X __ __ Old-fashioned
Importance scale	A scale that rates the importance of some attribute from "not at all important" to "extremely important."	"Airline food service to me is" Extremely important — Very important — Somewhat important — Not very important — Not at all important 1 ___ 2 ___ 3 ___ 4 ___ 5 ___
Rating scale	A scale that rates some attribute from "poor" to "excellent."	"Delta's food service is" Excellent — Very good — Good — Fair — Poor 1 ___ 2 ___ 3 ___ 4 ___ 5 ___
Intention-to-buy scale	A scale that describes the respondent's intentions to buy.	"If in-flight, first-run movie service were available on a long flight, I would" Definitely buy — Probably buy — Not certain — Probably not buy — Definitely not buy 1 ___ 2 ___ 3 ___ 4 ___ 5 ___

B. Open-End Questions

Name	Description	Example
Completely unstructured	A question that respondents can answer in an almost unlimited number of ways.	"What is your opinion of Delta Airlines?"
Word association	Words are presented, one at a time, and respondents mention the first word that comes to mind.	"What is the first word that comes to mind when you hear the following?" Airline _____ Delta _____ Travel _____
Sentence completion	Incomplete sentences are presented, one at a time, and respondents complete the sentence.	"When I choose an airline, the most important consideration in my decision is _____ "
Story completion	An incomplete story is presented, and respondents are asked to complete it.	"I flew Delta a few days ago. I noticed that the exterior and interior of the plane had very bright colors. This aroused in me the following thoughts and feelings." Now complete the story.
Picture completion	A picture of two characters is presented, with one making a statement. Respondents are asked to identify with the other and fill in the empty balloon.	Fill in the empty ballon.
Thematic Apperception Tests (TAT)	A picture is presented, and respondents are asked to make up a story about what they think is happening or may happen in the picture.	Make up a story about what you see.

IMPLEMENTING THE RESEARCH PLAN

The researcher next puts the marketing research plan into action. This involves collecting, processing, and analyzing the information. Data collection can be carried out by the company's marketing research staff or by outside firms. The company keeps more control over the collection process and data quality by using its own staff. However, outside firms that specialize in data collection often can do the job more quickly and at a lower cost.

The data collection phase of the marketing research process is generally the most expensive and the most subject to error. The researcher should watch fieldwork closely to make sure that the plan is implemented correctly and to guard against problems with contacting respondents, with respondents who refuse to cooperate or who give biased or dishonest answers, and with interviewers who make mistakes or take shortcuts.

active exercise ‹

Take a moment to consider some problems that market researchers face.

Researchers must process and analyze the collected data to isolate important information and findings. They need to check data from questionnaires for accuracy and completeness and code it for computer analysis. The researchers then tabulate the results and compute averages and other statistical measures.

INTERPRETING AND REPORTING THE FINDINGS

The researcher must now interpret the findings, draw conclusions, and report them to management. The researcher should not try to overwhelm managers with numbers and fancy statistical techniques. Rather, the researcher should present important findings that are useful in the major decisions faced by management.

However, interpretation should not be left only to the researchers. They are often experts in research design and statistics, but the marketing manager knows more about the problem and the decisions that must be made. In many cases, findings can be interpreted in different ways, and discussions between researchers and managers will help point to the best interpretations. The manager will also want to check that the research project was carried out properly and that all the necessary analysis was completed. Or, after seeing the findings, the manager may have additional questions that can be answered through further sifting of the data. Finally, the manager is the one who ultimately must decide what action the research suggests. The researchers may even make the data directly available to marketing managers so that they can perform new analyses and test new relationships on their own.

Interpretation is an important phase of the marketing process. The best research is meaningless if the manager blindly accepts faulty interpretations from the researcher. Similarly, managers may be biased—they might tend to accept research results that show what they expected and to reject those that they did not expect or hope for. Thus, managers and researchers must work together closely when interpreting research results, and both must share responsibility for the research process and resulting decisions.[22]

active concept check ‹

Now let's take a moment to test your knowledge of what you've just read.

[22]For a discussion of the importance of the relationship between market researchers and research users, see Christine Moorman, Gerald Zaltman, and Rohit Deshpande, "Relationships Between Providers and Users of Market Research: The Dynamics of Trust Within and Between Organizations,"*Journal of Marketing Research,* August 1992, pp. 314–28; Christine Moorman, Rohit Deshpande, and Gerald Zaltman, "Factors Affecting Trust in Market Research Relationships," *Journal of Marketing,* January 1993, pp. 81–101; Arlene Farber Sirkin, "Maximizing the Client–Researcher Partnership," *Marketing News,* September 13, 1994, p. 38; Pippa Considine, "Divided by a Common Cause," *Campaign,* September 19, 1997, p. 43; and Kevin P. Lonnie, "Researchers Must *Show* Their Findings to Clients," *Marketing News,* May 11, 1998, p. 4.

This section discusses marketing research in two special contexts: marketing research by small businesses and nonprofit organizations, and international marketing research. Finally, we look at public policy and ethics issues in marketing research.

MARKETING RESEARCH IN SMALL BUSINESSES AND NONPROFIT ORGANIZATIONS

Managers of small businesses and nonprofit organizations often think that marketing research can be done only by experts in large companies with big research budgets. But many of the marketing research techniques discussed in this chapter also can be used by smaller organizations in a less formal manner and at little or no expense.

Managers of small businesses and nonprofit organizations can obtain good marketing information simply by *observing* things around them. For example, retailers can evaluate new locations by observing vehicle and pedestrian traffic. They can monitor competitor advertising by collecting ads from local media. They can evaluate their customer mix by recording how many and what kinds of customers shop in the store at different times. In addition, many small business managers routinely visit their rivals and socialize with competitors to gain insights. Tom Coohill, a chef who owns two Atlanta restaurants, gives managers a food allowance to dine out and bring back ideas. Atlanta jeweler Frank Maier Jr., who often visits out-of-town rivals, spotted and copied a dramatic way of lighting displays.[23]

Managers can conduct informal *surveys* using small convenience samples. The director of an art museum can learn what patrons think about new exhibits by conducting informal focus groups—inviting small groups to lunch and having discussions on topics of interest. Retail salespeople can talk with customers visiting the store; hospital officials can interview patients. Restaurant managers might make random phone calls during slack hours to interview consumers about where they eat out and what they think of various restaurants in the area.

Managers also can conduct their own simple *experiments*. For example, by changing the themes in regular fund-raising mailings and watching the results, a nonprofit manager can find out much about which marketing strategies work best. By varying newspaper advertisements, a store manager can learn the effects of things such as ad size and position, price coupons, and media used.

Small organizations can obtain most of the secondary data available to large businesses. In addition, many associations, local media, chambers of commerce, and government agencies provide special help to small organizations. The U.S. Small Business Administration offers dozens of free publications and a Web site (**www.sbaonline.sba.gov**) that give advice on topics ranging from starting, financing, and expanding a small business to ordering business cards. Local newspapers often provide information on local shoppers and their buying patterns. Finally, small businesses can collect a considerable amount of information at very little cost on the Internet. They can scour competitor and customer Web sites and use Internet search engines to research specific companies and issues.

Many associations, media, and government agencies provide special help to small organizations. Here the U.S. Small Business Administration offers a Web site that gives advice on topics ranging from starting, financing, and expanding a small business to ordering business cards.

[23]"Business Bulletin: Studying the Competition," *Wall Street Journal,* March 19, 1995, pp. A1, A5.

In summary, secondary data collection, observation, surveys, and experiments can all be used effectively by small organizations with small budgets. Although these informal research methods are less complex and less costly, they still must be conducted carefully. Managers must think carefully about the objectives of the research, formulate questions in advance, recognize the biases introduced by smaller samples and less skilled researchers, and conduct the research systematically.[24]

INTERNATIONAL MARKETING RESEARCH

International marketing researchers follow the same steps as domestic researchers, from defining the research problem and developing a research plan to interpreting and reporting the results. However, these researchers often face more and different problems. Whereas domestic researchers deal with fairly homogenous markets within a single country, international researchers deal with differing markets in many different countries. These markets often vary greatly in their levels of economic development, cultures and customs, and buying patterns.

In many foreign markets, the international researcher has a difficult time finding good *secondary data*. Whereas U.S. marketing researchers can obtain reliable secondary data from dozens of domestic research services, many countries have almost no research services at all. Some of the largest international research services operate in many countries. For example, AC Nielsen Corporation, the world's largest marketing research company, has offices in more than 80 countries, with over 72 percent of its revenues coming from outside the United States. Forty-seven percent of the revenues of the world's 25 largest marketing research firms comes from outside their own countries.[25] However, most research firms operate in only a relative handful of countries. Thus, even when secondary information is available, it usually must be obtained from many different sources on a country-by-country basis, making the information difficult to combine or compare.

Because of the scarcity of good secondary data, international researchers often must collect their own primary data. Here again, researchers face problems not found domestically. For example, they may find it difficult simply to develop good samples. U.S. researchers can use current telephone directories, census tract data, and any of several sources of socioeconomic data to construct samples. However, such information is largely lacking in many countries.

Once the sample is drawn, the U.S. researcher usually can reach most respondents easily by telephone, by mail, or in person. Reaching respondents is often not so easy in other parts of the world. Researchers in Mexico cannot rely on telephone and mail data collection—most data collection is door to door and concentrated in three or four of the largest cities. Most surveys in Mexico bypass the large segment of the population in which native tribes speak languages other than Spanish. In some countries, few people have phones; for example, there are only thirty-two phones per thousand people in Argentina. In other countries, the postal system is notoriously unreliable. In Brazil, for instance, an estimated 30 percent of the mail is never delivered. In many developing countries, poor roads and transportation systems make certain areas hard to reach, making personal interviews difficult and expensive.[26]

Cultural differences from country to country cause additional problems for international researchers. Language is the most obvious obstacle. For example, questionnaires must be prepared in one language and then translated into the languages of each country researched. Responses then must

---

[24]See Nancy Levenburg and Tom Dandridge, "Can't Afford Research? Try Miniresearch," *Marketing News,* March 31, 1997, p. 19; and Nancy Levenburg, "Research Resources Exist for Small Businesses," *Marketing News,* January 4, 1999, p. 19.

[25]Honomichl, "Honomichl Global 25," pp. H1–H23; and the AC Nielsen Web page at www.acnielsen.com, February 2000.

[26]Many of the examples in this section, along with others, are found in Subhash C. Jain, *International Marketing Management,* 3rd ed. (Boston: PWS-Kent Publishing Company, 1990), pp. 334–39. Also see Jack Honomichl, "Research Cultures Are Different in Mexico, Canada," *Marketing News,* May 5, 1993, pp. 12–13; Naghi Namakforoosh, "Data Collection Methods Hold Key to Research in Mexico," *Marketing News,* August 29, 1994, p. 28; Ken Gofton, "Going Global with Research," *Marketing,* April 15, 1999, p. 35; and Jack Edmonston, "U.S., Overseas Differences Abound," *Advertising Age's Business Marketing,* January 1998, p. 32.

be translated back into the original language for analysis and interpretation. This adds to research costs and increases the risks of error.

Translating a questionnaire from one language to another is anything but easy. Many idioms, phrases, and statements mean different things in different cultures. For example, a Danish executive noted, "Check this out by having a different translator put back into English what you've translated from English. You'll get the shock of your life. I remember [an example in which] 'out of sight, out of mind' had become 'invisible things are insane.'"[27]

Buying roles and consumer decision processes vary greatly from country to country, further complicating international marketing research. Consumers in different countries also vary in their attitudes toward marketing research. People in one country may be very willing to respond; in other countries, nonresponse can be a major problem. For example, customs in some countries may prohibit people from talking with strangers. In certain cultures, research questions often are considered too personal. For example, in many Latin American countries, people may feel embarrassed to talk with researchers about their choices of shampoo, deodorant, or other personal care products. Even when respondents are *willing* to respond, they may not be *able* to because of high functional illiteracy rates. Middle-class people in developing countries often make false claims in order to appear well off. For example, in a study of tea consumption in India, over 70 percent of middle-income respondents claimed that they used one of several national brands. However, the researchers had good reason to doubt these results—over 60 percent of the tea sold in India is unbranded generic tea.

Despite these problems, the recent growth of international marketing has resulted in a rapid increase in the use of international marketing research. Global companies have little choice but to conduct such research. Although the costs and problems associated with international research may be high, the costs

[27]Jain, *International Marketing Management,* p. 338.

of not doing it—in terms of missed opportunities and mistakes—might be even higher. Once recognized, many of the problems associated with international marketing research can be overcome or avoided.

PUBLIC POLICY AND ETHICS IN MARKETING RESEARCH

Most marketing research benefits both the sponsoring company and its consumers. Through marketing research, companies learn more about consumers' needs, resulting in more satisfying products and services. However, the misuse of marketing research can also harm or annoy consumers. Two major public policy and ethics issues in marketing research are intrusions on consumer privacy and the misuse of research findings.

Intrusions on Consumer Privacy

Many consumers feel positively about marketing research and believe that it serves a useful purpose. Some actually enjoy being interviewed and giving their opinions. However, others strongly resent or even mistrust marketing research. A few consumers fear that researchers might use sophisticated techniques to probe our deepest feelings and then use this knowledge to manipulate our buying. Others may have been taken in by previous "research surveys" that actually turned out to be attempts to sell them something. Still other consumers confuse legitimate marketing research studies with telemarketing or database development efforts and say "no" before the interviewer can even begin. Most, however, simply resent the intrusion. They dislike mail or telephone surveys that are too long or too personal or that interrupt them at inconvenient times.

Increasing consumer resentment has become a major problem for the research industry. One recent poll found that 82 percent of Americans worry that they lack control over how businesses use their personal information, and 41 percent said that business had invaded their privacy. These concerns have led to lower survey response rates in recent years. One study found that 38 percent of Americans now refuse to be interviewed in an average survey, up dramatically from a decade ago. Another study found that 59 percent of consumers had refused to give information to a company because they thought it was not really needed or too personal, up from 42 percent just five years earlier.[28]

The research industry is considering several options for responding to this problem. One is to expand its "Your Opinion Counts" program to educate consumers about the benefits of marketing research and to distinguish it from telephone selling and database building. Another option is to provide a toll-free number that people can call to verify that a survey is legitimate. The industry also has considered adopting broad standards, perhaps based on Europe's International Code of Marketing and Social Research Practice. This code outlines researchers' responsibilities to respondents and to the general public. For example, it says that researchers should make their names and addresses available to participants, and it bans companies from representing activities such as database compilation or sales and promotional pitches as research.

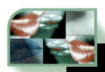

active poll <

Give your opinion on a question concerning the issue of customer privacy.

Misuse of Research Findings

Research studies can be powerful persuasion tools; companies often use study results as claims in their advertising and promotion. Today, however, many research studies appear to be little more than vehicles for pitching the sponsor's products. In fact, in some cases, the research surveys appear to have been designed just to produce the intended effect. Few advertisers openly rig their research designs or blatantly misrepresent the findings; most abuses tend to be subtle "stretches." Consider the following examples:[29]

[28]See "MRA Study Shows Refusal Rates Are Highest at Start of Process," *Marketing News,* August 16, 1993, p. A15; "Private Eyes," *Marketing Tools,* January–February 1996, pp. 31–32; William O. Bearden, Charles S. Madden, and Kelly Uscategui, "The Pool Is Drying Up," *Marketing Research,* Spring 1998, pp. 26–33; and "Survey Results Show Consumers Want Privacy," *Direct Marketing,* March 1999, p. 10.

[29]Cynthia Crossen, "Studies Galore Support Products and Positions, but Are They Reliable?" *Wall Street Journal,* November 14, 1991, pp. A1, A9. Also see Betsy Spethmann, "Cautious Consumers Have Surveyers Wary," *Advertising Age,* June 10, 1991, p. 34.

A study by Chrysler contends that Americans overwhelmingly prefer Chrysler to Toyota after test-driving both. However, the study included just 100 people in each of two tests. More importantly, none of the people surveyed owned a foreign car, so they appear to be favorably predisposed to U.S. cars.

A Black Flag survey asked: "A roach disk . . . poisons a roach slowly. The dying roach returns to the nest and after it dies is eaten by other roaches. In turn these roaches become poisoned and die. How effective do you think this type of product would be in killing roaches?" Not surprisingly, 79 percent said effective.

A poll sponsored by the disposable diaper industry asked: "It is estimated that disposable diapers account for less than 2 percent of the trash in today's landfills. In contrast, beverage containers, third-class mail, and yard waste are estimated to account for about 21 percent of the trash in landfills. Given this, in your opinion, would it be fair to ban disposable diapers?" Again, not surprisingly, 84 percent said no.

Thus, subtle manipulations of the study's sample, or the choice or wording of questions, can greatly affect the conclusions reached.

In others cases, so-called independent research studies actually are paid for by companies with an interest in the outcome. Small changes in study assumptions or in how results are interpreted can subtly affect the direction of the results. For example, at least four widely quoted studies compare the environmental effects of using disposable diapers to those of using cloth diapers. The two studies sponsored by the cloth diaper industry conclude that cloth diapers are more environmentally friendly. Not surprisingly, the other two studies, sponsored by the paper diaper industry, conclude just the opposite. Yet both appear to be correct *given* the underlying assumptions used.

Recognizing that surveys can be abused, several associations—including the American Marketing Association, the Council of American Survey Research Organizations, and the Marketing Research Association—have developed codes of research ethics and standards of conduct.[30] In the end, however, unethical or inappropriate actions cannot simply be regulated away. Each company must accept responsibility for policing the conduct and reporting of its own marketing research to protect consumers' best interests and its own.

> active concept check

Now let's take a moment to test your knowledge of what you've just read.

> Chapter Wrap-Up

Now that you've reached the end of the chapter, you may wish to explore the concepts you've been reading about in greater detail, or test yourself to see how well you've comprehended the material. In the box below you'll find a number of links. Click on any one of these links to find additional chapter resources.

[30]For example, see Betsy Peterson, "Ethics Revisited," *Marketing Research,* Winter 1996, pp. 47–48; and O. C. Ferrell, Michael D. Hartline, and Stephen W. McDaniel, "Codes of Ethics Among Corporate Research Departments, Marketing Research Firms, and Data Subcontractors: An Examination of a Three-Communities Metaphor," *Journal of Business Ethics,* April 1998, pp. 503–16. For discussion of a framework for ethical marketing research, see Naresh K. Malhotra and Gina L. Miller, "An Integrated Model of Ethical Decisions in Marketing Research," *Journal of Business Ethics,* February 1998, pp. 263–80.

> end-of-chapter resources

- Review of Concept Connections
- Practice Quiz
- Issues for Discussion
- Key Terms
- Marketing Applications
- Internet Connections
- Company Case

C H A P T E R 5

Consumer Markets and Consumer Buyer Behavior

 ## What's Ahead

Few brands engender such intense loyalty as that found in the hearts of Harley-Davidson owners. "The Harley audience is granitelike" in its devotion, laments the vice president of sales for competitor Yamaha. Observes the publisher of *American Iron,* an industry publication, "You don't see people tattooing Yamaha on their bodies." Each year, in early March, more than 400,000 Harley bikers rumble through the streets of Daytona Beach, Florida, to attend Harley-Davidson's Bike Week celebration. Bikers from across the nation lounge on their low-slung Harleys, swap biker tales, and sport T-shirts proclaiming "I'd rather push a Harley than drive a Honda."

Riding such intense emotions, Harley-Davidson has rumbled its way to the top of the fast-growing heavyweight motorcycle market. Harley's "Hogs" capture over one-fifth of all U.S. bike sales and more than half of the heavyweight segment. Both the segment and Harley's sales are growing rapidly. In fact, for several years running, sales have far outstripped supply, with customer waiting lists of up to three years for popular models and street prices running well above suggested list prices. "We've seen people buy a new Harley and then sell it in the parking lot for

$4,000 to $5,000 more," says one dealer. Since its initial public stock offering in 1986, by the year 2000, Harley-Davidson shares had split 4 times and were up more than 7,100 percent.

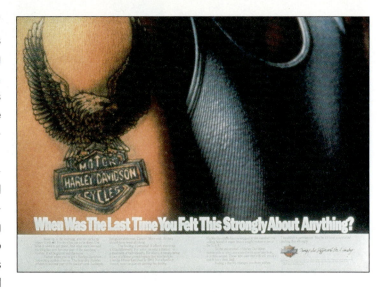

Harley-Davidson's marketers spend a great deal of time thinking about customers and their buying behavior. They want to know who their customers are, what they think and how they feel, and why they buy a Harley rather than a Yamaha or a Suzuki or a big Honda American Classic. What is it that makes Harley buyers so fiercely loyal? These are difficult questions; even Harley owners themselves don't know exactly what motivates their buying. But Harley management puts top priority on understanding customers and what makes them tick.

Who rides a Harley? You might be surprised. It's no longer the Hell's Angels crowd—the burly, black-leather-jacketed rebels and biker chicks who once made up Harley's core clientele. Motorcycles are attracting a new breed of riders—older, more affluent, and better educated. Harley now appeals more to "rubbies" (rich urban bikers) than to rebels. The average Harley customer is a 43-year-old husband with a median household income of $66,400. Harley's big, comfortable cruisers give these new consumers the easy ride, prestige, and twist-of-the-wrist power they want and can afford.

Harley-Davidson makes good bikes, and to keep up with its shifting market, the company has upgraded its showrooms and sales approaches. But Harley customers are buying a lot more than just a quality bike and a smooth sales pitch. To gain a better understanding of customers' deeper motivations, Harley-Davidson conducted focus groups in which it invited bikers to make cut-and-paste collages of pictures that expressed their feelings about Harley-Davidsons. (Can't you just see a bunch of hard-core bikers doing this?) It then mailed out 16,000 surveys containing a typical battery of psychological, sociological, and demographic questions as well as subjective questions such as "Is Harley more typified by a brown bear or a lion?" The research revealed seven core customer types: adventure-loving traditionalists, sensitive pragmatists, stylish status seekers, laid-back campers, classy capitalists, cool-headed loners, and cocky misfits. However, all owners appreciated their Harleys for the same basic reasons. "It didn't matter if you were the guy who swept the floors of the factory or if you were the CEO at that factory, the attraction to Harley was very similar," says a Harley executive. "Independence, freedom, and power were the universal Harley appeals."

These studies confirm that Harley customers are doing more than just buying motorcycles. They're making a lifestyle statement and displaying an attitude. As one analyst suggests, owning a Harley makes you "the toughest, baddest guy on the block. Never mind that [you're] a dentist or an accountant. You [feel] wicked astride all that power." Your Harley renews your spirits and announces your independence. As the Harley Web home page announces, "Thumbing the starter of a Harley-Davidson does a lot more than fire the engine. It fires the imagination." Adds a Harley dealer: "We sell a dream here. Our customers lead hardworking professional or computer-oriented lives. Owning a Harley removes barriers to meeting people on a casual basis, and it gives you maximum self-expression in your own space.

The classic look, the throaty sound, the very idea of a Harley—all contribute to its mystique. Owning this "American legend" makes you a part of something bigger, a member of the Harley family. The fact that you have to wait to get a Harley makes it all that much more satisfying to have one. In fact, the company deliberately restricts its output. "Our goal is to eventually run production at a level that's always one motorcycle short of demand," says Harley-Davidson's chief executive.

Such strong emotions and motivations are captured in a recent Harley-Davidson advertisement. The ad shows a close-up of an arm, the bicep adorned with a Harley-Davidson tattoo. The headline asks, "When was the last time you felt this strongly about anything?" The ad copy outlines the problem and suggests a solution:

Wake up in the morning and life picks up where it left off. You do what has to be done. Use what it takes to get there. And what once seemed exciting has now become part of the numbing routine. It all begins to feel the same. Except when you've got a Harley-Davidson. Something strikes a nerve. The heartfelt thunder rises up, refusing to become part of the background. Suddenly things are different. Clearer. More real. As they should have been all along. The feeling is personal. For some, owning a Harley is a statement of individuality. For others, owning a Harley means being a part of a home-grown legacy that was born in a tiny Milwaukee shed in 1903. . . . To the uninitiated, a Harley-Davidson motorcycle is associated with a certain look, a certain sound. Anyone who owns one will tell you it's much more than that. Riding a Harley changes you from within. The effect is permanent. Maybe it's time you started feeling this strongly. Things are different on a Harley.[1]

> objectives

Before you begin, take a moment to familiarize yourself with the key objectives of this chapter.

> gearing up

Before we begin our exploration this chapter, take a short warm-up test to see what you know about this topic.

The Harley-Davidson example shows that many different factors affect consumer buying behavior. Buying behavior is never simple, yet understanding it is the essential task of marketing management.

This chapter explores the dynamics of consumer behavior and the consumer market. **Consumer buying behavior** refers to the buying behavior of final consumers—individuals and households who buy goods and services for personal consumption. All of these final consumers combined make up the **consumer market.** The American consumer market consists of more than 273 million people who consume many trillions of dollars worth of goods and services each year, making it one of the most

---

[1]Quotes from Richard A. Melcher, "Tune-Up Time for Harley," *Business Week,* April 8, 1997, pp. 90–94; Ian P. Murphy, "Aided by Research, Harley Goes Whole Hog," *Marketing News,* December 2, 1996, pp. 16, 17; Dyan Machan, "Is the Hog Going Soft?" *Forbes,* March 10, 1997, pp. 114–19; and Linda Sandler, "Workspaces: Harley Shop," *Wall Street Journal,* April 21, 1999, p. B20; and the Harley-Davidson Web site (www.Harley-Davidson.com), September 1999. Also see Sarah Lorge, "Revving Up Customers," *Sales & Marketing Management,* June 1998, p. 15; and Leslie P. Norton, "Potholes Ahead?" *Barron's,* February 1, 1999, pp. 16–17.

attractive consumer markets in the world. The world consumer market consists of more than *6 billion* people. At present growth rates, the world population will reach almost 8 billion people by 2025.[2]

Consumers around the world vary tremendously in age, income, education level, and tastes. They also buy an incredible variety of goods and services. How these diverse consumers connect with each other and with other elements of the world around them impacts their choices among various products, services, and companies. Here we examine the fascinating array of factors that affect consumer behavior.

> Model of Consumer Behavior

Consumers make many buying decisions every day. Most large companies research consumer buying decisions in great detail to answer questions about what consumers buy, where they buy, how and how much they buy, when they buy, and why they buy. Marketers can study actual consumer purchases to find out what they buy, where, and how much. But learning about the *whys* of consumer buying behavior is not so easy—the answers are often locked deep within the consumer's head.

The central question for marketers is: How do consumers respond to various marketing efforts the company might use? The company that really understands how consumers will respond to different product features, prices, and advertising appeals has a great advantage over its competitors. The starting point is the stimulus–response model of buyer behavior shown in Figure 5.1. This figure shows that marketing and other stimuli enter the consumer's "black box" and produce certain responses. Marketers must figure out what is in the buyer's black box.[3]

Marketing stimuli consist of the four Ps: product, price, place, and promotion. Other stimuli include major forces and events in the buyer's environment: economic, technological, political, and cultural. All these inputs enter the buyer's black box, where they are turned into a set of observable buyer responses: product choice, brand choice, dealer choice, purchase timing, and purchase amount.

The marketer wants to understand how the stimuli are changed into responses inside the consumer's black box, which has two parts. First, the buyer's characteristics influence how he or she perceives and reacts to the stimuli. Second, the buyer's decision process itself affects the buyer's behavior. This chapter looks first at buyer characteristics as they affect buying behavior, and then discusses the buyer decision process.

active concept check <

Now let's take a moment to test your knowledge of what you've just read.

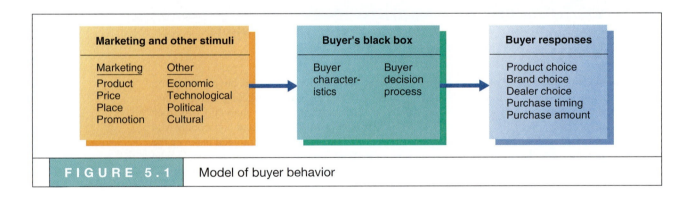

Marketing and other stimuli		Buyer's black box		Buyer responses
Marketing	**Other**	Buyer character- istics	Buyer decision process	Product choice
Product	Economic			Brand choice
Price	Technological			Dealer choice
Place	Political			Purchase timing
Promotion	Cultural			Purchase amount

FIGURE 5.1	Model of buyer behavior

[2]For current population estimates, see the U.S. and world POP clocks at www.census.gov.

[3]Several models of the consumer buying process have been developed by marketing scholars. For a summary, see Leon G. Schiffman and Leslie Lazar Kanuk, *Consumer Behavior,* 6th ed. (Upper Saddle River, NJ: Prentice Hall, 1997), pp. 560–64.

Consumer purchases are influenced strongly by cultural, social, personal, and psychological characteristics, as shown in Figure 5.2. For the most part, marketers cannot control such factors, but they must take them into account. We illustrate these characteristics for the case of a hypothetical consumer named Anna Flores. Anna is a married college graduate who works as a brand manager in a leading consumer packaged-goods company. She wants to find a new leisure-time activity that will provide some contrast to her working day. This need has led her to consider buying a camera and taking up photography. Many characteristics in her background will affect the way she evaluates cameras and chooses a brand.

CULTURAL FACTORS

Cultural factors exert the broadest and deepest influence on consumer behavior. The marketer needs to understand the role played by the buyer's *culture, subculture,* and *social class.*

Culture

Culture is the most basic cause of a person's wants and behavior. Human behavior is largely learned. Growing up in a society, a child learns basic values, perceptions, wants, and behaviors from the family and other important institutions. A child in the United States normally learns or is exposed to the following values: achievement and success, activity and involvement, efficiency and practicality, progress, material comfort, individualism, freedom, humanitarianism, youthfulness, and fitness and health.

Every group or society has a culture, and cultural influences on buying behavior may vary greatly from country to country. Failure to adjust to these differences can result in ineffective marketing or embarrassing mistakes. For example, business representatives of a U.S. community trying to market itself in Taiwan found this out the hard way. Seeking more foreign trade, they arrived in Taiwan bearing gifts of green baseball caps. It turned out that the trip was scheduled a month before Taiwan elections, and that green was the color of the political opposition party. Worse yet, the visitors learned after the fact that according to Taiwan culture, a man wears green to signify that his wife has been unfaithful. The head of the community delegation later noted, "I don't know whatever happened to those green hats, but the trip gave us an understanding of the extreme differences in our cultures."[4] International marketers must understand the culture in each international market and adapt their marketing strategies accordingly.

Anna Flores's cultural background will affect her camera buying decision. Anna's desire to own a camera may result from her being raised in a modern society that has developed camera technology and a whole set of consumer learnings and values. Anna knows what cameras are. She knows how to read instructions, and her society has accepted the idea of women photographers.

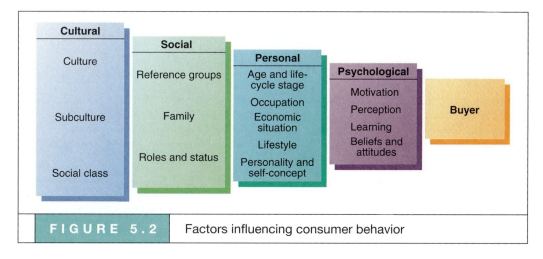

FIGURE 5.2 | Factors influencing consumer behavior

---

[4]For this and other examples of the effects of culture in international marketing, see Philip R. Cateora, *International Marketing,* 8th ed. (Homewood, IL: Irwin, 1993), chap. 4; Sak Onkvisit and John J. Shaw, *International Marketing: Analysis and Strategy,* 3rd ed. (Upper Saddle River, NJ: Prentice Hall, 1997), chap. 6; and Greg Gimba, "Color in Marketing: Shades of Meaning," *Marketing News,* March 16, 1998, p. 6.

Marketers are always trying to spot *cultural shifts* in order to discover new products that might be wanted. For example, the cultural shift toward greater concern about health and fitness has created a huge industry for exercise equipment and clothing, low-fat and more natural foods, and health and fitness services. The shift toward informality has resulted in more demand for casual clothing and simpler home furnishings. The increased desire for leisure time has resulted in more demand for convenience products and services, such as microwave ovens and fast food.

Subculture

Each culture contains smaller **subcultures,** or groups of people with shared value systems based on common life experiences and situations. Subcultures include nationalities, religions, racial groups, and geographic regions. Many subcultures make up important market segments, and marketers often design products and marketing programs tailored to their needs. Here are examples of four such important subculture groups.

Hispanic Consumers. The U.S. Hispanic market—Americans of Cuban, Mexican, Central American, South American, and Puerto Rican descent—consists of 29 million consumers who buy more than $348 billion worth of goods and services each year. Expected to number almost 40 million by the year 2010, Hispanics are easy to reach through the growing selection of Spanish-language broadcast and print media that cater to them.[5]

Hispanics have long been a target for marketers of food, beverages, and household care products. But as the segment's buying power increases, Hispanics are now emerging as an attractive market for pricier products such as computers, financial services, photography equipment, large appliances, life insurance, and automobiles. Hispanic consumers tend to buy more branded, higher quality products—generics don't sell well to Hispanics. Perhaps more important, Hispanics are very brand loyal, and they favor companies who show special interest in them. Because of the segment's strong brand loyalty, companies that get the first foothold have an important head start in this fast-growing market.

Sears makes a special effort to market to Hispanic American consumers, especially for the 20 percent of its stores that are located in heavily Hispanic neighborhoods:

Sears was one of the first credit card providers to market cards to Hispanics, helping the retailer to build a formidable database of Hispanic consumers. Sears currently markets heavily to this attractive segment. Last year, it spent some $25 million on advertising to Hispanics—more than any other retailer—and it recently launched a Spanish-language Web site. In addition to advertising through local Spanish radio stations and newspapers, local Sears stores in Hispanic neighborhoods periodically hang Spanish-language ads on the doorknobs of area homes. These neighborhoods also receive regular visits from a Fiesta Mobile, a colorful Winnebago that plays music, gives out prizes, and promotes the Sears credit card. Sears also sponsors major Hispanic cultural festivals and concerts. However, one of its most successful marketing efforts is its magazine *Nuestra Gente*—which means Our People—the nation's largest Spanish-language magazine. The magazine features articles about Hispanic celebrities alongside glossy spreads of Sears fashions. Using a list culled from its database, Sears has built up a controlled circulation of about 700,000. The magazine is free, but subscriptions are available only by request. As a result of this careful cultivation of Hispanic consumers, although Sears has lost sales in recent years to discount retailers, the Hispanic segment has remained steadfastly loyal.[6]

Targeting Hispanics may also provide an additional benefit. With the passage of the North American Free Trade Agreement (NAFTA)—which reduced trade barriers between the United States, Mexico, and Canada—U.S. and Mexican companies have sought new opportunities to market "pan-American" brands. Companies on both sides of the border see the U.S. Hispanic population as a bridge for spanning U.S. and Latin American markets.

African American Consumers. If the U.S. population of African American consumers were a separate nation, its buying power of $500 billion annually would rank twelfth in the free world.[7] The black population in the United States is growing in affluence and sophistication. Although more price

[5]For examples, see Nancy Coltun Webster, "Multicultural," *Advertising Age,* November 17, 1997, pp. S1–S2; Rachel X. Weissman, "Los Ninos Go Shopping," *American Demographics,* May 1999, pp. 37–38; and Helene Stapinski, "Generación Latino," *American Demographics,* July 1999, pp. 63–68.

[6]Calmetta Y. Coleman, "Attention Shoppers: Target Makes a Play for Minority Group Sears Has Cultivated," *Wall Street Journal,* April 12, 1999, p. A1.

[7]Webster, "Multicultural," p. S1.

conscious than other segments, blacks are also strongly motivated by quality and selection. They place more importance on brand names, are more brand loyal, and do less "shopping around."

In recent years, many companies have developed special products and services, packaging, and appeals to meet the needs of African Americans. Hallmark launched its Afrocentric brand, Mahogany, with only 16 cards in 1987; it offers 800 cards today. Other companies are moving away from creating separate products for African Americans. Instead, they are offering more inclusive product lines within the same brand that goes out to the general market. For example, Sara Lee discontinued its separate Color-Me-Natural line of L'eggs pantyhose for black women and now offers shades and sheer styles popular among black women as half of the company's general-focus subbrands.[8]

A wide variety of magazines, television channels, and other media now target black consumers. Marketers are also reaching out to the African American virtual community. Per capita, black consumers spend twice as much as white consumers for online services. African Americans are increasingly turning to Web sites like The Black World Today (**www.tbwt.com**), a black *USA Today* on the Internet that address black culture in ways that network and cable TV rarely do. Other popular sites include Urban Sports Network, Net Noir, Afronet, and Black Voices.[9]

Asian American Consumers.   Asian Americans, the fastest-growing and most affluent U.S. demographic segment, now number more than 10 million with spending power of $110 billion annually. Chinese constitute the largest group, followed by Filipinos, Japanese, Asian Indians, and Koreans. Asian American family income exceeds the national average by 19 percent.[10] Long-distance telephone companies and financial services marketers have long targeted Asian American consumers, but until recently, packaged-goods firms, automobile companies, retailers, and fast-food chains have lagged in this segment. Language and cultural traditions appear to be the biggest barriers. For example, 66 percent of Asian Americans are foreign born, and 56 percent of those five years and older

[8]See "L'eggs Joins New Approach in Marketing to African-American Women," *Supermarket Business,* June 1998, p. 81; Beth Belton, "Black Buying Power Soaring," *USA Today,* July 30, 1998, p. 1B; and Dana Canedy, "The Courtship of Black Consumers," *New York Times,* August 11, 1998, pp. D1, D2.

[9]See David Kiley, "Black Surfing," *Brandweek,* November 17, 1997, p. 36; Kim Cleland, "Narrow-Marketing Efforts Winning the Internet Savvy," *Advertising Age,* November 16, 1998, p. S26; and Chuck Ross, "BET Cries Foul, Hits Lack of Ad Commitment," *Advertising Age,* April 12, 1999, pp. S1, S16.

[10]Webster, "Multicultural," p. S1; and Saul Gitlin, "A Yen for Brands," *Brandweek,* January 5, 1998, p. 17.

do not speak English fluently. Still, because of the segment's rapidly growing buying power, many firms are now looking seriously at this market.[11]

The 50-Plus Market.   As the U.S. population ages, mature consumers are becoming a very attractive market. Now 75 million strong, the 50-and-older population will swell to 115 million in the next 25 years. Mature consumers are better off financially than younger consumer groups. Because seniors have more time and money, they are an ideal market for exotic travel, restaurants, high-tech home entertainment products, leisure goods and services, designer furniture and fashions, financial services, and health care services.

Their desire to look as young as they feel also makes more mature consumers good candidates for cosmetics and personal care products, health foods, fitness products, and other items that combat the effects of aging. The best strategy is to appeal to their active, multidimensional lives. For example, a recent Nike commercial features a senior weight lifter who proudly proclaims, "I'm not strong for my age. I'm strong!" Similarly, Kellogg aired a TV spot for All-Bran cereal in which individuals ranging in age from 53 to 81 are featured playing ice hockey, water skiing, running hurdles, and playing baseball, all to the tune of "Wild Thing." An Aetna commercial portrays a senior who, after retiring from a career as a lawyer, fulfills a life-long dream to become an archeologist.[12]

Anna Flores's buying behavior will be influenced by her subculture identification. These factors will affect her food preferences, clothing choices, recreation activities, and career goals. Subcultures attach different meanings to picture taking, and this could affect both Anna's interest in cameras and the brand she buys.

Social Class

Almost every society has some form of social class structure. **Social classes** are society's relatively permanent and ordered divisions whose members share similar values, interests, and behaviors. Social scientists have identified the seven American social classes (see Table 5.1).

Social class is not determined by a single factor, such as income, but is measured as a combination of occupation, income, education, wealth, and other variables. In some social systems, members of different classes are reared for certain roles and cannot change their social positions. In the United States, however, the lines between social classes are not fixed and rigid; people can move to a higher social class or drop into a lower one. Marketers are interested in social class because people within a given social class tend to exhibit similar buying behavior.[13]

Social classes show distinct product and brand preferences in areas such as clothing, home furnishings, leisure activity, and automobiles. Anna Flores's social class may affect her camera decision. If she comes from a high social class background, her family probably owned an expensive camera and she may have dabbled in photography.

SOCIAL FACTORS

A consumer's behavior also is influenced by social factors, such as the consumer's *small groups, family,* and *social roles* and *status.*

Groups

A person's behavior is influenced by many small **groups.** Groups that have a direct influence and to which a person belongs are called *membership groups.* In contrast, *reference groups* serve as direct (face-to-face) or indirect points of comparison or reference in forming a person's attitudes or behavior. People often are influenced by reference groups to which they do not belong. For example, an *aspirational group* is one to which the individual wishes to belong, as when a teenage basketball

[11]See Christy Fisher, "Marketers Straddle Asian-America Curtain," *Advertising Age,* November 7, 1994; John Steere, "How Asian-Americans Make Purchasing Decisions," *Marketing News,* March 13, 1995, p. 9; "Asian Demographics," *Media Week,* April 17, 1995, p. S1; and Brad Edmondson, "Asian Americans in 2001," *American Demographics,* February 1997, pp. 16–17.

[12]See Rick Adler, "Stereotypes Won't Work with Seniors Anymore," *Advertising Age,* November 11, 1996, p. 32; Richard Lee, "The Youth Bias in Advertising," *American Demographics,* January 1997, pp. 47–50; D. Allen Kerr, "Where There's Gray, There's Green," *Marketing News,* May 25, 1998, p. 2; Jeff Brazil, "You Talkin' to Me?" *American Demographics,* December 1998, pp. 55–59; Heather Chaplin, "Centrum's Self-Inflicted Silver Bullet," *American Demographics,* March 1999, pp. 68–69; and Kendra Parker, "Reaping What They've Sown," *American Demographics,* December 1999, pp. 34–37.

[13]For more on social class, see Leon G. Schiffman and Leslie L. Kanuk, *Consumer Behavior,* 6th ed. (Upper Saddle River, NJ: Prentice Hall, 1997), chap. 13; Michael R. Solomon, *Consumer Behavior,* 3rd ed. (Upper Saddle River, NJ: Prentice Hall, 1996), pp. 432–52; David Leonhardt, "Two-Tier Marketing," *Business Week,* March 17, 1997, p. 82; and Rebecca Piirto Heath, "The New Working Class," *American Demographics,* January 1998, pp. 51–55.

TABLE 5.1	Characteristics of Seven Major American Social Classes

Upper Uppers (Less Than 1 Percent)

Upper uppers are the social elite who live on inherited wealth and have well-known family backgrounds. They give large sums to charity, run debutante balls, own more than one home, and send their children to the finest schools. They are a market for jewelry, antiques, homes, and vacations. They often buy and dress conservatively rather than showing off their wealth. Although small in number, upper uppers serve as a reference group for others.

Lower Uppers (About 2 Percent)

Lower uppers have earned high income or wealth through exceptional ability in the professions or business. They usually begin in the middle class. They tend to be active in social and civic affairs and buy for themselves and their children the symbols of status, such as expensive homes, schools, swimming pools, and automobiles. They include the new rich who consume conspicuously to impress those below them. They want to be accepted in the upper-upper stratum, a status more likely to be achieved by their children than by themselves.

Upper Middles (12 Percent)

Upper middles possess neither family status nor unusual wealth. They are primarily concerned with "career." They have attained positions as professionals, independent businesspersons, and corporate managers. They believe in education and want their children to develop professional or administrative skills. They are joiners and highly civic-minded. They are the quality market for good homes, clothes, furniture, and appliances.

Middle Class (32 Percent)

The middle class is made up of average-pay white- and blue-collar workers who live on "the better side of town" and try to "do the proper things." To keep up with the trends, they often buy products that are popular. Most are concerned with fashion, seeking the better brand names. Better living means owning a nice home in a nice neighborhood with good schools. They believe in spending more money on worthwhile experiences for their children and aiming them toward a college education.

Working Class (38 Percent)

The working class consists of those who lead a "working-class lifestyle," whatever their income, school background, or job. They depend heavily on relatives for economic and emotional support, for advice on purchases, and for assistance in times of trouble. The working class maintains sharper sex role division and stereotyping.

Upper Lower (9 Percent)

Upper lowers are working (are not on welfare), although their living standard is just above poverty. They perform unskilled work for very poor pay although they strive toward a higher class. Often, upper lowers lack education. Although they fall near the poverty line financially, they manage to "present a picture of self-discipline" and "maintain some effort at cleanliness."

Lower Lowers (7 Percent)

Lower lowers are on welfare, visibly poverty stricken, and usually out of work or have "the dirtiest jobs." Often they are not interested in finding a job and are permanently dependent on public aid or charity for income. Their homes, clothes, and possessions are "dirty," "raggedy," and "broken-down."

Sources: See Richard P. Coleman, "The Continuing Significance of Social Class to Marketing," *Journal of Consumer Research,* December 1983, pp. 265–80, © Journal of Consumer Research, Inc., 1983; and Leon G. Shiffman and Leslie Lazar Kanuk, *Consumer Behavior,* 6th ed. (Upper Saddle River, NJ: Prentice Hall, 1997), p. 388.

player hopes to play someday for the Utah Jazz. Marketers try to identify the reference groups of their target markets. Reference groups expose a person to new behaviors and lifestyles, influence the person's attitudes and self-concept, and create pressures to conform that may affect the person's product and brand choices.

The importance of group influence varies across products and brands. It tends to be strongest when the product is visible to others whom the buyer respects. Manufacturers of products and brands subjected to strong group influence must figure out how to reach **opinion leaders**—people within a reference group who, because of special skills, knowledge, personality, or other characteristics, exert influence on others.

Many marketers try to identify opinion leaders for their products and direct marketing efforts toward them. In other cases, advertisements can simulate opinion leadership, thereby reducing the need for consumers to seek advice from others. For example, the hottest trends in teenage music, language, and fashion start in America's inner cities, then quickly spread to more mainstream youth in the suburbs. Thus, clothing companies who hope to appeal to these fickle and fashion-conscious youth often make a concerted effort to monitor urban opinion leaders' style and behavior. Levi-Strauss is a good example:

> In recent years, Levi-Strauss has been squeezed by the competition as teens and youth flock to designer labels and more "cool" brands. To revitalize sales for its Silver Tab line of clothing, the company's ad agency sent out employees to build a network of contacts familiar with the urban scene, including club-hoppers, stylists, photographers, and disk jockeys. The agency kept a scrapbook of people and looks and separated them into "tribes" defined by the music they like, including electronica, hip-hop and rap, and retro soul music. Its illustrated ads appealing to hip-hop and rap culture featured the statement "It's bangin', son," which means "cool," and teenagers clad in Silver Tab clothing—baggy pants, hip huggers, tiny tops—and wearing accessories such as nose rings, beepers, and chunky gold jewelry.[14]

The importance of group influence varies across products and brands. It tends to be strongest when the product is visible to others whom the buyer respects. Purchases of products that are bought and used privately are not much affected by group influences because neither the product nor the brand will be noticed by others. If Anna Flores buys a camera, both the product and the brand will be visible to others whom she respects, and her decision to buy the camera and her brand choice may be influenced strongly by some of her groups, such as friends who belong to a photography club.

Family

Family members can strongly influence buyer behavior. The family is the most important consumer buying organization in society, and it has been researched extensively. Marketers are interested in the roles and influence of the husband, wife, and children on the purchase of different products and services.

Husband–wife involvement varies widely by product category and by stage in the buying process. Buying roles change with evolving consumer lifestyles. In the United States, the wife traditionally has been the main purchasing agent for the family, especially in the areas of food, household products, and clothing. But with 70 percent of women holding jobs outside the home and the willingness of husbands to do more of the family's purchasing, all this is changing. For example, women now buy about 45 percent of all cars and men account for about 40 percent of food-shopping dollars.[15]

Such changes suggest that marketers who've typically sold their products to only women or only men are now courting the opposite sex. For example, with research revealing that women now account for nearly half of all hardware store purchases, home improvement retailers such as Home Depot and Builders Square have turned what once were intimidating warehouses into female-friendly retail outlets. The new Builders Square II outlets feature decorator design centers at the front of the store. To attract more women, Builders Square runs ads targeting women in *Home, House Beautiful, Woman's Day,* and *Better Homes and Gardens.* Home Depot even offers bridal registries.

Similarly, after research indicated that women now make up 34 percent of the luxury car market, Cadillac has started paying more attention to this important segment. Male car designers at Cadillac are going about their work with paper clips on their fingers to simulate what it feels like to operate buttons, knobs, and other interior features with longer fingernails. The Cadillac Catera features an air-

[14]Courteny Kane, "Advertising: TBWA/Chiat Day Brings 'Street Culture' to a Campaign for Levi-Strauss Silver Tab Clothing," *New York Times,* August 14, 1998, p. D8.

[15]Debra Goldman, "Spotlight Men," *Adweek,* August 13, 1990, pp. M1–M6; Nancy Ten Kate, "Who Buys the Pants in the Family?" *American Demographics,* January 1992, p. 12; and Laura Zinn, "Real Men Buy Paper Towels, Too," *Business Week,* November 9, 1992, pp. 75–76.

conditioned glove box to preserve such items as lipstick and film. Under the hood, yellow markings highlight where fluid fills go.[16]

Children may also have a strong influence on family buying decisions. Chevrolet recognizes these influences in marketing its Chevy Venture minivan. For example, it ran ads to woo these "back-seat consumers" in *Sports Illustrated for Kids,* which attracts mostly 8- to 14-year-old boys. "We're kidding ourselves when we think kids aren't aware of brands," says Venture's brand manager, adding that even she was surprised at how often parents told her that kids played a tie-breaking role in deciding which car to buy.[17]

In the case of expensive products and services, husbands and wives often make joint decisions. Anna Flores's husband may play an *influencer role* in her camera-buying decision. He may have an opinion about her buying a camera and about the kind of camera to buy. At the same time, she will be the primary decider, purchaser, and user.

Roles and Status

A person belongs to many groups—family, clubs, organizations. The person's position in each group can be defined in terms of both role and status. With her parents, Anna Flores plays the role of daughter; in her family, she plays the role of wife; in her company, she plays the role of brand manager. A *role* consists of the activities people are expected to perform according to the persons around them. Each of Anna's roles will influence some of her buying behavior.

Each role carries a *status* reflecting the general esteem given to it by society. People often choose products that show their status in society. For example, the role of brand manager has more status in our society than the role of daughter. As a brand manager, Anna will buy the kind of clothing that reflects her role and status.

> **active example**

Consider how one firm studied the behavioral factors associated with users of its products and then crafted its marketing messaged accordingly.

PERSONAL FACTORS

A buyer's decisions also are influenced by personal characteristics such as the buyer's *age* and *life-cycle stage, occupation, economic situation, lifestyle,* and *personality* and *self-concept.*

Age and Life-Cycle Stage

People change the goods and services they buy over their lifetimes. Tastes in food, clothes, furniture, and recreation are often age related. Buying is also shaped by the stage of the *family life cycle*—the stages through which families might pass as they mature over time. Table 5.2 lists the stages of the family life cycle. Marketers often define their target markets in terms of life-cycle stage and develop appropriate products and marketing plans for each stage. Traditional family life-cycle stages include young singles and married couples with children. Today, however, marketers are increasingly catering to a growing number of alternative, nontraditional stages such as unmarried couples, couples marrying later in life, childless couples, same-sex couples, single parents, extended parents (those with young adult children returning home), and others.

Occupation

A person's occupation affects the goods and services bought. Blue-collar workers tend to buy more rugged work clothes, whereas white-collar workers buy more business suits. Marketers try to identify the occupational groups that have an above-average interest in their products and services. A company

---

[16]Jeffery Zbar, "Hardware Builds Awareness among Women," *Advertising Age,* July 11, 1994, p. 18; and Alan Alder, "Purchasing Power Women's Buying Muscle Shops Up in Car Design, Marketing," *Chicago Tribune,* September 29, 1996, p. A21.

[17]David Leonhardt, "Hey Kids, Buy This," *Business Week,* June 30, 1997, pp. 62–67. Also see Kay M. Palan and Robert E. Wilkes, "Adolescent–Parent Interaction in Family Decisions," *Journal of Consumer Research,* September 1997, pp. 159–69; Chankon Kim and Hanjoon Lee, "Development of Family Triadic Measures for Children's Purchase Influence," *Journal of Marketing Research,* August 1997, pp. 307–21; and Judann Pollack, "Foods Targeting Children Aren't Just Child's Play," *Advertising Age,* March 1, 1999, p. 16.

TABLE 5.2	Family Life-Cycle Stages	
Young	**Middle-Aged**	**Older**
Single	Single	Older married
Married without children	Married without children	Older unmarried
Married with children	Married with children	
Divorced with children	Married without dependent children	
	Divorced without children	
	Divorced with children	
	Divorced without dependent children	

Sources: Adapted from Patrick E. Murphy and William A. Staples, "A Modernized Family Life Cycle," *Journal of Consumer Research,* June 1979, p. 16; © Journal of Consumer Research, Inc., 1979. Also see Leon G. Shiffman and Leslie Lazar Kanuk, *Consumer Behavior,* 6th ed. (Upper Saddle River, NJ: Prentice Hall, 1997), pp. 360–69.

can even specialize in making products needed by a given occupational group. Thus, computer software companies will design different products for brand managers, accountants, engineers, lawyers, and doctors.

Economic Situation

A person's economic situation will affect product choice. Anna Flores can consider buying an expensive Nikon if she has enough spendable income, savings, or borrowing power. Marketers of income-sensitive goods watch trends in personal income, savings, and interest rates. If economic indicators point to a recession, marketers can take steps to redesign, reposition, and reprice their products closely.

Lifestyle

People coming from the same subculture, social class, and occupation may have quite different lifestyles. **Lifestyle** is a person's pattern of living as expressed in his or her psychographics. It involves measuring consumers' major *AIO dimensions—activities* (work, hobbies, shopping, sports, social events), *interests* (food, fashion, family, recreation), and *opinions* (about themselves, social issues, business, products). Lifestyle captures something more than the person's social class or personality. It profiles a person's whole pattern of acting and interacting in the world.

Several research firms have developed lifestyle classifications. The most widely used is the SRI Consulting's *Values and Lifestyles (VALS)*™ typology (see Figure 5.3). VALS classifies people according to how they spend their time and money. It divides consumers into eight groups based on two major dimensions: self-orientation and resources. *Self-orientation* groups include *principle-oriented* consumers who buy based on their views of the world; *status-oriented* buyers who base their purchases on the actions and opinions of others; and *action-oriented* buyers who are driven by their desire for activity, variety, and risk taking. Consumers within each orientation are further classified into those with *abundant resources* and those with *minimal resources,* depending on whether they have high or low levels of income, education, health, self-confidence, energy, and other factors. Consumers with either very high or very low levels of resources are classified without regard to their self-orientations (actualizers, strugglers). Actualizers are people with so many resources that they can indulge in any or all self-orientations. In contrast, strugglers are people with too few resources to be included in any consumer orientation.

Iron City beer, a well-known brand in Pittsburgh, used VALS to update its image and improve sales. Iron City was losing sales—its aging core users were drinking less beer, and younger men weren't buying the brand. According to VALS research, experiencers drink the most beer, followed by strivers. To assess Iron City's image problems, the company interviewed men in these categories. It gave the men stacks of pictures of different kinds of people and asked them to identify first Iron City brand users and then people most like themselves. The men pictured Iron City drinkers as blue-collar steelworkers stopping off at the local bar. However, they saw themselves as more modern, hard working, and fun loving. They strongly rejected the outmoded, heavy-industry image of Pittsburgh. Based on this research, Iron City created ads linking its beer to the new self-image of target consumers. The

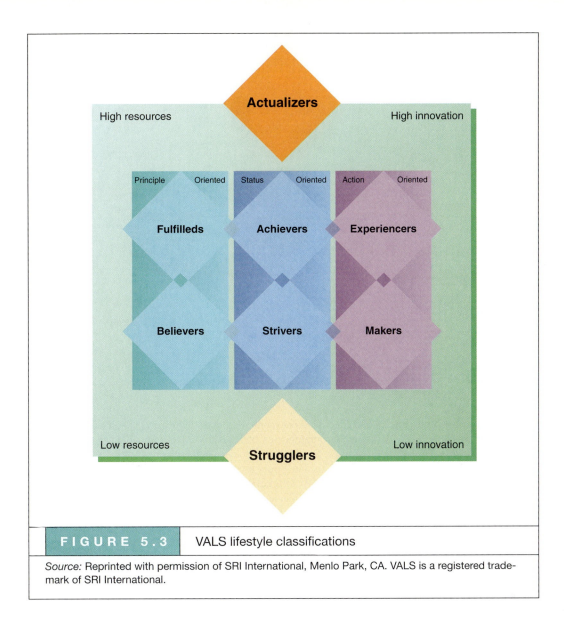

| FIGURE 5.3 | VALS lifestyle classifications |

Source: Reprinted with permission of SRI International, Menlo Park, CA. VALS is a registered trademark of SRI International.

ads mingled images of the old Pittsburgh with those of the new, dynamic city and scenes of young experiencers and strivers having fun and working hard. Within just one month of the start of the campaign, Iron City sales shot up by 26 percent.[18]

VALS can also be used to understand Internet behavior. SRIConsulting's 1999 Leading Edge survey showed that three-fourths of all Actualizers access the Internet but only one in six Believers do so. VALSalso shows differences in how VALSgroups use the Internet. For example, Actualizers and Fulfilleds are more likely to use the Internet to track investments whereas Experiencers and Strivers are more likely to visit chat sites. SRI's Web site (**future.sri.com**) allows visitors to complete the VALS questionnaire to determine their VALS type.[19] Others are developing tools for classifying consumers by "technology type."

Lifestyle classifications are by no means universal—they can vary significantly from country to country. Advertising agency McCann-Erikson London, for example, found the following British lifestyles: Avant Guardians (interested in change); Pontificators (traditionalists, very British);

[18]This and other examples of companies using VALS can be found in Rebecca Piirto, "Measuring Minds in the 1990s," *American Demographics,* December 1990, pp. 35–39; and Rebecca Piirto, "VALS the Second Time," *American Demographics,* July 1991, p. 6. For good discussions of other lifestyle topics, see Basil G. Englis and Michael Solomon, "To Be or Not to Be: Lifestyle Imagery, Reference Groups, and the Clustering of America," *Journal of Advertising,* March 1995, p. 13; and Tom Miller, "Global Segments from 'Strivers' to 'Creatives,'" *Marketing News,* July 20, 1998, p. 11.

[19]Piirto, "VALS the Second Time," p. 6; and Rebecca Piirto, "The Frontier of Psychographics," *American Demographics,* July 1996, pp. 38–43.

Lifestyles: Jeep targets people who want to "leave the civilized world behind."

Jeep
THERE'S ONLY ONE

Jeep 4x4s let people achieve the kind of happiness that can only come from leaving the civilized world far behind.
Contact us at 1-800-925-JEEP or www.jeep.com.

Jeep is a registered trademark of DaimlerChrysler.

Chameleons (follow the crowd); and Sleepwalkers (contented underachievers). The D'Arcy, Masius, Benton, & Bowles agency identified five categories of Russian consumers: Kuptsi (merchants), Cossacks, Students, Business Executives, and Russian Souls. Cossacks are characterized as ambitious, independent, and status seeking; Russian Souls as passive, fearful of choices, and hopeful. Thus, a typical Cossack might drive a BMW, smoke Dunhill cigarettes, and drink Remy Martin liquor, whereas a Russian Soul would drive a Lada, smoke Marlboros, and drink Smirnoff vodka.[20]

When used carefully, the lifestyle concept can help the marketer understand changing consumer values and how they affect buying behavior. Anna Flores, for example, can choose to live the role of a capable homemaker, a career woman, or a free spirit—or all three. She plays several roles, and the way she blends them expresses her lifestyle. If she becomes a professional photographer, this would change her lifestyle, in turn changing what and how she buys.

Personality and Self-Concept

Each person's distinct personality influences his or her buying behavior. **Personality** refers to the unique psychological characteristics that lead to relatively consistent and lasting responses to one's own environment. Personality is usually described in terms of traits such as self-confidence, dominance, sociability, autonomy, defensiveness, adaptability, and aggressiveness. Personality can be useful in analyzing consumer behavior for certain product or brand choices. For example, coffee marketers have discovered that heavy coffee drinkers tend to be high on sociability. Thus, to attract customers, Starbucks and other coffeehouses create environments in which people can relax and socialize over a cup of steaming coffee.

Many marketers use a concept related to personality—a person's *self-concept* (also called *self-image*). The basic self-concept premise is that people's possessions contribute to and reflect their identities; that is, "we are what we have." Thus, in order to understand consumer behavior, the marketer must first understand the relationship between consumer self-concept and possessions. For example, the founder and chief executive of Barnes & Noble, the nation's leading bookseller, notes that people buy books to support their self-images:

> People have the mistaken notion that the thing you do with books is read them. Wrong. . . . People buy books for what the purchase says about them—their taste, their cultivation, their trendiness. Their aim . . . is to connect themselves, or those to whom they give the books as gifts, with all the other refined owners of Edgar Allen Poe collections or sensitive owners of

---

[20]Stuart Elliot, "Sampling Tastes of a Changing Russia," *New York Times,* April 1, 1992, pp. D1, D19; and Miller, "Global Segments from 'Strivers' to 'Creatives,'" p. 11. For an excellent discussion of cross-cultural lifestyle systems, see Philip Kotler, Gary Armstrong, John Saunders, and Veronica Wong, *Principles of Marketing,* 2nd European ed. (London: Prentice Hall Europe, 1999), pp. 240–42.

Virginia Woolf collections. . . . [The result is that] you can sell books as consumer products, with seductive displays, flashy posters, an emphasis on the glamour of the book, and the fashionableness of the bestseller and the trendy author.[21]

Anna Flores may see herself as outgoing, creative, and active. Therefore, she will favor a camera that projects the same qualities. If the Nikon is promoted as a camera for outgoing, creative, and active people, then its brand image will match her self-image.

> ## active example

Learn more about this valuable marketing tool.

PSYCHOLOGICAL FACTORS

A person's buying choices are further influenced by four major psychological factors: *motivation, perception, learning,* and *beliefs* and *attitudes.*

Motivation

We know that Anna Flores became interested in buying a camera. Why? What is she *really* seeking? What *needs* is she trying to satisfy?

A person has many needs at any given time. Some are *biological,* arising from states of tension such as hunger, thirst, or discomfort. Others are *psychological,* arising from the need for recognition, esteem, or belonging. Most of these needs will not be strong enough to motivate the person to act at a given point in time. A need becomes a *motive* when it is aroused to a sufficient level of intensity. A **motive** (or *drive*) is a need that is sufficiently pressing to direct the person to seek satisfaction. Psychologists have developed theories of human motivation. Two of the most popular—the theories of Sigmund Freud and Abraham Maslow—have quite different meanings for consumer analysis and marketing.

Freud's Theory of Motivation. Freud assumed that people are largely unconscious about the real psychological forces shaping their behavior. He saw the person as growing up and repressing many urges. These urges are never eliminated or under perfect control; they emerge in dreams, in slips of the tongue, in neurotic and obsessive behavior, or ultimately in psychoses.

Thus, Freud suggests that a person does not fully understand his or her motivation. If Anna Flores wants to purchase an expensive camera, she may describe her motive as wanting a hobby or career. At a deeper level, she may be purchasing the camera to impress others with her creative talent. At a still deeper level, she may be buying the camera to feel young and independent again.

Motivation researchers collect in-depth information from small samples of consumers to uncover the deeper motives for their product choices. They use nondirective depth interviews and various "projective techniques" to throw the ego off guard—techniques such as word association, sentence completion, picture interpretation, and role playing. Motivation researchers have reached some interesting and sometimes odd conclusions about what may be in the buyer's mind regarding certain purchases. For example, one classic study concluded that consumers resist prunes because they are wrinkled looking and remind people of sickness and old age. Despite its sometimes unusual conclusions, motivation research remains a useful tool for marketers seeking a deeper understanding of consumer behavior.

Maslow's Theory of Motivation. Abraham Maslow sought to explain why people are driven by particular needs at particular times. Why does one person spend much time and energy on personal safety and another on gaining the esteem of others? Maslow's answer is that human needs are arranged in a hierarchy, from the most pressing to the least pressing. Maslow's hierarchy of needs is shown in Figure 5.4. In order of importance, they are *physiological* needs, *safety* needs, *social* needs, *esteem* needs, and *self-actualization* needs. A person tries to satisfy the most important need first. When that need is satisfied, it will stop being a motivator and the person will then try to satisfy the next most important need. For example, starving people (physiological need) will not take an interest

---

[21]Myron Magnet, "Let's Go for Growth," *Fortune,* March 7, 1994, p. 70. Also see Timothy R. Graeff, "Consumption Situations and the Effects of Brand Image on Consumers' Brand Evaluations," *Psychology and Marketing,* January 1997, pp. 49–70; Dun Gifford Jr., "Moving Beyond Loyalty," *Harvard Business Review,* March–April 1997, pp. 9–10; and Jennifer L. Aaker, "The Malleable Self: The Role of Self-Expression in Persuasion," *Journal of Marketing Research,* February 1999, pp. 45–57.

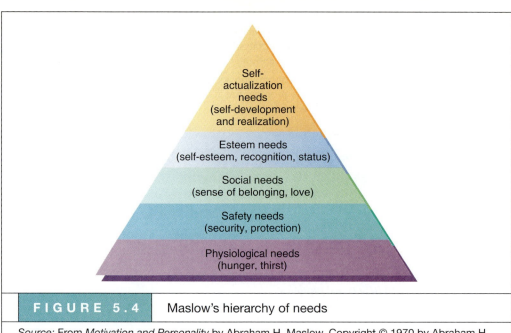

| FIGURE 5.4 | Maslow's hierarchy of needs |

Source: From *Motivation and Personality* by Abraham H. Maslow. Copyright © 1970 by Abraham H. Maslow. Copyright 1954, 1987 by Harper & Row Publishers, Inc. Reprinted by permission of Addison-Wesley Educational Publishers Inc. Also see Barbara Marx Hubbard, "Seeking Our Future Potentials," *The Futurist,* May 1998, pp. 29–32.

in the latest happenings in the art world (self-actualization needs), nor in how they are seen or esteemed by others (social or esteem needs), nor even in whether they are breathing clean air (safety needs). But as each important need is satisfied, the next most important need will come into play.

What light does Maslow's theory throw on Anna Flores's interest in buying a camera? We can guess that Anna has satisfied her physiological, safety, and social needs; they do not motivate her interest in cameras. Her camera interest might come from a strong need for more esteem. Or it might come from a need for self-actualization—she might want to be a creative person and express herself through photography.[22]

Perception

A motivated person is ready to act. How the person acts is influenced by his or her own perception of the situation. All of us learn by the flow of information through our five senses: sight, hearing, smell, touch, and taste. However, each of us receives, organizes, and interprets this sensory information in an individual way. **Perception** is the process by which people select, organize, and interpret information to form a meaningful picture of the world.

People can form different perceptions of the same stimulus because of three perceptual processes: selective attention, selective distortion, and selective retention. People are exposed to a great amount of stimuli every day. For example, the average person may be exposed to more than 1,500 ads in a single day. It is impossible for a person to pay attention to all these stimuli. *Selective attention*—the tendency for people to screen out most of the information to which they are exposed—means that marketers have to work especially hard to attract the consumer's attention.

Even noted stimuli do not always come across in the intended way. Each person fits incoming information into an existing mind-set. *Selective distortion* describes the tendency of people to interpret information in a way that will support what they already believe. Anna Flores may hear a salesperson mention some good and bad points about a competing camera brand. Because she already has a strong leaning toward Nikon, she is likely to distort those points in order to conclude that Nikon is the better camera. Selective distortion means that marketers must try to understand the mind-sets of consumers and how these will affect interpretations of advertising and sales information.

People also will forget much that they learn. They tend to retain information that supports their attitudes and beliefs. Because of *selective retention,* Anna is likely to remember good points made about the Nikon and to forget good points made about competing cameras. Because of selective exposure, distortion, and retention, marketers have to work hard to get their messages through. This fact explains why marketers use so much drama and repetition in sending messages to their market.

[22]See Barbara Marx Hubbard, "Seeking Our Future Potentials," *The Futurist,* May 1998, pp. 29–32.

Interestingly, although most marketers worry about whether their offers will be perceived at all, some consumers worry that they will be affected by marketing messages without even knowing it—through *subliminal advertising*. In 1957, a researcher announced that he had flashed the phrases "Eat popcorn" and "Drink Coca-Cola" on a screen in a New Jersey movie theater every five seconds for 1/300th of a second. He reported that although viewers did not consciously recognize these messages, they absorbed them subconsciously and bought 58 percent more popcorn and 18 percent more Coke. Suddenly advertisers and consumer-protection groups became intensely interested in subliminal perception. People voiced fears of being brainwashed, and California and Canada declared the practice illegal. Although the researcher later admitted to making up the data, the issue has not died. Some consumers still fear that they are being manipulated by subliminal messages.

> ## active exercise

Take a moment to consider the debate over subliminal advertising.

> ## active poll

Give your opinion on a question concerning consumer behavior.

Numerous studies by psychologists and consumer researchers have found no link between subliminal messages and consumer behavior. It appears that subliminal advertising simply doesn't have the power attributed to it by its critics. Most advertisers scoff at the notion of an industry conspiracy to manipulate consumers through "invisible" messages. As one advertising agency executive put it, "We have enough trouble persuading consumers using a series of up-front 30-second ads—how could we do it in 1/300th of a second?"

Learning

When people act, they learn. **Learning** describes changes in an individual's behavior arising from experience. Learning theorists say that most human behavior is learned. Learning occurs through the interplay of *drives, stimuli, cues, responses,* and *reinforcement.*

We saw that Anna Flores has a drive for self-actualization. A *drive* is a strong internal stimulus that calls for action. Her drive becomes a motive when it is directed toward a particular *stimulus object,* in this case a camera. Anna's response to the idea of buying a camera is conditioned by the surrounding cues. *Cues* are minor stimuli that determine when, where, and how the person responds. Seeing cameras in a shop window, hearing of a special sale price, and receiving her husband's support are all cues that can influence Anna's *response* to her interest in buying a camera.

Suppose Anna buys the Nikon. If the experience is rewarding, she will probably use the camera more and more. Her response to cameras will be *reinforced.* Then the next time she shops for a camera, binoculars, or some similar product, the probability is greater that she will buy a Nikon product.

The practical significance of learning theory for marketers is that they can build up demand for a product by associating it with strong drives, using motivating cues, and providing positive reinforcement.

Beliefs and Attitudes

Through doing and learning, people acquire beliefs and attitudes. These, in turn, influence their buying behavior. A **belief** is a descriptive thought that a person has about something. Anna Flores may believe that a Nikon camera takes great pictures, stands up well under hard use, and costs $450. These beliefs may be based on real knowledge, opinion, or faith, and may or may not carry an emotional charge. For example, Anna Flores's belief that a Nikon camera is heavy may or may not matter to her decision.

Marketers are interested in the beliefs that people formulate about specific products and services, because these beliefs make up product and brand images that affect buying behavior. If some of the beliefs are wrong and prevent purchase, the marketer will want to launch a campaign to correct them.

People have attitudes regarding religion, politics, clothes, music, food, and almost everything else. **Attitude** describes a person's relatively consistent evaluations, feelings, and tendencies toward an

Attitudes are difficult to change, but the National Fluid Milk Processors' wildly popular milk mustache campaign succeeded in changing attitudes toward milk.

object or idea. Attitudes put people into a frame of mind of liking or disliking things, of moving toward or away from them. Thus, Anna Flores may hold attitudes such as "Buy the best," "The Japanese make the best products in the world," and "Creativity and self-expression are among the most important things in life." If so, the Nikon camera would fit well into Anna's existing attitudes.

Attitudes are difficult to change. A person's attitudes fit into a pattern, and to change one attitude may require difficult adjustments in many others. Thus, a company should usually try to fit its products into existing attitudes rather than attempt to change attitudes. Of course, there are exceptions in which the great cost of trying to change attitudes may pay off handsomely:

By 1994, milk consumption had been in decline for 25 years. The general perception was that milk was unhealthy, outdated, just for kids, or good only with cookies and cake. Beginning in 1994, the National Fluid Milk Processors Education Program (MilkPEP) began a $55 million print ad campaign featuring milk be-mustached celebrities like Cindy Crawford, Danny DeVito, Patrick Ewing, and Ivana Trump with the tag line "Milk: Where's your mustache?" The campaign has not only been wildly popular, it has been successful as well—not only did it stop the decline, milk consumption actually increased. By 1999, the campaign was still running and MilkPEP had upped spending on it to $110 million. Although initially the target market was women in their twenties, the campaign has been expanded to other target markets and has gained cult status with teens, much to their parents' delight. Teens collect the print ads featuring celebrities ranging from music stars Hanson and Leann Rimes, supermodel Tyra Banks, and Garfield to sports idols such as Mark McGuire, Jeff Gordon, Pete Sampras, Gabriela Sabatini, and Dennis Rodman. (Says Dennis, "Three glasses a day give the average man all the calcium he needs. Maybe I should drink six.") "Milking" the success of the print ads, milk producers set up Club Milk on a Web site (www.whymilk.com) where they limit membership only to those who pledge they will drink three glasses of the white fluid a day.[23]

[23]Jill Venter, "Milk Mustache Campaign Is a Hit with Teens," *St. Louis Post-Dispatch,* April 1, 1998, p. E1; Dave Fusaro, "The Milk Mustache," *Dairy Foods,* April 1997, p. 75; Judann Pollack, "Milk: Kurt Graetzer," *Advertising Age,* June 30, 1997, p. S1; and the Milk: Where's Your Mustache Web site (www.whymilk.com), February 2000.

We can now appreciate the many forces acting on consumer behavior. The consumer's choice results from the complex interplay of cultural, social, personal, and psychological factors.

> **active concept check**

Now let's take a moment to test your knowledge of what you've just read.

> **Types of Buying Decision Behavior**

Buying behavior differs greatly for a tube of toothpaste, a tennis racket, an expensive camera, and a new car. More complex decisions usually involve more buying participants and more buyer deliberation. Figure 5.5 shows types of consumer buying behavior based on the degree of buyer involvement and the degree of differences among brands.[24]

COMPLEX BUYING BEHAVIOR

Consumers undertake **complex buying behavior** when they are highly involved in a purchase and perceive significant differences among brands. Consumers may be highly involved when the product is expensive, risky, purchased infrequently, and highly self-expressive. Typically, the consumer has much to learn about the product category. For example, a personal computer buyer may not know what attributes to consider. Many product features carry no real meaning: a "Pentium Pro chip," "super VGA resolution," or "megs of RAM."

This buyer will pass through a learning process, first developing beliefs about the product, then attitudes, and then making a thoughtful purchase choice. Marketers of high-involvement products must understand the information-gathering and evaluation behavior of high-involvement consumers. They need to help buyers learn about product-class attributes and their relative importance, and about what the company's brand offers on the important attributes. Marketers need to differentiate their brand's features, perhaps by describing the brand's benefits using print media with long copy. They must motivate store salespeople and the buyer's acquaintances to influence the final brand choice.

DISSONANCE-REDUCING BUYING BEHAVIOR

Dissonance-reducing buying behavior occurs when consumers are highly involved with an expensive, infrequent, or risky purchase, but see little difference among brands. For example, consumers buy-

	High involvement	Low involvement
Significant differences between brands	Complex buying behavior	Variety-seeking buying behavior
Few differences between brands	Dissonance-reducing buying behavior	Habitual buying behavior

FIGURE 5.5 Four types of buying behavior

Source: Adapted from Henry Assael, *Consumer Behavior and Marketing Action* (Boston: Kent Publishing Company, 1987), p. 87. Copyright © 1987 by Wadsworth, Inc. Printed by permission of Kent Publishing Company, a division of Wadsworth, Inc.

[24] See Henry Assael, *Consumer Behavior and Marketing Action* (Boston: Kent Publishing, 1987), chap. 4. An earlier classification of three types of consumer buying behavior—routine response behavior, limited problem solving, and extensive problem solving—can be found in John A. Howard and Jagdish Sheth, *The Theory of Consumer Behavior* (New York: John Wiley, 1969), pp. 27–28. Also see John A. Howard, *Consumer Behavior in Marketing Strategy* (Upper Saddle River, NJ: Prentice Hall, 1989).

ing carpeting may face a high-involvement decision because carpeting is expensive and self-expressive. Yet buyers may consider most carpet brands in a given price range to be the same. In this case, because perceived brand differences are not large, buyers may shop around to learn what is available, but buy relatively quickly. They may respond primarily to a good price or to purchase convenience.

After the purchase, consumers might experience *postpurchase dissonance* (after-sale discomfort) when they notice certain disadvantages of the purchased carpet brand or hear favorable things about brands not purchased. To counter such dissonance, the marketer's after-sale communications should provide evidence and support to help consumers feel good about their brand choices.

HABITUAL BUYING BEHAVIOR

Habitual buying behavior occurs under conditions of low consumer involvement and little significant brand difference. For example, take salt. Consumers have little involvement in this product category—they simply go to the store and reach for a brand. If they keep reaching for the same brand, it is out of habit rather than strong brand loyalty. Consumers appear to have low involvement with most low-cost, frequently purchased products.

In such cases, consumer behavior does not pass through the usual belief–attitude–behavior sequence. Consumers do not search extensively for information about the brands, evaluate brand characteristics, and make weighty decisions about which brands to buy. Instead, they passively receive information as they watch television or read magazines. Ad repetition creates *brand familiarity* rather than *brand conviction*. Consumers do not form strong attitudes toward a brand; they select the brand because it is familiar. Because they are not highly involved with the product, consumers may not evaluate the choice even after purchase. Thus, the buying process involves brand beliefs formed by passive learning, followed by purchase behavior, which may or may not be followed by evaluation.

Because buyers are not highly committed to any brands, marketers of low-involvement products with few brand differences often use price and sales promotions to stimulate product trial. In advertising for a low-involvement product, ad copy should stress only a few key points. Visual symbols and imagery are important because they can be remembered easily and associated with the brand. Ad campaigns should include high repetition of short-duration messages. Television is usually more effective than print media because it is a low-involvement medium suitable for passive learning. Advertising planning should be based on classical conditioning theory, in which buyers learn to identify a certain product by a symbol repeatedly attached to it.

Marketers can try to convert low-involvement products into higher-involvement ones by linking them to some involving issue. Procter & Gamble does this when it links Crest toothpaste to avoiding cavities. Or the product can be linked to some involving personal situation. Nestlé did this in its series of ads for Taster's Choice coffee, each consisting of a new soap-opera-like episode featuring the evolving romantic relationship between two neighbors. At best, these strategies can raise consumer involvement from a low to a moderate level. However, they are not likely to propel the consumer into highly involved buying behavior.

VARIETY-SEEKING BUYING BEHAVIOR

Consumers undertake **variety-seeking buying behavior** in situations characterized by low consumer involvement but significant perceived brand differences. In such cases, consumers often do a lot of brand switching. For example, when buying cookies, a consumer may hold some beliefs, choose a cookie brand without much evaluation, then evaluate that brand during consumption. But the next time, the consumer might pick another brand out of boredom or simply to try something different. Brand switching occurs for the sake of variety rather than because of dissatisfaction.

In such product categories, the marketing strategy may differ for the market leader and minor brands. The market leader will try to encourage habitual buying behavior by dominating shelf space, keeping shelves fully stocked, and running frequent reminder advertising. Challenger firms will encourage variety seeking by offering lower prices, special deals, coupons, free samples, and advertising that presents reasons for trying something new.

active concept check <

Now let's take a moment to test your knowledge of what you've just read.

DOES YOUR KID HAVE HUNDRED DOLLAR FEET AND A TEN DOLLAR HEAD?

Ah, kids today. Always going around with expensive sneakers and cheap bike helmets like they do. Hey, wait a second. That's your fault. Or is it?

Maybe it's more a statement of society. Sneakers are status. Helmets, well they're just some dumb safety thing moms—and in some cases, lawmakers—make kids wear. Or maybe it's simply a result of the little bugger wearing you down for the fancy shoes. Either way, let's get this straight. You don't want your kid wearing a cheesy helmet. You want your kid wearing a Bell helmet.

Because nobody makes a better helmet than us. It's been that way for 40 years or so. We pioneered the field of helmet safety—first with race car helmets, now with bike helmets, too. We developed our own safety tests, which we conducted in our own lab. And still do. Understandably, no other company has sold nearly as many helmets. And no other company is chosen by more race car drivers and pro cyclists. Many of whom have had the misfortune of proving firsthand how good our helmets are. With any luck, something your kid will never do.

If you spent more money on your kids' bike helmets than you did on their sneakers, don't read another word of this ad. We thought so.

COURAGE FOR YOUR HEAD. BELL HELMETS

Need recognition can be triggered by advertising. This ad asks an arresting question that alerts parents to the need for a high-quality bike helmet.

> The Buyer Decision Process

Now that we have looked at the influences that affect buyers, we are ready to look at how consumers make buying decisions. Figure 5.6 shows that the buyer decision process consists of five stages: *need recognition, information search, evaluation of alternatives, purchase decision,* and *postpurchase behavior.* Clearly, the buying process starts long before actual purchase and continues long after. Marketers need to focus on the entire buying process rather than on just the purchase decision.

The figure implies that consumers pass through all five stages with every purchase. But in more routine purchases, consumers often skip or reverse some of these stages. A woman buying her regular brand of toothpaste would recognize the need and go right to the purchase decision, skipping information search and evaluation. However, we use the model in Figure 5.6 because it shows all the considerations that arise when a consumer faces a new and complex purchase situation.

To illustrate this model, we will again follow Anna Flores and try to understand how she became interested in buying an expensive camera, and the stages she went through to make the final choice.

NEED RECOGNITION

The buying process starts with **need recognition**—the buyer recognizes a problem or need. The buyer senses a difference between his or her *actual* state and some *desired* state. The need can be triggered by *internal stimuli* when one of the person's normal needs—hunger, thirst, sex—rises to a level high enough to become a drive. A need can also be triggered by *external stimuli*. Anna Flores might have felt the need for a new hobby when her busy season at work slowed down, and she thought of cameras after talking to a friend about photography or seeing a camera ad. At this stage, the marketer should research consumers to find out what kinds of needs or problems arise, what brought them about, and how they led the consumer to this particular product.

By gathering such information, the marketer can identify the factors that most often trigger interest in the product and can develop marketing programs that involve these factors.

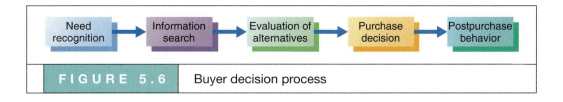

| Need recognition | → | Information search | → | Evaluation of alternatives | → | Purchase decision | → | Postpurchase behavior |

FIGURE 5.6   Buyer decision process

INFORMATION SEARCH

An aroused consumer may or may not search for more information. If the consumer's drive is strong and a satisfying product is near at hand, the consumer is likely to buy it then. If not, the consumer may store the need in memory or undertake an **information search** related to the need.

At one level, the consumer may simply enter *heightened attention*. Here Anna Flores becomes more receptive to information about cameras. She pays attention to camera ads, cameras used by friends, and camera conversations. Or Anna may go into *active information search,* in which she looks for reading material, phones friends, and gathers information in other ways. The amount of searching she does will depend on the strength of her drive, the amount of information she starts with, the ease of obtaining more information, the value she places on additional information, and the satisfaction she gets from searching.

The consumer can obtain information from any of several sources. These include *personal sources* (family, friends, neighbors, acquaintances), *commercial sources* (advertising, salespeople, dealers, packaging, displays, Web sites), *public sources* (mass media, consumer-rating organizations), and *experiential sources* (handling, examining, using the product). The relative influence of these information sources varies with the product and the buyer. Generally, the consumer receives the most information about a product from commercial sources—those controlled by the marketer. The most effective sources, however, tend to be personal. Commercial sources normally *inform* the buyer, but personal sources *legitimize* or *evaluate* products for the buyer.

People often ask others—friends, relatives, acquaintances, professionals—for recommendations concerning a product or service. Thus, companies have a strong interest in building such *word-of-mouth sources.* These sources have two chief advantages. First, they are convincing: Word of mouth is the only promotion method that is *of* consumers, *by* consumers, and *for* consumers. Having loyal, satisfied customers that brag about doing business with you is the dream of every business owner. Not only are satisfied customers repeat buyers, but they are also walking, talking billboards for your business. Second, the costs are low. Keeping in touch with satisfied customers and turning them into word-of-mouth advocates costs the business relatively little.[25]

As more information is obtained, the consumer's awareness and knowledge of the available brands and features increases. In her information search, Anna Flores learned about the many camera brands available. The information also helped her drop certain brands from consideration. A company must design its marketing mix to make prospects aware of and knowledgeable about its brand. It should carefully identify consumers' sources of information and the importance of each source. Consumers should be asked how they first heard about the brand, what information they received, and what importance they placed on different information sources.

EVALUATION OF ALTERNATIVES

We have seen how the consumer uses information to arrive at a set of final brand choices. How does the consumer choose among the alternative brands? The marketer needs to know about **alternative evaluation**—that is, how the consumer processes information to arrive at brand choices. Unfortunately, consumers do not use a simple and single evaluation process in all buying situations. Instead, several evaluation processes are at work.

The consumer arrives at attitudes toward different brands through some evaluation procedure. How consumers go about evaluating purchase alternatives depends on the individual consumer and the specific buying situation. In some cases, consumers use careful calculations and logical thinking. At other times, the same consumers do little or no evaluating; instead they buy on impulse and rely on intuition. Sometimes consumers make buying decisions on their own; sometimes they turn to friends, consumer guides, or salespeople for buying advice.

Suppose Anna Flores has narrowed her choices to four cameras. Also suppose that she is primarily interested in four attributes—picture quality, ease of use, camera size, and price. Anna has formed beliefs about how each brand rates on each attribute. Clearly, if one camera rated best on all the attributes, we could predict that Anna would choose it. However, the brands vary in appeal. Anna might base her buying decision on only one attribute, and her choice would be easy to predict. If she wants picture quality above everything, she will buy the camera that she thinks has the best picture quality. But most buyers consider several attributes, each with different importance. If we knew the importance weights that Anna assigns to each of the four attributes, we could predict her camera choice more reliably.

Marketers should study buyers to find out how they actually evaluate brand alternatives. If they know what evaluative processes go on, marketers can take steps to influence the buyer's decision.

---

[25]For more on word-of-mouth sources, see Philip Kotler, *Marketing Management: Analysis, Planning, Implementation, and Control,* 10th ed. (Upper Saddle River, NJ: Prentice Hall, 2000), p. 560.

A ROCKET SCIENTIST IN FLIP-FLOPS.

The technology of a serious camera. The spontaneity of a point-and-shoot. Now you don't have to choose between the two. The Nikon Pronea™ S is the best of both worlds. Serious camera technology. Compact size. Three picture formats. Interchangeable zoom lenses. At 16 ounces, it's one of the biggest things to happen to picture taking.

Nikon
WE TAKE THE WORLD'S GREATEST PICTURES® YOURS.

See the affordable Pronea S and Nikkor lenses at authorized dealers displaying this symbol. © 1998 Nikon Inc. www.nikonusa.com or call 1-800-NIKON-35.

Evaluating alternatives: In some cases, consumers use careful calculations; in others they do little or no evaluating. In the small print, this Nikon ad emphasizes its serious camera technology, compact size, three picture-taking formats, and interchangeable zoom lenses—"The technology of a serious camera. The spontaneity of a point-and-shoot."

PURCHASE DECISION

In the evaluation stage, the consumer ranks brands and forms purchase intentions. Generally, the consumer's **purchase decision** will be to buy the most preferred brand, but two factors can come between the purchase *intention* and the purchase *decision.* The first factor is the *attitudes of others.* If Anna Flores's husband feels strongly that Anna should buy the lowest priced camera, then the chances of Anna's buying a more expensive camera will be reduced.

The second factor is *unexpected situational factors.* The consumer may form a purchase intention based on factors such as expected income, expected price, and expected product benefits. However, unexpected events may change the purchase intention. Anna Flores may lose her job, some other purchase may become more urgent, or a friend may report being disappointed in her preferred camera. Or a close competitor may drop its price. Thus, preferences and even purchase intentions do not always result in actual purchase choice.

> video example

Take a moment to watch a group of managers discuss consumer behavior.

POSTPURCHASE BEHAVIOR

The marketer's job does not end when the product is bought. After purchasing the product, the consumer will be satisfied or dissatisfied and will engage in **postpurchase behavior** of interest to the marketer. What determines whether the buyer is satisfied or dissatisfied with a purchase? The answer lies in the relationship between the *consumer's expectations* and the product's *perceived performance.* If the product falls short of expectations, the consumer is disappointed; if it meets expectations, the consumer is satisfied; if it exceeds expectations, the consumer is delighted.

The larger the gap between expectations and performance, the greater the consumer's dissatisfaction. This suggests that sellers should make product claims that faithfully represent the product's performance so that buyers are satisfied. Some sellers might even understate performance levels to boost consumer satisfaction with the product. For example, Boeing's salespeople tend to be conservative when they estimate the potential benefits of their aircraft. They almost always underestimate fuel efficiency—they promise a 5 percent savings that turns out to be 8 percent. Customers are delighted with better-than-expected performance; they buy again and tell other potential customers that Boeing lives up to its promises.

Almost all major purchases result in **cognitive dissonance,** or discomfort caused by postpurchase conflict. After the purchase, consumers are satisfied with the benefits of the chosen brand and are glad to avoid the drawbacks of the brands not bought. However, every purchase involves compromise. Consumers feel uneasy about acquiring the drawbacks of the chosen brand and about losing the benefits of the brands not purchased. Thus, consumers feel at least some postpurchase dissonance for every purchase.[26]

Why is it so important to satisfy the customer? Such satisfaction is important because a company's sales come from two basic groups—*new customers* and *retained customers.* It usually costs more to attract new customers than to retain current ones, and the best way to retain current customers is to keep them satisfied. Customer satisfaction is a key to making lasting connections with consumers—to keeping and growing consumers and reaping their customer lifetime value. Satisfied customers buy a product again, talk favorably to others about the product, pay less attention to competing brands and advertising, and buy other products from the company. Many marketers go beyond merely *meeting* the expectations of customers—they aim to *delight* the customer. A delighted customer is even more likely to purchase again and to talk favorably about the product and company.

A dissatisfied consumer responds differently. Whereas, on average, a satisfied customer tells 3 people about a good product experience, a dissatisfied customer gripes to 11 people. In fact, one study showed that 13 percent of the people who had a problem with an organization complained about the company to more than 20 people.[27] Clearly, bad word of mouth travels farther and faster than good word of mouth and can quickly damage consumer attitudes about a company and its products.

Therefore, a company would be wise to measure customer satisfaction regularly. It cannot simply rely on dissatisfied customers to volunteer their complaints when they are dissatisfied. Some 96 percent of unhappy customers never tell the company about their problem. Companies should set up systems that *encourage* customers to complain. In this way, the company can learn how well it is doing and how it can improve. The 3M Company claims that over two-thirds of its new-product ideas come from listening to customer complaints. But listening is not enough—the company also must respond constructively to the complaints it receives.

active exercise <

Take a moment to think about how technology could affect the consumer buying process.

active concept check <

Now let's take a moment to test your knowledge of what you've just read.

[26]See Leon Festinger, *A Theory of Cognitive Dissonance* (Stanford, CA: Stanford University Press, 1957); Schiffman and Kanuk, *Consumer Behavior,* pp. 271–72; Jeff Stone, "A Radical New Look at Cognitive Dissonance," *The American Journal of Psychology,* Summer 1998, pp. 319–26; and Thomas R. Schultz, Elene Leveille, and Mark R. Lepper, "Free Choice and Cognitive Dissonance Revisited: Choosing 'Lesser Evils' Versus 'Greater Goods,'" *Personality and Social Psychology Bulletin,* January 1999, pp. 40–48.

[27]See Frank Rose, "Now Quality Means Service Too," *Fortune,* April 22, 1991, pp. 97–108; Chip Walker, "Word of Mouth," *American Demographics,* July 1995, p. 40; Thomas O. Jones and W. Earl Sasser Jr., "Why Satisfied Customers Defect," *Harvard Business Review,* November–December 1995, pp. 88–99; and Roger Sant, "Did He Jump or Was He Pushed?" *Marketing News,* May 12, 1997, pp. 2, 21.

We have looked at the stages buyers go through in trying to satisfy a need. Buyers may pass quickly or slowly through these stages, and some of the stages may even be reversed. Much depends on the nature of the buyer, the product, and the buying situation.

We now look at how buyers approach the purchase of new products. A **new product** is a good, service, or idea that is perceived by some potential customers as new. It may have been around for a while, but our interest is in how consumers learn about products for the first time and make decisions on whether to adopt them. We define the **adoption process** as "the mental process through which an individual passes from first learning about an innovation to final adoption,"[28] and *adoption* as the decision by an individual to become a regular user of the product.

STAGES IN THE ADOPTION PROCESS

Consumers go through five stages in the process of adopting a new product:

- *Awareness:* The consumer becomes aware of the new product, but lacks information about it.
- *Interest:* The consumer seeks information about the new product.
- *Evaluation:* The consumer considers whether trying the new product makes sense.
- *Trial:* The consumer tries the new product on a small scale to improve his or her estimate of its value.
- *Adoption:* The consumer decides to make full and regular use of the new product.

This model suggests that the new-product marketer should think about how to help consumers move through these stages. A manufacturer of large-screen televisions may discover that many consumers in the interest stage do not move to the trial stage because of uncertainty and the large investment. If these same consumers were willing to use a large-screen television on a trial basis for a small fee, the manufacturer should consider offering a trial-use plan with an option to buy.

> ## active example

Consider one case of how marketers address the information needs of buyers of new products.

INDIVIDUAL DIFFERENCES IN INNOVATIVENESS

People differ greatly in their readiness to try new products. In each product area, there are "consumption pioneers" and early adopters. Other individuals adopt new products much later. People can be classified into the adopter categories shown in Figure 5.7. After a slow start, an increasing number of people adopt the new product. The number of adopters reaches a peak and then drops off as fewer nonadopters remain. Innovators are defined as the first 2.5 percent of the buyers to adopt a new idea (those beyond two standard deviations from mean adoption time); the early adopters are the next 13.5 percent (between one and two standard deviations); and so forth.

The five adopter groups have differing values. *Innovators* are venturesome—they try new ideas at some risk. *Early adopters* are guided by respect—they are opinion leaders in their communities and adopt new ideas early but carefully. The *early majority* are deliberate—although they rarely are leaders, they adopt new ideas before the average person. The *late majority* are skeptical—they adopt an innovation only after a majority of people have tried it. Finally, *laggards* are tradition bound—they are suspicious of changes and adopt the innovation only when it has become something of a tradition itself.

This adopter classification suggests that an innovating firm should research the characteristics of innovators and early adopters and should direct marketing efforts toward them. In general, innovators tend to be relatively younger, better educated, and higher in income than later adopters and nonadopters. They are more receptive to unfamiliar things, rely more on their own values and judgment,

[28]The following discussion draws heavily from Everett M. Rogers, *Diffusion of Innovations,* 3rd ed. (New York: Free Press, 1983). Also see Hubert Gatignon and Thomas S. Robertson, "A Propositional Inventory for New Diffusion Research," *Journal of Consumer Research,* March 1985, pp. 849–67; and Rogers, *Diffusion of Innovations,* 4th ed. (New York: Free Press, 1995).

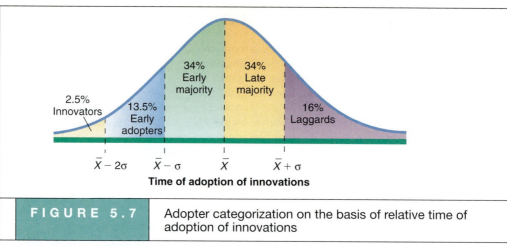

| FIGURE 5.7 | Adopter categorization on the basis of relative time of adoption of innovations |

Source: Everett M. Rogers, *Diffusion of Innovations,* 4th ed. (New York: Free Press, 1995). Copyright© 1995 by Everett M. Rogers. Copyright© 1962, 1971, 1983 by The Free Press. Reprinted with the permission of The Free Press, a Division of Simon & Schuster.

and are more willing to take risks. They are less brand loyal and more likely to take advantage of special promotions such as discounts, coupons, and samples.

INFLUENCE OF PRODUCT CHARACTERISTICS ON RATE OF ADOPTION

The characteristics of the new product affect its rate of adoption. Some products catch on almost overnight (Beanie Babies), whereas others take a long time to gain acceptance (high-density television, or HDTV). Five characteristics are especially important in influencing an innovation's rate of adoption. For example, consider the characteristics of HDTV in relation to the rate of adoption:

- *Relative advantage:* The degree to which the innovation appears superior to existing products. The greater the perceived relative advantage of using HDTV—say, in picture quality and ease of viewing—the sooner such HDTVs will be adopted.
- *Compatibility:* The degree to which the innovation fits the values and experiences of potential consumers. HDTV, for example, is highly compatible with the lifestyles found in upper-middle-class homes. However, it is not very compatible with the programming and broadcasting systems currently available to consumers.
- *Complexity:* The degree to which the innovation is difficult to understand or use. HDTVs are not very complex and, therefore, once programming is available and prices come down, will take less time to penetrate U.S. homes than more complex innovations.
- *Divisibility:* The degree to which the innovation may be tried on a limited basis. HDTVs are still very expensive. To the extent that people can lease them with an option to buy, their rate of adoption will increase.
- *Communicability:* The degree to which the results of using the innovation can be observed or described to others. Because HDTV lends itself to demonstration and description, its use will spread faster among consumers.

Other characteristics influence the rate of adoption, such as initial and ongoing costs, risk and uncertainty, and social approval. The new-product marketer has to research all these factors when developing the new product and its marketing program.

active concept check <

Now let's take a moment to test your knowledge of what you've just read.

Understanding consumer behavior is difficult enough for companies marketing within the borders of a single country. For companies operating in many countries, however, understanding and serving the needs of consumers can be daunting. Although consumers in different countries may have some things in common, their values, attitudes, and behaviors often vary greatly. International marketers must understand such differences and adjust their products and marketing programs accordingly.

Sometimes the differences are obvious. For example, in the United States, where most people eat cereal regularly for breakfast, Kellogg focuses its marketing on persuading consumers to select a Kellogg brand rather than a competitor's brand. In France, however, where most people prefer croissants and coffee or no breakfast at all, Kellogg advertising simply attempts to convince people that they should eat cereal for breakfast. Its packaging includes step-by-step instructions on how to prepare cereal. In India, where many consumers eat heavy, fried breakfasts and many consumers skip the meal altogether, Kellogg's advertising attempts to convince buyers to switch to a lighter, more nutritious breakfast diet.

Often, differences across international markets are more subtle. They may result from physical differences in consumers and their environments. For example, Remington makes smaller electric shavers to fit the smaller hands of Japanese consumers and battery-powered shavers for the British market, where few bathrooms have electrical outlets. Other differences result from varying customs. In Japan, for example, where humility and deference are considered great virtues, pushy, hard-hitting sales approaches are considered offensive. Failing to understand such differences in customs and behaviors from one country to another can spell disaster for a marketer's international products and programs.

Marketers must decide on the degree to which they will adapt their products and marketing programs to meet the unique cultures and needs of consumers in various markets. On the one hand, they want to standardize their offerings in order to simplify operations and take advantage of cost economies. On the other hand, adapting marketing efforts within each country results in products and programs that better satisfy the needs of local consumers. The question of whether to adapt or standardize the marketing mix across international markets has created a lively debate in recent years.

> ### active exercise

Consider how American car manufacturers are struggling to market their products abroad.

> ### active concept check

Now let's take a moment to test your knowledge of what you've just read.

> ### Chapter Wrap-Up

Now that you've reached the end of the chapter, you may wish to explore the concepts you've been reading about in greater detail, or test yourself to see how well you've comprehended the material. In the box below you'll find a number of links. Click on any one of these links to find additional chapter resources.

> end-of-chapter resources

- Review of Concept Connections
- Practice Quiz
- Issues for Discussion
- Key Terms
- Marketing Applications
- Internet Connections
- Company Case

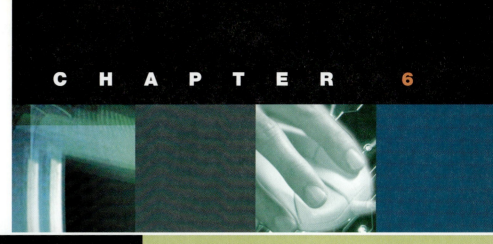

CHAPTER 6

Business Markets and Business Buyer Behavior

> ## What's Ahead

For more than 40 years, Gulfstream Aerospace Corporation has been the Rolls-Royce of corporate aviation. The original Gulfstream model—a twin-engine turboprop introduced in 1958—was the first jet designed expressly for corporate use. Gulfstream business jets come with price tags averaging $35 million. Identifying potential buyers isn't a problem—worldwide, only about 300 to 500 customers have the wherewithal to own and operate multimillion-dollar business aircraft. Customers include Disney, American Express, Coca-Cola, General Motors, IBM, and many others, including Bill Cosby and King Fahd of Saudi Arabia. Gulfstream's more difficult problems involve reaching key decision makers for jet purchases, understanding their complex motivations and decision processes, analyzing what factors will be important in their decisions, and designing marketing approaches.

Gulfstream recognizes the importance of *rational* motives and *objective* factors in buyers' decisions. Customers justify the expense of a corporate jet on utilitarian grounds, such as security, flexibility, responsiveness to customers, and efficient time use. A company buying a jet will evaluate Gulfstream aircraft on quality and performance, prices, operating costs, and service. At times, these "objective" factors may appear to be the only things that drive the buying decision. But having a superior product isn't enough to land the sale: Gulfstream also must consider the more subtle *human factors* that affect the choice of a jet.

The purchase process may be initiated by the chief executive officer (CEO), a board member wishing to increase efficiency or security, the company's chief pilot, or through Gulfstream efforts such as advertising or a sales visit. The CEO will be central in deciding whether to buy the jet, but he or she will be heavily influenced by the company's pilot, financial officer, and members of top management. The involvement of so many people in the purchase decision creates a group dynamic that Gulfstream must factor into its sales planning. Who makes up the buying group? How will the parties interact? Who will dominate and who submit? What priorities do the individuals have?

Each party in the buying process has subtle roles and needs. For example, the salespeople who try to impress both the CEO with depreciation schedules and the chief pilot with minimum runway statistics will almost certainly not sell a plane if they overlook the psychological and emotional components of the buying decision. The chief pilot, as an equipment expert, often has veto power over purchase decisions and may be able to stop the purchase of a certain brand of jet by simply expressing a negative opinion about, say, the plane's bad-

weather capabilities. In this sense, the pilot not only influences the decision but also serves as an information "gatekeeper" by advising management on the equipment to select. The users of the jet—middle and upper management of the buying company, important customers, and others—may have at least an indirect role in choosing the equipment. Although the corporate legal staff will handle the purchase agreement and the purchasing department will acquire the jet, these parties may have little to say about whether or how the plane will be obtained and which type will be selected.

According to one salesperson, in dealing with the CEO, the biggest factor is not the plane's hefty price tag, but its image. You need all the numbers for support, but if you can't find the kid inside the CEO and excite him or her with the raw beauty of the new plane, you'll never sell the equipment. If you sell the excitement, you sell the jet.

Some buying influences may come as a big surprise. Gulfstream may never really know who is behind the purchase of a plane. Although many people inside the customer company can be influential, the most important influence may turn out to be the CEO's spouse. The typical buyer spends about $4 million to outfit the plane's interior. This covers top-of-the-line stereo sound and video systems, a lavish galley, and a bewildering array of custom-made furnishings. To help with such decisions, many CEOs hire designers and bring their spouses along to planning sessions. As one salesperson notes, "Wives are behind the CEO's decisions on a lot of things, not just airplanes. . . . A crucial moment in a deal comes when the CEO's wife takes off her shoes and starts decorating the plane."

In some ways, selling corporate jets to business buyers is like selling cars and kitchen appliances to families. Gulfstream asks the same questions as consumer marketers: Who are the buyers and what are their needs? How do buyers make their buying decisions and what factors influence these decisions? What marketing program will be most effective? But the answers to these questions are usually different for the business buyer. Thus, Gulfstream faces many of the same challenges as consumer marketersand some additional ones. A solid understanding of the full dynamics of business buyer behavior has Gulfstream flying high these days. The company captures a lion's share of the top-of-the-line segment of the business-jet market and has amassed a $4.1 billion backlog of orders.[1]

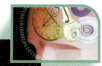

> ## objectives

Before you begin, take a moment to familiarize yourself with the key objectives of this chapter.

> ## gearing up

Before we begin our exploration this chapter, take a short warm-up test to see what you know about this topic.

In one way or another, most large companies sell to other organizations. Many companies, such as DuPont, Xerox, Boeing, Motorola, and countless other firms, sell *most* of their products to other businesses. Even large consumer-products companies, which make products used by final consumers, must first sell their products to other businesses. For example, General Mills makes many familiar consumer products—Cheerios, Betty Crocker cake mixes, Gold Medal flour, and others. But to sell these products to consumers, General Mills must first sell them to the wholesalers and retailers that serve the consumer market. General Mills also sells products such as specialty chemicals directly to other businesses.

The **business market** comprises all the organizations that buy goods and services for use in the production of other products and services that are sold, rented, or supplied to others. It also includes retailing and wholesaling firms that acquire goods for the purpose of reselling or renting them to others at a profit. In the **business buying process,** business buyers determine which products and services their organizations need to purchase, and then find, evaluate, and choose among alternative suppliers and brands. Companies that sell to other business organizations must do their best to understand business markets and business buyer behavior.

> ## Business Markets

The business market is *huge*. In fact, business markets involve far more dollars and items than do consumer markets. For example, think about the large number of business transactions involved in the production and sale of a single set of Goodyear tires. Various suppliers sell Goodyear the rubber, steel, equipment, and other goods that it needs to produce the tires. Goodyear then sells the finished tires to retailers, who in turn sell them to consumers. Thus, many sets of *business* purchases were made for only one set of *consumer* purchases. In addition, Goodyear sells tires as original equipment to manufacturers who install them on new vehicles, and as replacement tires to companies that maintain their own fleets of company cars, trucks, buses, or other vehicles.

> ## active example

Consider how one major corporation has tried to move into the huge and profitable business market.

[1]Portions adapted from Thomas V. Bonoma, "Major Sales: Who Really Does the Buying," *Harvard Business Review,* May–June 1982. Copyright © 1982 by the President and Fellows of Harvard College; all rights reserved. Quotes from John Huey, "The Absolute Best Way to Fly," *Fortune,* May 30, 1994, pp. 121–28; and Anthony Bianco, "Gulfstream's Pilot," *Business Week,* April 14, 1997, pp. 64–76. Also see "My First Gulfstream," *Vanity Fair,* October 1998, pp. 236–58; and Steven Lipin and Andy Pasztor, "Defense Firm Set to Acquire Gulfstream," *Wall Street Journal,* May 17, 1999, p. A3.

CHARACTERISTICS OF BUSINESS MARKETS

In some ways, business markets are similar to consumer markets. Both involve people who assume buying roles and make purchase decisions to satisfy needs. However, business markets differ in many ways from consumer markets. The main differences, shown in Table 6.1 and discussed below, are in the *market structure and demand,* the *nature of the buying unit,* and the *types of decisions and the decision process* involved.

Market Structure and Demand

The business marketer normally deals with *far fewer but far larger buyers* than the consumer marketer does. For example, when Goodyear sells replacement tires to final consumers, its potential market includes the owners of the millions of cars currently in use in the United States. But Goodyear's fate in the business market depends on getting orders from one of only a few large automakers. Even in large business markets, a few buyers normally account for most of the purchasing.

Business markets are also *more geographically concentrated.* More than half the nation's business buyers are concentrated in eight states: California, New York, Ohio, Illinois, Michigan, Texas, Pennsylvania, and New Jersey. Further, business demand is **derived demand**—it ultimately derives from the demand for consumer goods. General Motors buys steel because consumers buy cars. If consumer demand for cars drops, so will the demand for steel and all the other products used to make cars. Therefore, business marketers sometimes promote their products directly to final consumers to increase business demand. For example, Intel's long-running "Intel Inside" advertising campaign sells personal computer buyers on the virtues of Intel microprocessors. The increased demand for Intel chips boosts demand for the PCs containing them, and both Intel and its business partners win.

Many business markets have *inelastic demand;* that is, total demand for many business products is not affected much by price changes, especially in the short run. A drop in the price of leather will not cause shoe manufacturers to buy much more leather unless it results in lower shoe prices that, in turn, will increase consumer demand for shoes.

Finally, business markets have more *fluctuating demand.* The demand for many business goods and services tends to change more—and more quickly—than the demand for consumer goods and services does. A small percentage increase in consumer demand can cause large increases in business demand. Sometimes a rise of only 10 percent in consumer demand can cause as much as a 200 percent rise in business demand during the next period.

TABLE 6.1	Characteristics of Business Markets
Marketing Structure and Demand	
Business markets contain *fewer but larger buyers.*	
Business customers are *more geographically concentrated.*	
Business buyer demand is *derived* from final consumer demand.	
Demand in many business markets is more inelastic—not affected as much in the short run by price changes.	
Demand in business markets *fluctuates more,* and more quickly.	
Nature of the Buying Unit	
Business purchases involve *more buyers.*	
Business buying involves a *more professional purchasing effort.*	
Types of Decisions and the Decision Process	
Business buyers usually face *more complex buying decisions.*	
The business buying process is *more formalized.*	
In business buying, buyers and sellers work more closely together and build close long-run *relationships.*	

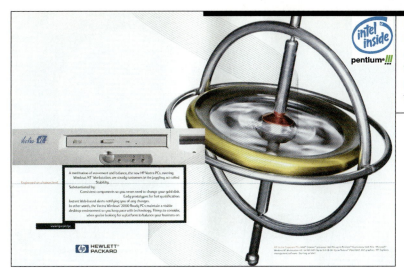

Derived demand: Intel's long-running "Intel Inside" logo advertising campaign boosts demand for Intel chips and for the PCs containing them. Now, HP and most other computer makers feature the logo in ads like this one.

Nature of the Buying Unit

Compared with consumer purchases, a business purchase usually involves *more decision participants* and a *more professional purchasing effort.* Often, business buying is done by trained purchasing agents who spend their working lives learning how to buy better. The more complex the purchase, the more likely that several people will participate in the decision-making process. Buying committees made up of technical experts and top management are common in the buying of major goods. As one observer notes, "It's a scary thought: Your customers may know more about your company and products than you do. . . . Companies are putting their best and brightest people on procurement patrol."[2] Therefore, business marketers must have well-trained salespeople to deal with well-trained buyers.

Types of Decisions and the Decision Process

Business buyers usually face *more complex* buying decisions than do consumer buyers. Purchases often involve large sums of money, complex technical and economic considerations, and interactions among many people at many levels of the buyer's organization. Because the purchases are more complex, business buyers may take longer to make their decisions. For example, the purchase of a large information technology system might take many months or more than a year to complete and could involve millions of dollars, thousands of technical details, and dozens of people ranging from top management to lower-level users.

The business buying process tends to be *more formalized* than the consumer buying process. Large business purchases usually call for detailed product specifications, written purchase orders, careful supplier searches, and formal approval. The buying firm might even prepare policy manuals that detail the purchase process.

Finally, in the business buying process, buyer and seller are often much *more dependent* on each other. Consumer marketers are often at a distance from their customers. In contrast, business marketers may roll up their sleeves and work closely with their customers during all stages of the buying process—from helping customers define problems, to finding solutions, to supporting after-sale operation. They often customize their offerings to individual customer needs. In the short run, sales go to suppliers who meet buyers' immediate product and service needs. However, business marketers also must build close *long-run* partnerships with customers. In recent years, relationships between customers and suppliers have been changing from downright adversarial to close and chummy:

Motoman, a leading supplier of industry robotic systems, and Stillwater Technologies, a contract tooling and machinery company and a key supplier to Motoman, are tightly integrated. Not only do they occupy office and manufacturing space in the same facility, they also link their telephone and computer systems and share a common lobby, conference room, and employee cafeteria. Philip Morrison, chairman and CEO of Motoman, says it's like "a joint venture without the paperwork." Short delivery distances are just one benefit of the unusual partnership. Also key is the fact that employees of both companies have ready

[2]Sarah Lorge, "Purchasing Power," *Sales & Marketing Management,* June 1998, pp. 43–46.

Business marketers often roll up their sleeves and work closely with their customers throughout the buying and consuming process. In this award-winning business-to-business ad, Fujitsu promises more than just high-tech products: "Our technology helps keep you moving upward. And our people won't let you down."

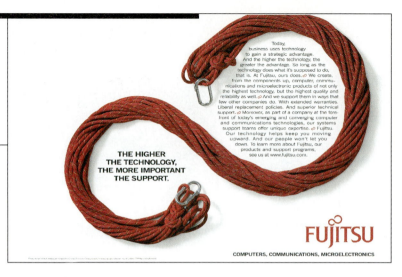

THE HIGHER
THE TECHNOLOGY,
THE MORE IMPORTANT
THE SUPPORT.

FUJITSU
COMPUTERS, COMMUNICATIONS, MICROELECTRONICS

access to each other and can share ideas on improving quality and reducing costs. This close relationship has also opened the door to new opportunities. Both companies had been doing work for Honda Motor Company, and Honda suggested that the two work together on systems projects. The symbiotic relationship makes the two bigger and better than they could be individually.[3]

In the long run, business marketers keep a customer's sales by meeting current needs *and* by working with customers to help them succeed with their own customers.

active exercise <

The business buying process is very different from the consumer buying process. Consider how one company manages business customers.

A MODEL OF BUSINESS BUYER BEHAVIOR

At the most basic level, marketers want to know how business buyers will respond to various marketing stimuli. Figure 6.1 shows a model of business buyer behavior. In this model, marketing and other stimuli affect the buying organization and produce certain buyer responses. As with consumer buying, the marketing stimuli for business buying consist of the four Ps: product, price, place, and promotion. Other stimuli include major forces in the environment: economic, technological, political, cultural, and competitive. These stimuli enter the organization and are turned into buyer responses: product or service choice; supplier choice; order quantities; and delivery, service, and payment terms. In order to design good marketing mix strategies, the marketer must understand what happens within the organization to turn stimuli into purchase responses.

Within the organization, buying activity consists of two major parts: the buying center, made up of all the people involved in the buying decision, and the buying decision process. The model shows that the buying center and the buying decision process are influenced by internal organizational, interpersonal, and individual factors as well as by external environmental factors.

video example <

Now that you have read about business markets, let's look at how real-life companies approach business markets.

[3] John H. Sheridan, "An Alliance Built on Trust," *Industry Week*, March 17, 1997, pp. 66–70.

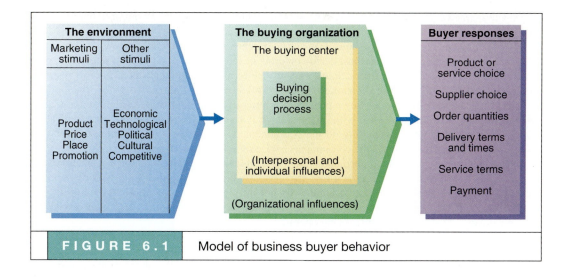

| FIGURE 6.1 | Model of business buyer behavior |

> active concept check

Now let's take a moment to test your knowledge of what you've just read.

> **Business Buyer Behavior**

The model in Figure 6.1 suggests four questions about business buyer behavior: What buying decisions do business buyers make? Who participates in the buying process? What are the major influences on buyers? How do business buyers make their buying decisions?

MAJOR TYPES OF BUYING SITUATIONS

There are three major types of buying situations.[4] At one extreme is the *straight rebuy,* which is a fairly routine decision. At the other extreme is the *new task,* which may call for thorough research. In the middle is the *modified rebuy,* which requires some research.

In a **straight rebuy,** the buyer reorders something without any modifications. It is usually handled on a routine basis by the purchasing department. Based on past buying satisfaction, the buyer simply chooses from the various suppliers on its list. "In" suppliers try to maintain product and service quality. They often propose automatic reordering systems so that the purchasing agent will save reordering time. "Out" suppliers try to offer something new or exploit dissatisfaction so that the buyer will consider them. They try to get their foot in the door with a small order and then enlarge their purchase share over time.

In a **modified rebuy,** the buyer wants to modify product specifications, prices, terms, or suppliers. The modified rebuy usually involves more decision participants than the straight rebuy. The in suppliers may become nervous and feel pressured to put their best foot forward to protect an account. Out suppliers may see the modified rebuy situation as an opportunity to make a better offer and gain new business.

A company buying a product or service for the first time faces a **new-task** situation. In such cases, the greater the cost or risk, the larger the number of decision participants and the greater their efforts to collect information will be. The new-task situation is the marketer's greatest opportunity and chal-

[4]Patrick J. Robinson, Charles W. Faris, and Yoram Wind, *Industrial Buying Behavior and Creative Marketing* (Boston: Allyn & Bacon, 1967). Also see Erin Anderson, Weyien Chu, and Barton Weitz, "Industrial Purchasing: An Empirical Exploration of the Buyclass Framework," *Journal of Marketing,* July 1987, pp. 71–86; Cynthia Webster, "Buying Involvement in Purchasing Success," *Industrial Marketing Management,* August 1993, p. 199; and Edward G. Brierty, Robert W. Eckles, and Robert R. Reeder, *Business Marketing,* 3rd ed. (Upper Saddle River, NJ: Prentice Hall, 1998), pp. 74–82.

lenge. The marketer not only tries to reach as many key buying influences as possible but also provides help and information.

The buyer makes the fewest decisions in the straight rebuy and the most in the new-task decision. In the new-task situation, the buyer must decide on product specifications, suppliers, price limits, payment terms, order quantities, delivery times, and service terms. The order of these decisions varies with each situation, and different decision participants influence each choice.

Many business buyers prefer to buy a packaged solution to a problem from a single seller. Called **systems buying,** this practice began with government buying of major weapons and communication systems. Instead of buying and putting all the components together, the government asked for bids from suppliers who would supply the components *and* assemble the package or system.

Sellers increasingly have recognized that buyers like this method and have adopted systems selling as a marketing tool. Systems selling is a two-step process. First, the supplier sells a group of interlocking products. For example, the supplier sells not only glue, but also applicators and dryers. Second, the supplier sells a system of production, inventory control, distribution, and other services to meet the buyer's need for a smooth-running operation.

Systems selling is a key business marketing strategy for winning and holding accounts. The contract often goes to the firm that provides the most complete solution to customers' problems. For example, Enron, the $31 billion energy company, is best known for providing the natural gas and electricity that its customers use to power their buildings. However, Enron has discovered that companies actually spend far more on the other elements of their energy systems, including energy equipment inside their facilities and the employees who maintain it, than on paying for the energy itself. To help customers meet their complete power management needs, Enron started Enron Energy Services (EES), a division that offers entire energy management solutions. Now, customers can turn over all of their energy management needs to Enron. The systems package includes both the power and all the interior workings: the boilers, chillers, heating, ventilation, and air-conditioning equipment. The idea is, if it has to do with managing buildings, keeping them lit and warm in the winter and cool in the summer, it should be Enron's domain. Such systems selling has produced stunning results for Enron: In only the past three years, EES's sales have grown sevenfold to more than $8 billion.[5]

PARTICIPANTS IN THE BUSINESS BUYING PROCESS

Who does the buying of the trillions of dollars' worth of goods and services needed by business organizations? The decision-making unit of a buying organization is called its **buying center:** all the individuals and units that participate in the business decision-making process.

The buying center includes all members of the organization who play any of five roles in the purchase decision process.[6]

- **Users** are members of the organization who will use the product or service. In many cases, users initiate the buying proposal and help define product specifications.
- **Influencers** often help define specifications and also provide information for evaluating alternatives. Technical personnel are particularly important influencers.
- **Buyers** have formal authority to select the supplier and arrange terms of purchase. Buyers may help shape product specifications, but their major role is in selecting vendors and negotiating. In more complex purchases, buyers might include high-level officers participating in the negotiations.
- **Deciders** have formal or informal power to select or approve the final suppliers. In routine buying, the buyers are often the deciders, or at least the approvers.
- **Gatekeepers** control the flow of information to others. For example, purchasing agents often have authority to prevent salespersons from seeing users or deciders. Other gatekeepers include technical personnel and even personal secretaries.

The buying center is not a fixed and formally identified unit within the buying organization. It is a set of buying roles assumed by different people for different purchases. Within the organization, the size and makeup of the buying center will vary for different products and for different buying situations. For some routine purchases, one person—say a purchasing agent—may assume all the buying center roles and serve as the only person involved in the buying decision. For more complex purchases, the buying center may include 20 or 30 people from different levels and departments in the

[5]Sarah Lorge, "Enron," *Sales & Marketing Management,* July 1999, pp. 48–52.

[6]Frederick E. Webster Jr. and Yoram Wind, *Organizational Buying Behavior* (Upper Saddle River, NJ: Prentice Hall, 1972), pp. 78–80. Also see Michael D. Hutt and Thomas Speh, *Business Marketing Management,* 4th ed. (Fort Worth, TX: Dryden Press, 1992), pp. 104–12; and James C. Anderson and James A. Narus, *Business Market Management: Understanding, Creating and Delivering Value* (Upper Saddle River, NJ: Prentice Hall, 1998), chap. 3.

organization. According to one survey, the average number of people involved in a buying decision ranges from about 3 (for services and items used in day-to-day operations) to almost 5 (for such high-ticket purchases as construction work and machinery). Another survey detected a trend toward team-based buying—87 percent of surveyed purchasing executives at Fortune 1000 companies expect teams of people from different functions to be making buying decisions in the year 2000.[7]

Business marketers working in global markets may face even greater levels of buying center influence. A study comparing the buying decision processes in the United States, Sweden, France, and Southeast Asia found that U.S. buyers may be lone eagles compared with their counterparts in some other countries. Sweden had the highest team buying effort, whereas the United States had the lowest, even though the Swedish and U.S. firms had very similar demographics. In making purchasing decisions, Swedish firms depended on technical staff, both their own and suppliers', much more than did the firms in other countries.[8]

The buying center concept presents a major marketing challenge. The business marketer must learn who participates in the decision, each participant's relative influence, and what evaluation criteria each decision participant uses. For example, Allegiance Healthcare Corporation, the large health care products and services company, sells disposable surgical gowns to hospitals. It identifies the hospital personnel involved in this buying decision as the vice president of purchasing, the operating room administrator, and the surgeons. Each participant plays a different role. The vice president of purchasing analyzes whether the hospital should buy disposable gowns or reusable gowns. If analysis favors disposable gowns, then the operating room administrator compares competing products and prices and makes a choice. This administrator considers the gown's absorbency, antiseptic quality, design, and cost, and normally buys the brand that meets requirements at the lowest cost. Finally, surgeons affect the decision later by reporting their satisfaction or dissatisfaction with the brand.

The buying center usually includes some obvious participants who are involved formally in the buying decision. For example, the decision to buy a corporate jet will probably involve the company's CEO, its chief pilot, a purchasing agent, some legal staff, a member of top management, and others formally charged with the buying decision. It may also involve less obvious, informal participants, some of whom may actually make or strongly affect the buying decision. Sometimes, even the people in the buying center are not aware of all the buying participants. As the Gulfstream example showed, the decision about which corporate jet to buy may actually be made by a corporate board member who has an interest in flying and who knows a lot about airplanes. This board member may work behind the scenes to sway the decision. Many business buying decisions result from the complex interactions of ever-changing buying center participants.

> **active example**

Business buying is a critical function. Read this example to see how one retail firm is transforming its purchase department to gain efficiencies.

MAJOR INFLUENCES ON BUSINESS BUYERS

Business buyers are subject to many influences when they make their buying decisions. Some marketers assume that the major influences are economic. They think buyers will favor the supplier who offers the lowest price or the best product or the most service. They concentrate on offering strong economic benefits to buyers. However, business buyers actually respond to both economic and personal factors. Far from being cold, calculating, and impersonal, business buyers are human and social as well. They react to both reason and emotion.

[7]For results of both surveys, see "I Think You Have a Great Product, but It's Not My Decision," *American Salesman,* April 1994, pp. 11–13; and Tim Minahan, "OEM Buying Survey—Part 2: Buyers Get New Roles but Keep Old Tasks," *Purchasing,* July 16, 1998, pp. 208–9. For more on influence strategies within buying centers, see R. Venkatesh, Ajay K. Kohli, and Gerald Zaltman, "Influence Strategies in Buying Centers," *Journal of Marketing,* October 1995, pp. 71–82; John Monoky, "Who Does the Buying?" *Industrial Distribution,* October 1995, p. 48; and David I. Gilliland and Wesley J. Johnson, "Toward a Model of Business-to-Business Marketing Communications Effects," *Industrial Marketing Management,* January 1997, pp. 15–29; and Philip L. Dawes, Don Y. Lee, and Grahame R. Dowling, "Information Control and Influence in Emergent Buying Centers," *Journal of Marketing,* July 1998, pp. 55–68.

[8]Melvin R. Matson and Esmail Salshi-Sangari, "Decision Making in Purchases of Equipment and Materials: A Four-Country Comparison," *International Journal of Physical Distribution & Logistics Management* 23, no. 8, 1993, pp. 16–30.

Today, most business-to-business marketers recognize that emotion plays an important role in business buying decisions. For example, you might expect that an advertisement promoting large trucks to corporate truck fleet buyers would stress objective technical, performance, and economic factors. However, a recent ad for Volvo heavy-duty trucks shows two drivers arm wrestling and claims, "It solves all your fleet problems. Except who gets to drive." It turns out that, in the face an industrywide driver shortage, the type of truck a fleet provides can help it to attract qualified drivers. The Volvo ad stresses the raw beauty of the truck and its comfort and roominess, features that make it more appealing to drivers. The ad concludes that Volvo trucks are "built to make fleets more profitable and drivers a lot more possessive."

When suppliers' offers are very similar, business buyers have little basis for strictly rational choice. Because they can meet organizational goals with any supplier, buyers can allow personal factors to play a larger role in their decisions. However, when competing products differ greatly, business buyers are more accountable for their choice and tend to pay more attention to economic factors. Figure 6.2 lists various groups of influences on business buyers—environmental, organizational, interpersonal, and individual.[9]

Environmental Factors

Business buyers are influenced heavily by factors in the current and expected *economic environment*, such as the level of primary demand, the economic outlook, and the cost of money. As economic uncertainty rises, business buyers cut back on new investments and attempt to reduce their inventories.

An increasingly important environmental factor is shortages in key materials. Many companies now are more willing to buy and hold larger inventories of scarce materials to ensure adequate supply. Business buyers also are affected by technological, political, and competitive developments in the environment. Culture and customs can strongly influence business buyer reactions to the marketer's behavior and strategies, especially in the international marketing environment. The business marketer must watch these factors, determine how they will affect the buyer, and try to turn these challenges into opportunities.

active example <

An important component of the environment that affects businesses is technology.

Organizational Factors

Each buying organization has its own objectives, policies, procedures, structure, and systems. The business marketer must know these *organizational factors* as thoroughly as possible. Questions such

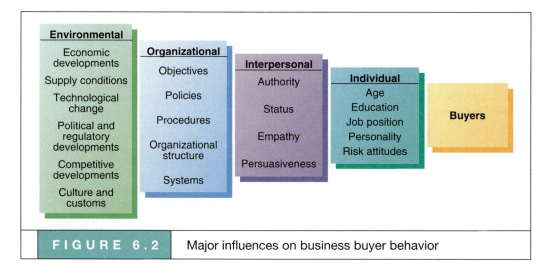

Environmental	**Organizational**	**Interpersonal**	**Individual**	
Economic developments	Objectives	Authority	Age	Buyers
Supply conditions	Policies	Status	Education	
Technological change	Procedures	Empathy	Job position	
Political and regulatory developments	Organizational structure	Persuasiveness	Personality	
Competitive developments	Systems		Risk attitudes	
Culture and customs				

FIGURE 6.2 | Major influences on business buyer behavior

[9]Webster and Wind, *Organizational Buying Behavior,* pp. 33–37. Also see Brierty, Eckles, and Reeder, *Business Marketing,* chap. 3.

as these arise: How many people are involved in the buying decision? Who are they? What are their evaluative criteria? What are the company's policies and limits on its buyers?

Interpersonal Factors

The buying center usually includes many participants who influence each other. The business marketer often finds it difficult to determine what kinds of *interpersonal factors* and group dynamics enter into the buying process. As one writer notes, "Managers do not wear tags that say 'decision maker' or 'unimportant person.' The powerful are often invisible, at least to vendor representatives."[10] Nor does the buying center participant with the highest rank always have the most influence. Participants may have influence in the buying decision because they control rewards and punishments, are well liked, have special expertise, or have a special relationship with other important participants. Interpersonal factors are often very subtle. Whenever possible, business marketers must try to understand these factors and design strategies that take them into account.

Individual Factors

Each participant in the business buying decision process brings in personal motives, perceptions, and preferences. These individual factors are affected by personal characteristics such as age, income, education, professional identification, personality, and attitudes toward risk. Also, buyers have different buying styles. Some may be technical types who make in-depth analyses of competitive proposals before choosing a supplier. Other buyers may be intuitive negotiators who are adept at pitting the sellers against one another for the best deal.

THE BUSINESS BUYING PROCESS

Table 6.2 lists the eight stages of the business buying process.[11] Buyers who face a new-task buying situation usually go through all stages of the buying process. Buyers making modified or straight rebuys may skip some of the stages. We will examine these steps for the typical new-task buying situation.

Problem Recognition

The buying process begins when someone in the company recognizes a problem or need that can be met by acquiring a specific product or service. **Problem recognition** can result from internal or external stimuli. Internally, the company may decide to launch a new product that requires new

TABLE 6.2	Major Stages of the Business Buying Process in Relation to Major Buying Situations		
	Buying Situations		
Stages of the Buying Process	**New Task**	**Modified Rebuy**	**Straight Rebuy**
1. Problem recognition	Yes	Maybe	No
2. General need description	Yes	Maybe	No
3. Product specification	Yes	Yes	Yes
4. Supplier search	Yes	Maybe	No
5. Proposal solicitation	Yes	Maybe	No
6. Supplier selection	Yes	Maybe	No
7. Order-routine specification	Yes	Maybe	No
8. Performance review	Yes	Yes	Yes

Source: Adapted from Patrick J. Robinson, Charles W. Faris, and Yoram Wind, *Industrial Buying and Creative Marketing* (Boston: Allyn & Bacon, 1967), p. 14

[10]Bonoma, "Major Sales," p. 114. Also see Ajay Kohli, "Determinants of Influence in Organizational Buying: A Contingency Approach," *Journal of Marketing,* July 1989, pp. 50–65.

[11]Robinson, Faris, and Wind, *Industrial Buying Behavior and Creative Marketing,* p. 14.

production equipment and materials. Or a machine may break down and need new parts. Perhaps a purchasing manager is unhappy with a current supplier's product quality, service, or prices. Externally, the buyer may get some new ideas at a trade show, see an ad, or receive a call from a salesperson who offers a better product or a lower price. In fact, in their advertising, business marketers often alert customers to potential problems and then show how their products provide solutions.

General Need Description

Having recognized a need, the buyer next prepares a **general need description** that describes the characteristics and quantity of the needed item. For standard items, this process presents few problems. For complex items, however, the buyer may have to work with others—engineers, users, consultants—to define the item. The team may want to rank the importance of reliability, durability, price, and other attributes desired in the item. In this phase, the alert business marketer can help the buyers define their needs and provide information about the value of different product characteristics.

Product Specification

The buying organization next develops the item's technical **product specifications,** often with the help of a value analysis engineering team. **Value analysis** is an approach to cost reduction in which components are studied carefully to determine if they can be redesigned, standardized, or made by less costly methods of production. The team decides on the best product characteristics and specifies them accordingly. Sellers, too, can use value analysis as a tool to help secure a new account. By showing buyers a better way to make an object, outside sellers can turn straight rebuy situations into new-task situations that give them a chance to obtain new business.

Supplier Search

The buyer now conducts a **supplier search** to find the best vendors. The buyer can compile a small list of qualified suppliers by reviewing trade directories, doing a computer search, or phoning other companies for recommendations. Today, more and more companies are turning to the Internet to find suppliers. For marketers, this has leveled the playing field—smaller suppliers have the same advantages as larger ones and can be listed in the same online catalogs for a nominal fee:

Worldwide Internet Solutions Network, better known as WIZnet (www.wiznet.net), has built an "interactive virtual library of business-to-business catalogs" that is global in coverage. At last report, its database included complete specifications for more than 10 million products and services from 45,000 manufacturers, distributors, and industrial service providers. For purchasing managers, who routinely receive a foot-high stack of mail each day, much of it catalogs, this kind of one-stop shopping will be an incredible time-saver (and price saver, because it allows easier comparison shopping). When told by a management consultant, "Do a search for 3.5-inch platinum ball valves available from a Michigan source," WIZnet found six Michigan sources for buying the exact product in about 15 seconds. More than just electric Yellow Pages, such as the Thomas Register or Industry.net, WIZnet includes all specifications for the products right in the system and offers secure e-mail to communicate directly with vendors to ask for requests for bids or to place an order. More than 10,000 product specs are added to WIZnet per week, and its database includes catalogs from Germany, Taiwan, the Czech Republic, and other countries.[12]

The newer the buying task, and the more complex and costly the item, the greater the amount of time the buyer will spend searching for suppliers. The supplier's task is to get listed in major directories and build a good reputation in the marketplace. Salespeople should watch for companies in the process of searching for suppliers and make certain that their firm is considered.

Many business buyers go to extremes in searching for and qualifying suppliers. Consider the hurdles that Xerox has set up in its qualifying suppliers:

Xerox qualifies only suppliers who meet ISO 9000 international quality standards (see chapter 18). But to win the company's top award—certification status—a supplier must first complete the Xerox Multinational Supplier Quality Survey. The survey requires the supplier to issue a quality assurance manual, adhere to continuous improvement principles, and demonstrate effective systems implementation. Once a supplier has been qualified, it must participate in Xerox's Continuous Supplier Involvement process, in which the two companies work together to create specifications for quality, cost, delivery times, and process capability. The final step toward certification requires a supplier to undergo additional quality training and an evaluation based on the same criteria as the Malcolm Baldrige National Quality Award. Not surprisingly, only 176 suppliers worldwide have achieved the 95 percent rating required for certification as a Xerox supplier.[13]

Proposal Solicitation

In the **proposal solicitation** stage of the business buying process, the buyer invites qualified suppliers to submit proposals. In response, some suppliers will send only a catalog or a salesperson. However, when the item is complex or expensive, the buyer will usually require detailed written proposals or formal presentations from each potential supplier.

Business marketers must be skilled in researching, writing, and presenting proposals in response to buyer proposal solicitations. Proposals should be marketing documents, not just technical documents. Presentations should inspire confidence and should make the marketer's company stand out from the competition.

Supplier Selection

The members of the buying center now review the proposals and select a supplier or suppliers. During **supplier selection,** the buying center often will draw up a list of the desired supplier attributes and

[12]John H. Sheridan, "Buying Globally Made Easier," *Industry Week,* February 2, 1998, pp. 63–64; and information accessed online at www.wiznet.net, September 1999.x

[13]See "Xerox Multinational Supplier Quality Survey," *Purchasing,* January 1995, p. 112.

Using the Internet to find suppliers: WIZnet's eCommerce Portal provides quick access to more than 45,000 manufacturers, distributors, and industrial service providers.

their relative importance. In one survey, purchasing executives listed the following attributes as most important in influencing the relationship between supplier and customer: quality products and services, on-time delivery, ethical corporate behavior, honest communication, and competitive prices. Other important factors include repair and servicing capabilities, technical aid and advice, geographic location, performance history, and reputation. The members of the buying center will rate suppliers against these attributes and identify the best suppliers.[14]

As part of the buyer selection process, buying centers must decide how many suppliers to use. In the past, many companies preferred a large supplier base to ensure adequate supplies and to obtain price concessions. These companies would insist on annual negotiations for contract renewal and would often shift the amount of business they gave to each supplier from year to year. Increasingly, however, companies are reducing the number of suppliers. Companies such as Ford, Motorola, and Allied Signal have cut the number of suppliers anywhere from 20 to 80 percent. These companies expect their preferred suppliers to work closely with them during product development and they value their suppliers' suggestions.

There is even a trend toward single sourcing, using one supplier. For example, whereas most newspapers rely on a variety of companies to supply the tons of newsprint they consume, the *Knoxville News-Sentinel* and the *New York Daily News* each rely on a single source for their newsprint.[15] With single sourcing there is only one supplier to handle and it is easier to control newsprint inventories. Using one source not only can translate into more consistent product performance, but it also allows press rooms to configure themselves for one particular kind of newsprint rather than changing presses for papers with different attributes.

Many companies, however, are still reluctant to use single sourcing. They fear that they may become too dependent on the single supplier or that the single-source supplier may become too comfortable in the relationship and lose its competitive edge. Some marketers have developed programs that address these concerns. For example, GC Electronics of Rockford, Illinois, has a "one source lowest price guarantee program," which promotes the reduced transaction and purchasing costs of using it as a single source. However, if after being with the program for a while, distributors can show that they could have gotten a better deal elsewhere, GC offers them a 6 percent rebate.[16]

[14]See "What Buyers Really Want," *Sales & Marketing Management,* October 1989, p. 30; "Purchasing Managers Sound Off," *Sales & Marketing Management,* February 1995, pp. 84–85; Thomas Y. Choi and Janet L. Hartley, "An Exploration of Supplier Selection Practices Across the Supply Chain," *Journal of Operations Management,* November 1996, pp. 333–43; Douglas M. Lambert, Ronald J. Adams, and Margaret A. Emmelhainz, "Supplier Selection Criteria in the Healthcare Industry: A Comparison of Importance and Performance," *International Journal of Purchasing and Materials Management,* Winter 1997, pp. 16–22; and Graig M. Gustin, Patricia J. Daugherty, and Alexander E. Ellinger, "Supplier Selection Decisions in Systems/Software," *International Journal of Purchasing and Materials Management,* Fall 1997, pp. 41–46.

[15]Donna Del Moro, "Single-Source Newsprint Supply," *Editor & Publisher,* October 25, 1997, pp. 42–45.

[16]See Kitty Vineyard, "Trends . . . in Single Sourcing," *Electrical Apparatus,* November 1996, p. 12; and Anne Millen Porter, "Supply Alliances Pose New Ethical Threats," *Purchasing,* May 20, 1999, pp. 20–23.

Order-Routine Specification

The buyer now prepares an **order-routine specification.** It includes the final order with the chosen supplier or suppliers and lists items such as technical specifications, quantity needed, expected time of delivery, return policies, and warranties. In the case of maintenance, repair, and operating items, buyers may use *blanket contracts* rather than periodic purchase orders. A blanket contract creates a long-term relationship in which the supplier promises to resupply the buyer as needed at agreed prices for a set time period. The seller holds the stock, and the buyer's computer automatically prints out an order to the seller when stock is needed. A blanket order eliminates the expensive process of renegotiating a purchase each time that stock is required. It also allows buyers to write more, but smaller, purchase orders, resulting in lower inventory levels and carrying costs.

Blanket contracting leads to more single-source buying and to buying more items from that source. This practice locks the supplier in tighter with the buyer and makes it difficult for other suppliers to break in unless the buyer becomes dissatisfied with prices or service.

Performance Review

In this stage, the buyer reviews supplier performance. The buyer may contact users and ask them to rate their satisfaction. The **performance review** may lead the buyer to continue, modify, or drop the arrangement. The seller's job is to monitor the same factors used by the buyer to make sure that the seller is giving the expected satisfaction.

We have described the stages that typically would occur in a new-task buying situation. The eight-stage model provides a simple view of the business buying decision process. The actual process is usually much more complex. In the modified rebuy or straight rebuy situation, some of these stages would be compressed or bypassed. Each organization buys in its own way, and each buying situation has unique requirements. Different buying center participants may be involved at different stages of the process. Although certain buying process steps usually do occur, buyers do not always follow them in the same order, and they may add other steps. Often, buyers will repeat certain stages of the process.

BUSINESS BUYING ON THE INTERNET

During the past few years, incredible advances in information technology have changed the face of the business-to-business marketing process. Increasingly, business buyers are purchasing all kinds of products and services electronically, either through electronic data interchange (EDI) links or on the Internet. Such "cyberpurchasing" gives buyers access to new suppliers, lowers purchasing costs, and hastens order processing and delivery. In turn, business marketers are connecting with customers online to share marketing information, sell products and services, provide customer support services, and maintain ongoing customer relationships. In addition to their own Web pages on the Internet, they are establishing extranets that link a company's communications and data with its regular suppliers and distributors.

So far, most of the products bought by businesses through Internet and extranet connections are MRO materials—maintenance, repair, and operations. For instance, Los Angeles County purchases everything from chickens to lightbulbs over the Internet. National Semiconductor has automated almost all of the company's 3,500 monthly requisitions to buy materials ranging from the sterile booties worn in its fabrication plants to state-of-the-art software. The actual dollar amount spent on these types of MRO materials pales in comparison to the amount spent for items like airplane parts, computer systems, and steel tubing. Yet, MRO materials make up 80 percent of all business orders, and the transaction costs for order processing are high. Thus, companies have much to gain by streamlining the MRO buying process on the Web.

General Electric, one of the world's biggest purchasers, plans to be buying *all* of its general operating and industrial supplies online within the next two years. Five years ago, GE set up its Trading Process Network—a central Web site through which all GE business units could make their purchases. The site was so successful that GE has now opened it up to other companies, creating a vast electronic cyberbuying clearinghouse.

The rapid growth business-to-business cyberbuying promises many benefits. The cyberbuying juggernaut promises to[17]

[17]See Robert Yoegel, "The Evolution of B-to-B Selling on the 'Net," *Target Marketing,* August 1998, p. 34; Andy Reinhardt in San Mateo, "Extranets: Log On, Link Up, Save Big," *Business Week,* June 22, 1998, p. 134; "To Byte the Hand That Feeds," *The Economist,* January 17, 1998, pp. 61–62; John Evan Frook, "Buying Behemoth—By Shifting $5B in Spending to Extranets, GE Could Ignite a Development Frenzy," *Internetweek,* August 17, 1998, p. 1; John Jesitus, "Procuring an Edge," *Industry Week,* June 23, 1997, pp. 56–62; Ken Brack, "Source of the Future," *Industrial Distribution,* October 1998, pp. 76–80; and James Carbone, "Internet Buying on the Rise," *Purchasing,* March 25, 1999, pp. 51–56.

- *Shave transaction costs* for both buyers and suppliers. A Web-powered purchasing program eliminates the paperwork associated with traditional requisition and ordering procedures. At National Semiconductor, the $75 to $250 cost of processing each paper-based requisition has been cut to just $3 per electronic order.

- *Reduce time between order and delivery:* Time savings are particularly dramatic for companies with many overseas suppliers. Adaptec, a leading supplier of computer storage, used an extranet to tie all of its Taiwanese chip suppliers together in a kind of virtual family. Now messages from Adaptec flow in seconds from its headquarters to its Asian partners, and Adaptec has reduced the time between the order and delivery of its chips from as long as 16 weeks to just 55 days—the same turnaround time for companies that build their own chips.

- *Create more efficient purchasing systems:* One key motivation for GE's massive move to online purchasing has been a desire to get rid of overlapping purchasing systems across its many divisions. "We have too many purchasing systems to count," said Randy Rowe, manager of GE's corporate initiatives group. "We're looking to enable each division to manage its purchasing on extranets with financial data [concentrated in] a centralized platform."

- *Forge more intimate relationships* between partners and buyers. Robert Mondavi Corporation puts satellite images of its vineyards out over its extranet so that its independent growers can pinpoint potential vineyard problems and improve the grapes Mondavi purchases from them.

- *Level the playing field* between large and small suppliers. By using Internet technology to establish secure, standing information links between companies, extranets have helped firms do business with smaller suppliers. Currently most large manufacturers use EDI to order supplies, because it provides a secure means of coding and exchanging standardized business forms. However, EDI is an expensive system; it can cost as much as $50,000 to add a single trading partner to an EDI network, compared to $1,000 for a company to join GE's Trading Process Network. Moving business-to-business commerce onto the Web also levels the playing field between local and foreign suppliers, because purchasers can source materials from suppliers all over the globe for no additional transaction cost.

The rapidly expanding use of cybersourcing, however, also presents some problems. Here are a few of the negatives:

- *Cut purchasing jobs* for millions of clerks and order processors. All these savings and efficiencies derived from cyberbuying don't come without a price. National Semiconductor reduced its purchasing staff by more than half when it took its purchasing activities online. On the other hand, for many purchasing professionals, going online means reducing drudgery and paperwork and spending more time managing inventory and working creatively with suppliers.

- *Erode supplier–buyer loyalty:* At the same time that the Web makes it possible for suppliers and customers to share business data and even collaborate on product design, it can also erode decades-old customer–supplier relationships. Many firms are using the Web to search for better suppliers. Japan Airlines (JAL) has used the Internet to post orders for in-flight materials such as plastic cups. On its Web site it posts drawings and specifications that will attract proposals from any firm that comes across the site, rather than from just the usual Japanese suppliers.

- *Create potential security disasters:* Over 80 percent of companies say security is the leading barrier to expanding electronic links with customers and partners. Although e-mail and home banking transactions can be protected through basic encryption, the secure environment that businesses need to carry out confidential interactions is still lacking. However, security is of such high priority that companies are spending millions of research dollars on it. Companies are creating their own defensive strategies for keeping hackers at bay. Cisco Systems, for example, specifies the types of routers, firewalls, and security procedures that its partners must use to safeguard extranet connections. In fact, the company goes even further—it sends its own security engineers to examine a partner's defenses and holds the partner liable for any security breach that originates from its computer.

active exercise <

Take a moment to consider how companies can use the Internet in their business-to-business strategies.

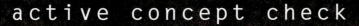

Now let's take a moment to test your knowledge of what you've just read.

> **Institutional and Government Markets**

So far, our discussion of organizational buying has focused largely on the buying behavior of business buyers. Much of this discussion also applies to the buying practices of institutional and government organizations. However, these two nonbusiness markets have additional characteristics and needs. In this final section, we address the special features of institutional and government markets.

INSTITUTIONAL MARKETS

The **institutional market** consists of schools, hospitals, nursing homes, prisons, and other institutions that provide goods and services to people in their care. Institutions differ from one another in their sponsors and in their objectives. For example, Humana hospitals are run for profit, whereas a non-profit Sisters of Charity Hospital provides health care to the poor and a government-run hospital might provide special services to veterans.

Many institutional markets are characterized by low budgets and captive patrons. For example, hospital patients have little choice but to eat whatever food the hospital supplies. A hospital purchasing agent has to decide on the quality of food to buy for patients. Because the food is provided as a part of a total service package, the buying objective is not profit. Nor is strict cost minimization the goal—patients receiving poor-quality food will complain to others and damage the hospital's reputation. Thus, the hospital purchasing agent must search for institutional-food vendors whose quality meets or exceeds a certain minimum standard and whose prices are low.

Many marketers set up separate divisions to meet the special characteristics and needs of institutional buyers. For example, Heinz produces, packages, and prices its ketchup and other products differently to better serve the requirements of hospitals, colleges, and other institutional markets.

GOVERNMENT MARKETS

The **government market** offers large opportunities for many companies, both big and small. In most countries, government organizations are major buyers of goods and services. In the United States alone, federal, state, and local governments contain more than 82,000 buying units. Government buying and business buying are similar in many ways. But there are also differences that must be understood by companies that wish to sell products and services to governments. To succeed in the government market, sellers must locate key decision makers, identify the factors that affect buyer behavior, and understand the buying decision process.

Government organizations typically require suppliers to submit bids, and normally they award the contract to the lowest bidder. In some cases, the government unit will make allowance for the supplier's superior quality or reputation for completing contracts on time. Governments will also buy on a negotiated contract basis, primarily in the case of complex projects involving major R&D costs and risks, and in cases where there is little competition.

Government organizations tend to favor domestic suppliers over foreign suppliers. A major complaint of multinationals operating in Europe is that each country shows favoritism toward its nationals in spite of superior offers that are made by foreign firms. The European Economic Commission is gradually removing this bias.

Like consumer and business buyers, government buyers are affected by environmental, organizational, interpersonal, and individual factors. One unique thing about government buying is that it is carefully watched by outside publics, ranging from Congress to a variety of private groups interested in how the government spends taxpayers' money. Because their spending decisions are subject to public review, government organizations require considerable paperwork from suppliers, who often complain about excessive paperwork, bureaucracy, regulations, decision-making delays, and frequent shifts in procurement personnel. Given all the red tape, why would any firm want to do business with the U.S. government? Here's how a consultant who has helped clients obtain more than $30 billion in government contracts answers that question:

When I hear that question, I tell the story of the businessman who buys a hardware store after moving to a small town. He asks his new employees who the biggest hardware customer in town is. He is surprised to learn that the customer isn't doing business with his store. When the owner asks why not, his employees say the customer is difficult to do business with and requires that a lot of forms be filled out. I point out that the same customer is probably very wealthy, doesn't bounce his checks, and usually does repeat business when satisfied. That's the type of customer the federal government can be.

Most governments provide would-be suppliers with detailed guides describing how to sell to the government. For example, the U.S. Small Business Administration prints a booklet entitled *U.S. Government Purchasing, Specifications, and Sales Directory,* which lists thousands of items most frequently purchased by the government and the specific agencies most frequently buying them. The Government Printing Office issues the *Commerce Business Daily,* which lists major current and planned purchases and recent contract awards, both of which can provide leads to subcontracting markets. The U.S. Commerce Department publishes *Business America,* which provides interpretations of government policies and programs and gives concise information on potential worldwide trade opportunities. In several major cities, the General Services Administration operates *Business Service Centers* with staffs to provide a complete education on the way government agencies buy, the steps that suppliers should follow, and the procurement opportunities available. Various trade magazines and associations provide information on how to reach schools, hospitals, highway departments, and other government agencies. Almost all of these government organizations and associations maintain Internet sites offering up-to-date information and advice.

Still, suppliers have to master the system and find ways to cut through the red tape. For example, the U.S. government has always been ADI Technology Corporation's most important client—federal contracts account for about 90 percent of its nearly $6 million in annual revenues. Yet managers at this small professional services company often shake their heads at all the work that goes into winning the coveted government contracts. A comprehensive bid proposal will run from 500 to 700 pages because of federal paperwork requirements. The company's president estimates that the firm has spent as much as $20,000, mostly in worker hours, to prepare a single bid proposal. Fortunately, government buying reforms are being put in place that will simplify contracting procedures and make bidding more attractive, particularly to smaller vendors. These reforms include more emphasis on buying commercial off-the-shelf items instead of items built to the government's specs, online communication with vendors to eliminate the massive paperwork, and a "debriefing" from the appropriate government agency for vendors who lose a bid, enabling them to increase their chances of winning the next time around.[18]

Noneconomic criteria also play a growing role in government buying. Government buyers are asked to favor depressed business firms and areas; small business firms; minority-owned firms; and business firms that avoid race, sex, or age discrimination. Sellers need to keep these factors in mind when deciding to seek government business.

Many companies that sell to the government have not been marketing oriented for a number of reasons. Total government spending is determined by elected officials rather than by any marketing effort to develop this market. Government buying has emphasized price, making suppliers invest their effort in technology to bring costs down. When the product's characteristics are specified carefully, product differentiation is not a marketing factor. Nor do advertising or personal selling matter much in winning bids on an open-bid basis.

Several companies, however, have established separate government marketing departments. Rockwell, Kodak, and Goodyear are examples. These companies anticipate government needs and projects, participate in the product specification phase, gather competitive intelligence, prepare bids carefully, and produce stronger communications to describe and enhance their companies' reputations. Other companies have set up customized marketing programs for government buyers. For example, Dell Computer has specific business units tailored to meet the needs of federal as well as state and local government buyers. Dell offers its customers tailor-made Web pages that include special pricing, online purchasing, and service and support for each city, state, and federal government entity.[19]

During the past decade, some of the government's buying has gone online. For example, *Commerce Business Daily* is now online (cbd.cos.com) and the two federal agencies that act as purchasing agents for the rest of government have launched World Wide Web–based catalogs. The

---

[18]Laura M. Litvan, "Selling to Uncle Sam: New, Easier Rules," *Nation's Business,* March 1995, pp. 46–48; and Edward Robinson, "The Pentagon Finally Learns to Shop," *Fortune,* December 21, 1998, pp. 174–83.

[19]For more on U.S. government buying, see Don Hill, "Who Says Uncle Sam's a Tough Sell?" *Sales & Marketing Management,* July 1988, pp. 56–60; Richard J. Wall and Carolyn M. Jones, "Navigating the Rugged Terrain of Government Contracts," *Internal Auditor,* April 1995, p. 32; and Wallace O. Keene, "New Bright Spot in Acquisition Reform," *Public Manager,* Spring 1999, pp. 45–46.

Dell Computer provides special Web pages for government buyers as well as individually customized sites for each city, state, or federal customer.

General Services Administration (www.gsa.gov) has set up an Advantage Web catalog, and the Defense Logistics Agency (www.dla.mil) offers one called Ascot. These Internet catalogs allow authorized defense and civilian agencies to buy everything from medical and office supplies to clothing through online purchasing. The GSA and DLA not only sell stocked merchandise through their Web sites but also create direct links between buyers and contract suppliers. For example, the branch of the DSA that sells 160,000 types of medical supplies to military forces transmits orders directly to vendors such as Bristol-Meyers. Such Internet systems promise to eliminate much of the hassle sometimes found in dealing with government purchasing.[20]

> **active poll**

Give your opinion on a question concerning the government buying process.

> **active concept check**

Now let's take a moment to test your knowledge of what you've just read.

> **Chapter Wrap-Up**

Now that you've reached the end of the chapter, you may wish to explore the concepts you've been reading about in greater detail, or test yourself to see how well you've comprehended the

[20]Ellen Messmer, "Feds Buy Online," *Network World,* April 15, 1996, p. 35; and "Government Surges Forward with Plans for Electronic Shopping Mall," *Supply Management,* March 18, 1999, p. 9. Also see Christina Couret, "Online Shopping Offers Governments 'Net' Gain," *The American City and County,* January 1999, pp. 20–23.

material. In the box below you'll find a number of links. Click on any one of these links to find additional chapter resources.

> end-of-chapter resources

- Review of Concept Connections
- Practice Quiz
- Issues for Discussion
- Key Terms
- Marketing Applications
- Internet Connections
- Company Case

Market Segmentation, Targeting, and Positioning for Competitive Advantage

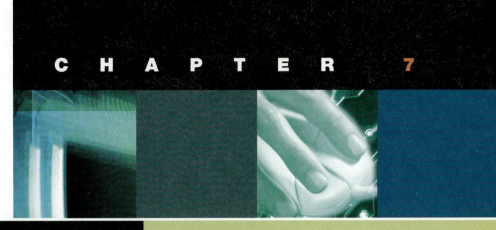

C H A P T E R 7

Chapter Outline

What's Ahead
Market Segmentation
   Levels of Market Segmentation
   Segmenting Consumer Markets
   Segmenting Business Markets
   Segmenting International Markets
   Requirements for Effective
   Segmentation
Market Targeting

Evaluating Market Segments
Selecting Market Segments
Socially Responsible Target
Marketing
Positioning for Competitive Advantage
   Choosing a Positioning Strategy
   Communicating and Delivering the
   Chosen Position
Chapter Wrap-Up

> What's Ahead

Procter & Gamble (P&G) sells eight brands of laundry detergent in the United States (Tide, Cheer, Bold, Gain, Era, Oxydol, Dreft, and Ivory Snow). It also sells six brands each of hand soap (Ivory, Safeguard, Camay, Oil of Olay, Zest, Coast) and shampoo (Pantene, Head & Shoulders, Ivory, Pert Plus, Vidal Sassoon, and Prell); four brands each of liquid dishwashing detergent (Dawn, Ivory, Joy, and Cascade), toothpaste (Crest, Gleam, Complete, and Denquel), and tissues and towels (Charmin, Bounty, Puffs, Royale); three brands each of floor cleaner (Spic & Span, Top Job, and Mr. Clean), deodorant (Secret, Sure, and Old Spice), and skin care potions (Oil of Olay, Noxema, and Clearasil); and two brands each of fabric softener (Downy and Bounce), disposable diapers (Pampers and Luvs), and cosmetics (Cover Girl and Max Factor). Moreover, P&G has many additional brands in each category for different international markets. For example, it sells 16 different laundry product brands in Latin America and 19 in Europe, the Middle East, and Africa. (See Procter & Gamble's Web site at *www.pg.com* for a full glimpse of the company's impressive lineup of familiar brands.)

   These P&G brands compete with one another on the same supermarket shelves. But why would P&G introduce several brands in one category instead of concentrating its resources on a single leading brand? The answer lies in the fact that different people want different *mixes of benefits* from the products they buy. Take laundry detergents as an example. People use laundry detergents to get their clothes clean. But they also want other things from their detergents—such as economy, bleaching power, fabric softening, fresh smell, strength or mildness, and lots of suds or only a few. We all want *some* of every one of these benefits from our detergent, but we may have different *priorities* for each benefit. To some people, cleaning and bleaching power are most important; to others, fabric softening matters most; still others want a mild, fresh-scented detergent. Thus, there are groups—or segments—of laundry detergent buyers, and each segment seeks a special combination of benefits.

Procter & Gamble has identified at least eight important laundry detergent segments, along with numerous subsegments, and has developed a different brand designed to meet the special needs of each. The eight P&G brands are positioned for different segments as follows:

- *Tide* "helps keep clothes looking like new." It's the all-purpose family detergent that is "tough on greasy stains." *Tide with Bleach* is "so powerful, it whitens down to the fiber."
- *Cheer with Triple Color Guard* is the "color expert." It guards against fading, color transfer, and fuzzy buildup. *Cheer Free* is "dermatologist tested . . . contains no irritating perfume or dye."
- *Bold* is the detergent with built-in fabric softener. It's "for clean, soft, fresh-smelling clothes." *Bold* liquid adds "the fresh fabric softener scent."
- *Gain,* originally P&G's "enzyme" detergent, was repositioned as the detergent that gives you clean, fresh-smelling clothes. It "cleans and freshens like sunshine. It's not just plain clean, it's Gain clean."
- *Era* has "built-in stain removers." It's "the power tool for stains."
- *Oxydol* contains "stain-seeking bleach." It "combines the cleaning power of detergents with the whitening power of nonchlorine bleach, so your whites sparkle and your clothes look bright." So "don't reach for the bleach—grab a box of Ox!"
- *Dreft* also "helps remove tough baby stains . . . for a clean you can trust." It's "pediatrician recommended and the first choice of mothers." It "doesn't remove the flame resistance of children's sleepwear."
- *Ivory Snow* is "ninety-nine and forty-four one hundredths percent pure." It "gently cleans fine washables and baby clothes . . . leaving them feeling soft." It provides "safe and gentle care in the gentle cycle."

Within each segment, Procter & Gamble has identified even *narrower* niches. For example, you can buy regular Tide (in powder or liquid form) or any of several formulations:

- *Tide with Bleach* helps to "keep your whites white and your colors bright," "kills 99.9 percent of bacteria."
- *Tide Clean Rinse* "goes beyond stain removal to prevent dingy buildup on clothes."
- *Tide Mountain Spring* lets you "bring the fresh clean scent of the great outdoors inside—the scent of crisp mountain air and fresh wildflowers."
- *Tide High Efficiency* is "formulated for high efficiency top-loading machines"—it prevents oversudsing.
- *Tide Free* "provides all the stain removal benefits without any dyes or perfumes."

By segmenting the market and having several detergent brands, Procter & Gamble has an attractive offering for consumers in all important preference groups. As a result, P&G is really cleaning up in the $4.3 billion U.S. laundry detergent market. Tide, by itself, captures a whopping 38 percent market share. All P&G brands combined take a 57 percent share of the market—two and one-half times that of nearest rival Unilever and much more than any single brand could obtain by itself.[1]

Companies today recognize that they cannot appeal to all buyers in the marketplace, or at least not to all buyers in the same way. Buyers are too numerous, too widely scattered, and too varied in their needs and buying practices. Moreover, the companies themselves vary widely in their abilities to serve different segments of the market. Rather than trying to compete in an entire market, sometimes against superior competitors, each company must identify the parts of the market that it can serve best and most profitably.

Thus, most companies are being more choosy about the customers with whom they wish to connect. Most have moved away from mass marketing and toward *market segmentation and targeting*—identifying market segments, selecting one or more of them, and developing products and marketing programs tailored to each. Instead of scattering their marketing efforts (the "shotgun" approach), firms are focusing on the buyers who have greater interest in the values they create best (the "rifle" approach).

Figure 7.1 shows the three major steps in target marketing. The first is **market segmentation**—dividing a market into smaller groups of buyers with distinct needs, characteristics, or behaviors who might require separate products or marketing mixes. The company identifies different ways to segment the market and develops profiles of the resulting market segments. The second step is **market targeting**—evaluating each market segment's attractiveness and selecting one or more of the market segments to enter. The third step is **market positioning**—setting the competitive positioning for the product and creating a detailed marketing mix. We discuss each of these steps in turn.

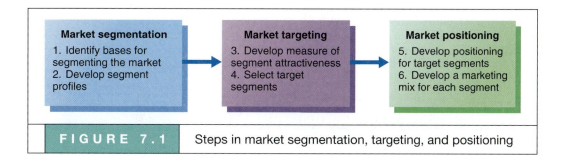

Market segmentation
1. Identify bases for segmenting the market
2. Develop segment profiles

Market targeting
3. Develop measure of segment attractiveness
4. Select target segments

Market positioning
5. Develop positioning for target segments
6. Develop a marketing mix for each segment

FIGURE 7.1   Steps in market segmentation, targeting, and positioning

[1]See Kerri Walsh, "Soaps and Detergents," *Chemical Week,* January 28, 1998, pp. 27–29; Christine Bittar, "P&G Sets Anti-Fade Plan for Ailing Powder Detergents: New SKUs," *Brandweek,* March 22, 1999, p. 4; and information accessed online from www.pg.com and www.tide.com, February 2000.

Markets consist of buyers, and buyers differ in one or more ways. They may differ in their wants, resources, locations, buying attitudes, and buying practices. Through market segmentation, companies divide large, heterogeneous markets into smaller segments that can be reached more efficiently and effectively with products and services that match their unique needs. In this section, we discuss five important segmentation topics: levels of market segmentation, segmenting consumer markets, segmenting business markets, segmenting international markets, and requirements for effective segmentation.

LEVELS OF MARKET SEGMENTATION

Because buyers have unique needs and wants, each buyer is potentially a separate market. Ideally, then, a seller might design a separate marketing program for each buyer. However, although some companies attempt to serve buyers individually, many others face larger numbers of smaller buyers and do not find complete segmentation worthwhile. Instead, they look for broader classes of buyers who differ in their product needs or buying responses. Thus, market segmentation can be carried out at several different levels. Figure 7.2 shows that companies can practice no segmentation (mass marketing), complete segmentation (micromarketing), or something in between (segment marketing or niche marketing).

Mass Marketing

Companies have not always practiced target marketing. In fact, for most of the 1900s, major consumer products companies held fast to *mass marketing*—mass producing, mass distributing, and mass promoting about the same product in about the same way to all consumers. Henry Ford epitomized this marketing strategy when he offered the Model T Ford to all buyers; they could have the car "in any color as long as it is black." Similarly, Coca-Cola at one time produced only one drink for the whole market, hoping it would appeal to everyone.

The traditional argument for mass marketing is that it creates the largest potential market, which leads to the lowest costs, which in turn can translate into either lower prices or higher margins. However, many factors now make mass marketing more difficult. For example, the world's mass markets have slowly splintered into a profusion of smaller segments—the baby boomers here, the GenXers there; here the Hispanic segment, there the African American segment; here working women, there single parents; here the Sun Belt, there the Rust Belt. Today, marketers find it very hard to create a single product or program that appeals to all of these diverse groups.

The proliferation of distribution channels and advertising media has also made it difficult to practice "one-size-fits-all" marketing. Today's consumers can shop at megamalls, superstores, or specialty shops; through mail catalogs or virtual stores on the Internet. They are bombarded with messages delivered via media ranging from old standards such as television, radio, magazines, newspapers, and telephone to newcomers like the Internet, fax, and e-mail. No wonder some have claimed that mass marketing is dying. Not surprisingly, many companies are retreating from mass marketing and turning to segmented marketing.

Segment Marketing

A company that practices **segment marketing** isolates broad segments that make up a market and adapts its offers to more closely match the needs of one or more segments. Thus, Marriott markets to a variety of segments—business travelers, families, and others—with packages adapted to their varying needs. GM has designed specific models for different income and age groups. In fact, it sells models for segments with varied *combinations* of age and income. For instance, GM designed its Buick Park Avenue for older, higher-income consumers.

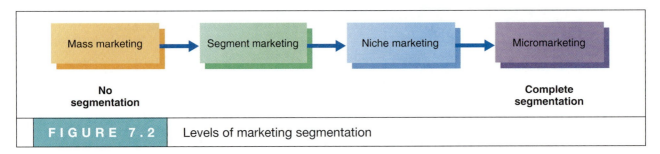

| Mass marketing | → | Segment marketing | → | Niche marketing | → | Micromarketing |

No segmentation   **Complete segmentation**

FIGURE 7.2   Levels of marketing segmentation

Segment marketing offers several benefits over mass marketing. The company can market more efficiently, targeting its products or services, channels, and communications programs toward only consumers that it can serve best and most profitably. The company can also market more effectively by fine-tuning its products, prices, and programs to the needs of carefully defined segments. The company may face fewer competitors if fewer competitors are focusing on this market segment.

Niche Marketing

Market segments are normally large, identifiable groups within a market—for example, luxury car buyers, performance car buyers, utility car buyers, and economy car buyers. **Niche marketing** focuses on subgroups within these segments. A *niche* is a more narrowly defined group, usually identified by dividing a segment into subsegments or by defining a group with a distinctive set of traits who may seek a special combination of benefits. For example, the utility vehicles segment might include light-duty pickup trucks and sport utility vehicles (SUVs). The sport utility vehicles subsegment might be further divided into standard SUV (as served by Ford and Chevrolet) and luxury SUV (as served by Lincoln and Lexus) niches.

Whereas segments are fairly large and normally attract several competitors, niches are smaller and normally attract only one or a few competitors. Niche marketers presumably understand their niches' needs so well that their customers willingly pay a price premium. For example, the luxurious Bentley gets a high price for its cars because its loyal buyers feel that no other automobile comes close to offering the product–service–membership benefits that Bentley does.

Niching offers smaller companies an opportunity to compete by focusing their limited resources on serving niches that may be unimportant to or overlooked by larger competitors. However, large companies also serve niche markets. For example, American Express offers not only its traditional green cards but also gold cards, corporate cards, and even platinum cards aimed at a niche consisting of the top-spending 1 percent of its 28 million cardholders.[2] Nike makes athletic gear for basketball, running, and soccer but also for smaller niches such as biking and street hockey.

In many markets today, niches are the norm. As an advertising agency executive observed, "There will be no market for products that everybody likes a little, only for products that somebody likes a lot." Other experts assert that companies will have to "niche or be niched."[3]

Micromarketing

Segment and niche marketers tailor their offers and marketing programs to meet the needs of various market segments. At the same time, however, they do not customize their offers to each individual customer. Thus, segment marketing and niche marketing fall between the extremes of mass marketing and micromarketing. **Micromarketing** is the practice of tailoring products and marketing programs to suit the tastes of specific individuals and locations. Micromarketing includes *local marketing* and *individual marketing*.

Local Marketing. **Local marketing** involves tailoring brands and promotions to the needs and wants of local customer groups—cities, neighborhoods, and even specific stores. Thus, retailers such as Sears and Wal-Mart routinely customize each store's merchandise and promotions to match its specific clientele. Citibank provides different mixes of banking services in its branches depending on neighborhood demographics. Kraft helps supermarket chains identify the specific cheese assortments and shelf positioning that will optimize cheese sales in low-income, middle-income, and high-income stores and in different ethnic communities.

Local marketing has some drawbacks. It can drive up manufacturing and marketing costs by reducing economies of scale. It can also create logistics problems as companies try to meet the varied requirements of different regional and local markets. Further, a brand's overall image might be diluted if the product and message vary too much in different localities. Still, as companies face increasingly fragmented markets, and as new supporting technologies develop, the advantages of local marketing often outweigh the drawbacks. Local marketing helps a company to market more effectively in the face of pronounced regional and local differences in community demographics and lifestyles. It also meets the needs of the company's first-line customers—retailers—who prefer more fine-tuned product assortments for their neighborhoods.

Individual Marketing. In the extreme, micromarketing becomes **individual marketing**—tailoring products and marketing programs to the needs and preferences of individual customers. Individual marketing has also been labeled *one-to-one marketing, customized marketing,* and *markets-of-one marketing.*[4]

The widespread use of mass marketing has obscured the fact that for centuries consumers were served as individuals: The tailor custom-made the suit, the cobbler designed shoes for the individual, the cabinetmaker made furniture to order. Today, however, new technologies are permitting many companies to return to customized marketing. More powerful computers, detailed databases, robotic production and flexible manufacturing, and immediate and interactive communication media such as e-mail, fax, and the Internet—all have combined to foster "mass customization." *Mass customization* is the process through which firms interact one-to-one with masses of customers to design products and services tailor-made to individual needs.

Thus, Dell Computer can deliver computers to individual customers loaded with customer-specified hardware and software. Peapod, the online grocery shopping and delivery service, lets customers create the virtual supermarket that best fits their individual needs. Ritz-Carlton Hotels creates custom-designed experiences for its delighted guests:

---

[2]Edward Baig, "Platinum Cards: Move Over AmEx," *Business Week,* August 19, 1996, p. 84; and "AmEx's No-Frills Snob Card," *Credit Card Management,* April 1997, pp. 12–14; and "AmEx Profit Up 25% in Quarter," *New York Times,* April 23, 1999, p. 4.

[3]Laurel Cutler, quoted in "Stars of the 1980s Cast Their Light," *Fortune,* July 3, 1989, p. 76; and Robert E. Linneman and John L. Stanton Jr., *Making Niche Marketing Work: How to Grow Bigger by Acting Smaller* (New York: McGraw-Hill, 1991).

[4]See Don Peppers and Martha Rogers, *The One-to-One Future: Building Relationships One Customer at a Time* (New York: Currency/Doubleday, 1993); B. Joseph Pine II, *Mass Customization* (Boston: Harvard Business School Press, 1993); B. Joseph Pine II, Don Peppers, and Martha Rogers, "Do You Want to Keep Your Customers Forever?" *Harvard Business Review,* March–April 1995, pp. 103–14; James H. Gilmore and B. Joseph Pine II, "The Four Faces of Customization," *Harvard Business Review,* January–February 1997, pp. 91–101; and Don Peppers, Martha Rogers, and Bob Dorf, "Is Your Company Ready for One-to-One Marketing?" *Harvard Business Review,* January–February 1999, pp. 151–60.

Check into any Ritz-Carlton hotel around the world, and you'll be amazed at how well the hotel's employees anticipate your slightest need. Without ever asking, they seem to know that you want a nonsmoking room with a king-size bed, a nonallergenic pillow, and breakfast with decaffeinated coffee in your room. How does Ritz-Carlton work this magic? The hotel employs a system that combines information technology and flexible operations to customize the hotel experience. At the heart of the system is a huge customer database, which contains information about guests gathered through the observations of hotel employees. Each day, hotel staffers—from those at the front desk to those in maintenance and housekeeping—discreetly record the unique habits, likes, and dislikes of each guest on small "guest preference pads." These observations are then transferred to a corporatewide "guest history database." Every morning, a "guest historian" at each hotel reviews the files of all new arrivals who have previously stayed at a Ritz-Carlton and prepares a list of suggested extra touches that might delight each guest. Guests have responded strongly to such markets-of-one service. Since inaugurating the guest-history system in 1992, Ritz-Carlton has boosted guest retention by 23 percent. An amazing 95 percent of departing guests report that their stay has been a truly memorable experience.

Business-to-business marketers are also finding new ways to customize their offerings. For example, Becton-Dickinson, a major medical supplier, offers to customize almost anything for its hospital customers. It offers custom-designed labeling, individual packaging, customized quality control, customized computer software, and customized billing. Motorola salespeople use a handheld computer to custom-design pagers following individual business customer wishes. The design data are transmitted to the Motorola factory and production starts within 17 minutes. The customized pagers are ready for shipment within two hours. John Deere manufactures seeding equipment that can be configured in more than 2 million versions to individual customer specifications. The seeders are produced one at a time, in any sequence, on a single production line.[5]

The move toward individual marketing mirrors the trend in consumer *self-marketing*. Increasingly, individual customers are taking more responsibility for determining which products and brands to buy. Consider two business buyers with two different purchasing styles. The first sees several salespeople, each trying to persuade him to buy his or her product. The second sees no salespeople but rather logs onto the Internet; searches for information on available products; interacts electronically with various suppliers, users, and product analysts; and then makes up her own mind about the best offer. The second purchasing agent has taken more responsibility for the buying process, and the marketer has had less influence over her buying decision.

As the trend toward more interactive dialogue and less advertising monologue continues, self-marketing will grow in importance. As more buyers look up consumer reports, join Internet product discussion forums, and place orders via phone or online, marketers will have to influence the buying process in new ways. They will need to involve customers more in all phases of the product development and buying processes, increasing opportunities for buyers to practice self-marketing. We will examine the trends toward one-to-one marketing and self-marketing further in chapter 17.

> **active example**

Consider another example of how consumer product companies can practice individual marketing.

SEGMENTING CONSUMER MARKETS

There is no single way to segment a market. A marketer has to try different segmentation variables, alone and in combination, to find the best way to view the market structure. Table 7.1 outlines the major variables that might be used in segmenting consumer markets. Here we look at the major *geographic, demographic, psychographic,* and *behavioral variables.*

---

[5]See Philip Kotler, *Kotler on Marketing* (New York: Free Press, 1999), pp. 149–50.

TABLE 7.1	Major Segmentation Variables for Consumer Markets

Geographic

World region or country Canada, Mexico	North America, Western Europe, Middle East, Pacific Rim, China, India,
Country region	Pacific, Mountain, West North Central, West South Central, East North Central, East South Central, South Atlantic, Middle Atlantic, New England
City or metro size	Under 5,000; 5,000–20,000; 20,000–50,000; 50,000–100,000; 100,000–250,000; 250,000–500,000; 500,000–1,000,000; 1,000,000–4,000,000; 4,000,000 or over
Density	Urban, suburban, rural
Climate	Northern, southern

Demographic

Age	Under 6, 6–11, 12–19, 20–34, 35–49, 50–64, 65+
Gender	Male, female
Family size	1–2, 3–4, 5+
Family life cycle	Young, single; young, married, no children; young, married with children; older, married with children; older, married, no children under 18; older, single; other
Income	Under $10,000; $10,000–$20,000; $20,000–$30,000; $30,000–$50,000; $50,000–$100,000; $100,000 and over
Occupation	Professional and technical; managers, officials, and proprietors; clerical, sales; craftspeople; supervisors; operatives; farmers; retired; students; homemakers; unemployed
Education	Grade school or less; some high school; high school graduate; some college; college graduate
Religion	Catholic, Protestant, Jewish, Muslim, Hindu, other
Race	Asian, Hispanic, Black, White
Generation	Baby boomer, Generation X, echo boomer
Nationality	North American, South American, British, French, German, Italian, Japanese

Psychographic

Social class	Lower lowers, upper lowers, working class, middle class, upper middles, lower uppers, upper uppers
Lifestyle	Achievers, strivers, strugglers
Personality	Compulsive, gregarious, authoritarian, ambitious

Behavioral

Occasions	Regular occasion, special occasion
Benefits	Quality, service, economy, convenience, speed
User status	Nonuser, ex-user, potential user, first-time user, regular user
Usage rate	Light user, medium user, heavy user
Loyalty status	None, medium, strong, absolute
Readiness stage	Unaware, aware, informed, interested, desirous, intending to buy
Attitude toward product	Enthusiastic, positive, indifferent, negative, hostile

Geographic segmentation: Home Depot is opening pint-size Villager's Hardware shops in smaller towns.

Geographic Segmentation

Geographic segmentation calls for dividing the market into different geographical units such as nations, regions, states, counties, cities, or neighborhoods. A company may decide to operate in one or a few geographical areas, or to operate in all areas but pay attention to geographical differences in needs and wants.

Many companies today are localizing their products, advertising, promotion, and sales efforts to fit the needs of individual regions, cities, and even neighborhoods. For example, Campbell sells Cajun gumbo soup in Louisiana and Mississippi and makes its nacho cheese soup spicier in Texas and California. P&G sells Ariel laundry detergent primarily in Los Angeles, San Diego, San Francisco, Miami, and south Texas—areas with larger concentrations of Hispanic consumers. In the South, where customers tend to arrive later in the day and stay longer, Starbucks offers more desserts and larger, more comfortable coffee shops.[6]

Other companies are seeking to cultivate as-yet untapped territory. For example, many large companies are fleeing the fiercely competitive major cities and suburbs to set up shop in small-town America. Hampton Inns has opened a chain of smaller-format motels in towns too small for its standard-size units. For example, Townsend, Tennessee, with a population of only 329, is small even by small-town standards. But looks can be deceiving. Situated on a heavily traveled and picturesque route between Knoxville and the Smoky Mountains, the village serves both business and vacation travelers. Hampton Inns opened a unit in Townsend and plans to open 100 more in small towns. It costs less to operate in these towns, and the company builds smaller units to match lower volume. The Townsend Hampton Inn, for example, has 54 rooms instead of the usual 135. Retailers from Home Depot to Saks Fifth Avenue are following suit. For example, Home Depot is testing four pint-size Villager's Hardware stores in New Jersey. Saks is implementing a new "Main Street" strategy, opening smaller stores in affluent suburbs and small towns that cannot support full-line Saks stores. Its new store in Greenwich, Connecticut, is less than one-third the size of regular stores found in malls and big cities.[7]

Demographic Segmentation

Demographic segmentation divides the market into groups based on variables such as age, gender, family size, family life cycle, income, occupation, education, religion, race, and nationality. Demographic factors are the most popular bases for segmenting customer groups. One reason is that consumer needs, wants, and usage rates often vary closely with demographic variables. Another is that demographic variables are easier to measure than most other types of variables. Even when market segments are first defined using other bases, such as benefits sought or behavior, their demographic characteristics must be known in order to assess the size of the target market and to reach it efficiently.

Age and Life-Cycle Stage.   Consumer needs and wants change with age. Some companies use **age and life-cycle segmentation,** offering different products or using different marketing approaches for different age and life-cycle groups. For example, McDonald's targets children, teens, adults, and seniors with different ads and media. Its ads to teens feature dance-beat music, adventure, and fast-paced cutting from scene to scene; ads to seniors are softer and more sentimental. Procter & Gamble

[6]Nelson D. Schwartz, "Still Perking After All These Years," *Fortune,* May 24, 1999, pp. 203–10.

[7]See Bruce Hager, "Podunk Is Beckoning," *Business Week,* December 2, 1991, p. 76; David Greisling, "The Boonies Are Booming," *Business Week,* October 9, 1995, pp. 104–10; Leah Nathans Spiro, "Saks Tries on a Petite," *Business Week,* October 7, 1997, p. 8; and Stephanie Anderson Forest, "Look Who's Thinking Small," *Business Week,* May 17, 1999, pp. 68–70.

boldly targets its Oil of Olay ProVital Series subbrand at women over 50 years of age. It's "specially designed to meet the increased moisturization needs of more mature skin."[8]

Sega, the computer games giant, which has typically focused on the teen market, is now targeting older customers. According to a Sega licensing executive, Sega's core market of 10- to 18-year-olds "sit in their bedrooms playing games for hours." Then, however, "they turn 18 and discover girls . . . and the computer gets locked away." To retain these young customers as they move into new life-cycle stages, Sega is launching a range of products for adults under its Sega Sports brand, including clothing, shoes, watches, and sports equipment such as Sega Sports–branded footballs and basketballs.[9]

Marketers must be careful to guard against stereotypes when using age and life-cycle segmentation. For example, although some 70-year-olds require wheelchairs, others play tennis. Similarly, whereas some 40-year-old couples are sending their children off to college, others are just beginning new families. Thus, age is often a poor predictor of a person's life cycle, health, work or family status, needs, and buying power. Companies marketing to mature consumers usually employ positive images and appeals. For example, ads for Oil of Olay ProVital feature attractive older spokeswomen and uplifting messages. "Many women 50 and older have told us that as they age, they feel more confident, wiser, and freer than ever before," observes Olay's marketing director. "These women are redefining beauty."[10]

Gender. **Gender segmentation** has long been used in clothing, cosmetics, toiletries, and magazines. For example, Procter & Gamble was among the first with Secret, a brand specially formulated for a woman's chemistry, packaged and advertised to reinforce the female image. Recently, other marketers have noticed opportunities for gender segmentation. For example, Merrill Lynch offers a *Financial Handbook for Women Investors* who want to "shape up their finances." Owens-Corning consciously aimed a major advertising campaign for home insulation at women after its study on women's role in home improvement showed that two-thirds were involved in materials installation, with 13 percent doing it themselves. Half the women surveyed compared themselves to Bob Vila, whereas less than half compared themselves to Martha Stewart.[11]

The automobile industry also uses gender segmentation extensively. Women buy half of all new cars sold in the United States and influence 80 percent of all new car purchasing decisions. "Selling to women should be no different than selling to men," notes one analyst. "But there are subtleties that make a difference." Women have different frames, less upper-body strength, and greater safety concerns. To address these issues, automakers are designing cars with hoods and trunks that are easier to open, seat belts that fit women better, and an increased emphasis on safety features. Male car designers at Cadillac now go about their work with paper clips on their fingers to simulate what it feels like to operate buttons, knobs, and other interior features with longer fingernails. The Cadillac Catera features an air-conditioned glove box to preserve such items as lipstick and film. Under the hood, yellow markings highlight where fluid fills go.[12]

A growing number of Web sites also target women. For example, the Girls On Network (www.girlson.com) appeals to 18- to 34-year-old women with hip, twenty somethings-style film, television, and book reviews and features. After only two years, this site has 100,000 members and averages 5 million page views per month. The leading women's online community, iVillage (www.iVillage.com), offers "real solutions for real women" and entreats visitors to "Join our community of smart, compassionate, real women." Various iVillage channels cover topics ranging from babies, food, fitness, pets, and relationships to careers, finance, and travel. The site now claims a membership of more than 1 million women across a broad demographic spectrum.[13]

Income. **Income segmentation** has long been used by the marketers of products and services such as automobiles, boats, clothing, cosmetics, financial services, and travel. Many companies target affluent consumers with luxury goods and convenience services. Stores such as Neiman Marcus pitch everything from expensive jewelry and fine fashions to glazed Australian apricots priced at $20 a

[8]Accessed online at www.olay.com/facecare/fcbodytips.htm, November 1999.

[9]"Sega to Target Adults with Brand Extensions," *Marketing Week,* March 12, 1998, p. 9.

[10]Pat Sloan and Jack Neff, "With Aging Baby Boomers in Mind, P&G, Den-Mat Plan Launches," *Advertising Age,* April 13, 1998, pp. 3, 38.

[11]Alice Z. Cuneo, "Advertisers Target Women, but Market Remains Elusive," *Advertising Age,* November 10, 1997, pp. 1, 24.

[12]See "Automakers Learn Better Roads to Women's Market," *Marketing News,* October 12, 1992, p. 2; Alan Alder, "Purchasing Power Women's Buying Muscle Shops Up in Car Design, Marketing," *Chicago Tribune,* September 29, 1996, p. 21A; Jean Halliday, "GM Taps Harris to Help Lure Women," *Advertising Age,* February 17, 1997, pp. 1, 37; and Mary Louis Quinlin, "Women: We've Come a Long Way, Maybe," *Advertising Age,* February 13, 1999, p. 46.

[13]"A Focus on Women at iVillage.com," *New York Times,* August 3, 1998, p. D6; Helene Stapinski, "Online Markets: You Go, Girls," *Sales & Marketing Management,* January 1999, pp. 47–48; and information accessed online at www.iVillage.com and www.girlson.com, February 2000.

Gender segmentation: A growing number of Web sites are targeting women, such as Oxygen Media's fresh and hip Girls On Web site for twentysomethings and iVillage, the leading women's online community.

pound. Prada's hot-selling black vinyl backpack sells for $450, and a front-row seat at a New York Knicks game at Madison Square Garden goes for $1,000.[14]

However, not all companies that use income segmentation target the affluent. Despite their lower spending power, the 25 percent of the nation's households that earn less that $25,000 per year offer an attractive market. For example, Greyhound Lines, with its inexpensive nationwide bus network, targets lower-income consumers. Almost half of its revenues come from people with annual incomes under $15,000. Many retailers also target this group, including chains such as Family Dollar, Dollar General, and Dollar Tree stores. When Family Dollar real estate experts scout locations for new stores, they look for lower-middle-class neighborhoods where people wear less expensive shoes and drive old cars that drip a lot of oil. The typical Family Dollar customer's household earns about $25,000 a year, and the average customer spends only about $8 per trip to the store. Yet the store's low-income strategy has made it one of the most profitable discount chains in the country.[15]

> video example

Take a moment to watch a group of managers discuss segmentation and targeting strategies.

Psychographic Segmentation

Psychographic segmentation divides buyers into different groups based on social class, lifestyle, or personality characteristics. People in the same demographic group can have very different psychographic makeups.

[14]See "The Wealthy," *Advertising Age,* April 3, 1995, p. S28; David Leonhardt, "Two-Tiered Marketing," *Business Week,* March 17, 1997, pp. 82–90; and Rebecca Piirto Heath, "Life on Easy Street," *American Demographics,* April 1997, pp. 33–37.

[15]Brian Bremner, "Looking Downscale Without Looking Down," *Business Week,* October 8, 1990, pp. 62–67; Cyndee Miller, "The Have-Nots: Firms with the Right Products and Services Succeed Among Low-Income Consumers," *Marketing News,* August 1, 1994, pp. 1, 2; Wendy Zellner, "Leave the Driving to Lentzsch," *Business Week,* March 18, 1996, pp. 66–67; and Anne Faircloth, "Value Retailers Go Dollar for Dollar," *Fortune,* July 6, 1998, pp. 164–66.

In chapter 5, we discussed how the products people buy reflect their *lifestyles*. As a result, marketers often segment their markets by consumer lifestyles. For example, Duck Head apparel targets a casual student lifestyle claiming, "You can't get them old until you get them new." One forward-looking grocery store found that segmenting its self-service meat products by lifestyle had a big payoff:

> Walk by the refrigerated self-service meat cases of most grocery stores and you'll usually find the offering grouped by type of meat. Pork is here, lamb is there, and chicken is over there. However, a Nashville, Tennessee, Kroger supermarket decided to experiment and offer groupings of different meats by lifestyle. For instance, the store had a section called "Meals in Minutes," one called "Cookin' Lite," another, filled with prepared products like hot dogs and ready-made hamburger patties, called "Kids Love This Stuff," and one called "I Like to Cook." By focusing on lifestyle needs and not on protein categories, Kroger's test store encouraged habitual beef and pork buyers to consider lamb and veal as well. As a result, the 16-foot service case has seen a substantial improvement in both sales and profits.[16]

Marketers also have used *personality* variables to segment markets. For example, the marketing campaign for Honda's Helix and Elite motor scooters *appears* to target hip and trendy 22-year-olds. But it is *actually* aimed at a much broader personality group. One ad, for example, shows a delighted child bouncing up and down on his bed while the announcer says, "You've been trying to get there all your life." The ad reminds viewers of the euphoric feelings they got when they broke away from authority and did things their parents told them not to do. It suggests that they can feel that way again by riding a Honda scooter. Thus, Honda is appealing to the rebellious, independent kid in all of us. As Honda notes on its Web page, "Fresh air, freedom, and flair—on a Honda scooter, every day is independence day!" In fact, more than half of Honda's scooter sales are to young professionals and older buyers—15 percent are purchased by the over-50 group.[17]

Behavioral Segmentation

Behavioral segmentation divides buyers into groups based on their knowledge, attitudes, uses, or responses to a product. Many marketers believe that behavior variables are the best starting point for building market segments.

Lifestyle segmentation: Duck Head targets a casual student lifestyle, claiming, "You can't get them old until you get them new."

HUNDREDS OF BORING LECTURES. A SUMMER FRAMING HOUSES. A FIGHT AT A REPLACE-MENTS CONCERT. 5 FAKE ID'S. BACKPACKING IN THE COHUTTAS. HELL WEEK. A STRING OF DEADBEAT ROOMMATES. ONE DULL POCKETKNIFE.

---

[16] "Lifestyle Marketing," *Progressive Grocer,* August 1997, pp. 107–10; and Philip Kotler, *Marketing Management: Analysis, Planning, Implementation, and Control,* 10th ed. (Upper Saddle River, NJ: Prentice Hall, 2000), pp. 266–67.

[17] See Laurie Freeman and Cleveland Horton, "Spree: Honda's Scooters Ride the Cutting Edge," *Advertising Age,* September 5, 1985, pp. 3, 35; "Scooter Wars," *Cycle World,* February 1998, p. 26; and Honda's Web site at www.hondamotorcycle.com/scooter, November 1999.

Occasions.   Buyers can be grouped according to occasions when they get the idea to buy, actually make their purchase, or use the purchased item. **Occasion segmentation** can help firms build up product usage. For example, orange juice is most often consumed at breakfast, but orange growers have promoted drinking orange juice as a cool and refreshing drink at other times of the day. In contrast, Coca-Cola's "Coke in the Morning" advertising campaign attempts to increase Coke consumption by promoting the beverage as an early morning pick-me-up. Some holidays, such as Mother's Day and Father's Day, were originally promoted partly to increase the sale of candy, flowers, cards, and other gifts. Many food marketers prepare special offers and ads for holiday occasions. For example, Beatrice Foods runs special Thanksgiving and Christmas ads for Reddi-wip during November and December, months that account for 30 percent of all whipped cream sales.

Kodak, Konica, Fuji, and other camera makers use occasion segmentation in designing and marketing their single-use cameras. By mixing lenses, film speeds, and accessories, they have developed special disposable cameras for about any picture-taking occasion, from underwater photography to taking baby pictures.

Standing on the edge of the Grand Canyon? Try Konica's Panoramic, which features a 17mm lens that takes in nearly 100 degrees horizontally. Going rafting, skiing, or snorkeling? You need Kodak's Max Sport, a rugged camera that can be used underwater to 14 feet. It has big knobs and buttons that let you use it with gloves. Want some pictures of the baby? Kodak offers a model equipped with a short focal-length lens and fast film requiring less light for parents who would like to take snapshots of their darlings without the disturbing flash. Need to check out your golf swing? Just point and shoot the QuickSnap Golf disposable camera, which snaps off eight frames per click showing how your body and club do during the swing. In one Japanese catalog aimed at young women, Kodak sells a package of five pastel-colored cameras, including a version with a fish-eye lens to create a rosy, romantic glow.[18]

[18]See Mark Maremont, "The Hottest Thing Since the Flashbulb," *Business Week,* September 7, 1992; Bruce Nussbaum, "A Camera in a Wet Suit," *Business Week,* June 2, 1997, p. 109; Dan Richards, "The Smartest Disposable Cameras," *Travel Holiday,* December 1998, p. 20; and "Point and Click," *Golf Magazine,* February 1999, p. 102.

Benefits Sought.   A powerful form of segmentation is to group buyers according to the different *benefits* that they seek from the product. **Benefit segmentation** requires finding the major benefits people look for in the product class, the kinds of people who look for each benefit, and the major brands that deliver each benefit. For example, one study of the benefits derived from travel uncovered three major market segments: those who travel to get away and be with family, those who travel for adventure or educational purposes, and people who enjoy the "gambling" and "fun" aspects of travel.[19]

One of the best examples of benefit segmentation was conducted in the toothpaste market (see Table 7.2). Research found four benefit segments: economic, medicinal, cosmetic, and taste. Each benefit group had special demographic, behavioral, and psychographic characteristics. For example, the people seeking to prevent decay tended to have large families, were heavy toothpaste users, and were conservative. Each segment also favored certain brands. Most current brands appeal to one of these segments. For example, Crest toothpaste stresses protection and appeals to the family segment, whereas Aim looks and tastes good and appeals to children.

User Status.   Markets can be segmented into groups of nonusers, ex-users, potential users, first-time users, and regular users of a product. For example, one study found that blood donors are low in self-esteem, low risk takers, and more highly concerned about their health; nondonors tend to be the opposite on all three dimensions. This suggests that social agencies should use different marketing approaches for keeping current donors and attracting new ones. A company's market position also influences its focus. Market share leaders focus on attracting potential users, whereas smaller firms focus on attracting current users away from the market leader.

Usage Rate.   Markets can also be segmented into light, medium, and heavy product users. Heavy users are often a small percentage of the market but account for a high percentage of total consumption. Marketers usually prefer to attract one heavy user to their product or service rather than several light users. For example, a recent study of U.S.-branded ice cream buyers showed that heavy users make up only 18 percent of all buyers but consume 55 percent of all the ice cream sold. On average, these heavy users pack away 13 gallons of ice cream per year versus only 2.4 gallons for light users. Similarly, a travel industry study showed that frequent users of travel agents for vacation travel are more involved, more innovative, more knowledgeable, and more likely to be opinion leaders than less frequent users. Heavy users take more trips and gather more information about

TABLE 7.2	Benefit Segmentation of the Toothpaste Market			
Benefit Segments	**Demographics**	**Behavior**	**Psychographics**	**Favored Brands**
Economic (low price)	Men	Heavy users	High autonomy, value oriented	Brands on sale
Medicinal (decay prevention)	Large families	Heavy users	Hypochondriacal, conservative	Crest
Cosmetic (bright teeth)	Teens, young adults	Smokers	High sociability, active	Aqua-Fresh, Ultra Brite
Taste (good tasting)	Children	Spearmint lovers	High self-involvement hedonistic	Colgate, Aim

Source: Adapted from Russell J. Haley, "Benefit Segmentation: A Decision-Oriented Research Tool," *Journal of Marketing,* July 1968, pp. 30–35. Also see Haley, "Benefit Segmentation: Backwards and Forwards," *Journal of Advertising Research,* February–March 1984, pp. 19–25; and Haley, "Benefit Segmentation—20 Years Later," *Journal of Consumer Marketing* Vol. 1, 1984, pp. 5–14.

[19]Stowe Shoemaker, "Segmenting the U.S. Travel Market According to Benefits Realized," *Journal of Travel Research,* Winter 1994, pp. 8–21.

vacation travel from newspapers, magazines, books, and travel shows. Clearly, a travel agency would benefit by directing its marketing efforts toward heavy users, perhaps using telemarketing and special promotions.[20]

Loyalty Status. A market can also be segmented by consumer loyalty. Consumers can be loyal to brands (Tide), stores (Wal-Mart), and companies (Ford). Buyers can be divided into groups according to their degree of loyalty. Some consumers are completely loyal—they buy one brand all the time. Others are somewhat loyal—they are loyal to two or three brands of a given product or favor one brand while sometimes buying others. Still other buyers show no loyalty to any brand. They either want something different each time they buy or they buy whatever's on sale.

A company can learn a lot by analyzing loyalty patterns in its market. It should start by studying its own loyal customers. Suppose Colgate finds that its loyal toothpaste buyers are more middle class, have larger families, and are more health conscious. These characteristics pinpoint the target market for Colgate. By studying its less loyal buyers, the company can detect which brands are most competitive with its own. If many Colgate buyers also buy Crest, Colgate can attempt to improve its positioning against Crest, possibly by using direct-comparison advertising. By looking at customers who are shifting away from its brand, the company can learn about its marketing weaknesses. As for nonloyals, the company may attract them by putting its brand on sale.

Using Multiple Segmentation Bases

Marketers rarely limit their segmentation analysis to only one or a few variables. Rather, they are increasingly using multiple segmentation bases in an effort to identify smaller, better-defined target groups. Thus, a bank may not only identify a group of wealthy retired adults but also, within that group, distinguish several segments depending on their current income, assets, savings and risk preferences, and lifestyles.

Companies often begin by segmenting their markets using a single base, then expand using other bases. Consider PageNet, the paging services provider, which found itself competing against communications giants such as Southwestern Bell and Pacific Telesis in the pager market:

> PageNet couldn't boast unique technology. Moreover, it was already competing on price, charging about 20 percent less than competitors. Instead, PageNet used smart segmentation to boost its competitive advantage. At first, it used geographic segmentation, targeting markets in Ohio and its home state of Texas where local competitors were vulnerable to PageNet's aggressive pricing. Once these markets were secure, the company targeted new geographical segments that promised the best growth potential. But PageNet's segmenting strategy didn't end with geography. The company next profiled major paging service user groups and targeted the most promising ones, such as salespeople, messengers, and service people. Flush with success, PageNet next used lifestyle segmentation to target additional consumer groups, such as parents who leave their babies with sitters, commuters who are out of reach while traveling to and from work, and elderly people living alone whose families want to keep an eye on them. The results of this multiple segmentation strategy: PageNet's subscriber base has expanded at a rate of 50 percent annually over the past 10 years. Now, with 10 million subscribers and sales approaching $1 billion, PageNet is the nation's largest wireless messaging and information services company.[21]

One of the most promising developments in multivariable segmentation is "geodemographic" segmentation. Several business information services have arisen to help marketing planners link U.S. Census data with lifestyle patterns to better segment their markets down to zip codes, neighborhoods, and even city blocks.

---

[20]See Ronald E. Goldsmith, Leisa Reinecke, and Mark Bonn, "An Empirical Study of Heavy Users of Travel Agencies," *Journal of Travel Research,* Summer 1994, pp. 38–43; and Warren Thayer, "Target Heavy Buyers!" *Frozen Food Age,* March 1998, pp. 22–24.

[21]Norton Paley, "Cut Out for Success," *Sales & Marketing Management,* April 1994, pp. 43–44; Erick Schonfeld, "Paging Investors for a Smart Call," *Fortune,* January 15, 1996, p. 117; Michael J. Himowitz, "A Pager That Talks," *Fortune,* May 11, 1998, pp. 168–70; Joe Strupp, "Bloomberg Puts Stock in PageNet," *Editor & Publisher,* May 22, 1999, p. 16; and information from www.pagenet.com, November 1999.

SEGMENTING BUSINESS MARKETS

Consumer and business marketers use many of the same variables to segment their markets. Business buyers can be segmented geographically, demographically (industry, company size), or by benefits sought, user status, usage rate, and loyalty status. Yet, as Table 7.3 shows, business marketers also use some additional variables, such as customer *operating characteristics, purchasing approaches, situational factors,* and *personal characteristics.* The table lists major questions that business marketers should ask in determining which customers they want to serve.

By going after segments instead of the whole market, companies have a much better chance to deliver value to consumers and to receive maximum rewards for close attention to consumer needs. Thus, Hewlett-Packard's Computer Systems Division targets specific industries that promise the best growth prospects, such as telecommunications and financial services. Its "red team" sales force specializes in developing and serving major customers in these targeted industries.[22] Within the chosen industry, a company can further segment by *customer size* or *geographic location.* For example, Hewlett-Packard's "blue team" telemarkets to smaller accounts and to those that don't fit neatly into the strategically targeted industries on which HP focuses.

A company might also set up separate systems for dealing with larger or multiple-location customers. For example, Steelcase, a major producer of office furniture, first segments customers into 10 industries, including banking, insurance, and electronics. Next, company salespeople work with independent Steelcase dealers to handle smaller, local, or regional Steelcase customers in each segment. But many national, multiple-location customers, such as Exxon or IBM, have special needs that may reach beyond the scope of individual dealers. So Steelcase uses national accounts managers to help its dealer networks handle its national accounts.

Within a given target industry and customer size, the company can segment by purchase approaches and criteria. As in consumer segmentation, many marketers believe that buying behavior and *benefits* provide the best basis for segmenting business markets.[23]

SEGMENTING INTERNATIONAL MARKETS

Few companies have either the resources or the will to operate in all, or even most, of the countries that dot the globe. Although some large companies, such as Coca-Cola or Sony, sell products in as many as 200 countries, most international firms focus on a smaller set. Operating in many countries presents new challenges. Different countries, even those that are close together, can vary dramatically in their economic, cultural, and political makeup. Thus, just as they do within their domestic markets, international firms need to group their world markets into segments with distinct buying needs and behaviors.

Companies can segment international markets using one or a combination of several variables. They can segment by *geographic location,* grouping countries by regions such as Western Europe, the Pacific Rim, the Middle East, or Africa. Geographic segmentation assumes that nations close to one another will have many common traits and behaviors. Although this is often the case, there are many exceptions. For example, although the United States and Canada have much in common, both differ culturally and economically from neighboring Mexico. Even within a region, consumers can differ widely. For example, many U.S. marketers think that all Central and South American countries are the same, including their 400 million inhabitants. However, the Dominican Republic is no more like Brazil than Italy is like Sweden. Many Latin Americans don't speak Spanish, including 140 million

---

[22]Daniel S. Levine, "Justice Served," *Sales & Marketing Management,* May 1995, pp. 53–61.

[23]For more on segmenting business markets, see John Berrigan and Carl Finkbeiner, *Segmentation Marketing: New Methods for Capturing Business* (New York: HarperBusiness, 1992); Rodney L. Griffith and Louis G. Pol, "Segmenting Industrial Markets," *Industrial Marketing Management* no. 23, 1994, pp. 39–46; Stavros P. Kalafatis and Vicki Cheston, "Normative Models and Practical Applications of Segmentation in Business Markets," *Industrial Marketing Management,* November 1997, pp. 519–30; and James C. Anderson and James A. Narus, *Business Market Management* (Upper Saddle River, NJ: Prentice Hall, 1999), pp. 44–47.

TABLE 7.3	Major Segmentation Variables for Business Markets

Demographics

Industry: Which industries that buy this product should we focus on?

Company size: What size companies should we focus on?

Location: What geographical areas should we focus on?

Operating Variables

Technology: What customer technologies should we focus on?

User–nonuser status: Should we focus on heavy, medium, or light users or nonusers?

Customer capabilities: Should we focus on customers needing many services or few services?

Purchasing Approaches

Purchasing function organization: Should we focus on companies with highly centralized or decentralized purchasing?

Power structure: Should we focus on companies that are engineering dominated, financially dominated, or marketing dominated?

Nature of existing relationships: Should we focus on companies with which we already have strong relationships or simply go after the most desirable companies?

General purchase policies: Should we focus on companies that prefer leasing? Service contracts? Systems purchases? Sealed bidding?

Purchasing criteria: Should we focus on companies that are seeking quality? Service? Price?

Situational Factors

Urgency: Should we focus on companies that need quick delivery or service?

Specific application: Should we focus on certain applications of our product rather than all applications?

Size of order: Should we focus on large or small orders?

Personal Characteristics

Buyer–seller similarity: Should we focus on companies whose people and values are similar to ours?

Attitudes toward risk: Should we focus on risk-taking or risk-avoiding customers?

Loyalty: Should we focus on companies that show high loyalty to their suppliers?

Source: Adapted from Thomas V. Bonoma and Benson P. Shapiro, *Segmenting the Industrial Market* (Lexington, MA: Lexington Books, 1983). Also see John Berrigan and Carl Finkbeiner, *Segmentation Marketing: New Methods for Capturing Business* (New York: HarperBusiness, 1992).

Portuguese-speaking Brazilians and the millions in other countries who speak a variety of Indian dialects.

World markets can also be segmented on the basis of economic factors. For example, countries might be grouped by population income levels or by their overall level of economic development.[24] Some countries, such as the United States, Britain, France, Germany, Japan, Canada, Italy, and Russia, have established, highly industrialized economies. Other countries have newly industrialized or developing economies (Singapore, Taiwan, Korea, Brazil, Mexico). Still others are less developed

[24]For example, see Philemon Oyewole, "Country Segmentation of the International Market Using ICP-Based Consumption Patterns," *Journal of Global Marketing,* 11, no. 4, 1998, pp. 75–94.

(China, India). A company's economic structure shapes its population's product and service needs and, therefore, the marketing opportunities it offers.

Countries can be segmented by political and legal factors such as the type and stability of government, receptivity to foreign firms, monetary regulations, and the amount of bureaucracy. Such factors can play a crucial role in a company's choice of which countries to enter and how. *Cultural factors* can also be used, grouping markets according to common languages, religions, values and attitudes, customs, and behavioral patterns.

Segmenting international markets on the basis of geographic, economic, political, cultural, and other factors assumes that segments should consist of clusters of countries. However, many companies use a different approach called **intermarket segmentation**. Using this approach, they form segments of consumers who have similar needs and buying behavior even though they are located in different countries. For example, Mercedes-Benz targets the world's well-to-do, regardless of their country. MTV targets the world's teenagers. One study of more than 6,500 teenagers from 26 countries showed that teens around the world live surprisingly parallel lives. As one expert notes, "From Rio to Rochester, teens can be found enmeshed in much the same regimen: . . . drinking Coke, . . . dining on Big Macs, and surfin' the Net on their computers."[25] The world's teens have a lot *in common:* They study, shop, and sleep. They are exposed to many of the same major issues: love, crime, homelessness, ecology, and working parents. In many ways, they have more in common with each other than with their parents. MTV bridges the gap between cultures, appealing to what teens around the world have in common.[26]

REQUIREMENTS FOR EFFECTIVE SEGMENTATION

Clearly, there are many ways to segment a market, but not all segmentations are effective. For example, buyers of table salt could be divided into blond and brunette customers. But hair color obviously does not affect the purchase of salt. Furthermore, if all salt buyers bought the same amount of salt each month, believed that all salt is the same, and wanted to pay the same price, the company would not benefit from segmenting this market.

To be useful, market segments must be:

- *Measurable:* The size, purchasing power, and profiles of the segments can be measured. Certain segmentation variables are difficult to measure. For example, there are 32.5 million left-handed people in the United States—almost equaling the entire population of Canada. Yet few products are targeted toward this left-handed segment. The major problem may be that the segment is hard to identify and measure. There are no data on the demographics of lefties, and the U.S. Census Bureau does not keep track of left-handedness in its surveys. Private data companies keep reams of statistics on other demographic segments but not on left-handers.

- *Accessible:* The market segments can be effectively reached and served. Suppose a fragrance company finds that heavy users of its brand are single men and women who stay out late and socialize a lot. Unless this group lives or shops at certain places and is exposed to certain media, its members will be difficult to reach.

- *Substantial:* The market segments are large or profitable enough to serve. A segment should be the largest possible homogenous group worth pursuing with a tailored marketing program. It would not pay, for example, for an automobile manufacturer to develop cars for persons whose height is under four feet.

- *Differentiable:* The segments are conceptually distinguishable and respond differently to different marketing mix elements and programs. If married and unmarried women respond similarly to a sale on perfume, they do not constitute separate segments.

- *Actionable:* Effective programs can be designed for attracting and serving the segments. For example, although one small airline identified seven market segments, its staff was too small to develop separate marketing programs for each segment.

active concept check

Now let's take a moment to test your knowledge of what you've just read.

[25]Cyndee Miller, "Teens Seen as the First Truly Global Consumers," *Advertising Age,* March 27, 1995, p. 9.

[26]Shawn Tully, "Teens: The Most Global Market of All," *Fortune,* May 16, 1994, pp. 90–97. Also see Matthew Klein, "Teen Green," *American Demographics,* February 1998, p. 39.

Market segmentation reveals the firm's market segment opportunities. The firm now has to evaluate the various segments and decide how many and which ones to target. We now look at how companies evaluate and select target segments.

EVALUATING MARKET SEGMENTS

In evaluating different market segments, a firm must look at three factors: segment size and growth, segment structural attractiveness, and company objectives and resources. The company must first collect and analyze data on current segment sales, growth rates, and expected profitability for various segments. It will be interested in segments that have the right size and growth characteristics. But are not always the most attractive ones for every company. Smaller companies may lack the skills and resources needed to serve the larger segments or may find these segments too competitive. Such companies may select segments that are smaller and less attractive, in an absolute sense, but that are potentially more profitable for them.

The company also needs to examine major structural factors that affect long-run segment attractiveness.[27] For example, a segment is less attractive if it already contains many strong and aggressive *competitors*. The existence of many actual or potential *substitute products* may limit prices and the profits that can be earned in a segment. The relative *power of buyers* also affects segment attractiveness. Buyers with strong bargaining power relative to sellers will try to force prices down, demand more services, and set competitors against one another—all at the expense of seller profitability. Finally, a segment may be less attractive if it contains *powerful suppliers* who can control prices or reduce the quality or quantity of ordered goods and services.

Even if a segment has the right size and growth and is structurally attractive, the company must consider its own objectives and resources in relation to that segment. Some attractive segments could be dismissed quickly because they do not mesh with the company's long-run objectives. Even if a segment fits the company's objectives, the company must consider whether it possesses the skills and resources it needs to succeed in that segment. If the company lacks the strengths needed to compete successfully in a segment and cannot readily obtain them, it should not enter the segment. Even if the company possesses the *required* strengths, it needs to employ skills and resources *superior* to those of the competition in order to really win in a market segment. The company should enter only segments in which it can offer superior value and gain advantages over competitors.

SELECTING MARKET SEGMENTS

After evaluating different segments, the company must now decide which and how many segments to serve. This is the problem of *target market selection*. A **target market** consists of a set of buyers who share common needs or characteristics that the company decides to serve. Figure 7.3 shows that the firm can adopt one of three market-coverage strategies: *undifferentiated marketing, differentiated marketing,* and *concentrated marketing.*

Undifferentiated Marketing

Using an **undifferentiated marketing** (or mass-marketing) strategy, a firm might decide to ignore market segment differences and go after the whole market with one offer. This mass-marketing strategy focuses on what is *common* in the needs of consumers rather than on what is *different*. The company designs a product and a marketing program that will appeal to the largest number of buyers. It relies on mass distribution and mass advertising, and it aims to give the product a superior image in people's minds. As noted earlier in the chapter, most modern marketers have strong doubts about this strategy. Difficulties arise in developing a product or brand that will satisfy all consumers. Moreover, mass marketers often have trouble competing with more focused firms that do a better job of satisfying the need of specific segments and niches.

Differentiated Marketing

Using a **differentiated marketing** strategy, a firm decides to target several market segments or niches and designs separate offers for each. General Motors tries to produce a car for every "purse, purpose, and personality." Nike offers athletic shoes for a dozen or more different sports, from running, fenc-

---

[27]See Michael Porter, *Competitive Advantage* (New York: Free Press, 1985), pp. 4–8, 234–36.

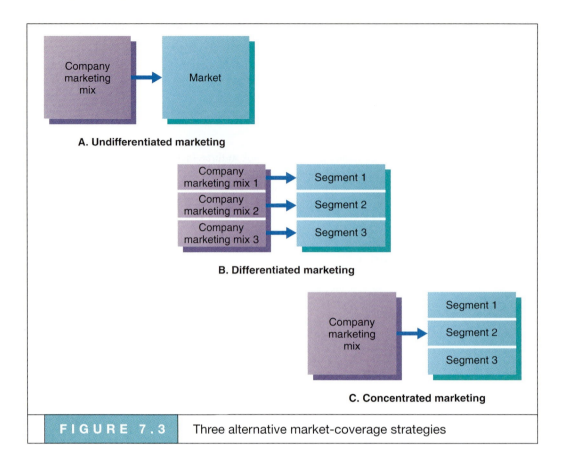

A. Undifferentiated marketing

B. Differentiated marketing

C. Concentrated marketing

| FIGURE 7.3 | Three alternative market-coverage strategies |

ing, and aerobics to bicycling and baseball. Estée Lauder offers dozens of different products aimed at carefully defined niches:

> The four best-selling prestige perfumes in the United States belong to Estée Lauder. So do seven of the top ten prestige makeup products and eight of the ten best-selling prestige skin care products. Estée Lauder is an expert in creating differentiated brands that serve the tastes of different market segments. There's the original Estée Lauder brand, which appeals to older, junior league types. Then there's Clinique, perfect for the middle-aged mom with a GMC Suburban and no time to waste. Then there's the hip M.A.C. line, which boasts as its spokesmodel RuPaul, a 6-foot, 7-inch drag queen. For the New Age type, there's upscale Aveda, with its aromatherapy line and earthy Origins, which the company expects will become a $1 billion brand. The company even offers downscale brands, such as Jane by Sassaby, for teens at Wal-Mart and Rite Aid.[28]

By offering product and marketing variations, these companies hope for higher sales and a stronger position within each market segment. Developing a stronger position within several segments creates more total sales than undifferentiated marketing across all segments. Procter & Gamble gets more total market share with eight brands of laundry detergent than it could with only one. But differentiated marketing also increases the costs of doing business. A firm usually finds it more expensive to develop and produce, say, 10 units of 10 different products than 100 units of one product. Developing separate marketing plans for the separate segments requires extra marketing research, forecasting, sales analysis, promotion planning, and channel management. Trying to reach different market segments with different advertising increases promotion costs. Thus, the company must weigh increased sales against increased costs when deciding on a differentiated marketing strategy.

Concentrated Marketing

A third market-coverage strategy, **concentrated marketing,** is especially appealing when company resources are limited. Instead of going after a small share of a large market, the firm goes after a large share of one or a few segments or niches. For example, Oshkosh Truck is the world's largest producer

[28]Nina Munk, "Why Women Find Lauder Mesmerizing," *Fortune,* May 25, 1998, pp. 97–106.

Concentrated marketing: Oshkosh Truck has found its niche as the world's largest producer of airport rescue trucks and front-loading concrete mixers.

of airport rescue trucks and front-loading concrete mixers. Tetra sells 80 percent of the world's tropical fish food, and Steiner Optical captures 80 percent of the world's military binoculars market.

Today, the low cost of setting up shop on the Internet makes it even more profitable to serve seemingly minuscule niches. Small businesses, in particular, are realizing riches from serving small niches on the Web. Here are two "Webpreneurs" who achieved astonishing results:[29]

Ostrichesonline.com. Whereas Internet giants like music retailer CDnow and bookseller Amazon.com have yet to even realize a profit, Steve Warrington is earning a six-figure income online selling ostriches and every product derived from them (www.ostrichesonline.com). Launched for next to nothing on the Web, Warrington's business generated $4 million in sales last year. The site tells visitors everything they ever wanted to know about ostriches and much, much more—it supplies ostrich facts, ostrich pictures, an ostrich farm index, and a huge ostrich database and reference index. Visitors to the site can buy ostrich meat, feathers, leather jackets, videos, eggshells, and skin care products derived from ostrich body oil.

Mesomorphosis.com. At the age of 26, Millard Baker, a clinical psychology graduate student at the University of South Florida, launched a Web-based business selling body building supplements and oils (www.mesomorphosis.com). Although other Web sites peddled similar products, few offered articles and content, so Millard Baker added these elements to his site. Mesomorphosis.com has now grown into a full-fledged Internet publication as well as an online store. It provides subscribers with "scientifically-based articles about body building so that [they] can make informed decisions about training, nutrition, and supplementation." How successful is this Web nicher? Baker now pulls in more than $25,000 a month.

Concentrated marketing provides an excellent way for small new businesses to get a foothold against larger, more resourceful competitors. For example, Southwest Airlines began by concentrating on serving intrastate, no-frills commuters. PageNet got off to a successful start by concentrating on

[29]Paul Davidson, "Entrepreneurs Reap Riches from Net Niches," *USA Today,* April 20, 1998, p. B3; and information accessed online from www.ostrichesonline.com and www.mesomorphosis. com, February 2000.

limited geographic areas. Wal-Mart got its start by bringing everyday low prices to small town and rural areas.

Through concentrated marketing, firms achieve strong market positions in the segments or niches they serve because of their greater knowledge of the segments' needs and the special reputations they acquire. They also enjoy many operating economies because of specialization in production, distribution, and promotion. If the segment is well chosen, firms can earn a high rate of return on their investments.

At the same time, concentrated marketing involves higher-than-normal risks. The particular market segment can turn sour. Or larger competitors may decide to enter the same segment. For example, California Cooler's success in the wine cooler segment attracted many large competitors, causing the original owners to sell to a larger company that had more marketing resources. For these reasons, many companies prefer to diversify in several market segments.

Choosing a Market-Coverage Strategy

Many factors need to be considered when choosing a market-coverage strategy. Which strategy is best depends on *company resources*. When the firm's resources are limited, concentrated marketing makes the most sense. The best strategy also depends on the degree of *product variability*. Undifferentiated marketing is more suited for uniform products such as grapefruit or steel. Products that can vary in design, such as cameras and automobiles, are more suited to differentiation or concentration. The *product's life-cycle stage* also must be considered.

When a firm introduces a new product, it is practical to launch only one version, and undifferentiated marketing or concentrated marketing makes the most sense. In the mature stage of the product life cycle, however, differentiated marketing begins to make more sense. Another factor is *market variability*. If most buyers have the same tastes, buy the same amounts, and react the same way to marketing efforts, undifferentiated marketing is appropriate. Finally, *competitors' marketing strategies* are important. When competitors use differentiated or concentrated marketing, undifferentiated marketing can be suicidal. Conversely, when competitors use undifferentiated marketing, a firm can gain an advantage by using differentiated or concentrated marketing.

active example <

Consider some issues raised by the practice of ethnic segmentation.

SOCIALLY RESPONSIBLE TARGET MARKETING

Smart targeting helps companies to be more efficient and effective by focusing on the segments that they can satisfy best and most profitably. Targeting also benefits consumers—companies reach specific groups of consumers with offers carefully tailored to satisfy their needs. However, target marketing sometimes generates controversy and concern. Issues usually involve the targeting of vulnerable or disadvantaged consumers with controversial or potentially harmful products.

For example, over the years, the cereal industry has been heavily criticized for its marketing efforts directed toward children. Critics worry that premium offers and high-powered advertising appeals presented through the mouths of lovable animated characters will overwhelm children's defenses. The marketers of toys and other children's products have been similarly battered, often with good justification. Some critics have even called for a complete ban on advertising to children. To encourage responsible advertising to children, the Children's Advertising Review Unit, the advertising industry's self-regulatory agency, has published extensive children's advertising guidelines that recognize the special needs of child audiences.

Cigarette, beer, and fast-food marketers have also generated much controversy in recent years by their attempts to target inner-city minority consumers. For example, McDonald's and other chains have drawn criticism for pitching their high-fat, salt-laden fare to low-income, inner-city residents who are much more likely than suburbanites to be heavy consumers. R.J. Reynolds took heavy flak in the early 1990s when it announced plans to market Uptown, a menthol cigarette targeted toward low-income blacks. It quickly dropped the brand in the face of a loud public outcry and heavy pressure from black leaders. G. Heileman Brewing made a similar mistake with PowerMaster, a potent malt liquor. Because malt liquor had become the drink of choice among many in the inner city, Heileman focused its marketing efforts for PowerMaster on inner-city blacks. However, this group suffers disproportionately from liver diseases brought on by alcohol, and the inner city is already plagued by alcohol-related problems such as crime and violence. Thus, Heileman's targeting decision drew substantial criticism.[30]

The meteoric growth of the Internet and other carefully targeted direct media has raised fresh concerns about potential targeting abuses. The Internet allows increasing refinement of audiences and, in turn, more precise targeting. This might help makers of questionable products or deceptive advertisers to more readily victimize the most vulnerable audiences. As one expert observes, "In theory, an audience member could have tailor-made deceptive messages sent directly to his or her computer screen."[31]

Not all attempts to target children, minorities, or other special segments draw such criticism. In fact, most provide benefits to targeted consumers. For example, Colgate-Palmolive's Colgate Junior toothpaste has special features designed to get children to brush longer and more often—it's less foamy, has a milder taste, contains sparkles, and exits the tube in a star-shaped column.

Golden Ribbon Playthings has developed a highly acclaimed and very successful black character doll named "Huggy Bean" targeted toward minority consumers. Huggy comes with books and toys that connect her with her African heritage. Many cosmetics companies have responded to the special needs of minority segments by adding products specifically designed for African American, Hispanic, or Asian women. Black-owned ICE theaters noticed that although moviegoing by blacks has surged, there are few inner-city theaters. The chain has opened a theater in Chicago's South Side as well as two other Chicago theaters, and it plans to open in four more cities this year. ICE partners with the black communities in which it operates theaters, using local radio stations to promote films and featuring favorite food items at concession stands.[32]

Thus, in market targeting, the issue is not really who is targeted but rather *how* and for *what*. Controversies arise when marketers attempt to profit at the expense of targeted segments—when they unfairly target vulnerable segments or target them with questionable products or tactics. Socially responsible marketing calls for segmentation and targeting that serve not just the interests of the company but also the interests of those targeted.

> active exercise

Take a moment to consider the impact of technology on market segmentation.

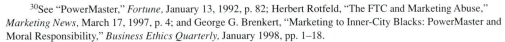

> active poll

Take a moment to give your opinion on a question concerning target marketing.

> active concept check

Now let's take a moment to test your knowledge of what you've just read.

---

[30]See "PowerMaster," *Fortune,* January 13, 1992, p. 82; Herbert Rotfeld, "The FTC and Marketing Abuse," *Marketing News,* March 17, 1997, p. 4; and George G. Brenkert, "Marketing to Inner-City Blacks: PowerMaster and Moral Responsibility," *Business Ethics Quarterly,* January 1998, pp. 1–18.

[31]Joseph Turow, "Breaking Up America: The Dark Side of Target Marketing," *American Demographics,* November 1997, pp. 51–54.

[32]Roger O. Crockett, "They're Lining Up for Flicks in the 'Hood," *Business Week,* June 8, 1998, pp. 75–76.

Once a company has decided which segments of the market it will enter, it must decide what positions it wants to occupy in those segments. A **product's position** is the way the product is *defined by consumers* on important attributes—the place the product occupies in consumers' minds relative to competing products. Positioning involves implanting the brand's unique benefits and differentiation in customers' minds. Thus, Tide is positioned as a powerful, all-purpose family detergent; Ivory Snow is positioned as the gentle detergent for fine washables and baby clothes. In the automobile market, Toyota Tercel and Subaru are positioned on economy, Mercedes and Cadillac on luxury, and Porsche and BMW on performance. Volvo positions powerfully on safety.

Consumers are overloaded with information about products and services. They cannot reevaluate products every time they make a buying decision. To simplify the buying process, consumers organize products into categories—they "position" products, services, and companies in their minds. A product's position is the complex set of perceptions, impressions, and feelings that consumers have for the product compared with competing products. Consumers position products with or without the help of marketers. But marketers do not want to leave their products' positions to chance. They must *plan* positions that will give their products the greatest advantage in selected target markets, and they must design marketing mixes to create these planned positions.

CHOOSING A POSITIONING STRATEGY

Some firms find it easy to choose their positioning strategy. For example, a firm well known for quality in certain segments will go for this position in a new segment if there are enough buyers seeking quality. But in many cases, two or more firms will go after the same position. Then, each will have to find other ways to set itself apart. Each firm must differentiate its offer by building a unique bundle of benefits that appeals to a substantial group within the segment.

The positioning task consists of three steps: identifying a set of possible competitive advantages upon which to build a position, choosing the right competitive advantages, and selecting an overall positioning strategy. The company must then effectively communicate and deliver the chosen position to the market.

Identifying Possible Competitive Advantages

The key to winning and keeping customers is to understand their needs and buying processes better than competitors do and to deliver more value. To the extent that a company can position itself as providing superior value to selected target markets it gains **competitive advantage.** But solid positions cannot be built on empty promises. If a company positions its product as *offering* the best quality and service, it must then *deliver* the promised quality and service. Thus, positioning begins with actually *differentiating* the company's marketing offer so that it will give consumers more value than competitors' offers do.

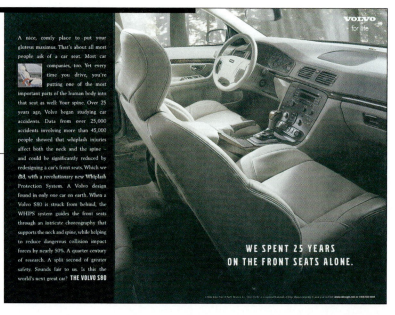

Competitive advantages: Volvo positions powerfully on safety: All most people want from a car seat is "a nice, comfy place to put your gluteus maximus." However, when a Volvo is struck from behind, a sophisticated system "guides the front seats through an intricate choreography that supports the neck and spine, while helping to reduce dangerous collision impact forces."

To find points of differentiation, marketers must think through the customer's entire experience with the company's product or service. An alert company can find ways to differentiate itself at every point where it comes in contact with customers.[33] In what specific ways can a company differentiate its offer from those of competitors? A company or market offer can be differentiated along the lines of *product, services, channels, people,* or *image.*

Product differentiation takes place along a continuum. At one extreme we find physical products that allow little variation: chicken, steel, aspirin. Yet even here some meaningful differentiation is possible. For example, Perdue claims that its branded chickens are better—fresher and more tender— and gets a 10 percent price premium based on this differentiation. At the other extreme are products that can be highly differentiated, such as automobiles, commercial machinery, and furniture. Such products can be differentiated on features, performance, or style and design. Thus, Volvo provides new and better safety features; Whirlpool designs its dishwasher to run more quietly; Bose speakers are positioned on striking design characteristics. Similarly, companies can differentiate their products on such attributes as *consistency, durability, reliability,* or *repairability.*

Beyond differentiating its physical product, a firm can also differentiate the services that accompany the product. Some companies gain *services differentiation* through speedy, convenient, or careful *delivery.* For example, BancOne has opened full-service branches in supermarkets to provide location convenience along with Saturday, Sunday, and weekday-evening hours. *Installation* can also differentiate one company from another, as can *repair* services. Many an automobile buyer will gladly pay a little more and travel a little farther to buy a car from a dealer that provides top-notch repair service. Some companies differentiate their offers by providing *customer training service* or *consulting services*—data, information systems, and advising services that buyers need. For example, McKesson Corporation, a major drug wholesaler, consults with its 12,000 independent pharmacists to help them set up accounting, inventory, and computerized ordering systems. By helping its customers compete better, McKesson gains greater customer loyalty and sales.

Firms that practice *channel differentiation* gain competitive advantage through the way they design their channel's coverage, expertise, and performance. Caterpillar's success in the construction-equipment industry is based on superior channels. Its dealers worldwide are renowned for their top-notch service. Dell Computer and Avon distinguish themselves by their high-quality direct channels. Iams pet food achieves success by going against tradition, distributing its products only through veterinarians and pet stores.

Companies can gain a strong competitive advantage through *people differentiation*—hiring and training better people than their competitors do. Thus, Disney people are known to be friendly and upbeat. Singapore Airlines enjoys an excellent reputation largely because of the grace of its flight attendants. IBM offers people who make sure that the solution customers want is the solution they get: "People Who Think. People Who Do. People Who Get It." People differentiation requires that a company select its customer-contact people carefully and train them well. For example, Disney trains its theme park people thoroughly to ensure that they are competent, courteous, and friendly. From the hotel check-in agents, to the monorail drivers, to the ride attendants, to the people who sweep Main Street USA, each employee understands the importance of understanding customers, communicating with them clearly and cheerfully, and responding quickly to their requests and problems. Each is carefully trained to "make a dream come true."

Even when competing offers look the same, buyers may perceive a difference based on company or brand *image differentiation.* A company or brand image should convey the product's distinctive benefits and positioning. Developing a strong and distinctive image calls for creativity and hard work. A company cannot plant an image in the public's mind overnight using only a few advertisements. If Ritz-Carlton means quality, this image must be supported by everything the company says and does. *Symbols*—such as McDonald's golden arches, the Prudential rock, or the Pillsbury doughboy—can provide strong company or brand recognition and image differentiation. The company might build a brand around a famous person, as Nike did with its Air Jordan basketball shoes. Some companies even become associated with colors, such as IBM (blue), Campbell (red and white), or Kodak (red and yellow). The chosen symbols, characters, and other image elements must be communicated through advertising that conveys the company's or brand's personality.

Choosing the Right Competitive Advantages

Suppose a company is fortunate enough to discover several potential competitive advantages. It now must choose the ones on which it will build its positioning strategy. It must decide *how many* differences to promote and *which ones.*

---

[33]For an interesting discussion of finding ways to differentiate marketing offers, see Ian C. MacMillan and Rita Gunther McGrath, "Discovering New Points of Differentiation," *Harvard Business Review,* July–August 1997, pp. 133–45.

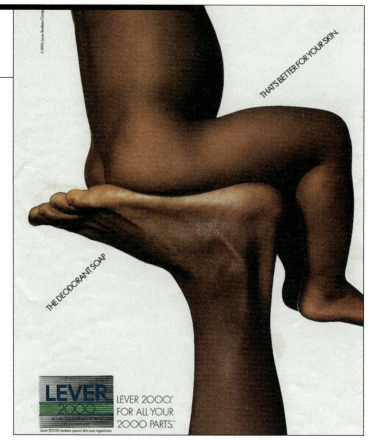

Unilever positioned its best-selling Lever 2000 soap on three benefits in one: cleansing, deodorizing, and moisturizing benefits. It's good "for all your 2000 parts."

How Many Differences to Promote? Many marketers think that companies should aggressively promote only one benefit to the target market. Ad man Rosser Reeves, for example, said a company should develop a *unique selling proposition (USP)* for each brand and stick to it. Each brand should pick an attribute and tout itself as "number one" on that attribute. Buyers tend to remember number one better, especially in an overcommunicated society. Thus, Crest toothpaste consistently promotes its anticavity protection and Volvo promotes safety. A company that hammers away at one of these positions and consistently delivers on it probably will become best known and remembered for it.

Other marketers think that companies should position themselves on more than one differentiating factor. This may be necessary if two or more firms are claiming to be the best on the same attribute. Today, in a time when the mass market is fragmenting into many small segments, companies are trying to broaden their positioning strategies to appeal to more segments. For example, Unilever introduced the first three-in-one bar soap—Lever 2000—offering cleansing, deodorizing, *and* moisturizing benefits. Clearly, many buyers want all three benefits, and the challenge was to convince them that one brand can deliver all three. Judging from Lever 2000's outstanding success, Unilever easily met the challenge. However, as companies increase the number of claims for their brands, they risk disbelief and a loss of clear positioning.

In general, a company needs to avoid three major positioning errors. The first is *underpositioning*—failing to ever really position the company at all. Some companies discover that buyers have only a vague idea of the company or that they do not really know anything special about it. The second error is *overpositioning*—giving buyers too narrow a picture of the company. Thus, a consumer might think that the Steuben glass company makes only fine art glass costing $1,000 and up, when in fact it makes affordable fine glass starting at around $50. Finally, companies must avoid *confused positioning*—leaving buyers with a confused image of a company. For example, over the past decade, Burger King has fielded six separate advertising campaigns, with themes ranging from "Herb the nerd doesn't eat here" to "Sometimes you've got to break the rules" and "BK Tee Vee." This barrage of positioning statements has left consumers confused and Burger King with poor sales and profits.

Which Differences to Promote? Not all brand differences are meaningful or worthwhile; not every difference makes a good differentiator. Each difference has the potential to create company costs as well as customer benefits. Therefore, the company must carefully select the ways in which it will distinguish itself from competitors. A difference is worth establishing to the extent that it satisfies the following criteria:

- *Important:* The difference delivers a highly valued benefit to target buyers.
- *Distinctive:* Competitors do not offer the difference, or the company can offer it in a more distinctive way.
- *Superior:* The difference is superior to other ways that customers might obtain the same benefit.
- *Communicable:* The difference is communicable and visible to buyers.
- *Preemptive:* Competitors cannot easily copy the difference.
- *Affordable:* Buyers can afford to pay for the difference.
- *Profitable:* The company can introduce the difference profitably.

Many companies have introduced differentiations that failed one or more of these tests. The Westin Stamford hotel in Singapore advertises that it is the world's tallest hotel, a distinction that is not important to many tourists—in fact, it turns many off. Polaroid's Polarvision, which produced instantly developed home movies, bombed too. Although Polarvision was distinctive and even preemptive, it was inferior to another way of capturing motion, namely, camcorders. When Pepsi introduced clear Crystal Pepsi some years ago, customers were unimpressed. Although the new drink was distinctive, consumers didn't see "clarity" as an important benefit in a soft drink. Thus, choosing competitive advantages upon which to position a product or service can be difficult, yet such choices may be crucial to success.

Selecting an Overall Positioning Strategy

Consumers typically choose products and services that give them the greatest value. Thus, marketers want to position their brands on the key benefits that they offer relative to competing brands. The full positioning of a brand is called the brand's **value proposition**—the full mix of benefits upon which the brand is positioned. It is the answer to the customer's question "Why should I buy your brand?" Volvo's value proposition hinges on safety but also includes reliability, roominess, and styling, all for a price that is higher than average but seems fair for this mix of benefits.

Figure 7.4 shows possible value propositions upon which a company might position its products. In the figure, the five green cells represent winning value propositions—positioning that gives the company competitive advantage. The orange cells, however, represent losing value propositions, and the center cell represents at best a marginal proposition. In the following sections, we discuss the five winning value propositions companies can use to position their products: more for more, more for the same, the same for less, less for much less, and more for less.[34]

More for More.   "More for more" positioning involves providing the most upscale product or service and charging a higher price to cover the higher costs. Ritz-Carlton Hotels, Mont Blanc writing instruments, Mercedes-Benz automobiles—each claims superior quality, craftsmanship, durability,

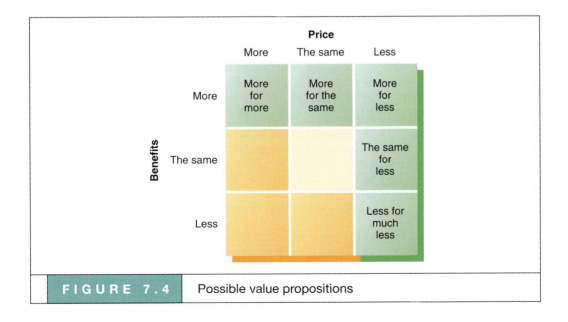

FIGURE 7.4   Possible value propositions

[34]See Philip Kotler, *Kotler on Marketing* (Upper Saddle River, NJ: Prentice Hall, 1999), pp. 59–63.

performance, or style and charges a price to match. Not only is the marketing offer high in quality, it also offers prestige to the buyer. It symbolizes status and a lofty lifestyle. Often, the price difference exceeds the actual increment in quality.

Sellers offering "only the best" can be found in every product and service category, from hotels, restaurants, food, and fashion to cars and kitchen appliances. Consumers are sometimes surprised, even delighted, when a new competitor enters a category with an unusually high-priced brand. Starbucks coffee entered as a very expensive brand in a largely commodity category; Häagen-Dazs came in as a premium ice cream brand at a price never before charged. In general, companies should be on the lookout for opportunities to introduce a "much more for much more" brand in any underdeveloped product or service category. For example, William-Sonoma's hottest-selling item this year is the $369 Dualit Toaster, a hand-assembled appliance that keeps toast warm for 10 minutes.[35]

Yet "more for more" brands can be vulnerable. They often invite imitators who claim the same quality but at a lower price. Luxury goods that sell well during good times may be at risk during economic downturns when buyers become more cautious in their spending.

More for the Same.   Companies can attack a competitor's more for more positioning by introducing a brand offering comparable quality but at a lower price. For example, Toyota introduced its Lexus line with a "more for the same" value proposition. Its headline read: "Perhaps the first time in history that trading a $72,000 car for a $36,000 car could be considered trading up." It communicated the high quality of its new Lexus through rave reviews in car magazines, through a widely distributed videotape showing side-by-side comparisons of Lexus and Mercedes-Benz automobiles, and through surveys showing that Lexus dealers were providing customers with better sales and service experiences than were Mercedes dealerships. Many Mercedes-Benz owners switched to Lexus, and the Lexus repurchase rate has been 60 percent, twice the industry average.

The Same for Less.   Offering "the same for less" can be a powerful value proposition—everyone likes a good deal. For example, Amazon.com sells the same book titles as its brick-and-mortar competitors but at lower prices, and Dell Computer offers equivalent quality at a better "price for performance." Discounts stores such as Wal-Mart and "category killers" such as Best Buy, Circuit City, and Sportmart also use this positioning. They don't claim to offer different or better products. Instead, they offer many of the same brands as department stores and specialty stores but at deep discounts based on superior purchasing power and lower-cost operations.

Other companies develop imitative but lower-priced brands in an effort to lure customers away from the market leader. For example, Advanced Micro Devices (AMD) and Cyrix make less expensive versions of Intel's market-leading microprocessor chips. Many personal computer companies make "IBM clones" and claim to offer the same performance at lower prices.

Less for Much Less.   A market almost always exists for products that offer less and therefore cost less. Few people need, want, or can afford "the very best" in everything they buy. In many cases, consumers will gladly settle for less than optimal performance or give up some of the bells and whistles in exchange for a lower price. For example, many travelers seeking lodgings prefer not to pay for what they consider unnecessary extras, such as a pool, cable television, attached restaurant, or mints on the pillow. Motel chains such as Motel 6 suspend some of these amenities and charge less accordingly.

"Less for much less" positioning involves meeting consumers' lower performance or quality requirements at a much lower price. For example, Family Dollar and Dollar General stores offer more affordable goods at very low prices. Sam's Club warehouse stores offer less merchandise selection and consistency, and much lower levels of service; as a result, they charge rock-bottom prices. Southwest Airlines, the nation's most profitable air carrier, also practices less for much less positioning. It charges incredibly low prices by not serving food, not assigning seats, and not using travel agents.

More for Less.   Of course, the winning value proposition would be to offer "more for less." Many companies claim to do this. For example, Dell Computer claims to have better products *and* lower prices for a given level of performance. Procter & Gamble claims that its laundry detergents provide the best cleaning *and* everyday low prices. In the short run, some companies can actually achieve such lofty positions. For example, when it first opened for business, Home Depot had arguably the best product selection and service *and* at the lowest prices compared to local hardware stores and other home improvement chains.

Yet in the long run, companies will find it very difficult to sustain such best-of-both positioning. Offering more usually costs more, making it difficult to deliver on the "for less" promise. Companies that try to deliver both may lose out to more focused competitors. For example, facing determined competition from Lowes stores, Home Depot must now decide whether it wants to compete primarily on superior service or on lower prices.

---

[35]Mercedes M. Cardona and Jack Neff, "Everything's at a Premium," *Advertising Age,* August 2, 1999, pp. 12, 15.

All said, each brand must adopt a positioning strategy designed to serve the needs and wants of its target markets. "More for more" will draw one target market, "less for much less" will draw another, and so on. Thus, in any market, there is usually room for many different companies, each successfully occupying different positions.

The important thing is that each company must develop its own winning positioning strategy, one that makes it special to its target consumers. Offering only "the same for the same" provides no competitive advantage, leaving the firm in the middle of the pack. Companies offering one of the three losing value propositions—"the same for more," "less for more," and "less for the same"—will inevitably fail. Here, customers soon realize that they've been underserved, tell others, and abandon the brand.

> **active example**

Take a moment to explore one company's choice of a positioning strategy.

COMMUNICATING AND DELIVERING THE CHOSEN POSITION

Once it has chosen a position, the company must take strong steps to deliver and communicate the desired position to target consumers. All the company's marketing mix efforts must support the positioning strategy. Positioning the company calls for concrete action, not just talk. If the company decides to build a position on better quality and service, it must first *deliver* that position. Designing the marketing mix—product, price, place, and promotion—essentially involves working out the tactical details of the positioning strategy. Thus, a firm that seizes on a "for more" position knows that it must produce high-quality products, charge a high price, distribute through high-quality dealers, and advertise in high-quality media. It must hire and train more service people, find retailers who have a good reputation for service, and develop sales and advertising messages that broadcast its superior service. This is the only way to build a consistent and believable "more for more" position.

Companies often find it easier to come up with a good positioning strategy than to implement it. Establishing a position or changing one usually takes a long time. In contrast, positions that have taken years to build can quickly be lost. Once a company has built the desired position, it must take care to maintain the position through consistent performance and communication. It must closely monitor and adapt the position over time to match changes in consumer needs and competitors' strategies. However, the company should avoid abrupt changes that might confuse consumers. Instead, a product's position should evolve gradually as it adapts to the ever-changing marketing environment.

> **active example**

Take a moment to explore how some well-known companies deliver their chosen market positions.

> **active concept check**

Now let's take a moment to test your knowledge of what you've just read.

> **video exercise**

Apply what you have learned in this chapter to a realistic case.

Now that you've reached the end of the chapter, you may wish to explore the concepts you've been reading about in greater detail, or test yourself to see how well you've comprehended the material. In the box below you'll find a number of links. Click on any one of these links to find additional chapter resources.

> **end-of-chapter resources**

- Review of Concept Connections
- Practice Quiz
- Issues for Discussion
- Key Terms
- Marketing Applications
- Internet Connections
- Company Case

C H A P T E R 8

Product and Services Strategy

> What's Ahead

Each year, cosmetics companies sell billions of dollars' worth of potions, lotions, and fragrances to consumers around the world. In one sense, these products are no more than

5
own your mind and body*

careful mixtures of oils and chemicals that have nice scents and soothing properties. But the cosmetics companies know that they sell much more than just mixtures of ingredients—they sell the promise of what these concoctions will do for the people who use them.

Of course, in the cosmetics business, like anywhere else, quality and performance contribute to success or failure. For example, perfume marketers agree, "No smell; no sell." However, $180-an-ounce perfume may cost no more than $10 to produce. Thus, to perfume consumers, many things beyond the scent and a few dollars' worth of ingredients add to a perfume's allure. For instance, a perfume's packaging is an important product attribute—the package and bottle are the most real symbols of the perfume and its image. The *name* is also important—fragrance names such as Obsession, Passion, Gossip, Wildheart, Opium, Joy, White Linen, Youth Dew, and Eternity suggest that the perfumes will do something more than just make you smell better.

What *is* the promise of cosmetics? The following account by a *New York Times* reporter suggests the extent to which cosmetics take on meaning far beyond their physical makeup.

Last week I bathed in purple water (*I Trust* bubble bath, made by Philosophy) and powdered up with pink powder (*Rebirth,* by 5S, "to renew the spirit and recharge the soul"). My moisturizer was *Bliss* (Chakra VII by Aveda, for "the joyful enlightenment and soaring of the spirit"); my nail polish was *Spiritual* (by Tony and Tina, "to aid connection with the higher self"). My teeth were clean, my heart was open—however, my bathroom was so crowded with bottles and brochures, the latest tools and totems from the human potential movement, that I could hardly find my third eye.

If you are looking for enlightenment in all the wrong places, cosmetics companies are eager to help. Because today, feeling good is the new religion. And cosmetics companies are the newest of the new prophets, turning the old notion of hope in a jar on its head.

"Cosmetics are our satellite to the divine!" This is what you'll hear from Tony and Tina, for example. Tony and Tina (Anthony Gillis and Cristina Bornstein) are nice young artists. He's from London, she grew up in New York. Chakra nail polish, which they invented for an installation at the Gershwin Gallery in Manhattan two years ago, was intended as an ironic commentary on the beauty business. But then a friend suggested they get into the beauty business, and now Tony and Tina have a $2 million cosmetics company with a mission statement: "To aid in the evolution of human consciousness." Their products include nail polishes (Vibrational Remedies) in colors meant to do nice things to your chakras, as well as body glitter and hair mascara, lipstick and eyeshadow. You can buy them at Fred Segal, Nordstrom, and Bloomingdale's, where last month they outsold Hard Candy and Urban Decay. "We think color therapy is going to be the new medicine," said Tony.

Rainbows are proliferating as rapidly in the New Age as angels once did. Philosophy, a three-year-old Arizona company, makes a sort of head/heart kit—"a self-help program," the company insists—called the *Rainbow Connection.* You pay $45 for seven bottles of colored bubble bath in a metal box. "Choose your colored bath according to the area of your emotional life that needs attention, i.e., self-love, self-worth," the brochure reads. "My role as I see it," said Christina Carlino, Philosophy's founder, "is to help you stay on your destiny path. It's not about what you look like. Beauty is defined by your deeds."

5S, a new sprout of the Japanese cosmetics company Shiseido, offers a regimen that plays, the company says, on the "fundamental and mythical significance of 5" (Five Pillars of Islam, Five Classics of Confucianism, and so on) and which is organized into emotional rather than physical categories. At the 5S store in SoHo, you don't buy things for dry skin, you buy things that are "energizing" or "nurturing" or "adoring." The company also believes in color therapy. Hence, *Rebirth,* products tinted "nouveau pink" (the color of bubble gum). A customer can achieve rebirth with 5S pink soap, pink powder, and pink toner.

Here are products that are not intended to make you look better, but to make you act better, feel better, and be a better person. You don't need a month's visit to India to find your higher self; you need only buy this bubble bath, that lipstick, this night cream. The beauty business's old come-on (trap your man!) has been swept away in favor of a new pitch: I don't have wrinkles anymore. I've got a chakra blockage.

Of course, who knew about chakras before Aveda? In 1989, the plant-based, eco-friendly cosmetics company Aveda trademarked Chakras I through VII to use as titles for moisturizers and scents. Chakra products were perhaps a little ahead of their time back then. However, the purchase of Aveda nine months ago by the Estée Lauder Companies, the General Motors of the cosmetics world, suggests that the pendulum of history has finally caught up. "Aveda isn't a marketing idea," says Jeanette Wagner, the vice chairperson of Estée Lauder. "It is a passionately held belief." Estée Lauder plans to extend the Aveda concept through "lifestyle" stores built with sustainable woods and nontoxic elements, selling "beauty, health, lifestyle, you name it." "From my point of view," Wagner says, "the appeal is first the spirituality, and then the products."

All this might sound like only so much flimflam, but the underlying point is legitimate. The success of such brands affirms that products really are more than just the physical entities. When a woman buys cosmetics, she really does buy much, much more than just oils, chemicals, and fragrances. The cosmetic's image, its promises and positioning, its ingredients, its name and package, the company that makes it, the stores that sell it—all become a part of the total cosmetic product. When Aveda, Philosophy, and 5S sell cosmetics, they sell more than just tangible goods. They sell lifestyle, self-expression, exclusivity, and spirituality; achievement, success, and status; romance, passion, and fantasy; memories, hopes, and dreams.[1]

> # objectives

Before you begin, take a moment to familiarize yourself with the key objectives of this chapter.

> # gearing up

Before we begin our exploration this chapter, take a short warm-up test to see what you know about this topic.

Clearly, cosmetics are more than just cosmetics when Aveda sells them. This chapter begins with a deceptively simple question: *What is a product?* After answering this question, we look at ways to classify products in consumer and business markets. Then we discuss the important decisions that marketers make regarding individual products, product lines, and product mixes. Finally, we examine the characteristics and marketing requirements of a special form of product—services.

> ## What Is a Product?

A Sony CD player, a Ford Taurus, a Costa Rican vacation, a Caffé Mocha at Starbucks, Charles Schwab online investment services, and advice from your family doctor—all are products. We define

[1]Excerpt adapted from Penelope Green, "Spiritual Cosmetics. No Kidding," *New York Times,* January 10, 1999, p. 1.

a **product** as anything that can be offered to a market for attention, acquisition, use, or consumption and that might satisfy a want or need. Products include more than just tangible goods. Broadly defined, products include physical objects, services, events, persons, places, organizations, ideas, or mixes of these entities. Thus, throughout this text, we use the term *product* broadly to include any or all of these entities.

Because of their importance in the world economy, we give special attention to services. **Services** are a form of product that consist of activities, benefits, or satisfactions offered for sale that are essentially intangible and do not result in the ownership of anything. Examples are banking, hotel, tax preparation, and home repair services. We will look at services more closely in a section at the end of this chapter.

PRODUCTS, SERVICES, AND EXPERIENCES

A company's offer to the marketplace often includes both tangible goods and services. Each component can be a minor or a major part of the total offer. At one extreme, the offer may consist of a *pure tangible good,* such as soap, toothpaste, or salt—no services accompany the product. At the other extreme are *pure services,* for which the offer consists primarily of a service. Examples include a doctor's exam or financial services. Between these two extremes, however, many goods and services combinations are possible.

active example <

Even one of life's basic necessities, such as drinking water, could be a product. Read below how two beverage giants are trying to profit by selling drinking water.

For example, a company's offer may consist of a *tangible good with accompanying services.* Ford offers more than just automobiles. Its offer also includes repair and maintenance services, warranty fulfillment, showrooms and waiting areas, and a host of other support services. A *hybrid offer* consists of equal parts of goods and services. For instance, people patronize restaurants both for their food and their service. A *service with accompanying minor goods* consists of a major service along with supporting goods. For example, American Airlines passengers primarily buy transportation service, but the trip also includes some tangibles, such as food, drinks, and an airline magazine. The service also requires a capital-intensive good—an airplane—for its delivery, but the primary offer is a service.

Today, as products and services become more and more commoditized, many companies are moving to a new level in creating value for their customers. To differentiate their offers, they are developing and delivering total customer *experiences.* Whereas products are tangible and services are intangible, experiences are memorable. Whereas products and services are external, experiences are personal and take place in the minds of individual consumers. Companies that market experiences realize that customers are really buying much more than just products and services. They are buying what those offers will *do* for them—the experiences they gain in purchasing and consuming these products and services.

LEVELS OF PRODUCT

Product planners need to think about products and services on three levels. The most basic level is the *core product,* which addresses the question *What is the buyer really buying?* As Figure 8.1 illustrates, the core product stands at the center of the total product. It consists of the core, problem-solving benefits that consumers seek when they buy a product or service. A woman buying lipstick buys more than lip color. Charles Revson of Revlon saw this early: "In the factory, we make cosmetics; in the store, we sell hope." Ritz-Carlton Hotels knows that it offers its guests more than simply rooms for rent—it provides "memorable travel experiences." Thus, when designing products, marketers must first define the core of *benefits* the product will provide to consumers. They must understand the total customer *experience* that surrounds the purchase and use of the product.

The product planner must next build an *actual product* around the core product. Actual products may have as many as five characteristics: a quality level, features, design, a brand name, and packaging. For example, a Sony camcorder is an actual product. Its name, parts, styling, features, packaging, and other attributes have all been combined carefully to deliver the core benefit—a convenient, high-quality way to capture important moments.

Finally, the product planner must build an *augmented product* around the core and actual products by offering additional consumer services and benefits. Sony must offer more than just a camcorder. It

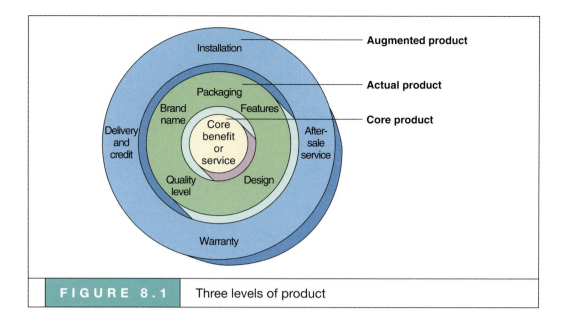

| FIGURE 8.1 | Three levels of product |

must provide consumers with a complete solution to their picture-taking problems. Thus, when consumers buy a Sony camcorder, Sony and its dealers also might give buyers a warranty on parts and workmanship, instructions on how to use the camcorder, quick repair services when needed, and a toll-free telephone number to call if they have problems or questions.

Therefore, a product is more than a simple set of tangible features. Consumers tend to see products as complex bundles of benefits that satisfy their needs. When developing products, marketers first must identify the *core* consumer needs the product will satisfy. They must then design the *actual* product and find ways to *augment* it in order to create the bundle of benefits that will best satisfy consumers.

> video exercise

Take a moment to watch a group of managers discuss strategy at different product levels.

> active concept check

Now let's take a moment to test your knowledge of what you've just read.

> Product Classifications

Products and services fall into two broad classes based on the types of consumers that use them—*consumer products* and *industrial products*. Broadly defined, products also include other marketable entities such as experiences, organizations, persons, places, and ideas.

CONSUMER PRODUCTS

Consumer products are those bought by final consumers for personal consumption. Marketers usually classify these goods further based on how consumers go about buying them. Consumer products include *convenience products, shopping products, specialty products,* and *unsought products.* These products differ in the ways consumers buy them and therefore in how they are marketed (see Table 8.1).

TABLE 8.1   Marketing Considerations for Consumer Products

Marketing Considerations	Type of Consumer Product			
	Convenience	**Shopping**	**Specialty**	**Unsought**
Customer buying behavior	Frequent purchase, little planning, little comparison or shopping effort, low customer involvement	Less frequent purchase, much planning and shopping effort, comparison of brands on price, quality, style	Strong brand preference and loyalty, special purchase effort, little comparison of brands, low price sensitivity	Little product awareness, knowledge (or, if aware, little or even negative interest)
Price	Low Price	Higher price	High price	Varies
Distribution	Widespread distribution, convenient locations	Selective distribution in fewer outlets	Exclusive distribution in only one or a few outlets per market area	Varies
Promotion	Mass promotion by the producer	Advertising and personal selling by both producer and resellers	More carefully targeted promotion by both producer and resellers	Aggressive advertising and personal selling by producer and resellers
Examples	Toothpaste, magazines, laundry detergent	Major appliances, televisions, furniture, clothing	Luxury goods, such as Rolex watches or fine crystal	Life insurance, Red Cross blood donations

Convenience products are consumer products and services that the customer usually buys frequently, immediately, and with a minimum of comparison and buying effort. Examples include soap, candy, newspapers, and fast food. Convenience products are usually low priced, and marketers place them in many locations to make them readily available when customers need them.

Shopping products are less frequently purchased consumer products and services that customers compare carefully on suitability, quality, price, and style. When buying shopping products and services, consumers spend much time and effort in gathering information and making comparisons. Examples include furniture, clothing, used cars, major appliances, and hotel and motel services. Shopping products marketers usually distribute their products through fewer outlets but provide deeper sales support to help customers in their comparison efforts.

Specialty products are consumer products and services with unique characteristics or brand identification for which a significant group of buyers is willing to make a special purchase effort. Examples include specific brands and types of cars, high-priced photographic equipment, designer clothes, and the services of medical or legal specialists. A Lamborghini automobile, for example, is a specialty product because buyers are usually willing to travel great distances to buy one. Buyers normally do not compare specialty products. They invest only the time needed to reach dealers carrying the wanted products.

Unsought products are consumer products that the consumer either does not know about or knows about but does not normally think of buying. Most major new innovations are unsought until the consumer becomes aware of them through advertising. Classic examples of known but unsought products and services are life insurance and blood donations to the Red Cross. By their very nature, unsought products require a lot of advertising, personal selling, and other marketing efforts.

INDUSTRIAL PRODUCTS

Industrial products are those purchased for further processing or for use in conducting a business. Thus, the distinction between a consumer product and an industrial product is based on the *purpose* for which the product is bought. If a consumer buys a lawn mower for use around home, the lawn mower is a consumer product. If the same consumer buys the same lawn mower for use in a landscaping business, the lawn mower is an industrial product.

The three groups of industrial products and services include materials and parts, capital items, and supplies and services. *Materials and parts* include raw materials and manufactured materials and parts. Raw materials consist of farm products (wheat, cotton, livestock, fruits, vegetables) and natural products (fish, lumber, crude petroleum, iron ore). Manufactured materials and parts consist of com-

Business services: ServiceMaster supplies business services for a wide range of organizations. This advertisement to schools and colleges offers services ranging from custodial, grounds, technology, and energy management services to maintenance and food services.

ponent materials (iron, yarn, cement, wires) and component parts (small motors, tires, castings). Most manufactured materials and parts are sold directly to industrial users. Price and service are the major marketing factors; branding and advertising tend to be less important.

> ## active example

Consider how one industrial-products firm has benefited from changes in consumer demand.

Capital items are industrial products that aid in the buyer's production or operations, including installations and accessory equipment. Installations consist of major purchases such as buildings (factories, offices) and fixed equipment (generators, drill presses, large computer systems, elevators). Accessory equipment includes portable factory equipment and tools (hand tools, lift trucks) and office equipment (fax machines, desks). They have a shorter life than installations and simply aid in the production process.

The final group of business products is *supplies and services*. Supplies include operating supplies (lubricants, coal, paper, pencils) and repair and maintenance items (paint, nails, brooms). Supplies are the convenience products of the industrial field because they are usually purchased with a minimum of effort or comparison. Business services include maintenance and repair services (window cleaning, computer repair) and business advisory services (legal, management consulting, advertising). Such services are usually supplied under contract.

ORGANIZATIONS, PERSONS, PLACES, AND IDEAS

In addition to tangible products and services, in recent years marketers have broadened the concept of a product to include other "marketable entities"—namely, organizations, persons, places, and ideas.

Organizations often carry out activities to "sell" the organization itself. *Organization marketing* consists of activities undertaken to create, maintain, or change the attitudes and behavior of target consumers toward an organization. Both profit and nonprofit organizations practice organization marketing. Business firms sponsor public relations or corporate advertising campaigns to polish their images. *Corporate image advertising* is a major tool companies use to market themselves to various publics. For example, Lucent puts out ads with the tag line, "We make the things that make communications work." IBM wants to establish itself as the company to turn to for "e-Business Solutions." Similarly, nonprofit organizations, such as churches, colleges, charities, museums, and performing arts groups, market their organizations in order to raise funds and attract members or patrons.

People can also be thought of as products. *Person marketing* consists of activities undertaken to create, maintain, or change attitudes or behavior toward particular people. All kinds of people and organizations practice person marketing. Presidents must be skillful in marketing themselves, their parties, and their platforms to get needed votes and program support. Entertainers and sports figures use marketing to promote their careers and improve their impact and incomes. Professionals such as doctors, lawyers, accountants, and architects market themselves in order to build their reputations and increase business. Business leaders use person marketing as a strategic tool to develop their companies' fortunes as well as their own. Businesses, charities, sports teams, fine arts groups, religious groups, and other organizations also use person marketing. Creating or associating with well-known personalities often helps these organizations achieve their goals better. Thus, brands such as Nike, Gatorade, McDonald's, Ball Park hot dogs, and Hanes have invested millions of dollars to link themselves with Michael Jordan.

Place marketing involves activities undertaken to create, maintain, or change attitudes or behavior toward particular places. Thus, cities, states, regions, and even entire nations compete to attract tourists, new residents, conventions, and company offices and factories. For example, today, almost every city, state, and country markets its tourist attractions. Texas has advertised "It's Like a Whole Other Country," Michigan has touted "YES M!CH!GAN—Great Lakes, Great Times," and New York State shouts "I Love New York!"[2] Stratford, Ontario, in Canada was a little-known town with one big marketing asset—its name and a river called Avon. This became the basis for an annual Shakespeare festival, which put Stratford on the tourist map. Most states and nations also operate industrial development offices that try to sell companies on the advantages of locating new plants in their states. For example, Ireland is an outstanding place marketer. The Irish Development Agency has attracted over 1,100 companies to locate their plants in Ireland. At the same time, the Irish Tourist Board has built a flourishing tourism business, and the Irish Export Board has created attractive markets for Irish exports.[3]

Ideas can also be marketed. In one sense, all marketing is the marketing of an idea, whether it be the general idea of brushing your teeth or the specific idea that Crest provides the most effective decay prevention. Here, however, we narrow our focus to the marketing of *social ideas,* such as public health campaigns to reduce smoking, alcoholism, drug abuse, and overeating; environmental campaigns to promote wilderness protection, clean air, and conservation; and other campaigns such as family planning, human rights, and racial equality. This area has been called **social marketing,** which includes the creation and implementation of programs seeking to increase the acceptability of a social idea, cause, or practice within targeted groups.

The Ad Council of America has developed dozens of social advertising campaigns, including classics such as "Smokey Bear," "Keep America Beautiful," "Join the Peace Corps," "Don't Drive Drunk," and "Say No to Drugs." It now represents 35 causes, ranging from antidiscrimination, child abuse prevention, education reform, and youth fitness to recycling and organ donation (see www.adcouncil.org). But social marketing involves much more than just advertising. Many public marketing campaigns fail because they assign advertising the primary role and fail to develop and use all the marketing mix tools.[4]

---

[2]Check out the tourism Web pages of these states at www.TravelTex.com, www.michigan.org, and www.iloveny.state.ny.us.

[3]See Philip Kotler, Irving J. Rein, and Donald Haider, *Marketing Places: Attracting Investment, Industry, and Tourism to Cities, States, and Nations* (New York: Free Press, 1993), pp. 202, 273.

[4]See V. Rangan Kasturi, Sohel Karim, and Sheryl K. Sandberg, "Do Better at Doing Good," *Harvard Business Review,* May–June 1996, pp. 42–54; Alan R. Andreasen, *Marketing Social Change: Changing Behavior to Promote Health, Social Development, and the Environment* (San Francisco: Jossey-Bass, 1995); Rance Crain, "Ruth Wooden Wheels and Deals to Lure Ad Council Sponsors," *Advertising Age,* March 9, 1998, p. 34; Alan R. Andreasen, Rob Gould, and Karen Gutierrez, "Social Marketing Has a New Champion," Advertising Age, February 7, 2000, p. 38 and information accessed online at www.adcouncil.org, February 2000.

Place marketing: The Irish Tourist Board has built a flourishing tourism business— "Awaken to a different world, Ireland!"

> ## active concept check

Now let's take a moment to test your knowledge of what you've just read.

> ## Individual Product Decisions

Figure 8.2 shows the important decisions in the development and marketing of individual products and services. We will focus on decisions about *product attributes, branding, packaging, labeling,* and *product support services.*

PRODUCT ATTRIBUTES

Developing a product or service involves defining the benefits that it will offer. These benefits are communicated and delivered by product attributes such as *quality, features,* and *style and design.*

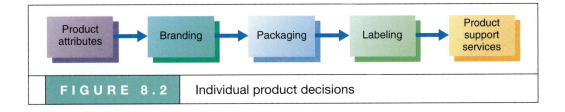

FIGURE 8.2   Individual product decisions

Product Quality

Quality is one of the marketer's major positioning tools. **Product quality** has two dimensions—level and consistency. In developing a product, the marketer must first choose a *quality level* that will support the product's position in the target market. Here, product quality means *performance quality*—the ability of a product to perform its functions. For example, a Rolls-Royce provides higher performance quality than a Chevrolet: It has a smoother ride, handles better, and lasts longer. Companies rarely try to offer the highest possible performance quality level—few customers want or can afford the high levels of quality offered in products such as a Rolls-Royce automobile, a Sub Zero refrigerator, or a Rolex watch. Instead, companies choose a quality level that matches target market needs and the quality levels of competing products.

Beyond quality level, high quality also can mean high levels of quality *consistency*. Here, product quality means *conformance quality*—freedom from defects and *consistency* in delivering a targeted level of performance. All companies should strive for high levels of conformance quality. In this sense, a Chevrolet can have just as much quality as a Rolls-Royce. Although a Chevy doesn't perform as well as a Rolls, it can as consistently deliver the quality that customers pay for and expect.

During the past two decades, a renewed emphasis on quality has spawned a global quality movement. Most firms implemented "total quality management" (TQM) programs, efforts to improve product and process quality constantly in every phase of their operations. Recently, however, the total quality management movement has drawn criticism. Too many companies viewed TQM as a magic cure-all and created token total quality programs that applied quality principles only superficially. Today, companies are taking a "return on quality" approach, viewing quality as an investment and holding quality efforts accountable for bottom-line results.[5]

Beyond simply reducing product defects, the ultimate goal of total quality is to improve customer satisfaction and value. For example, when Motorola first began its total quality program in the early 1980s, its goal was to drastically reduce manufacturing defects. Later, however, Motorola's quality concept evolved into one of *customer-defined quality* and *total customer satisfaction.* "Quality," noted Motorola's vice president of quality, "has to do something for the customer. . . . Our definition of a defect is 'if the customer doesn't like it, it's a defect.'" Similarly, Siemens defines quality this way: "Quality is when our customers come back and our products don't."[6] As more and more companies have moved toward such customer-driven definitions of quality, their TQM programs are evolving into customer satisfaction and customer retention programs.

Thus, many companies today have turned customer-driven quality into a potent strategic weapon. They create customer satisfaction and value by consistently and profitably meeting customers' needs and preferences for quality. In fact, quality has now become a competitive necessity—in the twenty-first century, only companies with the best quality will thrive.

Product Features

A product can be offered with varying features. A stripped-down model, one without any extras, is the starting point. The company can create higher-level models by adding more features. Features are a competitive tool for differentiating the company's product from competitors' products. Being the first producer to introduce a needed and valued new feature is one of the most effective ways to compete.

How can a company identify new features and decide which ones to add to its product? The company should periodically survey buyers who have used the product and ask these questions: How do you like the product? Which specific features of the product do you like most? Which features could we add to improve the product? The answers provide the company with a rich list of feature ideas. The company can then assess each feature's *value* to customers versus its *cost* to the company. Features that customers value little in relation to costs should be dropped; those that customers value highly in relation to costs should be added.

Product Style and Design

Another way to add customer value is through distinctive *product style and design.* Some companies have reputations for outstanding style and design, such as Black & Decker in cordless appliances and tools, Steelcase in office furniture and systems, Bose in audio equipment, and Ciba Corning in med-

---

[5]See Roland T. Rust, Anthony J. Zahorik, and Timothy L. Keiningham, "Return on Quality (ROQ): Making Service Quality Financially Accountable," *Journal of Marketing,* April 1995, pp. 58–70; Valerie A. Zeithaml, Leonard L. Berry, and A. Parasuraman, "The Behavioral Consequences of Service Quality," *Journal of Marketing,* April 1996, pp. 31–46; Otis Port, "The Baldrige's Other Reward," *Business Week,* March 10, 1997, p. 75; and George Thorne, "TQM Connects All Segments of Marketing," *Advertising Age's Business Marketing,* March 1998, p. 34.

[6]Philip Kotler, *Kotler on Marketing* (New York: Free Press, 1999), p. 17.

The dramatic iMac—with its sleek, egg-shaped, single-unit monitor and hard drive in a futuristic translucent casing—won raves for design and lured buyers in droves.

The thrill of surfing.
The agony of choosing a color.

Hop on an iMac and in just ten minutes you could be surfing the internet and e-mailing everyone and their brother. Now for the hard part: what color will it be? www.apple.com Think different.

ical equipment. Design can be one of the most powerful competitive weapons in a company's marketing arsenal.

Design is a larger concept than style. *Style* simply describes the appearance of a product. Styles can be eye catching or yawn producing. A sensational style may grab attention and produce pleasing aesthetics, but it does not necessarily make the product *perform* better. Unlike style, *design* is more than skin deep—it goes to the very heart of a product. Good design contributes to a product's usefulness as well as to its looks.

Good style and design can attract attention, improve product performance, cut production costs, and give the product a strong competitive advantage in the target market. For example, consider Apple's iMac personal computer:

> Who said that computers have to be beige and boxy? Apple's iMac, is anything but. The iMac features a sleek, egg-shaped monitor and hard drive, all in one unit, in a futuristic translucent turquoise casing. There's no clunky tower or desktop hard drive to clutter up your office area. There's also no floppy drive—with more and more software being distributed via CDs or the Internet, Apple thinks the floppy is on the verge of extinction. Featuring one-button Internet access, this is a machine designed specifically for cruising the Internet (that's what the "i" in "iMac" stands for). The dramatic iMac won raves for design and lured buyers in droves. Only one month after the iMac hit the stores in the summer of 1998, it was the number-two best-selling computer. By mid-1999, it had sold more than a million units, marking Apple's reemergence as a legitimate contender in the personal computer industry.[7]

BRANDING

Perhaps the most distinctive skill of professional marketers is their ability to create, maintain, protect, and enhance brands of their products and services. A **brand** is a name, term, sign, symbol, or design, or a combination of these, that identifies the maker or seller of a product or service. Consumers view a brand as an important part of a product, and branding can add value to a product. For example, most consumers would perceive a bottle of White Linen perfume as a high-quality, expensive product. But the same perfume in an unmarked bottle would likely be viewed as lower in quality, even if the fragrance were identical.

BRAND

Branding has become so strong that today hardly anything goes unbranded. Salt is packaged in branded containers, common nuts and bolts are packaged with a distributor's label, and automobile

---

[7]See "Hot R.I.P.: The Floppy Disk," *Rolling Stone,* August 20, 1998, p. 86; Owen Edwards, "Beauty and the Box," *Forbes,* October 5, 1998, p. 131; Bob Woods, "iMac Drives Apple's Q2 Results," *Computer Dealer News,* April 30, 1999, p. 39; and Eleftheria Parpis, "Show Toppers," *Adweek,* May 10, 1999, pp. 31–32.

parts—spark plugs, tires, filters—bear brand names that differ from those of the automakers. Even fruits, vegetables, and poultry are branded—Sunkist oranges, Dole pineapples, Chiquita bananas, Fresh Express salad greens, and Perdue chickens.

Branding helps buyers in many ways. Brand names help consumers identify products that might benefit them. Brands also tell the buyer something about product quality. Buyers who always buy the same brand know that they will get the same features, benefits, and quality each time they buy. Branding also gives the seller several advantages. The brand name becomes the basis on which a whole story can be built about a product's special qualities. The seller's brand name and trademark provide legal protection for unique product features that otherwise might be copied by competitors. Branding also helps the seller to segment markets. For example, General Mills can offer Cheerios, Wheaties, Total, Lucky Charms, and many other cereal brands, not just one general product for all consumers.

Brand Equity

Brands vary in the amount of power and value they have in the marketplace. A powerful brand has high **brand equity.** Brands have higher brand equity to the extent that they have higher brand loyalty, name awareness, perceived quality, strong brand associations, and other assets such as patents, trademarks, and channel relationships.

A brand with strong brand equity is a very valuable asset. Measuring the actual equity of a brand name is difficult. However, according to one estimate, the brand equity of Coca-Cola is $84 billion, Microsoft is $57 billion, and IBM is $44 billion. Other brands rating among the world's most valuable include McDonald's, Disney, Sony, Kodak, Intel, Gillette, and Budweiser.[8]

Although we normally think of brand equity as something accruing to products, service companies also prize it. As Wall Street competition intensifies, financial service companies are spending millions on their brand names in order to attract investors. Just as Coke wants you to reach for its soda when you're thirsty, Merrill Lynch and Charles Schwab want you to call them when you need financial know-how. Hence, brand-building advertising by financial services companies has soared in recent years.

High brand equity provides a company with many competitive advantages. A powerful brand enjoys a high level of consumer brand awareness and loyalty. Because consumers expect stores to carry the brand, the company has more leverage in bargaining with resellers. Because the brand name carries high credibility, the company can more easily launch line and brand extensions, as when Coca-Cola leveraged its well-known brand to introduce Diet Coke or when Procter & Gamble introduced Ivory dishwashing detergent. Above all, a powerful brand offers the company some defense against fierce price competition.

video example <

Take a moment to consider the importance companies place on building and protecting strong brands.

Some analysts see brands as *the* major enduring asset of a company, outlasting the company's specific products and facilities. Yet every powerful brand really represents a set of loyal customers. Therefore, the fundamental asset underlying brand equity is *customer equity.* This suggests that the proper focus of marketing planning is that of extending *loyal customer lifetime value,* with brand management serving as a major marketing tool.

Branding poses challenging decisions to the marketer. Figure 8.3 shows the key branding decisions.

Brand Name Selection

A good name can add greatly to a product's success. However, finding the best brand name is a difficult task. It begins with a careful review of the product and its benefits, the target market, and proposed marketing strategies.

[8]Kathleen Morris, "The Name's the Thing," *Business Week,* November 15, 1999, pp. 36–39. Also see David A. Aaker, *Managing Brand Equity* (New York: Free Press, 1991); Terry Lefton and Weston Anson, "How Much Is Your Brand Worth?" *Brandweek,* January 26, 1996, pp. 43–44; Kevin Lane Keller, *Strategic Brand Management: Building, Measuring, and Managing Brand Equity* (Upper Saddle River, NJ: Prentice Hall, 1997); and David Kiley, "Q&A: Brand Value Rx," *Brandweek,* March 23, 1998, pp. 36–40.

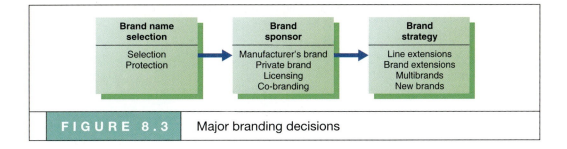

FIGURE 8.3 Major branding decisions

Desirable qualities for a brand name include the following: (1) It should suggest something about the product's benefits and qualities. Examples: DieHard, Easy-Off, Craftsman, Sunkist, Spic and Span, Snuggles, Merrie Maids, and OFF! bug spray. (2) It should be easy to pronounce, recognize, and remember. Short names help. Examples: Tide, Aim, Puffs. But longer ones are sometimes effective. Examples: "Love My Carpet" carpet cleaner, "I Can't Believe It's Not Butter" margarine, Better Business Bureau. (3) The brand name should be distinctive. Examples: Taurus, Kodak, Exxon. (4) The name should translate easily into foreign languages. Before spending $100 million to change its name to Exxon, Standard Oil of New Jersey tested several names in 54 languages in more than 150 foreign markets. It found that the name Enco referred to a stalled engine when pronounced in Japanese. (5) It should be capable of registration and legal protection. A brand name cannot be registered if it infringes on existing brand names.

Once chosen, the brand name must be protected. Many firms try to build a brand name that will eventually become identified with the product category. Brand names such as Kleenex, Levi's, Jell-O, Scotch Tape, Formica, and Fiberglas have succeeded in this way. However, their very success may threaten the company's rights to the name. Many originally protected brand names, such as cellophane, aspirin, nylon, kerosene, linoleum, yo-yo, trampoline, escalator, thermos, and shredded wheat, are now generic names that any seller can use.

Brand Sponsor

A manufacturer has four sponsorship options. The product may be launched as a *manufacturer's brand* (or national brand), as when Kellogg and IBM sell their output under their own manufacturer's brand names. Or the manufacturer may sell to resellers who give it a *private brand* (also called a *store brand* or *distributor brand*). Although most manufacturers create their own brand names, others market *licensed brands*. Finally, two companies can join forces and *co-brand* a product.

Manufacturer's Brands Versus Private Brands. Manufacturers' brands have long dominated the retail scene. In recent times, however, an increasing number of retailers and wholesalers have created their own **private brands** (or **store brands**). For example, Sears has created several names— DieHard batteries, Craftsman tools, Kenmore appliances, Weatherbeater paints. Wal-Mart offers its own Sam's American Choice and Great Value brands of beverages and food products to compete against major national brands. BASF Wyandotte, the world's second-largest antifreeze maker, sells its Alugard antifreeze through intermediaries that market the product under about 80 private brands, including Kmart, True Value, Pathmark, and Rite Aid. Private brands can be hard to establish and costly to stock and promote. However, they also yield higher profit margins for the reseller, and they give resellers exclusive products that cannot be bought from competitors, resulting in greater store traffic and loyalty.

In the so-called *battle of the brands* between manufacturers' and private brands, retailers have many advantages. They control what products they stock, where they go on the shelf, and which ones they will feature in local circulars. They charge manufacturers **slotting fees**—payments demanded by retailers before they will accept new products and find "slots" for them on the shelves. Retailers price their store brands lower than comparable manufacturers' brands, thereby appealing to budget-conscious shoppers, especially in difficult economic times. Most shoppers believe that store brands are often made by one of the larger manufacturers anyway.

As store brands improve in quality and as consumers gain confidence in their store chains, store brands are posing a strong challenge to manufacturers' brands. Consider the case of Loblaws, the Canadian supermarket chain. Its President's Choice Decadent Chocolate Chip Cookies brand is now the leading cookie brand in Canada. Loblaws' private label President's Choice cola racks up 50 percent of Loblaws' canned cola sales. Based on this success, the private label powerhouse has expanded into a wide range of food categories. For example, it now offers more than 2,500 food items under the President's Choice label, ranging from cookies, paper, and frozen desserts to prepared foods and boxed meats. The brand has become so popular that Loblaw now licenses it to retailers across the

Store brands: Loblaws's President's Choice brand has become so popular that the company now licenses it to retailers across the United States and in eight other countries where Loblaws has no stores of its own.

United States and eight other countries where Loblaws has no stores of its own. For example, President's Choice Decadent Chocolate Chip Cookies are now sold by Jewel Food Stores in Chicago, where they are the number-one seller, beating out even Nabisco's Chips Ahoy brand.[9]

In U.S. supermarkets, taken as a single brand, private-label products are the number-one, -two, or -three brand in over 40 percent of all grocery product categories. In all, they capture over a 20 percent share of U.S. supermarket sales. Private labels are even more prominent in Europe, accounting for as much as 36 percent of supermarket sales in Britain and 24 percent in France. French retail giant Carrefour sells more than 3,000 in-house brands, ranging from cooking oil to car batteries. To fend off private brands, leading brand marketers will have to invest in R&D to bring out new brands, new features, and continuous quality improvements. They must design strong advertising programs to maintain high awareness and preference. They must find ways to "partner" with major distributors in a search for distribution economies and improved joint performance.[10]

Licensing. Most manufacturers take years and spend millions to create their own brand names. However, some companies license names or symbols previously created by other manufacturers, names of well-known celebrities, characters from popular movies and books—for a fee, any of these can provide an instant and proven brand name. Apparel and accessories sellers pay large royalties to adorn their products—from blouses to ties, and linens to luggage—with the names or initials of well-known fashion innovators such as Calvin Klein, Tommy Hilfiger, Gucci, or Armani. Sellers of children's products attach an almost endless list of character names to clothing, toys, school supplies, linens, dolls, lunch boxes, cereals, and other items. The character names range from classics such as Sesame Street, Disney, Peanuts, Winnie the Pooh, the Muppets, Scooby Doo, and Dr. Seuss characters to the more recent Teletubbies, Pokemon, Powderpuff Girls, Rugrats, and Blue's Clues characters. Almost half of all retail toy sales come from products based on television shows and movies such as *The Rugrats, Scooby Doo, Star Trek,* or *Star Wars.*

Name and character licensing has grown rapidly in recent years. Annual retail sales of licensed products in the United States and Canada has grown from only $4 billion in 1977 to $55 billion in

[9]Emily DeNitto, "They Aren't Private Labels Anymore—They're Brands," *Advertising Age,* September 13, 1993, p. 8; Warren Thayer, "Loblaws Exec Predicts: Private Labels to Surge," *Frozen Food Age,* May 1996, p. 1; "President's Choice Continues Brisk Pace," *Frozen Food Age,* March 1998, pp. 17–18; David Dunne and Chakravarthi Narasimhan, "The New Appeal of Private Labels," *Harvard Business Review,* May–June 1999, pp. 41–52; and Jack Neff, "Wal-Mart Stores Go Private Label," *Advertising Age,* November 29, 1999, pp. 1, 34.

[10]See Patrick Oster, "The Eurosion of Brand Loyalty," *Business Week,* July 19, 1993, p. 22; Marcia Mogelonsky, "When Stores Become Brands," *American Demographics,* February 1995, pp. 32–38; John A. Quelch and David Harding, "Brands Versus Private Labels: Fighting to Win," *Harvard Business Review,* January–February 1996, pp. 99–109; Stephanie Thompson, "Private Label Marketers Getting Savvier to Consumption Trends," *Brandweek,* November 24, 1997, p. 9; and David Dunne and Chakravarthi Narasimhan, "The New Appeal of Private Labels," *Harvard Business Review,* May–June 1999, pp. 41–52.

1987 and more than $71 billion today. The fastest-growing licensing category is corporate brand licensing, as more and more for-profit and nonprofit organizations are licensing their names to generate additional revenues and brand recognition. Even the Vatican engages in licensing: Heavenly images from its art collection, architecture, frescoes, and manuscripts are now imprinted on such earthy objects as T-shirts, ties, glassware, candles, and ornaments.[11]

Many companies have mastered the art of peddling their established brands and characters. For example, through savvy marketing, Warner Brothers has turned Bugs Bunny, Daffy Duck, Foghorn Leghorn, and its more than 100 other *Looney Tunes* characters into the world's favorite cartoon brand. The *Looney Tunes* license, arguably the most sought-after nonsports license in the industry, generates $4 billion in annual retail sales by more than 225 licensees. Warner Brothers has yet to tap the full potential of many of its secondary characters. The Tazmanian Devil, for example, initially appeared in only five cartoons. But through cross-licensing agreements with organizations such as Harley-Davidson and the NFL, Taz has become something of a pop icon. Warner Brothers sees similar potential for Michigan Frog or Speedy Gonzales for the Hispanic market.[12]

Co-Branding.   Although companies have been **co-branding** products for many years, there has been a recent resurgence in co-branded products. Co-branding occurs when two established brand names of different companies are used on the same product. For example, Nabisco joined with Pillsbury to create Pillsbury Oreo Bars baking mix and with Kraft Foods' Post cereal division to create Oreo O's cereal. Kellogg joined forces with ConAgra to co-brand Healthy Choice from Kellogg's cereals. Ford and Eddie Bauer co-branded a sport utility vehicle—the Ford Explorer, Eddie Bauer edition. General Electric worked with Culligan to develop its Water by Culligan Profile Performance refrigerator with a built-in Culligan water filtration system. Mattel teamed with Coca-Cola to market Soda Fountain Sweetheart Barbie. In most co-branding situations, one company licenses another company's well-known brand to use in combination with its own.

Co-branding offers many advantages. Because each brand dominates in a different category, the combined brands create broader consumer appeal and greater brand equity. Co-branding also allows a company to expand its existing brand into a category it might otherwise have difficulty entering alone. For example, by licensing its Healthy Choice brand to Kellogg, ConAgra entered the breakfast segment with a solid product. In return, Kellogg could leverage the broad awareness of the Healthy Choice name in the cereal category.

Co-branding also has limitations. Such relationships usually involve complex legal contracts and licenses. Co-branding partners must carefully coordinate their advertising, sales promotion, and other marketing efforts. Finally, when co-branding, each partner must trust the other will take good care of its brand. As one Nabisco manager puts it, "Giving away your brand is a lot like giving away your child—you want to make sure everything is perfect."[13]

Brand Strategy

A company has four choices when it comes to brand strategy (see Figure 8.4). It can introduce *line extensions* (existing brand names extended to new forms, sizes, and flavors of an existing product category), *brand extensions* (existing brand names extended to new product categories), *multibrands* (new brand names introduced in the same product category), or *new brands* (new brand names in new product categories).

Line Extensions.   **Line extensions** occur when a company introduces additional items in a given product category under the same brand name, such as new flavors, forms, colors, ingredients, or package sizes. Thus, Dannon introduced several line extensions, including seven new yogurt flavors, a fat-free yogurt, and a large, economy-size yogurt. The vast majority of new-product activity consists of line extensions.

[11]See Silvia Sansoni, "Gucci, Armani, and . . . John Paul II?" *Business Week,* May 13, 1996, p. 61; Bart A. Lazar, "Licensing Gives Known Brands New Life," *Advertising Age,* February 16, 1998, p. 8; Robert Oas, "Licensed Merchandise Sales Decrease, but Corporate Merchandise Is on the Rise," *Potentials,* April 1999, p. 8; and Laura Petrecca, "'Corporate Brands' Put Licensing in the Spotlight," *Advertising Age,* June 14, 1999, p. 1.

[12]Terry Lefton, "Warner Brothers' Not Very Looney Path to Licensing Gold," *Brandweek,* February 14, 1994, pp. 36–37; Robert Scally, "Warner Builds Brand Presence, Strengthens 'Tunes' Franchise," *Discount Store News,* April 6, 1998, p. 33; and Adrienne Mand, "Comet Cursors Bring WB Characters to Web," *Adweek,* April 19, 1999, p. 113.

[13]Phil Carpenter, "Some Cobranding Caveats to Obey," *Marketing News,* November 7, 1994, p. 4; Karen Benezra, "Coke, Mattel Ink Pact for Collectable Barbie," *Brandweek,* October 14, 1996, p. 5; Tobi Elkin, "Brand Builders," *Brandweek,* February 2, 1998, pp. 16–18; Stephanie Thompson, "Brand Buddies," *Brandweek,* February 23, 1998, pp. 22–30; and Gabrielle Solomon, "Co-Branding Alliances: Arranged Marriages Made by Marketers," *Fortune,* October 12, 1998, p. 188.

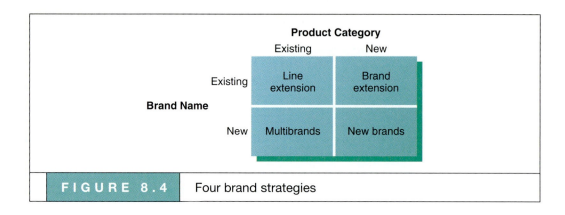

		Product Category	
		Existing	New
Brand Name	Existing	Line extension	Brand extension
	New	Multibrands	New brands

FIGURE 8.4 Four brand strategies

A company might introduce line extensions as a low-cost, low-risk way to introduce new products in order to meet consumer desires for variety, to utilize excess capacity, or simply to command more shelf space from resellers. However, line extensions involve some risks. An overextended brand name might lose its specific meaning or heavily extended brands can cause consumer confusion or frustration. A consumer buying cereal at the local supermarket will be confronted by more than 150 brands, up to 30 different brands, flavors, and sizes of oatmeal alone. By itself, Quaker offers its original Quaker Oats, several flavors of Quaker instant oatmeal, and several dry cereals such as Oatmeal Squares, Toasted Oats, and Toasted Oats—Honey Nut. Another risk is that sales of an extension may come at the expense of other items in the line. A line extension works best when it takes sales away from competing brands, not when it "cannibalizes" the company's other items.

Brand Extensions. A **brand extension** involves the use of a successful brand name to launch new or modified products in a new category. Mattel has extended its incredibly popular and enduring Barbie Doll brand into new categories ranging from Barbie home furnishings, Barbie cosmetics, and Barbie electronics to Barbie books, Barbie sporting goods, and even a Barbie band—Beyond Pink. Honda uses its company name to cover different products such as its automobiles, motorcycles, snowblowers, lawn mowers, marine engines, and snowmobiles. This allows Honda to advertise that it can fit "six Hondas in a two-car garage." Swiss Army brand sunglasses, Disney Cruise Lines, Cosmopolitan low-fat dairy products, Century 21 home improvements, and Brinks home security systems—all are brand extensions.

video example <

Take a moment to watch how one company approaches the process of implementing brand extension.

A brand extension gives a new product instant recognition and faster acceptance. It also saves the high advertising costs usually required to build a new brand name. At the same time, a brand extension strategy involves some risk. Brand extensions such as Bic pantyhose, Heinz pet food, Life Savers gum, and Clorox laundry detergent met early deaths. The extension may confuse the image of the main brand. For example, when clothing retailer Gap saw competitors targeting its value-conscious customers with Gap-like fashions at lower prices, it began testing Gap Warehouse, which sold merchandise at a cut below Gap quality and price. However, the connection confused customers and eroded Gap image. As a result, the company renamed the stores Old Navy Clothing Company, a brand that has become enormously successful.[14]

If a brand extension fails, it may harm consumer attitudes toward the other products carrying the same brand name. Further, a brand name may not be appropriate to a particular new product, even if it is well made and satisfying—would you consider buying Texaco milk or Alpo chili? A brand name

---

[14]See David Aaker, "Should You Take Your Brand to Where the Action Is?" *Harvard Business Review,* September–October 1997, pp. 135–45; Zeynep Gurhan-Canli and Durairaj Maheswaran, "The Effects of Extensions on Brand Name Dilution and Enhancement," *Journal of Marketing,* November 1998, pp. 464–73; and Lauren Goldstein, "Barbie's Secret Plan for World Domination," *Fortune,* November 23, 1998, pp. 38–39.

may lose its special positioning in the consumer's mind through overuse. Companies that are tempted to transfer a brand name must research how well the brand's associations fit the new product.[15]

Multibrands. Companies often introduce additional brands in the same category. Thus, P&G markets many different brands in each of its product categories. *Multibranding* offers a way to establish different features and appeal to different buying motives. It also allows a company to lock up more reseller shelf space. Or the company may want to protect its major brand by setting up *flanker* or *fighter brands*. For example, Seiko uses different brand names for its higher-priced watches (Seiko Lasalle) and lower-priced watches (Pulsar) to protect the flanks of its mainstream Seiko brand. Finally, companies may develop separate brand names for different regions or countries, perhaps to suit different cultures or languages. For example, Procter & Gamble dominates the U.S. laundry detergent market with Tide, which in all its forms captures over a 40 percent market share. Outside North America, however, P&G leads the detergent category with its Ariel brand, now Europe's number-two packaged-goods brand behind Coca-Cola. In the United States, P&G targets Ariel to Hispanic markets.

A major drawback of multibranding is that each brand might obtain only a small market share, and none may be very profitable. The company may end up spreading its resources over many brands instead of building a few brands to a highly profitable level. These companies should reduce the number of brands they sell in a given category and set up tighter screening procedures for new brands.

New Brands. A company may create a new brand name when it enters a new product category for which none of the company's current brand names are appropriate. For example, Japan's Matsushita uses separate names for its different families of products: Technics, Panasonic, National, and Quasar. Or, a company might believe that the power of its existing brand name is waning and a new brand name is needed. Finally, the company may obtain new brands in new categories through acquisitions. For example, S.C. Johnson & Son—marketer of Pledge furniture polish, Glade air freshener, Raid insect spray, Edge shaving gel, and many other well-known brands—added several new powerhouse brands through its acquisition of Drackett Company, including Windex, Drano, and Vanish toilet bowl cleaner.

As with multibranding, offering too many new brands can result in a company spreading its resources too thin. In some industries, such as consumer packaged goods, consumers and retailers have become concerned that there are already too many brands, with too few differences between them. Thus, Procter & Gamble, Frito-Lay, and other large consumer-product marketers are now pursuing *megabrand* strategies—weeding out weaker brands and focusing their marketing dollars only on brands that can achieve the number-one or -two market share positions in their categories.

PACKAGING

Packaging involves designing and producing the container or wrapper for a product. The package may include the product's primary container (the tube holding Colgate toothpaste); a secondary package that is thrown away when the product is about to be used (the cardboard box containing the tube of Colgate); and the shipping package necessary to store, identify, and ship the product (a corrugated box carrying six dozen tubes of Colgate toothpaste). Labeling, printed information appearing on or with the package, is also part of packaging.

Traditionally, the primary function of the package was to contain and protect the product. In recent times, however, numerous factors have made packaging an important marketing tool. Increased competition and clutter on retail store shelves means that packages must now perform many sales tasks—from attracting attention, to describing the product, to making the sale. Companies are realizing the power of good packaging to create instant consumer recognition of the company or brand. For example, in an average supermarket, which stocks 15,000 to 17,000 items, the typical shopper passes by some 300 items per minute, and 53 percent of all purchases are made on impulse. In this highly competitive environment, the package may be the seller's last chance to influence buyers. It becomes a "five-second commercial." The Campbell Soup Company estimates that the average shopper sees its familiar red and white can 76 times a year, creating the equivalent of $26 million worth of advertising. The package can also reinforce the product's positioning. Coca-Cola's familiar contour bottle speaks

[15]For more on the use of line and brand extensions and consumer attitudes toward them, see David A. Aaker and Kevin L. Keller, "Consumer Evaluations of Brand Extensions," *Journal of Marketing,* January 1990, pp. 27–41; Susan M. Broniarczyk and Joseph W. Alba, "The Importance of Brand in Brand Extension," *Journal of Marketing Research,* May 1994, pp. 214–28; Srinivas K. Reddy, Susan L. Holak, and Subodh Bhat, "To Extend or Not to Extend: Success Determinants of Line Extensions," *Journal of Marketing Research,* May 1994, pp. 243–62; Deborah Roedder John, Barbara Loken, and Christopher Joiner, *Journal of Marketing,* January 1998, pp. 19–32; and Gurrhan-Canli and Maheswaran, "The Effects of Extensions on Brand Name Dilution and Enhancement," pp. 464–73.

volumes about the product inside. "Even in a shadow, people know it's a Coke," observes a packaging expert. "It's a beautiful definition of how a package can influence the way a consumer perceives a product. People taste Coke differently from a contour bottle versus a generic package."[16]

Innovative packaging can give a company an advantage over competitors. Liquid Tide quickly attained a 10 percent share of the heavy-duty detergent market, partly because of the popularity of its container's innovative drip-proof spout and cap. In contrast, poorly designed packages can cause headaches for consumers and lost sales for the company. For example, Planters Lifesavers Company recently attempted to use innovative packaging to create an association between fresh-roasted peanuts and fresh-roasted coffee. It packaged its Fresh Roast Salted Peanuts in vacuum-packed "Brik-Pacs," similar to those used for ground coffee. Unfortunately, the coffeelike packaging worked too well: Consumers mistook the peanuts for a new brand of flavored coffee and ran them through supermarket coffee-grinding machines, creating a gooey mess, disappointed customers, and lots of irate store managers.[17]

Developing a good package for a new product requires making many decisions. First, the company must establish the *packaging concept,* which states what the package should *be* or *do* for the product. Should it mainly offer product protection, introduce a new dispensing method, suggest certain qualities about the product, or something else? Decisions then must be made on specific elements of the package, such as size, shape, materials, color, text, and brand mark. These elements must work together to support the product's position and marketing strategy. The package must be consistent with the product's advertising, pricing, and distribution.

In recent years, product safety has also become a major packaging concern. We have all learned to deal with hard-to-open "childproof" packages. After the rash of product tampering scares during the 1980s, most drug producers and food makers are now putting their products in tamper-resistant packages. In making packaging decisions, the company also must heed growing environmental concerns and make decisions that serve society's interests as well as immediate customer and company objectives. Shortages of paper, aluminum, and other materials suggest that marketers should try to reduce packaging. Many packages end up as broken bottles and crumpled cans littering the streets and coun-

Environmentally responsible packaging: Tetra Pak advertises the benefits of its packaging to consumers directly and initiates recycling programs to save the environment. As this ad to producers suggests, it's "more than just a package."

[16]See Joan Holleran, "Packaging Speaks Volumes," *Beverage Industry,* February 1998, p. 30.

[17]Robert M. McMath, "Chock Full of (Pea)nuts," *American Demographics,* April 1997, p. 60.

tryside. All of this packaging creates a major problem in solid waste disposal, requiring huge amounts of labor and energy.

Fortunately, many companies have gone "green." For example, S.C. Johnson repackaged Agree Plus shampoo in a stand-up pouch using 80 percent less plastic. P&G eliminated outer cartons from its Secret and Sure deodorants, saving 3.4 million pounds of paperboard per year. Tetra Pak, a major Swedish multinational company, provides an example of the power of innovative packaging that takes environmental concerns into account.

> Tetra Pak invented an "aseptic" package that enables milk, fruit juice, and other perishable liquid foods to be distributed without refrigeration or preservatives. Not only is this packaging more environmentally responsible, it also provides economic and distribution advantages. Aseptic packaging allows companies to distribute beverages over a wider area without investing in refrigerated trucks and warehouses. Supermarkets can carry Tetra Pak packaged products on ordinary shelves, allowing them to save expensive refrigerator space. Tetra's motto is "a package should save more than it cost." Tetra Pak promotes the benefits of its packaging to consumers directly and even initiates recycling programs to save the environment.

LABELING

Labels may range from simple tags attached to products to complex graphics that are part of the package. They perform several functions. At the very least, the label *identifies* the product or brand, such as the name Sunkist stamped on oranges. The label might also *describe* several things about the product—who made it, where it was made, when it was made, its contents, how it is to be used, and how to use it safely. Finally, the label might *promote* the product through attractive graphics.

There has been a long history of legal concerns about packaging and labels. The Federal Trade Commission Act of 1914 held that false, misleading, or deceptive labels or packages constitute unfair competition. Labels can mislead customers, fail to describe important ingredients, or fail to include needed safety warnings. As a result, several federal and state laws regulate labeling. The most prominent is the Fair Packaging and Labeling Act of 1966, which set mandatory labeling requirements, encouraged voluntary industry packaging standards, and allowed federal agencies to set packaging regulations in specific industries.

Labeling has been affected in recent times by *unit pricing* (stating the price per unit of standard measure), *open dating* (stating the expected shelf life of the product), and *nutritional labeling* (stating the nutritional values in the product). The Nutritional Labeling and Educational Act of 1990 requires sellers to provide detailed nutritional information on food products, and recent sweeping actions by the Food and Drug Administration regulate the use of health-related terms such as *low-fat, light,* and *high-fiber.* Sellers must ensure that their labels contain all the required information.

PRODUCT SUPPORT SERVICES

Customer service is another element of product strategy. A company's offer to the marketplace usually includes some services, which can be a minor or a major part of the total offer. Later in the chapter, we will discuss services as products in themselves. Here, we discuss *product support services*—services that augment actual products. More and more companies are using product support services as a major tool in gaining competitive advantage.

A company should design its product and support services to profitably meet the needs of target customers. The first step is to survey customers periodically to assess the value of current services and to obtain ideas for new ones. For example, Cadillac holds regular focus group interviews with owners and carefully watches complaints that come into its dealerships. From this careful monitoring, Cadillac has learned that buyers are very upset by repairs that are not done correctly the first time.

Once the company has assessed the value of various support services to customers, it must next assess the costs of providing these services. It can then develop a package of services that will both delight customers and yield profits to the company. For example, based on its consumer interviews, Cadillac has set up a system directly linking each dealership with a group of 10 engineers who can help walk mechanics through difficult repairs. Such actions helped Cadillac jump, in one year, from fourteenth to seventh in independent rankings of service.[18]

---

[18]Bro Uttal, "Companies That Serve You Best," *Fortune,* December 7, 1987, p. 116. For an excellent discussion of support services, see James C. Anderson and James A. Narus, "Capturing the Value of Supplementary Services," *Harvard Business Review,* January–February 1995, pp. 75–83.

Many companies are now using the Internet to provide support services that were not possible before. For example, Kaiser-Permanente, the nation's largest health maintenance organization (HMO), has rolled out a Web site that lets members register online for office visits and send e-mail questions to nurses and pharmacists (and get responses within 24 hours). Kaiser also plans to give members access to lab results and pharmaceutical refills online. Similarly, American Airlines provides a support Web site for its frequent flier members. Members can streamline the booking process by creating profiles of their home airports, usual routes, and seating and meal preferences for themselves and their families. Beyond using the site to book tickets, members can check the status of their frequent flier accounts and take advantage of special member fares. Moreover, using these profiles, American can, say, offer discounts on flights to Disney World for parents whose children's school vacations start in a few weeks.[19]

PRODUCT DECISIONS AND SOCIAL RESPONSIBILITY

Product decisions have attracted much public attention. When making such decisions, marketers should consider carefully a number of public policy issues and regulations involving acquiring or dropping products, patent protection, product quality and safety, and product warranties.

Regarding the addition of new products, the government may prevent companies from adding products through acquisitions if the effect threatens to lessen competition. Companies dropping products must be aware that they have legal obligations, written or implied, to their suppliers, dealers, and customers who have a stake in the discontinued product. Companies must also must obey U.S. patent laws when developing new products. A company cannot make its product illegally similar to another company's established product.

Manufacturers must comply with specific laws regarding product quality and safety. The Federal Food, Drug, and Cosmetic Act protects consumers from unsafe and adulterated food, drugs, and cosmetics. Various acts provide for the inspection of sanitary conditions in the meat- and poultry-processing industries. Safety legislation has been passed to regulate fabrics, chemical substances, automobiles, toys, and drugs and poisons. The Consumer Product Safety Act of 1972 established a Consumer Product Safety Commission, which has the authority to ban or seize potentially harmful products and set severe penalties for violation of the law.

If consumers have been injured by a product that has been designed defectively, they can sue manufacturers or dealers. Product liability suits are now occurring in federal and state courts at the rate of almost 110,000 per year, with individual awards often running in the millions of dollars.[20] This phenomenon has resulted in huge increases in product liability insurance premiums, causing big problems in some industries. Some companies pass these higher rates along to consumers by raising prices. Others are forced to discontinue high-risk product lines.

Many manufacturers offer written product warranties to convince customers of their products' quality. To protect consumers, Congress passed the Magnuson-Moss Warranty Act in 1975. The act requires that full warranties meet certain minimum standards, including repair "within a reasonable time and without charge" or a replacement or full refund if the product does not work "after a reasonable number of attempts" at repair. Otherwise, the company must make it clear that it is offering only a limited warranty. The law has led several manufacturers to switch from full to limited warranties and others to drop warranties altogether as a marketing tool.

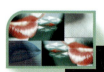

active poll   <

Take a moment to give your opinion on a question concerning product liability.

[19]Heather Green, "A Cyber Revolt in Health Care," *Business Week,* October 19, 1998, pp. 154–56; Robert D. Hof, "Now It's Your Web," *Business Week,* October 5, 1998, pp. 164–76; and George V. Hulme, Help! Companies Are Turning to Their Call Centers to Improve Customer Service on the Web," *Sales and Marketing Management,* February 2000, pp. 79–84.

[20]See Paula Mergenbagen, "Product Liability: Who Sues?" *American Demographics,* June 1995, p. 48; "Support Urged for Product Liability Reform," *Industrial Distribution,* April 1997, p. SA3; Owen Ullmann, "Product Liability Deadlock," *Business Week,* January 12, 1998, p. 51; and "A Primer on Product Liability Laws," *Purchasing,* May 6, 1999, pp. 32–34.

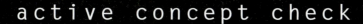

> active concept check

Now let's take a moment to test your knowledge of what you've just read.

> Product Line Decisions

We have looked at product strategy decisions such as branding, packaging, labeling, and support services for individual products and services. But product strategy also calls for building a product line. A **product line** is a group of products that are closely related because they function in a similar manner, are sold to the same customer groups, are marketed through the same types of outlets, or fall within given price ranges. For example, Nike produces several lines of athletic shoes, Motorola produces several lines of telecommunications products, and AT&T offers several lines of long-distance telephone services. In developing product line strategies, marketers face a number of tough decisions.

The major product line decision involves *product line length*—the number of items in the product line. The line is too short if the manager can increase profits by adding items; the line is too long if the manager can increase profits by dropping items. Product line length is influenced by company objectives and resources.

Product lines tend to lengthen over time. The sales force and distributors may pressure the product manager for a more complete line to satisfy their customers. Or, the manager may want to add items to the product line to create growth in sales and profits. However, as the manager adds items, several costs rise: design and engineering costs, inventory costs, manufacturing changeover costs, transportation costs, and promotional costs to introduce new items. Eventually top management calls a halt to the mushrooming product line. Unnecessary or unprofitable items will be pruned from the line in a major effort to increase overall profitability. This pattern of uncontrolled product line growth followed by heavy pruning is typical and may repeat itself many times.

The company must manage its product lines carefully. It can systematically increase the length of its product line in two ways: by *stretching* its line and by *filling* its line. *Product line stretching* occurs when a company lengthens its product line beyond its current range. The company can stretch its line downward, upward, or both ways.

Many companies initially locate at the upper end of the market and later stretch their lines *downward*. A company may stretch downward to plug a market hole that otherwise would attract a new competitor or to respond to a competitor's attack on the upper end. Or it may add low-end products because it finds faster growth taking place in the low-end segments. Mercedes-Benz stretched downward for all these reasons. Facing a slow-growth luxury car market and attacks by Japanese automakers on its high-end positioning, Mercedes-Benz successfully introduced its C-Class cars at $30,000 without harming its ability to sell other Mercedes-Benz for $100,000 or more. In a joint venture with Switzerland's Swatch watchmaker, Mercedes-Benz launched the $10,000 Smart microcompact car, an environmentally correct second car. Just 7.5 feet long, and affectionately dubbed the "Swatchmobile," the Smart is "designed for two people and a crate of beer."[21]

> active example

Take a moment to explore how one prominent firm is practicing downward extension.

Companies at the lower end of the market may want to stretch their product lines *upward*. Sometimes, companies stretch upward in order to add prestige to their current products. They may be attracted by a faster growth rate or higher margins at the higher end, or they may simply want to position themselves as full-line manufacturers. Thus, each of the leading Japanese auto companies intro-

---

[21]John Templeman, "A Mercedes in Every Driveway?" *Business Week,* August 26, 1996, pp. 38–40; and Sam Pickens and Dagmar Mussey, "Swatch Taps Zurich Shop to Develop Euro Car Ads," *Advertising Age,* May 19, 1997, p. 32.

Product line stretching: Mercedes introduced several smaller, lower-priced models, including the $10,000 Smart microcompact car in a joint venture with Swatch. Affectionately dubbed the "Swatchmobile," the Smart is "designed for two people and a crate of beer."

duced an upmarket automobile: Toyota launched Lexus; Nissan launched Infinity; and Honda launched Acura. They used entirely new names rather than their own names. Other companies have included their own names in moving upmarket. For example, Gallo introduced Ernest and Julio Gallo Varietals and priced these wines at more than twice the price of its regular wines. General Electric introduced GE Profile brand appliances targeted at the select few households earning more than $100,000 per year and living in houses valued at more than $400,000.[22]

Companies in the middle range of the market may decide to stretch their lines in *both directions.* Marriott did this with its hotel product line. Along with regular Marriott hotels, it added the Marriott Marquis line to serve the upper end of the market, and the Springhill Suites and Fairfield Inn lines to serve the moderate and lower ends. Each branded hotel line is aimed at a different target market. Marriott Marquis aims to attract and please top executives; Marriotts, middle managers; Courtyards, salespeople and other "road warriors"; and Fairfield Inns, vacationers and business travelers on a tight travel budget. Marriott's Residence Inn provides a home away from home for people who travel for a living, who are relocating, or who are on assignment and need inexpensive temporary lodging. The major risk with this strategy is that some travelers will trade down after finding that the lower-price hotels in the Marriott chain give them pretty much everything they want. However, Marriott would rather capture its customers who move downward than lose them to competitors.

An alternative to product line stretching is *product line filling*—adding more items within the present range of the line. There are several reasons for product line filling: reaching for extra profits, satisfying dealers, using excess capacity, being the leading full-line company, and plugging holes to keep out competitors. Thus, Sony filled its Walkman line by adding solar-powered and waterproof Walkmans and an ultralight model that attaches to a sweatband for joggers, bicyclers, tennis players, and other exercisers. However, line filling is overdone if it results in cannibalization and customer confusion. The company should ensure that new items are noticeably different from existing ones.

active concept check   <

Now let's take a moment to test your knowledge of what you've just read.

> ## Product Mix Decisions

An organization with several product lines has a product mix. A **product mix** (or **product assortment**) consists of all the product lines and items that a particular seller offers for sale. Avon's product mix consists of four major product lines: cosmetics, jewelry, fashions, and household items. Each product line consists of several sublines. For example, cosmetics breaks down into lipstick, eyeliner, powder, and so on. Each line and subline has many individual items. Altogether, Avon's product mix

[22]See Aaker, "Should You Take Your Brand to Where the Action Is?" pp. 135–43.

includes 1,300 items. In contrast, a typical Kmart stocks 15,000 items, 3M markets more than 60,000 products, and General Electric manufactures as many as 250,000 items.

A company's product mix has four important dimensions: width, length, depth, and consistency. Product mix *width* refers to the number of different product lines the company carries. For example, Procter & Gamble markets a fairly wide product mix consisting of many product lines, including paper, food, household cleaning, medicinal, cosmetics, and personal care products. Product mix *length* refers to the total number of items the company carries within its product lines. P&G typically carries many brands within each line. For example, it sells eight laundry detergents, six hand soaps, six shampoos, and four dishwashing detergents.

Product line *depth* refers to the number of versions offered of each product in the line. Thus, P&G's Crest toothpaste comes in three sizes and two formulations (paste and gel). Finally, the *consistency* of the product mix refers to how closely related the various product lines are in end use, production requirements, distribution channels, or some other way. P&G's product lines are consistent insofar as they are consumer products that go through the same distribution channels. The lines are less consistent insofar as they perform different functions for buyers.

> ## active exercise

Take a moment to consider the practical relevance of product mix decisions.

These product mix dimensions provide the handles for defining the company's product strategy. The company can increase its business in four ways. It can add new product lines, thus widening its product mix. In this way, its new lines build on the company's reputation in its other lines. The company can lengthen its existing product lines to become a more full-line company. Or it can add more versions of each product and thus deepen its product mix. Finally, the company can pursue more product line consistency—or less—depending on whether it wants to have a strong reputation in a single field or in several fields.

> ## active concept check

Now let's take a moment to test your knowledge of what you've just read.

> ## Services Marketing

One of the major world trends in recent years has been the dramatic growth of services. As a result of rising affluence, more leisure time, and the growing complexity of products that require servicing, the United States has become the world's first service economy. Services now generate 74 percent of U.S. gross domestic product. Whereas service jobs accounted for 55 percent of all U.S. jobs in 1970, by 1993 they accounted for 79 percent of total employment. Services are growing even faster in the world economy, making up a quarter of the value of all international trade. In fact, a variety of service industries—from banking, insurance, and communications to transportation, travel, and entertainment—now accounts for well over 60 percent of the economy in developed countries around the world.[23]

Service industries vary greatly. *Governments* offer services through courts, employment services, hospitals, loan agencies, military services, police and fire departments, postal service, regulatory agencies, and schools. *Private nonprofit organizations* offer services through museums, charities, churches, colleges, foundations, and hospitals. A large number of *business organizations* offer services—airlines, banks, hotels, insurance companies, consulting firms, medical and law practices, enter-

---

[23]See Ronald Henkoff, "Service Is Everybody's Business," *Fortune,* June 27, 1994, pp. 48–60; Adrian Palmer and Catherine Cole, *Services Marketing: Principles and Practice* (Upper Saddle River, NJ: Prentice Hall, 1995), pp. 56–60; Valerie Zeithaml and Mary Jo Bitner, *Services Marketing* (New York: McGraw-Hill, 1996), pp. 8–9; and Michael van Biema and Bruce Greenwald, "Managing Our Way to Higher Service-Sector Productivity," *Harvard Business Review,* July–August 1997, pp. 87–95.

tainment companies, real estate firms, advertising and research agencies, and retailers. Some service businesses are very large, with total sales and assets in the billions of dollars. There are also tens of thousands of smaller service providers.

NATURE AND CHARACTERISTICS OF A SERVICE

A company must consider four special service characteristics when designing marketing programs: *intangibility, inseparability, variability,* and *perishability.* These characteristics are summarized in Figure 8.5 and discussed in the following sections.

Service intangibility means that services cannot be seen, tasted, felt, heard, or smelled before they are bought. For example, people undergoing cosmetic surgery cannot see the result before the purchase. Airline passengers have nothing but a ticket and the promise that they and their luggage will arrive safely at the intended destination, hopefully at the same time. To reduce uncertainty, buyers look for "signals" of service quality. They draw conclusions about quality from the place, people, price, equipment, and communications that they can see. Therefore, the service provider's task is to make the service tangible in one or more ways. Whereas product marketers try to add intangibles to their tangible offers, service marketers try to add tangibles to their intangible offers.

Physical goods are produced, then stored, later sold, and still later consumed. In contrast, services are first sold, then produced and consumed at the same time. **Service inseparability** means that services cannot be separated from their providers, whether the providers are people or machines. If a service employee provides the service, then the employee is a part of the service. Because the customer is also present as the service is produced, *provider–customer interaction* is a special feature of services marketing. Both the provider and the customer affect the service outcome.

Service variability means that the quality of services depends on who provides them as well as when, where, and how they are provided. For example, some hotels—say, Marriott—have reputations for providing better service than others. Still, within a given Marriott hotel, one registration-desk employee may be cheerful and efficient, whereas another standing just a few feet away may be unpleasant and slow. Even the quality of a single Marriott employee's service varies according to his or her energy and frame of mind at the time of each customer encounter.

Service perishability means that services cannot be stored for later sale or use. Some doctors charge patients for missed appointments because the service value existed only at that point and disappeared when the patient did not show up. The perishability of services is not a problem when demand is steady. However, when demand fluctuates, service firms often have difficult problems. For example, because of rush-hour demand, public transportation companies have to own much more equipment than they would if demand were even throughout the day. Thus, service firms often design strategies for producing a better match between demand and supply. For instance, hotels and resorts charge lower prices in the off-season to attract more guests. Restaurants hire part-time employees to serve during peak periods.

active exercise >

Let's now look at an example of a service organization using tangible cues for promoting its intangible service.

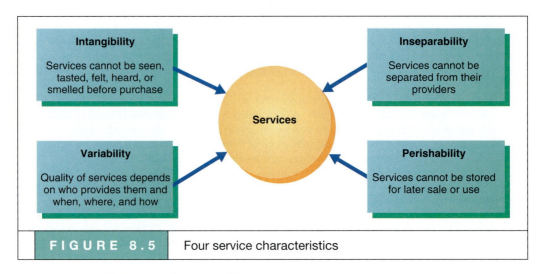

| FIGURE 8.5 | Four service characteristics |

MARKETING STRATEGIES FOR SERVICE FIRMS

Just like manufacturing businesses, good service firms use marketing to position themselves strongly in chosen target markets. Southwest Airlines positions itself as a no-frills, short-haul airline charging very low fares. Ritz-Carlton Hotels positions itself as offering a memorable experience that "enlivens the senses, instills well-being, and fulfills even the unexpressed wishes and needs of our guests." These and other service firms establish their positions through traditional marketing mix activities.

However, because services differ from tangible products, they often require additional marketing approaches. In a product business, products are fairly standardized and can sit on shelves waiting for customers. But in a service business, the customer and frontline service employee *interact* to create the service. Thus, service providers must interact effectively with customers to create superior value during service encounters. Effective interaction, in turn, depends on the skills of frontline service employees and on the service production and support processes backing these employees.

The Service-Profit Chain

Successful service companies focus their attention on *both* their customers and their employees. They understand the **service-profit chain,** which links service firm profits with employee and customer satisfaction. This chain consists of five links:[24]

- *Internal service quality:* superior employee selection and training, a quality work environment, and strong support for those dealing with customers, which results in . . .
- *Satisfied and productive service employees:* more satisfied, loyal, and hard-working employees, which results in . . .
- *Greater service value:* more effective and efficient customer value creation and service delivery, which results in . . .
- *Satisfied and loyal customers:* satisfied customers who remain loyal, repeat purchase, and refer other customers, which results in . . .
- *Healthy service profits and growth:* superior service firm performance.

Therefore, reaching service profits and growth goals begins with taking care of those who take care of customers.

All of this suggests that service marketing requires more than just traditional external marketing using the four Ps. Figure 8.6 shows that service marketing also requires *internal marketing* and *interactive marketing*. **Internal marketing** means that the service firm must effectively train and motivate its customer-contact employees and all the supporting service people to work as a *team* to provide customer satisfaction. For the firm to deliver consistently high service quality, marketers must get everyone in the organization to practice a customer orientation. In fact, internal marketing must *precede* external marketing.

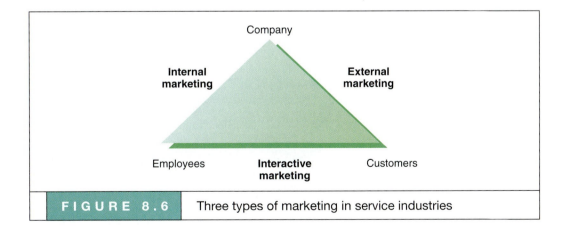

| FIGURE 8.6 | Three types of marketing in service industries |

[24]See James L. Heskett, Thomas O. Jones, Gary W. Loveman, W. Earl Sasser Jr., and Leonard A. Schlesinger, "Putting the Service-Profit Chain to Work," *Harvard Business Review,* March–April, 1994, pp. 164–74; and James L. Heskett, W. Earl Sasser Jr., and Leonard A. Schlesinger, *The Service Profit Chain: How Leading Companies Link Profit and Growth to Loyalty, Satisfaction, and Value* (New York: Free Press, 1997). Also see Anthony J. Rucci, Steven P. Kirn, and Richard T. Quinn, "The Employee–Customer–Profit Chain at Sears," *Harvard Business Review,* January–February 1998, pp. 83–97.

Interactive marketing means that service quality depends heavily on the quality of the buyer–seller interaction during the service encounter. In product marketing, product quality often depends little on how the product is obtained. But in services marketing, service quality depends on both the service deliverer and the quality of the delivery. Service marketers cannot assume that they will satisfy the customer simply by providing good technical service. They have to master interactive marketing skills as well.

Today, as competition and costs increase, and as productivity and quality decrease, more service marketing sophistication is needed. Service companies face three major marketing tasks: They want to increase their *competitive differentiation, service quality,* and *productivity.*

Managing Service Differentiation

In these days of intense price competition, service marketers often complain about the difficulty of differentiating their services from those of competitors. To the extent that customers view the services of different providers as similar, they care less about the provider than the price.

The solution to price competition is to develop a differentiated offer, delivery, and image. The *offer* can include innovative features that set one company's offer apart from competitors' offers. For example, airlines have introduced innovations such as in-flight movies, advance seating, air-to-ground telephone service, and frequent flier award programs to differentiate their offers. British Airways even offers international travelers a sleeping compartment, hot showers, and cooked-to-order breakfasts.

Service companies can differentiate their service *delivery* by having more able and reliable customer-contact people, by developing a superior physical environment in which the service product is delivered, or by designing a superior delivery process. For example, many banks offer their customers electronic home banking as a better way to access banking services than having to drive, park, and wait in line.

Finally, service companies also can work on differentiating their *images* through symbols and branding. For example, the Harris Bank of Chicago adopted the lion as its symbol on its stationery, in its advertising, and even as stuffed animals offered to new depositors. The well-known Harris lion confers an image of strength on the bank. Other well-known service symbols include The Travelers' red umbrella, Merrill Lynch's bull, and Allstate's "good hands."

Service companies differentiate their images through symbols and branding. Note the now very familiar "Allstate: You're in good hands" brand and symbol at the bottom of this ad.

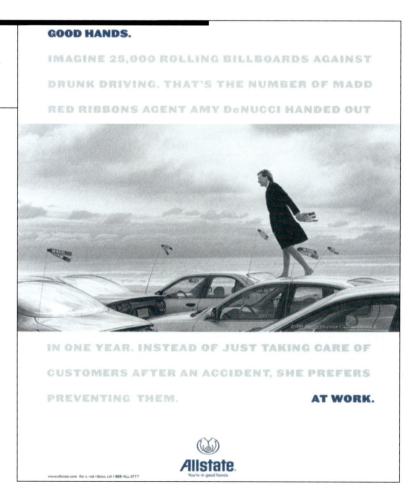

GOOD HANDS.

IMAGINE 25,000 ROLLING BILLBOARDS AGAINST DRUNK DRIVING. THAT'S THE NUMBER OF MADD RED RIBBONS AGENT AMY DeNUCCI HANDED OUT

IN ONE YEAR. INSTEAD OF JUST TAKING CARE OF CUSTOMERS AFTER AN ACCIDENT, SHE PREFERS PREVENTING THEM. **AT WORK.**

Allstate.
You're in good hands.

Managing Service Quality

One of the major ways a service firm can differentiate itself is by delivering consistently higher quality than its competitors do. Like manufacturers before them, most service industries have now joined the total quality movement. Like product marketers, service providers need to identify the expectations of target customers concerning service quality. Unfortunately, service quality is harder to define and judge than is product quality. For instance, it is harder to get agreement on the quality of a haircut than on the quality of a hair dryer. Customer retention is perhaps the best measure of quality—a service firm's ability to hang onto its customers depends on how consistently it delivers value to them.[25]

Service companies want to ensure that customers will receive consistently high-quality service in every service encounter. However, unlike product manufacturers who can adjust their machinery and inputs until everything is perfect, service quality will always vary, depending on the interactions between employees and customers. Problems will inevitably occur. As hard as they try, even the best companies will have an occasional late delivery, burned steak, or grumpy employee. However, although a company cannot always prevent service problems, it can learn to recover from them. Good *service recovery* can turn angry customers into loyal ones. In fact, good recovery can win more customer purchasing and loyalty than if things had gone well in the first place. Therefore, companies should take steps not only to provide good service every time but also to recover from service mistakes when they do occur.[26]

The first step is to *empower* frontline service employees—to give them the authority, responsibility, and incentives they need to recognize, care about, and tend to customer needs. At Marriott, for example, well-trained employees are given the authority to do whatever it takes, on the spot, to keep guests happy. They are also expected to help management ferret out the cause of guests' problems and to inform managers of ways to improve overall hotel service and guests' comfort.[27]

Studies of well-managed service companies show that they share a number of common virtues regarding service quality. Top service companies are *customer obsessed* and set *high service quality standards.* They do not settle merely for good service; they aim for 100 percent defect-free service. A 98 percent performance standard may sound good but, using this standard, 64,000 Federal Express packages would be lost each day, 10 words would be misspelled on each printed page, 400,000 prescriptions would be misfilled daily, and drinking water would be unsafe 8 days a year.[28]

Top service firms also *watch service performance closely,* both their own and that of competitors. They use methods such as comparison shopping, customer surveys, and suggestion and complaint forms. For example, General Electric sends out 700,000 response cards each year to households that rate their service people's performance. Citibank takes regular measures of "ART"—accuracy, responsiveness, and timeliness—and sends out employees who act as customers to check on service quality.

Good service companies also communicate their concerns about service quality to employees and provide performance feedback. At Federal Express, quality measurements are everywhere. When employees walk in the door in the morning, they see the previous week's on-time percentages. Then, the company's in-house television station gives them detailed breakdowns of what happened yesterday and any potential problems for the day ahead.

> **video exercise**

Take a moment to consider the challenges of managing service quality.

---

[25]For excellent discussions of service quality, see A. Parasuraman, Valerie A. Zeithaml, and Leonard L. Berry, "A Conceptual Model of Service Quality and Its Implications for Future Research," *Journal of Marketing,* Fall 1985, pp. 41–50; J. Joseph Cronin Jr. and Steven A. Taylor, "Measuring Service Quality: A Reexamination and Extension," *Journal of Marketing,* July 1992, pp. 55–68; Parasuraman, Zeithaml, and Berry, "Reassessment of Expectations as a Comparison Standard in Measuring Service Quality: Implications for Further Research," *Journal of Marketing,* January 1994, pp. 111–24; Zeithaml, Berry, and Parasuraman, "The Behavioral Consequences of Service Quality," pp. 31–46; and "Service Competitiveness: An Anglo-U.S. Study," *Business Strategy Review* 8, no. 1, 1997, pp. 7–22.

[26]See Erika Rasmusson, "Winning Back Angry Customers," *Sales & Marketing Management,* October 1997, p. 131; and Stephen S. Tax, Stephen W. Brown, and Murali Chandrashekaran, "Customer Evaluations of Service Complaint Experiences: Implications for Relationship Marketing," *Journal of Marketing,* April 1998, pp. 60–76.

[27]Ronald Henkoff, "Finding and Keeping the Best Service Workers," *Fortune,* October 3, 1994, pp. 110–22.

[28]See James L. Heskett, W. Earl Sasser Jr., and Christopher W. L. Hart, *Service Breakthroughs* (New York: Free Press, 1990).

Managing Service Productivity

With their costs rising rapidly, service firms are under great pressure to increase service productivity. They can do so in several ways. The service providers can train current employees better or hire new ones who will work harder or more skillfully. Or the service providers can increase the quantity of their service by giving up some quality. Doctors working for health maintenance organizations (HMOs) have moved toward handling more patients and giving less time to each. The provider can "industrialize the service" by adding equipment and standardizing production, as in McDonald's assembly-line approach to fast-food retailing.

Finally, the service provider can harness the power of technology. Although we often think of technology's power to save time and costs in manufacturing companies, it also has great—and often untapped—potential to make service workers more productive. Consider this example:[29]

> Using a help-desk computerized system called Apriori, Storage Dimensions (SD) can answer customer service questions on the spot. When a customer calls Storage Dimensions with a problem, the operator inputs keywords. If the customer's question has been asked and answered before by others, as so many have, a solution document "bubbles up" to the top of the PC screen and customer's problems get solved on the spot. Since installing Apriori, SD has reduced problem resolution time from an average of two hours to twenty minutes. As an added bonus, the company has also used information gleaned during the "help" conversations to generate sales leads and product development ideas.

Similarly, a well-designed Web site can allow customers to obtain buying information, narrow their purchase options, or even make a purchase directly, saving service provider time. For example, personal computer buyers can visit the Dell Web site (**www.Dell.com**), review the characteristics of various Dell models, check out prices, and organize their questions ahead of time. Even if they choose to call a Dell telesales representative rather than buying via the Web site, they are better informed and require less personal service.

However, companies must avoid pushing productivity so hard that doing so reduces quality. Attempts to industrialize a service or to cut costs can make a service company more efficient in the short run but reduce its longer run ability to innovate, maintain service quality, or respond to consumer needs and desires. In some cases, service providers accept reduced productivity in order to create more service differentiation or quality.

active concept check <

Now let's take a moment to test your knowledge of what you've just read.

> ## International Product and Services Marketing

International product and service marketers face special challenges. First, they must figure out what products and services to introduce and in which countries. Then, they must decide how much to standardize or adapt their products and services for world markets. On the one hand, companies would like to standardize their offerings. Standardization helps a company to develop a consistent worldwide image. It also lowers manufacturing costs and eliminates duplication of research and development, advertising, and product design efforts. On the other hand, consumers around the world differ in their cultures, attitudes, and buying behaviors. Markets also vary in their economic conditions, competition, legal requirements, and physical environments. Companies must usually respond to these differences by adapting their product offerings. Something as simple as an electrical outlet can create big product problems:

[29]Nilly Landau, "Are You Being Served?" *International Business,* March 1995, pp. 38–40; and Omar A. El Sawy, "Redesigning the Customer Support Process for the Electronic Economy: Insights from Storage Dimensions," *MIS Quarterly,* December 1997, pp. 457–83. Also see Michael van Biema and Bruce Greenwald, "Managing Our Way to Higher Service-Sector Productivity," *Harvard Business Review,* July–August 1997, pp. 87–95.

Those who have traveled across Europe know the frustration of electrical plugs, different voltages, and other annoyances of international travel. . . . Philips, the electrical appliance manufacturer, has to produce 12 kinds of irons to serve just its European market. The problem is that Europe does not have a universal [electrical] standard. The ends of irons bristle with different plugs for different countries. Some have three prongs, others two; prongs protrude straight or angled, round or rectangular, fat, thin, and sometimes sheathed. There are circular plug faces, squares, pentagons, and hexagons. Some are perforated and some are notched. One French plug has a niche like a keyhole; British plugs carry fuses.[30]

Packaging also presents new challenges for international marketers. Packaging issues can be subtle. For example, names, labels, and colors may not translate easily from one country to another. A firm using yellow flowers in its logo might fare well in the United States but meet with disaster in Mexico, where a yellow flower symbolizes death or disrespect. Similarly, although Nature's Gift might be an appealing name for gourmet mushrooms in America, it would be deadly in Germany, where *gift* means poison. Packaging may also have to be tailored to meet the physical characteristics of consumers in various parts of the world. For instance, soft drinks are sold in smaller cans in Japan to fit the smaller Japanese hand better. Thus, although product and package standardization can produce benefits, companies must usually adapt their offerings to the unique needs of specific international markets.

Service marketers also face special challenges when going global. Some service industries have a long history of international operations. For example, the commercial banking industry was one of the first to grow internationally. Banks had to provide global services in order to meet the foreign exchange and credit needs of their home country clients wanting to sell overseas. In recent years, many banks have become truly global operations. Germany's Deutsche Bank, for example, has branches in 41 countries. Thus, for its clients around the world who wish to take advantage of growth opportunities created by German reunification, Deutsche Bank can raise money not just in Frankfurt but also in Zurich, London, Paris, and Tokyo.

> ## active example

Take a moment to explore the strategies U.S. car makers are planning in order to gain a foothold for their products in the Asian market.

The travel industry also moved naturally into international operations. American hotel and airline companies grew quickly in Europe and Asia during the economic expansion that followed World War II. Credit card companies soon followed—the early worldwide presence of American Express has now been matched by Visa and MasterCard. Business travelers and vacationers like the convenience, and they have now come to expect that their credit cards will be honored wherever they go.

Professional and business services industries such as accounting, management consulting, and advertising have only recently globalized. The international growth of these firms followed the globalization of the manufacturing companies they serve. For example, as their client companies began to employ global marketing and advertising strategies, advertising agencies and other marketing services firms responded by globalizing their own operations.

Retailers are among the latest service businesses to go global. As their home markets become saturated with stores, American retailers such as Wal-Mart, Kmart, Toys "R" Us, Office Depot, Saks Fifth Avenue, and Disney are expanding into faster growing markets abroad. For example, every year since 1995, Wal-Mart has entered a new country; its international division's sales have now skyrocketed to more than $12 billion. Foreign retailers are making similar moves. The Japanese retailer Yaohan now operates the largest shopping center in Asia, the 21-story Nextage Shanghai Tower in China, and Carrefour of France is the leading retailer in Brazil and Argentina. Asian shoppers now buy American products in Dutch-owned Makro stores, now Southeast Asia's biggest store group with sales in the region of more than $2 billion.[31]

Service companies wanting to operate in other countries are not always welcomed with open arms. Whereas manufacturers usually face straightforward tariff, quota, or currency restrictions when attempting to sell their products in another country, service providers are likely to face more subtle barriers. In some cases, rules and regulations affecting international service firms reflect the host

[30]Philip Cateora, *International Marketing,* 8th ed. (Homewood, IL: Irwin, 1993), p. 270.

[31]See Carla Rapoport, "Retailers Go Global," *Fortune,* February 20, 1995, pp. 102–8; "Top 200 Global Retailers," *Stores,* January 1998, pp. S5–S12; Jeffery Adler, "The Americanization of Global Retailing," *Discount Merchandiser,* February 1998, p. 102; and Tony Lisanti, "Europe's Abuzz over Wal-Mart," *Discount Store News,* May 3, 1999, p. 11.

country's traditions. In others, they appear to protect the country's own fledgling service industries from large global competitors with greater resources. In still other cases, however, the restrictions seem to have little purpose other than to make entry difficult for foreign service firms.

A Turkish law, for example, forbids international accounting firms from bringing capital into the country to set up offices and requires them to use the names of local partners in their marketing rather than their own internationally known company names. To audit the books of a multinational company's branch in Buenos Aires, an accountant must have the equivalent of a high school education in Argentinean geography and history. In New Delhi, India, international insurance companies are not allowed to sell property and casualty policies to the country's fast-growing business community or life insurance to its huge middle class.[32]

Despite such difficulties, the trend toward growth of global service companies will continue, especially in banking, airlines, telecommunications, and professional services. Today service firms are no longer simply following their manufacturing customers. Instead, they are taking the lead in international expansion.

active concept check   <

Now let's take a moment to test your knowledge of what you've just read.

> Chapter Wrap-Up

Now that you've reached the end of the chapter, you may wish to explore the concepts you've been reading about in greater detail, or test yourself to see how well you've comprehended the material. In the box below you'll find a number of links. Click on any one of these links to find additional chapter resources.

> end-of-chapter resources

- Review of Concept Connections
- Practice Quiz
- Issues for Discussion
- Key Terms
- Marketing Applications
- Internet Connections
- Company Case

---

[32]Lee Smith, "What's at Stake in the Trade Talks," *Fortune,* August 27, 1990, pp. 76–77.

New-Product Development and Product Life-Cycle Strategies

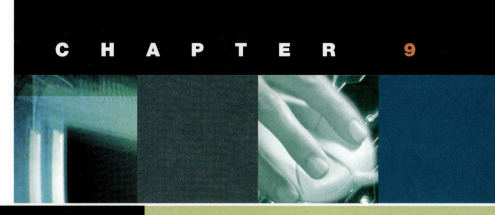

Chapter Outline

> What's Ahead

"New products!" declares Gillette's chairman and CEO Alfred M. Zeien. "That's the name of the game." Since its founding in 1901, Gillette's heavy commitment to innovation has kept the company razor sharp. Gillette is best known for its absolute dominance of the razor-and-blades market. However, all of its divisions—Duracell batteries, Gillette toiletries and cosmetics (Right Guard, Soft & Dri), stationery products (Parker, Paper Mate, and Waterman pens), Oral-B toothbrushes, and Braun electrical appliances—share common traits: Each is profitable, fast growing, number one worldwide in its markets, and anchored by a steady flow of innovative new-product offerings. Zeien predicts that 50 percent of Gillette's new products will soon come from products that didn't exist five years ago—that's twice the level of innovation found at the average consumer-products company. "Gillette is a new-product machine," says one Wall Street analyst.

New products don't just happen at Gillette. New-product success starts with a company-wide culture that supports innovation. Whereas many companies try to protect their successful current products, Gillette encourages innovations that will cannibalize its established product hits. "They know that if they don't bring out a new zinger, someone else will," observes an industry consultant. Gillette also accepts blunders and dead ends as a normal part of creativity and innovation. It knows that it must generate dozens of new-product ideas to get just one success in the marketplace. The company scorns what CEO Zeien calls "putting blue dots in the soap powder"—attaching superficial frills to existing products and labeling them innovations. However, Gillette strongly encourages its people to take creative risks in applying cutting-edge technologies to find substantial improvements that make life easier for customers.

New-product development is complex and expensive, but Gillette's mastery of the process has put the company in a class of its own. For example, Gillette spent $275 million on designing and developing its Sensor family of razors, garnering 29 patents along the way. It spent an incredible $1 billion on the development of Sensor's successor, the triple-bladed Mach3, and applied for 35 more patents. Competing brands Bic and Wilkinson have managed to claim significant shares of the disposable-razor market, and Shick, Norelco, and Remington compete effectively in electric razors with Gillette's Braun unit. But Gillette, with its stunning technological superiority, operates with virtually no competition worldwide in the burgeoning cartridge-razor sector. Backed by Gillette's biggest new-product launch ever, the Mach3 strengthened the company's stranglehold on this market. Within only a few months of its introduction, the new razor and blades were number-one sellers.

At Gillette, it seems that almost everyone gets involved in one way or another with new-product development. Even people who don't participate directly in the product design and development are likely to be pressed into service testing prototypes. Every working day at Gillette, 200 volunteers from various departments come to work unshaven, troop to the second floor of the company's gritty South Boston manufacturing and research plant, and enter small booths with a sink and mirror. There they take instructions from technicians on the other side of a small window as to which razor, shaving cream, or aftershave to use. The volunteers evaluate razors for sharpness of blade, smoothness of glide, and ease of handling. When finished, they enter their judgments into a computer. In a nearby shower room, women perform the same ritual on their legs, underarms, and what the company delicately refers to as the "bikini area." "We bleed so you'll get a good shave at home," says one Gillette employee.

Gillette also excels at bringing new products to market. The company understands that, once introduced, fledgling products need generous manufacturing and marketing support to thrive in the hotly competitive consumer products marketplace. To deliver the required support, Gillette has devised a formula that calls for R&D, capital investment, and advertising expenditures—which it refers to collectively as "growth drivers"—to rise in combination at least as fast as sales. Last year, spending on these growth drivers rose 16 percent as compared with a 12 percent rise in sales. The company spent a staggering $300 million on introductory advertising and marketing for the Mach3 alone.

Thus, over the decades, superior new products have been the cornerstone of Gillette's amazing success. The company commands the loyalty of more than 700 million shavers in 200 countries around the globe. These customers have purchased hundreds of millions of Gillette razors and billions of blades, giving Gillette more than 70 percent of the wet-shave market in the United States and 72 percent of the $7 billion worldwide market. Last year, Gillette was named by the American Marketing Association as its New Product Marketer of the Year.

Gillette's new-product prowess is so much a part of its image that it has even become the stuff of jokes. Quips down-home humorist Dave Barry, "One day soon the Gillette Company will announce the development of a razor that, thanks to a computer microchip, can actually travel ahead in time and shave beard hairs that don't even exist yet."[1]

> ## objectives

Before you begin, take a moment to familiarize yourself with the key objectives of this chapter.

> ## gearing up

Before we begin our exploration this chapter, take a short warm-up test to see what you know about this topic.

A company has to be good at developing and managing new products. Every product seems to go through a life cycle—it is born, goes through several phases, and eventually dies as newer products come along that better serve consumer needs. This product life cycle presents two major challenges: First, because all products eventually decline, a firm must be good at developing new products to replace aging ones (the problem of *new-product development*). Second, the firm must be good at adapting its marketing strategies in the face of changing tastes, technologies, and competition as products pass through life-cycle stages (the problem of *product life-cycle strategies*). We first look at the problem of finding and developing new products and then at the problem of managing them successfully over their life cycles.

> ### New-Product Development Strategy

Given the rapid changes in consumer tastes, technology, and competition, companies must develop a steady stream of new products and services. A firm can obtain new products in two ways. One is through *acquisition*—by buying a whole company, a patent, or a license to produce someone else's product. The other is through **new-product development** in the company's own research and development department. By *new products* we mean original products, product improvements, product modifications, and new brands that the firm develops through its own research and development efforts. In this chapter, we concentrate on new-product development.

Innovation can be very risky. Ford lost $350 million on its Edsel automobile; RCA lost $580 million on its SelectaVision videodisc player; and Texas Instruments lost a staggering $660 million before withdrawing from the home computer business. Other costly product failures from sophisticated companies include New Coke (Coca-Cola Company), Eagle Snacks (Anheuser-Busch), Zap Mail electronic mail (Federal Express), Polarvision instant movies (Polaroid), Premier "smokeless" cigarettes (R.J. Reynolds), Clorox detergent (Clorox Company), and Arch Deluxe sandwiches (McDonald's).[2]

New products continue to fail at a disturbing rate. One source estimates that new consumer packaged goods (consisting mostly of line extensions) fail at a rate of 80 percent. Another study suggested that of the staggering 25,000 new consumer food, beverage, beauty, and health care products to hit the

---

[1]Quotes from Lawrence Ingrassia, "Taming the Monster: How Big Companies Can Change," *Wall Street Journal,* December 10, 1992, pp. A1, A6; William H. Miller, "Gillette's Secret to Sharpness," *Industry Week,* January 3, 1994, pp. 24–30; Linda Grant, "Gillette Knows Shaving—and How to Turn Out Hot New Products," *Fortune,* October 14, 1996, pp. 207–10; and Dana Canedy, "Gillette's Strengths in Razors Undone by Troubles Abroad," *New York Times,* June 19, 1999, p. 3. Also see William C. Symonds, "Would You Spend $1.50 for a Razor Blade?" *Business Week,* April 27, 1998, p. 46; James Heckman, "Razor Sharp: Adding Value, Making Noise with Mach3 Intro," *Marketing News,* March 29, 1999, pp. E4, E13; and William C. Symonds, "The Big Trim at Gillette," *Business Week,* November 8, 1999, p. 42.

[2]For these and other examples, see Cliff Edwards, "Where Have All the Edsels Gone?" *Greensboro News Record,* May 24, 1999, p. B6.

market each year, only 40 percent will be around five years later. Moreover, failure rates for new industrial products may be as high as 30 percent.[3] Why do so many new products fail? There are several reasons. Although an idea may be good, the market size may have been overestimated. Perhaps the actual product was not designed as well as it should have been. Or maybe it was incorrectly positioned in the market, priced too high, or advertised poorly. A high-level executive might push a favorite idea despite poor marketing research findings. Sometimes the costs of product development are higher than expected, and sometimes competitors fight back harder than expected.

Because so many new products fail, companies are anxious to learn how to improve their odds of new-product success. One way is to identify successful new products and find out what they have in common. Another is to study new-product failures to see what lessons can be learned. Various studies suggest that new-product success depends on developing a *unique superior product*, one with higher quality, new features, and higher value in use. Another key success factor is a *well-defined product concept* prior to development, in which the company carefully defines and assesses the target market, the product requirements, and the benefits before proceeding. Other success factors have also been suggested—senior management commitment, relentless innovation, and a smoothly functioning new-product development process.[4] In all, to create successful new products, a company must understand its consumers, markets, and competitors and develop products that deliver superior value to customers.

So companies face a problem—they must develop new products, but the odds weigh heavily against success. The solution lies in strong new-product planning and in setting up a systematic *new-product development process* for finding and growing new products. Figure 9.1 shows the eight major steps in this process.

active example <

Consider an example of how firms deal with the cost of new-product development.

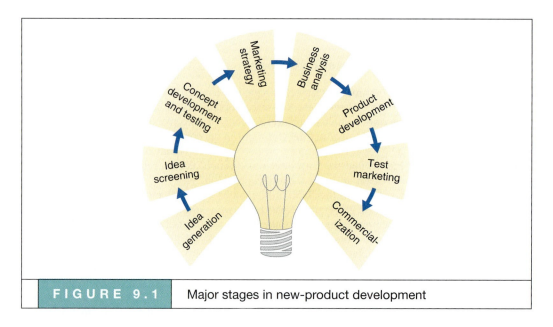

| FIGURE 9.1 | Major stages in new-product development |

[3]See Robert G. Cooper, "New Product Success in Industrial Firms," *Industrial Marketing Management,* 1992, pp. 215–23; William Bolding, Ruskin Morgan, and Richard Staelin, "Pulling the Plug to Stop the New Product Drain," *Journal of Marketing Research,* February 1997, pp. 164–76; Constance Gustke, "Built to Last," *Sales & Marketing Management,* August 1997, pp. 78–83; Philip Kotler, *Kotler on Marketing* (New York: Free Press, 1999), p. 51; and Martha Wirth Fellman, "Number of New Products Keeps Rising," *Marketing News,* March 29, 1999, p. 3.

[4]See Robert G. Cooper and Elko J. Kleinschmidt, *New Product: The Key Factors in Success* (Chicago: American Marketing Association, 1990); X. Michael Song and Mark E. Perry, "A Cross-National Comparative Study of New Product Development Processes: Japan and the United States," *Journal of Marketing,* April 1997, pp. 1–18; Jerry Wind and Vijay Mahajan, "Issues and Opportunities in New Product Development," *Journal of Marketing Research,* February 1997, pp. 1–12; Jean-Marie Martino, "Not Only to Succeed but to Endure," *Across the Board,* January 1998, p. 55; and Don H. Lester, "Critical Success Factors for New Product Development," *Research Technology Management,* January–February 1998, pp. 36–43.

IDEA GENERATION

New-product development starts with **idea generation**—the systematic search for new-product ideas. A company typically has to generate many ideas in order to find a few good ones. At Gillette, of every 45 carefully developed new-product ideas, 3 make it into the development stage and only 1 eventually reaches the marketplace. DuPont has found that it can take as many as 3,000 raw ideas to produce just 2 winning commercial products, and pharmaceutical companies may require 6,000 to 8,000 starting ideas for every successful commercial new product.[5]

Major sources of new-product ideas include internal sources, customers, competitors, distributors and suppliers, and others. Using *internal sources,* the company can find new ideas through formal research and development. It can pick the brains of its executives, scientists, engineers, manufacturing, and salespeople. Some companies have developed successful "intrapreneurial" programs that encourage employees to think up and develop new-product ideas. For example, 3M's well-known "15 percent rule" allows employees to spend 15 percent of their time "bootlegging"—working on projects of personal interest whether or not those projects directly benefit the company. The spectacularly successful Post-it notes evolved out of this program. Similarly, Texas Instruments's IDEA program provides funds for employees who pursue their own ideas. Among the successful new products to come out of the IDEA program was TI's Speak 'n' Spell, the first children's toy to contain a microchip. Many other speaking toys followed, ultimately generating several hundred million dollars for TI.[6]

Good new-product ideas also come from watching and listening to *customers.* The company can analyze customer questions and complaints to find new products that better solve consumer problems. The company can conduct surveys or focus groups to learn about consumer needs and wants. Or company engineers or salespeople can meet with and work alongside customers to get suggestions and ideas. For example, United States Surgical Corporation (USSC) has developed most of its surgical instruments by working closely with surgeons. The company was quick to pick up on early experiments in laparoscopy—surgery performed by inserting a tiny TV camera into the body along with slim, long-handled instruments. USSC now captures about 58 percent of the single-use laparoscopy market.[7]

Finally, consumers often create new products and uses on their own, and companies can benefit by finding these products and putting them on the market. Customers can also be a good source of ideas for new product uses that can expand the market for and extend the life of current products. For example, Avon capitalized on new uses discovered by consumers for its Skin-So-Soft bath oil and moisturizer. For years, customers have been spreading the word that Skin-So-Soft bath oil is also a terrific bug repellent. Whereas some consumers were content simply to bathe in water scented with the fragrant oil, others carried it in their backpacks to mosquito-infested campsites or kept a bottle on the deck of their beach houses. Now, Avon offers a complete line of Skin-So-Soft Bug Guard products, including Bug Guard Plus, a combination moisturizer, insect repellent, and sunscreen.[8]

Competitors are another good source of new-product ideas. Companies watch competitors' ads and other communications to get clues about their new products. They buy competing new products, take them apart to see how they work, analyze their sales, and decide whether they should bring out a new product of their own. Finally, *distributors and suppliers* contribute many good new-product ideas. Resellers are close to the market and can pass along information about consumer problems and new-product possibilities. Suppliers can tell the company about new concepts, techniques, and materials that can be used to develop new products. Other idea sources include trade magazines, shows, and seminars; government agencies; new-product consultants; advertising agencies; marketing research firms; university and commercial laboratories; and inventors.

The search for new-product ideas should be systematic rather than haphazard. Otherwise, few new ideas will surface and many good ideas will sputter in and die. Top management can avoid these problems by installing an *idea management system* that directs the flow of new ideas to a central point where they can be collected, reviewed, and evaluated. In setting up such a system, the company can do any or all of the following:[9]

- Appoint a respected senior person to be the company's idea manager.

[5]See Grant, "Gillette Knows Shaving—and How to Turn Out Hot New Products," pp. 207–10; Rosabeth Moss Kanter, "Don't Wait to Innovate," *Sales & Marketing Management,* February 1997, pp. 22–24; and Greg A. Stevens and James Burley, "3,000 Raw Ideas Equals 1 Commercial Success!" *Research-Technology Management,* May–June 1997, pp. 16–27.

[6]See Tim Stevens, "Idea Dollars," *Industry Week,* February 16, 1998, pp. 47–49.

[7]For this and other examples, see Jennifer Reese, "Getting Hot Ideas from Customers," *Fortune,* May 18, 1992, pp. 86–87; and Ken Miller, "Where You Really Need to Hear Customers," *Brandweek,* January 20, 1998, p. 17.

[8]Pam Weisz, "Avon's Skin-So-Soft Bugs Out," *Brandweek,* June 6, 1994, p. 4; and information accessed online at www.avon.com, September 1999.

[9]Kotler, *Kotler on Marketing,* pp. 43–44.

"Intrapreneurial" programs encourage employees to think up and develop new product ideas. 3M's spectacularly successful Post-it notes evolved out of such a program.

- Create a multidisciplinary idea management committee consisting of people from R&D, engineering, purchasing, operations, finance, and sales and marketing to meet regularly and evaluate proposed new-product and service ideas.
- Set up a toll-free number for anyone who wants to send a new idea to the idea manager.
- Encourage all company stakeholders—employees, suppliers, distributors, dealers— to send their ideas to the idea manager.
- Set up formal recognition programs to reward those who contribute the best new ideas.

The idea manager approach yields two favorable outcomes. First, it helps create an innovation-oriented company culture. It shows that top management supports, encourages, and rewards innovation. Second, it will yield a larger number of ideas among which will be found some especially good ones. As the system matures, ideas will flow more freely. No longer will good ideas wither for the lack of a sounding board or a senior product advocate.

IDEA SCREENING

The purpose of idea generation is to create a large number of ideas. The purpose of the succeeding stages is to *reduce* that number. The first idea-reducing stage is **idea screening,** which helps spot good ideas and drop poor ones as soon as possible. Product development costs rise greatly in later stages, so the company wants to go ahead only with the product ideas that will turn into profitable products. As one marketing executive suggests, "Three executives sitting in a room can get 40 good ideas ricocheting off the wall in minutes. The challenge is getting a steady stream of good ideas out of the labs and creativity campfires, through marketing and manufacturing, and all the way to consumers."[10]

[10]Brian O'Reilly, "New Ideas, New Products," Fortune, March 3, 1997, pp. 61–64.

Many companies require their executives to write up new-product ideas on a standard form that can be reviewed by a new-product committee. The write-up describes the product, the target market, and the competition. It makes some rough estimates of market size, product price, development time and costs, manufacturing costs, and rate of return. The committee then evaluates the idea against a set of general criteria. For example, at Kao Company, the large Japanese consumer-products company, the committee asks questions such as these: Is the product truly useful to consumers and society? Is it good for our particular company? Does it mesh well with the company's objectives and strategies? Do we have the people, skills, and resources to make it succeed? Does it deliver more value to customers than do competing products? Is it easy to advertise and distribute? Many companies have well-designed systems for rating and screening new-product ideas.

CONCEPT DEVELOPMENT AND TESTING

An attractive idea must be developed into a **product concept.** It is important to distinguish between a product idea, a product concept, and a product image. A *product idea* is an idea for a possible product that the company can see itself offering to the market. A *product concept* is a detailed version of the idea stated in meaningful consumer terms. A *product image* is the way consumers perceive an actual or potential product.

Concept Development

DaimlerChrysler is getting ready to commercialize its experimental fuel-cell-powered electric car. This car's low-polluting fuel-cell system runs directly off liquid hydrogen. It is highly fuel efficient (75 percent more efficient than gasoline engines) and gives the new car an environmental advantage over standard internal combustion engine cars. DaimlerChrysler is currently road testing its NECAR 4 (New Electric Car) subcompact prototype and plans to deliver the first fuel-cell cars to customers in 2004. Based on the tiny Mercedes A-Class, the car accelerates quickly, reaches speeds of 90 miles per hour, and has a 280-mile driving range, giving it a huge edge over battery-powered electric cars that travel only about 80 miles before needing 3 to 12 hours of recharging.[11]

DaimlerChrysler's task is to develop this new product into alternative product concepts, find out how attractive each concept is to customers, and choose the best one. It might create the following product concepts for the fuel-cell electric car:

Concept 1	A moderately priced subcompact designed as a second family car to be used around town. The car is ideal for running errands and visiting friends.
Concept 2	A medium-cost sporty compact appealing to young people.
Concept 3	An inexpensive subcompact "green" car appealing to environmentally conscious people who want practical transportation and low pollution.

DaimlerChrysler's task is to develop its fuel-cell powered electric car into alternative product concepts, find out how attractive each is to customers, and choose the best one.

[11]See "DaimlerChrysler Plans '04 Launch of Fuel Cell Car," *Ward's Auto World,* April 1999, p. 25; and William J. Cook, "A Mercedes for the Future," *U.S. News & World Report,* March 29, 1999, p. 62.

Concept Testing

Concept testing calls for testing new-product concepts with groups of target consumers. The concepts may be presented to consumers symbolically or physically. Here, in words, is concept 3:

> An efficient, fun-to-drive, fuel-cell-powered electric subcompact car that seats four. This high-tech wonder runs on liquid hydrogen, providing practical and reliable transportation with almost no pollution. It goes up to 90 miles per hour and, unlike battery-powered electric cars, it never needs recharging. It's priced, fully equipped, at $20,000.

For some concept tests, a word or picture description might be sufficient. However, a more concrete and physical presentation of the concept will increase the reliability of the concept test. Today, some marketers are finding innovative ways to make product concepts more real to consumer subjects. For example, some are using virtual reality to test product concepts. Virtual reality programs use computers and sensory devices (such as gloves or goggles) to simulate reality. For example, a designer of kitchen cabinets can use a virtual reality program to help a customer "see" how his or her kitchen would look and work if remodeled with the company's products. Although virtual reality is still in its infancy, its applications are increasing daily.[12]

After being exposed to the concept, consumers then may be asked to react to it by answering questions such as those in Table 9.1. The answers will help the company decide which concept has the strongest appeal. For example, the last question asks about the consumer's intention to buy. Suppose 10 percent of the consumers said they "definitely" would buy and another 5 percent said "probably." The company could project these figures to the full population in this target group to estimate sales volume. Even then, the estimate is uncertain because people do not always carry out their stated intentions.

Many firms routinely test new-product concepts with consumers before attempting to turn them into actual new products. For example, each month Richard Saunders, Inc.'s Acu-Poll research system tests 35 new-product concepts in person on 100 nationally representative grocery store shoppers. In recent polls, Nabisco's Oreo Chocolate Cones concept received a rare A1 rating, meaning that consumers think it is an outstanding concept that they would try and buy. Lender's Bake at Home Bagels were also a big hit. Other product concepts didn't fare so well. Nubrush Anti-Bacterial Toothbrush Spray disinfectant, from Applied Microdontics, received an F. Consumers found Nubrush to be overpriced, and most don't think they have a problem with "infected" toothbrushes. Another concept that fared poorly was Chef Williams 5 Minute Marinade, which comes with a syringe customers use to inject the marinade into meats. "I can't see that on grocery shelves," comments an Acu-Poll executive. Some consumers might find the thought of injecting something into meat a bit repulsive, and "it's just so politically incorrect to have this syringe on there."[13]

TABLE 9.1	Questions for Fuel-Cell Electric Car Concept Test

1. Do you understand the concept of a fuel-cell-powered electric car?
2. Do you believe the claims about the car's performance?
3. What are the major benefits of the fuel-cell-powered electric car compared with a conventional car?
4. What are its advantages compared with a batter-powered electric car?
5. What improvements in the car's features would you suggest?
6. For what uses would you prefer a fuel-cell-powered electric car to a conventional car?
7. What would be a reasonable price to charge for the car?
8. Who would be involved in your decision to buy such a car? Who would drive it?
9. Would you buy such a car? (Definitely, probably, probably not, definitely not)

---

[12]See Raymond R. Burke, "Virtual Reality Shopping: Breakthrough in Marketing Research," *Harvard Business Review,* March–April 1996, pp. 120–31; Brian Silverman, "Get 'Em While They're Hot," *Sales & Marketing Management,* February 1997, pp. 47–52; and Mike Hoffman, "Virtual Shopping," *Inc.,* July 1998, p. 88.

[13]Adrienne Ward Fawcett, "Oreo Cones Make Top Grade in Poll," Advertising Age, June 14, 1993, p. 30; "Fat-Free Cupcakes? OK; Frozen Incetea Bars? Nope." *Marketing News,* February 12, 1996, p. 14; and Becky Ebenkamp, "The New Gold Standards," *Brandweek,* April 19, 1999, p. 34.

Take a moment to watch how a company approaches the process of product development.

MARKETING STRATEGY DEVELOPMENT

Suppose DaimlerChrysler finds that concept 3 for the fuel-cell-powered electric car tests best. The next step is **marketing strategy development,** designing an initial marketing strategy for introducing this car to the market.

The *marketing strategy statement* consists of three parts. The first part describes the target market; the planned product positioning; and the sales, market share, and profit goals for the first few years. Thus:

> The target market is younger, well-educated, moderate-to-high-income individuals, couples, or small families seeking practical, environmentally responsible transportation. The car will be positioned as more economical to operate, more fun to drive, and less polluting than today's internal combustion engine cars, and as less restricting than battery-powered electric cars, which must be recharged regularly. The company will aim to sell 100,000 cars in the first year, at a loss of not more than $15 million. In the second year, the company will aim for sales of 120,000 cars and a profit of $25 million.

The second part of the marketing strategy statement outlines the product's planned price, distribution, and marketing budget for the first year:

> The fuel-cell-powered electric car will be offered in three colors—red, white, and blue—and will have optional air-conditioning and power-drive features. It will sell at a retail price of $20,000—with 15 percent off the list price to dealers. Dealers who sell more than 10 cars per month will get an additional discount of 5 percent on each car sold that month. An advertising budget of $20 million will be split 50–50 between national and local advertising. Advertising will emphasize the car's fun and low emissions. During the first year, $100,000 will be spent on marketing research to find out who is buying the car and their satisfaction levels.

The third part of the marketing strategy statement describes the planned long-run sales, profit goals, and marketing mix strategy:

> DaimlerChrysler intends to capture a 3 percent long-run share of the total auto market and realize an after-tax return on investment of 15 percent. To achieve this, product quality will start high and be improved over time. Price will be raised in the second and third years if competition permits. The total advertising budget will be raised each year by about 10 percent. Marketing research will be reduced to $60,000 per year after the first year.

BUSINESS ANALYSIS

Once management has decided on its product concept and marketing strategy, it can evaluate the business attractiveness of the proposal. **Business analysis** involves a review of the sales, costs, and profit projections for a new product to find out whether they satisfy the company's objectives. If they do, the product can move to the product development stage.

To estimate sales, the company might look at the sales history of similar products and conduct surveys of market opinion. It can then estimate minimum and maximum sales to assess the range of risk. After preparing the sales forecast, management can estimate the expected costs and profits for the product, including marketing, R&D, operations, accounting, and finance costs. The company then uses the sales and costs figures to analyze the new product's financial attractiveness.

PRODUCT DEVELOPMENT

So far, for many new-product concepts, the product may have existed only as a word description, a drawing, or perhaps a crude mock-up. If the product concept passes the business test, it moves into **product development.** Here, R&D or engineering develops the product concept into a physical product. The product development step, however, now calls for a large jump in investment. It will show whether the product idea can be turned into a workable product.

The R&D department will develop and test one or more physical versions of the product concept. R&D hopes to design a prototype that will satisfy and excite consumers and that can be produced quickly and at budgeted costs. Developing a successful prototype can take days, weeks, months, or even years. Often, products undergo rigorous functional tests to make sure that they perform safely and effectively. Here are some examples of such functional tests:[14]

A scuba-diving Barbie doll must swim and kick for 15 straight hours to satisfy Mattel that she will last at least one year. But because Barbie may find her feet in small owners' mouths rather than in the bathtub, Mattel has devised another, more torturous test: Barbie's feet are clamped by two steel jaws to make sure that her skin doesn't crack—and choke—potential owners.

At Shaw Industries, temps are paid $5 an hour to pace up and down 5 long rows of sample carpets for up to 8 hours a day, logging an average of 14 miles each. One regular reads 3 mysteries a week while pacing and shed 40 pounds in 2 years. Shaw Industries counts walkers' steps and figures that 20,000 steps equal several years of average carpet wear.

Acting on behalf of manufacturers, the Buyers Laboratory in Hackensack, New Jersey, an independent office products testing lab, tests the writing quality of ballpoint, felt-tip, and roller-ball pens. Its 50-pound "pen rig" measures a pen's life span. The range fluctuates, but a medium-tip, made-in-the-U.S.A. ballpoint might last for 7,775 feet. In general, pens that blob, skip, and dot receive low ratings. Which pens fail the test altogether? "Some points are so fine they cut through the paper," says one supervisor, "and some felt-tips wear down long before the ink runs out."

The prototype must have the required functional features and also convey the intended psychological characteristics. The electric car, for example, should strike consumers as being well built, comfortable, and safe. Management must learn what makes consumers decide that a car is well built. To some consumers, this means that the car has "solid-sounding" doors. To others, it means that the car is able to withstand heavy impact in crash tests. Consumer tests are conducted in which consumers test-drive the car and rate its attributes.

active example <

Take a moment to explore one recent new-product initiative.

TEST MARKETING

If the product passes functional and consumer tests, the next step is **test marketing,** the stage at which the product and marketing program are introduced into more realistic market settings. Test marketing gives the marketer experience with marketing the product before going to the great expense of full introduction. It lets the company test the product and its entire marketing program—positioning strategy, advertising, distribution, pricing, branding and packaging, and budget levels.

The amount of test marketing needed varies with each new product. Test marketing costs can be enormous, and it takes time that may allow competitors to gain advantages. When the costs of developing and introducing the product are low, or when management is already confident about the new product, the company may do little or no test marketing. Companies often do not test-market simple line extensions or copies of successful competitor products. For example, Procter & Gamble introduced its Folger's decaffeinated coffee crystals without test marketing, and Pillsbury rolled out Chewy granola bars and chocolate-covered Granola Dipps with no standard test market. However, when introducing a new product requires a big investment, or when management is not sure of the product or marketing program, a company may do a lot of test marketing. For instance, Lever USA

---

[14]See Faye Rice, "Secrets of Product Testing," *Fortune,* November 28, 1994, pp. 172–74.

spent two years testing its highly successful Lever 2000 bar soap in Atlanta before introducing it internationally. Frito-Lay did eighteen months of testing in three markets on at least five formulations before introducing its Baked Lays line of low-fat snacks.[15]

The costs of test marketing can be high, but they are often small when compared with the costs of making a major mistake. For example, Nabisco's launch of one new product without testing had disastrousand soggy—results:[16]

Nabisco hit a marketing home run with its Teddy Grahams, teddy-bear-shaped graham crackers in several different flavors. So, the company decided to extend Teddy Grahams into a new area. In 1989, it introduced chocolate, cinnamon, and honey versions of Breakfast Bears Graham Cereal. When the product came out, however, consumers didn't like the taste enough, so the product developers went back to the kitchen and modified the formula. But they didn't test it. The result was a disaster. Although the cereal may have tasted better, it no longer stayed crunchy in milk, as the advertising on the box promised. Instead, it left a gooey mess of graham mush on the bottom of cereal bowls. Supermarket managers soon refused to restock the cereal, and Nabisco executives decided it was too late to reformulate the product again. So a promising new product was killed through haste to get it to market.

When using test marketing, consumer products companies usually choose one of three approaches—standard test markets, controlled test markets, or simulated test markets.

Standard Test Markets

Using standard test markets, the company finds a small number of representative test cities, conducts a full marketing campaign in these cities, and uses store audits, consumer and distributor surveys, and other measures to gauge product performance. The results are used to forecast national sales and profits, discover potential product problems, and fine-tune the marketing program.

Standard test markets have some drawbacks. They can be very costly and they may take a long time—some last as long as three years. Moreover, competitors can monitor test market results or even interfere with them by cutting their prices in test cities, increasing their promotion, or even buying up the product being tested. Finally, test markets give competitors a look at the company's new product well before it is introduced nationally. Thus, competitors may have time to develop defensive strategies, and may even beat the company's product to the market. For example, while Clorox was still test marketing its new detergent with bleach in selected markets, P&G launched Tide with Bleach nationally. Tide with Bleach quickly became the segment leader; Clorox later withdrew its detergent.

Despite these disadvantages, standard test markets are still the most widely used approach for major market testing. However, many companies today are shifting toward quicker and cheaper controlled and simulated test marketing methods.

Controlled Test Markets

Several research firms keep controlled panels of stores that have agreed to carry new products for a fee. Controlled test marketing systems like Nielsen's Scantrack and Information Resources, Inc.'s (IRI) BehaviorScan track individual behavior from the television set to the checkout counter. IRI keeps panels of 2,000 to 3,000 shoppers in 6 carefully selected markets.[17] It measures TV viewing in each panel household and can send special commercials to panel member television sets. Panel consumers buy from cooperating stores and show identification cards when making purchases.

Within test stores, IRI controls such factors as shelf placement, price, and in-store promotions. Detailed electronic scanner information on each consumer's purchases is fed into a central computer, where it is combined with the consumer's demographic and TV viewing information and reported daily. Thus, BehaviorScan can provide store-by-store, week-by-week reports on the sales of new products being tested. Because the scanners record the specific purchases of individual consumers, the system also can provide information on repeat purchases and the ways that different types of consumers are reacting to the new product, its advertising, and various other elements of the marketing program.

[15]Judann Pollack, "Baked Lays," *Advertising Age*, June 24, 1996, p. S2.

[16]See Robert McMath, "To Test or Not to Test," *Advertising Age*, June 1998, p. 64.

[17]Information on BehaviorScan accessed online at www.infores.com/ public/prodserv/AB/bscan.htm, February 2000.

IRI's BehaviorScan provides an in-market laboratory for testing new products and marketing programs under highly controlled yet real-world conditions.

Controlled test markets usually cost less than standard test markets and take less time (6 months to a year). A typical BehaviorScan test takes 16 to 24 months to complete. However, some companies are concerned that the limited number of small cities and panel consumers used by the research services may not be representative of their products' markets or target consumers. As in standard test markets, controlled test markets allow competitors to get a look at the company's new product.

Simulated Test Markets

Companies can also test new products in a simulated shopping environment. The company or research firm shows ads and promotions for a variety of products, including the new product being tested, to a sample of consumers. It gives consumers a small amount of money and invites them to a real or laboratory store where they may keep the money or use it to buy items. The researchers note how many consumers buy the new product and competing brands. This simulation provides a measure of trial and the commercial's effectiveness against competing commercials. The researchers then ask consumers the reasons for their purchase or nonpurchase. Some weeks later, they interview the consumers by phone to determine product attitudes, usage, satisfaction, and repurchase intentions. Using sophisticated computer models, the researchers then project national sales from results of the simulated test market. Recently, some marketers have begun to use interesting new high-tech approaches to simulated test market research, such as virtual reality and the Internet.

Simulated test markets overcome some of the disadvantages of standard and controlled test markets. They usually cost much less, can be run in eight weeks, and keep the new product out of competitors' view. Yet, because of their small samples and simulated shopping environments, many marketers do not think that simulated test markets are as accurate or reliable as larger, real-world tests. Still, simulated test markets are used widely, often as "pretest" markets. Because they are fast and inexpensive, they can be run to quickly assess a new product or its marketing program. If the pretest results are strongly positive, the product might be introduced without further testing. If the results are very poor, the product might be dropped or substantially redesigned and retested. If the results are promising but indefinite, the product and marketing program can be tested further in controlled or standard test markets.

COMMERCIALIZATION

Test marketing gives management the information needed to make a final decision about whether to launch the new product. If the company goes ahead with **commercialization**—introducing the new product into the market—it will face high costs. The company will have to build or rent a manufacturing facility. It may have to spend, in the case of a new consumer packaged good, between $10 million and $200 million for advertising, sales promotion, and other marketing efforts in the first year.

The company launching a new product must first decide on introduction *timing*. If DaimlerChrysler's new fuel-cell electric car will eat into the sales of the company's other cars, its introduction may be delayed. If the car can be improved further, or if the economy is down, the company may wait until the following year to launch it.

Next, the company must decide *where* to launch the new product—in a single location, a region, the national market, or the international market. Few companies have the confidence, capital, and capacity to launch new products into full national or international distribution. They will develop a planned *market rollout* over time. In particular, small companies may enter attractive cities or regions one at a time. Larger companies, however, may quickly introduce new models into several regions or into the full national market.

Companies with international distribution systems may introduce new products through global rollouts. Colgate-Palmolive uses a "lead-country" strategy. For example, it launched its Palmolive Optims shampoo and conditioner first in Australia, the Philippines, Hong Kong, and Mexico, then rapidly rolled it out into Europe, Asia, Latin America, and Africa. However, international companies are increasingly introducing their new products in swift global assaults. Procter & Gamble did this with its Pampers Phases line of disposable diapers, which it had on the shelf in 90 countries within just 12 months of introduction. Such rapid worldwide expansion solidified the brand's market position before foreign competitors could react. P&G has since mounted worldwide introductions of several other new products.[18]

> video exercise

Take a moment to watch a group of managers discuss new product development strategy.

SPEEDING UP NEW-PRODUCT DEVELOPMENT

Many companies organize their new-product development process into the orderly sequence of steps shown in Figure 9.1, starting with idea generation and ending with commercialization. Under this **sequential product development** approach, one company department works individually to complete its stage of the process before passing the new product along to the next department and stage. This orderly, step-by-step process can help bring control to complex and risky projects. But it also can be dangerously slow. In fast-changing, highly competitive markets, such slow-but-sure product development can result in product failures, lost sales and profits, and crumbling market positions. "Speed to market" and reducing new-product development cycle time have become pressing concerns to companies in all industries.

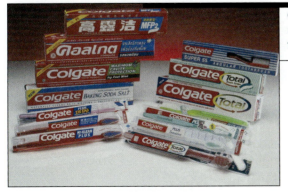

Colgate-Palmolive introduces its new products internationally using a "lead country" strategy, launching the product first in a few important regions, followed by a swift global rollout.

[18]Jennifer Lawrence, "P&G Rushes on Global Diaper Rollout," *Advertising Age*, October 14, 1991, p. 6; Bill Saporito, "Behind the Tumult at P&G," *Fortune*, March 7, 1994, pp. 75–82; and George M. Chryssochoidis, "Rolling Out New Products Across Country Markets: An Empirical Study of Causes of Delays," *The Journal of Product Innovation Management*, January 1998, pp. 16–41.

In order to get their new products to market more quickly, many companies are adopting a faster, team-oriented approach called **simultaneous (or team-based) product development.** Under this approach, company departments work closely together, overlapping the steps in the product development process to save time and increase effectiveness. Instead of passing the new product from department to department, the company assembles a team of people from various departments that stays with the new product from start to finish. Such teams usually include people from the marketing, finance, design, manufacturing, and legal departments, and even supplier and customer companies.

Top management gives the product development team general strategic direction but no clear-cut product idea or work plan. It challenges the team with stiff and seemingly contradictory goals—"turn out carefully planned and superior new products, but do it quickly"—and then gives the team whatever freedom and resources it needs to meet the challenge. In the sequential process, a bottleneck at one phase can seriously slow the entire project. In the simultaneous approach, if one functional area hits snags, it works to resolve them while the team moves on.

The Allen-Bradley Company, a maker of industrial controls, realized tremendous benefits by using simultaneous development. Under its old sequential approach, the company's marketing department handed off a new-product idea to designers, who worked in isolation to prepare concepts that they then passed along to product engineers. The engineers, also working by themselves, developed expensive prototypes and handed them off to manufacturing, which tried to find a way to build the new product. Finally, after many years and dozens of costly design compromises and delays, marketing was asked to sell the new product, which it often found to be too high priced or sadly out of date. Now, all of Allen-Bradley's departments work together to develop new products. The results have been astonishing. For example, the company recently developed a new electrical control in just two years; under the old system, it would have taken six years.

Black & Decker used the simultaneous approach—what it calls "concurrent engineering"—to develop its Quantum line of tools targeted toward serious do-it-yourselfers. B&D assigned a "fusion team," called Team Quantum and consisting of 85 Black & Decker employees from around the world, to get the right product line to customers as quickly as possible. The team included engineers, finance people, marketers, designers, and others from the United States, Britain, Germany, Italy, and Switzerland. From idea to launch, including 3 months of consumer research, the team developed the highly acclaimed Quantum line in only 12 months.

The simultaneous approach does have some limitations. Superfast product development can be riskier and more costly than the slower, more orderly sequential approach. Moreover, it often creates increased organizational tension and confusion. The company also must take care that rushing a product to market doesn't adversely affect its quality—the objective is not just to create products faster, but to create them *better* and faster. Despite these drawbacks, in rapidly changing industries facing increasingly shorter product life cycles, the rewards of fast and flexible product development far exceed the risks. Companies that get new and improved products to the market faster than competitors often gain a dramatic competitive edge. They can respond more quickly to emerging consumer tastes and charge higher prices for more advanced designs. As one auto industry executive states, "What we

A Black & Decker "fusion team" developed the highly acclaimed Quantum tool line in only 12 months. The team included 85 marketers, engineers, finance people, and others from the United States, Britain, Germany, Italy, and Switzerland.

want to do is get the new car approved, built, and in the consumer's hands in the shortest time possible. . . . Whoever gets there first gets all the marbles."[19]

> **active poll**

Give your opinion on a question concerning new-product development.

> **active concept check**

Now let's take a moment to test your knowledge of what you've just read.

> Product Life-Cycle Strategies

After launching the new product, management wants the product to enjoy a long and happy life. Although it does not expect the product to sell forever, the company wants to earn a decent profit to cover all the effort and risk that went into launching it. Management is aware that each product will have a life cycle, although the exact shape and length is not known in advance.

Figure 9.2 shows a typical **product life cycle (PLC),** the course that a product's sales and profits take over its lifetime. The product life cycle has five distinct stages:

1. *Product development* begins when the company finds and develops a new-product idea. During product development, sales are zero and the company's investment costs mount.

2. *Introduction* is a period of slow sales growth as the product is introduced in the market. Profits are nonexistent in this stage because of the heavy expenses of product introduction.

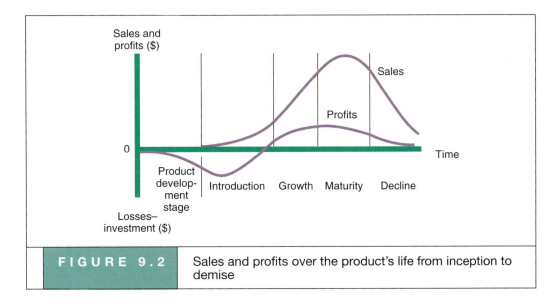

| FIGURE 9.2 | Sales and profits over the product's life from inception to demise |

[19]For a good review of research on new-product development, see Shona L. Brown and Kathleen M. Eisenhardt, "Product Development: Past Research, Present Findings, and Future Directions," Academy of Management Review, April 1995, pp. 343–78; Jerry Wind and Vijay Mahajan, "Issues and Opportunities in New Product Development," *Journal of Marketing Research,* February 1997, pp. 1–12; Durward K. Sobek II, Jeffrey K. Liker, and Allen C. Ward, "Another Look at How Toyota Integrates Product Development," *Harvard Business Review,* July–August 1998, pp. 36–49; and Susanne Willsey, "Taking These 7 Steps Will Help You Launch a New Product," *Marketing News,* March 29, 1999, p. 17.

3. *Growth* is a period of rapid market acceptance and increasing profits.

4. *Maturity* is a period of slowdown in sales growth because the product has achieved acceptance by most potential buyers. Profits level off or decline because of increased marketing outlays to defend the product against competition.

5. *Decline* is the period when sales fall off and profits drop.

Not all products follow this product life cycle. Some products are introduced and die quickly; others stay in the mature stage for a long, long time. Some enter the decline stage and are then cycled back into the growth stage through strong promotion or repositioning.

The PLC concept can describe a product class (gasoline-powered automobiles), a *product form* (minivans), or a *brand* (the Ford Taurus). The PLC concept applies differently in each case. Product classes have the longest life cycles—the sales of many product classes stay in the mature stage for a long time. Product forms, in contrast, tend to have the standard PLC shape. Product forms such as "cream deodorants," the "dial telephone," and "phonograph records" passed through a regular history of introduction, rapid growth, maturity, and decline. A specific brand's life cycle can change quickly because of changing competitive attacks and responses. For example, although teeth-cleaning products (product class) and toothpastes (product form) have enjoyed fairly long life cycles, the life cycles of specific brands have tended to be much shorter.

The PLC concept also can be applied to what are known as styles, fashions, and fads. Their special life cycles are shown in Figure 9.3. A style is a basic and distinctive mode of expression. For example, styles appear in homes (colonial, ranch), clothing (formal, casual), and art (realist, surrealist, abstract). Once a style is invented, it may last for generations, passing in and out of vogue. A style has a cycle showing several periods of renewed interest. A **fashion** is a currently accepted or popular style in a given field. For example, the "preppie look" in the clothing of the 1980s gave way to the casual and layered look of the 1990s. Fashions tend to grow slowly, remain popular for a while, then decline slowly.

Fads are fashions that enter quickly, are adopted with great zeal, peak early, and decline very quickly. They last only a short time and tend to attract only a limited following. "Pet rocks" have become the classic example of a fad. Upon hearing his friends complain about how expensive it was to care for their dogs, advertising copywriter Gary Dahl joked about his pet rock and was soon writing a spoof of a dog-training manual for it. Soon Dahl was selling some 1.5 million ordinary beach pebbles at $4 a pop. Yet the fad, which broke in October 1975, had sunk like a stone by the next February. Dahl's advice to those who want to succeed with a fad, "Enjoy it while it lasts." Other examples of fads include Rubik's Cubes and lava lamps. Most fads do not survive for long because they normally do not satisfy a strong need or satisfy it well.[20]

The PLC concept can be applied by marketers as a useful framework for describing how products and markets work. But using the PLC concept for forecasting product performance or for developing marketing strategies presents some practical problems.[21] For example, managers may have trouble identifying which stage of the PLC the product is in, pinpointing when the product moves into the

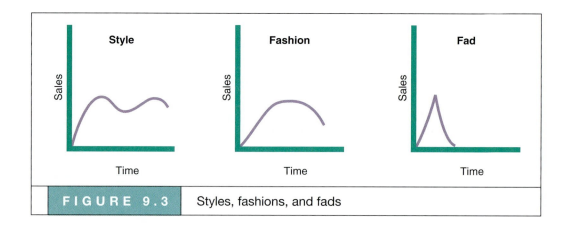

| FIGURE 9.3 | Styles, fashions, and fads |

[20]See Martin G. Letscher, "How to Tell Fads from Trends," American Demographics, December 1994, pp. 38–45; John Grossmann, "A Follow-up on Four Fabled Frenzies," *Inc.*, October 1994, pp. 66–67; and David Stipp, "The Theory of Fads," *Fortune*, October 14, 1996, pp. 49–52.

[21]See George S. Day, "The Product Life Cycle: Analysis and Applications Issues," Journal of Marketing, Fall 1981, pp. 60–67; Chuck Ryan and Walter E. Riggs, "Redefining the Product Life Cycle: The Five-Element Product Wave," *Business Horizons,* September–October 1996, pp. 33–40; and Carole R. Hedden, "The Circle of (Product) Life," *American Demographics,* September 1996, pp. 26–30.

CHANGE IS BAD

UNCHANGED **HERSHEY'S** MILK CHOCOLATE SINCE 1899

Product life cycle: Companies want their products to enjoy long and happy life cycles. Hershey's chocolate bars have been "unchanged since 1899."

next stage, and determining the factors that affect the product's movement through the stages. In practice, it is difficult to forecast the sales level at each PLC stage, the length of each stage, and the shape of the PLC curve.

Using the PLC concept to develop marketing strategy also can be difficult because strategy is both a cause and a result of the product's life cycle. The product's current PLC position suggests the best marketing strategies, and the resulting marketing strategies affect product performance in later life-cycle stages. Yet, when used carefully, the PLC concept can help in developing good marketing strategies for different stages of the product life cycle.

We looked at the product development stage of the product life cycle in the first part of the chapter. We now look at strategies for each of the other life-cycle stages.

> ## active exercise

Consider how one prominent company's product life-cycle strategy.

> ## Introduction Stage

The **introduction stage** starts when the new product is first launched. Introduction takes time, and sales growth is apt to be slow. Well-known products such as instant coffee, frozen orange juice, and powdered coffee creamers lingered for many years before they entered a stage of rapid growth.

In this stage, as compared to other stages, profits are negative or low because of the low sales and high distribution and promotion expenses. Much money is needed to attract distributors and build their inventories. Promotion spending is relatively high to inform consumers of the new product and get them to try it. Because the market is not generally ready for product refinements at this stage, the company and its few competitors produce basic versions of the product. These firms focus their selling on those buyers who are the readiest to buy.

A company, especially the market pioneer, must choose a launch strategy that is consistent with the intended product positioning. It should realize that the initial strategy is just the first step in a grander marketing plan for the product's entire life cycle. If the pioneer chooses its launch strategy to make a "killing," it will be sacrificing long-run revenue for the sake of short-run gain. As the pioneer moves through later stages of the life cycle, it will have to continuously formulate new pricing, promotion, and other marketing strategies. It has the best chance of building and retaining market leadership if it plays its cards correctly from the start.[22]

GROWTH STAGE

If the new product satisfies the market, it will enter a **growth stage,** in which sales will start climbing quickly. The early adopters will continue to buy, and later buyers will start following their lead, especially if they hear favorable word of mouth. Attracted by the opportunities for profit, new competitors will enter the market. They will introduce new product features, and the market will expand. The increase in competitors leads to an increase in the number of distribution outlets, and sales jump just to build reseller inventories. Prices remain where they are or fall only slightly. Companies keep their promotion spending at the same or a slightly higher level. Educating the market remains a goal, but now the company must also meet the competition.

Profits increase during the growth stage, as promotion costs are spread over a large volume and as unit manufacturing costs fall. The firm uses several strategies to sustain rapid market growth as long as possible. It improves product quality and adds new product features and models. It enters new market segments and new distribution channels. It shifts some advertising from building product awareness to building product conviction and purchase, and it lowers prices at the right time to attract more buyers.

In the growth stage, the firm faces a trade-off between high market share and high current profit. By spending a lot of money on product improvement, promotion, and distribution, the company can capture a dominant position. In doing so, however, it gives up maximum current profit, which it hopes to make up in the next stage.

active example   <

Consider how the Internet influenced the development of a new product.

MATURITY STAGE

At some point, a product's sales growth will slow down, and the product will enter a **maturity stage.** This maturity stage normally lasts longer than the previous stages, and it poses strong challenges to marketing management. Most products are in the maturity stage of the life cycle, and therefore most of marketing management deals with the mature product.

The slowdown in sales growth results in many producers with many products to sell. In turn, this overcapacity leads to greater competition. Competitors begin marking down prices, increasing their advertising and sales promotions, and upping their R&D budgets to find better versions of the product. These steps lead to a drop in profit. Some of the weaker competitors start dropping out, and the industry eventually contains only well-established competitors.

Although many products in the mature stage appear to remain unchanged for long periods, most successful ones are actually evolving to meet changing consumer needs. Product managers should do more than simply ride along with or defend their mature products—a good offense is the best defense. They should consider modifying the market, product, and marketing mix.

In *modifying the market*, the company tries to increase the consumption of the current product. It looks for new users and market segments, as when Johnson & Johnson targeted the adult market with its baby powder and shampoo. The manager also looks for ways to increase usage among present customers. Campbell does this by offering recipes and convincing consumers that "soup is good food." Or

[22]For an interesting discussion of how brand performance is affected by the product life-cycle stage at which the brand enters the market, see Venkatesh Shankar, Gregory S. Carpenter, and Lekshman Krishnamurthi, "The Advantages of Entry in the Growth Stage of the Product Life Cycle: An Empirical Analysis," Journal of Marketing Research, May 1999, pp. 269–76.

the company may want to reposition the brand to appeal to a larger or faster-growing segment, as Arrow did when it introduced its new line of casual shirts and announced, "We're loosening our collars."

The company might also try *modifying the product*—changing characteristics such as quality, features, or style to attract new users and to inspire more usage. It might improve the product's quality and performance—its durability, reliability, speed, or taste. Or it might add new features that expand the product's usefulness, safety, or convenience. For example, Sony keeps adding new styles and features to its Walkman and Discman lines, and Volvo adds new safety features to its cars. Finally, the company can improve the product's styling and attractiveness. Thus, car manufacturers restyle their cars to attract buyers who want a new look. The makers of consumer food and household products introduce new flavors, colors, ingredients, or packages to revitalize consumer buying.

Finally, the company can try *modifying the marketing mix*—improving sales by changing one or more marketing mix elements. It can cut prices to attract new users and competitors' customers. It can launch a better advertising campaign or use aggressive sales promotions—trade deals, cents-off, premiums, and contests. The company can also move into larger market channels, using mass merchandisers, if these channels are growing. Finally, the company can offer new or improved services to buyers.

DECLINE STAGE

The sales of most product forms and brands eventually dip. The decline may be slow, as in the case of oatmeal cereal, or rapid, as in the case of phonograph records. Sales may plunge to zero, or they may drop to a low level where they continue for many years. This is the **decline stage.**

Sales decline for many reasons, including technological advances, shifts in consumer tastes, and increased competition. As sales and profits decline, some firms withdraw from the market. Those remaining may prune their product offerings. They may drop smaller market segments and marginal trade channels, or they may cut the promotion budget and reduce their prices further.

Carrying a weak product can be very costly to a firm, and not just in profit terms. There are many hidden costs. A weak product may take up too much of management's time. It often requires frequent price and inventory adjustments. It requires advertising and sales force attention that might be better used to make "healthy" products more profitable. A product's failing reputation can cause customer concerns about the company and its other products. The biggest cost may well lie in the future. Keeping weak products delays the search for replacements, creates a lopsided product mix, hurts current profits, and weakens the company's foothold on the future.

For these reasons, companies need to pay more attention to their aging products. The firm's first task is to identify those products in the decline stage by regularly reviewing sales, market shares, costs, and profit trends. Then, management must decide whether to maintain, harvest, or drop each of these declining products.

Management may decide to *maintain* its brand without change in the hope that competitors will leave the industry. For example, Procter & Gamble made good profits by remaining in the declining liquid soap business as others withdrew. Or management may decide to reposition or reformulate the brand in hopes of moving it back into the growth stage of the product life cycle. For instance, after watching sales of its Tostitos tortilla chips plunge 50 percent from their mid-1980s high, Frito-Lay reformulated the chips by doubling their size, changing their shape from round to triangular, and using white corn flour instead of yellow. The new Tostitos Restaurant Style Tortilla Chips have ridden the crest of the recent Tex-Mex food craze's record revenues. Similarly, facing a slumping market, Vlasic reinvented the sliced pickle:

Pickle consumption has been declining about 2 percent a year since the 1980s, but following successful new-product introductions, sales generally get a prolonged boost. Vlasic began its quest for a blockbuster pickle in the mid-1990s after focus groups revealed that people hate it when pickle slices slither out the sides of hamburgers and sandwiches. At first the company decided to slice its average pickles horizontally into strips and marketed them as "Sandwich Stackers." The only problem was that the strips usually contained the soft seedy part of the cucumber, not the crunchy part. The company then embarked on "Project Frisbee," an effort to create a giant pickle chip. In 1998, after years of research and development, Vlasic created a cucumber ten times larger than the traditional pickle cucumber. The pickle slice, or "chip," is large enough to cover the entire surface of a hamburger and is stacked a dozen high in jars. The Sandwich Stackers line now accounts for about 20 percent of Vlasic's pickle sales.[23]

[23]Vanessa O'Connell, "Food: After Years of Trial and Error, a Pickle Slice That Stays Put," Wall Street Journal, October 6, 1998, p. B1; "Vlasic's Hamburger-Size Pickles," *Wall Street Journal,* October 5, 1998, p. A26; and "Vlasic Foods International FY2000 New Products," accessed online at www.vlasic.com, July 1999.

Management may decide to *harvest* the product, which means reducing various costs (plant and equipment, maintenance, R&D, advertising, sales force) and hoping that sales hold up. If successful, harvesting will increase the company's profits in the short run. Or management may decide to *drop* the product from the line. It can sell it to another firm or simply liquidate it at salvage value. If the company plans to find a buyer, it will not want to run down the product through harvesting.

Table 9.2 summarizes the key characteristics of each stage of the product life cycle. The table also lists the marketing objectives and strategies for each stage.[24]

active example

Take a moment to explore an industry that is in the decline stage of PLC.

TABLE 9.2	Summary of Product Life-Cycle Characteristics, Objectives, and Strategies			
Characteristics	**Introduction**	**Growth**	**Maturity**	**Decline**
Sales	Low sales	Rapidly rising sales	Peak sales	Declining sales
Costs	High cost per customer	Average cost per customer	Low cost per customer	Low cost per customer
Profits	Negative	Rising profits	High profits	Declining profits
Customers	Innovators	Early adopters	Middle majority	Laggards
Competitors	Few	Growing number	Stable number beginning to decline	Declining number
Marketing Objectives				
	Create product awareness and trial	Maximize market share	Maximize profit while defending market share	Reduce expenditure and milk the brand
Strategies				
Product	Offer a basic product	Offer product extensions, service, warranty	Diversify brand and models	Phase out weak items
Price	Use cost-plus	Price to penetrate market	Price to match or beat competitors	Cut price
Distribution	Build selective distribution	Build intensive distribution	Build more intensive distribution	Go selective: phase out unprofitable outlets
Advertising	Build product awareness among early adopters and dealers	Build awareness and interest in the mass market	Stress brand differences and benefits	Reduce to level needed to retain hard-core loyals
Sales Promotion	Use heavy sales promotion to entice trial	Reduce to take acvantage of heavy consumer demand	Increase to encourage brand switching	Reduce to minimal level

Source: Philip Kotler, *Marketing Management: Analysis, Planning, Implementation, and Control,* 10th ed. (Upper Saddle River, NJ: Prentice Hall, 2000), p. 316.

[24]For a more comprehensive discussion of marketing strategies over the course of the product life cycle, see Philip Kotler, Marketing Management, 10th ed. (Upper Saddle River, NJ: Prentice Hall, 2000), pp. 303–23.

> active concept check

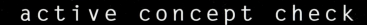

Now let's take a moment to test your knowledge of what you've just read.

> Chapter Wrap-Up

Now that you've reached the end of the chapter, you may wish to explore the concepts you've been reading about in greater detail, or test yourself to see how well you've comprehended the material. In the box below you'll find a number of links. Click on any one of these links to find additional chapter resources.

> end-of-chapter resources

- Review of Concept Connections
- Practice Quiz
- Issues for Discussion
- Key Terms
- Marketing Applications
- Internet Connections
- Company Case

Pricing Products: Pricing Considerations and Approaches

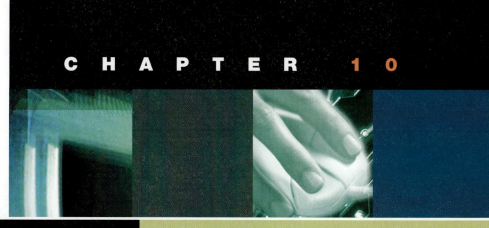

> What's Ahead

For decades preceding 1995, Kellogg was beloved on Wall Street—it was a virtual money machine. The cereal giant's 1995 sales of $7 billion represented its fifty-first straight year of rising revenues. Over the previous 30 years, Kellogg's sales had grown at one and a half times the industry growth rate and its share of the U.S. cereal market had consistently exceeded 40 percent. Over the preceding decade, annual returns to shareholders had averaged 19 percent, with gross margins running as high as 55 percent. In 1995, Kellogg held a 42 percent worldwide market share, with a 48 percent share in Asia and Europe and a mind-blowing 69 percent share in Latin America. Things, it seemed, could only get better for Kellogg.

Behind these dazzling numbers, however, Kellogg's cereal empire had begun to lose its luster. Much of its recent success, it now appears, had come at the expense of cereal customers. Kellogg's recent gains—and those of major competitors General Mills, Post, and Quaker—had come not from innovative new products, creative marketing programs, and operational improvements that added value for customers. Instead, these gains had come almost entirely from price increases that padded the sales and profits of the cereal makers.

Throughout most of the 1980s and early 1990s, Kellogg had boosted profit margins by steadily raising prices on its Rice Krispies, Special K, Raisin Bran, and Frosted Flakes—often twice a year. For example, by early 1996, a 14-ounce box of Raisin Bran that sold for $2.39 in 1985 was going for as much as $4.00 to $5.00, but with little or no change in the costs of the materials making up the cereal or its packaging. Since World War II, no food category had had more price increases than cereal. The price increases were very profitable for Kellogg and the other cereal companies—on average, the cereal makers were reaping more than twice the operating margins of the food industry as a whole. However, the relentless price increases became increasingly difficult for customers to swallow.

So, not surprisingly, in 1994 the cereal industry's pricing policies began to backfire as frustrated consumers retaliated with a quiet fury. Cereal buyers began shifting away from branded cereals toward cheaper private-label brands; by 1995, private labels were devouring 10 percent of the American cereal market, up from a little more than 5 percent only five years earlier. Worse, many Americans switched to less expensive, more portable handheld breakfast foods, such as bagels, muffins, and breakfast bars. As a result, total American cereal sales began falling off by 3 to 4 percent a year. Kellogg's sales and profits sagged and its U.S. market

share dropped to 36 percent. By early 1996, after what most industry analysts viewed as years of outrageous and self-serving pricing policies, Kellogg and the other cereal makers faced a full-blown crisis.

Post Cereals was the first competitor to break away. Belated research showed that exorbitant pricing was indeed the cause of the industry's doldrums. "Every statistic, every survey we took only showed that our customers were becoming more and more dissatisfied," said Mark Leckie, then general manager of Post Cereals. "You can see them walking down cereal aisles, clutching fistfuls of coupons and looking all over the shelves, trying to match them with a specific brand." To boost its soggy sales, in April 1996 Post slashed the prices on its 22 cereal brands an average of 20 percent—a surprise move that rocked the industry.

At first, Kellogg, General Mills, and Quaker held stubbornly to their premium prices. However, cereal buyers began switching in droves to Post's lower-priced brands—Post quickly stole 4 points from Kellogg's market share alone. Kellogg and the others had little choice but to follow Post's lead. Kellogg announced price cuts averaging 19 percent on two-thirds of all brands sold in the United States, marking the start of what would become a long and costly industry price war. In recanting their previous pricing excesses, the cereal makers swung wildly in the opposite direction, caught up in layoffs, plant closings, and other cost-cutting measures and fresh rounds of price cutting. "It reminds me of one of those World War I battles where there's all this firing but when the smoke clears you can't tell who won," noted an industry analyst. In fact, it appears that nobody won, as the fortunes of all competitors suffered.

Kellogg was perhaps the hardest hit of the major competitors. Post Cereal's parent company, consumer-foods powerhouse Philip Morris, derived only about 2 percent of its sales and profits from cereals and could easily offset the losses elsewhere. However, Kellogg, which counted on domestic cereal sales for 42 percent of its revenues and 43 percent of its operating profits, suffered enormously. Its operating margins were halved, and even after lowering its prices, Kellogg's revenues and profits continued to decline.

Now, several years after the initial price rollbacks, Kellogg and the cereal industry are still feeling the aftershocks. Entering the new millennium, the total American cereal market is growing at a meager 1 percent a year, private brands now capture an impressive 18 percent market share, and alternative breakfast foods continue their strong growth. Kellogg's market share has slumped to 32 percent, down from 42 percent in 1988, and its sales and profits are flat. During the past several years, Kellogg has watched its stock price languish while the stock market as a whole has more than tripled.

Recently, Kellogg and the other cereal titans have quietly begun pushing ahead with modest price increases. The increases are needed, they argue, to fund the product innovation and marketing support necessary to stimulate growth in the stagnant cereal category. But there's an obvious risk. Consumers have long memories, and if the new products and programs aren't exciting enough, the higher prices may well push consumers further toward less expensive private-label cereals and alternative breakfast foods. "It's almost a no-win situation," says another analyst.

Despite its problems, Kellogg remains the industry leader. The Kellogg brand name is still one of the world's best known and most respected. Kellogg's recent initiatives to cut costs, get reacquainted with its customers, and develop innovative new products and marketing programs—all of which promise to add value for customers rather than simply cutting prices—has Wall Street cautiously optimistic about Kellogg's future. But events of the past five years teach an important lesson. When setting prices, as when making any other marketing decisions, a company can't afford to focus on its own costs and profits. Instead, it must focus on customers' needs and the value they receive from the company's total marketing offer. If a company doesn't give customers full value for the price they're paying, they'll go elsewhere. In this case, Kellogg stole profits by steadily raising prices without also increasing customer value. Customers paid the price in the short run—but Kellogg is paying the price in the long run.[1]

> objectives

Before you begin, take a moment to familiarize yourself with the key objectives of this chapter.

> gearing up

Before we begin our exploration this chapter, take a short warm-up test to see what you know about this topic.

> video example

Listen to how marketers talk about the price of their products.

All profit organizations and many nonprofit organizations must set prices on their products or services. *Price* goes by many names:

[1]See John Greenwald, "Cereal Showdown," *Time,* April 29, 1996, p. 60; "Cereal Thriller," *The Economist,* June 15, 1996, p. 59; Gretchen Morgenson, "Denial in Battle Creek," *Forbes,* October 7, 1996, p. 44; Judann Pollack, "Post's Price Play Rocked Category, but Did It Work?" *Advertising Age,* December 1, 1997, p. 24; Carleen Hawn, "General Mills Tests Limits," *Forbes,* April 6, 1998, p. 48; Judann Pollack, "Price Cuts Unsettling to Cereal Business," *Advertising Age,* September 28, 1998, p. S10; Rekha Balu, "Kellogg Increases Prices on Majority of Cereal Brands," *Wall Street Journal,* December 15, 1998, p. B23; Susan Pulliam, "Kellogg, Long Treated as Stale by Wall Street, Shows Signs of Putting Some Snap in Its Walk," *Wall Street Journal,* February 16, 1999, pp. C2, C3; Terril Yue Jones, "Outside the Box," *Forbes,* June 14, 1999, pp. 52–53; and Amy Kover, "Why the Cereal Business Is Soggy." *Fortune,* March 6, 2000.

Price is all around us. You pay *rent* for your apartment, *tuition* for your education, and a *fee* to your physician or dentist. The airline, railway, taxi, and bus companies charge you a *fare;* the local utilities call their price a *rate;* and the local bank charges you *interest* for the money you borrow. The price for driving your car on Florida's Sunshine Parkway is a *toll,* and the company that insures your car charges you a *premium.* The guest lecturer charges an *honorarium* to tell you about a government official who took a *bribe* to help a shady character steal *dues* collected by a trade association. Clubs or societies to which you belong may make a special *assessment* to pay unusual expenses. Your regular lawyer may ask for a *retainer* to cover her services. The "price" of an executive is a *salary,* the price of a salesperson may be a *commission,* and the price of a worker is a *wage.* Finally, although economists would disagree, many of us feel that *income taxes* are the price we pay for the privilege of making money.[2]

In the narrowest sense, **price** is the amount of money charged for a product or service. More broadly, price is the sum of all the values that consumers exchange for the benefits of having or using the product or service. Historically, price has been the major factor affecting buyer choice. This is still true in poorer nations, among poorer groups, and with commodity products. However, nonprice factors have become more important in buyer-choice behavior in recent decades.

Throughout most of history, prices were set by negotiation between buyers and sellers. *Fixed price* policies—setting one price for all buyers—is a relatively modern idea that arose with the development of large-scale retailing at the end of the nineteenth century. Now, some one hundred years later, the Internet promises to reverse the fixed pricing trend and take us back to an era of *dynamic pricing*— charging different prices depending on individual customers and situations. The Internet, corporate networks, and wireless setups are connecting sellers and buyers as never before. Web sites like Compare.Net and PriceScan.com allow buyers to quickly and easily compare products and prices. Online auction sites like eBay.com and Amazon.com make it easy for buyers and sellers to negotiate prices on thousands of items—from refurbished computers to antique tin trains. At the same time, new technologies allow sellers to collect detailed data about customers' buying habits, preferences—even spending limits—so they can tailor their products and prices.[3]

Price is the only element in the marketing mix that produces revenue; all other elements represent costs. Price is also one of the most flexible elements of the marketing mix. Unlike product features and channel commitments, price can be changed quickly. At the same time, pricing and price competition is the number-one problem facing many marketing executives. Yet, as the chapter-opening Kellogg example illustrates, many companies do not handle pricing well. The most common mistakes are pricing that is too cost oriented rather than customer-value oriented; prices that are not revised often enough to reflect market changes; pricing that does not take the rest of the marketing mix into account; and prices that are not varied enough for different products, market segments, and purchase occasions.

In this chapter and the next, we focus on the problem of setting prices. This chapter looks at the factors marketers must consider when setting prices and at general pricing approaches. In the next chapter, we examine pricing strategies for new-product pricing, product mix pricing, price adjustments for buyer and situational factors, and price changes.

> Factors to Consider When Setting Prices

A company's pricing decisions are affected by both internal company factors and external environmental factors (see Figure 10.1).[4]

INTERNAL FACTORS AFFECTING PRICING DECISION

Internal factors affecting pricing include the company's marketing objectives, marketing mix strategy, costs, and organizational considerations.

Marketing Objectives

Before setting price, the company must decide on its strategy for the product. If the company has selected its target market and positioning carefully, then its marketing mix strategy, including price,

---

[2]See David J. Schwartz, *Marketing Today: A Basic Approach,* 3rd ed. (New York: Harcourt Brace Jovanovich, 1981), pp. 270–73.

[3]See Amy E. Cortese, "Good-Bye to Fixed Pricing?" *Business Week,* May 4, 1998, pp. 71–84; Robert D. Hof, "The Buyer Always Wins," *Business Week,* March 22, 1999, pp. EB26–EB28; and Robert D. Hof, "Going, Going, Gone," *Business Week,* April 12, 1999, pp. 30–32.

[4]For an excellent discussion of factors affecting pricing decisions, see Thomas T. Nagle and Reed K. Holden, *The Strategy and Tactics of Pricing,* 2nd ed. (Upper Saddle River, NJ: Prentice Hall, Inc., 1995), chap. 1.

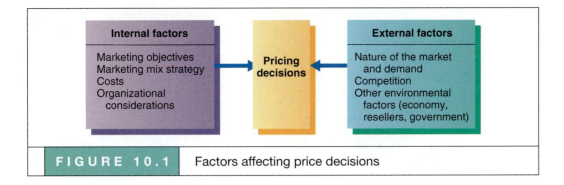

FIGURE 10.1 Factors affecting price decisions

will be fairly straightforward. For example, if General Motors decides to produce a new sports car to compete with European sports cars in the high-income segment, this suggests charging a high price. Motel 6, Econo Lodge, and Red Roof Inn have positioned themselves as motels that provide economical rooms for budget-minded travelers; this position requires charging a low price. Thus, pricing strategy is largely determined by decisions on market positioning.

At the same time, the company may seek additional objectives. The clearer a firm is about its objectives, the easier it is to set price. Examples of common objectives are *survival, current profit maximization, market share leadership,* and *product quality leadership.*

Companies set *survival* as their major objective if they are troubled by too much capacity, heavy competition, or changing consumer wants. To keep a plant going, a company may set a low price, hoping to increase demand. In this case, profits are less important than survival. As long as their prices cover variable costs and some fixed costs, they can stay in business. However, survival is only a short-term objective. In the long run, the firm must learn how to add value that consumers will pay for or face extinction.

Many companies use *current profit maximization* as their pricing goal. They estimate what demand and costs will be at different prices and choose the price that will produce the maximum current profit, cash flow, or return on investment. In all cases, the company wants current financial results rather than long-run performance. Other companies want to obtain *market share leadership.* They believe that the company with the largest market share will enjoy the lowest costs and highest long-run profit. To become the market share leader, these firms set prices as low as possible.

> ## active example

Consider how one major corporation benefited from current profit maximization.

A company might decide that it wants to achieve *product quality leadership.* This normally calls for charging a high price to cover higher performance quality and the high cost of R&D. For example, Hewlett-Packard focuses on the high-quality, high-price end of the hand-held calculator market. Gillette's product superiority lets it price its Mach3 razor cartridges at a 50 percent premium over its own SensorExcel and competitors' cartridges. Maytag has long built high-quality washing machines and priced them higher. Its ads use the long-running Maytag slogan "Built to last longer" and feature the lonely Maytag repairman (who's lonely because no one ever calls him for service). The ads point out that washers are custodians of what is often a $300 to $400 load of clothes, making them worth the higher price tag. For instance, at $1,099, Maytag's new Neptune, a front-loading washer without an agitator, sells for double what most other washers cost because the company's marketers claim that it uses less water and electricity and prolongs the life of clothing by being less abrasive.[5]

A company might also use price to attain other, more specific objectives. It can set prices low to prevent competition from entering the market or set prices at competitors' levels to stabilize the market. Prices can be set to keep the loyalty and support of resellers or to avoid government intervention. Prices can be reduced temporarily to create excitement for a product or to draw more customers into a retail store. One product may be priced to help the sales of other products in the company's line.

---

[5]See Steve Gelsi, "Spin-Cycle Doctor," *Brandweek,* March 10, 1997, pp. 38–40. Tim Stevens, "From Reliable to 'Wow,'" *Industry Week,* June 22, 1998, pp. 22–26; and William C. Symonds, "'Build a Better Mousetrap' Is No Claptrap," *Business Week,* February 1, 1999, p. 47.

Product-quality leadership: Maytag targets the higher quality end of the appliance market. Its ads use the long-running slogan "Built to last longer" and feature Ol' Lonely, the Maytag repairman.

Thus, pricing may play an important role in helping to accomplish the company's objectives at many levels.

Nonprofit and public organizations may adopt a number of other pricing objectives. A university aims for *partial cost recovery,* knowing that it must rely on private gifts and public grants to cover the remaining costs. A nonprofit hospital may aim for *full cost recovery* in its pricing. A nonprofit theater company may price its productions to fill the maximum number of theater seats. A social service agency may set a *social price* geared to the varying income situations of different clients.

Marketing Mix Strategy

Price is only one of the marketing mix tools that a company uses to achieve its marketing objectives. Price decisions must be coordinated with product design, distribution, and promotion decisions to form a consistent and effective marketing program. Decisions made for other marketing mix variables may affect pricing decisions. For example, producers using many resellers who are expected to support and promote their products may have to build larger reseller margins into their prices. The decision to position the product on high-performance quality will mean that the seller must charge a higher price to cover higher costs.

Companies often position their products on price and then base other marketing mix decisions on the prices they want to charge. Here, price is a crucial product-positioning factor that defines the product's market, competition, and design. Many firms support such price-positioning strategies with a technique called **target costing,** a potent strategic weapon. Target costing reverses the usual process of first designing a new product, determining its cost, and then asking, "Can we sell it for that?" Instead, it starts with an ideal selling price based on customer considerations, then targets costs that will ensure that the price is met.

The original Swatch watch provides a good example of target costing. Rather than starting with its own costs, Swatch surveyed the market and identified an unserved segment of watch buyers who wanted "a low-cost fashion accessory that also keeps time." Armed with this information about market needs, Swatch set out to give consumers the watch they wanted at a price they were willing to pay, and it managed the new product's costs accordingly. Like most watch buyers, targeted consumers were concerned about precision, reliability, and durability. However, they were also concerned about fashion and affordability. To keep costs down, Swatch designed fashionable simpler watches that contained fewer parts and that were constructed from high-tech but less expensive materials. It then developed a revolutionary automated process for mass producing the new watches and exercised strict cost controls throughout the manufacturing process. By managing costs carefully, Swatch was able to create a watch that offered just the right blend of fashion and function at a price consumers were willing to pay. As a result of its initial major success, consumers have placed increasing value on Swatch products, allowing the company to introduce successively higher-priced designs.[6]

Other companies deemphasize price and use other marketing mix tools to create *nonprice* positions. Often, the best strategy is not to charge the lowest price, but rather to differentiate the marketing offer to make it worth a higher price. For example, for years Johnson Controls, a producer of

[6]See Timothy M. Laseter, "Supply Chain Management The Ins and Outs of Target Costing," *Purchasing,* March 12, 1998, pp. 22–25. Also check out the Swatch Web page at www.swatch.com.

climate-control systems for office buildings, used initial price as its primary competitive tool. However, research showed that customers were more concerned about the total cost of installing and maintaining a system than about its initial price. Repairing broken systems was expensive, time-consuming, and risky. Customers had to shut down the heat or air conditioning in the whole building, disconnect a lot of wires, and face the dangers of electrocution. Johnson decided to change its strategy. It designed an entirely new system called "Metasys." To repair the new system, customers need only pull out an old plastic module and slip in a new one—no tools required. Metasys costs more to make than the old system, and customers pay a higher initial price, but it costs less to install and maintain. Despite its higher asking price, the new Metasys system brought in $500 million in revenues in its first year.[7]

Thus, the marketer must consider the total marketing mix when setting prices. If the product is positioned on nonprice factors, then decisions about quality, promotion, and distribution will strongly affect price. If price is a crucial positioning factor, then price will strongly affect decisions made about the other marketing mix elements. However, even when featuring price, marketers need to remember that customers rarely buy on price alone. Instead, they seek products that give them the best value in terms of benefits received for the price paid. Thus, in most cases, the company will consider price along with all the other marketing-mix elements when developing the marketing program.

Costs

Costs set the floor for the price that the company can charge for its product. The company wants to charge a price that both covers all its costs for producing, distributing, and selling the product and delivers a fair rate of return for its effort and risk. A company's costs may be an important element in its pricing strategy. Many companies, such as Southwest Airlines, Wal-Mart, and Union Carbide, work to become the "low-cost producers" in their industries. Companies with lower costs can set lower prices that result in greater sales and profits.

Types of Costs. A company's costs take two forms, fixed and variable. **Fixed costs** (also known as overhead) are costs that do not vary with production or sales level. For example, a company must pay each month's bills for rent, heat, interest, and executive salaries, whatever the company's output. **Variable costs** vary directly with the level of production. Each personal computer produced by Compaq involves a cost of computer chips, wires, plastic, packaging, and other inputs. These costs tend to be the same for each unit produced. They are called variable because their total varies with the number of units produced. **Total costs** are the sum of the fixed and variable costs for any given level of production. Management wants to charge a price that will at least cover the total production costs at a given level of production. The company must watch its costs carefully. If it costs the company more than competitors to produce and sell its product, the company will have to charge a higher price or make less profit, putting it at a competitive disadvantage.

Costs at Different Levels of Production. To price wisely, management needs to know how its costs vary with different levels of production. For example, suppose Texas Instruments (TI) has built a plant to produce 1,000 calculators per day. Figure 10.2a shows the typical short-run average cost curve (SRAC). It shows that the cost per calculator is high if TI's factory produces only a few per day. But as production moves up to 1,000 calculators per day, average cost falls. This is because fixed costs are

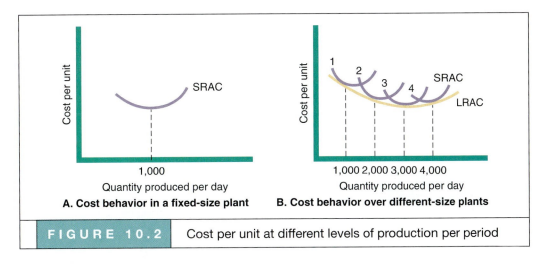

A. Cost behavior in a fixed-size plant

B. Cost behavior over different-size plants

| FIGURE 10.2 | Cost per unit at different levels of production per period |

[7]Brian Dumaine, "Closing the Innovation Gap," *Fortune,* December 2, 1991, pp. 56–62.

spread over more units, with each one bearing a smaller share of the fixed cost. TI can try to produce more than 1,000 calculators per day, but average costs will increase because the plant becomes inefficient. Workers have to wait for machines, the machines break down more often, and workers get in each other's way.

If TI believed it could sell 2,000 calculators a day, it should consider building a larger plant. The plant would use more efficient machinery and work arrangements. Also, the unit cost of producing 2,000 calculators per day would be lower than the unit cost of producing 1,000 units per day, as shown in the long-run average cost (LRAC) curve (Figure 10.2b). In fact, a 3,000-unit capacity plant would even be more efficient, according to Figure 10.2b. But a 4,000-unit daily production plant would be less efficient because of increasing diseconomies of scale—too many workers to manage, paperwork slows things down, and so on. Figure 10.2b shows that a 3,000-unit daily production plant is the best size to build if demand is strong enough to support this level of production.

Costs as a Function of Production Experience. Suppose TI runs a plant that produces 3,000 calculators per day. As TI gains experience in producing calculators, it learns how to do it better. Workers learn shortcuts and become more familiar with their equipment. With practice, the work becomes better organized, and TI finds better equipment and production processes. With higher volume, TI becomes more efficient and gains economies of scale. As a result, average cost tends to fall with accumulated production experience. This is shown in Figure 10.3.[8] Thus, the average cost of producing the first 100,000 calculators is $10 per calculator. When the company has produced the first 200,000 calculators, the average cost has fallen to $9. After its accumulated production experience doubles again to 400,000, the average cost is $7. This drop in the average cost with accumulated production experience is called the **experience curve** (or the **learning curve**).

If a downward-sloping experience curve exists, this is highly significant for the company. Not only will the company's unit production cost fall, but it will fall faster if the company makes and sells more during a given time period. But the market has to stand ready to buy the higher output. To take advantage of the experience curve, TI must get a large market share early in the product's life cycle. This suggests the following pricing strategy. TI should price its calculators low; its sales will then increase, and its costs will decrease through gaining more experience, and then it can lower its prices further.

Some companies have built successful strategies around the experience curve. For example, Bausch & Lomb solidified its position in the soft contact lens market by using computerized lens design and steadily expanding its one Soflens plant. As a result, its market share climbed steadily to 65 percent. However, a single-minded focus on reducing costs and exploiting the experience curve will not always work. Experience curve pricing carries some major risks. The aggressive pricing might give the product a cheap image. The strategy also assumes that competitors are weak and not willing to fight it out by meeting the company's price cuts. Finally, while the company is building volume under one technology, a competitor may find a lower-cost technology that lets it start at prices lower than the market leader's, who still operates on the old experience curve.

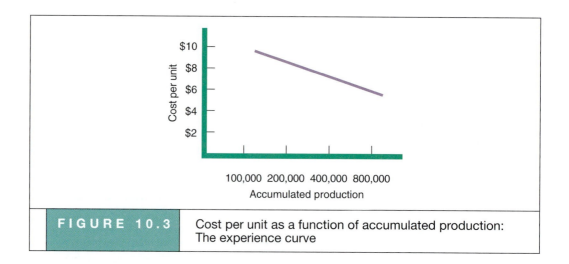

| FIGURE 10.3 | Cost per unit as a function of accumulated production: The experience curve |

[8]Here accumulated production is drawn on a semilog scale so that equal distances represent the same percentage increase in output.

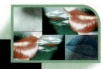

Organizational Considerations

Management must decide who within the organization should set prices. Companies handle pricing in a variety of ways. In small companies, prices are often set by top management rather than by the marketing or sales departments. In large companies, pricing is typically handled by divisional or product line managers. In industrial markets, salespeople may be allowed to negotiate with customers within certain price ranges. Even so, top management sets the pricing objectives and policies, and it often approves the prices proposed by lower-level management or salespeople. In industries in which pricing is a key factor (aerospace, railroads, oil companies), companies often have a pricing department to set the best prices or help others in setting them. This department reports to the marketing department or top management. Others who have an influence on pricing include sales managers, production managers, finance managers, and accountants.

EXTERNAL FACTORS AFFECTING PRICING DECISIONS

External factors that affect pricing decisions include the nature of the market and demand, competition, and other environmental elements.

The Market and Demand

Whereas costs set the lower limit of prices, the market and demand set the upper limit. Both consumer and industrial buyers balance the price of a product or service against the benefits of owning it. Thus, before setting prices, the marketer must understand the relationship between price and demand for its product. In this section, we explain how the price–demand relationship varies for different types of markets and how buyer perceptions of price affect the pricing decision. We then discuss methods for measuring the price–demand relationship.

Pricing in Different Types of Markets.   The seller's pricing freedom varies with different types of markets. Economists recognize four types of markets, each presenting a different pricing challenge.

Under *pure competition,* the market consists of many buyers and sellers trading in a uniform commodity such as wheat, copper, or financial securities. No single buyer or seller has much effect on the going market price. A seller cannot charge more than the going price because buyers can obtain as much as they need at the going price. Nor would sellers charge less than the market price because they can sell all they want at this price. If price and profits rise, new sellers can easily enter the market. In a purely competitive market, marketing research, product development, pricing, advertising, and sales promotion play little or no role. Thus, sellers in these markets do not spend much time on marketing strategy.

Under *monopolistic competition,* the market consists of many buyers and sellers who trade over a range of prices rather than a single market price. A range of prices occurs because sellers can differentiate their offers to buyers. Either the physical product can be varied in quality, features, or style, or the accompanying services can be varied. Buyers see differences in sellers' products and will pay different prices for them. Sellers try to develop differentiated offers for different customer segments and, in addition to price, freely use branding, advertising, and personal selling to set their offers apart. For example, H.J. Heinz, Vlasic, and several other national brands of pickles compete with dozens of regional and local brands, all differentiated by price and nonprice factors. In services, Kinko's differentiates its offer through strong branding and advertising, reducing the impact of pricing. Because there are many competitors in such markets, each firm is less affected by competitors' marketing strategies than in oligopolistic markets.

Under *oligopolistic competition,* the market consists of a few sellers who are highly sensitive to each other's pricing and marketing strategies. The product can be uniform (steel, aluminum) or nonuniform (cars, computers). There are few sellers because it is difficult for new sellers to enter the market. Each seller is alert to competitors' strategies and moves. If a steel company slashes its price by 10 percent, buyers will quickly switch to this supplier. The other steelmakers must respond by lowering their prices or increasing their services. An oligopolist is never sure that it will gain anything

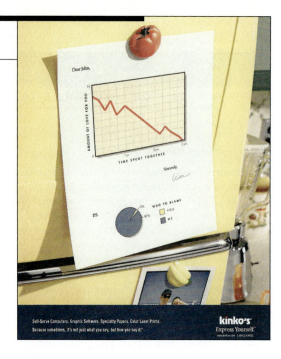

permanent through a price cut. In contrast, if an oligopolist raises its price, its competitors might not follow this lead. The oligopolist then would have to retract its price increase or risk losing customers to competitors.

In a *pure monopoly,* the market consists of one seller. The seller may be a government monopoly (the U.S. Postal Service), a private regulated monopoly (a power company), or a private nonregulated monopoly (DuPont when it introduced nylon). Pricing is handled differently in each case. A government monopoly can pursue a variety of pricing objectives. It might set a price below cost because the product is important to buyers who cannot afford to pay full cost. Or the price might be set either to cover costs or to produce good revenue. It can even be set quite high to slow down consumption. In a regulated monopoly, the government permits the company to set rates that will yield a "fair return," one that will let the company maintain and expand its operations as needed. Nonregulated monopolies are free to price at what the market will bear. However, they do not always charge the full price for a number of reasons: a desire to not attract competition, a desire to penetrate the market faster with a low price, or a fear of government regulation.[9]

Consumer Perceptions of Price and Value. In the end, the consumer will decide whether a product's price is right. Pricing decisions, like other marketing mix decisions, must be buyer oriented. When consumers buy a product, they exchange something of value (the price) to get something of value (the benefits of having or using the product). Effective, buyer-oriented pricing involves understanding how much value consumers place on the benefits they receive from the product and setting a price that fits this value.

A company often finds it hard to measure the values customers will attach to its product. For example, calculating the cost of ingredients in a meal at a fancy restaurant is relatively easy. But assigning a value to other satisfactions such as taste, environment, relaxation, conversation, and status is very hard. These values will vary both for different consumers and different situations. Still, consumers will use these values to evaluate a product's price. If customers perceive that the price is greater than the product's value, they will not buy the product. If consumers perceive that the price is below the product's value, they will buy it, but the seller loses profit opportunities.

active exercise

Consider some consequences of changing consumer perceptions of price and value.

[9]See Luis M. B. Cabral, David J. Salant, and Glenn A. Woroch, "Monopoly Pricing with Network Externalities," *International Journal of Industrial Organization,* February 1999, pp. 199–214.

Analyzing the Price–Demand Relationship. Each price the company might charge will lead to a different level of demand. The relationship between the price charged and the resulting demand level is shown in the **demand curve** in Figure 10.4. The demand curve shows the number of units the market will buy in a given time period at different prices that might be charged. In the normal case, demand and price are inversely related; that is, the higher the price, the lower the demand. Thus, the company would sell less if it raised its price from P_1 to P_2. In short, consumers with limited budgets probably will buy less of something if its price is too high.

In the case of prestige goods, the demand curve sometimes slopes upward. Consumers think that higher prices mean more quality. For example, Gibson Guitar Corporation recently toyed with the idea of lowering its prices to compete more effectively with Japanese rivals like Yamaha and Ibanez. To its surprise, Gibson found that its instruments didn't sell as well at lower prices. "We had an inverse [price–demand relationship]," noted Gibson's chief executive officer. "The more we charged, the more product we sold." Gibson's slogan promises: "The world's finest musical instruments." It turns out that low prices simply aren't consistent with "Gibson's century old tradition of creating investment-quality instruments that represent the highest standards of imaginative design and masterful craftsmanship."[10] Still, if the company charges too high a price, the level of demand will be lower.

Most companies try to measure their demand curves by estimating demand at different prices. The type of market makes a difference. In a monopoly, the demand curve shows the total market demand resulting from different prices. If the company faces competition, its demand at different prices will depend on whether competitors' prices stay constant or change with the company's own prices.

In measuring the price–demand relationship, the market researcher must not allow other factors affecting demand to vary. For example, if Sony increased its advertising at the same time that it lowered its television prices, we would not know how much of the increased demand was due to the lower prices and how much was due to the increased advertising. The same problem arises if a holiday weekend occurs when the lower price is set—more gift giving over the holidays causes people to buy more televisions. Economists show the impact of nonprice factors on demand through shifts in the demand curve rather than movements along it.

> ## active example

Take a moment to consider the price-demand relationship in the sports world.

Price Elasticity of Demand. Marketers also need to know **price elasticity**—how responsive demand will be to a change in price. Consider the two demand curves in Figure 10.4. In Figure 10.4a, a price increase from P_1 to P_2 leads to a relatively small drop in demand from Q_1 to Q_2. In Figure 10.4b, however, the same price increase leads to a large drop in demand from Q'_1 to Q'_2. If demand hardly changes with a small change in price, we say the demand is *inelastic*. If demand changes

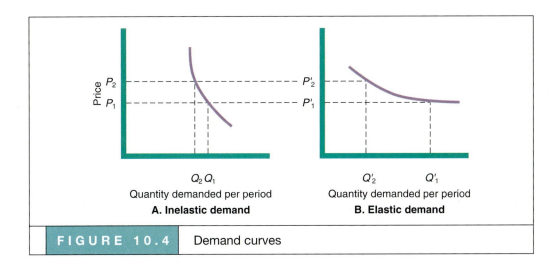

| FIGURE 10.4 | Demand curves |

---

[10]Joshua Rosenbaum, "Guitar Maker Looks for a New Key," *Wall Street Journal,* February 11, 1998, p. B1; and information obtained online from www.gibson.com, February 2000.

greatly, we say the demand is *elastic*. The price elasticity of demand is given by the following formula:

$$\text{Price Elasticity of Demand} = \frac{\%\ \text{Change in Quantity Demanded}}{\%\ \text{Change in Price}}$$

Suppose demand falls by 10 percent when a seller raises its price by 2 percent. Price elasticity of demand is therefore –5 (the minus sign confirms the inverse relation between price and demand) and demand is elastic. If demand falls by 2 percent with a 2 percent increase in price, then elasticity is –1. In this case, the seller's total revenue stays the same: The seller sells fewer items but at a higher price that preserves the same total revenue. If demand falls by 1 percent when price is increased by 2 percent, then elasticity is –1/2 and demand is inelastic. The less elastic the demand, the more it pays for the seller to raise the price.

What determines the price elasticity of demand? Buyers are less price sensitive when the product they are buying is unique or when it is high in quality, prestige, or exclusiveness. They are also less price sensitive when substitute products are hard to find or when they cannot easily compare the quality of substitutes. Finally, buyers are less price sensitive when the total expenditure for a product is low relative to their income or when the cost is shared by another party.[11]

If demand is elastic rather than inelastic, sellers will consider lowering their price. A lower price will produce more total revenue. This practice makes sense as long as the extra costs of producing and selling more do not exceed the extra revenue. At the same time, most firms want to avoid pricing that turns their products into commodities. In recent years, forces such as deregulation and the instant price comparisons afforded by the Internet and other technologies have increased consumer price sensitivity, turning products ranging from telephones and computers to new automobiles into commodities in consumers' eyes. Marketers need to work harder than ever to differentiate their offerings when a dozen competitors are selling virtually the same product at a comparable or lower price. More than ever, companies need to understand the price sensitivity of their customers and prospects and the trade-offs people are willing to make between price and product characteristics. In the words of marketing consultant Kevin Clancy, those who target only the price sensitive are "leaving money on the table."

Even in the energy marketplace, where you would think that a kilowatt is a kilowatt is a kilowatt, some utility companies are beginning to wake up to this fact. They are differentiating their power, branding it, marketing it, and providing unique services to customers, even if it means higher prices. For example, Green Mountain Power (GMP), a small Vermont utility, is approaching the deregulated consumer energy marketplace with the firm belief that even kilowatt hours can be differentiated. GMP conducted extensive marketing research and uncovered a large segment of prospects who were not only concerned with the environment but were willing to support their attitudes with dollars. Because GMP is a "green" power provider—a large percentage of its power is hydroelectric— customers had an opportunity to ease the environmental burden by purchasing GMP power. GMP has already participated in two residential power-selling pilot projects in Massachusetts and New Hampshire, successfully competing against "cheaper" brands that focused on more price-sensitive consumers.[12]

Competitors' Costs, Prices, and Offers

Another external factor affecting the company's pricing decisions is competitors' costs and prices and possible competitor reactions to the company's own pricing moves. A consumer who is considering the purchase of a Canon camera will evaluate Canon's price and value against the prices and values of comparable products made by Nikon, Minolta, Pentax, and others. In addition, the company's pricing strategy may affect the nature of the competition it faces. If Canon follows a high-price, high-margin strategy, it may attract competition. A low-price, low-margin strategy, however, may stop competitors or drive them out of the market.

Canon needs to benchmark its costs against its competitors' costs to learn whether it is operating at a cost advantage or disadvantage. It also needs to learn the price and quality of each competitor's offer. Once Canon is aware of competitors' prices and offers, it can use them as a starting point for its own pricing. If Canon's cameras are similar to Nikon's, it will have to price close to Nikon or lose sales. If Canon's cameras are not as good as Nikon's, the firm will not be able to charge as much. If Canon's products are better than Nikon's, it can charge more. Basically, Canon will use price to position its offer relative to the competition.

[11]See Nagle and Holden, *The Strategy and Tactics of Pricing,* chap. 4.

[12]Kevin J. Clancy, "At What Profit Price?" *Brandweek,* June 23, 1997, pp. 24–28; and information obtained from www.gmpvt.com, February 2000.

Other External Factors

When setting prices, the company also must consider other factors in its external environment. *Economic conditions* can have a strong impact on the firm's pricing strategies. Economic factors such as boom or recession, inflation, and interest rates affect pricing decisions because they affect both the costs of producing a product and consumer perceptions of the product's price and value. The company must also consider what impact its prices will have on other parties in its environment. How will *resellers* react to various prices? The company should set prices that give resellers a fair profit, encourage their support, and help them to sell the product effectively. The *government* is another important external influence on pricing decisions. Finally, *social concerns* may have to be taken into account. In setting prices, a company's short-term sales, market share, and profit goals may have to be tempered by broader societal considerations.

> ## active example

Consider how one big corporation addressed external pricing factors.

> ## active concept check

Now let's take a moment to test your knowledge of what you've just read.

> ## General Pricing Approaches

The price the company charges will be somewhere between one that is too low to produce a profit and one that is too high to produce any demand. Figure 10.5 summarizes the major considerations in setting price. Product costs set a floor to the price; consumer perceptions of the product's value set the ceiling. The company must consider competitors' prices and other external and internal factors to find the best price between these two extremes.

Companies set prices by selecting a general pricing approach that includes one or more of three sets of factors. We examine these approaches: the *cost-based approach* (cost-plus pricing, break-even analysis, and target profit pricing); the *buyer-based approach* (value-based pricing); and the *competition-based approach* (going-rate and sealed-bid pricing).

COST-BASED PRICING

Cost-Plus Pricing

The simplest pricing method is **cost-plus pricing**—adding a standard markup to the cost of the product. Construction companies, for example, submit job bids by estimating the total project cost and

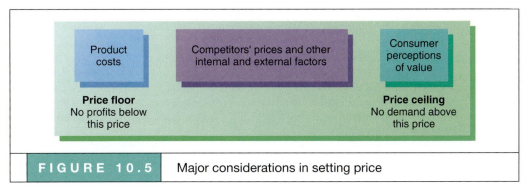

Product costs	Competitors' prices and other internal and external factors	Consumer perceptions of value
Price floor No profits below this price		**Price ceiling** No demand above this price

FIGURE 10.5   Major considerations in setting price

adding a standard markup for profit. Lawyers, accountants, and other professionals typically price by adding a standard markup to their costs. Some sellers tell their customers they will charge cost plus a specified markup; for example, aerospace companies price this way to the government.

To illustrate markup pricing, suppose a toaster manufacturer had the following costs and expected sales:

Variable cost	$10
Fixed costs	$300,000
Expected unit sales	50,000

Then the manufacturer's cost per toaster is given by:

$$\text{Unit Cost} = \text{Variable Cost} + \frac{\text{Fixed Costs}}{\text{Unit Sales}} = \$10 + \frac{\$300,000}{50,000} = \$16$$

Now suppose the manufacturer wants to earn a 20 percent markup on sales. The manufacturer's markup price is given by:[13]

$$\text{Markup Price} = \frac{\text{Unit Cost}}{(1 - \text{Desired Return on Sales})} = \frac{\$16}{1 - 0.2} = \$20$$

The manufacturer would charge dealers $20 a toaster and make a profit of $4 per unit. The dealers, in turn, will mark up the toaster. If dealers want to earn 50 percent on sales price, they will mark up the toaster to $40 ($20 + 50% of $40). This number is equivalent to a *markup on cost* of 100 percent ($20/$20).

Does using standard markups to set prices make sense? Generally, no. Any pricing method that ignores demand and competitor prices is not likely to lead to the best price. Suppose the toaster manufacturer charged $20 but sold only 30,000 toasters instead of 50,000. Then the unit cost would have been higher because the fixed costs are spread over fewer units, and the realized percentage markup on sales would have been lower. Markup pricing works only if that price actually brings in the expected level of sales.

Still, markup pricing remains popular for many reasons. First, sellers are more certain about costs than about demand. By tying the price to cost, sellers simplify pricing—they do not have to make frequent adjustments as demand changes. Second, when all firms in the industry use this pricing method, prices tend to be similar and price competition is thus minimized. Third, many people feel that cost-plus pricing is fairer to both buyers and sellers. Sellers earn a fair return on their investment but do not take advantage of buyers when buyers' demand becomes great.

Break-even Analysis and Target Profit Pricing

Another cost-oriented pricing approach is **break-even pricing** (or a variation called **target profit pricing.**) The firm tries to determine the price at which it will break even or make the target profit it is seeking. Such pricing is used by General Motors, which prices its automobiles to achieve a 15 to 20 percent profit on its investment. This pricing method is also used by public utilities, which are constrained to make a fair return on their investment.

Target pricing uses the concept of a *break-even chart,* which shows the total cost and total revenue expected at different sales volume levels. Figure 10.6 shows a break-even chart for the toaster manufacturer discussed here. Fixed costs are $300,000 regardless of sales volume. Variable costs are added to fixed costs to form total costs, which rise with volume. The total revenue curve starts at zero and rises with each unit sold. The slope of the total revenue curve reflects the price of $20 per unit.

The total revenue and total cost curves cross at 30,000 units. This is the *break-even volume.* At $20, the company must sell at least 30,000 units to break even; that is, for total revenue to cover total cost. Break-even volume can be calculated using the following formula:

$$\text{Break-even Volume} = \frac{\text{Fixed Cost}}{\text{Price} - \text{Variable Cost}} = \frac{\$300,000}{\$20 - \$10} = 30,000$$

If the company wants to make a target profit, it must sell more than 30,000 units at $20 each. Suppose the toaster manufacturer has invested $1,000,000 in the business and wants to set price to earn a 20 percent return, or $200,000. In that case, it must sell at least 50,000 units at $20 each. If the company charges a higher price, it will not need to sell as many toasters to achieve its target return. But the market may not buy even this lower volume at the higher price. Much depends on the price elasticity and competitors' prices.

---

[13]The arithmetic of markups and margins is discussed in Appendix 2, "Marketing Arithmetic."

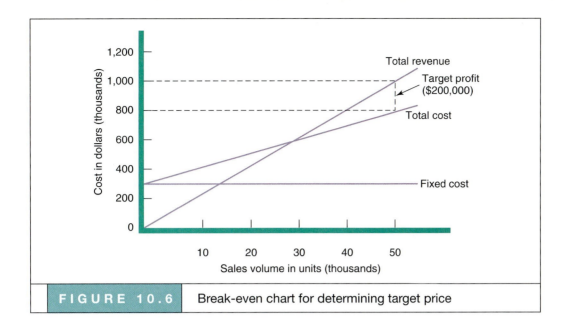

The manufacturer should consider different prices and estimate break-even volumes, probable demand, and profits for each. This is done in Table 10.1. The table shows that as price increases, break-even volume drops (column 2). But as price increases, demand for the toasters also falls off (column 3). At the $14 price, because the manufacturer clears only $4 per toaster ($14 less $10 in variable costs), it must sell a very high volume to break even. Even though the low price attracts many buyers, demand still falls below the high break-even point, and the manufacturer loses money. At the other extreme, with a $22 price the manufacturer clears $12 per toaster and must sell only 25,000 units to break even. But at this high price, consumers buy too few toasters, and profits are negative. The table shows that a price of $18 yields the highest profits. Note that none of the prices produce the manufacturer's target profit of $200,000. To achieve this target return, the manufacturer will have to search for ways to lower fixed or variable costs, thus lowering the break-even volume.

VALUE-BASED PRICING

An increasing number of companies are basing their prices on the product's perceived value. **Value-based pricing** uses buyers' perceptions of value, not the seller's cost, as the key to pricing. Value-based pricing means that the marketer cannot design a product and marketing program and then set the price. Price is considered along with the other marketing mix variables *before* the marketing program is set.

Figure 10.7 compares cost-based pricing with value-based pricing. Cost-based pricing is product driven. The company designs what it considers to be a good product, totals the costs of making the product, and sets a price that covers costs plus a target profit. Marketing must then convince buyers

TABLE 10.1 Break-even Volume and Profits at Different Prices

(1) Price	(2) Unit Demand Needed to Break Even	(3) Expected Unit Demand at Given Price	(4) Total Revenues (1) × (3)	(5) Total costs*	(6) Profit (4) − (5)
$14	75,000	71,000	$ 994,000	$1,010,000	−$ 16,000
16	50,000	67,000	1,072,000	970,000	102,000
18	37,500	60,000	1,080,000	900,000	180,000
20	30,000	42,000	840,000	720,000	120,000
22	25,000	23,000	506,000	530,000	−24,000

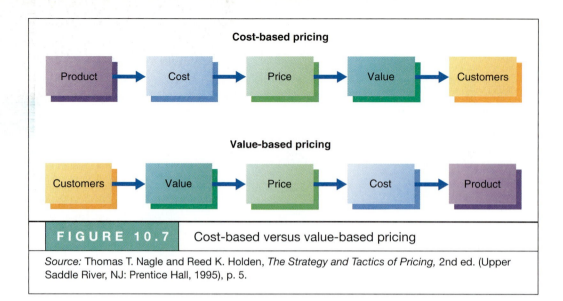

| FIGURE 10.7 | Cost-based versus value-based pricing |

Source: Thomas T. Nagle and Reed K. Holden, *The Strategy and Tactics of Pricing,* 2nd ed. (Upper Saddle River, NJ: Prentice Hall, 1995), p. 5.

that the product's value at that price justifies its purchase. If the price turns out to be too high, the company must settle for lower markups or lower sales, both resulting in disappointing profits.

Value-based pricing reverses this process. The company sets its target price based on customer perceptions of the product value. The targeted value and price then drive decisions about product design and what costs can be incurred. As a result, pricing begins with analyzing consumer needs and value perceptions, and price is set to match consumers' perceived value.

A company using value-based pricing must find out what value buyers assign to different competitive offers. However, measuring perceived value can be difficult. Sometimes, consumers are asked how much they would pay for a basic product and for each benefit added to the offer. Or a company might conduct experiments to test the perceived value of different product offers. If the seller charges more than the buyers' perceived value, the company's sales will suffer. Many companies overprice their products, and their products sell poorly. Other companies underprice. Underpriced products sell very well, but they produce less revenue than they would have if price were raised to the perceived-value level.

During the past decade, marketers have noted a fundamental shift in consumer attitudes toward price and quality. Many companies have changed their pricing approaches to bring them into line with changing economic conditions and consumer price perceptions. According to Jack Welch, CEO of General Electric, "The value decade is upon us. If you can't sell a top-quality product at the world's best price, you're going to be out of the game. . . . The best way to hold your customers is to constantly figure out how to give them more for less."[14]

Thus, more and more, marketers have adopted **value pricing** strategies—offering just the right combination of quality and good service at a fair price. In many cases, this has involved the introduction of less expensive versions of established, brand-name products. Campbell introduced its Great Starts Budget frozen-food line, Holiday Inn opened several Holiday Express budget hotels, Revlon's Charles of the Ritz offered the Express Bar collection of affordable cosmetics, and fast-food restaurants such as Taco Bell and McDonald's offered "value menus." In other cases, value pricing has involved redesigning existing brands in order to offer more quality for a given price or the same quality for less.

In many business-to-business marketing situations, the pricing challenge is to find ways to maintain the company's *pricing power*—its power to maintain or even raise prices without losing market share. To retain pricing power—to escape price competition and to justify higher prices and margins—a firm must retain or build the value of its marketing offer. This is especially true for suppliers of commodity products, which are characterized by little differentiation and intense price competition. In such cases, many companies adopt *value-added* strategies. Rather than cutting prices to match competitors, they attach value-added services to differentiate their offers and thus support higher margins.[15]

An important type of value pricing at the retail level is *everyday low pricing (EDLP)*. EDLP involves charging a constant, everyday low price with few or no temporary price discounts. In con-

[14]See Philip Kotler, *Kotler on Marketing* (New York: Free Press, 1999), p. 54.

[15]See Darren McDermott, "Cost-Consciousness Beats 'Pricing Power,' " *Wall Street Journal,* May 3, 1999, p. A1.

trast, *high–low pricing* involves charging higher prices on an everyday basis but running frequent promotions to temporarily lower prices on selected items below the EDLP level.[16] In recent years, high–low pricing has given way to EDLP in retail settings ranging from Saturn car dealerships to upscale department stores such as Nordstrom. Retailers adopt EDLP for many reasons, the most important of which is that constant sales and promotions are costly and have eroded consumer confidence in the credibility of everyday shelf prices. Consumers also have less time and patience for such time-honored traditions as watching for supermarket specials and clipping coupons.

The king of EDLP is Wal-Mart, which practically defined the concept. Except for a few sale items every month, Wal-Mart promises everyday low prices on everything it sells. In contrast, Sears's attempts at EDLP in 1989 failed. To offer everyday low prices, a company must first have everyday low costs. Wal-Mart's EDLP strategy works well because its expenses are only 15 percent of sales. Sears, however, was spending 29 percent of sales to cover administrative and other overhead costs. As a result, Sears now offers everyday *fair* pricing, under which it tries to offer customers differentiated products at a consistent, fair price with fewer markdowns.

COMPETITION-BASED PRICING

Consumers will base their judgments of a product's value on the prices that competitors charge for similar products. One form of **competition-based pricing** is *going-rate pricing*, in which a firm bases its price largely on competitors' prices, with less attention paid to its own costs or to demand. The firm might charge the same, more, or less than its major competitors. In oligopolistic industries that sell a commodity such as steel, paper, or fertilizer, firms normally charge the same price. The smaller firms follow the leader: They change their prices when the market leader's prices change, rather than when their own demand or costs change. Some firms may charge a bit more or less, but they hold the amount of difference constant. Thus, minor gasoline retailers usually charge a few cents less than the major oil companies, without letting the difference increase or decrease.

Going-rate pricing is quite popular. When demand elasticity is hard to measure, firms feel that the going price represents the collective wisdom of the industry concerning the price that will yield a fair return. They also feel that holding to the going price will prevent harmful price wars.

Competition-based pricing is also used when firms *bid* for jobs. Using *sealed-bid pricing,* a firm bases its price on how it thinks competitors will price rather than on its own costs or on the demand. The firm wants to win a contract, and winning the contract requires pricing less than other firms. Yet the firm cannot set its price below a certain level. It cannot price below cost without harming its position. In contrast, the higher the company sets its price above its costs, the lower its chance of getting the contract.

> **video exercise**

Apply what you learned in this section to a fictional case.

> **active concept check**

Now let's take a moment to test your knowledge of what you've just read.

> **Chapter Wrap-Up**

Now that you've reached the end of the chapter, you may wish to explore the concepts you've been reading about in greater detail, or test yourself to see how well you've comprehended the material. In the box below you'll find a number of links. Click on any one of these links to find additional chapter resources.

---

[16]See Stephen J. Hoch, Xavier Drèze, and Mary E. Purk, "EDLP, Hi-Lo, and Margin Arithmetic," *Journal of Marketing,* October 1994, pp. 16–27.

> end-of chapter resources

- **Review of Concept Connections**
- **Practice Quiz**
- **Issues for Discussion**
- **Key Terms**
- **Marketing Applications**
- **Internet Connections**
- **Company Case**

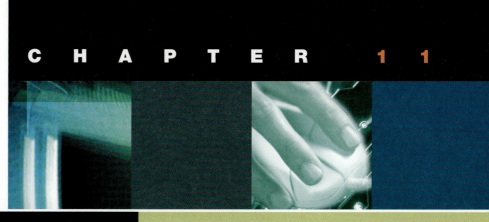

CHAPTER 11

Pricing Products: Pricing strategies

 ## What's Ahead

Procter & Gamble, the huge consumer packaged-goods producer, is part of a complex food industry distribution channel consisting of producers, wholesale food distributors, and grocery retailers. In early 1992, P&G's relations with many of its resellers took a decided turn for the worse. "We think that [P&G] will end up where most dictators end up—in trouble," fumed the chairman of Stop & Shop, a chain of 119 groceries in the Northeast. Hundreds of miles away, the assistant manager of Paulbeck's SuperValu in International Falls, Minnesota, shared these harsh feelings: "We should drop their top dogs—like half the sizes of Tide—and say 'Now see who put you on the shelf and who'll take you off of it.' "

The cause of the uproar was P&G's new everyday fair-pricing policy, tabbed "value pricing" by the company. Under this sweeping new plan, the company began phasing out most of the large promotional discounts that it had offered resellers in the past. At the same time, it lowered its everyday wholesale list prices for these products by 10 percent to 25 percent. P&G insists that price fluctuations and promotions had gotten out of hand. During the previous decade, average trade discounts had more than tripled. Some 44 percent of all marketing dollars spent by manufacturers went to trade promotions, up from 24 percent only a decade earlier.

Manufacturers had come to rely on price-oriented trade promotions to differentiate their brands and boost short-term sales. In turn, wholesalers and retail chains were conditioned to wait for manufacturers' "deals." Many per-fected "forward buying"—stocking up during manufacturers' price promotions on far more merchandise than they could sell, then reselling it to consumers at higher prices once the promotion was over. Such forward buying created costly production and distri-bution inefficiencies. P&G's factories had to gear up to meet the resulting huge demand swings. Meanwhile, supermarkets needed more buyers to find the best prices and extra warehouses to store and handle mer-chandise bought "on deal." The industry's "promotion sickness" also infected con-sumers. Wildly fluctuating retail prices eroded brand loyalty by teaching consumers to shop for what's on sale, rather than to assess the merits of each brand.

Through value pricing, P&G sought to restore the price integrity of its brands and to begin weaning the industry and consumers from discount pricing. But the strategy came into conflict with the pricing strategies of P&G's distribution channels. Discounts are the bread and butter of many retailers and wholesalers, who had used products purchased from P&G at special low prices for weekly sales to lure value-minded consumers into supermarkets or stores. In other cases, retailers and wholesalers relied on the discounts to pad their profits through forward buying. Although the average costs of products to resellers remained unchanged, resellers lost promotional dollars that they—not P&G—controlled. Thus, the new system gave P&G greater control over how its products were marketed but reduced retailer and wholesaler pricing flexi-bility.

P&G's new strategy was risky. It alienated some of the very businesses that sell its wares to the public, and it gave competitors an opportunity to take advantage of the ban on promotions by highlighting their own specials. P&G counted on its enormous market clout—retailers could ill afford, the company hoped, to eliminate heavily advertised and immensely popular brands such as Tide detergent, Crest toothpaste, Folgers coffee, Pantene shampoo, and Ivory soap. But even P&G's size and power were sorely tested. Some large chains such as A&P, Safeway, and Rite Aid drugstores began pruning out selected P&G sizes or dropping marginal brands such as Prell and Gleem. Certified Grocers, a Midwestern wholesaler, dropped about 50 of the 300 P&G varieties it stocked. Numerous other chains considered moving P&G brands from prime, eye-level space to less visible shelves, stocking more profitable private-label brands and competitors' products in P&G's place. SuperValu, the nation's largest wholesaler, which also runs retail stores, added surcharges to some P&G products and pared back orders to make up for profits it says it lost.

Despite these strong reactions, P&G stayed the course with its bold new pricing approach, and the strategy appears to be paying off. After an initial drop in sales and market shares, P&G's products in most categories are again growing steadily and producing healthier profits. The company claims that under the new pricing scheme it cut list prices an average of 6 per-cent across its product portfolio, saving consumers $6 billion. Given this success at home, P&G later introduced value pricing to its European markets. It received the same blistering response from European retailers that it had received from U.S. retailers five years earlier. For example, Germany's largest retailer, Rewe, and its major supermarket chain, Spar, immediately "delisted" several P&G brands, including Ariel, Vizir, and Lenor laundry products, Bess toilet paper, and

Tempo tissues. As happened in the United States, initial European sales and market shares dipped as angry retailers responded.

P&G's struggle to reshape the industry's distorted pricing system demonstrates the dynamic forces shaping today's pricing decisions. Ideally, P&G should set its prices at the level that will reflect and enhance the value consumers perceive in its brands. But such value is difficult to assess. Which offers more value: higher regular prices with frequent sales or lower everyday prices? What impact will each pricing strategy have on consumer perceptions of brand quality? P&G's pricing decisions would be difficult enough if the company had only to set its own prices and gauge customer reactions. However, P&G's pricing decisions affect not just its own sales and profits but those of its marketing partners as well. Thus, P&G must work with resellers to find the pricing strategy that is best for all. In the end, customers will judge whether prices accurately reflect the value they receive. Which is the best pricing strategy? Customers will vote with their food-budget dollars.[1]

> objectives

Before you begin, take a moment to familiarize yourself with the key objectives of this chapter.

> gearing up

Before we begin our exploration this chapter, take a short warm-up test to see what you know about this topic.

As the Procter & Gamble example illustrates, pricing decisions are subject to an incredibly complex array of environmental and competitive forces. A company sets not a single price, but rather a *pricing structure* that covers different items in its line. This pricing structure changes over time as products move through their life cycles. The company adjusts product prices to reflect changes in costs and demand and to account for variations in buyers and situations. As the competitive environment changes, the company considers when to initiate price changes and when to respond to them.

This chapter examines the major dynamic pricing strategies available to management. In turn, we look at *new-product pricing strategies* for products in the introductory stage of the product life cycle, *product mix pricing strategies* for related products in the product mix, *price-adjustment strategies* that account for customer differences and changing situations, and strategies for initiating and responding to *price changes*.[2]

[1]Portions adapted from Valerie Reitman, "Retail Resistance: Eliminated Discounts on P&G Goods Annoy Many Who Sell Them," *Wall Street Journal,* August 11, 1992, pp. A1, A3. Also see Zachary Schiller, "Not Everyone Loves a Supermarket Special," *Business Week,* February 17, 1992, pp. 64–68; Karen Benezra, "Beyond Value," *Brandweek,* October 7, 1996, pp. 14–16; Dagmar Mussey, "Heat's on Value Pricing," *Advertising Age International,* January 1997, pp. i21–i22; and Cathy Bond, "P&G's Gamble: Price or Promotion?" *Marketing,* February 13, 1997, pp. 30–33. For additional interesting insights, see Kusum L. Aliwadi, Donald R. Lehmann, and Scott A. Neslin, "Understanding Market Response to a Long-Term Change in Marketing Mix: An Analysis of P&G's Value Pricing Strategy," working paper, Dartmouth University, August 5, 1999.

[2]For a comprehensive discussion of pricing strategies, see Thomas T. Nagle and Reed K. Holden, *The Strategy and Tactics of Pricing,* 2nd ed. (Upper Saddle River, NJ: Prentice Hall, 1995). Also see Joshua D. Libresco, "The Pricing Game, Have I Got a Deal for You," *Marketing News,* December 8, 1997, p. 10.

Pricing strategies usually change as the product passes through its life cycle. The introductory stage is especially challenging. Companies bringing out a new product face the challenge of setting prices for the first time. They can choose between two broad strategies: *market-skimming pricing* and *market-penetration pricing.*

MARKET-SKIMMING PRICING

Many companies that invent new products initially set high prices to "skim" revenues layer by layer from the market. Intel is a prime user of this strategy, called **market-skimming pricing.** One analyst describes Intel's pricing strategy this way: "The chip giant introduces a new, higher-margin microprocessor every 12 months and sends older models down the food chain to feed demand at lower price points."[3] When Intel first introduces a new computer chip, it charges as much as $1,000 for each chip, a price that makes it *just* worthwhile for some segments of the market to adopt computers containing the chip. The new chips power top-of-the-line PCs and servers purchased by customers who just can't wait. As initial sales slow down, and as competitors threaten to introduce similar chips, Intel lowers the price to draw in the next price-sensitive layer of customers. Prices eventually bottom out at less than $200 per chip, making the chip a hot mass-market processor. In this way, Intel skims a maximum amount of revenue from the various segments of the market.[4]

Market skimming makes sense only under certain conditions. First, the product's quality and image must support its higher price, and enough buyers must want the product at that price. Second, the costs of producing a smaller volume cannot be so high that they cancel the advantage of charging more. Finally, competitors should not be able to enter the market easily and undercut the high price.

active exercise <

Consider the importance of market-skimming pricing for companies engaged in significant R&D.

MARKET-PENETRATION PRICING

Rather than setting a high initial price to *skim* off small but profitable market segments, some companies use **market-penetration pricing.** They set a low initial price in order to *penetrate* the market quickly and deeply—to attract a large number of buyers quickly and win a large market share. The high sales volume results in falling costs, allowing the company to cut its price even further. For example, Dell used penetration pricing to enter the personal computer market, selling high-quality computer products through lower-cost direct channels. Its sales soared when IBM, Compaq, Apple, and other competitors selling through retail stores could not match its prices. Wal-Mart and other discount retailers also use penetration pricing.

Several conditions must be met for this low-price strategy to work. First, the market must be highly price sensitive so that a low price produces more market growth. Second, production and distribution costs must fall as sales volume increases. Finally, the low price must help keep out the competition, and the penetration pricer must maintain its low-price position—otherwise, the price advantage may be only temporary. For example, Dell faced difficult times when IBM and Compaq established their own direct distribution channels. However, through its dedication to low production and distribution costs, Dell has retained its price advantage and established itself as the industry's fastest-growing computer maker and number two in personal computers behind Compaq.

active concept check <

Now let's take a moment to test your knowledge of what you've just read.

[3]Andy Reinhardt, "Pentium: The Next Generation," *Business Week,* May 12, 1997, pp. 42–43.

[4]See Marcia Savage, "Intel Set to Slash Pentium II Prices," *Computer Reseller News,* February 8, 1999, pp. 1, 10.

The strategy for setting a product's price often has to be changed when the product is part of a product mix. In this case, the firm looks for a set of prices that maximizes the profits on the total product mix. Pricing is difficult because the various products have related demand and costs and face different degrees of competition. We now take a closer look at the five product mix pricing situations summarized in Table 11.1.

PRODUCT LINE PRICING

Companies usually develop product lines rather than single products. For example, Snapper makes many different lawn mowers, ranging from simple walk-behind versions priced at $259.95, $299.95, and $399.95, to elaborate riding mowers priced at $1,000 or more. Each successive lawn mower in the line offers more features. Kodak offers not just one type of film, but an assortment, including regular Kodak film, higher-priced Kodak Royal Gold film for special occasions, and still higher-priced Advantix APS film for Advanced Photo System cameras. It offers each of these brands in a variety of sizes and film speeds. In **product line pricing,** management must decide on the price steps to set between the various products in a line.

The price steps should take into account cost differences between the products in the line, customer evaluations of their different features, and competitors' prices. In many industries, sellers use well-established *price points* for the products in their line. Thus, men's clothing stores might carry men's suits at three price levels: $185, $325, and $495. The customer will probably associate low-, average-, and high-quality suits with the three price points. Even if the three prices are raised a little, men normally will buy suits at their own preferred price points. The seller's task is to establish perceived quality differences that support the price differences.

OPTIONAL-PRODUCT PRICING

Many companies use **optional-product pricing**—offering to sell optional or accessory products along with their main product. For example, a car buyer may choose to order power windows, cruise control, and a CD changer. Pricing these options is a sticky problem. Automobile companies have to decide which items to include in the base price and which to offer as options. Until recent years, General Motors' normal pricing strategy was to advertise a stripped-down model at a base price to pull people into showrooms and then devote most of the showroom space to showing option-loaded cars at higher prices. The economy model was stripped of so many comforts and conveniences that most buyers rejected it. More recently, however, GM and other U.S. carmakers have followed the example of the Japanese and German automakers and included in the sticker price many useful items previously sold only as options. The advertised price now often represents a well-equipped car.

CAPTIVE-PRODUCT PRICING

Companies that make products that must be used along with a main product are using **captive-product pricing.** Examples of captive products are razor blades, camera film, video games, and computer software. Producers of the main products (razors, cameras, video game consoles, and computers) often price them low and set high markups on the supplies. Thus, Polaroid prices its cameras low because it makes its money on the film it sells. Gillette sells low-priced razors but makes money on

TABLE 11.1	Product Mix Pricing Strategies
Strategy	**Description**
Product line pricing	Setting price steps between product line items
Optional-product pricing	Pricing optional or accessory products sold with the main product
Captive-product pricing	Pricing products that must be used with the main product
By-product pricing	Pricing low-value by-products to get rid of them
Product bundle pricing	Pricing bundles of products sold together

Product line pricing: Kodak makes many different types of film priced at different levels.

the replacement cartridges. U-Haul rents out trucks at low rates but commands high margins on accessories such as boxes, pads, insurance, and storage space rental. Nintendo sells its game consoles at low prices and makes money on video game titles. In fact, whereas Nintendo's margins on its consoles run a mere 1 percent to 5 percent, margins on its game cartridges run close to 45 percent. Video game sales contribute more than half the company's profits.[5]

In the case of services, this strategy is called *two-part pricing.* The price of the service is broken into a *fixed fee* plus a *variable usage rate.* Thus, a telephone company charges a monthly rate—the fixed fee—plus charges for calls beyond some minimum number—the variable usage rate. Amusement parks charge admission plus fees for food, midway attractions, and rides over a minimum. Theaters charge admission, then generate additional revenues from concessions. The service firm must decide how much to charge for the basic service and how much for the variable usage. The fixed amount should be low enough to induce usage of the service; profit can be made on the variable fees.

BY-PRODUCT PRICING

In producing processed meats, petroleum products, chemicals, and other products, there are often by-products. If the by-products have no value and if getting rid of them is costly, this will affect the pricing of the main product. Using **by-product pricing,** the manufacturer will seek a market for these by-products and should accept any price that covers more than the cost of storing and delivering them. This practice allows the seller to reduce the main product's price to make it more competitive. By-products can even turn out to be profitable. For example, many lumber mills have begun to sell bark chips and sawdust profitably as decorative mulch for home and commercial landscaping.

Sometimes, companies don't realize how valuable their by-products are. For example, most zoos don't realize that one of their by-products—their occupants' manure—can be an excellent source of additional revenue. But the Zoo-Doo Compost Company has helped many zoos understand the costs and opportunities involved with these by-products. Zoo-Doo licenses its name to zoos and receives royalties on manure sales. "Many zoos don't even know how much manure they are producing or the cost of disposing of it," explains president and founder Pierce Ledbetter. Zoos are often so pleased with any savings they can find on disposal that they don't think to move into active by-product sales. However, sales of the fragrant by-product can be substantial. So far, novelty sales have been the largest, with tiny containers of Zoo Doo (and even "Love, Love Me Doo" valentines) available in 160 zoo stores and 700 additional retail outlets. You can also buy Zoo Doo products online ("the easiest way to buy our crap," says Zoo Doo). For the long-term market, Zoo-Doo looks to organic gardeners who buy 15 to 70 pounds of manure at a time. Zoo-Doo is already planning a "Dung of the Month" club to reach this lucrative by-products market.[6]

[5]Seanna Browder, "Nintendo: At the Top of Its Game," *Business Week,* June 9, 1997, pp. 72–73; and Orit Gadiesh and James L. Gilbert, "Profit Pools: A Fresh Look at Strategy," *Harvard Business Review,* May–June 1999, p. 140.

[6]Susan Krafft, "Love, Love Me Doo," *American Demographics,* June 1994, pp. 15–16; Damon Darlin, "Zoo Doo," *Forbes,* May 22, 1995, p. 92; and the Zoo Doo Web site (www.zoodoo.com), March 2000.

By-product pricing: Zoo Doo sells tiny containers of zoo "by-products"—even "Love Me Doo" valentines—through 160 zoo stores and 700 additional retail outlets.

> active example

Consider an example of by-product pricing.

PRODUCT BUNDLE PRICING

Using **product bundle pricing,** sellers often combine several of their products and offer the bundle at a reduced price. Thus, theaters and sports teams sell season tickets at less than the cost of single tickets; hotels sell specially priced packages that include room, meals, and entertainment; computer makers include attractive software packages with their personal computers. Price bundling can promote the sales of products consumers might not otherwise buy, but the combined price must be low enough to get them to buy the bundle.[7]

> active concept check

Now let's take a moment to test your knowledge of what you've just read.

> Price-Adjustment Strategies

Companies usually adjust their basic prices to account for various customer differences and changing situations. Table 11.2 summarizes six price-adjustment strategies: *discount and allowance pricing, segmented pricing, psychological pricing, promotional pricing, geographical pricing,* and *international pricing.*

---

[7]See Nagle and Holden, *The Strategy and Tactics of Pricing,* pp. 225–28; and Manjit S. Yadav and Kent B. Monroe, "How Buyers Perceive Savings in a Bundle Price: An Examination of a Bundle's Transaction Value," *Journal of Marketing Research,* August 1993, pp. 350–58.

TABLE 11.2	Price-Adjustment Strategies
Strategy	**Description**
Discount and allowance pricing	Reducing prices to reward customer responses such as paying early or promoting the product
Segmented pricing	Adjusting prices to allow for differences in customers, products, or locations
Psychological pricing	Adjusting prices for psychological effect
Promotional pricing	Temporarily reducing prices to increase short-run sales
Geographical pricing	Adjusting prices to account for the geographic location of customers
International pricing	Adjusting prices for international markets

DISCOUNT AND ALLOWANCE PRICING

Most companies adjust their basic price to reward customers for certain responses, such as early payment of bills, volume purchases, and off-season buying. These price adjustments—called *discounts* and *allowances*—can take many forms.

A **cash discount** is a price reduction to buyers who pay their bills promptly. A typical example is "2/10, net 30," which means that although payment is due within 30 days, the buyer can deduct 2 percent if the bill is paid within 10 days. The discount must be granted to all buyers meeting these terms. Such discounts are customary in many industries and help to improve the sellers' cash situation and reduce bad debts and credit-collection costs.

A **quantity discount** is a price reduction to buyers who buy large volumes. A typical example might be "$10 per unit for less than 100 units, $9 per unit for 100 or more units." By law, quantity discounts must be offered equally to all customers and must not exceed the seller's cost savings associated with selling large quantities. These savings include lower selling, inventory, and transportation expenses. Discounts provide an incentive to the customer to buy more from one given seller, rather than from many different sources.

A **functional discount** (also called a *trade discount*) is offered by the seller to trade channel members who perform certain functions, such as selling, storing, and record keeping. Manufacturers may offer different functional discounts to different trade channels because of the varying services they perform, but manufacturers must offer the same functional discounts within each trade channel.

A **seasonal discount** is a price reduction to buyers who buy merchandise or services out of season. For example, lawn and garden equipment manufacturers offer seasonal discounts to retailers during the fall and winter months to encourage early ordering in anticipation of the heavy spring and summer selling seasons. Hotels, motels, and airlines will offer seasonal discounts in their slower selling periods. Seasonal discounts allow the seller to keep production steady during an entire year.

Allowances are another type of reduction from the list price. For example, *trade-in allowances* are price reductions given for turning in an old item when buying a new one. Trade-in allowances are most common in the automobile industry but are also given for other durable goods. *Promotional allowances* are payments or price reductions to reward dealers for participating in advertising and sales support programs.

active example <

Consider an example of discount and allowance pricing.

SEGMENTED PRICING

Companies will often adjust their basic prices to allow for differences in customers, products, and locations. In **segmented pricing,** the company sells a product or service at two or more prices, even though the difference in prices is not based on differences in costs.

Segmented pricing takes several forms. Under *customer-segment* pricing, different customers pay different prices for the same product or service. Museums, for example, will charge a lower admission for students and senior citizens. Under *product-form pricing,* different versions of the product are priced differently but not according to differences in their costs. For instance, Black & Decker prices its most expensive iron at $54.98, which is $12 more than the price of its next most expensive iron. The top model has a self-cleaning feature, yet this extra feature costs only a few more dollars to make. Using *location pricing,* a company charges different prices for different locations, even though the cost of offering at each location is the same. For instance, theaters vary their seat prices because of audience preferences for certain locations, and state universities charge higher tuition for out-of-state students. Finally, using *time pricing,* a firm varies its price by the season, the month, the day, and even the hour. Public utilities vary their prices to commercial users by time of day and weekend versus weekday. The telephone company offers lower off-peak charges, and resorts give seasonal discounts.

For segmented pricing to be an effective strategy, certain conditions must exist. The market must be segmentable, and the segments must show different degrees of demand. Members of the segment paying the lower price should not be able to turn around and resell the product to the segment paying the higher price. Competitors should not be able to undersell the firm in the segment being charged the higher price. Nor should the costs of segmenting and watching the market exceed the extra revenue obtained from the price difference. Of course, the segmented pricing must also be legal. Most importantly, segmented prices should reflect real differences in customers' perceived value. Otherwise, in the long run, the practice will lead to customer resentment and ill will.

PSYCHOLOGICAL PRICING

Price says something about the product. For example, many consumers use price to judge quality. A $100 bottle of perfume may contain only $3 worth of scent, but some people are willing to pay the $100 because this price indicates something special.

In using **psychological pricing,** sellers consider the psychology of prices and not simply the economics. For example, one study of the relationship between price and quality perceptions of cars found that consumers perceive higher-priced cars as having higher quality.[8] By the same token, higher-quality cars are perceived to be even higher priced than they actually are. When consumers can judge the quality of a product by examining it or by calling on past experience with it, they use price less to judge quality. When consumers cannot judge quality because they lack the information or skill, price becomes an important quality signal:

Psychological pricing: What do the prices marked on this tag suggest about the product and buying situation?

[8]See Gary M. Erickson and Johnny K. Johansson, "The Role of Price in Multi-Attribute Product Evaluations," *Journal of Consumer Research,* September 1985, pp. 195–99.

Heublein produces Smirnoff, America's leading vodka brand. Some years ago, Smirnoff was attacked by another brand. Wolfschmidt, priced at one dollar less per bottle, claimed to have the same quality as Smirnoff. To hold on to market share, Heublein considered either lowering Smirnoff's price by one dollar or holding Smirnoff's price but increasing advertising and promotion expenditures. Either strategy would lead to lower profits and it seemed that Heublein faced a no-win situation. At this point, however, Heublein's marketers thought of a third strategy. They *raised* the price of Smirnoff by one dollar! Heublein then introduced a new brand, Relska, to compete with Wolfschmidt. Moreover, it introduced yet another brand, Popov, priced even *lower* than Wolfschmidt. This clever strategy positioned Smirnoff as the elite brand and Wolfschmidt as an ordinary brand, producing a large increase in Heublein's overall profits. The irony is that Heublein's three brands are pretty much the same in taste and manufacturing costs. Heublein knew that a product's price signals its quality. Using price as a signal, Heublein sells roughly the same product at three different quality positions.

Another aspect of psychological pricing is **reference prices**—prices that buyers carry in their minds and refer to when looking at a given product. The reference price might be formed by noting current prices, remembering past prices, or assessing the buying situation. Sellers can influence or use these consumers' reference prices when setting price. For example, a company could display its product next to more expensive ones in order to imply that it belongs in the same class. Department stores often sell women's clothing in separate departments differentiated by price: Clothing found in the more expensive department is assumed to be of better quality. Companies can also influence consumers' reference prices by stating high manufacturer's suggested prices, by indicating that the product was originally priced much higher, or by pointing to a competitor's higher price.

Even small differences in price can suggest product differences. Consider a stereo priced at $300 compared to one priced at $299.95. The actual price difference is only 5 cents, but the psychological difference can be much greater. For example, some consumers will see the $299.95 as a price in the $200 range rather than the $300 range. The $299.95 will more likely be seen as a bargain price, whereas the $300 price suggests more quality. Some psychologists argue that each digit has symbolic and visual qualities that should be considered in pricing. Thus, 8 is round and even and creates a soothing effect, whereas 7 is angular and creates a jarring effect.[9]

active exercise

Consider the role psychology plays in an interesting case of pricing.

PROMOTIONAL PRICING

With **promotional pricing,** companies will temporarily price their products below list price and sometimes even below cost. Promotional pricing takes several forms. Supermarkets and department stores will price a few products as *loss leaders* to attract customers to the store in the hope that they will buy other items at normal markups. Sellers will also use *special-event pricing* in certain seasons to draw more customers. Thus, linens are promotionally priced every January to attract weary Christmas shoppers back into stores.

Manufacturers will sometimes offer *cash rebates* to consumers who buy the product from dealers within a specified time; the manufacturer sends the rebate directly to the customer. Rebates have been popular with automakers and producers of durable goods and small appliances, but they are also used

[9]For more reading on reference prices and psychological pricing, see K. N. Rajendran and Gerard J. Tellis, "Contextual and Temporal Components of Reference Price," *Journal of Marketing,* January 1994, pp. 22–34; Richard A. Briesch, Lakshman Krishnamurthi, Tridib Mazumdar, and S. P. Raj, "A Comparative Analysis of Reference Price Models," *Journal of Consumer Research,* September 1997, pp. 202–14; John Huston and Nipoli Kamdar, "$9.99: Can 'Just-Below' Pricing Be Reconciled with Rationality?" *Eastern Economic Journal,* Spring 1996, pp. 137–45; Robert M. Schindler and Patrick N. Kirby, "Patterns of Right-Most Digits Used in Advertised Prices: Implications for Nine-Ending Effects," *Journal of Consumer Research,* September 1997, pp. 192–201; Michel Wedel and Peter S. H. Leeflang, "A Model for the Effects of Psychological Pricing in Gabor-Granger Price Studies," *Journal of Economic Psychology,* April 1998, pp. 237–60; and Dhruv Grewal, Kent B. Monroe, Chris Janiszewski, and Donald R. Lichtenstein, "A Range Theory of Price Perception," *Journal of Consumer Research,* March 1999, pp. 353–68.

with consumer packaged goods. Some manufacturers offer *low-interest financing, longer warranties,* or *free maintenance* to reduce the consumer's "price." This practice has recently become a favorite of the auto industry. Or, the seller may simply offer *discounts* from normal prices to increase sales and reduce inventories.

Promotional pricing, however, can have adverse effects. Used too frequently and copied by competitors, price promotions can create "deal-prone" customers who wait until brands go on sale before buying them. Or, constantly reduced prices can erode a brand's value in the eyes of customers. Marketers sometimes use price promotions as a quick fix instead of sweating through the difficult process of developing effective longer-term strategies for building their brands. In fact, one observer notes that price promotions can be downright addicting to both the company and the customer: "Price promotions are the brand equivalent of heroin: easy to get into but hard to get out of. Once the brand and its customers are addicted to the short-term high of a price cut it is hard to wean them away to real brand building. . . . But continue and the brand dies by 1,000 cuts."[10]

Jack Trout, a well-known marketing author and consultant, cautions that some categories tend to self-destruct by always being on sale. Discount pricing has become routine for a surprising number of companies. Furniture, automobile tires, and many other categories of goods are rarely sold at anything near list price, and when automakers get rebate happy, the market just sits back and waits for a deal. Even Coca-Cola and Pepsi, two of the world's most popular brands, engage in regular price wars that ultimately tarnish their brand equity. Trout offers several "Commandments of Discounting," such as "Thou shalt not offer discounts because everyone else does," "Thou shalt be creative with your discounting," "Thou shalt put time limits on the deal," and "Thou shalt stop discounting as soon as you can."[11] The point is that promotional pricing can be an effective means of generating sales in certain circumstances but can be damaging if taken as a steady diet.

GEOGRAPHICAL PRICING

A company also must decide how to price its products for customers located in different parts of the country or world. Should the company risk losing the business of more distant customers by charging them higher prices to cover the higher shipping costs? Or should the company charge all customers the same prices regardless of location? We will look at five geographical pricing strategies for the following hypothetical situation:

> The Peerless Paper Company is located in Atlanta, Georgia, and sells paper products to customers all over the United States. The cost of freight is high and affects the companies from whom customers buy their paper. Peerless wants to establish a geographical pricing policy. It is trying to determine how to price a $100 order to three specific customers: Customer A (Atlanta); Customer B (Bloomington, Indiana), and Customer C (Compton, California).

One option is for Peerless to ask each customer to pay the shipping cost from the Atlanta factory to the customer's location. All three customers would pay the same factory price of $100, with Customer A paying, say, $10 for shipping; Customer B, $15; and Customer C, $25. Called **FOB-origin pricing,** this practice means that the goods are placed *free on board* (hence, *FOB*) a carrier. At that point the title and responsibility pass to the customer, who pays the freight from the factory to the destination. Because each customer picks up its own cost, supporters of FOB pricing feel that this is the fairest way to assess freight charges. The disadvantage, however, is that Peerless will be a high-cost firm to distant customers.

Uniform-delivered pricing is the opposite of FOB pricing. Here, the company charges the same price plus freight to all customers, regardless of their location. The freight charge is set at the average freight cost. Suppose this is $15. Uniform-delivered pricing therefore results in a higher charge to the Atlanta customer (who pays $15 freight instead of $10) and a lower charge to the Compton customer (who pays $15 instead of $25). Although the Atlanta customer would prefer to buy paper from another local paper company that uses FOB-origin pricing, Peerless has a better chance of winning over the California customer. Other advantages of uniform-delivered pricing are that it is fairly easy to administer and it lets the firm advertise its price nationally.

Zone pricing falls between FOB-origin pricing and uniform-delivered pricing. The company sets up two or more zones. All customers within a given zone pay a single total price; the more distant the

[10]Tim Ambler, "Kicking Price Promotion Habit Is Like Getting Off Heroin—Hard," *Marketing,* May 27, 1999, p. 24.

[11]Jack Trout, "Prices: Simple Guidelines to Get Them Right," *The Journal of Business Strategy,* November–December 1998, pp. 13–16.

zone, the higher the price. For example, Peerless might set up an East Zone and charge $10 freight to all customers in this zone, a Midwest Zone in which it charges $15, and a West Zone in which it charges $25. In this way, the customers within a given price zone receive no price advantage from the company. For example, customers in Atlanta and Boston pay the same total price to Peerless. The complaint, however, is that the Atlanta customer is paying part of the Boston customer's freight cost.

Using **basing-point pricing,** the seller selects a given city as a "basing point" and charges all customers the freight cost from that city to the customer location, regardless of the city from which the goods are actually shipped. For example, Peerless might set Chicago as the basing point and charge all customers $100 plus the freight from Chicago to their locations. This means that an Atlanta customer pays the freight cost from Chicago to Atlanta, even though the goods may be shipped from Atlanta. If all sellers used the same basing-point city, delivered prices would be the same for all customers and price competition would be eliminated. Industries such as sugar, cement, steel, and automobiles used basing-point pricing for years, but this method has become less popular today. Some companies set up multiple basing points to create more flexibility: They quote freight charges from the basing-point city nearest to the customer.

Finally, the seller who is anxious to do business with a certain customer or geographical area might use **freight-absorption pricing.** Using this strategy, the seller absorbs all or part of the actual freight charges in order to get the desired business. The seller might reason that if it can get more business, its average costs will fall and more than compensate for its extra freight cost. Freight-absorption pricing is used for market penetration and to hold on to increasingly competitive markets.

INTERNATIONAL PRICING

Companies that market their products internationally must decide what prices to charge in the different countries in which they operate. In some cases, a company can set a uniform worldwide price. For example, Boeing sells its jetliners at about the same price everywhere, whether in the United States, Europe, or a third-world country. However, most companies adjust their prices to reflect local market conditions and cost considerations.

The price that a company should charge in a specific country depends on many factors, including economic conditions, competitive situations, laws and regulations, and development of the wholesaling and retailing system. Consumer perceptions and preferences also may vary from country to country, calling for different prices. Or the company may have different marketing objectives in various world markets, which require changes in pricing strategy. For example, Sony might introduce a new product into mature markets in highly developed countries with the goal of quickly gaining mass-market share—this would call for a penetration-pricing strategy. In contrast, it might enter a less developed market by targeting smaller, less price-sensitive segments; in this case, market-skimming pricing makes sense.

Costs play an important role in setting international prices. Travelers abroad are often surprised to find that goods that are relatively inexpensive at home may carry outrageously higher price tags in other countries. A pair of Levi's selling for $30 in the United States goes for about $63 in Tokyo and $88 in Paris. A McDonald's Big Mac selling for a modest $2.25 here costs $5.75 in Moscow, and an Oral-B toothbrush selling for $2.49 at home costs $10.00 in China. Conversely, a Gucci handbag going for only $60 in Milan, Italy, fetches $240 in the United States. In some cases, such *price escalation* may result from differences in selling strategies or market conditions. In most instances, however, it is simply a result of the higher costs of selling in foreign markets—the additional costs of modifying the product, higher shipping and insurance costs, import tariffs and taxes, costs associated with exchange-rate fluctuations, and higher channel and physical distribution costs.

For example, Campbell found that its distribution costs in the United Kingdom were 30 percent higher than in the United States. U.S. retailers typically purchase soup in large quantities—48-can cases of a single soup by the dozens, hundreds, or carloads. In contrast, English grocers purchase soup in small quantities—typically in 24-can cases of *assorted* soups. Each case must be handpacked for shipment. To handle these small orders, Campbell had to add a costly extra wholesale level to its European channel. The smaller orders also mean that English retailers order two or three times as often as their U.S. counterparts, bumping up billing and order costs. These and other factors caused Campbell to charge much higher prices for its soups in the United Kingdom.[12]

Thus, international pricing presents some special problems and complexities. We discuss international pricing issues in more detail in chapter 19.

[12]Philip R. Cateora, *International Marketing,* 7th ed. (Homewood, IL: Richard D. Irwin, 1990), p. 540. Also see S. Tamer Cavusgil, "Pricing for Global Markets," *Columbia Journal of World Business,* Winter 1996, pp. 66–78; and Sak Onkvisit and John R. Shaw, *International Marketing: Analysis and Strategy* (Upper Saddle River, NJ: Prentice Hall, 1997), chap. 16.

Now let's take a moment to test your knowledge of what you've just read.

> Price Changes

After developing their pricing structures and strategies, companies often face situations in which they must initiate price changes or respond to price changes by competitors.

INITIATING PRICE CHANGES

In some cases, the company may find it desirable to initiate either a price cut or a price increase. In both cases, it must anticipate possible buyer and competitor reactions.

Initiating Price Cuts

Several situations may lead a firm to consider cutting its price. One such circumstance is excess capacity. In this case, the firm needs more business and cannot get it through increased sales effort, product improvement, or other measures. It may drop its "follow-the-leader pricing"—charging about the same price as its leading competitor—and aggressively cut prices to boost sales. But as the airline, construction equipment, fast-food, and other industries have learned in recent years, cutting prices in an industry loaded with excess capacity may lead to price wars as competitors try to hold on to market share.

Another situation leading to price changes is falling market share in the face of strong price competition. Several American industries—automobiles, consumer electronics, cameras, watches, and steel, for example—lost market share to Japanese competitors whose high-quality products carried lower prices than did their American counterparts. In response, American companies resorted to more aggressive pricing action. A company may also cut prices in a drive to dominate the market through lower costs. Either the company starts with lower costs than its competitors or it cuts prices in the hope of gaining market share that will further cut costs through larger volume. Bausch & Lomb used an aggressive low-cost, low-price strategy to become an early leader in the competitive soft contact lens market.

Initiating Price Increases

A successful price increase can greatly increase profits. For example, if the company's profit margin is 3 percent of sales, a 1 percent price increase will increase profits by 33 percent if sales volume is unaffected. A major factor in price increases is cost inflation. Rising costs squeeze profit margins and lead companies to pass cost increases along to customers. Another factor leading to price increases is overdemand: When a company cannot supply all its customers' needs, it can raise its prices, ration products to customers, or both.

Companies can increase their prices in a number of ways to keep up with rising costs. Prices can be raised almost invisibly by dropping discounts and adding higher-priced units to the line. Or prices can be pushed up openly. In passing price increases on to customers, the company must avoid being perceived as a price gouger. Companies also need to think of who will bear the brunt of increased prices. As the Kellogg example in the previous chapter suggests, customer memories are long, and they will eventually turn away from companies or even whole industries that they perceive as charging excessive prices.

There are some techniques for avoiding this problem. One is to maintain a sense of fairness surrounding any price increase. Price increases should be supported with a company communication program telling customers why prices are being increased and customers should be given advance notice so they can do forward buying or shop around. Making low-visibility price moves first is also a good technique: Eliminating discounts, increasing minimum order sizes, curtailing production of low-margin products are some examples. Contracts or bids for long-term projects should contain escalator clauses based on such factors as increases in recognized national price indexes. The company sales force should help business customers find ways to economize.[13]

---

[13]Eric Mitchell, "How Not to Raise Prices," *Small Business Reports,* November 1990, pp. 64–67.

Wherever possible, the company should consider ways to meet higher costs or demand without raising prices. For example, it can consider more cost-effective ways to produce or distribute its products. It can shrink the product instead of raising the price, as candy bar manufacturers often do. It can substitute less expensive ingredients or remove certain product features, packaging, or services. Or it can "unbundle" its products and services, removing and separately pricing elements that were formerly part of the offer. IBM, for example, now offers training and consulting as separately priced services.

Buyer Reactions to Price Changes

Whether the price is raised or lowered, the action will affect buyers, competitors, distributors, and suppliers and may interest government as well. Customers do not always interpret prices in a straightforward way. They may view a price *cut* in several ways. For example, what would you think if Sony were suddenly to cut its VCR prices in half? You might think that these VCRs are about to be replaced by newer models or that they have some fault and are not selling well. You might think that Sony is abandoning the VCR business and may not stay in this business long enough to supply future parts. You might believe that quality has been reduced. Or you might think that the price will come down even further and that it will pay to wait and see.

Similarly, a price *increase,* which would normally lower sales, may have some positive meanings for buyers. What would you think if Sony *raised* the price of its latest VCR model? On the one hand, you might think that the item is very "hot" and may be unobtainable unless you buy it soon. Or you might think that the VCR is an unusually good value. On the other hand, you might think that Sony is greedy and charging what the traffic will bear.[14]

Competitor Reactions to Price Changes

A firm considering a price change has to worry about the reactions of its competitors as well as its customers. Competitors are most likely to react when the number of firms involved is small, when the product is uniform, and when the buyers are well informed.

How can the firm anticipate the likely reactions of its competitors? If the firm faces one large competitor, and if the competitor tends to react in a set way to price changes, that reaction can be easily anticipated. But if the competitor treats each price change as a fresh challenge and reacts according to its self-interest, the company will have to figure out just what makes up the competitor's self-interest at the time.

The problem is complex because, like the customer, the competitor can interpret a company price cut in many ways. It might think the company is trying to grab a larger market share, that the company is doing poorly and trying to boost its sales, or that the company wants the whole industry to cut prices to increase total demand.

Buyer reactions to price changes: What would you think if the price of Joy was suddenly cut in half?

[14]For an interesting discussion of buyer perceptions of price increases, see Margaret C. Campbell, "Perceptions of Price Unfairness: Antecedents and Consequences," *Journal of Marketing Research,* May 1999, pp. 187–99.

When there are several competitors, the company must guess each competitor's likely reaction. If all competitors behave alike, this amounts to analyzing only a typical competitor. In contrast, if the competitors do not behave alike—perhaps because of differences in size, market shares, or policies— then separate analyses are necessary. However, if some competitors will match the price change, there is good reason to expect that the rest will also match it.

> video example

Before you explore this topic in depth, observe how one prominent company deals with the challenge of responding to competitors' lower prices.

RESPONDING TO PRICE CHANGES

Here we reverse the question and ask how a firm should respond to a price change by a competitor. The firm needs to consider several issues: Why did the competitor change the price? Was it to take more market share, to use excess capacity, to meet changing cost conditions, or to lead an industry-wide price change? Is the price change temporary or permanent? What will happen to the company's market share and profits if it does not respond? Are other companies going to respond? What are the competitor's and other firms' responses to each possible reaction likely to be?

Besides these issues, the company must make a broader analysis. It has to consider its own product's stage in the life cycle, the product's importance in the company's product mix, the intentions and resources of the competitor, and the possible consumer reactions to price changes. The company cannot always make an extended analysis of its alternatives at the time of a price change, however. The competitor may have spent much time preparing this decision, but the company may have to react within hours or days. About the only way to cut down reaction time is to plan ahead for both possible competitor's price changes and possible responses.

Figure 11.1 shows the ways a company might assess and respond to a competitor's price cut. Once the company has determined that the competitor has cut its price and that this price reduction is likely to harm company sales and profits, it might simply decide to hold its current price and profit margin. The company might believe that it will not lose too much market share, or that it would lose too much profit if it reduced its own price. It might decide that it should wait and respond when it has more information on the effects of the competitor's price change. For now, it might be willing to hold on to good customers, while giving up the poorer ones to the competitor. The argument against this holding strategy, however, is that the competitor may get stronger and more confident as its sales increase and that the company might wait too long to act.

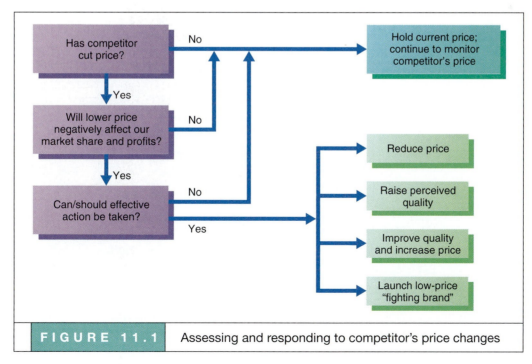

| FIGURE 11.1 | Assessing and responding to competitor's price changes |

If the company decides that effective action can and should be taken, it might make any of four responses. First, it could *reduce its price* to match the competitor's price. It may decide that the market is price sensitive and that it would lose too much market share to the lower-priced competitor. Or it might worry that recapturing lost market share later would be too hard. Cutting the price will reduce the company's profits in the short run. Some companies might also reduce their product quality, services, and marketing communications to retain profit margins, but this will ultimately hurt long-run market share. The company should try to maintain its quality as it cuts prices.

Alternatively, the company might maintain its price but *raise the perceived quality* of its offer. It could improve its communications, stressing the relative quality of its product over that of the lower-price competitor. The firm may find it cheaper to maintain price and spend money to improve its perceived value than to cut price and operate at a lower margin.

Or, the company might *improve quality and increase price,* moving its brand into a higher-price position. The higher quality justifies the higher price, which in turn preserves the company's higher margins. Or the company can hold price on the current product and introduce a new brand at a higher-price position.

Finally, the company might launch a low-price "fighter brand." Often, one of the best responses is to add lower-price items to the line or to create a separate lower-price brand. This is necessary if the particular market segment being lost is price sensitive and will not respond to arguments of higher quality. Thus, when challenged on price by store brands and other low-price entrants, Procter & Gamble turned a number of its brands into fighter brands, including Luvs disposable diapers, Joy dishwashing detergent, and Camay beauty soap. In response to price pressures, Miller cut the price of its High Life brand by 20 percent in most markets, and sales jumped 9 percent in less than a year.[15]

Fighter brands: When challenged on price by store brands and other low-priced entrants, Procter & Gamble turned a number of its brands into fighting brands, including Luvs disposable diapers.

Luvs just loves to save you money.

Put your baby in Luvs and save a small bundle. You may not have noticed, but we've reduced our price! Luvs Ultra Leakguards are the lowest priced national brand.

And Luvs doesn't just save you money, we also help save you from embarrassing messy leaks thanks to our special Leakguard System. Now Luvs gets to the bottom of leaks... without getting to the bottom of your pocketbook.

Prices may vary. Based on a survey of national retail prices past three months ending 4/3/94.

Luvs gets to the bottom of Leaks.

LOW PRICE
Luvs
Ultra Leakguards

[15]Jonathon Berry and Zachary Schiller, "Attack of the Fighting Brands," *Business Week,* May 2, 1994, p. 125; and Jeff Ansell, "Luvs," *Advertising Age,* June 30, 1997, p. S16.

> **video exercise**

Consider the challenge of responding to price changes through a fictional case.

> **active concept check**

Now let's take a moment to test your knowledge of what you've just read.

> Public Policy and Pricing

Price competition is a core element of our free-market economy. In setting prices, companies are not usually free to charge whatever prices they wish. Many federal, state, and even local laws govern the rules of fair play in pricing. In addition, companies must consider broader societal pricing concerns. The most important pieces of legislation affecting pricing are the Sherman, Clayton, and Robinson-Patman acts, initially adopted to curb the formation of monopolies and to regulate business practices that might unfairly restrain trade. Because these federal statutes can be applied only to interstate commerce, some states have adopted similar provisions for companies that operate locally.

> **active example**

Consider an example of how government regulation can affect pricing.

Figure 11.2 shows the major public policy issues in pricing. These include potentially damaging pricing practices within a given level of the channel (price-fixing and predatory pricing) and across levels of the channel (retail price maintenance, discriminatory pricing, and deceptive pricing).[16]

PRICING WITHIN CHANNEL LEVELS

Federal legislation on *price-fixing* states that sellers must set prices without talking to competitors. Otherwise, price collusion is suspected. Price-fixing is illegal per se—that is, the government does not accept any excuses for price-fixing. Companies found guilty of such practices can receive heavy fines. For example, when the U.S. Justice Department recently found that Archer Daniels Midland Company and three of its competitors had met regularly in the early 1990s to illegally fix prices, the four companies paid more than $100 million to settle the charges.[17]

Even a simple conversation between competitors can have serious consequences. For example, during the early 1980s, American Airlines and Braniff were immersed in a price war in the Texas market. In the heat of the battle, American's CEO, Robert Crandall, called the president of Braniff and said, "Raise your . . . fares 20 percent. I'll raise mine the next morning. You'll make more money and I will, too." Fortunately for Crandall, the Braniff president warned him off, saying, "We can't talk about pricing!" As it turns out, the phone conversation had been recorded, and the U.S. Justice Department began action against Crandall and American for price-fixing. The charges were eventu-

---

[16]For an excellent discussion of these issues, see Dhruv Grewel and Larry D. Compeau, "Pricing and Public Policy: A Research Agenda and Overview of Special Issue," *Journal of Marketing and Public Policy,* Spring 1999, pp. 3–10.

[17]David Barboza, "Archer Daniels Executive Said to Tell of Price-Fixing Talks with Cargill Counterpart," *New York Times,* June 17, 1999, p. 6.

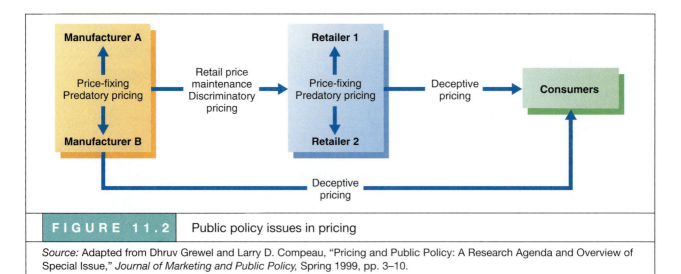

FIGURE 11.2 Public policy issues in pricing

Source: Adapted from Dhruv Grewel and Larry D. Compeau, "Pricing and Public Policy: A Research Agenda and Overview of Special Issue," *Journal of Marketing and Public Policy,* Spring 1999, pp. 3–10.

ally dropped—the courts ruled that because Braniff had rejected Crandall's proposal, no actual collusion had occurred and that a proposal to fix prices was not an actual violation of the law. Still, as part of the settlement, for two years Crandall was required to keep a detailed log of his conversations with fellow airline chiefs.[18] Such cases have made most executives very reluctant to discuss prices in any way with competitors.

Sellers are also prohibited from using *predatory pricing*—selling below cost with the intention of punishing a competitor or gaining higher long-run profits by putting competitors out of business. This protects small sellers from larger ones who might sell items below cost temporarily or in a specific locale to drive them out of business. The biggest problem is determining just what constitutes predatory pricing behavior. Selling below cost to sell off excess inventory is not considered predatory; selling below cost to drive out competitors is. Thus, the same action may or may not be predatory depending on intent, and intent can be very difficult to determine or prove.

In recent years, several large and powerful companies have been accused of this practice. For example, Wal-Mart has been sued by dozens of small competitors charging that it lowered prices in their specific areas to drive them out of business. In another case, the Justice Department sued American Airlines in 1999 for allegedly using predatory pricing to muscle three small competitors—Vanguard Airlines, Sun Jet, and Western Pacific—out of its huge Dallas–Fort Worth hub. American contended that it was just being a tough competitor.[19] Giant Microsoft has also been a Justice Department target:

> When Microsoft targets a market for domination, it frequently wins over customers with an irresistible offer: free products. In 1996, Microsoft started giving away Internet Explorer, its Web browser—and in some cases arguably even "paid" people to use it by offering free software and marketing assistance. The strategy was crucial in wresting market dominance from Netscape Communications Corporation. Netscape constantly revised its pricing structure but "better than free" is not the most appealing sales pitch. Most of Microsoft's giveaways were offered as part of its effort to gain share in the interactive corporate computing market. For instance, the company offered free Web server software to customers who purchase the Windows NT network operating system. Netscape was selling a higher-powered version of the same software for $4,100. Although such pricing and promotion strategies might be viewed as shrewd marketing by some, competitors saw them as purely predatory. They noted that in the past, once Microsoft had use these tactics to gain a lion's share of the market, it had tended to raise prices *above* market levels. For example, the wholesale price it charged PC makers for its Windows operating system (in which is bundled the Internet Explorer) has doubled during the past seven years.[20]

[18]Holman W. Jenkins Jr., "Business World: Flying the 'Angry' Skies," *Wall Street Journal,* April 29, 1998, p. A23.

[19]John Greenwald, "Bird of Prey," *Time,* May 24, 1999, p. 66.

[20]Mike France, "Does Predatory Pricing Make Microsoft a Predator?" *Business Week,* November 23, 1998, pp. 130–32.

PRICING ACROSS CHANNEL LEVELS

The Robinson-Patman Act seeks to prevent unfair *price discrimination* by ensuring that sellers offer the same price terms to customers at a given level of trade. For example, every retailer is entitled to the same price terms from a given manufacturer, whether the retailer is Sears or the local bicycle shop. However, price discrimination is allowed if the seller can prove that its costs are different when selling to different retailers—for example, that it costs less per unit to sell a large volume of bicycles to Sears than to sell a few bicycles to a local dealer. Or the seller can discriminate in its pricing if the seller manufactures different qualities of the same product for different retailers. The seller has to prove that these differences are proportional. Price differentials may also be used to "match competition" in "good faith," provided the price discrimination is temporary, localized, and defensive rather than offensive.

Resale price maintenance is also prohibited—a manufacturer cannot require dealers to charge a specified retail price for its product. Although the seller can propose a manufacturer's *suggested* retail price to dealers, it cannot refuse to sell to a dealer who takes independent pricing action, nor can it punish the dealer by shipping late or denying advertising allowances. For example, in 1996 the Federal Trade Commission (FTC) charged that New Balance had engaged in fixing resale prices for its athletic shoes. Its agreements with retailers required that the retailers raise the price of New Balance products, maintain prices at levels set by New Balance, and not discount the products.

Deceptive pricing occurs when a seller states prices or price savings that mislead consumers or are not actually available to consumers. This might involve bogus reference or comparison prices, as when a retailer sets artificially high "regular" prices then announces "sale" prices close to its previous everyday prices. Such comparison pricing is widespread:

> Open any Sunday newspaper and find hundreds of such promotions being offered by a variety of retailers, such as supermarkets, office supply stores, furniture stores, computer stores, appliance stores, pharmacies and drug stores, car dealers, department stores, and others. Surf the Internet and see similar price promotions. Watch the shopping channels on television and find more of the same. It seems that, today, selling prices rarely stand alone. Instead retailers are using an advertised reference price (e.g., regular price, original price, manufacturer's suggested price) to suggest that buyers will save money if they take advantage of the "deal" being offered.[21]

Such claims are legal if they are truthful. However, the FTC's *Guides Against Deceptive Pricing* warns sellers not to advertise a price reduction unless it is a saving from the usual retail price, not to advertise "factory" or "wholesale" prices unless such prices are what they are claimed to be, and not to advertise comparable value prices on imperfect goods.

Other deceptive pricing issues include *scanner fraud* and price confusion. The widespread use of scanner-based computer checkouts has lead to increasing complaints of retailers overcharging their customers. Most of these overcharges result from poor management—from a failure to enter current or sale prices into the system. Other cases, however, involve intentional overcharges. *Price confusion* results when firms employ pricing methods that make it difficult for consumers to understand just what price they are really paying. For example, consumers are sometimes mislead regarding the real price of a home mortgage or car leasing agreement. In other cases, important pricing details may be buried in the "fine print."

Many federal and state statutes regulate against deceptive pricing practices. For example, the Automobile Information Disclosure Act requires automakers to attach a statement to new car windows stating the manufacturer's suggested retail price, the prices of optional equipment, and the dealer's transportation charges. However, reputable sellers go beyond what is required by law. Treating customers fairly and making certain that they fully understand prices and pricing terms is an important part of building strong and lasting customer relationships.[22]

[21]Grewel and Compeau, "Pricing and Public Policy: A Research Agenda and Overview of Special Issue," p. 8.

[22]For more on public policy and pricing, see Louis W. Stern and Thomas L. Eovaldi, *Legal Aspects of Marketing Strategy* (Upper Saddle River, NJ: Prentice Hall, 1984), chap. 5; Robert J. Posch, *The Complete Guide to Marketing and the Law* (Upper Saddle River, NJ: Prentice Hall, 1988), chap. 28; Nagle and Holden, *The Strategy and Tactics of Pricing*, chap. 14; Joseph P. Guiltinan and Gregory Gunlach, "Aggressive and Predatory Pricing: A Framework for Analysis," *Journal of Marketing*, July 1996, pp. 87–102; Bruce Upbin, "Vindication," *Forbes*, November 17, 1997, pp. 52–56; and Grewel and Compeau, "Pricing and Public Policy: A Research Agenda and Overview of Special Issue," pp. 3–10

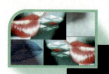

active poll   <

Give your opinion on a question concerning a common pricing practice.

active concept check   <

Now let's take a moment to test your knowledge of what you've just read.

> **Chapter Wrap-Up**

Now that you've reached the end of the chapter, you may wish to explore the concepts you've been reading about in greater detail, or test yourself to see how well you've comprehended the material. In the box below you'll find a number of links. Click on any one of these links to find additional chapter resources.

> ## end-of-chapter resources

- **Review of Concept Connections**
- **Practice Quiz**
- **Issues for Discussion**
- **Key Terms**
- **Marketing Applications**
- **Internet Connections**
- **Company Case**

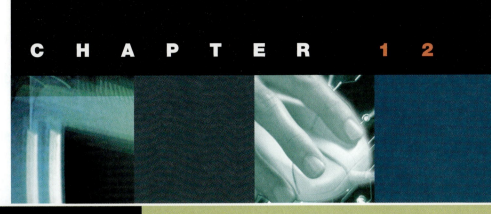

C H A P T E R 1 2

Distribution Channels and Logistics Management

Chapter Outline

What's Ahead

The Nature of Distribution Channels

    Why Are Marketing Intermediaries Used?

    Distribution Channel Functions

    Number of Channel Levels

Channel Behavior and Organization

    Channel Behavior

    Vertical Marketing Systems

    Horizontal Marketing Systems

    Hybrid Marketing Systems

    Changing Channel Organization

Channel Design Decisions

    Analyzing Consumer Service Needs

    Setting Channel Objectives and Constraints

    Identifying Major Alternatives

Evaluating the Major Alternatives

Designing International Distribution Channels

Channel Management Decisions

    Selecting Channel Members

    Motivating Channel Members

    Evaluating Channel Members

Public Policy and Distribution Decisions

Physical Distribution and Logistics Management

    Nature and Importance of Physical Distribution and Marketing Logistics

    Goals of the Logistics System

    Major Logistics Functions

    Integrated Logistics Management

    Third-Party Logistics

Chapter Wrap-Up

> What's Ahead

For more than half a century, Caterpillar has dominated the world's markets for heavy construction and mining equipment. Its familiar yellow tractors, crawlers, loaders, and trucks are a common sight at any construction area. With sales of $21 billion, Caterpillar is half again as large as its nearest competitor. It now captures over a 40 percent share of the world's heavy-construction equipment market, selling more than 300 products in nearly 200 countries. Caterpillar has posted 6 straight record years of record sales.

Many factors contribute to Caterpillar's enduring success—high-quality products, flexible and efficient manufacturing, a steady stream of innovative new products, and a lean organization that is responsive to customer needs. Although Caterpillar charges premium prices for its equipment, its high-quality and trouble-free operation provide greater long-term value. Yet these are not the most important reasons for Caterpillar's dominance. Instead, Caterpillar Chairman and CEO Glen Barton credits the company's focus on customers and its worldwide distribution system, which does a superb job of taking care of every customer need. Former CEO Donald Fites agrees: "The biggest reason for Caterpillar's success has been our system of distribution and product support and the close customer relationships its fosters. . . . The backbone of that system is our 195 dealers around the world who sell and service our [equipment]."

Caterpillar's dealers provide a wide range of important services to customers. Fites summarizes:

> After the product leaves our door, the dealers take over. They are the ones on the front-line. They're the ones who live with the product for its lifetime. They're the ones customers see. Although we offer financing and insurance, they arrange those deals for customers. They're out there making sure that when a machine is delivered, it's in the condition it's supposed to be in. They're out there training a customer's operators. They service a product frequently throughout its life, carefully monitoring a machine's health and scheduling repairs to prevent costly downtime. The customer . . . knows that there is a $20-billion-plus company called Caterpillar. But the dealers create the image of a company that doesn't just stand behind its products but with its products, anywhere in the world. Our dealers are the reason that our motto—Buy the Iron, Get the Company—is not an empty slogan.

Caterpillar's dealers build strong customer relationships in their communities. "Our independent dealer in Novi, Michigan, or in Bangkok, Thailand, knows so much more about the requirements of customers in those locations than a huge corporation like Caterpillar could," says Fites. Competitors often bypass their dealers and sell directly to big customers to cut costs or make more profits for themselves. However, Caterpillar wouldn't think of going around its dealers. "The knowledge of the local market and the close relations with customers that our dealers provide are worth every penny," he asserts with passion. "We'd rather cut off our right arm than sell directly to customers and bypass our dealers."

Caterpillar and its dealers work in close harmony to find better ways to bring value to customers. Says Fites, "We genuinely treat our system and theirs as one." The entire system is linked by a single worldwide computer network. For example, working at their desktop computers, Caterpillar managers can check to see how many Cat machines in the world are waiting for parts. Closely linked dealers play a vital role in almost every aspect of Caterpillar's operations, from product design and delivery, to product service and support, to market intelligence and customer feedback.

In the heavy-equipment industry, in which equipment downtime can mean big losses, Caterpillar's exceptional service gives it a huge advantage in winning and keeping customers. For example, consider Freeport-McMoRan, a Cat customer that operates one of the world's largest copper and gold mines, 24 hours a day, 365 days a year. High in the mountains of Indonesia, the mine is accessible only by aerial cableway or helicopter. Freeport-McMoRan relies on more than 500 pieces of Caterpillar mining and construction equipment—worth several hundred million dollars—including loaders, tractors, and mammoth 240-ton, 2,000-plus-horsepower trucks. Many of these machines cost well over $1 million apiece. When equipment breaks down, Freeport-McMoRan loses money fast. Thus, Freeport-McMoRan gladly pays a premium price for machines and service on which it can count. It knows that it can count on Caterpillar and its outstanding distribution network for superb support.

The close working relationship between Caterpillar and its dealers comes down to more than just formal contracts and business agreements. According to Fites, the powerful partnership rests on a handful of basic principles and practices:

- *Dealer profitability:* Caterpillar's rule: "Share the gain as well as the pain." When times are good, Caterpillar shares the bounty with its dealers rather than trying to grab all the riches for itself. When times are bad, Caterpillar protects its dealers. For example, in the mid-1980s, facing a depressed global construction-equipment market and cutthroat competition, Caterpillar sheltered its dealers by absorbing much of the economic damage. It lost almost $1 billion in just three years but didn't lose a single dealer. In contrast, competitors' dealers struggled and many failed. As a result, Caterpillar emerged with its distribution system intact and its competitive position stronger than ever.

- *Extraordinary dealer support:* Nowhere is this support more apparent than in the company's parts delivery system, the fastest and most reliable in the industry. Caterpillar maintains 22 parts facilities around the world, which stock 320,000 different parts and ship 84,000 items per day, about one per second every day of the year. In turn, dealers have made huge investments in inventory, warehouses, fleets of trucks, service bays, diagnostic and service equipment, and information technology. Together, Caterpillar and its dealers guarantee parts delivery within 48 hours anywhere in the world. The company ships 80 percent of parts orders immediately and 99 percent on the same day the order is received. In contrast, it's not unusual for competitors' customers to wait four or five days for a part.

- *Communications:* Caterpillar communicates with its dealers—fully, frequently, and honestly. According to Fites, "There are no secrets between us and our dealers. We have the financial statements and key operating data of every dealer in the world. . . . In addition, virtually all Caterpillar and dealer employees have real-time access to continually updated databases of service information, sales trends and forecasts, customer satisfaction surveys, and other critical data. . . . [Moreover,] virtually everyone from the youngest design engineer to the CEO now has direct contact with somebody in our dealer organizations."

- *Dealer performance:* Caterpillar does all it can to ensure that its dealerships are run well. It closely monitors each dealership's sales, market position, service capability, financial situation, and other performance measures. It genuinely wants each dealer to succeed, and when it sees a problem, it jumps in to help. As a result, Caterpillar dealerships, many of which are family businesses, tend to be stable and profitable. The average Caterpillar dealership has remained in the hands of the same family for more than 50 years. Some actually predate the 1925 merger that created Caterpillar.

- *Personal relationships:* In addition to more formal business ties, Cat forms close personal ties with its dealers in a kind of family relationship. Fites relates the following example: "When I see Chappy Chapman, a retired executive vice-president . . ., out on the golf course, he always asks about particular dealers or about their children, who may be running the business now. And every time I see those dealers, they inquire, 'How's Chappy?' That's the sort of relationship we have. . . . I consider the majority of dealers personal friends."

Thus, Caterpillar's superb distribution system serves as a major source of competitive advantage. The system is built on a firm base of mutual trust and shared dreams. Caterpillar and its dealers feel a deep pride in what they are accomplishing together. As Fites puts it, "There's a camaraderie among our dealers around the world that really makes it more than just a financial arrangement. They feel that what they're doing is good for the world because they are part of an organization that makes, sells, and tends to the machines that make the world work."[1]

objectives   <

Before you begin, take a moment to familiarize yourself with the key objectives of this chapter.

gearing up   <

Before we begin our exploration this chapter, take a short warm-up test to see what you know about this topic.

Marketing channel decisions are among the most important decisions that management faces. A company's channel decisions are linked with every other marketing decision. The company's pricing depends on whether it uses mass merchandisers or high-quality specialty stores. The firm's sales force and advertising decisions depend on how much persuasion, training, motivation, and support the dealers need. Whether a company develops or acquires certain new products may depend on how well those products fit the capabilities of its channel members.

Companies often pay too little attention to their distribution channels, however, sometimes with damaging results. In contrast, many companies have used imaginative distribution systems to *gain* a competitive advantage. Federal Express's creative and imposing distribution system made it the leader in the small-package delivery industry. General Electric gained a strong advantage in selling its major appliances by supporting its dealers with a sophisticated computerized order-processing and delivery system. Dell Computer revolutionized its industry by selling personal computers directly to consumers rather than through retail stores. Charles Schwab & Company pioneered the delivery of financial services via the Internet.

Distribution channel decisions often involve long-term commitments to other firms. For example, companies such as Ford, IBM, or McDonald's can easily change their advertising, pricing, or promotion programs. They can scrap old products and introduce new ones as market tastes demand. But when they set up distribution channels through contracts with franchisees, independent dealers, or large retailers, they cannot readily replace these channels with company-owned stores if conditions change. Therefore, management must design its channels carefully, with an eye on tomorrow's likely selling environment as well as today's.

This chapter examines four major questions concerning distribution channels: What is the nature of distribution channels? How do channel firms interact and organize to do the work of the channel? What problems do companies face in designing and managing their channels? What role does physical distribution play in attracting and satisfying customers? In chapter 13, we will look at distribution channel issues from the viewpoint of retailers and wholesalers.

[1]Quotes from Donald V. Fites, "Make Your Dealers Your Partners," *Harvard Business Review,* March–April 1996, pp. 84–95; and De Ann Weimer, "A New Cat on the Hot Seat," *Business Week,* March 1998, pp. 56–62. Also see Peter Elstrom, "This Cat Keeps on Purring," *Business Week,* January 20, 1997, pp. 82–84; "Caterpillar CEO Optimistic About Company's Future," press release accessed online at www.cat.com, April 14, 1999; and "Best Sales Forces: Caterpillar," *Sales & Marketing Management,* July 1999, p. 64.

Most producers use intermediaries to bring their products to market. They try to forge a **distribution channel**—a set of interdependent organizations involved in the process of making a product or service available for use or consumption by the consumer or business user.[2]

WHY ARE MARKETING INTERMEDIARIES USED?

Why do producers give some of the selling job to intermediaries? After all, doing so means giving up some control over how and to whom the products are sold. The use of intermediaries results from their greater efficiency in making goods available to target markets. Through their contacts, experience, specialization, and scale of operation, intermediaries usually offer the firm more than it can achieve on its own.

Figure 12.1 shows how using intermediaries can provide economies. Figure 12.1a shows three manufacturers, each using direct marketing to reach three customers. This system requires nine different contacts. Figure 12.1b shows the three manufacturers working through one distributor, who contacts the three customers. This system requires only six contacts. In this way, intermediaries reduce the amount of work that must be done by both producers and consumers.

From the economic system's point of view, the role of marketing intermediaries is to transform the assortments of products made by producers into the assortments wanted by consumers. Producers make narrow assortments of products in large quantities, but consumers want broad assortments of products in small quantities. In the distribution channels, intermediaries buy large quantities from many producers and break them down into the smaller quantities and broader assortments wanted by consumers. Thus, intermediaries play an important role in matching supply and demand.

The concept of distribution channels is not limited to the distribution of tangible products. Producers of services and ideas also face the problem of making their output available to target populations. In the private sector, retail stores, hotels, banks, and other service providers take great care to make their services conveniently available to target customers. In the public sector, service organizations and agencies develop "educational distribution systems" and "health care delivery systems" for reaching sometimes widely dispersed populations. Hospitals must be located to serve various patient populations, and schools must be located close to the children who need to be taught. Communities must locate their fire stations to provide rapid response to fires and polling stations must be placed where people can vote conveniently.

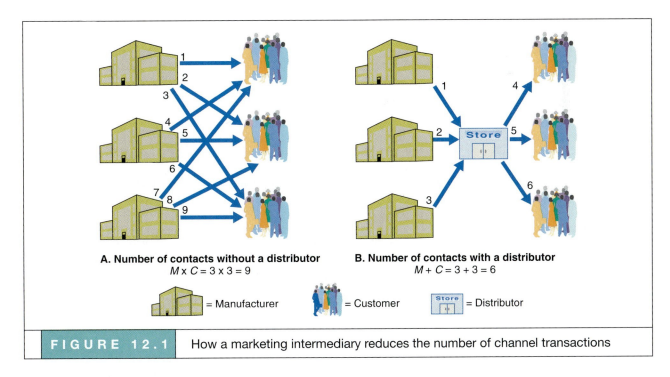

A. Number of contacts without a distributor
$M \times C = 3 \times 3 = 9$

B. Number of contacts with a distributor
$M + C = 3 + 3 = 6$

= Manufacturer   = Customer   = Distributor

FIGURE 12.1   How a marketing intermediary reduces the number of channel transactions

[2]See Louis Stern, Adel I. El-Ansary, and Anne Coughlin, *Marketing Channels,* 5th ed. (Upper Saddle River, NJ: Prentice Hall, 1996), p. 3.

DISTRIBUTION CHANNEL FUNCTIONS

The distribution channel moves goods and services from producers to consumers. It overcomes the major time, place, and possession gaps that separate goods and services from those who would use them. Members of the marketing channel perform many key functions. Some help to complete transactions:

- *Information:* gathering and distributing marketing research and intelligence information about actors and forces in the marketing environment needed for planning and aiding exchange.
- *Promotion:* developing and spreading persuasive communications about an offer.
- *Contact:* finding and communicating with prospective buyers.
- *Matching:* shaping and fitting the offer to the buyer's needs, including activities such as manufacturing, grading, assembling, and packaging.
- *Negotiation:* reaching an agreement on price and other terms of the offer so that ownership or possession can be transferred.

Others help to fulfill the completed transactions:

- *Physical distribution:* transporting and storing goods.
- *Financing:* acquiring and using funds to cover the costs of the channel work.
- *Risk taking:* assuming the risks of carrying out the channel work.

The question is not *whether* these functions need to be performed—they must be—but rather *who* will perform them. To the extent that the manufacturer performs these functions, its costs go up and its prices have to be higher. At the same time, when some of these functions are shifted to intermediaries, the producer's costs and prices may be lower, but the intermediaries must charge more to cover the costs of their work. In dividing the work of the channel, the various functions should be assigned to the channel members who can perform them most efficiently and effectively to provide satisfactory assortments of goods to target consumers.

video exercise   <

Consider a fictional case of distribution management.

NUMBER OF CHANNEL LEVELS

Distribution channels can be described by the number of channel levels involved. Each layer of marketing intermediaries that performs some work in bringing the product and its ownership closer to the final buyer is a **channel level.** Because the producer and the final consumer both perform some work, they are part of every channel. We use the *number of intermediary levels* to indicate the *length* of a channel. Figure 12.2a shows several consumer distribution channels of different lengths.

Channel 1, called a **direct marketing channel,** has no intermediary levels. It consists of a company selling directly to consumers. For example, Avon, Amway, and Tupperware sell their products door to door or through home and office sales parties; Lands' End and Fingerhut sell products direct through mail order, telephone, or at their Web sites; and Singer sells its sewing machines through its own stores. The remaining channels in Figure 12.2a are **indirect marketing channels.** Channel 2 contains one intermediary level. In consumer markets, this level is typically a retailer. For example, the makers of televisions, cameras, tires, furniture, major appliances, and many other products sell their goods directly to large retailers such as Wal-Mart and Sears, which then sell the goods to final consumers. Channel 3 contains two intermediary levels, a wholesaler and a retailer. This channel is often used by small manufacturers of food, drugs, hardware, and other products. Channel 4 contains three intermediary levels. In the meatpacking industry, for example, jobbers buy from wholesalers and sell to smaller retailers who generally are not served by larger wholesalers. Distribution channels with even more levels are sometimes found, but less often. From the producer's point of view, a greater number of levels means less control and greater channel complexity.

Figure 12.2b shows some common business distribution channels. The business marketer can use its own sales force to sell directly to business customers. It can also sell to industrial distributors, who in turn sell to business customers. It can sell through manufacturer's representatives or its own sales branches to business customers, or it can use these representatives and branches to sell through industrial distributors. Thus, business markets commonly include multilevel distribution channels.

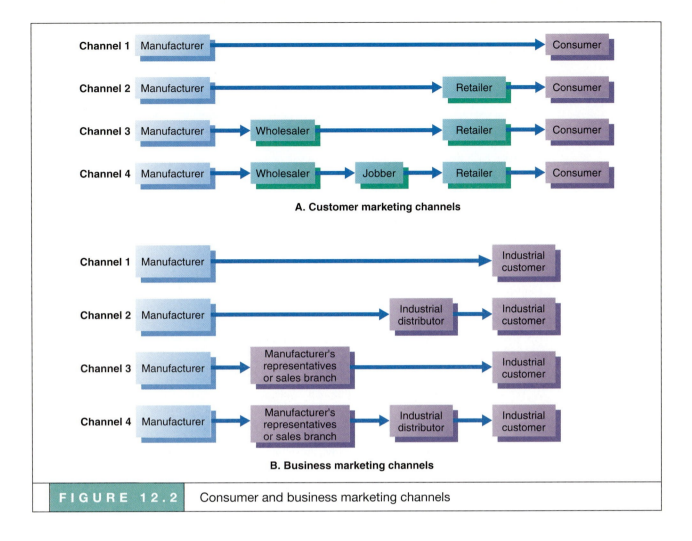

A. Customer marketing channels

B. Business marketing channels

FIGURE 12.2 Consumer and business marketing channels

All of the institutions in the channel are connected by several types of *flows*. These include the *physical flow* of products, the *flow of ownership*, the *payment flow*, the *information flow*, and the *promotion flow*. These flows can make even channels with only one or a few levels very complex.

> active concept check

Now let's take a moment to test your knowledge of what you've just read.

> ## Channel Behavior and Organization

Distribution channels are more than simple collections of firms tied together by various flows. They are complex behavioral systems in which people and companies interact to accomplish individual, company, and channel goals. Some channel systems consist only of informal interactions among loosely organized firms; others consist of formal interactions guided by strong organizational structures. Moreover, channel systems do not stand still—new types of intermediaries emerge and whole new channel systems evolve. Here we look at channel behavior and at how members organize to do the work of the channel.

CHANNEL BEHAVIOR

A distribution channel consists of firms that have banded together for their common good. Each channel member is dependent on the others. For example, a Ford dealer depends on the Ford Motor

Company to design cars that meet consumer needs. In turn, Ford depends on the dealer to attract consumers, persuade them to buy Ford cars, and service cars after the sale. The Ford dealer also depends on other dealers to provide good sales and service that will uphold the reputation of Ford and its dealer body. In fact, the success of individual Ford dealers depends on how well the entire Ford distribution channel competes with the channels of other auto manufacturers.

Each channel member plays a role in the channel and specializes in performing one or more functions. For example, Compaq's role is to produce personal computers that consumers will like and to create demand through national advertising. Best Buy's role is to display these Compaq computers in convenient locations, to answer buyers' questions, and to close sales. The channel will be most effective when each member is assigned the tasks it can do best.

Ideally, because the success of individual channel members depends on overall channel success, all channel firms should work together smoothly. They should understand and accept their roles, coordinate their goals and activities, and cooperate to attain overall channel goals. By cooperating, they can more effectively sense, serve, and satisfy the target market.

However, individual channel members rarely take such a broad view. They are usually more concerned with their own short-run goals and their dealings with those firms closest to them in the channel. Cooperating to achieve overall channel goals sometimes means giving up individual company goals. Although channel members are dependent on one another, they often act alone in their own short-run best interests. They often disagree on the roles each should play—on who should do what and for what rewards. Such disagreements over goals and roles generate **channel conflict.**

Horizontal conflict occurs among firms at the same level of the channel. For instance, some Ford dealers in Chicago might complain about other dealers in the city who steal sales from them by being too aggressive in their pricing and advertising or by selling outside their assigned territories. Or Holiday Inn franchisees might complain about other Holiday Inn franchisees overcharging guests or giving poor service, hurting the overall Holiday Inn image.

Vertical conflict, conflicts between different levels of the same channel, is even more common. For example, McDonald's came into conflict with some of its California dealers when its aggressive expansion plans called for placing new stores in areas that took business from existing locations. Similarly, office furniture maker Herman Miller created conflict with its dealers when it opened an online store—**www.hmstore.com**—and began selling its products directly to customers. Although Herman Miller believed that the Web site was reaching only smaller customers who weren't being served by current channels, dealers complained loudly. To help resolve the conflict, Herman Miller embarked on a communication campaign to educate dealers on how the online efforts would help them rather than hurt them.[3]

Some conflict in the channel takes the form of healthy competition. Such competition can be good for the channel—without it, the channel could become passive and noninnovative. But sometimes conflict can damage the channel, as it did in the case of Motorola's StarTAC phone. For the channel as a whole to perform well, each channel member's role must be specified and channel conflict must be managed. Cooperation, role assignment, and conflict management in the channel are attained through strong channel leadership. The channel will perform better if it includes a firm, agency, or mechanism that has the power to assign roles and manage conflict.

active example <

Look at how some big retailers are managing channel conflict.

VERTICAL MARKETING SYSTEMS

Historically, distribution channels have been loose collections of independent companies, each showing little concern for overall channel performance. These *conventional distribution channels* have lacked strong leadership and have been troubled by damaging conflict and poor performance. One of the biggest recent channel developments has been the *vertical marketing systems* that have emerged to challenge conventional marketing channels. Figure 12.3 contrasts the two types of channel arrangements.

[3]Greg Burns, "Fast-Food Fight," *Business Week,* June 2, 1997, pp. 34–36; Patricia Sellers, "McDonald's Starts Over," *Fortune,* June 22, 1998, pp. 34–35; and Rochelle Garner, "Mad as Hell," *Sales & Marketing Management,* June 1999, pp. 55–59.

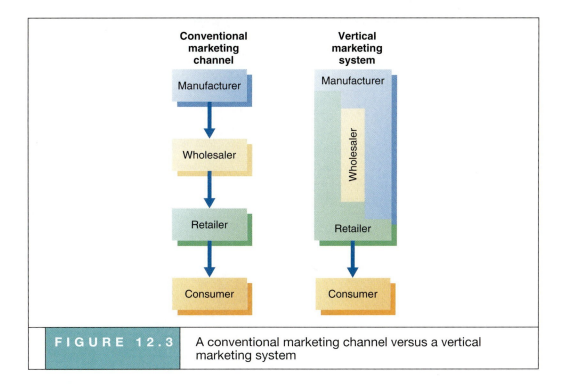

FIGURE 12.3 A conventional marketing channel versus a vertical marketing system

A **conventional distribution channel** consists of one or more independent producers, wholesalers, and retailers. Each is a separate business seeking to maximize its own profits, even at the expense of profits for the system as a whole. No channel member has much control over the other members, and no formal means exists for assigning roles and resolving channel conflict. In contrast, a **vertical marketing system (VMS)** consists of producers, wholesalers, and retailers acting as a unified system. One channel member owns the others, has contracts with them, or wields so much power that they must all cooperate. The VMS can be dominated by the producer, wholesaler, or retailer. Vertical marketing systems came into being to control channel behavior and manage channel conflict.

We look now at three major types of VMSs: *corporate, contractual,* and *administered.* Each uses a different means for setting up leadership and power in the channel. We now take a closer look at each type of VMS.

Corporate VMS

A **corporate VMS** combines successive stages of production and distribution under single ownership. Coordination and conflict management are attained through regular organizational channels. For example, Sears obtains over 50 percent of its goods from companies that it partly or wholly owns. Giant Food Stores operates an ice-making facility, a soft drink bottling operation, an ice cream plant, and a bakery that supplies Giant stores with everything from bagels to birthday cakes.

E. J. Gallo, the world's largest wine maker, grows its own grapes to produce wine, which it pours into Gallo-made bottles topped with caps produced in Gallo's wholly owned Midcal Aluminum Company plant. Gallo's Fairbanks Trucking Company hauls wine out of Gallo wineries and raw materials back in. The raw materials include lime from Gallo's quarry near Sacramento. Thus, Gallo participates in every aspect of producing and selling "short of whispering in the ear of each imbiber."

Contractual VMS

A **contractual VMS** consists of independent firms at different levels of production and distribution who join together through contracts to obtain more economies or sales impact than each could achieve alone. Coordination and conflict management are attained through contractual agreements among channel members. There are three types of contractual VMSs: wholesaler-sponsored voluntary chains, retailer cooperatives, and franchise organizations.

In *wholesaler-sponsored voluntary chains,* wholesalers organize voluntary chains of independent retailers to help them compete with large chain organizations. The wholesaler develops a program in which independent retailers standardize their selling practices and achieve buying economies that let the group compete effectively with chain organizations. Examples include the Independent Grocers Alliance (IGA), Western Auto, and Do it Best hardwares.

Contractual VMS: Hardware wholesaler Do it Best Corp. has organized a voluntary chain of 4,400 independently owned hardware stores, helping them to compete with large chain organizations.

In *retailer cooperatives,* retailers organize a new, jointly owned business to carry on wholesaling and possibly production. Members buy most of their goods through the retailer co-op and plan their advertising jointly. Profits are passed back to members in proportion to their purchases. Examples include Certified Grocers, Associated Grocers, and Ace Hardware.

In **franchise organizations,** a channel member called a *franchiser* links several stages in the production-distribution process. The more than 500,000 franchise operations in the United States now account for nearly $760 billion in sales, about 40 percent of all U.S. retail sales.[4] Almost every kind of business has been franchised—from motels and fast-food restaurants to dental centers and dating services, from wedding consultants and maid services to funeral homes and fitness centers.

There are three forms of franchises. The first form is the *manufacturer-sponsored retailer franchise system,* as found in the automobile industry. Ford, for example, licenses dealers to sell its cars; the dealers are independent businesspeople who agree to meet various conditions of sales and service. The second type of franchise is the *manufacturer-sponsored wholesaler franchise system,* as found in the soft drink industry. Coca-Cola, for example, licenses bottlers (wholesalers) in various markets who buy Coca-Cola syrup concentrate and then carbonate, bottle, and sell the finished product to retailers in local markets. The third franchise form is the *service-firm-sponsored retailer franchise system,* in which a service firm licenses a system of retailers to bring its service to consumers. Examples are found in the auto-rental business (Hertz, Avis); the fast-food service business (McDonald's, Burger King); and the motel business (Holiday Inn, Ramada Inn).

The fact that most consumers cannot tell the difference between contractual and corporate VMSs shows how successfully the contractual organizations compete with corporate chains. Chapter 13 presents a fuller discussion of the various contractual VMSs.

Administered VMS

An **administered VMS** coordinates successive stages of production and distribution, not through common ownership or contractual ties but through the size and power of one of the parties. In an *administered VMS,* leadership is assumed by one or a few dominant channel members. Manufacturers

[4]See Stern, El-Ansary, and Coughlin, *Marketing Channels,* p. 251.

of a top brand can obtain strong trade cooperation and support from resellers. For example, General Electric, Procter & Gamble, and Kraft can command unusual cooperation from resellers regarding displays, shelf space, promotions, and price policies. Large retailers like Wal-Mart and Barnes & Noble can exert strong influence on the manufacturers that supply the products they sell.

HORIZONTAL MARKETING SYSTEMS

Another channel development is the **horizontal marketing system,** in which two or more companies at one level join together to follow a new marketing opportunity. By working together, companies can combine their capital, production capabilities, or marketing resources to accomplish more than any one company could alone. Companies might join forces with competitors or noncompetitors. They might work with each other on a temporary or permanent basis, or they may create a separate company. For example, the Lamar Savings Bank of Texas arranged to locate its savings offices and automated teller machines in Safeway stores. Lamar gained quicker market entry at a low cost, and Safeway was able to offer in-store banking convenience to its customers.

Such channel arrangements also work well globally. For example, because of its excellent coverage of international markets, Nestlé jointly sells General Mills cereal brands in markets outside North America. Coca-Cola and Nestlé formed a joint venture to market ready-to-drink coffee and tea worldwide. Coke provides worldwide experience in marketing and distributing beverages, and Nestlé contributes two established brand names—Nescafé and Nestea. Similarly, Coca-Cola and Procter & Gamble have created distribution systems linking Coca-Cola soft drinks and Pringles potato crisps in global markets. Seiko Watch's distribution partner in Japan, K. Hattori, markets Schick's razors there, giving Schick the leading market share in Japan, despite Gillette's overall strength in many other markets.[5]

HYBRID MARKETING SYSTEMS

In the past, many companies used a single channel to sell to a single market or market segment. Today, with the proliferation of customer segments and channel possibilities, more and more companies have

Horizontal marketing systems: Nestlé jointly sells General Mills cereal brands in markets outside North America.

[5]See Allan J. Magrath, "Collaborative Marketing Comes of Age—Again," *Sales & Marketing Management,* September 1991, pp. 61–64; Andrew E. Serwer, "What Price Loyalty?" *Fortune,* January 10, 1995, pp. 103–4; and Judann Pollack and Louise Kramer, "Coca-Cola and Pringles Eye Global Brand Linkup," *Advertising Age,* June 15, 1998, pp. 1, 73.

adopted *multichannel distribution systems*—often called **hybrid marketing channels.** Such multi-channel marketing occurs when a single firm sets up two or more marketing channels to reach one or more customer segments. The use of hybrid channel systems has increased greatly in recent years.

Figure 12.4 shows a hybrid channel. In the figure, the producer sells directly to consumer segment 1 using direct-mail catalogs and telemarketing and reaches consumer segment 2 through retailers. It sells indirectly to business segment 1 through distributors and dealers and to business segment 2 through its own sales force.

IBM uses such a hybrid channel effectively. For years, IBM sold computers only through its own sales force, which sold its large systems to business customers. However, the market for computers and information technology has now exploded into a profusion of products and services for dozens of segments and niches, ranging from large corporate buyers to small businesses to home and home office buyers. As a result, IBM has had to dramatically rethink the way it goes to market. To serve the diverse needs of these many segments, IBM added 18 new channels in less than 10 years. For example, in addition to selling through the vaunted IBM sales force, IBM also sells through a comprehensive network of distributors and value-added resellers, which sell IBM computers, systems, and services to a variety of special business segments. Final customers can buy IBM personal computers from specialty computer stores or any of several large retailers, including Wal-Mart, Circuit City, and Office Depot. IBM uses telemarketing to service the needs of small and medium-size business. Both business and final consumers can buy online from the company's ShopIBM Web site (**www.direct.ibm.com**).[6]

Hybrid channels offer many advantages to companies facing large and complex markets. With each new channel, the company expands its sales and market coverage and gains opportunities to tailor its products and services to the specific needs of diverse customer segments. But such hybrid channel systems are harder to control, and they generate conflict as more channels compete for customers and sales. For example, when IBM began selling directly to customers through catalogs, telemarketing, and its own Web site, many of its retail dealers cried "unfair competition" and threatened to drop the IBM line or to give it less emphasis. Many outside salespeople felt that they were being undercut by the new "inside channels."

active example   <

Consider how the Internet is promoting the use of hybrid channels in several industries.

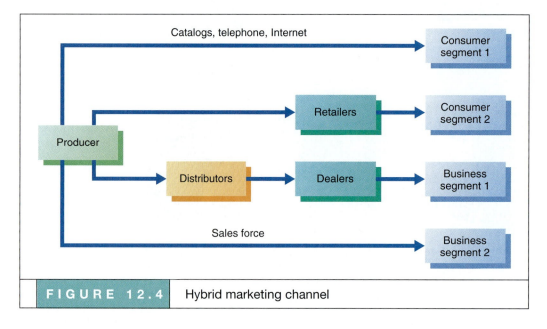

| FIGURE 12.4 | Hybrid marketing channel |

[6]See Rowland T. Moriarity and Ursula Moran, "Managing Hybrid Marketing Systems," *Harvard Business Review,* November–December 1990, pp. 146–55; Frank V. Cespedes and E. Raymond Corey, "Managing Multiple Channels," *Business Horizons,* July–August 1990, pp. 67–77; Geoffrey Brewer, "Lou Gerstner Has His Hands Full," *Sales & Marketing Management,* May 1998, pp. 36–41; and the ShopIBM Web site at www.direct.ibm.com.

Hybrid channels: In addition to its sales force, IBM sells through distributors and value-added resellers, specialty computer stores and large retailers, telemarketing, and its ShopIBM Web site.

CHANGING CHANNEL ORGANIZATION

Changes in technology and the explosive growth of direct and online marketing are having a profound impact on the nature and design of marketing channels. One major trend is toward **disintermediation**—a big term with a clear message and important consequences. Disintermediation means that more and more, product and service producers are bypassing intermediaries and going directly to final buyers, or that radically new types of channel intermediaries are emerging to displace traditional ones.

Thus, in many industries, traditional intermediaries are dropping by the wayside. For example, companies like Dell Computer are selling directly to final buyers, eliminating retailers from their marketing channels. E-commerce merchants are growing rapidly in number and size, displacing traditional brick-and-mortar retailers. Consumers can buy flowers from 1-800-Flowers.com; books, videos, CDs, toys, and other goods from Amazon.com; household products from Wal-Mart; groceries from Peapod.com or webvan.com; clothes from Gap or Eddie Bauer; and consumer electronics from buy.com, all without ever visiting a store.

Disintermediation presents problems and opportunities for both producers and intermediaries. To avoid being swept aside, traditional intermediaries must find new ways to add value in the supply chain. To remain competitive, product and service producers must develop new channel opportunities, such as Internet and other direct channels. However, developing these new channels often brings them into direct competition with their established channels, resulting in conflict. To ease this problem, companies often look for ways to make going direct a plus for both the company and its channel partners:

> Going direct is rarely an all-or-nothing proposition. For example, to trim costs and add business, Hewlett-Packard opened three direct-sales Web sites—Shopping Village (for consumers), HP Commerce Center (for businesses buying from authorized resellers), and Electronic Solutions Now (for existing contract customers). However, to avoid conflicts with its established reseller channels, HP forwards all its Web orders to resellers, who complete the orders, ship the products, and get the commissions. In this way, HP gains the advantages of direct selling but also boosts business for resellers.

However, although this compromise system reduces conflicts, it also creates inefficiencies. "That all sounds great and everyone's happy," says a distribution consultant, "but kicking the customer over to the reseller . . . is a lot more expensive than letting customers order directly from the manufacturer. HP is spending a fair chunk of change to set this up, plus the business partner still wants eight percent margins for getting the product to the customer."[7] To be truly efficient in the long run, HP eventually will have to find ways for its resellers to add value or drop them from the direct channel.

[7]See Garner, "Mad as Hell," pp. 55–61.

active concept check   ◀

Now let's take a moment to test your knowledge of what you've just read.

▶ Channel Design Decisions

We now look at several channel decisions manufacturers face. In designing marketing channels, manufacturers struggle between what is ideal and what is practical. A new firm with limited capital usually starts by selling in a limited market area. Deciding on the *best* channels might not be a problem: The problem might simply be how to convince one or a few good intermediaries to handle the line.

If successful, the new firm might branch out to new markets through the existing intermediaries. In smaller markets, the firm might sell directly to retailers; in larger markets, it might sell through distributors. In one part of the country, it might grant exclusive franchises; in another, it might sell through all available outlets. In this way, channel systems often evolve to meet market opportunities and conditions. However, for maximum effectiveness, channel analysis and decision making should be more purposeful. Designing a channel system calls for analyzing consumer service needs, setting channel objectives and constraints, identifying major channel alternatives, and evaluating them.

ANALYZING CONSUMER SERVICE NEEDS

As noted previously, marketing channels can be thought of as *customer value delivery systems* in which each channel member adds value for the customer. Thus, designing the distribution channel starts with finding out what targeted consumers want from the channel. Do consumers want to buy from nearby locations or are they willing to travel to more distant centralized locations? Would they rather buy in person, over the phone, through the mail, or via the Internet? Do they value breadth of assortment or do they prefer specialization? Do consumers want many add-on services (delivery, credit, repairs, installation) or will they obtain these elsewhere? The faster the delivery, the greater the assortment provided, and the more add-on services supplied, the greater the channel's service level.

But providing the fastest delivery, greatest assortment, and most services may not be possible or practical. The company and its channel members may not have the resources or skills needed to provide all the desired services. Also, providing higher levels of service results in higher costs for the channel and higher prices for consumers. The company must balance consumer service needs not only against the feasibility and costs of meeting these needs but also against customer price preferences. The success of off-price and discount retailing shows that consumers are often willing to accept lower service levels if this means lower prices.

SETTING CHANNEL OBJECTIVES AND CONSTRAINTS

Channel objectives should be stated in terms of the desired service level of target consumers. Usually, a company can identify several segments wanting different levels of channel service. The company should decide which segments to serve and the best channels to use in each case. In each segment, the company wants to minimize the total channel cost of meeting customer service requirements.

The company's channel objectives are also influenced by the nature of the company, its products, marketing intermediaries, competitors, and the environment. For example, the company's size and financial situation determine which marketing functions it can handle itself and which it must give to intermediaries. Companies selling perishable products may require more direct marketing to avoid delays and too much handling. In some cases, a company may want to compete in or near the same outlets that carry competitors' products. In other cases, producers may avoid the channels used by competitors. Avon, for example, set up a profitable door-to-door selling operation rather than going head to head with other cosmetics makers for scarce positions in retail stores. Finally, environmental factors such as economic conditions and legal constraints may affect channel objectives and design. For example, in a depressed economy, producers want to distribute their goods in the most economical way, using shorter channels and dropping unneeded services that add to the final price of the goods.

IDENTIFYING MAJOR ALTERNATIVES

When the company has defined its channel objectives, it should next identify its major channel alternatives in terms of *types* of intermediaries, the *number* of intermediaries, and the *responsibilities* of each channel member.

Types of Intermediaries

A firm should identify the types of channel members available to carry out its channel work. For example, suppose a manufacturer of test equipment has developed an audio device that detects poor mechanical connections in machines with moving parts. Company executives think this product would have a market in all industries in which electric, combustion, or steam engines are made or used. The company's current sales force is small, and the problem is how best to reach these different industries. The following channel alternatives might emerge from management discussion:

Company sales force: Expand the company's direct sales force. Assign outside salespeople to territories and have them contact all prospects in the area or develop separate company sales forces for different industries. Or, add an inside telesales operation in which telephone salespeople handle small or midsize companies.

Manufacturer's agency: Hire manufacturer's agents—independent firms whose sales forces handle related products from many companies—in different regions or industries to sell the new test equipment.

Industrial distributors: Find distributors in the different regions or industries who will buy and carry the new line. Give them exclusive distribution, good margins, product training, and promotional support.

Number of Marketing Intermediaries

Companies must also determine the number of channel members to use at each level. Three strategies are available: intensive distribution, exclusive distribution, and selective distribution.

Producers of convenience products and common raw materials typically seek **intensive distribution**—a strategy in which they stock their products in as many outlets as possible. These goods must be available where and when consumers want them. For example, toothpaste, candy, and other similar items are sold in millions of outlets to provide maximum brand exposure and consumer convenience. Procter & Gamble, Coca-Cola, and other consumer goods companies distribute their products in this way.

By contrast, some producers purposely limit the number of intermediaries handling their products. The extreme form of this practice is **exclusive distribution,** in which the producer gives only a limited number of dealers the exclusive right to distribute its products in their territories. Exclusive distribution is often found in the distribution of new automobiles and prestige women's clothing. For example, Bentley dealers are few and far between—even large cities may have only one or two dealers. By granting exclusive distribution, Bentley gains stronger distributor selling support and more control over dealer prices, promotion, credit, and services. Exclusive distribution also enhances the car's image and allows for higher markups.

Between intensive and exclusive distribution lies **selective distribution**—the use of more than one, but fewer than all, of the intermediaries who are willing to carry a company's products. Most television, furniture, and small-appliance brands are distributed in this manner. For example, Maytag, Whirlpool, and General Electric sell their major appliances through dealer networks and selected large retailers. By using selective distribution, they do not have to spread their efforts over many outlets, including many marginal ones. They can develop good working relationships with selected channel members and expect a better-than-average selling effort. Selective distribution gives producers good market coverage with more control and less cost than does intensive distribution.

> ## active exercise

Apply the concepts you've learned so far to the work of some prominent companies.

Responsibilities of Channel Members

The producer and intermediaries need to agree on the terms and responsibilities of each channel member. They should agree on price policies, conditions of sale, territorial rights, and specific services to be performed by each party. The producer should establish a list price and a fair set of discounts for intermediaries. It must define each channel member's territory, and it should be careful about where it places new resellers. Mutual services and duties need to be spelled out carefully, especially in franchise and exclusive distribution channels. For example, McDonald's provides franchisees with promotional support, a record-keeping system, training, and general management assistance. In turn, franchisees must meet company standards for physical facilities, cooperate with new promotion programs, provide requested information, and buy specified food products.

EVALUATING THE MAJOR ALTERNATIVES

Suppose a company has identified several channel alternatives and wants to select the one that will best satisfy its long-run objectives. Each alternative should be evaluated against economic, control, and adaptive criteria.

Using *economic criteria,* a company compares the likely profitability of different channel alternatives. It estimates the sales that each channel would produce and the costs of selling different volumes through each channel. The company must also consider *control issues.* Using intermediaries usually means giving them some control over the marketing of the product, and some intermediaries take more control than others. Other things being equal, the company prefers to keep as much control as possible. Finally, the company must apply *adaptive criteria.* Channels often involve long-term commitments to other firms, making it hard to adapt the channel to the changing marketing environment. The company wants to keep the channel as flexible as possible. Thus, to be considered, a channel involving long-term commitment should be greatly superior on economic and control grounds.

active example

Take a moment to see how some prominent companies approached the evaluation of alternatives.

DESIGNING INTERNATIONAL DISTRIBUTION CHANNELS

International marketers face many additional complexities in designing their channels. Each country has its own unique distribution system that has evolved over time and changes very slowly. These channel systems can vary widely from country to country. Thus, global marketers must usually adapt their channel strategies to the existing structures within each country. In some markets, the distribution system is complex and hard to penetrate, consisting of many layers and large numbers of intermediaries. Consider Japan:

> The Japanese distribution system stems from the early seventeenth century when cottage industries and a [quickly growing] urban population spawned a merchant class. . . . Despite Japan's economic achievements, the distribution system has remained remarkably faithful to its antique pattern. . . . [It] encompasses a wide range of wholesalers and other agents, brokers, and retailers, differing more in number than in function from their American counterparts. There are myriad tiny retail shops. An even greater number of wholesalers supplies goods to them, layered tier upon tier, many more than most U.S. executives would think necessary. For example, soap may move through three wholesalers plus a sales company after it leaves the manufacturer before it ever reaches the retail outlet. A steak goes from rancher to consumers in a process that often involves a dozen middle agents. . . . The distribution network . . . reflects the traditionally close ties among many Japanese companies . . . [and places] much greater emphasis on personal relationships with users. . . . Although [these channels appear] inefficient and cumbersome, they seem to serve the Japanese customer well. . . . Lacking much storage space in their small homes, most Japanese homemakers shop several times a week and prefer convenient [and more personal] neighborhood shops.[8]

[8]Subhash C. Jain, *International Marketing Management,* 3rd ed. (Boston, MA: PWS-Kent Publishing, 1990), pp. 489–91. Also see Emily Thornton, "Revolution in Japanese Retailing," *Fortune,* February 7, 1994, pp. 143–47; and "Ever-Shorter Channels—Wholesale Industry Restructures," *Focus Japan,* July–August 1997, pp. 3–4.

Many Western firms have had great difficulty breaking into the closely knit, tradition-bound Japanese distribution network.

At the other extreme, distribution systems in developing countries may be scattered and inefficient, or altogether lacking. For example, China and India would appear to be huge markets, each with populations in the hundreds of millions. In reality, however, these markets are much smaller than the population numbers suggest. Because of inadequate distribution systems in both countries, most companies can profitably access only a small portion of the population located in each country's most affluent cities.[9]

Thus, international marketers face a wide range of channel alternatives. Designing efficient and effective channel systems between and within various country markets poses a difficult challenge. We discuss international distribution decisions further in chapter 19.

> active concept check

Now let's take a moment to test your knowledge of what you've just read.

> **Channel Management Decisions**

Once the company has reviewed its channel alternatives and decided on the best channel design, it must implement and manage the chosen channel. Channel management calls for selecting and motivating individual channel members and evaluating their performance over time.

SELECTING CHANNEL MEMBERS

Producers vary in their ability to attract qualified marketing intermediaries. Some producers have no trouble signing up channel members. For example, when Toyota first introduced its Lexus line in the United States, it had no trouble attracting new dealers. In fact, it had to turn down many would-be resellers. In some cases, the promise of exclusive or selective distribution for a desirable product will draw plenty of applicants.

[9]For examples, see Philip Cateora, *International Marketing,* 7th ed. (Homewood, IL: Richard D. Irwin, 1990), pp. 570–71; and Dexter Roberts, "Blazing Away at Foreign Brands," *Business Week,* May 12, 1997, p. 58.

At the other extreme are producers who have to work hard to line up enough qualified intermediaries. When Polaroid started, for example, it could not get photography stores to carry its new cameras, and it had to go to mass-merchandising outlets. Similarly, when the U.S. Time Company first tried to sell its inexpensive Timex watches through regular jewelry stores, most jewelry stores refused to carry them. The company then managed to get its watches into mass-merchandise outlets. This turned out to be a wise decision because of the rapid growth of mass merchandising.

When selecting intermediaries, the company should determine what characteristics distinguish the better ones. It will want to evaluate each channel member's years in business, other lines carried, growth and profit record, cooperativeness, and reputation. If the intermediaries are sales agents, the company will want to evaluate the number and character of other lines carried and the size and quality of the sales force. If the intermediary is a retail store that wants exclusive or selective distribution, the company will want to evaluate the store's customers, location, and future growth potential.

MOTIVATING CHANNEL MEMBERS

Once selected, channel members must be motivated continuously to do their best. The company must sell not only *through* the intermediaries but *to* them. Most companies see their intermediaries as first-line customers. Some use the carrot-and-stick approach: At times they offer *positive* motivators such as higher margins, special deals, premiums, cooperative advertising allowances, display allowances, and sales contests. At other times they use *negative* motivators, such as threatening to reduce margins, to slow down delivery, or to end the relationship altogether. A producer using this approach usually has not done a good job of studying the needs, problems, strengths, and weaknesses of its distributors.

More advanced companies try to forge long-term partnerships with their distributors to create a marketing system that meets the needs of both the manufacturer *and* the distributors. Thus, Procter & Gamble and Wal-Mart work together to create superior value for final consumers. They jointly plan merchandising goals and strategies, inventory levels, and advertising and promotion plans. Similarly, GE Appliances works closely with its independent dealers to help them be successful in selling the company's products. In managing its channels, a company must convince distributors that they can make their money by being part of an advanced marketing system.[10]

EVALUATING CHANNEL MEMBERS

The producer must regularly check the channel member's performance against standards such as sales quotas, average inventory levels, customer delivery time, treatment of damaged and lost goods, cooperation in company promotion and training programs, and services to the customer. The company should recognize and reward intermediaries who are performing well. Those who are performing poorly should be assisted or, as a last resort, replaced. A company may periodically "requalify" its intermediaries and prune the weaker ones.

Finally, manufacturers need to be sensitive to their dealers. Those who treat their dealers lightly risk not only losing their support but also causing some legal problems. The next section describes various rights and duties pertaining to manufacturers and their channel members.

active example <

Consider how one prominent company evaluates its channel members.

[10]See James A. Narus and James C. Anderson, "Turn Your Industrial Distributors into Partners," *Harvard Business Review,* March–April 1986, pp. 66–71; Jan B. Heide, "Interorganizational Governance in Marketing Channels," *Journal of Marketing,* January 1994, pp. 71–85; Nirmalya Kumar, "The Power of Trust in Manufacturer–Retailer Relationships," *Harvard Business Review,* November–December 1996, pp. 92–106; James A. Narus and James C. Anderson, "Rethinking Distribution," *Harvard Business Review,* July–August 1996, pp. 112–20; and James C. Anderson and James A. Narus, *Business Market Management* (Upper Saddle River, NJ: Prentice Hall, 1999), pp. 276–88.

> **active concept check**
Now let's take a moment to test your knowledge of what you've just read.

> **Public Policy and Distribution Decisions**

For the most part, companies are legally free to develop whatever channel arrangements suit them. In fact, the laws affecting channels seek to prevent the exclusionary tactics of some companies that might keep another company from using a desired channel. Most channel law deals with the mutual rights and duties of the channel members once they have formed a relationship.

Many producers and wholesalers like to develop exclusive channels for their products. When the seller allows only certain outlets to carry its products, this strategy is called *exclusive distribution*. When the seller requires that these dealers not handle competitors' products, its strategy is called *exclusive dealing*. Both parties can benefit from exclusive arrangements: The seller obtains more loyal and dependable outlets, and the dealers obtain a steady source of supply and stronger seller support. But exclusive arrangements also exclude other producers from selling to these dealers. This situation brings exclusive dealing contracts under the scope of the Clayton Act of 1914. They are legal as long as they do not substantially lessen competition or tend to create a monopoly and as long as both parties enter into the agreement voluntarily.

Exclusive dealing often includes *exclusive territorial agreements*. The producer may agree not to sell to other dealers in a given area or the buyer may agree to sell only in its own territory. The first practice is normal under franchise systems as a way to increase dealer enthusiasm and commitment. It is also perfectly legal—a seller has no legal obligation to sell through more outlets than it wishes. The second practice, whereby the producer tries to keep a dealer from selling outside its territory, has become a major legal issue.

Producers of a strong brand sometimes sell it to dealers only if the dealers will take some or all of the rest of the line. This is called full-line forcing. Such *tying agreements* are not necessarily illegal, but they do violate the Clayton Act if they tend to lessen competition substantially. The practice may prevent consumers from freely choosing among competing suppliers of these other brands.

Finally, producers are free to select their dealers, but their right to terminate dealers is somewhat restricted. In general, sellers can drop dealers "for cause." However, they cannot drop dealers if, for example, the dealers refuse to cooperate in a doubtful legal arrangement, such as exclusive dealing or tying agreements.[11]

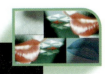

> **active example**
Consider some of the implications of distribution decisions for public policy.

> **active poll**
Give your opinion on a question concerning public policy and distribution decisions.

[11]For a full discussion of laws affecting marketing channels, see Stern, El-Ansary, and Coughlin, *Marketing Channels,* chap. 8.

> Physical Distribution and Logistics Management

In today's global marketplace, selling a product is sometimes easier than getting it to customers. Companies must decide on the best way to store, handle, and move their products and services so that they are available to customers in the right assortments, at the right time, and in the right place. Logistics effectiveness has a major impact on both customer satisfaction and company costs. Here we consider the *nature and importance of marketing logistics, goals of the logistics system, major logistics functions,* and the need for *integrated logistics management.*

NATURE AND IMPORTANCE OF PHYSICAL DISTRIBUTION AND MARKETING LOGISTICS

To some managers, physical distribution means only trucks and warehouses. But modern logistics is much more than this. **Physical distribution**—or **marketing logistics**—involves planning, implementing, and controlling the physical flow of materials, final goods, and related information from points of origin to points of consumption to meet customer requirements at a profit. In short, it involves getting the right product to the right customer in the right place at the right time.

Traditional physical distribution typically started with products at the plant and then tried to find low-cost solutions to get them to customers. However, today's marketers prefer *market logistics* thinking, which starts with the marketplace and works backward to the factory. Logistics addresses not only the problem of outbound distribution (moving products from the factory to customers) but also the problem of inbound distribution (moving products and materials from suppliers to the factory). It involves the management of entire *supply chains,* value-added flows from suppliers to final users, as shown in Figure 12.5. Thus, the logistics manager's task is to coordinate activities of suppliers, purchasing agents, marketers, channel members, and customers. These activities include forecasting, information systems, purchasing, production planning, order processing, inventory, warehousing, and transportation planning.

Companies today are placing greater emphasis on logistics for several reasons. First, customer service and satisfaction have become the cornerstones of marketing strategy, and distribution is an important customer service element. More and more, companies are finding that they can attract and keep customers by giving better service or lower prices through better physical distribution.

Second, logistics is a major cost element for most companies. According to one study, in a recent year American companies "spent $670 billion—a gaping 10.5 percent of gross domestic product—to wrap, bundle, load, unload, sort, reload, and transport goods."[12] About 15 percent of an average product's price is accounted for by shipping and transport alone. Poor physical distribution decisions result in high costs. Improvements in physical distribution efficiency can yield tremendous cost savings for both the company and its customers.

Third, the explosion in product variety has created a need for improved logistics management. For example, in 1911 the typical A&P grocery store carried only 270 items. The store manager could keep track of this inventory on about 10 pages of notebook paper stuffed in a shirt pocket. Today, the average A&P carries a bewildering stock of more than 16,700 items.[13] Ordering, shipping, stocking, and controlling such a variety of products presents a sizable logistics challenge.

Finally, improvements in information technology have created opportunities for major gains in distribution efficiency. The increased use of computers, point-of-sale scanners, uniform product codes, satellite tracking, electronic data interchange (EDI), and electronic funds transfer (EFT) has allowed companies to create advanced systems for order processing, inventory control and handling, and transportation routing and scheduling.

---

[12]Ronald Henkoff, "Delivering the Goods," *Fortune,* November 18, 1994, pp. 64–78. Also see Shlomo Maital, "The Last Frontier of Cost Reduction," *Across the Board,* February 1994, pp. 51–52.

[13]Maital, "The Last Frontier of Cost Reduction," p. 52.

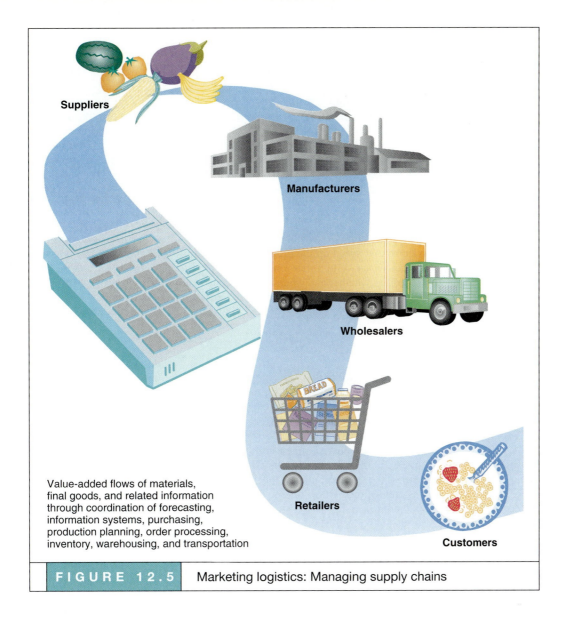

Suppliers

Manufacturers

Wholesalers

Retailers

Customers

Value-added flows of materials,
final goods, and related information
through coordination of forecasting,
information systems, purchasing,
production planning, order processing,
inventory, warehousing, and transportation

FIGURE 12.5 Marketing logistics: Managing supply chains

GOALS OF THE LOGISTICS SYSTEM

Some companies state their logistics objective as providing maximum customer service at the least cost. Unfortunately, no logistics system can *both* maximize customer service *and* minimize distribution costs. Maximum customer service implies rapid delivery, large inventories, flexible assortments, liberal returns policies, and other services—all of which raise distribution costs. In contrast, minimum distribution costs imply slower delivery, smaller inventories, and larger shipping lots—which represent a lower level of overall customer service.

The goal of the marketing logistics system should be to provide a targeted level of customer service at the least cost. A company must first research the importance of various distribution services to its customers and then set desired service levels for each segment. The company normally will want to offer at least the same level of service as its competitors do. But the objective is to maximize *profits,* not sales. Therefore, the company must weigh the benefits of providing higher levels of service against the costs. Some companies offer less service than their competitors and charge a lower price. Other companies offer more service and charge higher prices to cover higher costs.

MAJOR LOGISTICS FUNCTIONS

Given a set of logistics objectives, the company is ready to design a logistics system that will minimize the cost of attaining these objectives. The major logistics functions include *order processing, warehousing, inventory management*, and *transportation.*

Order Processing

Orders can be submitted in many ways—by mail or telephone, through salespeople, or via computer and EDI. In some cases, the suppliers might actually generate orders for their customers:

> One Kmart quick response program calls for selected suppliers to manage the retailer's inventory replenishment for their products. Kmart transmits daily records of product sales to the vendor, who analyzes the sales information, comes up with an order, and sends it back to Kmart through EDI. Once in Kmart's system, the order is treated as though Kmart itself created it. Says a Kmart executive, "We don't modify the order, and we don't question it. . . . Our relationship with those vendors is such that we trust them to create the type of order that will best meet our inventory needs."[14]

Once received, orders must be processed quickly and accurately. Both the company and its customers benefit when order processing is carried out efficiently. Most companies now use computerized order-processing systems that speed up the order–shipping–billing cycle. For example, General Electric operates a computer-based system that, on receipt of a customer's order, checks the customer's credit standing as well as whether and where the items are in stock. The computer then issues an order to ship, bills the customer, updates the inventory records, sends a production order for new stock, and relays the message back to the salesperson that the customer's order is on its way—all in less than 15 seconds.

Warehousing

Every company must store its goods while they wait to be sold. A storage function is needed because production and consumption cycles rarely match. For example, Snapper, Toro, and other lawn mower manufacturers must produce all year long and store up their product for the heavy spring and summer buying seasons. The storage function overcomes differences in needed quantities and timing.

A company must decide on *how many* and *what types* of warehouses it needs and *where* they will be located. The company might use either *storage warehouses* or *distribution centers*. Storage warehouses store goods for moderate to long periods. **Distribution centers** are designed to move goods rather than just store them. They are large and highly automated warehouses designed to receive goods from various plants and suppliers, take orders, fill them efficiently, and deliver goods to customers as quickly as possible. For example, Wal-Mart operates huge distribution centers. One center, which serves the daily needs of 165 Wal-Mart stores, contains some 28 acres of space under a single roof. Laser scanners route as many as 190,000 cases of goods per day along 11 miles of conveyer belts, and the center's 1,000 workers load or unload 310 trucks daily.[15]

Warehousing facilities and equipment technology have improved greatly in recent years. Older, multistoried warehouses with outdated materials-handling methods are facing competition from newer, single-storied *automated warehouses* with advanced materials-handling systems under the control of a central computer. In these warehouses, only a few employees are necessary. Computers read orders and direct lift trucks, electric hoists, or robots to gather goods, move them to loading docks, and issue invoices. These warehouses have reduced worker injuries, labor costs, theft, and breakage and have improved inventory control.

Inventory

Inventory levels also affect customer satisfaction. The major problem is to maintain the delicate balance between carrying too much inventory and carrying too little. Carrying too much inventory results in higher-than-necessary inventory-carrying costs and stock obsolesence. Carrying too little may result in stock outs, costly emergency shipments or production, and customer dissatisfaction. In making inventory decisions, management must balance the costs of carrying larger inventories against resulting sales and profits.

During the past decade, many companies have greatly reduced their inventories and related costs through *just-in-time* logistics systems. Through such systems, producers and retailers carry only small inventories of parts or merchandise, often only enough for a few days of operations. New stock arrives exactly when needed, rather than being stored in inventory until being used. Just-in-time systems require accurate forecasting along with fast, frequent, and flexible delivery so that new supplies

---

[14]See "Linking with Vendors for Just-in-Time Service," *Chain Store Age Executive,* June 1993, pp. 22A–24A; Ken Cottrill, "Reforging the Supply Chain," *The Journal of Business Strategy,* November–December 1997, pp. 35–39; and "Kmart to Outsource Most EDI Tasks," *Chain Store Age,* April 1998, pp. 74–76.

[15]John Huey, "Wal-Mart: Will It Take Over the World?" *Fortune,* January 30, 1989, pp. 52–64. Also see "Distribution Centers," *Chain Store Age,* October 1996, pp. 4–10.

will be available when needed. However, these systems result in substantial savings in inventory-carrying and handling costs.

Transportation

Marketers need to take an interest in their company's *transportation* decisions. The choice of transportation carriers affects the pricing of products, delivery performance, and condition of the goods when they arrive—all of which will affect customer satisfaction. In shipping goods to its warehouses, dealers, and customers, the company can choose among five transportation modes: rail, truck, water, pipeline, and air.

Railroads are the nation's largest carrier, accounting for 26 percent of total cargo ton-miles moved.[16] They are one of the most cost-effective modes for shipping large amounts of bulk products—coal, sand, minerals, farm and forest products—over long distances. In recent years, railroads have increased their customer services by designing new equipment to handle special categories of goods, providing flatcars for carrying truck trailers by rail (piggyback), and providing in-transit services such as the diversion of shipped goods to other destinations en route and the processing of goods en route. Thus, after decades of losing out to truckers, railroads appear ready for a comeback.[17]

Trucks have increased their share of transportation steadily and now account for 24 percent of total cargo ton-miles (over 52 percent of actual tonnage). They account for the largest portion of transportation *within* cities as opposed to *between* cities. Each year in the United States, trucks travel more than 600 billion miles—equal to nearly 1.3 million round trips to the moon—carrying 2.5 billion tons

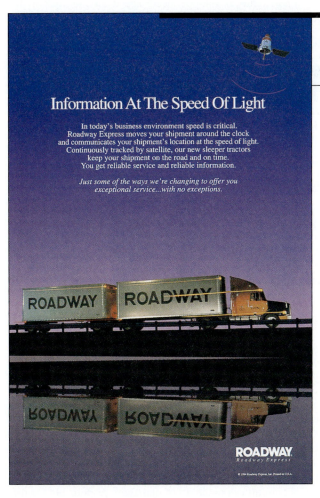

Roadway and other trucking firms have added many services in recent years, such as satellite tracking of shipments and sleeper tractors that keep freight moving around the clock.

---

[16]For statistics on freight shipments, see *Transportation Statistics Annual Report: 1998,* U.S. Department of Transportation, Bureau of Transportation Statistics, (Washington, DC: 1998). A copy can be obtained from www.fed-stats.gov.

[17]Shawn Tully, "Comeback Ahead for Railroads," *Fortune,* June 17, 1991, pp. 107–13; and Joseph Weber, "Highballing Toward Two Big Railroads," *Business Week,* March 17, 1997, pp. 32–33.

of freight.[18] Trucks are highly flexible in their routing and time schedules, and they can usually offer faster service than railroads. They are efficient for short hauls of high-value merchandise. Trucking firms have added many services in recent years. For example, Roadway Express now offers satellite tracking of shipments and sleeper tractors that move freight around the clock.

Water carriers transport large amounts of goods by ships and barges on U.S. coastal and inland waterways. Mississippi River barges alone account for 15 percent of the freight shipped in the United States. Although the cost of water transportation is very low for shipping bulky, low-value, nonperishable products such as sand, coal, grain, oil, and metallic ores, water transportation is the slowest mode and may be affected by the weather.

Pipelines are a specialized means of shipping petroleum, natural gas, and chemicals from sources to markets. Most pipelines are used by their owners to ship their own products.

Although *air* carriers transport less than 1 percent of the nation's goods, they are becoming more important as a transportation mode. Air freight rates are much higher than rail or truck rates, but air freight is ideal when speed is needed or distant markets have to be reached. Among the most frequently air-freighted products are perishables (fresh fish, cut flowers) and high-value, low-bulk items (technical instruments, jewelry). Companies find that air freight also reduces inventory levels, packaging costs, and the number of warehouses needed.

Shippers increasingly are using **intermodal transportation**—combining two or more modes of transportation. *Piggyback* describes the use of rail and trucks; *fishyback,* water and trucks; *trainship,* water and rail; and *airtruck,* air and trucks. Combining modes provides advantages that no single mode can deliver. Each combination offers advantages to the shipper. For example, not only is piggyback cheaper than trucking alone but it also provides flexibility and convenience.

In choosing a transportation mode for a product, shippers must balance many considerations: speed, dependability, availability, cost, and others. Thus, if a shipper needs speed, air and truck are the prime choices. If the goal is low cost, then water or pipeline might be best.

active example   <

Read more about an important player in the rail transportation industry: The Union Pacific Railroad.

INTEGRATED LOGISTICS MANAGEMENT

Today, more and more companies are adopting the concept of **integrated logistics management.** This concept recognizes that providing better customer service and trimming distribution costs requires *teamwork,* both inside the company and among all the marketing channel organizations. Inside, the company's various functional departments must work closely together to maximize the company's own logistics performance. Outside, the company must integrate its logistics system with those of its suppliers and customers to maximize the performance of the entire distribution system.

Cross-Functional Teamwork Inside the Company

In most companies, responsibility for various logistics activities is assigned to many different functional units—marketing, sales, finance, manufacturing, purchasing. Too often, each function tries to optimize its own logistics performance without regard for the activities of the other functions. However, transportation, inventory, warehousing, and order-processing activities interact, often in an inverse way. For example, lower inventory levels reduce inventory-carrying costs. But they may also reduce customer service and increase costs from stock outs, back orders, special production runs, and costly fast-freight shipments. Because distribution activities involve strong trade-offs, decisions by different functions must be coordinated to achieve superior overall logistics performance.

The goal of integrated logistics management is to harmonize all of the company's distribution decisions. Close working relationships among functions can be achieved in several ways. Some companies have created permanent logistics committees made up of managers responsible for different physical distribution activities. Companies can also create management positions that link the logistics activities of functional areas. For example, Procter & Gamble has created supply man-

---

[18]See "Trucking Deregulation: A Ten-Year Anniversary," *Fortune,* August 13, 1990, pp. 25–35; and Brian O'Reilly and Alicia Hills Moore, "On the Road Again," *Fortune,* April 27, 1998, pp. 182–95.

agers, who manage all of the supply chain activities for each of its product categories. Many companies have a vice president of logistics with cross-functional authority. The important thing is that the company coordinate its logistics and marketing activities to create high market satisfaction at a reasonable cost.

Building Channel Partnerships

The members of a distribution channel are linked closely in delivering customer satisfaction and value. One company's distribution system is another company's supply system. The success of each channel member depends on the performance of the entire supply chain. For example, Wal-Mart can charge the lowest prices at retail only if its entire supply chain—consisting of thousands of merchandise suppliers, transport companies, warehouses, and service providers—operates at maximum efficiency.

Companies must do more than improve their own logistics. They must also work with other channel members to improve whole-channel distribution. Today, smart companies are coordinating their logistics strategies and building strong partnerships with suppliers and customers to improve customer service and reduce channel costs.

These channel partnerships can take many forms. Many companies have created *cross-functional, cross-company teams.* For example, Procter & Gamble has a team of almost 100 people living in Bentonville, Arkansas, home of Wal-Mart. The P&Gers work with their counterparts at Wal-Mart to jointly find ways to squeeze costs out of their distribution system. Working together benefits not only P&G and Wal-Mart but also their final consumers. Haggar Apparel Company has a similar system called "multiple points of contact," in which a Haggar team works with JCPenney people at corporate, divisional, and store levels. As a result of this partnership, JCPenney now receives Haggar merchandise within 18 days of placing an order—10 days fewer than its next-best supplier. Haggar ships the merchandise "floor ready"—hangered and pretagged—reducing the time it takes JCPenney to move the stock from receiving docks to the sales floor from four days to just one.[19]

Other companies partner through *shared projects.* For example, many larger retailers are working closely with suppliers on in-store programs. Home Depot allows key suppliers to use its stores as a testing ground for new merchandising programs. The suppliers spend time at Home Depot stores watching how their product sells and how customers relate to it. They then create programs specially tailored to Home Depot and its customers. Western Publishing Group, publisher of "Little Golden Books" for children, formed a similar partnership with Toys "R" Us. Western and the giant toy retailer coordinated their marketing strategies to create minibookstore sections—called Books "R" Us—within each Toys "R" Us store. Toys "R" Us provides the locations, space, and customers; Western serves as distributor, consolidator, and servicer for the Books "R" Us program.[20] Clearly, both the supplier and customer benefit from such partnerships.

Channel partnerships may also take the form of *information sharing* and *continuous inventory replenishment* systems. Companies manage their supply chains through information. Suppliers link up with customers to share information and coordinate their logistics decisions. Here are just two examples:

> The Branded Apparel division of giant Sara Lee Corporation says that retailer Dayton Hudson's willingness to share information with suppliers separates this company from its competitors. Dayton's Global Merchandising System (GMS), its supply chain management system, consists of more than 60 applications, including forecasting, ordering, and trend analysis. A Dayton company, such as Target stores, can use GMS to order a certain number of sweatshirts from Sara Lee Branded Apparel without specifying more than style. As the delivery date draws near, Target analyzes trends for colors and sizes. Based on those forecasts, Sara Lee makes trial lots and Target starts to sell them. If customers buy more navy sweatshirts than initially predicted, Target adjusts its order. The result: Both Sara Lee and Target have fewer goods in inventory while at the same time doing a better job of meeting customer preferences, which in turn results in fewer markdowns.[21]

[19]See Sandra J. Skrovan, "Partnering with Vendors: The Ties That Bind," *Chain Store Age Executive,* January 1994, pp. 6MH–9MH; Robert D. Buzzell and Gwen Ortmeyer, "Channel Partnerships Streamline Distribution," *Sloan Management Review,* March 22, 1995, p. 85; and Ken Cottrill, "Reforging the Supply Chain," *The Journal of Business Strategy,* November–December 1997, pp. 35–39.

[20]Skrovan, "Partnering with Vendors," p. 6MH; and Susan Caminiti, "After You Win, the Fun Begins," *Fortune,* May 2, 1994, p. 76.

[21]Tom Stein and Jeff Sweat, "Killer Supply Chains—Six Companies Are Using Supply Chains to Transform the Way They Do Business," *Information Week,* November 11, 1998, p. 36.

Western Publishing Group partners with Toys "R" Us to create mini-bookstore sections—called Books "R" Us—within each store. Toys "R" Us provides the space and customers; Western serves as distributor and servicer for the Books "R" Us sections.

Bailey Controls, a manufacturer of control systems for big factories, from steel and paper mills to chemical and pharmaceutical plants, . . . treats some of its suppliers almost like departments of its own plants. Bailey has plugged two of its main electronics suppliers into itself. Future Electronics is hooked in through an electronic data interchange system. Every week, Bailey electronically sends Future its latest forecasts of what materials it will need for the next six months so that Future can stock up in time. Bailey itself stocks only enough inventory for a few days of operation, as opposed to the three or four months' worth it used to carry. Whenever a bin of parts falls below a designated level, a Bailey employee passes a laser scanner over the bin's bar code, instantly alerting Future to send the parts at once. Arrow Electronics . . . is plugged in even more closely: It has a warehouse in Bailey's factory, stocked according to Bailey's twice-a-month forecasts. Bailey provides the space, Arrow the warehouseman and the $500,000 of inventory.[22]

Today, as a result of such partnerships, many companies have switched from *anticipatory-based distribution systems* to *response-based distribution systems.*[23] In anticipatory distribution, the company produces the amount of goods called for by a sales forecast. It builds and holds stock at various supply points, such as the plant, distribution centers, and retail outlets. A response-based distribution system, in contrast, is *customer triggered.* The producer continuously builds and replaces stock as orders arrive. It produces what is currently selling. For example, Japanese carmakers take orders for cars, then produce and ship them within four days. Benetton, the Italian fashion house, uses a *quick-*

[22]Myron Magnet, "The New Golden Rule of Business," *Fortune,* February 21, 1994, pp. 60–64. For a related example, see Justin Martin, "Are You as Good as You Think You Are?" *Fortune,* September 1996, pp. 145–46.

[23]Based on an address by Professor Donald J. Bowersox at Michigan State University on August 5, 1992. For a general discussion of improving supply chain performance, see Marshall L. Fisher, "What Is the Right Supply Chain for Your Product?" *Harvard Business Review,* March–April 1997, pp. 105–16.

response system, dyeing its sweaters in the colors that are currently selling instead of trying to guess far in advance which colors people will want. Producing for order rather than for forecast substantially cuts down inventory costs and risks.

THIRD-PARTY LOGISTICS

Over 90 percent of U.S. businesses perform their own logistics functions. However, a growing number of firms now outsource some or all their logistics to **third-party logistics providers** such as Ryder Systems, UPS Worldwide Logistics, FedEx Logistics, Roadway Logistics Services, or Emory Global Logistics. Such integrated logistics companies perform any or all of the functions required to get their clients' product to market. For example, Emory's Global Logistics unit provides clients with coordinated, single-source logistics services including supply chain management, customized information technology, inventory control, warehousing, transportation management, customer service and fulfillment, and freight auditing and control. Last year, U.S. manufacturers and distributors spent more than $39 billion on third-party logistics (also called *outsourced logistics* or *contract logistics*) services, and the market is expected to grow by at least 20 percent per year through the year 2004.[24]

Companies may use third-party logistics providers for several reasons. First, because getting the product to market is their main focus, these providers can often do it more efficiently and at lower cost than clients whose strengths lie elsewhere. According to one study, outsourcing warehousing alone typically results in 10 percent to 15 percent cost savings. Another expert estimates that companies can save 15 percent to 25 percent in their total logistics costs by outsourcing.[25] Second, outsourcing logistics frees a company to focus more intensely on its core business. Finally, integrated logistics companies understand increasingly complex logistics environments. This can be especially helpful to companies attempting to expand their global market coverage. For example, companies

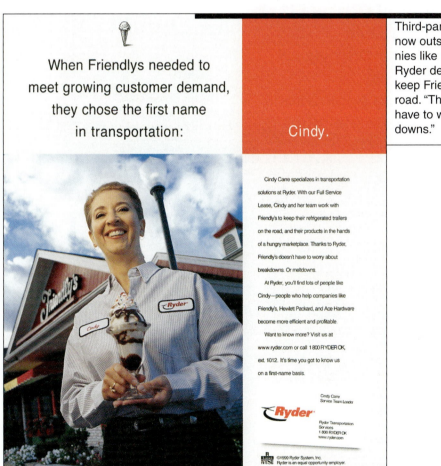

When Friendlys needed to meet growing customer demand, they chose the first name in transportation: Cindy.

Cindy Carre specializes in transportation solutions at Ryder. With our Full Service Lease, Cindy and her team work with Friendly's to keep their refrigerated trailers on the road, and their products in the hands of a hungry marketplace. Thanks to Ryder, Friendly's doesn't have to worry about breakdowns. Or meltdowns.

At Ryder, you'll find lots of people like Cindy—people who help companies like Friendly's, Hewlett Packard, and Ace Hardware become more efficient and profitable.

Want to know more? Visit us at www.ryder.com or call 1 800 RYDER OK ext. 1012. It's time you got to know us on a first-name basis.

Third-party logistics: Many companies are now outsourcing logistics tasks to companies like Ryder Integrated Logistics. Here, Ryder describes a system it designed to keep Friendly's refrigerated trucks on the road. "Thanks to Ryder, Friendly's doesn't have to worry about breakdowns. Or meltdowns."

[24]Brian Milligan, "New Study Says 3PL Services Keep Growing," *Purchasing,* June 3, 1999, pp. 89–90.

[25] See Martha Celestino, "Choosing a Third-Party Logistics Provider," *World Trade,* July 1999, pp. 54–56.

distributing their products across Europe face a bewildering array of environmental restrictions that affect logistics, including packaging standards, truck size and weight limits, and noise and emissions pollution controls. By outsourcing its logistics, a company can gain a complete pan-European distribution system without incurring the costs, delays, and risks associated with setting up its own system.[26]

active concept check   <

Now let's take a moment to test your knowledge of what you've just read.

> Chapter Wrap-Up

Now that you've reached the end of the chapter, you may wish to explore the concepts you've been reading about in greater detail, or test yourself to see how well you've comprehended the material. In the box below you'll find a number of links. Click on any one of these links to find additional chapter resources.

> end-of-chapter resources

- Review of Concept Connections
- Practice Quiz
- Issues for Discussion
- Key Terms
- Marketing Applications
- Internet Connections
- Company Case

[26]See Stern, El-Ansary, and Coughlin, *Marketing Channels,* p. 160; and Sandor Boyson, Thomas Corsi, Martin Dresner, and Elliott Rabinovich, "Managing Effective Third Party Logistics Relationships: What Does It Take?" *Journal of Business Logistics,* 20, no. 1, 1999, pp. 73–101.

C H A P T E R 13

Retailing and Wholesaling

> What's Ahead

Home Depot, the giant do-it-yourself home improvement retail chain, is one of the world's hottest retailers. It's one of a breed of retailers called *category killers*—giant retailers that offer a huge selection of merchandise in a single product category at such low prices that they destroy the competition. At first glance, a cavernous Home Depot store doesn't look like much. With its cement floors and drafty, warehouselike interior, the store offers all the atmosphere of an airplane hangar. But the chances are good that you'll find exactly what you're looking for, priced to make it a real value. Home Depot carries a huge assortment of more than 35,000 items—anything and everything related to home improvement. Its prices run 20 to 30 percent below those of local hardware stores.

Home Depot provides more than the right products at the right prices, however. Perhaps the best part of shopping at Home Depot is the high quality of its customer service. Home Depot is

more than just customer driven—it's customer *obsessed.* In the words of cofounder and chief executive Bernie Marcus, "All of our people understand what the Holy Grail is. It's not the bottom line. It's an almost blind, passionate commitment to taking care of customers." Arthur Blank, Home Depot's other cofounder and president, gives all new store managers the following six pieces of advice: "Serve the customer, serve the customer, serve the customer, serve the customer, serve the customer. And number 6, kick [butt]."

Bernie Marcus and Arthur Blank founded Home Depot with the simple mission of helping customers solve their home improvement problems. Their goal: "To take ham-handed homeowners who lack the confidence to do more than screw in a lightbulb and transform them into Mr. and Ms. Fixits." Accomplishing this mission takes more than simply peddling the store's products and taking the customers' money. It means building lasting customer relationships.

Bernie and Arthur understand the importance of customer satisfaction. They calculate that a satisfied customer is worth more than $25,000 in customer lifetime value ($38 per store visit, times 30 visits per year, times about 22 years of patronage). Customer satisfaction, in turn, results from interactions with well-trained, highly motivated employees who consistently provide good value and high-quality service. "The most important part of our formula," says Arthur, "is the quality of caring that takes place in our stores between the employee and the customer." Thus, at Home Depot, taking care of customers begins with taking care of employees.

Home Depot attracts the best salespeople by paying above-average salaries; then it trains them thoroughly. All employees take regular "product knowledge" classes to gain hands-on experience with problems customers will face. When it comes to creating customer value and satisfaction, Home Depot treats its employees as partners. All full-time employees receive at least 7 percent of their annual salary in company stock. As a result, Home Depot employees take ownership in the business of serving customers. Each employee wears a bright orange apron that says, "Hello, I'm _____ , a Home Depot stockholder. Let me help you."

Bernie and Arthur have become energetic crusaders in the cause of customer service. For example, four Sundays a year at 6:30 A.M., the two don their own orange aprons and air *Breakfast with Bernie and Art*—a good old-fashioned revival broadcast live over closed-circuit TV to the company's more than 100,000 employees nationwide. According to one account, "Bernie regularly rouses his disciples with the following: 'Where do you go if you want a job?' They yell back: 'Sears . . . Lowe's . . . Builders Square.' 'Where do you go if you want a *career?*' 'HOME DEPOT!' they roar. At times, when the excitement becomes feverish, Marcus has been known to grab a resisting Blank, plant a noisy kiss on his cheek, and exclaim, 'Arthur, I love you!'"

Home Depot avoids the high-pressure sales techniques used by some retailers. Instead, it encourages salespeople to build long-term relationships with customers—to spend whatever time it takes, visit after visit, to solve customer problems. Home Depot pays employees a straight salary so that they can spend as much time as necessary with customers without worrying about making the sale. Bernie Marcus declares, "The day I'm dead with an apple in my mouth is the day we'll pay commissions." In fact, rather than pushing customers to *overspend,* employees are trained to help customers spend *less* than they expected. "I love it when shoppers tell me they were prepared to spend $150 and our people showed them how to do the job for four or five bucks," says Bernie.

Home Depot has also extended its high-grade relationship-building efforts to the Internet. In addition to selling goods online, the company's Web site also offers plenty of how-to tips for household projects: how to fix it, build it, grow it, decorate it, or install it. It provides useful tools, such as calculators for figuring out how much paint or wallpaper is needed to cover a given amount of space. Home Depot also sends e-mail to regular site users alerting them to how-to workshops or other events at nearby stores.

Taking care of customers has made Home Depot one of today's most successful retailers. Founded in 1978, in little more than 20 years it has grown explosively to become the nation's largest do-it-yourself chain, with more than 820 stores reaping more than $30 billion in sales. Home Depot sales have grown 36 percent annually over the past decade, with 10-year average annual returns to shareholders of almost 45 percent. The company's stock price has rocketed up 28,000 percent—yes, 28,000 percent—since the company went public in 1981! In fact, a current problem in some stores is too many customers—some outlets are generating an astounding $600 of sales per square foot (compared with Wal-Mart at $250 and Kmart at $150). This has created problems with clogged aisles, stock outs, too few salespeople, and long checkout lines. Although many retailers would welcome this kind of problem, it bothers Bernie and Arthur greatly, and they've quickly taken corrective action. Continued success, they know, depends on the passionate pursuit of customer satisfaction. Bernie will tell you, "Every customer has to be treated like your mother, your father, your sister, or your brother." You certainly wouldn't want to keep your mother waiting in line.[1]

> objectives

Before you begin, take a moment to familiarize yourself with the key objectives of this chapter.

> gearing up

Before we begin our exploration this chapter, take a short warm-up test to see what you know about this topic.

[1]Quotes in this Home Depot tale are from Patricia Sellers, "Companies That Serve You Best," *Fortune,* May 31, 1993, pp. 74–88; and Patricia Sellers, "Can Home Depot Fix Its Sagging Stock?" *Fortune,* March 4, 1996, pp. 139–46. Also see Graham Button, "The Man Who Almost Walked Out on Ross Perot," *Forbes,* November 22, 1993, pp. 68–76; Roy S. Johnson, "Home Depot Renovates," *Fortune,* November 23, 1998, pp. 200–12; Thomas H. Nodine, "Home Depot's Leading Indicators of Value," *Harvard Business Review,* March–April 1999, p. 100; "Home Depot to Sell Wares on Site Beginning in the Fall," *Wall Street Journal,* June 30, 1999, p. A4; and Bernie Marcus, Arthur Blank, and Bob Andelman, *Built from Scratch: How a Couple of Regular Guys Grew the Home Depot from Nothing to $30 Billion* (New York: Random House, 1999).

The Home Depot story provides many insights into the workings of one of today's most successful retailers. This chapter looks at *retailing* and *wholesaling*. In the first section, we look at the nature and importance of retailing, major types of store and nonstore retailers, the decisions retailers make, and the future of retailing. In the second section, we discuss these same topics as they relate to wholesalers.

> Retailing

What is retailing? We all know that Wal-Mart, Sears, and Kmart are retailers, but so are Avon representatives, Amazon.com, the local Holiday Inn, and a doctor seeing patients. **Retailing** includes all the activities involved in selling goods or services directly to final consumers for their personal, non-business use. Many institutions—manufacturers, wholesalers, and retailers—do retailing. But most retailing is done by **retailers:** businesses whose sales come *primarily* from retailing.

Although most retailing is done in retail stores, in recent years *nonstore retailing* has been growing much faster than has store retailing. Nonstore retailing includes selling to final consumers through direct mail, catalogs, telephone, home TV shopping shows, home and office parties, door-to-door contact, vending machines, online services and the Internet, and other direct retailing approaches. We discuss such direct-marketing approaches in detail in chapter 17. In this chapter, we focus on store retailing.

> Types of Retailers

Retail stores come in all shapes and sizes, and new retail types keep emerging. The most important types of retail stores are described in Table 13.1 and discussed in the following sections. They can be classified in terms of several characteristics, including the *amount of service* they offer, the breadth and depth of their *product lines,* the *relative prices* they charge, and how they are organized.

AMOUNT OF SERVICE

Different products require different amounts of service, and customer service preferences vary. Retailers may offer one of three levels of service—self-service, limited service, and full service.

Self-service retailers serve customers who are willing to perform their own "locate-compare-select" process to save money. Self-service is the basis of all discount operations and is typically used by sellers of convenience goods (such as supermarkets) and nationally branded, fast-moving shopping goods (such as Best Buy or Service Merchandise).

Limited-service retailers, such as Sears or JCPenney, provide more sales assistance because they carry more shopping goods about which customers need information. Their increased operating costs result in higher prices. In *full-service retailers,* such as specialty stores and first-class department stores, salespeople assist customers in every phase of the shopping process. Full-service stores usually carry more specialty goods for which customers like to be "waited on." They provide more services resulting in much higher operating costs, which are passed along to customers as higher prices.

active example

> **Take a moment to consider the possible fate of customer service.**

PRODUCT LINE

Retailers also can be classified by the length and breadth of their product assortments. Some retailers, such as **specialty stores,** carry narrow product lines with deep assortments within those lines. Today, specialty stores are flourishing. The increasing use of market segmentation, market targeting, and product specialization has resulted in a greater need for stores that focus on specific products and segments.

In contrast, **department stores** carry a wide variety of product lines. In recent years, department stores have been squeezed between more focused and flexible specialty stores on the one hand, and more efficient, lower-priced discounters on the other. In response, many have added "bargain base-

TABLE 13.1 Major Types of Retailers

Type	Description	Examples
Specialty stores	Carry a narrow product line with a deep assortment within that line: apparel stores, sporting-goods stores, furniture stores, florists, and bookstores. Specialty stores can be subclassified by the degree of narrowness in their product line. A clothing store would be a *single-line store*; a men's clothing store would be a *limited-line store*; and a men's custom-shirt store would be a *superspecialty store*.	Athlete's Foot (sport shoes only), Tall Men (tall men's clothing), The Limited (women's clothing), The Body Shop (cosmetics and bath supplies)
Department stores	Carry several product lines—typically clothing, home furnishings, and household goods—with each line operated as a separate department managed by specialist buyers or merchandisers.	Sears, Saks Fifth Avenue, Marshall Fields, May's, JCPenney, Nordstrom, Macy's
Supermarkets	Relatively large, low-cost, low-margin, high-volume, self-service operations designed to serve the consumers total needs for food, laundry, and household maintenance products.	Safeway, Kroger, A&P, Winn-Dixie, Publix, Food Lion, Vons, Jewel
Convenience stores	Relatively small stores that are located near residential areas, open long hours seven days a week, and carry a limited line of high-turnover convenience products. Their long hours and their use by consumers mainly for "fill-in" purchases make them relatively high-price operations.	7-Eleven, Circle K, Stop-N-Go, White Hen Pantry
Superstores	Larger stores that aim at meeting consumers' total needs for routinely purchased food and nonfood items. They include *supercenters*, combined supermarket and discount stores, which feature cross-merchandising. They also include so-called *category killers* that carry a very deep assortment of a particular line. Another superstore variation is *hypermarkets*, huge stores that combine supermarket, discount, and warehouse retailing to sell routinely purchased goods as well as furniture, large and small appliances, clothing, and many other items.	*Supercenters:* Wal-Mart Supercenters, and Super Kmart Centers; *Category killers:* Toys "R" Us (toys), Petsmart (pet supplies), Staples (office supplies), Home Depot (home improvements), Best Buy (consumer electronics); *Hypermarkets:* Carrefour (France), Pyrca (Spain), Meijer's (Netherlands)
Discount stores	Sell standard merchandise at lower prices by accepting lower margins and selling higher volumes. A true discount store *regularly* sells its merchandise at lower prices, offering mostly national brands, not inferior goods. Discount retailers include both general merchandise and specialty merchandise stores.	*General discount stores:* Wal-Mart, Kmart, Target; *Specialty discount stores:* Circuit City (electronics), Crown Book (books)
Off-price retailers	Sell a changing and unstable collection of higher-quality merchandise, often leftover goods, overruns, and irregulars obtained at reduced prices from manufacturers or other retailers. They buy at less-than-regular wholesale prices and charge consumers less than retail. They include three main types:	
Independent off-price retailers	Owned and run either by entrepreneurs or by divisions of larger retail corporations.	T.J. Maxx, Filene's Basement, Loehmann's, Hit or Miss
Factory outlets	Owned and operated by manufacturers and normally carry the manufacturer's surplus, discontinued, or irregular goods. Such outlets increasingly group together in *factory outlet malls*, where dozens of outlet stores offer prices as much as 50 percent below retail on a broad range of items.	Mikasa (dinnerware), Dexter (shoes), Ralph Lauren and Liz Claiborne (upscale apparel)
Warehouse clubs (or wholesale clubs)	Sell a limited selection of brand-name grocery items, appliances, clothing, and a hodgepodge of other goods at deep discounts to members who pay $25 to $50 annual membership fees. They serve small businesses and other club members out of huge, low-overhead, warehouselike facilities and offer few frills or services.	Wal-Mart-owned Sam's Club, Costco, BJ's Wholesale Club

ments" and promotional events to meet the discount threat. Others have set up store brand programs, "boutiques" and "designer shops" (such as Tommy Hilfiger or Polo shops within department stores), and other store formats that compete with specialty stores. Still others are trying mail-order, telephone, and Web site selling. Service remains the key differentiating factor. Department stores such as Nordstrom, Saks, Neiman Marcus, and other high-end department stores are doing well by emphasizing high-quality service.

Supermarkets are the most frequently shopped type of retail store. Today, however, they are facing slow sales growth because of slower population growth and an increase in competition from convenience stores, discount food stores, and superstores. Supermarkets also have been hit hard by the rapid growth of out-of-home eating. Thus, most supermarkets are making improvements to attract more customers. In the battle for "share of stomachs," most large supermarkets have moved upscale, providing from-scratch bakeries, gourmet deli counters, and fresh seafood departments. Others are cutting costs, establishing more efficient operations, and lowering prices in order to compete more effectively with food discounters.

Convenience stores are small stores that carry a limited line of high-turnover convenience goods. In the 1990s, the convenience store industry suffered from overcapacity as its primary market of young, blue-collar men shrunk. As a result, many chains have redesigned their stores with female customers in mind. They are dropping the image of a "truck stop" where men go to buy beer, cigarettes, and magazines, and instead offer fresh, prepared foods and cleaner, safer environments. Many convenience chains also are experimenting with micromarketing—tailoring each store's merchandise to the specific needs of its surrounding neighborhood. For example, a Stop-N-Go in an affluent neighborhood carries fresh produce, gourmet pasta sauces, chilled Evian water, and expensive wines. Stop-N-Go stores in Hispanic neighborhoods carry Spanish-language magazines and other goods catering to the specific needs of Hispanic consumers.[2]

Superstores are much larger than regular supermarkets and offer a large assortment of routinely purchased food products, nonfood items, and services. Examples include Safeway's Pak 'N Pay and Pathmark Super Centers. Wal-Mart, Kmart, and other discount retailers are now opening *supercenters,* combination food and discount stores that emphasize cross-merchandising. For example, at a Super Kmart Center, toasters are above the fresh-baked bread, kitchen gadgets are across from produce, and infant centers carry everything from baby food to clothing. Supercenters are growing in the United States at an annual rate of 25 percent, compared with a supermarket industry growth rate of only 1 percent. Wal-Mart, which opened its first supercenter in 1988, had opened more than 700 such stores by 2000, capturing almost two-thirds of all supercenter volume. By 2005, the retailing giant will likely be operating 1,200 to 1,500 supercenters.[3]

Recent years have also seen the explosive growth of superstores that are actually giant specialty stores, the so-called **category killers.** They feature stores the size of airplane hangers that carry a very deep assortment of a particular line with a knowledgeable staff. Category killers are prevalent in a wide range of categories, including books, baby gear, toys, electronics, home improvement products, linens and towels, party goods, sporting goods, even pet supplies. Another superstore variation, *hypermarkets,* are huge superstores, perhaps as large as *six* football fields. Although hypermarkets have been very successful in Europe and other world markets, they have met with little success in the United States.

Finally, for some retailers, the product line is actually a service. Service retailers include hotels and motels, banks, airlines, colleges, hospitals, movie theaters, tennis clubs, bowling alleys, restaurants, repair services, hair care shops, and dry cleaners. Service retailers in the United States are growing faster than product retailers.

RELATIVE PRICES

Retailers can also be classified according to the prices they charge. Most retailers charge regular prices and offer normal-quality goods and customer service. Others offer higher-quality goods and service at higher prices. The retailers that feature low prices are discount stores, "off-price" retailers, and catalog showrooms (see Table 13.1).

---

[2] See "Stop-N-Go Micromarkets New Upscale Mix," *Chain Store Age Executive,* January 1990, p. 145; Matt Nannery, "Convenience Stores Get Fresh," *Chain Store Age,* August 1996, pp. 18A–19A; Wendy Zellner, "How Classy Can 7-Eleven Get?" *Business Week,* September 1, 1997, pp. 74–75; and "Convenience Stores," *Chain Store Age,* January 1998, pp. 8A–9A.

[3] "Traditional Discount Stores Take a Back Seat to Supercenters," *Discount Store News,* March 3, 1997, p. 43; and Laura Liebeck, "After a Long Warm-Up, Large Units Ready to Race," *Discount Store News,* June 7, 1999, pp. 89, 128.

Discount Stores

A **discount store** sells standard merchandise at lower prices by accepting lower margins and selling higher volume. The early discount stores cut expenses by offering few services and operating in warehouselike facilities in low-rent, heavily traveled districts. In recent years, facing intense competition from other discounters and department stores, many discount retailers have "traded up." They have improved decor, added new lines and services, and opened suburban branches, which have led to higher costs and prices.

Off-Price Retailers

When the major discount stores traded up, a new wave of **off-price retailers** moved in to fill the low-price, high-volume gap. Ordinary discounters buy at regular wholesale prices and accept lower margins to keep prices down. In contrast, off-price retailers buy at less-than-regular wholesale prices and charge consumers less than retail. Off-price retailers can be found in all areas, from food, clothing, and electronics to no-frills banking and discount brokerages.

The three main types of off-price retailers are *independents, factory outlets,* and *warehouse clubs*. **Independent off-price retailers** are either owned and run by entrepreneurs or are divisions of larger retail corporations. Although many off-price operations are run by smaller independents, most large off-price retailer operations are owned by bigger retail chains. Examples include Loehmann's (owned by Associated Dry Goods, owner of Lord & Taylor), Filene's Basement (Federated Department Stores), and T.J. Maxx (TJX Cos).

Factory outlets—such as the Burlington Coat Factory Warehouse, Manhattan's Brand Name Fashion Outlet, and the factory outlets of Levi-Strauss, Carters, and Ship 'n' Shore—sometimes group together in *factory outlet malls* and *value-retail centers,* where dozens of outlet stores offer prices as low as 50 percent below retail on a wide range of items. Whereas outlet malls consist primarily of manufacturers' outlets, value-retail centers combine manufacturers' outlets with off-price retail stores and department store clearance outlets. Factory outlet malls have become one of the hottest growth areas in retailing.

The malls now are moving upscale, narrowing the gap between factory outlets and more traditional forms of retailers. As the gap narrows, the discounts offered by outlets are getting smaller. However, a growing number of factory outlets now feature brands such as Coach, Esprit, Liz Claiborne, Calvin Klein, and Nike, causing department stores to protest to the manufacturers of these brands. Given their higher costs, the department stores have to charge more than the off-price outlets. Manufacturers counter that they send last year's merchandise and seconds to the factory outlet malls, not the new merchandise that they supply to the department stores. The malls are also located far from urban areas, making travel to them more difficult. Still, the department stores are concerned about the growing number of shoppers willing to make weekend trips to stock up on branded merchandise at substantial savings.[4]

Warehouse clubs (or *wholesale clubs,* or *membership warehouses*), such as Sam's Club and Costco, operate in huge, drafty, warehouselike facilities and offer few frills. Customers themselves must wrestle furniture, heavy appliances, and other large items to the checkout line. Such clubs make no home deliveries and accept no credit cards, but they do offer rock-bottom prices. Warehouse clubs took the country by storm in the 1980s, but growth slowed considerably in the 1990s as a result of growing competition among warehouse store chains and effective reactions by supermarkets and discount stores.[5]

> **video example**

Consider how firms could classify their competitors into different retail categories.

---

[4]See Duke Ratliff, "Evolution of Off-Price Retailers," *Discount Merchandising,* March 1996, pp. 22–30; Roberta Maynard, "A Growing Outlet for Small Firms," *Nation's Business,* August 1996, pp. 45–48; Charles V. Bagli, "Discount Mania," *New York Times,* April 5, 1998, p. 12; and Howard Banks, "The Malling of Europe," *Forbes,* February 22, 1999, p. 66.

[5]"Warehouse Clubs Experience Renewed Sales Growth," *Discount Store News,* March 9, 1998, pp. 7, 10; Robert Scally, "Costco Ready to Grow Clubs and Expand Private Label," *Discount Store News,* February 8, 1999, pp. 1, 72; and Laura Liebeck, "New Leader Hopes to Take Member Club Out of Middle Ground," *Discount Store News,* June 7, 1999, pp. 92, 139.

RETAIL ORGANIZATIONS

Although many retail stores are independently owned, an increasing number are banding together under some form of corporate or contractual organization. The major types of retail organizations—*corporate chains, voluntary chains* and *retailer cooperatives, franchise organizations,* and *merchandising conglomerates*—are described in Table 13.2.

Chain stores are two or more outlets that are commonly owned and controlled. They have many advantages over independents. Their size allows them to buy in large quantities at lower prices. They can afford to hire corporate-level specialists to deal with areas such as pricing, promotion, merchandising, inventory control, and sales forecasting. Corporate chains gain promotional economies because their advertising costs are spread over many stores and over a large sales volume.

The great success of corporate chains caused many independents to band together in one of two forms of contractual associations. One is the *voluntary chain*—a wholesaler-sponsored group of independent retailers that engages in group buying and common merchandising. The other form of contractual association is the *retailer cooperative*—a group of independent retailers that bands together to set up a jointly owned, central wholesale operation and conducts joint merchandising and promotion efforts. These organizations give independents the buying and promotion economies they need to meet the prices of corporate chains.

Another form of contractual retail organization is a **franchise.** The main difference between franchise organizations and other contractual systems (voluntary chains and retail cooperatives) is that franchise systems are normally based on some unique product or service; on a method of doing business; or on the trade name, goodwill, or patent that the franchiser has developed. Franchising has been prominent in fast foods, video stores, health or fitness centers, haircutting, auto rentals, motels, travel agencies, real estate, and dozens of other product and service areas.

TABLE 13.2	Major Types of Retail Organizations	
Type	**Description**	**Examples**
Corporate chain stores	Two or more outlets that are commonly owned and controlled, employ central buying and merchandising, and sell similar lines of merchandise. Corporate chains appear in all types of retailing, but they are strongest in department stores, variety stores, food stores, drugstores, shoe stores, and women's clothing stores.	Tower Records, CVS Pharmacy, Pottery Barn (dinnerware and home furnishings)
Voluntary chains	Wholesaler-sponsored groups of independent retailers engaged in bulk buying and common merchandising.	Independent Grocers Alliance (IGA), Sentry Hardwares, Western Auto, True Value
Retailer cooperatives	Groups of independent retailers who set up a central buying organization and conduct joint promotion efforts.	Associated Grocers (groceries), ACE (hardware)
Franchise organizations	Contractual association between a *franchiser* (a manufacturer, wholesaler, or service organization) and *franchisees* (independent businesspeople who buy the right to own and operate one or more units in the franchise system). Franchise organizations are normally based on some unique product, service, or method of doing business, or on a trade name or patent, or on goodwill that the franchiser has developed.	McDonald's, Subway, Pizza Hut, Jiffy Lube, Meineke Mufflers, 7-Eleven
Merchandising conglomerates	A free-form corporation that combines several diversified retailing lines and forms under central ownership, along with some integration of their distribution and management functions.	Dayton-Hudson, the Venator Group

> ## active exercise

Consider some issues raised by the growth of franchise ownership.

Finally, *merchandising conglomerates* are corporations that combine several different retailing forms under central ownership. Examples include Dayton-Hudson, JCPenney, and the Venator Group. For example, Dayton-Hudson operates Target (upscale discount stores), Mervyn's (middle-market apparel and soft goods), and three department stores—Dayton's, Hudson's, and Marshall Fields. The Venator Group owns numerous specialty chains, including Foot Locker, Northern Reflections, Champs Sports, Afterthoughts (targeting American teenage girls), Eastbay (catalog and online sales), and a dozen others. Diversified retailing, which provides superior management systems and economies that benefit all the separate retail operations, is likely to increase in the new millennium.

> ## active concept check

Now let's take a moment to test your knowledge of what you've just read.

> ## Retailer Marketing Decisions

Retailers are searching for new marketing strategies to attract and hold customers. In the past, retailers attracted customers with unique products, more or better services than their competitors offered, or credit cards. Today, national-brand manufacturers, in their drive for volume, have placed their branded goods everywhere. Thus, stores offer more similar assortments—national brands are found not only in department stores but also in mass-merchandise and off-price discount stores. As a result, stores are looking more and more alike.

Service differentiation among retailers has also eroded. Many department stores have trimmed their services, whereas discounters have increased theirs. Customers have become smarter and more price sensitive. They see no reason to pay more for identical brands, especially when service differences are shrinking. For all these reasons, many retailers today are rethinking their marketing strategies.

As shown in Figure 13.1, retailers face major marketing decisions about their *target markets* and *positioning, product assortment and services, price, promotion,* and *place.*

TARGET MARKET AND POSITIONING DECISION

Retailers first must define their target markets and then decide how they will position themselves in these markets. Should the store focus on upscale, midscale, or downscale shoppers? Do target shop-

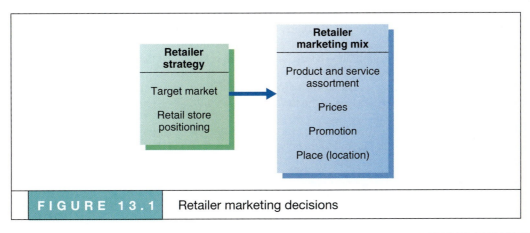

FIGURE 13.1 Retailer marketing decisions

pers want variety, depth of assortment, convenience, or low prices? Until they define and profile their markets, retailers cannot make consistent decisions about product assortment, services, pricing, advertising, store decor, or any of the other decisions that must support their positions.

Too many retailers fail to define their target markets and positions clearly. They try to have "something for everyone" and end up satisfying no market well. In contrast, successful retailers define their target markets well and position themselves strongly. For example, in 1963, Leslie H. Wexner borrowed $5,000 from his aunt to create *The Limited,* which started as a single store targeted to young, fashion-conscious women. All aspects of the store—clothing assortment, fixtures, music, colors, personnel—were orchestrated to match the target consumer. He continued to open more stores, but a decade later his original customers were no longer in the "young" group. To catch the new "youngs," he started the Limited Express. Over the years, he has started or acquired other highly targeted store chains, including Lane Bryant, Victoria's Secret, Lerner, Express, Structure, Bath & Body Works, and others to reach new segments. Today The Limited, Inc. operates more than 5,300 stores in several different segments of the market, with sales of almost $10 billion.[6]

Even large stores such as Wal-Mart, Sears, Kmart, and Target must define their major target markets in order to design effective marketing strategies. In fact, in recent years, thanks to strong targeting and positioning, Wal-Mart has zoomed past Sears and Kmart to become the world's largest retailer. How can any discounter hope to compete with the likes of huge and dominating Wal-Mart? Again, the answer is good targeting and positioning. For example, rather than facing Wal-Mart head-on, Target aims for a seemingly oxymoronic niche—the "upscale discount" segment.

Target—or Tar-*zhay* as many fans call it—has developed its own distinct interpretation of the discount retailing. "Going to Target is a cool experience, and everybody now considers it cool to save money," says one retailing consultant. "On the other hand, is it cool to save at Kmart, at Wal-Mart? I don't think so." Wal-Mart and other rival "marts" achieve growth with expanded stores, inventory prowess, and rock-bottom prices. But Target isn't Wal-Mart, the giant that wooed suburbia with its acres of guns and gummy bears. And it definitely isn't Kmart, which still seems downscale despite its Martha Stewart tea-towel sets. Target's aim is more subtle: Stick to low prices, of course, but rise above the discount fray with upmarket style and design and higher-grade service. In other words, price like a discounter, but don't think like one. Target's ability to position itself as an upscale alternative really separates it from its mass-merchant peers. The payoff is that Target's "expect more, pay less" creed is appealing to more affluent consumers than those frequenting other discounters. The chain's average customer is typically female, 40, and college educated, with a household income approaching $50,000. On average, Target customers spend $40 a visit, almost twice that of other mass merchants. With nearly 1,000 stores nationwide, Target accounted for an impressive 75 percent of parent company Dayton-Hudson's sales and earnings. "People used to say, 'Ooh, a Nordstrom's coming to town,' " says another consultant. "Those same people now say, 'Ooh, we're getting a Target!' "[7]

PRODUCT ASSORTMENT AND SERVICES DECISION

Retailers must decide on three major product variables: *product assortment, services mix,* and *store atmosphere.*

The retailer's *product assortment* should match target shoppers' expectations. In its quest to differentiate itself from competitors, a retailer can use any of several product-differentiation strategies. For one, it can offer merchandise that no other competitor carries—its own private brands or national brands on which it holds exclusives. For example, The Limited designs most of the clothes carried by its store and Saks gets exclusive rights to carry a well-known designer's labels. Second, the retailer can feature blockbuster merchandising events—Bloomingdale's is known for running spectacular shows featuring goods from a certain country, such as India or China. Or the retailer can offer surprise merchandise, as when Loehmann's offers surprise assortments of seconds, overstocks, and closeouts. Finally, the retailer can differentiate itself by offering a highly targeted product assortment—Lane Bryant carries goods in larger sizes; Brookstone offers an unusual assortment of gadgets in what amounts to an adult toy store.

Retailers also must decide on a *services mix* to offer customers. The old mom-and-pop grocery stores offered home delivery, credit, and conversation—services that today's supermarkets ignore.

---

[6]Rebecca Quick, "Limited to Spin Off Chain as It Disposes of Its Noncore Businesses," *Wall Street Journal,* May 4, 1999, p. B10; and information accessed online from www.limited.com, February 2000.

[7]Based on Shelly Branch, "How Target Got Hot," *Fortune,* May 24, 1999, pp. 169–74.

Target—or Tar-zhay as many fans call it—has developed its own distinct positioning as an "upscale discounter." Its trendy ads appeal to more affluent consumers who spend more than twice as much per visit as those frequenting other discounters. Its familiar bulls-eye design is a registered trademark.

The services mix is one of the key tools of nonprice competition for setting one store apart from another.

The *store's atmosphere* is another element in its product arsenal. Every store has a physical layout that makes moving around in it either hard or easy. Each store has a "feel"; one store is cluttered, another charming, a third plush, a fourth somber. The store must have a planned atmosphere that suits the target market and moves customers to buy.

> video example

Watch how a company approaches the issue of store layout and atmosphere.

Increasingly, retailers are turning their stores into theaters that transport customers into unusual, exciting shopping environments. For example, Barnes & Noble uses atmospherics to turn shopping for books into entertainment. It has found that "to consumers, shopping is a social activity. They do it to mingle with others in a prosperous-feeling crowd, to see what's new, to enjoy the theatrical dazzle of the display, to treat themselves to something interesting or unexpected." Thus, Barnes & Noble stores are designed with "enough woody, traditional, soft-colored library touches to please book lovers; enough sophisticated modern architecture and graphics, sweeping vistas, and stylish displays to satisfy fans of the theater of consumption. And for everyone, plenty of space, where they can meet other people and feel at home. . . . [Customers] settle in at heavy chairs and tables to browse through piles of books; they fill the cafes [designed] to increase the festivities. . . ." As one Barnes & Noble executive notes: "The feel-good part of the store, the quality of life contribution, is a big part of the success."[8]

[8]Myron Magnet, "Let's Go for Growth," *Fortune,* March 7, 1994, pp. 60–72. Also see Dierdre Donahue, "Bookstores: A Haven for the Intellect," *USA Today,* July 10, 1997, pp. D1, D2; and Christina Nifong, "Beyond Browsing," *Raleigh News & Observer,* May 25, 1999, p. E1.

Perhaps the most dramatic conversion of stores into theater is the Mall of America near Minneapolis. Containing more than 500 specialty stores, the mall is a veritable playground. Under a single roof, it shelters a seven-acre Knott's Berry Farm amusement park featuring 23 rides and attractions, an ice-skating rink, an Underwater World featuring hundreds of marine specimens and a dolphin show, and a two-story miniature golf course. One of the stores, Oshman Supersports USA, features a basketball court, a boxing gym, a baseball batting cage, a 50-foot archery range, and a simulated ski slope.[9]

All of this confirms that retail stores are much more than simply assortments of goods. They are environments to be experienced by the people who shop in them. Store atmospheres offer a powerful tool by which retailers can differentiate their stores from those of competitors.

PRICE DECISION

A retailer's price policy is a crucial positioning factor and must be decided in relation to its target market, its product and service assortment, and its competition. All retailers would like to charge high markups and achieve high volume, but the two seldom go together. Most retailers seek *either* high markups on lower volume (most specialty stores) *or* low markups on higher volume (mass merchandisers and discount stores). Thus, Bijan's on Rodeo Drive in Beverly Hills prices men's suits starting at $1,000 and shoes at $400—it sells a low volume but makes a hefty profit on each sale. At the other extreme, T.J. Maxx sells brand-name clothing at discount prices, settling for a lower margin on each sale but selling at a much higher volume.

PROMOTION DECISION

Retailers use the normal promotion tools—advertising, personal selling, sales promotion, public relations, and direct marketing—to reach consumers. They advertise in newspapers, magazines, radio, and television. Advertising may be supported by newspaper inserts and direct-mail pieces. Personal selling requires careful training of salespeople in how to greet customers, meet their needs, and handle their complaints. Sales promotions may include in-store demonstrations, displays, contests, and visiting celebrities. Public relations activities, such as press conferences and speeches, store openings, special events, newsletters, magazines, and public service activities, are always available to retailers. Many retailers have also set up Web sites, offering customers information and other features and sometimes selling merchandise directly.

PLACE DECISION

Retailers often cite three critical factors in retailing success: *location, location,* and *location*! A retailer's location is key to its ability to attract customers. The costs of building or leasing facilities have a major impact on the retailer's profits. Thus, site-location decisions are among the most important the retailer makes. Small retailers may have to settle for whatever locations they can find or afford. Large retailers usually employ specialists who select locations using advanced methods. Two of the savviest location experts in recent years have been the off-price retailer T.J. Maxx and toy-store giant Toys "R" Us. Both put the majority of their new locations in rapidly growing areas where the population closely matches their customer base. The undisputed winner in the "place race" has been Wal-Mart, whose strategy of being the first mass merchandiser to locate in small and rural markets was one of the key factors in its phenomenal early success.

active example   <

Take a moment to read more about retail location decisions.

Most stores today cluster together to increase their customer pulling power and to give consumers the convenience of one-stop shopping. *Central business districts* were the main form of retail cluster until the 1950s. Every large city and town had a central business district with department stores, specialty stores, banks, and movie theaters. When people began to move to the sub-

---

[9]"It's Not Just a Mall. It's Mallville, U.S.A.," *New York Times Magazine,* February 8, 1998, p. 19; Kristen Ostendorf, "Not Wed to Tradition," Gannett News Service, January 5, 1998; and "The History of Mall of America," www.mallofamerica.com, February 2000.

urbs, however, these central business districts, with their traffic, parking, and crime problems, began to lose business. Downtown merchants opened branches in suburban shopping centers, and the decline of the central business districts continued. In recent years, many cities have joined with merchants to try to revive downtown shopping areas by building malls and providing underground parking.

A **shopping center** is a group of retail businesses planned, developed, owned, and managed as a unit. A *regional shopping center,* the largest and most dramatic shopping center, contains from 40 to over 200 stores. It is like a covered minidowntown and attracts customers from a wide area. A *community shopping center* contains between 15 and 40 retail stores. It normally contains a branch of a department store or variety store, a supermarket, specialty stores, professional offices, and sometimes a bank. Most shopping centers are *neighborhood shopping centers* or *strip malls* that generally contain between 5 and 15 stores. They are close and convenient for consumers. They usually contain a supermarket, perhaps a discount store, and several service stores—dry cleaner, self-service laundry, drugstore, video-rental outlet, barber or beauty shop, hardware store, or other stores.

Combined, all shopping centers now account for about one-third of all retail sales, but they may have reached their saturation point. Through the past decade, on average, consumers have been going to traditional malls less often, staying a shorter period of time, and visiting fewer stores. Why are people using shopping malls less? First, with more dual-income households, people have less time to shop. "You have two workers in every family and no one has time to go to the mall for four hours anymore," observes one industry analyst. "People who used to go to the mall 20 times a year now go two or three times."[10]

Second, shoppers appear to be tiring of traditional malls, which are too big, too crowded, and too much alike. Today's large malls offer great selection but are less comfortable and convenient. Finally, today's consumers have many alternatives to traditional malls, ranging from online shopping to so-called *power centers.* These huge unenclosed shopping centers consist of a long strip of retail stores, including large, free-standing anchors such as Wal-Mart, Home Depot, Best Buy, Michaels, OfficeMax, and CompUSA. Each store has its own entrance with parking directly in front for shoppers who wish to visit only one store. Power centers have increased rapidly during the past few years to challenge traditional indoor malls. "Malls have been hit hard by competition from street shopping and from recent retail innovations—especially power centers," concludes the analyst. "And . . . malls in the same city may no longer be differentiated by their anchors; they seem to have the same stores. Add to all this the emergence of Internet shopping, and the concept of the shopping mall is beginning to look dated."[11] Thus, despite the recent development of many new "megamalls," such as the spectacular Mall of America, the current trend is toward value-oriented outlet malls, power centers, and smaller malls located in medium-size and smaller cities in fast-growing areas such as the Southwest.

Shopping centers: The spectacular Mall of America contains more than 500 stores, 45 restaurants, 7 theaters, and a 7-acre indoor theme park. It attracts more than 35 million visitors a year.

[10]Steven Bergsman, "Slow Times at Sherman Oaks: What's Ailing the Big Malls of America?" *Barron's,* May 17, 1999, p. 39.

[11]Ibid., p. 39.

active exercise   <

Consider how one company has tried to reshape the experience of the shopping.

active concept check   <

Now let's take a moment to test your knowledge of what you've just read.

> ## The Future of Retailing

Retailers operate in a harsh and fast-changing environment, which offers threats as well as opportunities. For example, the industry suffers from chronic overcapacity, resulting in fierce competition for customer dollars. Consumer demographics, lifestyles, and shopping patterns are changing rapidly, as are retailing technologies. To be successful, then, retailers will have to choose target segments carefully and position themselves strongly. They will have to take the following retailing developments into account as they plan and execute their competitive strategies.

NEW RETAIL FORMS AND SHORTENING RETAIL LIFE CYCLES

New retail forms continue to emerge to meet new situations and consumer needs, but the life cycle of new retail forms is getting shorter. Department stores took about 100 years to reach the mature stage of the life cycle; more recent forms, such as warehouse stores, reached maturity in about 10 years. In such an environment, seemingly solid retail positions can crumble quickly. Of the top 10 discount retailers in 1962 (the year that Wal-Mart and Kmart began), not one still exists today.

Consider the Price Club, the original warehouse store chain. When Sol Price opened his first warehouse store outside San Diego in 1976, he launched a retailing revolution. Selling everything from tires and office supplies to five-pound tubs of peanut butter at superlow prices, his store chain was generating $2.6 billion a year in sales within 10 years. But Price refused to expand beyond its California base. As the industry quickly matured, Price ran headlong into wholesale clubs run by such retail giants as Wal-Mart and Kmart. Only 17 years later, in a stunning reversal of fortune, a faltering Price sold out to competitor Costco. Price's rapid rise and fall "serves as a stark reminder to mass-market retailers that past success means little in a fiercely competitive and rapidly changing industry."[12] Thus, retailers can no longer sit back with a successful formula. To remain successful, they must keep adapting.

Many retailing innovations are partially explained by the **wheel of retailing concept**.[13] According to this concept, many new types of retailing forms begin as low-margin, low-price, low-status operations. They challenge established retailers that have become "fat" by letting their costs and margins increase. The new retailers' success leads them to upgrade their facilities and offer more services. In turn, their costs increase, forcing them to increase their prices. Eventually, the new retailers become like the conventional retailers they replaced. The cycle begins again when still newer types of retailers evolve with lower costs and prices. The wheel of retailing concept seems to explain the initial success and later troubles of department stores, supermarkets, and discount stores, and the recent success of off-price retailers.

---

[12]Amy Barrett, "A Retailing Pacesetter Pulls Up Lame," *Business Week,* July 12, 1993, pp. 122–23.

[13]See Malcolm P. McNair and Eleanor G. May, "The Next Revolution of the Retailing Wheel," *Harvard Business Review,* September–October 1978, pp. 81–91; Stephen Brown, "The Wheel of Retailing: Past and Future," *Journal of Retailing,* Summer 1990, pp. 143–47; Stephen Brown, "Variations on a Marketing Enigma: The Wheel of Retailing Theory," *The Journal of Marketing Management* 7, no. 2, 1991, pp. 131–55; Stanley C. Hollander, "The Wheel of Retailing," reprinted in *Marketing Management,* Summer 1996, pp. 63–66; and Jennifer Negley, "Retrenching, Reinventing and Remaining Relevant," *Discount Store News,* April 5, 1999, p. 11.

GROWTH OF NONSTORE RETAILING

Although most retailing still takes place the old-fashioned way across countertops in stores, consumers now have an array of alternatives, including mail order, television, phone, and online shopping. "Some Americans never face a single crowd at holiday time; they do all of their gift shopping via phone or computer. A few may never even talk to a human being; they can punch in their order and credit card numbers on a Web site and have gifts delivered to recipients. This might remove some of the personal touch from the process, but it sure saves time."[14] Although such advances may threaten some traditional retailers, they offer exciting opportunities for others. Most store retailers are now actively exploring direct retailing channels.

INCREASING INTERTYPE COMPETITION

Today's retailers increasingly face competition from many different forms of retailers. For example, a consumer can buy CDs at specialty music stores, discount music stores, electronics superstores, general merchandise discount stores, video-rental outlets, and through dozens of Web sites. They can buy books at stores ranging from independent local bookstores to discount stores such as Wal-Mart, superstores such as Barnes & Noble or Borders, or Web sites such as Amazon.com. When it comes to brand-name appliances, department stores, discount stores, off-price retailers, or electronics superstores all compete for the same customers. Suggests one industry expert, "What we're seeing is cross-shopping—consumers buying one item at Neiman Marcus and another at Wal-Mart or General Dollar."[15]

The competition between chain superstores and smaller, independently owned stores has become particularly heated. Because of their bulk buying power and high sales volume, chains can buy at lower costs and thrive on smaller margins. The arrival of a superstore can quickly force nearby independents out of business. For example, the decision by Best Buy, the electronics superstore, to sell CDs as loss leaders at rock-bottom prices pushed a number of specialty record store chains into bankruptcy.[16] Yet the news is not all bad for smaller companies. Many small, independent retailers are thriving. Independents are finding that sheer size and marketing muscle are often no match for the personal touch small stores can provide or the specialty niches that small stores fill for a devoted customer base.

THE RISE OF MEGARETAILERS

The rise of huge mass merchandisers and specialty superstores, the formation of vertical marketing systems and buying alliances, and a rash of retail mergers and acquisitions have created a core of superpower megaretailers. Through their superior information systems and buying power, these giant retailers are able to offer better merchandise selections, good service, and strong price savings to consumers. As a result, they grow even larger by squeezing out their smaller, weaker competitors. The megaretailers also are shifting the balance of power between retailers and producers. A relative handful of retailers now controls access to enormous numbers of consumers, giving them the upper hand in their dealings with manufacturers. For example, in the United States, Wal-Mart's revenues are more than three times those of Procter & Gamble. Wal-Mart can, and often does, use this power to wring concessions from P&G and other suppliers.[17]

> **active poll**

Give your opinion regarding the impact of megaretailers on other businesses.

[14]Diane Crispell, "Retailing's Next Decade," *American Demographics,* May 1997, p. 9. Also see Barbara Martinez, "REIT Interest: Will the Internet Kill All the Shopping Centers?" *Wall Street Journal,* February 17, 1999, p. B12.

[15]Stephanie Anderson Forest and Keith Naughton, "I'll Take That and That and That and . . . ," *Business Week,* June 22, 1998, p. 38.

[16]Tim Carvell, "The Crazy Record Business: These Prices Really Are Insane," *Fortune,* August 4, 1997, pp. 109–16.

[17]See Nirmalya Kumar, "The Power of Trust in Manufacturer–Retailer Relationships," *Harvard Business Review,* November–December 1996, pp. 92–106; and "The Fortune 500," *Fortune,* April 26, 1999, p. F1.

GROWING IMPORTANCE OF RETAIL TECHNOLOGY

Retail technologies are becoming critically important as competitive tools. Progressive retailers are using computers to produce better forecasts, control inventory costs, order electronically from suppliers, send e-mail between stores, and even sell to customers within stores. They are adopting checkout scanning systems, online transaction processing, electronic funds transfer, electronic data interchange, in-store television, and improved merchandise-handling systems.

One innovative scanning system now in use is the shopper scanner, a radarlike system that counts store traffic. When a New Jersey Saks Fifth Avenue used one such system, ShopperTrak, it learned that there was a shopper surge between the hours of 11 A.M. and 3 P.M. To better handle the shopper flow, the store varied lunch hours for its counter clerks. Pier One Imports uses the same system to test, among other things, the impact of newspaper ads on store traffic. By combining traffic and sales data, retailers say they can find out how well the store converts browsers into buyers.[18]

Perhaps the most startling advances in retailing technology concern the ways in which today's retailers are connecting with customers:

> In the past, life was simple. Retailers connected with their customers through stores, through their salespeople, through the brands and packages they sold, and through direct mail and advertising in the mass media. But today, life is more complex. There are dozens of new ways to attract and engage consumers. . . . Indeed, even if one omits the obvious—the Web—retailers are still surrounded by technical innovations that promise to redefine the way they and manufacturers interact with customers. Consider, as just a sampling, touch screen kiosks, electronic shelf labels and signs, handheld shopping assistants, smart cards, self-scanning systems, virtual reality displays, and intelligent agents. So, if we ask the question, Will technology change the way [retailers] interface with customers in the future? The answer has got to be yes.[19]

GLOBAL EXPANSION OF MAJOR RETAILERS

Retailers with unique formats and strong brand positioning are increasingly moving into other countries. Many are expanding internationally to escape mature and saturated home markets. Over the years, several giant U.S. retailers—McDonald's, Gap, Toys "R" Us—have become globally prominent as a result of their great marketing prowess. Others, such as Wal-Mart and Kmart, are rapidly establishing a global presence. Wal-Mart, which now operates more than 700 stores in 8 countries abroad, sees exciting global potential. Its international division racked up 1999 sales of more than $12 billion, an increase of 63 percent over the previous year. Here's what happened when it recently opened two new stores in Shenzhen, China:[20]

> [Customers came] by the hundreds of thousands—up to 175,000 on Saturdays alone—to China's first Wal-Mart Supercenter and Sam's Club. They broke the display glass to snatch out chickens at one store and carted off all the big-screen TVs before the other store had been open an hour. The two outlets . . . were packed on Day One and have been bustling ever since.

However, U.S retailers are still significantly behind Europe and Asia when it comes to global expansion. Only 18 percent of the top U.S. retailers operate globally, compared to 40 percent of European retailers and 31 percent of Asian retailers. Among foreign retailers that have gone global are Britain's Marks and Spencer, Italy's Benetton, France's Carrefour hypermarkets, Sweden's IKEA home furnishings stores, and Japan's Yaohan supermarkets.[21] Marks and Spencer, which started out as a penny bazaar in 1884, grew into a chain of variety stores over the decades and now has a thriving string of 150 franchised stores around the world, which sell mainly its private-label clothes. It also runs a major food business. IKEA's well-constructed but fairly inexpensive furniture has proven very popular in the United States, where shoppers often spend an entire day in an IKEA store.

[18]"Business Bulletin: Shopper Scanner," *Wall Street Journal,* February 18, 1995, pp. A1, A5; and Kenneth Labich, "Attention Shoppers: This Man Is Watching You," *Fortune,* July 19, 1999, pp. 131–34.

[19]Regina Fazio Maruca, "Retailing: Confronting the Challenges that Face Bricks-and-Mortar Stores," *Harvard Business Review,* July–August 1999, pp. 159–68.

[20]James Cox, "Red-Letter Day as East Meets West in the Aisles," *USA Today,* September 11, 1996, p. B1; "Everybody's Hometown Store," Wal-Mart 1999 Annual Report, accessed online at www.walmart.com/corporate/annual_1999; and Jeremy Kahn, "Wal-Mart Goes Shopping in Europe," *Fortune,* June 7, 1999, pp. 105–12.

[21]Shelby D. Coolidge, "Facing Saturated Home Markets, Retailers Look to Rest of World," *Christian Science Monitor,* February 14, 1994, p. 7; Carla Rapoport, "Retailers Go Global," *Fortune,* February 20, 1995, pp. 102–8; and Joseph H. Ellis, "Global Retailing's Winners and Losers," *Chain Store Age,* December 1997, pp. 27–29.

Consider the potential challenges and rewards of global expansion.

RETAIL STORES AS "COMMUNITIES" OR "HANGOUTS"

With the rise in the number of people living alone, working at home, or living in isolated and sprawling suburbs, there has been a resurgence of establishments that, regardless of the product or service they offer, also provide a place for people to get together. These places include cafes, tea shops, juice bars, bookshops, superstores, children's play spaces, brew pubs, and urban greenmarkets. Brew pubs such as New York's Zip City Brewing and Seattle's Trolleyman Pub (run by Red Hook Brewery) offer tastings and a place to pass the time. The Discovery Zone, a chain of children's play spaces, offers indoor spaces where kids can go wild without breaking anything and stressed-out parents can exchange stories. Today's bookstores have become part bookstore, part library, and part living room.

> Welcome to today's bookstore. The one featuring not only shelves and cash registers but also cushy chairs and coffee bars. It's where backpack-toting high school students come to do homework, where retirees thumb through the gardening books and parents read aloud to their toddlers. If no one actually buys books, that's just fine, say bookstore owners and managers. They're offering something grander than ink and paper, anyway. They're selling comfort, relaxation, community.[22]

Denver's two Tattered Cover Bookstores host more than 250 events annually, from folk dancing to women's meetings.

> ## active concept check

Now let's take a moment to test your knowledge of what you've just read.

Stores as communities: Today's bookstores offer something grander than just ink and paper—they're selling comfort, relaxation, and community.

[22]Christina Nifong, "Beyond Browsing," *Raleigh News & Observer,* May 25, 1999, p. E1.

Wholesaling includes all activities involved in selling goods and services to those buying for resale or business use. We call **wholesalers** those firms engaged *primarily* in wholesaling activity.

Wholesalers buy mostly from producers and sell mostly to retailers, industrial consumers, and other wholesalers. But why are wholesalers used at all? For example, why would a producer use wholesalers rather than selling directly to retailers or consumers? Quite simply, wholesalers are often better at performing one or more of the following channel functions:

- *Selling and promoting:* Wholesalers' sales forces help manufacturers reach many small customers at a low cost. The wholesaler has more contacts and is often more trusted by the buyer than the distant manufacturer.

- *Buying and assortment building:* Wholesalers can select items and build assortments needed by their customers, thereby saving the consumers much work.

- *Bulk-breaking:* Wholesalers save their customers money by buying in carload lots and breaking bulk (breaking large lots into small quantities).

- *Warehousing:* Wholesalers hold inventories, thereby reducing the inventory costs and risks of suppliers and customers.

- *Transportation:* Wholesalers can provide quicker delivery to buyers because they are closer than the producers.

- *Financing:* Wholesalers finance their customers by giving credit, and they finance their suppliers by ordering early and paying bills on time.

- *Risk bearing:* Wholesalers absorb risk by taking title and bearing the cost of theft, damage, spoilage, and obsolescence.

- *Market information:* Wholesalers give information to suppliers and customers about competitors, new products, and price developments.

- *Management services and advice:* Wholesalers often help retailers train their salesclerks, improve store layouts and displays, and set up accounting and inventory control systems.

video example <

Take a moment to watch how one company provides transportation support for businesses.

Wholesalers fall into three major groups (see Table 13.3): *merchant wholesalers, brokers* and *agents,* and *manufacturers' sales branches and offices.* **Merchant wholesalers** are the largest single group of wholesalers, accounting for roughly 50 percent of all wholesaling. Merchant wholesalers include two broad types: full-service wholesalers and limited-service wholesalers. *Full-service wholesalers* provide a full set of services, whereas the various *limited-service wholesalers* offer fewer services to their suppliers and customers. The several different types of limited-service wholesalers perform varied specialized functions in the distribution channel.

Brokers and *agents* differ from merchant wholesalers in two ways: They do not take title to goods, and they perform only a few functions. Like merchant wholesalers, they generally specialize by product line or customer type. A **broker** brings buyers and sellers together and assists in negotiation. **Agents** represent buyers or sellers on a more permanent basis. *Manufacturers' agents* (also called manufacturers' representatives) are the most common type of agent wholesaler. The third major type of wholesaling is that done in **manufacturers' sales branches and offices** by sellers or buyers themselves rather than through independent wholesalers.

active concept check <

Now let's take a moment to test your knowledge of what you've just read.

TABLE 13.3	Major Types of Wholesalers

Type	Description
Merchant wholesalers	Independently owned businesses that take title to the merchandise they handle. In different trades they are called *jobbers, distributors,* or *mill supply houses.* Include full-service wholesalers and limited-service wholesalers:
Full-service wholesalers	Provide a full line of services: carrying stock, maintaining a sales force, offering credit, making deliveries, and providing management assistance. There are two types:
Wholesale merchants	Sell primarily to retailers and provide a full range of services. *General-merchandise wholesalers* carry several merchandise lines, whereas *general-line wholesalers* carry one or two lines in greater depth. *Specialty wholesalers* specialize in carrying only part of a line. (Examples: health food wholesalers, seafood wholesalers.)
Industrial distributors	Sell to manufacturers rather than to retailers. Provide several services, such as carrying stock, offering credit, and providing delivery. May carry a broad range of merchandise, a general line, or a specialty line.
Limited-service wholesalers	Offer fewer services than full-service wholesalers. Limited-service wholesalers are of several types:
Cash-and-carry wholesalers	Carry a limited line of fast-moving goods and sell to small retailers for cash. Normally do not deliver. Example: A small fish store retailer may drive to a cash-and-carry fish wholesaler, buy fish for cash, and bring the merchandise back to the store.
Truck wholesalers (or truck jobbers)	Perform primarily a selling and delivery function. Carry a limited line of semiperishable merchandise (such as milk, bread, snack foods), which they sell for cash as they make their rounds to supermarkets, small groceries, hospitals, restaurants, factory cafeterias, and hotels.
Drop shippers	Do not carry inventory or handle the product. On receiving an order, they select a manufacturer, who ships the merchandise directly to the customer. The drop shipper assumes title and risk from the time the order is accepted to its delivery to the customer. They operate in bulk industries, such as coal, lumber, and heavy equipment.
Rack jobbers	Serve grocery and drug retailers, mostly in nonfood items. They send delivery trucks to stores, where the delivery people set up toys, paperbacks, hardware items, health and beauty aids, or other items. They price the goods, keep them fresh, set up point-of-purchase displays, and keep inventory records. Rack jobbers retain title to the goods and bill the retailers only for the goods sold to consumers.
Producers' cooperatives	Owned by farmer members and assemble farm produce to sell in local markets. The co-op's profits are distributed to members at the end of the year. They often attempt to improve product quality and promote a co-op brand name, such as Sun Maid raisins, Sunkist oranges, or Diamond walnuts.
Mail-order wholesalers	Send catalogs to retail, industrial, and institutional customers featuring jewelry, cosmetics, specialty foods, and other small items. Maintain no outside sales force. Main customers are businesses in small outlying areas. Orders are filled and sent by mail, truck, or other transportation.
Brokers and agents	Do not take title to goods. Main function is to facilitate buying and selling, for which they earn a commission on the selling price. Generally, specialize by product line or customer types.

Type	Description
Brokers	Chief function is bringing buyers and sellers together and assisting in negotiation. They are paid by the party who hired them, and do not carry inventory, get involved in financing, or assume risk. Examples: food brokers, real estate brokers, insurance brokers, and security brokers.
Agents	Represent either buyers or sellers on a more permanent basis than brokers do. There are several types:
Manufacturers' agents	Represent two or more manufacturers of complementary lines. A formal written agreement with each manufacturer covers pricing, territories, order handling, delivery service and warranties, and commission rates. Often used in such lines as apparel, furniture, and electrical goods. Most manufacturers' agents are small businesses, with only a few skilled salespeople as employees. They are hired by small manufacturers who cannot afford their own field sales forces, and by large manufacturers who use agents to open new territories or to cover territories that cannot support full-time salespeople.
Selling agents	Have contractual authority to sell a manufacturer's entire output. The manufacturer either is not interested in the selling function or feels unqualified. The selling agent serves as a sales department and has significant influence over prices, terms, and conditions of sale. Found in product areas such as textiles, industrial machinery and equipment, coal and coke, chemicals, and metals.
Purchasing agents	Generally have a long-term relationship with buyers and make purchases for them, often receiving, inspecting, warehousing, and shipping the merchandise to the buyers. They provide helpful market information to clients and help them obtain the best goods and prices available.
Commission merchants	Take physical possession of products and negotiate sales. Normally, they are not employed on a long-term basis. Used most often in agricultural marketing by farmers who do not want to sell their own output and do not belong to producers' cooperatives. The commission merchant takes a truckload of commodities to a central market, sells it for the best price, deducts a commission and expenses, and remits the balance to the producer.
Manufacturers' and retailers' branches and offices	Wholesaling operations conducted by sellers or buyers themselves rather than through independent wholesalers. Separate branches and offices can be dedicated to either sales or purchasing.
Sales branches and offices	Set up by manufacturers to improve inventory control, selling, and promotion. Sales branches carry inventory and are found in industries such as lumber and automotive equipment and parts. Sales offices do not carry inventory and are most prominent in dry-goods and notions industries.
Purchasing offices	Perform a role similar to that of brokers or agents but are part of the buyer's organization. Many retailers set up purchasing offices in major market centers such as New York and Chicago.

> Wholesaler Marketing Decisions

Wholesalers have experienced mounting competitive pressures in recent years. They have faced new sources of competition, more demanding customers, new technologies, and more direct-buying programs on the part of large industrial, institutional, and retail buyers. As a result, they have had to improve their strategic decisions on target markets and positioning, and on the marketing mix—product assortments and services, price, promotion, and place (see Figure 13.2).

TARGET MARKET AND POSITIONING DECISION

Like retailers, wholesalers must define their target markets and position themselves effectively—they cannot serve everyone. They can choose a target group by size of customer (only large retailers), type of customer (convenience food stores only), need for service (customers who need credit), or other factors. Within the target group, they can identify the more profitable customers, design stronger offers, and build better relationships with them. They can propose automatic reordering systems, set up management-training and advising systems, or even sponsor a voluntary chain. They can discourage less profitable customers by requiring larger orders or adding service charges to smaller ones.

MARKETING MIX DECISIONS

Like retailers, wholesalers must decide on product assortment and services, prices, promotion, and place. The wholesaler's "product" is the assortment of *products and services* that it offers. Wholesalers are under great pressure to carry a full line and to stock enough for immediate delivery. But this practice can damage profits. Wholesalers today are cutting down on the number of lines they carry, choosing to carry only the more profitable ones. Wholesalers are also rethinking which services count most in building strong customer relationships and which should be dropped or charged for. The key is to find the mix of services most valued by their target customers.

Price is also an important wholesaler decision. Wholesalers usually mark up the cost of goods by a standard percentage—say, 20 percent. Expenses may run 17 percent of the gross margin, leaving a profit margin of 3 percent. In grocery wholesaling, the average profit margin is often less than 2 percent. Wholesalers are trying new pricing approaches. They may cut their margin on some lines in order to win important new customers. They may ask suppliers for special price breaks when they can turn them into an increase in the supplier's sales.

Although *promotion* can be critical to wholesaler success, most wholesalers are not promotion minded. Their use of trade advertising, sales promotion, personal selling, and public relations is largely scattered and unplanned. Many are behind the times in personal selling—they still see selling as a single salesperson talking to a single customer instead of as a team effort to sell, build, and service major accounts. Wholesalers also need to adopt some of the nonpersonal promotion techniques used by retailers. They need to develop an overall promotion strategy and to make greater use of supplier promotion materials and programs.

Finally, *place* is important—wholesalers must choose their locations and facilities carefully. Wholesalers typically locate in low-rent, low-tax areas and tend to invest little money in their buildings, equipment, and systems. As a result, their materials-handling and order-processing systems are often outdated. In recent years, however, large and progressive wholesalers are reacting to rising costs by investing in automated warehouses and online ordering systems. Orders are fed from the retailer's system directly into the wholesaler's computer, and the items are picked up by mechanical devices and automatically taken to a shipping platform where they are assembled. Most large wholesalers use computers to carry out accounting, billing, inventory control, and forecasting. Modern wholesalers are adapting their services to the needs of target customers and finding cost-reducing methods of doing business.

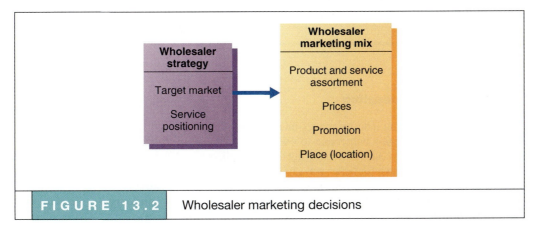

FIGURE 13.2 Wholesaler marketing decisions

Merchant wholesalers: A typical Fleming Companies, Inc., whole-sale food distribution center. The average Fleming warehouse contains 500,000 square feet of floor space (with 30-foot-high ceilings), carries 16,000 different food items, and serves 150 to 200 retailers within a 500-mile radius.

video example <

Take a moment to watch how CanGo faces some of its distribution challenges.

active concept check <

Now let's take a moment to test your knowledge of what you've just read.

> **Trends in Wholesaling**

As the thriving wholesaling industry moves into the twenty-first century, it faces considerable challenges. The industry remains vulnerable to one of the most enduring trends of the 1990s—fierce resistance to price increases and the winnowing out of suppliers based on cost and quality. Progressive wholesalers constantly watch for better ways to meet the changing needs of their suppliers and target customers. They recognize that, in the long run, their only reason for existence comes from adding value by increasing the efficiency and effectiveness of the entire marketing channel. To achieve this goal, they must constantly improve their services and reduce their costs.

McKesson HBOC, the nation's leading wholesaler of pharmaceuticals, health and beauty care, and home health care products, provides an example of progressive wholesaling. To survive, McKesson HBOC had to remain more cost-effective than manufacturers' sales branches. Thus, the company automated its 36 warehouses, established direct computer links with 225 drug manufacturers, designed a computerized accounts-receivable program for pharmacists, and provided drugstores with computer terminals for ordering inventories. Retailers can even use the McKesson HBOC computer system to maintain medical profiles on their customers. Thus, McKesson HBOC has delivered better value to both manufacturers and retail customers.

One study predicts several developments in the wholesaling industry.[23] Geographic expansion will require that distributors learn how to compete effectively over wider and more diverse areas. Consolidation will significantly reduce the number of wholesaling firms. Surviving wholesalers will grow larger, primarily through acquisition, merger, and geographic expansion. The trend toward vertical integration, in which manufacturers try to control their market share by owning the intermediaries that bring their goods to market, remains strong. In health care, for instance, drug makers have purchased drug-distribution and pharmacy-management companies. This trend began in 1993 when drug-industry giant Merck acquired Medco Containment Services, a drug-benefits manager and mail-order distributor. The surviving wholesaler-distributors in this sector and in others will be bigger and will provide more services for their customers.[24]

The distinction between large retailers and large wholesalers continues to blur. Many retailers now operate formats such as wholesale clubs and hypermarkets that perform many wholesale functions. In return, many large wholesalers are setting up their own retailing operations. SuperValu and Fleming, both leading food wholesalers, now operate their own retail outlets. In fact, SuperValu, the nation's largest food wholesaling company, is also the country's eleventh largest food retailer. Almost 30 percent of the company's $17.4 billion in sales comes from its Bigg's, Cub Foods, Shop 'n Save, Farm Fresh, Hornbacher's, Save-A-Lot, Laneco, and Scott's supermarket operations.[25]

> ## active example

Consider how one prominent firm has successfully gone straight to the consumer.

Wholesalers will continue to increase the services they provide to retailers—retail pricing, cooperative advertising, marketing and management information reports, accounting services, online transactions, and others. Rising costs on the one hand, and the demand for increased services on the other, will put the squeeze on wholesaler profits. Wholesalers who do not find efficient ways to deliver value to their customers will soon drop by the wayside. However, the increased use of computerized, automated, and Internet systems will help wholesalers to contain the costs of ordering, shipping, and inventory holding, boosting their productivity.

Finally, facing slow growth in their domestic markets and such developments as the North American Free Trade Agreement, many large wholesalers are now going global. For example, in 1991, McKesson HBOC bought out its Canadian partner, Provigo. The company now receives about 3 percent of its total revenues from Canada.

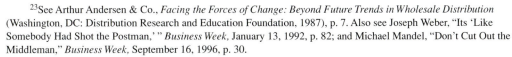

> ## active concept check

Now let's take a moment to test your knowledge of what you've just read.

[23]See Arthur Andersen & Co., *Facing the Forces of Change: Beyond Future Trends in Wholesale Distribution* (Washington, DC: Distribution Research and Education Foundation, 1987), p. 7. Also see Joseph Weber, "Its 'Like Somebody Had Shot the Postman,'" *Business Week,* January 13, 1992, p. 82; and Michael Mandel, "Don't Cut Out the Middleman," *Business Week,* September 16, 1996, p. 30.

[24]Richard A. Melcher, "The Middlemen Stay on the March," *Business Week,* January 9, 1995, p. 87.

[25]Facts accessed online from www.supervalu.com, February 2000.

Now that you've reached the end of the chapter, you may wish to explore the concepts you've been reading about in greater detail, or test yourself to see how well you've comprehended the material. In the box below you'll find a number of links. Click on any one of these links to find additional chapter resources.

> ## end-of-chapter resources

- Review of Concept Connections
- Practice Quiz
- Issues for Discussion
- Key Terms
- Marketing Applications
- Internet Connections
- Company Case

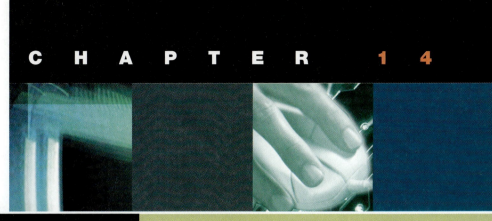

CHAPTER 14

Integrated Marketing Communications Strategy

Chapter Outline

> What's Ahead

Jim Lesinski, director of Marketing Communications and Research for Volvo Trucks North America, first proposed putting an ad for Volvo's heavy-duty trucks on the Super Bowl in 1994. His bosses at Swedish parent AB Volvo, who were not familiar with the hype and frenzy that surrounds American football, must have thought he'd gone a little ditzy. "How much will it cost?" they asked. "About $1.3 million in media costs," replied Lesinski, "plus another $500,000 or so to produce the ad." "And how long and how often will the ad run?" they asked. "Just once," said Lesinski, "for 30 seconds." With eyebrows raised and mouths agape, Volvo's top management respectfully rejected Lesinski's proposal.

In fact, early on, Lesinski himself had some doubts. *Did* it make sense to spend almost a third of his annual marketing budget on a single ad? Given the narrow target market for Volvo's huge, $120,000 trucks, *was* it wise to advertise in the granddaddy of mass-media spectacles, amidst the glitzy showcase ads run by big-spending consumer-product companies selling to the masses? Volvo Trucks' target market constituted a mere 1 percent of the total Super Bowl audience. Moreover, no other heavy-duty truck manufacturer was advertising on television, let alone on the Super Bowl.

But the more he thought about it, the more convinced Lesinski became. Volvo had been selling heavy trucks in the United States since 1981 under a variety of nameplates, including Volvo, Autocar, and White/GMC. Its early trucks lacked quality, sold at relatively low prices, and had gained a reputation as low-status "fleet trucks." In recent years, however, Volvo Trucks had consolidated its various nameplates under the Volvo brand and had

developed a new line of premium trucksthe VN Series. These new Volvo trucks were superior to competing premium brands in overall quality, design, safety, and driving comfort. Now, all that remained was to raise Volvo Trucks' old low-status image to match the new high-quality reality. That task, Lesinski knew, would take something dramatic—something like the Super Bowl. He persisted and finally won approval to place a single ad in the 1998 Super Bowl.

The target market for heavy-duty trucks consists of truck fleet buyers and independent owner-operators. However, truck drivers themselves are perhaps the most important buying influence. The industry faces a severe driver shortage, and firms perceived as having better-performing, more comfortable, higher-status trucks have a big edge in attracting and holding good drivers. As a result, truck buyers are swayed by driver perceptions. Thus, Lesinski's communications goal was to improve the image of Volvo's VN Series trucks, not just among truck buyers but also among drivers. No other event reaches this audience more completely than the Super Bowl. In fact, nearly 70 percent of all truck drivers watch some or all of an average Super Bowl game.

Still, Jim Lesinski knew that a single Super Bowl ad, by itself, wasn't likely to have much lasting impact on buyer and driver perceptions. Instead—and this is the real story—he designed a comprehensive, carefully targeted, four-month integrated promotional campaign, with Super Bowl advertising as its centerpiece (see figure below). Called *The Best Drive in the Game Sweepstakes,* the promotion offered truck drivers a chance to win a new Volvo VN770 truck worth $120,000. Lesinski began promoting the Best Drive sweepstakes in September 1997, using a wide range of carefully coordinated media, including trucker magazines and radio stations. Drivers could enter the sweepstakes by responding to print or radio ads, by visiting a Volvo Truck dealer or participating truck stop, or by clicking onto the Volvo Trucks Web site (a large proportion of truckers use the Internet regularly to schedule loads). To create additional interest, Volvo Trucks sponsored a national truck tour, consisting of two caravans of three VN770s each, that visited major truck stops around the country, encouraging truck drivers to enter the Best Drive sweepstakes and giving them a chance to experience a new Volvo VN770 firsthand.

The campaign attracted more than 48,700 entrants. Each entrant received a wallet-size entry card with one of 40 "Volvo Truths" printed on it—each emphasizing a key VN770 positioning point. If the phrase on a driver's card matched the winning phrase revealed in the Super Bowl commercial, the driver became a finalist eligible for the grand prize. To further encourage drivers to watch the commercial, Volvo Trucks sponsored Super Bowl parties at 40 Flying J truck stops around the country. It also had Volvo VN770s at each truck stop so that drivers could see the truck that was causing all the commotion.

On Super Bowl Sunday 1998, Jim Lesinski found himself at a Greensboro, North Carolina, truck stop, anxiously awaiting the fourth-quarter airing of his ad. He sat shoulder to shoulder with a standing-room-only crowd of truckers, clustered around a lounge television with their Best Drive wallet cards in hand. To Lesinski's dismay, a clever ad for Tabasco Sauce preceded the Volvo ad (remember the exploding mosquito?) and the crowd was still laughing as the Volvo commercial began. Lesinski still remembers counting off the missed seconds (at a cost of some $60,000 apiece!) waiting for the group to settle their attention on his ad.

The Volvo Trucks ad itself used soft humor to make the quality point. It featured an experienced and approachable professional driver named Gus, driving a new Volvo VN770 down a desert highway. Gus talked sagely about "what 30 years on the road have taught me," and advised "always run the best truck you can." During the 30-second spot, the scenes shifted to show both the sleek, handsome exterior of the truck and its luxurious interior. "But success hasn't spoiled me," Gus concluded. "I still put my pants on one leg at a time." As Gus delivered this last line, a uniformed butler approached from the sleeper area of the truck, presenting a small silver box on a pillow. "Your toothpick, sir," he intoned. The winning phrase, "Volvo—Drive Safely," appeared on the screen as the commercial ended.

To Jim's enormous relief, the drivers at the truck stop seemed to really like the commercial. They were pleased that it portrayed professional truck drivers and their huge, sometimes scary trucks in positive light. More importantly, the ad got the drivers buzzing about the VN770 truck and the winning phrase. In the month following the Super Bowl, the 10 finalists holding winning phrases received all-expense-paid trips to the trucking industry's premier trade show, the Mid-America Truck Show in Louisville, Kentucky. Volvo stole the show, sponsoring a Brooks and Dunn concert at which company officials held an on-stage drawing in front of 20,000 truckers to select the grand prize winner.

In all, the Best Drive in the Game Sweepstakes cost Volvo Trucks North America $2.4 million $1.8 million for the ad alone. Was it worth the cost? Lesinski and his bosses at AB Volvo cer-

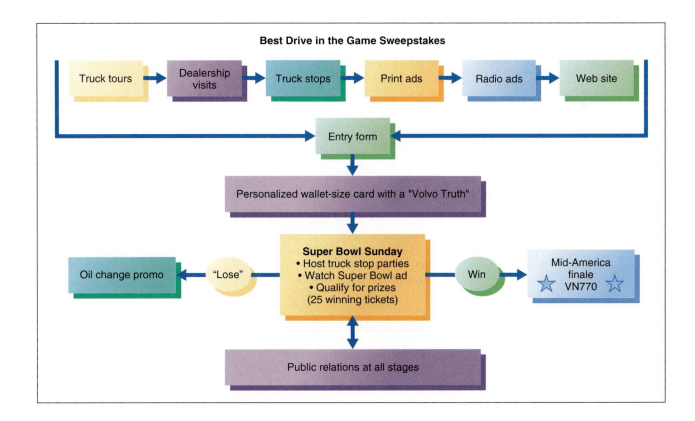

tainly think so. Later research showed that the campaign had a sizable, positive impact on both trucker and public perceptions. More than 30 million U.S. adults recalled seeing the Super Bowl ad. Just that one ad created a 98 percent increase in the general public's awareness of Volvo trucks and significantly improved public perceptions of Volvo drivers as intelligent, safe, successful, and friendly.

Perhaps more importantly, the ad was viewed by 1.4 million truck drivers, almost half the target market. Twenty-three percent of these drivers talked about the ad with someone else, generating more than 325,000 conversations about the commercial. After the Best Drive campaign, substantially higher proportions of drivers and buyers perceive the Volvo VN770 as being like a "Hilton" rather than a "Motel 6," and as a "sleek, aerodynamic, friendly vehicle" versus a "work truck." The campaign created 30 percent driver preference for Volvo trucks, higher than preferences for competitors Freightliner (25 percent), Peterbilt (23 percent), and Kenworth (16 percent). By the end of 1998, sales of Volvo trucks were up 44.5 percent compared with the previous year; market share rose 2.5 points to 12 percent. Based on these results, Volvo Trucks North America sponsored a repeat promotion, *The Best Drive in the Game II,* the following year, including a brand new ad in the 1999 Super Bowl.

Why did the Best Drive promotion work so well? Success resulted from much, much more than just a single Super Bowl ad. "The ad was definitely the main attraction," says Jim Lesinski, "but it was really just the lure that pulled drivers into the full Best Drive promotion and got them into our trucks." By blending Super Bowl advertising with a full slate of other carefully targeted ads, promotions, and events, Lesinski created a complete integrated marketing communications campaign that had a larger and more lasting impact than any single ad could ever have achieved.[1]

objectives <

Before you begin, take a moment to familiarize yourself with the key objectives of this chapter.

gearing up <

Before we begin our exploration this chapter, take a short warm-up test to see what you know about this topic.

Modern marketing calls for more than just developing a good product, pricing it attractively, and making it available to target customers. Companies must also *communicate* with current and prospective customers, and what they communicate should not be left to chance. For most companies, the question is not *whether* to communicate, but *how much to spend* and *in what ways.* All of their communications efforts must be blended into a consistent and coordinated communications program.

> The Marketing Communications Mix

A company's total **marketing communications mix**—also called its **promotion mix**—consists of the specific blend of advertising, personal selling, sales promotion, public relations, and direct-marketing

---

[1]Based on information supplied by Jim Lesinski at Volvo Trucks North America.

tools that the company uses to pursue its advertising and marketing objectives. Definitions of the five major promotion tools follow:[2]

Advertising: Any paid form of nonpersonal presentation and promotion of ideas, goods, or services by an identified sponsor.

Personal selling: Personal presentation by the firm's sales force for the purpose of making sales and building customer relationships.

Sales promotion: Short-term incentives to encourage the purchase or sale of a product or service.

Public relations: Building good relations with the company's various publics by obtaining favorable publicity, building up a good corporate image, and handling or heading off unfavorable rumors, stories, and events.

Direct marketing: Direct connections with carefully targeted individual consumers to both obtain an immediate response and cultivate lasting customer relationships—the use of telephone, mail, fax, e-mail, the Internet, and other tools to communicate directly with specific consumers.

Each category involves specific tools. For example, advertising includes print, broadcast, outdoor, and other forms. Personal selling includes sales presentations, trade shows, and incentive programs. Sales promotion includes point-of-purchase displays, premiums, discounts, coupons, specialty advertising, and demonstrations. Direct marketing includes catalogs, telemarketing, fax, kiosks, the Internet, and more. Thanks to technological breakthroughs, people can now communicate through traditional media (newspapers, radio, telephone, television), as well as through newer media forms (fax machines, cellular phones, pagers, and computers). The new technologies have encouraged more companies to move from mass communication to more targeted communication and one-to-one dialogue.

> **active example**

Take a moment to read about how, in some product categories, the advertising dollars are moving from one element of the promotional mix to another.

At the same time, communication goes beyond these specific promotion tools. The product's design, its price, the shape and color of its package, and the stores that sell it—*all* communicate something to buyers. Thus, although the promotion mix is the company's primary communication activity, the entire marketing mix—promotion *and* product, price, and place—must be coordinated for the greatest communication impact.

In this chapter, we begin by examining the rapidly changing marketing communications environment, the concept of integrated marketing communications, and the marketing communication process. Next, we discuss the factors that marketing communicators must consider in shaping an overall communication mix. Finally, we summarize the legal, ethical, and social responsibility issues in marketing communications. In chapter 15, we look at *mass-communication tools*—advertising, sales promotion, and public relations. Chapter 16 examines the *sales force* as a communication and promotion tool.

> **active concept check**

Now let's take a moment to test your knowledge of what you've just read.

> **Integrated Marketing Communications**

During the past several decades, companies around the world have perfected the art of mass marketing—selling highly standardized products to masses of customers. In the process, they have developed effective mass-media advertising techniques to support their mass-marketing strategies. These companies routinely invest millions of dollars in the mass media, reaching tens of millions of cus-

---

[2]The first four of these definitions are adapted from Peter D. Bennett, *Dictionary of Marketing Terms* (Chicago: American Marketing Association, 1995).

tomers with a single ad. However, as we move into the twenty-first century, marketing managers face some new marketing communications realities.

THE CHANGING COMMUNICATIONS ENVIRONMENT

Two major factors are changing the face of today's marketing communications. First, as mass markets have fragmented, marketers are shifting away from mass marketing. More and more, they are developing focused marketing programs designed to build closer relationships with customers in more narrowly defined micromarkets. Second, vast improvements in information technology are speeding the movement toward segmented marketing. Today's information technology helps marketers to keep closer track of customer needs—more information about consumers at the individual and household levels is available than ever before. New technologies also provide new communications avenues for reaching smaller customer segments with more tailored messages.

The shift from mass marketing to segmented marketing has had a dramatic impact on marketing communications. Just as mass marketing gave rise to a new generation of mass-media communications, the shift toward one-to-one marketing is spawning a new generation of more specialized and highly targeted communications efforts.[3]

Given this new communications environment, marketers must rethink the roles of various media and promotion mix tools. Mass-media advertising has long dominated the promotion mixes of con-

The relatively few mass magazines of past decades have been replaced today by thousands of magazines targeting special-interest audiences. HMF alone publishes these and more than 20 other magazines reaching 17 different markets and more than 47 million readers, not to mention a wide range of online, broadcast, outdoor, and other media.

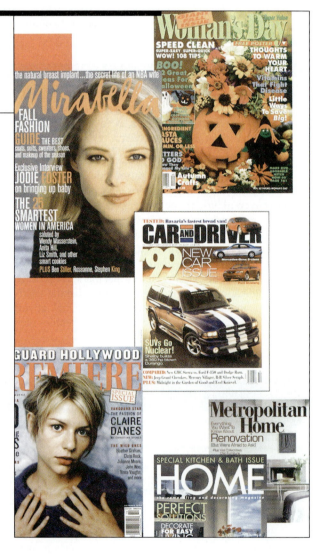

[3]For more discussion, see Don E. Schultz, Stanley I. Tannenbaum, and Robert F. Lauterborn, *Integrated Marketing Communication* (Chicago, IL: NTC, 1992), pp. 11, 17; Larry Percy, *Strategies for Implementing Integrated Marketing Communication* (Chicago, IL: NTC, 1997); and James R. Ogdan, *Developing a Creative and Innovative Integrated Marketing Communications Plan* (Upper Saddle River, NJ: Prentice Hall, 1998).

sumer product companies. However, although television, magazines, and other mass media remain very important, their dominance is now declining. *Market* fragmentation has resulted in *media* fragmentation—in an explosion of more focused media that better match today's targeting strategies. For example, in 1975 what used to be the three major TV networks (ABC, CBS, and NBC) attracted 82 percent of the 24-hour viewing audience. By 1995 that number had dropped to only 35 percent, as cable television and satellite broadcasting systems offered advertisers dozens or even hundreds of alternative channels that reach smaller, specialized audiences. It's expected to drop even further, down to 25 percent by the year 2005. Similarly, the relatively few mass magazines of the 1940s and 1950s—*Look, Life, Saturday Evening Post*—have been replaced by more than 18,600 special-interest magazines reaching more focused audiences. Beyond these channels, advertisers are making increased use of new, highly targeted media, ranging from video screens on supermarket shopping carts to CD-ROM catalogs and Web sites on the Internet.[4]

More generally, advertising appears to be giving way to other elements of the promotion mix. In the glory days of mass marketing, consumer product companies spent the lion's share of their promotion budgets on mass-media advertising. Today, media advertising captures only about 26 percent of total promotion spending.[5] The rest goes to various sales promotion activities, which can be focused more effectively on individual consumer and trade segments. They are using a richer variety of focused communication tools in an effort to reach their diverse target markets. In all, companies are doing less *broadcasting* and more *narrowcasting*.

> **active exercise**

Take a moment to consider the effects of media fragmentation.

THE NEED FOR INTEGRATED MARKETING COMMUNICATIONS

The shift from mass marketing to targeted marketing, and the corresponding use of a richer mixture of communication channels and promotion tools, poses a problem for marketers. Consumers are being exposed to a greater variety of marketing communications from and about the company from a broader array of sources. However, customers don't distinguish between message sources the way marketers do. In the consumer's mind, advertising messages from different media such as television, magazines, or online sources blur into one. Messages delivered via different promotional approaches—such as advertising, personal selling, sales promotion, public relations, or direct marketing—all become part of a single message about the company. Conflicting messages from these different sources can result in confused company images and brand positions.

All too often, companies fail to integrate their various communications channels. The result is a hodgepodge of communications to consumers. Mass advertisements say one thing, a price promotion sends a different signal, a product label creates still another message, company sales literature says something altogether different, and the company's Web site seems out of sync with everything else.

The problem is that these communications often come from different company sources. Advertising messages are planned and implemented by the advertising department or advertising agency. Personal selling communications are developed by sales management. Other functional specialists are responsible for public relations, sales promotion, direct marketing, online sites, and other forms of marketing communications. Recently, such functional separation has been a major problem for many companies and their Internet communications activities, which are often split off into separate organizational units. "These new, forward-looking, high-tech functional groups, whether they exist as part of an established organization or as a separate new business operation, commonly are located in separate space, apart from the traditional operation," observes one IMC expert. "They generally are populated by young, enthusiastic, technologically proficient people with a burning desire to 'change the world,'" he adds, but "the separation and the lack of cooperation and cohesion" can be a *dis*integrating force in marketing communications.

[4]Michael Kubin, "Simple Days of Retailing on TV Are Long Gone," *Marketing News,* February 17, 1997, pp. 2, 13; Elizabeth Lesly Stevens and Ronald Glover, "The Entertainment Glut," *Business Week,* February 16, 1998, pp. 88–95; Ronald Glover, "If These Shows Are Hits, Why Do They Hurt So Much?" *Business Week,* April 13, 1998, p. 36; Stuart Elliott, "Fewer Viewers, More Commercials," *New York Times,* June 8, 1999, p. 1; Joe Mandese, "Networks Facing a Most Uncertain Fate," *Advertising Age,* February 14, 2000, pp. 54, 516; and information accessed online at www.magazine.org, March 2000.

[5]"Promotion Practices Condensed," *Potentials,* November 1998, p. 6.

In the past, no one person was responsible for thinking through the communication roles of the various promotion tools and coordinating the promotion mix. Today, however, more companies are adopting the concept of **integrated marketing communications (IMC).** Under this concept, as illustrated in Figure 14.1, the company carefully integrates and coordinates its many communications channels to deliver a clear, consistent, and compelling message about the organization and its products.[6] As one marketing executive puts it, "IMC builds a strong brand identity in the marketplace by tying together and reinforcing all your images and messages. IMC means that all your corporate messages, positioning and images, and identity are coordinated across all [marketing communications] venues. It means that your PR materials say the same thing as your direct mail campaign, and your advertising has the same 'look and feel' as your Web site."[7]

The IMC solution calls for recognizing all contact points where the customer may encounter the company, its products, and its brands. Each *brand contact* will deliver a message, whether good, bad, or indifferent. The company must strive to deliver a consistent and positive message at all contact points.

To help implement integrated marketing communications, some companies appoint a marketing communications director or *marcom manager*—who has overall responsibility for the company's communications efforts. Integrated marketing communications produces better communications consistency and greater sales impact. It places the responsibility in someone's hands—where none existed before—to unify the company's image as it is shaped by thousands of company activities. It leads to a total marketing communication strategy aimed at showing how the company and its products can help customers solve their problems.

active concept check <

Now let's take a moment to test your knowledge of what you've just read.

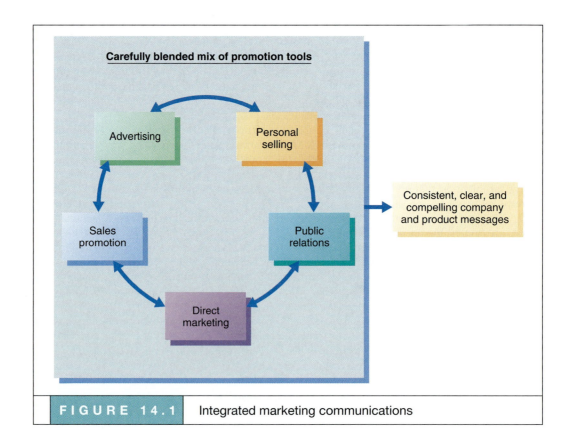

| FIGURE 14.1 | Integrated marketing communications |

---

[6]See Schultz, Tannenbaum, and Lauterborn, *Integrated Marketing Communication,* chaps. 3 and 4.

[7]P. Griffith Lindell, "You Need Integrated Attitude to Develop IMC," *Marketing News,* May 26, 1997, p. 6.

Integrated marketing communications involves identifying the target audience and shaping a well-coordinated promotional program to elicit the desired audience response. Too often, marketing communications focus on overcoming immediate awareness, image, or preference problems in the target market. But this approach to communication has limitations: It is too short term and too costly, and most messages of this type fall on deaf ears. Today, marketers are moving toward viewing communications as *managing the customer relationship over time,* during the preselling, selling, consuming, and postconsumption stages. Because customers differ, communications programs need to be developed for specific segments, niches, and even individuals. Given the new interactive communications technologies, companies must ask not only "How can we reach our customers?" but also "How can we find ways to let our customers reach us?"

Thus, the communications process should start with an audit of all the potential contacts target customers may have with the company and its brands. For example, someone purchasing a new computer may talk to others, see television ads, read articles and ads in newspapers and magazines, visit various Web sites, and try out computers in one or more stores. The marketer needs to assess the influence that each of these communications experiences will have at different stages of the buying process. This understanding will help marketers allocate their communication dollars more efficiently and effectively.

To communicate effectively, marketers need to understand how communication works. Communication involves the nine elements shown in Figure 14.2. Two of these elements are the major parties in a communication—the *sender* and the *receiver.* Another two are the major communication tools—the *message* and the *media.* Four more are major communication functions—*encoding, decoding, response,* and *feedback.* The last element is *noise* in the system. Definitions of these elements follow and are applied to an ad for Hewlett-Packard (HP) color copiers.

- *Sender:* The *party sending the message* to another party—here, HP.
- *Encoding:* The process of *putting thought into symbolic form*—HP's advertising agency assembles words and illustrations into an advertisement that will convey the intended message.
- *Message:* The *set of symbols* that the sender transmits—the actual HP copier ad.
- *Media:* The *communication channels* through which the message moves from sender to receiver—in this case, the specific magazines that HP selects.
- *Decoding:* The process by which the receiver *assigns meaning to the symbols* encoded by the sender—a consumer reads the HP copier ad and interprets the words and illustrations it contains.
- *Receiver:* The *party receiving the message* sent by another party—the home office or business customer who reads the HP copier ad.
- *Response:* The *reactions of the receiver* after being exposed to the message—any of hundreds of possible responses, such as the consumer is more aware of the attributes of HP copiers, actually buys an HP copier, or does nothing.

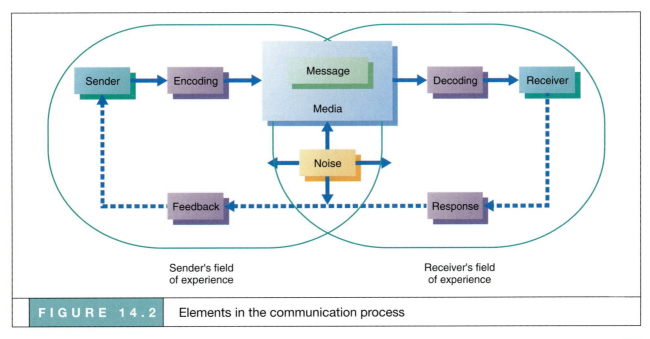

FIGURE 14.2 | Elements in the communication process

- *Feedback:* The part of the *receiver's response communicated back to the sender*—HP research shows that consumers are struck by and remember the ad, or consumers write or call HP praising or criticizing the ad or HP's products.

- *Noise:* The *unplanned static or distortion* during the communication process, which results in the receiver's getting a different message than the one the sender sent—the consumer it distracted while reading the magazine and misses the HP ad or its key points.

active example <

Consider how two companies are trying to relate better to the "fields of experience" of minority consumers.

For a message to be effective, the sender's encoding process must mesh with the receiver's decoding process. Thus, the best messages consist of words and other symbols that are familiar to the receiver. The more the sender's field of experience overlaps with that of the receiver, the more effective the message is likely to be. Marketing communicators may not always *share* their consumer's field of experience. For example, an advertising copywriter from one social stratum might create ads for consumers from another stratum—say, blue-collar workers or wealthy business owners. However, to communicate effectively, the marketing communicator must *understand* the consumer's field of experience.

This model points out several key factors in good communication. Senders need to know what audiences they wish to reach and what responses they want. They must be good at encoding messages that take into account how the target audience decodes them. They must send messages through media that reach target audiences, and they must develop feedback channels so that they can assess the audience's response to the message.

active concept check <

Now let's take a moment to test your knowledge of what you've just read.

> ### Steps in Developing Effective Communication

We now examine the steps in developing an effective integrated communications and promotion program. The marketing communicator must do the following: Identify the target audience; determine the communication objectives; design a message; choose the media through which to send the message; select the message source; and collect feedback.

IDENTIFYING THE TARGET AUDIENCE

A marketing communicator starts with a clear target audience in mind. The audience may be potential buyers or current users, those who make the buying decision or those who influence it. The audience may be individuals, groups, special publics, or the general public. The target audience will heavily affect the communicator's decisions on *what* will be said, *how* it will be said, *when* it will be said, *where* it will be said, and *who* will say it.

DETERMINING THE COMMUNICATION OBJECTIVES

Once the target audience has been defined, the marketing communicator must decide what response is sought. Of course, in many cases, the final response is *purchase*. But purchase is the result of a long process of consumer decision making. The marketing communicator needs to know where the target audience now stands and to what stage it needs to be moved. The target audience may be in any of six **buyer-readiness stages,** the stages consumers normally pass through on their way to making a purchase. These stages include *awareness, knowledge, liking, preference, conviction,* and *purchase* (see Figure 14.3).

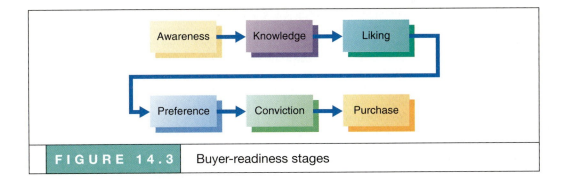

FIGURE 14.3 Buyer-readiness stages

The marketing communicator's target market may be totally unaware of the product, know only its name, or know one or a few things about it. The communicator must first build *awareness* and *knowledge*. For example, when Nissan introduced its Infiniti automobile line, it began with an extensive "teaser" advertising campaign to create name familiarity. Initial ads for the Infiniti created curiosity and awareness by showing the car's name but not the car. Later ads created knowledge by informing potential buyers of the car's high quality and many innovative features.

Assuming target consumers *know* the product, how do they *feel* about it? Once potential buyers knew about the Infiniti, Nissan's marketers wanted to move them through successively stronger stages of feelings toward the car. These stages included *liking* (feeling favorable about the Infiniti), *preference* (preferring Infiniti to other car brands), and *conviction* (believing that Infiniti is the best car for them). Infiniti marketers used a combination of the promotion mix tools to create positive feelings and conviction. Advertising extolled the Infiniti's advantages over competing brands. Press releases

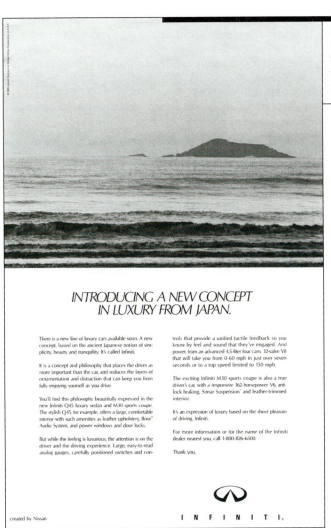

Moving consumers toward purchase: Nissan created awareness for Infiniti using teaser ads that didn't show the car. Later ads created liking, preference, and conviction by comparing the Infiniti's features to those of competitors.

and other public relations activities stressed the car's innovative features and performance. Dealer salespeople told buyers about options, value for the price, and after-sale service.

Finally, some members of the target market might be convinced about the product, but not quite get around to making the *purchase*. Potential Infiniti buyers might have decided to wait for more information or for the economy to improve. The communicator must lead these consumers to take the final step. Actions might include offering special promotional prices, rebates, or premiums. Salespeople might call or write to selected customers, inviting them to visit the dealership for a special showing. The Infiniti Web site (www.infiniti.com) tells potential buyers, "Own one and you'll understand," explains various financing options, and invites them to visit the local dealer's showroom.

Of course, marketing communications alone cannot create positive feelings and purchases for Infiniti. The car itself must provide superior value for the customer. In fact, outstanding marketing communications can actually speed the demise of a poor product. The more quickly potential buyers learn about the poor product, the more quickly they become aware of its faults. Thus, good marketing communication calls for "good deeds followed by good words."

video example
<

Consider the objectives of a familiar ad campaign.

DESIGNING A MESSAGE

Having defined the desired audience response, the communicator turns to developing an effective message. Ideally, the message should get *Attention,* hold *Interest,* arouse *Desire,* and obtain *Action* (a framework known as the *AIDA model*). In practice, few messages take the consumer all the way from awareness to purchase, but the AIDA framework suggests the desirable qualities of a good message. In putting the message together, the marketing communicator must decide what to say (*message content*) and how to say it (*message structure* and *format*).

active example
<

Take a moment to read about a novel way of attracting viewer attention.

Message Content

The communicator has to figure out an appeal or theme that will produce the desired response. There are three types of appeals: rational, emotional, and moral. *Rational appeals* relate to the audience's self-interest. They show that the product will produce the desired benefits. Examples are messages showing a product's quality, economy, value, or performance. Thus, in its ads, Mercedes offers automobiles that are "engineered like no other car in the world," stressing engineering design, performance, and safety.

Emotional appeals attempt to stir up either negative or positive emotions that can motivate purchase. Communicators may use positive emotional appeals such as love, pride, joy, and humor. For example, advocates for humorous messages claim that they attract more attention and create more liking and belief in the sponsor. Consider the recent series of ads from Hartford Financial Services Group:

> The insurer's new . . . ads use humor to talk about what for most people is either a deadly serious or eternally boring subject. New slogan: "Whatever life brings. Bring it on." In [one] spot, a kangaroo escapes from the zoo and starts bouncing through a crowd. "Possibility one: He flattens your car. Your Hartford auto policy covers the damage. Possibility two: He flattens your hot dog stand. Your Hartford small-business insurance helps you rebuild. Possibility three: He flattens your Great Aunt Edna. Might we suggest investing your inheritance in one of our top-selling annuities?" Funny, no? Hartford's chairman and chief executive . . . thinks so.

"Insurance ads often portray fires—mishaps if you will," he says. Now, "there is nothing humorous about a fire or a hurricane," he quickly adds. But "because everybody's ads are so serious" in the insurance business "we thought it would be neat if we portrayed a more energetic, confident, invigorating attitude to life. We wanted people to remember us, and we thought humor would bring that out." Insurance "is such a low-interest category, bordering on no interest," adds [an executive at Hartford's ad agency]. . . . "Creatively, you better make people cry or make them laugh, or it's not going to be memorable," she says. Hartford says consumer tests found the company's message—that it's in the financial-services industry and not just in insurance—came through clearly. What's more, she says, the ads "seemed to warm up the company's personality, and we want people to identify with us."[8]

Cliff Freeman, the adman responsible for a decade's worth of humorous Little Caesars' "Pizza, Pizza" ads, as well as more recent side splitters for companies like Staples and Outpost.com, contend that "Humor is a great way to bound out of the starting gate. When you make people laugh, and they feel good after seeing the commercial, they like the association with the product." But others maintain that humor can detract from comprehension, wear out its welcome fast, and overshadow the product.[9]

Communicators can also use negative emotional appeals, such as fear, guilt, and shame that get people to do things they should (brush their teeth, buy new tires) or to stop doing things they shouldn't (smoke, drink too much, eat fatty foods). For example, a Crest ad invokes mild fear when it claims, "There are some things you just can't afford to gamble with" (cavities). Etonic ads ask, "What would you do if you couldn't run?" They go on to note that Etonic athletic shoes are designed to avoid injuries—they're "built so you can last." The American Academy of Dermatology advertises, "One in every five Americans will develop skin cancer. Don't be the one."

Moral appeals are directed to the audience's sense of what is "right" and "proper." They are often used to urge people to support social causes such as a cleaner environment, better race relations, equal rights for women, and aid to the disadvantaged. An example of a moral appeal is the March of Dimes appeal, "God made you whole. Give to help those He didn't."

> ### active example

Consider how one company plans to use emotional appeal in its ad campaigns.

Message Structure

The communicator must also decide how to handle three message structure issues. The first is whether to draw a conclusion or leave it to the audience. Early research showed that drawing a conclusion was usually more effective. More recent research, however, suggests that in many cases the advertiser is better off asking questions and letting buyers come to their own conclusions. The second message structure issue is whether to present a one-sided argument (mentioning only the product's strengths) or a two-sided argument (touting the product's strengths while also admitting its shortcomings). Usually, a one-sided argument is more effective in sales presentations—except when audiences are highly educated or likely to hear opposing claims, or when the communicator has a negative association to overcome. In this spirit, Heinz ran the message "Heinz Ketchup is slow good" and Listerine ran the message "Listerine tastes bad twice a day."[10] In such cases, two-sided messages can enhance the advertiser's credibility and make buyers more resistant to competitor attacks. The third message structure issue is whether to present the strongest arguments first or last. Presenting them first gets strong attention but may lead to an anticlimactic ending.

Message Format

The marketing communicator also needs a strong *format* for the message. In a print ad, the communicator has to decide on the headline, copy, illustration, and color. To attract attention, advertisers can

[8]Sally Beatty, " 'Serious' Super Bowl Advertisers to Try Humor in Making Pitches," *Wall Street Journal,* January 28, 1999, p. B16.

[9]Kevin Goldman, "Advertising: Knock, Knock. Who's There? The Same Old Funny Ad Again," *Wall Street Journal,* November 2, 1993, p. B10; Melanie Wells, "Little Caesars Ads Aim for Pizza Lust," *USA Today,* November 16, 1998, p. 8B; and "Comedy Dominates the Best," *Advertising Age,* May 31, 1999, p. S2.

[10]See Ayn E. Crowley and Wayne D. Hoyer, "An Integrative Framework for Understanding Two-Sided Persuasion," *Journal of Consumer Research,* March 1994, pp. 561–74.

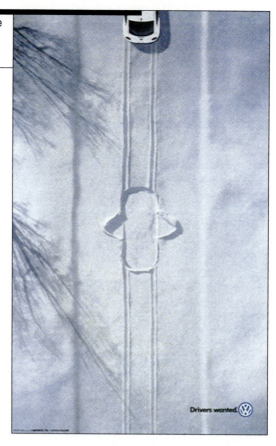

Message format: To attract attention, advertisers can use distinctive formats, novelty, and eye-catching pictures, as in this award-winning Volkswagen ad.

use novelty and contrast; eye-catching pictures and headlines; distinctive formats; message size and position; and color, shape, and movement. If the message is to be carried over the radio, the communicator has to choose words, sounds, and voices. The "sound" of an announcer promoting banking services should be different from one promoting quality furniture.

If the message is to be carried on television or in person, then all these elements plus body language have to be planned. Presenters plan their facial expressions, gestures, dress, posture, and hairstyle. If the message is carried on the product or its package, the communicator has to watch texture, scent, color, size, and shape. For example, color plays a major communication role in food preferences. When consumers sampled four cups of coffee that had been placed next to brown, blue, red, and yellow containers (the coffee samples were identical, but the consumers did not know this), 75 percent felt that the coffee next to the brown container tasted too strong; nearly 85 percent judged the coffee next to the red container to be the richest; nearly everyone felt that the coffee next to the blue container was mild; and the coffee next to the yellow container was judged as weak. Thus, if a coffee company wants to communicate that its coffee is rich, it should probably use a red container along with label copy boasting the coffee's rich taste.[11]

CHOOSING MEDIA

The communicator now must select *channels of communication*. There are two broad types of communication channels—*personal* and *nonpersonal*.

Personal Communication Channels

In **personal communication channels,** two or more people communicate directly with each other. They might communicate face to face, over the telephone, through the mail, or even through an Internet "chat." Personal communication channels are effective because they allow for personal addressing and feedback.

Some personal communication channels are controlled directly by the company. For example, company salespeople contact buyers in the target market. But other personal communications about

---

[11]Philip Kotler, *Marketing Management: Analysis, Planning, Implementation, and Control,* 10th ed. (Upper Saddle River, NJ: Prentice Hall, 2000), p. 559.

the product may reach buyers through channels not directly controlled by the company. These might include independent experts—consumer advocates, consumer buying guides, and others—making statements to target buyers. Or they might be neighbors, friends, family members, and associates talking to target buyers. This last channel, known as **word-of-mouth influence,** has considerable effect in many product areas.

Personal influence carries great weight for products that are expensive, risky, or highly visible. For example, buyers of automobiles and major appliances often go beyond mass-media sources to seek the opinions of knowledgeable people.

Companies can take steps to put personal communication channels to work for them. For example, they can create *opinion leaders*—people whose opinions are sought by others—by supplying certain people with the product on attractive terms. For instance, they can work through community members such as local radio personalities, class presidents, and heads of local organizations. They can use influential people in their advertisements or develop advertising that has high "conversation value."

Nonpersonal Communication Channels

Nonpersonal communication channels are media that carry messages without personal contact or feedback. They include major media, atmospheres, and events. Major *media* include print media (newspapers, magazines, direct mail), broadcast media (radio, television), display media (billboards, signs, posters), and online media (online services, Web sites). *Atmospheres* are designed environments that create or reinforce the buyer's leanings toward buying a product. Thus, lawyers' offices and banks are designed to communicate confidence and other qualities that might be valued by their clients. *Events* are staged occurrences that communicate messages to target audiences. For example, public relations departments arrange press conferences, grand openings, shows and exhibits, public tours, and other events.

Nonpersonal communication affects buyers directly. In addition, using mass media often affects buyers indirectly by causing more personal communication. Communications first flow from television, magazines, and other mass media to opinion leaders and then from these opinion leaders to others. Thus, opinion leaders step between the mass media and their audiences and carry messages to people who are less exposed to media. This suggests that mass communicators should aim their messages directly at opinion leaders, letting them carry the message to others.

SELECTING THE MESSAGE SOURCE

In either personal or nonpersonal communication, the message's impact on the target audience is also affected by how the audience views the communicator. Messages delivered by highly credible sources are more persuasive. Thus, marketers hire celebrity endorsers—well-known athletes, actors, and even cartoon characters—to deliver their messages. Many food companies promote to doctors, dentists, and other health care providers to motivate these professionals to recommend their products to patients.

Campbell Soup Company did this to promote its Intelligent Quisine (IQ) meal plan program of prepackaged, healthy frozen entrées and snacks delivered weekly via UPS to customers' homes. The 40 or so meals are tailored to nutritional guidelines limiting fat, cholesterol, and salt. To win over physicians, Campbell consulted with the American Heart Association and the American Diabetes Association and sponsored research on the program's effectiveness. Campbell salespeople visit health care professionals regularly, urging them to recommend the Intelligent Quisine program to their patients.[12]

COLLECTING FEEDBACK

After sending the message, the communicator must research its effect on the target audience. This involves asking the target audience members whether they remember the message, how many times they saw it, what points they recall, how they felt about the message, and their past and present attitudes toward the product and company. The communicator would also like to measure behavior resulting from the message—how many people bought a product, talked to others about it, or visited the store.

Feedback on marketing communications may suggest changes in the promotion program or in the product offer itself. For example, US Airways uses television and newspaper advertising to inform area consumers about the airline, its routes, and its fares. Suppose feedback research shows that 80 percent of all fliers in an area recall seeing the airline's ads and are aware of its flights and prices.

---

[12]Joseph Weber, "Now, Campbell's Makes House Calls," *Business Week,* June 16, 1997, pp. 144–46; and Chad Kaydo, "Selling a Lifestyle Change," *Sales & Marketing Management,* December 1997, p. 95.

Sixty percent of these aware fliers have flown US Airways, but only 20 percent of those who tried it were satisfied. These results suggest that although promotion is creating *awareness,* the airline isn't giving consumers the *satisfaction* they expect. Therefore, US Airways needs to improve its service while staying with the successful communication program. In contrast, suppose the research shows that only 40 percent of area consumers are aware of the airline, only 30 percent of those aware have tried it, but 80 percent of those who have tried it return. In this case, US Airways needs to strengthen its promotion program to take advantage of its power to create customer satisfaction.

active concept check   <

Now let's take a moment to test your knowledge of what you've just read.

> ### Setting the Total Promotion Budget and Mix

We have looked at the steps in planning and sending communications to a target audience. But how does the company decide on the total *promotion budget* and its division among the major promotional tools to create the *promotion mix?* By what process does it blend the tools to create integrated marketing communications? We now look at these questions.

SETTING THE TOTAL PROMOTION BUDGET

One of the hardest marketing decisions facing a company is how much to spend on promotion. John Wanamaker, the department store magnate, once said, "I know that half of my advertising is wasted, but I don't know which half. I spent $2 million for advertising, and I don't know if that is half enough or twice too much." Thus, it is not surprising that industries and companies vary widely in how much they spend on promotion. Promotion spending may be 20 to 30 percent of sales in the cosmetics industry and only 2 or 3 percent in the industrial machinery industry. Within a given industry, both low and high spenders can be found.[13]

How does a company decide on its promotion budget? We look at four common methods used to set the total budget for advertising: the *affordable method,* the *percentage-of-sales method,* the *competitive-parity method,* and the *objective-and-task method.*[14]

Affordable Method

Some companies use the **affordable method:** They set the promotion budget at the level they think the company can afford. Small businesses often use this method, reasoning that the company cannot spend more on advertising than it has. They start with total revenues, deduct operating expenses and capital outlays, and then devote some portion of the remaining funds to advertising.

Unfortunately, this method of setting budgets completely ignores the effects of promotion on sales. It tends to place advertising last among spending priorities, even in situations in which advertising is critical to the firm's success. It leads to an uncertain annual promotion budget, which makes long-range market planning difficult. Although the affordable method can result in overspending on advertising, it more often results in underspending.

Percentage-of-Sales Method

Other companies use the **percentage-of-sales method,** setting their promotion budget at a certain percentage of current or forecasted sales. Or they budget a percentage of the unit sales price. The percentage-of-sales method has advantages. It is simple to use and helps management think about the relationships between promotion spending, selling price, and profit per unit.

[13]"1999 Advertising-to-Sales Ratios for the 200 Largest Ad Spending Industries," *Advertising Age,* June 28, 1999, p. 58.

[14]For more on setting promotion budgets, see George S. Low and Jakki J. Mohr, "Brand Managers' Perceptions of the Marketing Communications Budget Allocation Process," Marketing Science Institute, Report No. 98-105, March 1998; and J. Thomas Russell and W. Ronald Lane, *Kleppner's Advertising Procedure,* 14th ed. (Upper Saddle River, NJ: Prentice Hall, 1999), chap. 6.

Despite these claimed advantages, however, the percentage-of-sales method has little to justify it. It wrongly views sales as the *cause* of promotion rather than as the *result.* "A study in this area found good correlation between investments in advertising and the strength of the brands concerned—but it turned out to be effect and cause, not cause and effect. . . . The strongest brands had the highest sales and could afford the biggest investments in advertising!"[15] Thus, the percentage-of-sales budget is based on availability of funds rather than on opportunities. It may prevent the increased spending sometimes needed to turn around falling sales. Because the budget varies with year-to-year sales, long-range planning is difficult. Finally, the method does not provide any basis for choosing a *specific* percentage, except what has been done in the past or what competitors are doing.

Competitive-Parity Method

Still other companies use the **competitive-parity method,** setting their promotion budgets to match competitors' outlays. They monitor competitors' advertising or get industry promotion spending estimates from publications or trade associations, and then set their budgets based on the industry average.

Two arguments support this method. First, competitors' budgets represent the collective wisdom of the industry. Second, spending what competitors spend helps prevent promotion wars. Unfortunately, neither argument is valid. There are no grounds for believing that the competition has a better idea of what a company should be spending on promotion than does the company itself. Companies differ greatly, and each has its own special promotion needs. Finally, there is no evidence that budgets based on competitive parity prevent promotion wars.

> ### active exercise

Business thrives on information. Consider what a firm could do with information about competitors' ad budgets.

Objective-and-Task Method

The most logical budget-setting method is the **objective-and-task method,** whereby the company sets its promotion budget based on what it wants to accomplish with promotion. This budgeting method entails (1) defining specific promotion objectives, (2) determining the tasks needed to achieve these objectives, and (3) estimating the costs of performing these tasks. The sum of these costs is the proposed promotion budget.

The objective-and-task method forces management to spell out its assumptions about the relationship between dollars spent and promotion results. But it is also the most difficult method to use. Often, it is hard to figure out which specific tasks will achieve specific objectives. For example, suppose Sony wants 95 percent awareness for its latest camcorder model during the six-month introductory period. What specific advertising messages and media schedules should Sony use to attain this objective? How much would these messages and media schedules cost? Sony management must consider such questions, even though they are hard to answer.

SETTING THE OVERALL PROMOTION MIX

The company now must divide the total promotion budget among the major promotion tools—advertising, personal selling, sales promotion, public relations, and direct marketing. The concept of integrated marketing communications suggests that it must blend the promotion tools carefully into a coordinated *promotion mix.* But how does the company determine what mix of promotion tools it will use? Companies within the same industry differ greatly in the design of their promotion mixes. For example, Avon spends most of its promotion funds on personal selling and direct marketing, whereas Revlon spends heavily on consumer advertising. Compaq Computer relies on advertising and promotion to retailers, whereas Dell Computer uses only direct marketing. We now look at factors that influence the marketer's choice of promotion tools.

[15]David Allen, "Excessive Use of the Mirror," *Management Accounting,* June 1966, p. 12. Also see Laura Petrecca, "4A's Will Study Financial Return on Ad Spending," *Advertising Age,* April 7, 1997, pp. 3, 52; and Dana W. Hayman and Don E. Schultz, "How Much Should You Spend on Advertising," *Advertising Age,* April 26, 1999, p. 32.

The Nature of Each Promotion Tool

Each promotion tool has unique characteristics and costs. Marketers must understand these characteristics in selecting their tools.

Advertising. Advertising can reach masses of geographically dispersed buyers at a low cost per exposure, and it enables the seller to repeat a message many times. For example, television advertising can reach huge audiences. More than 127 million Americans tuned into the most recent Super Bowl and about 78 million people watched at least part of the past Academy Awards broadcast. "If you want to get to the mass audience," says a media services executive, "broadcast TV is where you have to be." He adds, "For anybody introducing anything who has to lasso an audience in a hurry—a new product, a new campaign, a new movie—the networks are still the biggest show in town."[16]

Beyond its reach, large-scale advertising says something positive about the seller's size, popularity, and success. Because of advertising's public nature, consumers tend to view advertised products as more legitimate. Advertising is also very expressive—it allows the company to dramatize its products through the artful use of visuals, print, sound, and color. On the one hand, advertising can be used to build up a long-term image for a product (such as Coca-Cola ads). On the other hand, advertising can trigger quick sales (as when Sears advertises a weekend sale).

Advertising also has some shortcomings. Although it reaches many people quickly, advertising is impersonal and cannot be as directly persuasive as company salespeople. For the most part, advertising can carry on only a one-way communication with the audience, and the audience does not feel that it has to pay attention or respond. In addition, advertising can be very costly. Although some advertising forms, such as newspaper and radio advertising, can be done on smaller budgets, other forms, such as network TV advertising, require very large budgets.

Personal Selling. Personal selling is the most effective tool at certain stages of the buying process, particularly in building up buyers' preferences, convictions, and actions. It involves personal interaction between two or more people, so each person can observe the other's needs and characteristics and make quick adjustments. Personal selling also allows all kinds of relationships to spring up, ranging from a matter-of-fact selling relationship to personal friendship. The effective salesperson keeps the customer's interests at heart in order to build a long-term relationship. Finally, with personal selling the buyer usually feels a greater need to listen and respond, even if the response is a polite "no thank you."

These unique qualities come at a cost, however. A sales force requires a longer-term commitment than does advertising—advertising can be turned on and off, but sales force size is harder to change. Personal selling is also the company's most expensive promotion tool, costing companies $165 on average per sales call.[17] U.S. firms spend up to three times as much on personal selling as they do on advertising.

Sales Promotion. Sales promotion includes a wide assortment of tools—coupons, contests, cents-off deals, premiums, and others—all of which have many unique qualities. They attract consumer attention, offer strong incentives to purchase, and can be used to dramatize product offers and to boost sagging sales. Sales promotions invite and reward quick response—whereas advertising says, "Buy our product," sales promotion says, "Buy it now." Sales promotion effects are often short lived, however, and often are not as effective as advertising or personal selling in building long-run brand preference.

Public Relations. Public relations is very believable—news stories, features, and events seem more real and believable to readers than ads do. Public relations can also reach many prospects who avoid salespeople and advertisements—the message gets to the buyers as "news" rather than as a sales-directed communication. As with advertising, public relations can dramatize a company or product. Marketers tend to underuse public relations or to use it as an afterthought. Yet a well-thought-out public relations campaign used with other promotion mix elements can be very effective and economical.

Direct Marketing. Although there are many forms of direct marketing— telemarketing, direct mail, electronic marketing, online marketing, and others—they all share four distinctive characteristics. Direct marketing is *nonpublic:* The message is normally addressed to a specific person. Direct marketing also is *immediate* and *customized:* Messages can be prepared very quickly, and they can be tailored to appeal to specific consumers. Finally, direct marketing is *interactive:* It allows a dialogue between the marketing and the consumer, and messages can be altered depending on the consumer's response. Thus, direct marketing is well suited to highly targeted marketing efforts and to building one-to-one customer relationships.

---

[16]Stuart Elliott, "Fewer Viewers, More Commercials," *New York Times,* June 8, 1999, p. 1.

[17]Michele Marchetti, "The Costs of Doing Business," *Sales & Marketing Management,* September 1999, p. 56.

Promotion Mix Strategies

Marketers can choose from two basic promotion mix strategies—*push* promotion or *pull* promotion. Figure 14.4 contrasts the two strategies. The relative emphasis on the specific promotion tools differs for push and pull strategies. A **push strategy** involves "pushing" the product through distribution channels to final consumers. The producer directs its marketing activities (primarily personal selling and trade promotion) toward channel members to induce them to carry the product and to promote it to final consumers. Using a **pull strategy,** the producer directs its marketing activities (primarily advertising and consumer promotion) toward final consumers to induce them to buy the product. If the pull strategy is effective, consumers will then demand the product from channel members, who will in turn demand it from producers. Thus, under a pull strategy, consumer demand "pulls" the product through the channels.

Some small industrial goods companies use only push strategies; some direct-marketing companies use only pull. However, most large companies use some combination of both. For example, Frito-Lay uses mass-media advertising to pull its products and a large sales force and trade promotions to push its products through the channels. In recent years, consumer goods companies have been decreasing the pull portions of their promotion mixes in favor of more push.

Companies consider many factors when developing their promotion mix strategies, including *type of product–market* and the *product life-cycle stage.* For example, the importance of different promotion tools varies between consumer and business markets. Consumer goods companies usually "pull" more, putting more of their funds into advertising, followed by sales promotion, personal selling, and then public relations. In contrast, business-to-business marketers tend to "push" more, putting more of their funds into personal selling, followed by sales promotion, advertising, and public relations. In general, personal selling is used more heavily with expensive and risky goods and in markets with fewer and larger sellers.

The effects of different promotion tools also vary with stages of the product life cycle. In the introduction stage, advertising and public relations are good for producing high awareness, and sales promotion is useful in promoting early trial. Personal selling must be used to get the trade to carry the product. In the growth stage, advertising and public relations continue to be powerful influences, whereas sales promotion can be reduced because fewer incentives are needed. In the mature stage, sales promotion again becomes important relative to advertising. Buyers know the brands, and advertising is needed only to remind them of the product. In the decline stage, advertising is kept at a reminder level, public relations is dropped, and salespeople give the product only a little attention. Sales promotion, however, might continue strong.

INTEGRATING THE PROMOTION MIX

Having set the promotion budget and mix, the company must now take steps to see that all of the promotion mix elements are smoothly integrated. Here is a checklist for integrating the firm's marketing communications.[18]

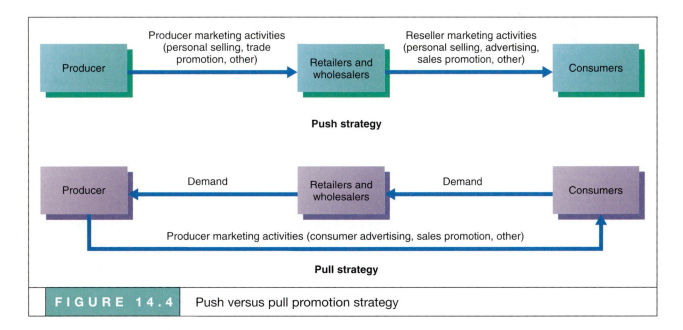

FIGURE 14.4   Push versus pull promotion strategy

[18]Based on Matthew P. Gonring, "Putting Integrated Marketing Communications to Work Today," *Public Relations Quarterly,* Fall 1994, pp. 45–48.

- *Analyze trends—internal and external—that can affect your company's ability to do business:* Look for areas where communications can help the most. Determine the strengths and weaknesses of each communications function. Develop a combination of promotional tactics based on these strengths and weaknesses.

- *Audit the pockets of communications spending throughout the organization:* Itemize the communications budgets and tasks and consolidate these into a single budgeting process. Reassess all communications expenditures by product, promotional tool, stage of the life cycle, and observed effect.

- *Identify all contact points for the company and its brands:* Work to ensure that communications at each point are consistent with your overall communications strategy and that your communications efforts are occurring when, where, and how your *customers* want them.

- *Team up in communications planning:* Engage all communications functions in joint planning. Include customers, suppliers, and other stakeholders at every stage of communications planning.

- *Create compatible themes, tones, and quality across all communications media:* Make sure each element carries your unique primary messages and selling points. This consistency achieves greater impact and prevents the unnecessary duplication of work across functions.

- *Create performance measures that are shared by all communications elements:* Develop systems to evaluate the combined impact of all communications activities.

- *Appoint a director responsible for the company's persuasive communications efforts:* This move encourages efficiency by centralizing planning and creating shared performance measures.

video example <

Watch this video to take a look at how on company approaches the issue of IMC.

active concept check <

Now let's take a moment to test your knowledge of what you've just read.

 Socially Responsible Marketing Communication

In shaping its promotion mix, a company must be aware of the large body of legal and ethical issues surrounding marketing communications. Most marketers work hard to communicate openly and honestly with consumers and resellers. Still, abuses may occur, and public policy makers have developed a substantial body of laws and regulations to govern advertising, sales promotion, personal selling, and direct-marketing activities. In this section, we discuss issues regarding advertising, sales promotion, and personal selling. Issues regarding direct marketing are addressed in chapter 17.

ADVERTISING AND SALES PROMOTION

By law, companies must avoid false or deceptive advertising. Advertisers must not make false claims, such as suggesting that a product cures something when it does not. They must avoid ads that have the capacity to deceive, even though no one actually may be deceived. An automobile cannot be advertised as getting 32 miles per gallon unless it does so under typical conditions, and a diet bread cannot be advertised as having fewer calories simply because its slices are thinner.

Sellers must avoid bait-and-switch advertising that attracts buyers under false pretenses. For example, a large retailer advertised a sewing machine at $179. However, when consumers tried to buy the advertised machine, the seller downplayed its features, placed faulty machines on showroom floors, understated the machine's performance, and took other actions in an attempt to switch buyers to a more expensive machine. Such actions are both unethical and illegal.

A company's trade promotion activities also are closely regulated. For example, under the Robinson-Patman Act, sellers cannot favor certain customers through their use of trade promotions. They must make promotional allowances and services available to all resellers on proportionately equal terms.

Beyond simply avoiding legal pitfalls, such as deceptive or bait-and-switch advertising, companies can use advertising to encourage and promote socially responsible programs and actions. For example, State Farm joined with the National Council for Social Studies, National Science Teachers Association, and other national teachers' organizations to create a Good Neighbor Award to recognize primary and secondary teachers for innovation, leadership, and involvement in their profession. State Farm promotes the award through a series of print advertisements. Similarly, Caterpillar is one of several companies and environmental groups forming the Tropical Forest Foundation, which is working to save the great Amazon rain forest. It uses advertising to promote the cause and its involvement.

> ## active poll

Give your opinion on a question concerning advertising claims.

PERSONAL SELLING

A company's salespeople must follow the rules of "fair competition." Most states have enacted deceptive sales acts that spell out what is not allowed. For example, salespeople may not lie to consumers or mislead them about the advantages of buying a product. To avoid bait-and-switch practices, salespeople's statements must match advertising claims.

Different rules apply to consumers who are called on at home versus those who go to a store in search of a product. Because people called on at home may be taken by surprise and may be especially vulnerable to high-pressure selling techniques, the Federal Trade Commission (FTC) has adopted a *three-day cooling-off rule* to give special protection to customers who are not seeking products. Under this rule, customers who agree in their own homes to buy something costing more than $25 have 72 hours in which to cancel a contract or return merchandise and get their money back, no questions asked.

Much personal selling involves business-to-business trade. In selling to businesses, salespeople may not offer bribes to purchasing agents or to others who can influence a sale. They may not obtain or use technical or trade secrets of competitors through bribery or industrial espionage. Finally, salespeople must not disparage competitors or competing products by suggesting things that are not true.[19]

> ## active example

Take a moment to read how one company is proactively making its promotions more socially responsible.

> ## active concept check

Now let's take a moment to test your knowledge of what you've just read.

[19]For more on the legal aspects of promotion, see Louis W. Stern and Thomas I. Eovaldi, *Legal Aspects of Marketing Policy* (Upper Saddle River, NJ: Prentice Hall, 1984), chaps. 7 and 8; Robert J. Posch, *The Complete Guide to Marketing and the Law* (Upper Saddle River, NJ: Prentice Hall, 1988), chaps. 15 to 17; and William Wells, John Burnett, and Sandra Moriarty, *Advertising Principles and Practice,* 4th ed. (Upper Saddle River, NJ: Prentice Hall, 1998), chap. 2.

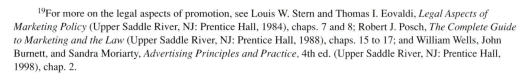

Now that you've reached the end of the chapter, you may wish to explore the concepts you've been reading about in greater detail, or test yourself to see how well you've comprehended the material. In the box below you'll find a number of links. Click on any one of these links to find additional chapter resources.

> end-of-chapter resources

- Review of Concept Connections
- Practice Quiz
- Issues for Discussion
- Key Terms
- Marketing Applications
- Internet Connections
- Company Case

CHAPTER 15

Advertising, Sales Promotion, and Public Relations

> What's Ahead

The senior marketing manager for M&M/Mars knew she was on to something when she got a call from her daughter at school. It seems that the kids in her daughter's class were picking up the phrase, "Not going anywhere for a while? Grab a Snickers." This was music to the woman behind the now highly successful Snickers advertising campaign.

In its "Not going anywhere for a while?" theme—later simplified to "Hungry? Why Wait?"—Snickers had found the elusive "big idea"—a creative approach that turns a solid advertising strategy into a great ad campaign. During the past three years, the idea has become the basis for a series of wonderfully engaging, award-winning commercials that spill over with brand personality. Such commercials are crucial in today's cluttered and chaotic TV advertising environment, in which the average U.S. adult is exposed to as many as 247 ads a day. Before an ad can even start to communicate a selling proposition, it must first break through the din of commercials and other distractions to capture viewer attention. Humor is often the best clutter buster, and the Snickers ads are delightfully funny.

The campaign has consisted of several humorous variations on a central premise: Through circumstances beyond their control, characters in the ads find themselves stuck in one place for a long time, without access to a meal. The first spot in the campaign featured Buffalo Bills coach Marv Levy—who had taken teams to the Super Bowl four times without a win—lecturing his players that nobody would leave until they figured out how to win the big game. The ad was funny. It was also very expensive—football stars don't come cheap. So the creative team at BBDO Worldwide, the Snickers ad agency, set out to reduce production ex-penses. "We have a great idea," said the ad agency's creative director to his team. "Let's simplify it." The team responded with five new spots that not only cost less to produce but also allowed more effective use of 15-second media slots versus 30-second ones, thus saving on media costs as well. The lower budget created a kind of modesty and simplicity in the Snickers campaign that made the new ads even more appealing than the original.

One of these ads, set in a football locker room, took a good-natured poke at political correctness. In the ad, a gruff, crew-cut head coach announces, "Listen up. This year we gotta be a little more 'politically correct' with the team prayer." He turns to a priest standing behind him and says, "Hit it, Padre." The priest begins his prayer, but before he can go on, the coach butts in to introduce a second clergyman. "All right, Rabbi. Let's go." The rabbi too is cut off, this time in favor of a Native American spiritualist, who in turn gives way to a Buddhist monk. "That was very touching," growls the coach. As the camera pans the room to reveal a long line of spiritual leaders waiting to bless the team, the voice-over says, "Not going anywhere for a while? Grab a Snickers."

Some may take the Snickers campaign as comedy for comedy's sake, but beneath the funny lines is a very serious selling proposition. The stakes are high and so is the investment—M&M/Mars spends tens of millions of dollars each year on advertising for Snickers. The campaign's objective is to advance Snickers' long-time hunger-satisfaction positioning—it's what to eat to satisfy your between-meal hunger. Previous advertising portrayed idealized role models such as firefighters and investigative reporters scarfing down Snickers bars before committing nougat-fortified acts of heroism. Those ads were neither entertaining nor relevant to the brand's primary target market of males 18 to 22 years old. The new ads are both. They give Snickers a less serious tone and position the brand more credibly and believably as a hunger-relieving stop-gap measure. "We moved [our positioning] from [damping] a preoccupying hunger to satisfying hunger in an enjoyable way," says the senior marketing manager.

Perhaps the most memorable ad was "Chefs." The ad opens with Clarence, the "Chiefs'" elderly end zone painter, painstakingly reproducing the team logo beneath the goal posts. As he steps back finally to admire his work, a player walks up behind him. "Hey, that's great," says the beefy player, "but who are the Chefs?" Yes, he left out the "i," which is amusing, but his reaction is hilarious. "Great googily moogily," he grumbles. (It's a line one member of the ad team remembered hearing an old uncle exclaim.) Disgusted that he's not going anywhere for a while, he gnaws on a Snickers.

A more recent ad taps the old gag of an umpire needing eyeglasses. A long-suffering but patient optometrist deals with a ref in a striped shirt who keeps seeing cows on the letter chart. "No, there are no cows," says the doctor gently. Meanwhile, his bored assistant looks outside the examination room to see a dozen officials in the waiting room. As the announcer asks "Hungry? Why Wait?" the assistant takes a big chomp out of a super-size Snickers bar.

Lots of people *are* chomping a Snickers, it would appear. The aggressive ad campaign has helped make Snickers one of the best-performing candy and snack brands in the country. The campaign seems to have captured the minds and imaginations of American consumers. "Enjoy-ability, memorability, and awareness of the thing have gone through the roof," says the director of marketing for the brand.

Thus, the Snickers advertising campaign amounts to much more than just funny ads. Bob Garfield, ad reviewer for *Advertising Age,* concludes, "The annals of advertising record very few . . . enduring 'big ideas,' but soon you may add to the list [Hungry? Why Wait?]. . . . As the campaign inexorably develops—and it will, over many years—this [big] idea will be revealed to have more than charm. It will have depth, scope, and the endless power of surprise. So grab a Snickers and enjoy. This advertising isn't going away for a long, long, time." In 1999, for the third year in a row, a Snickers "Hungry? Why Wait?" ad was selected as the Ad Age Best TV Spot in the packaged-goods category.[1]

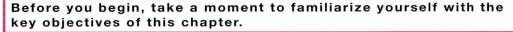

> objectives

Before you begin, take a moment to familiarize yourself with the key objectives of this chapter.

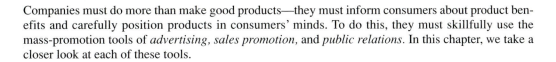

> gearing up

Before we begin our exploration this chapter, take a short warm-up test to see what you know about this topic.

Companies must do more than make good products—they must inform consumers about product benefits and carefully position products in consumers' minds. To do this, they must skillfully use the mass-promotion tools of *advertising, sales promotion,* and *public relations.* In this chapter, we take a closer look at each of these tools.

> Advertising

Advertising can be traced back to the very beginnings of recorded history. Archaeologists working in the countries around the Mediterranean Sea have dug up signs announcing various events and offers. The Romans painted walls to announce gladiator fights, and the Phoenicians painted pictures promoting their wares on large rocks along parade routes. A Pompeii wall painting praised a politician and asked for votes. During the Golden Age in Greece, town criers announced the sale of cattle, crafted items, and even cosmetics. An early "singing commercial" went as follows: "For eyes that are shining, for cheeks like the dawn/For beauty that lasts after girlhood is gone/For prices in reason, the woman who knows/Will buy her cosmetics from Aesclyptos."

Modern advertising, however, is a far cry from these early efforts. U.S. advertisers now run up an estimated annual advertising bill of more than $212 billion; worldwide ad spending exceeds $414 billion.[2] Although advertising is used mostly by business firms, it also is used by a wide range of nonprofit organizations, professionals, and social agencies that advertise their causes to various target publics. In fact, the twenty-fifth largest advertising spender is a nonprofit organization—the U.S. government. Advertising is a good way to inform and persuade, whether the purpose is to sell Coca-Cola worldwide or to get consumers in a developing nation to drink milk or use birth control.

Large national advertisers spend huge amounts to position their brands and influence buyers. General Motors, the nation's top advertiser, spends $2.9 billion annually in the United States

[1]Portions adapted from "The Marketing 100: Snickers' Santa Cruz Hughes," *Advertising Age,* June 30, 1997, p. S32; Bob Garfield, "Snickers Ads Grab the Elusive 'Big Idea,'" *Advertising Age,* September 2, 1996, p. 37; Bob Garfield, "Best TV: Snickers," *Advertising Age,* May 26, 1997, p. S1; and "A Sure Thing? Hunger Pangs Have One Answer: Snickers Satisfies," *Advertising Age,* May 31, 1999, pp. S2, S12.

[2]Robert J. Coen, "Spending Spree," *Advertising Age Special Issue: The Advertising Century,* 1999, p. 126.

alone. Number-two Procter & Gamble spends $2.7 billion in the United States and more than twice that amount worldwide.[3] Other major spenders are found in the retailing, auto, food, and entertainment industries. Advertising as a percentage of sales varies greatly by industry. For example, percentage spending is low in the auto industry but high in food, drugs, toiletries, and cosmetics.

Marketing management must make four important decisions when developing an advertising program (see Figure 15.1): *setting advertising objectives, setting advertising budgets, developing advertising strategy (message decisions and media decisions), and evaluating advertising campaigns.*

SETTING ADVERTISING OBJECTIVES

The first step is to set *advertising objectives.* These objectives should be based on past decisions about the target market, positioning, and marketing mix, which define the job that advertising must do in the total marketing program.

An **advertising objective** is a specific communication *task* to be accomplished with a specific *target* audience during a specific period of *time.* Advertising objectives can be classified by primary purpose—whether the aim is to *inform, persuade,* or *remind.* Table 15.1 lists examples of each of these objectives.

Informative advertising is used heavily when introducing a new product category. In this case, the objective is to build primary demand. Thus, producers of CD players first informed consumers of the sound and convenience benefits of CDs. *Persuasive advertising* becomes more important as competition increases. Here, the company's objective is to build selective demand. For example, once CD players were established, Sony began trying to persuade consumers that *its* brand offered the best quality for their money.

Some persuasive advertising has become *comparative advertising,* in which a company directly or indirectly compares its brand with one or more other brands. Comparative advertising has been used for products ranging from soft drinks and computers to batteries, pain relievers, long-distance telephone services, car rentals, and credit cards. For example, in its classic comparative campaign, Avis positioned itself against market-leading Hertz by claiming, "We're number two, so we try harder." More recently, Buick ran a "Century Challenge" campaign in which it compared the Buick Century directly against the Ford Taurus and other midsize cars. The aggressive ads take jabs at Taurus's smaller truck and at aspects of the Toyota Camry and Honda Accord that Buick contends compare unfavorably with its Century. In its long-running comparative campaign, Visa has advertised, "American Express is offering you a new credit card, but you don't have to accept it. Heck, 7 million merchants don't." American Express has responded with ads bashing Visa, noting that AmEx's cards offer benefits not available with Visa's regular card, such as rapid replacement of lost cards and higher

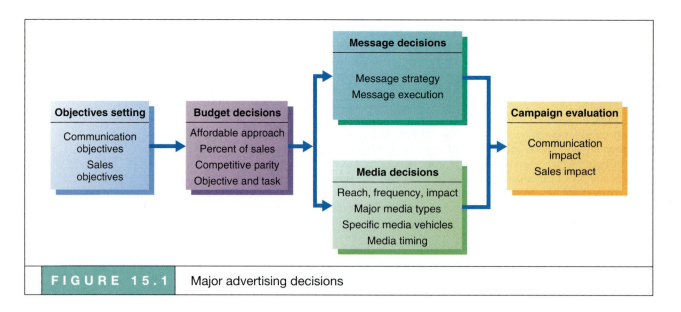

| FIGURE 15.1 | Major advertising decisions |

---

[3]Statistical information in this section on advertising's size and composition draws from information accessed online from http://adage.com/dataplace, December 1999.

TABLE 15.1	Possible Advertising Objectives

To Inform

Telling the market about a new product	Describing available services
Suggesting new uses for a product	Correcting false impressions
Informing the market of a price change	Reducing buyers' fears
Explaining how the product works	Building a company image

To Persuade

Building brand preference	Persuading customers to purchase now
Encouraging switching to your brand	Persuading customers to receive a sales call
Changing customer perceptions of product attributes	

To Remind

Reminding customers that the product may be needed in the near future	Keeping the product in customers' minds during off-seasons
Reminding customers where to buy the product	Maintaining top-of-mind product awareness

Comparative advertising: This ad compares Tylenol—very favorably—to Excedrin.

credit limits. As often happens with comparative advertising, both sides complain that the other's ads are misleading.[4]

Reminder advertising is important for mature products—it keeps consumers thinking about the product. Expensive Coca-Cola ads on television are designed primarily to remind people about Coca-Cola, not to inform or persuade them.

active exercise <

Consider the challenges of setting advertising objectives.

SETTING THE ADVERTISING BUDGET

After determining its advertising objectives, the company next sets its *advertising budget* for each product. Four commonly used methods for setting promotion budgets are discussed in chapter 14. Here we discuss some specific factors that should be considered when setting the advertising budget.

A brand's advertising budget often depends on its *stage in the product life cycle*. For example, new products typically need large advertising budgets to build awareness and to gain consumer trial. In contrast, mature brands usually require lower budgets as a ratio to sales. *Market share* also impacts the amount advertising needed: Because building the market or taking share from competitors requires larger advertising spending than does simply maintaining current share, high-share brands usually need more advertising spending as a percentage of sales. Also, brands in a market with many competitors and high advertising clutter must be advertised more heavily to be noticed above the noise in the market. Undifferentiated brands—those that closely resemble other brands in their product class (beer, soft drinks, laundry detergents)—may require heavy advertising to set them apart. When the product differs greatly from competitors, advertising can be used to point out the differences to consumers.

No matter what method is used, setting the advertising budget is no easy task. How does a company know if it is spending the right amount? Some critics charge that large consumer packaged-goods firms tend to spend too much on advertising and business-to-business marketers generally underspend on advertising. They claim that, on the one hand, the large consumer companies use lots of image advertising without really knowing its effects. They overspend as a form of "insurance" against not spending enough. On the other hand, business advertisers tend to rely too heavily on their sales forces to bring in orders. They underestimate the power of company and product image in pre-selling to industrial customers. Thus, they do not spend enough on advertising to build customer awareness and knowledge.

Companies such as Coca-Cola and Kraft have built sophisticated statistical models to determine the relationship between promotional spending and brand sales, and to help determine the "optimal investment" across various media. Still, because so many factors affect advertising effectiveness, some controllable and others not, measuring the results of advertising spending remains an inexact science. In most cases, managers must rely on large doses of judgment along with more quantitative analysis when setting advertising budgets.[5]

DEVELOPING ADVERTISING STRATEGY

Advertising strategy consists of two major elements: creating advertising *messages* and selecting advertising *media*. In the past, companies often viewed media planning as secondary to the message-creation process. The creative department first created good advertisements, then the media department selected the best media for carrying these advertisements to desired target audiences. This often caused friction between creatives and media planners.

[4]See Dhruv Grewel, Sukumar Kavanoor, Edward F. Fern, Carolyn Costley, and James Barnes, "Comparative Versus Noncomparative Advertising: A Meta-Analysis," *Journal of Marketing,* October 1997, pp. 1–15; "Attribute Upgrading Through Across-Class, Within-Category Comparison Advertising," *Journal of Advertising Research,* March–April 1998, pp. 6–16; Stuart Van Auken and Arthur J. Adams, "Across- Versus Within-Class Comparative Advertising: Insights into Prestige Class Anchoring," *Psychology & Marketing,* August 1999, p. 429–50; and Jeff Green, "Buick Aims 'Challenge' at Rivals," *Brandweek,* June 21, 1999, p. 10.

[5]See Andrew Ehrenberg, Neil Barnard, and John Scriven, "Justifying Our Advertising Budgets," *Marketing & Research Today,* February 1997, pp. 38–44; and Dana W. Hayman and Don E. Schultz, "How Much Should You Spend on Advertising?" *Advertising Age,* April 26, 1999, p. 32.

Today, however, media fragmentation, soaring media costs, and more focused target marketing strategies have promoted the importance of the media-planning function. In some cases, an advertising campaign might start with a great message idea, followed by the choice of appropriate media. In other cases, however, a campaign might begin with a good media opportunity, followed by advertisements designed to take advantage of that opportunity. Increasingly, companies are realizing the benefits of planning these two important elements *jointly.*

Thus, more and more advertisers are orchestrating a closer harmony between their messages and the media that deliver them. Media planning is no longer an after-the-fact complement to a new ad campaign. Media planners are now working more closely than ever with creatives to allow media selection to help shape the creative process, often before a single ad is written. In some cases, media people are even initiating ideas for new campaigns.

Among the more noteworthy ad campaigns based on tight media-creative partnerships is the pioneering campaign for Absolut vodka, marketed by Seagram.

The Absolut team and its ad agency meet once each year with a slew of magazines to set Absolut's media schedule. The schedule consists of up to 100 magazines, ranging from consumer and business magazines to theater playbills. The agency's creative department is charged with creating media-specific ads. The result is a wonderful assortment of very creative ads for Absolut, tightly targeted to audiences of the media in which they appear. For example, an "Absolut Bravo" ad in playbills has roses adorning a clear bottle, whereas business magazines contain an "Absolut Merger" foldout. In New York–area magazines, "Absolut Manhattan" ads feature a satellite photo of Manhattan, with Central Park assuming the distinctive outline of an Absolut bottle. In Chicago, the windy city, ads show an Absolut bottle with the letters on the label blown askew. An "Absolute Primary" ad run during the political season featured the well-known bottle spattered with mud. In some cases, the creatives even developed ads for magazines not yet on the schedule, such as a clever "Absolut Centerfold" ad for *Playboy* magazine. The ad portrayed a clear, unadorned playmate bottle ("11-inch bust, 11-inch waist, 11-inch hips"). In all, Absolut has developed

Media planners for Absolut vodka work with creatives to design ads targeted to specific media audiences. "Absolut Bravo" appears in theater playbills. "Absolut Chicago" targets the Windy City.

more than 500 ads for the almost two-decade-old campaign. At a time of soaring media costs and cluttered communication channels, a closer cooperation between creative and media people has paid off handsomely for Absolut. Largely as a result of its breakthrough advertising, Absolut now captures a 63 percent share of the imported vodka market.[6]

Creating the Advertising Message

No matter how big the budget, advertising can succeed only if commercials gain attention and communicate well. Good advertising messages are especially important in today's costly and cluttered advertising environment. The average number of television channels beamed into U.S. homes has skyrocketed from 3 in 1950 to 47 today, and consumers have 18,600 magazines from which to choose.[7] Add the countless radio stations and a continuous barrage of catalogs, direct-mail and online ads, and out-of-home media, and consumers are being bombarded with ads at home, at work, and at all points in between.

If all this advertising clutter bothers some consumers, it also causes big problems for advertisers. Take the situation facing network television advertisers. They regularly pay $200,000 or more for 30 seconds of advertising time during a popular prime-time program, even more if it's an especially popular program such as *ER* ($545,000 per 30-second spot), *Friends* ($510,000), *Frasier* ($466,000 per spot), *The Drew Carey Show* ($370,000), or a mega-event such as the Super Bowl (more than $1.6 million).[8] Then, their ads are sandwiched in with a clutter of some 60 other commercials, announcements, and network promotions per hour.

Until recently, television viewers were pretty much a captive audience for advertisers. Viewers had only a few channels from which to choose. But with the growth in cable and satellite TV, VCRs, and remote-control units, today's viewers have many more options. They can avoid ads by watching commercial-free cable channels. They can "zap" commercials by pushing the fast-forward button during taped programs. With remote control, they can instantly turn off the sound during a commercial or "zip" around the channels to see what else is on. In fact, a recent study found that half of all television viewers now switch channels when the commercial break starts.[9]

Thus, just to gain and hold attention, today's advertising messages must be better planned, more imaginative, more entertaining, and more rewarding to consumers. "Today we have to entertain and not just sell, because if you try to sell directly and come off as boring or obnoxious, people are going to press the remote on you," points out one advertising executive. "When most TV viewers are armed with remote channel switchers, a commercial has to cut through the clutter and seize the viewers in one to three seconds, or they're gone," comments another.[10] Some advertisers even create intentionally controversial ads to break through the clutter and gain attention for their products.

video example   <

Watch a group of executives discuss the creative strategy for a well-known ad campaign.

Message Strategy.   The first step in creating effective advertising messages is to decide what general message will be communicated to consumers—to plan a *message strategy*. The purpose of advertising is to get consumers to think about or react to the product or company in a certain way. People will react only if they believe that they will benefit from doing so. Thus, developing an effective message strategy begins with identifying customer *benefits* that can be used as advertising

[6]Information from Gary Levin, "'Meddling' in Creative More Welcome," *Advertising Age,* April 9, 1990, pp. S4, S8; Lynne Roberts, "New Media Choice: Absolut Vodka," *Marketing,* April 9, 1998, p. 12; Eleftheria Parpis, "TBWA: Absolut," *Adweek,* November 9, 1998, p. 172; and the Q&A section at www.absolutvodka.com, March 2000.

[7]"Swimming the Channels," *American Demographics,* June 1998, p. 37; and information obtained online at www.magazine.org, February 2000.

[8]"1999–2000 Network TV Price Estimates," *Advertising Age,* September 20, 1999, p. 12.

[9]Richard Cook, "Tackling the Problem of Increased TV Zapping," *Campaign,* September 25, 1998, p. 16.

[10]Edward A. Robinson, "Frogs, Bears, and Orgasms: Think Zany If You Want to Reach Today's Consumers," *Fortune,* June 9, 1997, pp. 153–56. Also see Marc Gunther, "What's Wrong with This Picture?" *Fortune,* January 12, 1998, pp. 107–14; John Consoli, "A Crescendo of Clutter," *Mediaweek,* March 16, 1998, pp. 4–5 and Chuck Ross, "TV Commercial Clutter Has Ad Buyers Worried," *Advertising Age,* December 6, 1999, p. 77.

appeals. Ideally, advertising message strategy will follow directly from the company's broader positioning strategy.

Message strategy statements tend to be plain, straightforward outlines of benefits and positioning points that the advertiser wants to stress. The advertiser must next develop a compelling *creative concept*—or *"big idea"*—that will bring the message strategy to life in a distinctive and memorable way. At this stage, simple message ideas become great ad campaigns. Usually, a copywriter and art director will team up to generate many creative concepts, hoping that one of these concepts will turn out to be the big idea. The creative concept may emerge as a visualization, a phrase, or a combination of the two.

The creative concept will guide the choice of specific appeals to be used in an advertising campaign. *Advertising appeals* should have three characteristics: First, they should be *meaningful,* pointing out benefits that make the product more desirable or interesting to consumers. Second, appeals must be *believable*—consumers must believe that the product or service will deliver the promised benefits. However, the most meaningful and believable benefits may not be the best ones to feature. Appeals should also be *distinctive*—they should tell how the product is better than the competing brands. For example, the most meaningful benefit of owning a wristwatch is that it keeps accurate time, yet few watch ads feature this benefit. Instead, based on the distinctive benefits they offer, watch advertisers might select any of a number of advertising themes. For years, Timex has been the affordable watch that "Takes a lickin' and keeps on tickin'." In contrast, Swatch has featured style and fashion, and Rolex stresses luxury and status.

Message Execution.   The advertiser now has to turn the big idea into an actual ad execution that will capture the target market's attention and interest. The creative people must find the best style, tone, words, and format for executing the message. Any message can be presented in different *execution styles,* such as the following:

- *Slice of life:* This style shows one or more "typical" people using the product in a normal setting. For example, two mothers at a picnic discuss the nutritional benefits of Jif peanut butter.

- *Lifestyle:* This style shows how a product fits in with a particular lifestyle. For example, an ad for Mongoose mountain bikes shows a serious biker traversing remote and rugged but beautiful terrain and states, "There are places that are so awesome and so killer that you'd like to tell the whole world about them. But please, *don't.*"

- *Fantasy:* This style creates a fantasy around the product or its use. For instance, many ads are built around dream themes. Gap even introduced a perfume named Dream. Ads show a woman sleeping blissfully and suggests that the scent is "the stuff that clouds are made of."

- *Mood or image:* This style builds a mood or image around the product, such as beauty, love, or serenity. No claim is made about the product except through suggestion. Bermuda tourism ads create such moods.

- *Musical:* This style shows one or more people or cartoon characters singing about the product. For example, one of the most famous ads in history was a Coca-Cola ad built around the song "I'd Like to Teach the World to Sing."

- *Personality symbol:* This style creates a character that represents the product. The character might be *animated* (the Jolly Green Giant, Cap'n Crunch, Garfield the Cat) or *real* (the Marlboro man, Ol' Lonely the Maytag repairman, Betty Crocker, Morris the 9-Lives Cat, Taco Bell's Chihuahua).

Execution styles: Harley-Davidson uses humor to get its "the legend rolls on" message across.

- *Technical expertise:* This style shows the company's expertise in making the product. Thus, Maxwell House shows one of its buyers carefully selecting coffee beans, and Gallo tells about its many years of wine-making experience.

- *Scientific evidence:* This style presents survey or scientific evidence that the brand is better or better liked than one or more other brands. For years, Crest toothpaste has used scientific evidence to convince buyers that Crest is better than other brands at fighting cavities.

- *Testimonial evidence or endorsement:* This style features a highly believable or likable source endorsing the product. It could be ordinary people saying how much they like a given product ("My doctor said Mylanta") or a celebrity presenting the product. Many companies use actors or sports celebrities as product endorsers.

The advertiser also must choose a *tone* for the ad. Procter & Gamble always uses a positive tone: Its ads say something very positive about its products. P&G usually avoids humor that might take attention away from the message. In contrast, Taco Bell ads use humor, in the form of an odd but cute little Chihuahua that has put the phrase "Yo quiero Taco Bell," along with millions of tacos, on the tongues of U.S. consumers.

The advertiser must use memorable and attention-getting *words* in the ad. For example, rather than claiming simply that "a BMW is a well-engineered automobile," BMW uses more creative and higher-impact phrasing: "The ultimate driving machine." Instead of stating plainly that Hanes socks last longer than less expensive ones, Hanes suggests, "Buy cheap socks and you'll pay through the toes." It's not that Häagen-Dazs is "a good-tasting luxury ice cream," it's "Our passport to indulgence: passion in a touch, perfection in a cup, summer in a spoon, one perfect moment."

Finally, *format* elements make a difference on an ad's impact as well as on its cost. A small change in ad design can make a big difference in its effect. The *illustration* is the first thing the reader notices—it must be strong enough to draw attention. Next, the *headline* must effectively entice the right people to read the copy. Finally, the *copy*—the main block of text in the ad—must be simple but strong and convincing. Moreover, these three elements must effectively work *together.*

Selecting Advertising Media

The major steps in media selection are (1) deciding on *reach, frequency,* and *impact;* (2) choosing among major *media types;* (3) selecting specific *media vehicles;* and (4) deciding on *media timing.*

Deciding on Reach, Frequency, and Impact. To select media, the advertiser must decide what reach and frequency are needed to achieve advertising objectives. *Reach* is a measure of the *percentage* of people in the target market who are exposed to the ad campaign during a given period of time. For example, the advertiser might try to reach 70 percent of the target market during the first three months of the campaign. *Frequency* is a measure of how many *times* the average person in the target market is exposed to the message. For example, the advertiser might want an average exposure frequency of three. The advertiser also must decide on the desired *media impact*—the *qualitative value* of a message exposure through a given medium. For example, for products that need to be demonstrated, messages on television may have more impact than messages on radio because television uses sight *and* sound. The same message in one magazine (say, *Newsweek*) may be more believable than in another (say, *The National Enquirer*). In general, the more reach, frequency, and impact the advertiser seeks, the higher the advertising budget will have to be.

Choosing Among Major Media Types. The media planner has to know the reach, frequency, and impact of each of the major media types. As summarized in Table 15.2, the major media types are newspapers, television, direct mail, radio, magazines, outdoor, and the Internet. Each medium has advantages and limitations.

Media planners consider many factors when making their media choices. The *media habits of target consumers* will affect media choice—advertisers look for media that reach target consumers effectively. So will the *nature of the product*—for example, fashions are best advertised in color magazines, and automobile performance is best demonstrated on television. Different *types of messages* may require different media. A message announcing a major sale tomorrow will require radio or newspapers; a message with a lot of technical data might require magazines, direct mailings, or an online ad and Web site. *Cost* is another major factor in media choice. For example, network television is very expensive, whereas newspaper or radio advertising costs much less but also reaches fewer consumers. The media planner looks both at the total cost of using a medium and at the cost per thousand exposures—the cost of reaching 1,000 people using the medium.

Media impact and cost must be reexamined regularly. For a long time, television and magazines have dominated in the media mixes of national advertisers, with other media often neglected. Recently, however, the costs and clutter of these media have gone up, audiences have declined, and marketers are adopting strategies beamed at narrower segments. As a result, advertisers are increas-

TABLE 15.2	Profiles of Major Media Types	
Medium	**Advantages**	**Limitations**
Newspapers	Flexibility; timeliness; good local market coverage; broad acceptability; high believability	Short-life; poor reproduction quality; small pass-along audience
Television	Good mass-market coverage; low cost per exposure; combines sight, sound, and motion; appealing to the senses	High absolute costs; high clutter; fleeting exposure; less audience selectivity
Direct mail	High audience selectivity; flexibility; no ad competition within the same medium; allows personalization	Relatively high cost per exposure, "junk mail" image
Radio	Good local acceptance; high geographic and demographic selectivity; low cost	Audio only, fleeting exposure; low attention ("the half-heard" medium); fragmented audiences
Magazines	High geographic and demographic selectivity; credibility and prestige; high-quality reproduction; long life and good pass-along readership	Long ad purchase lead time; high cost; no guarantee of position
Outdoor	Flexibility; high repeat exposure; low cost; low message competition; good positional selectivity	Little audience selectivity; creative limitations
Internet	High selectivity; low cost; immediacy; interactive capabilities	Small, demographically skewed audience; relatively low impact; audience controls exposure

ingly turning to alternative mediaranging from cable TV and outdoor advertising to parking meters and shopping carts—that cost less and target more effectively.

> **active exercise**

Take a moment to consider the challenges of media buying.

Selecting Specific Media Vehicles. The media planner now must choose the best *media vehicles*—specific media within each general media type. For example, television vehicles include *ER* and *ABC World News Tonight*. Magazine vehicles include *Newsweek, People, In Style,* and *Sports Illustrated.*

Media planners must compute the cost per thousand persons reached by a vehicle. For example, if a full-page, four-color advertisement in *Time* costs $162,000 and *Time's* readership is 4 million people, the cost of reaching each group of 1,000 persons is $40. The same advertisement in *Business Week* may cost only $81,000 but reach only 875,000 persons—at a cost per thousand of about $93. The media planner ranks each magazine by cost per thousand and favor those magazines with the lower cost per thousand for reaching target consumers.[11]

The media planner must also consider the costs of producing ads for different media. Whereas newspaper ads may cost very little to produce, flashy television ads may cost millions. On average, U.S. advertisers pay $308,000 to produce a single 30-second television commercial. A few years ago, Nike paid a cool $2 million to make a single ad called "The Wall."[12]

[11]For current magazines rates and circulations, see each magazine's media kit, accessed through www.magazine-data.com.

[12]See *Television Production Cost Survey* (New York: American Association of Advertising Agencies, 1998); and the 4A's Web site at www.aaaa.org/resources.

In selecting media vehicles, the media planner must balance media cost measures against several media impact factors. First, the planner should balance costs against the media vehicle's *audience quality*. For a baby lotion advertisement, for example, *New Parents* magazine would have a high-exposure value; *Gentlemen's Quarterly* would have a low-exposure value. Second, the media planner should consider *audience attention*. Readers of *Vogue,* for example, typically pay more attention to ads than do *Newsweek* readers. Third, the planner should assess the vehicle's *editorial quality*—*Time* and the *Wall Street Journal* are more believable and prestigious than *The National Enquirer.*

Deciding on Media Timing. The advertiser must also decide how to schedule the advertising over the course of a year. Suppose sales of a product peak in December and drop in March. The firm can vary its advertising to follow the seasonal pattern, to oppose the seasonal pattern, or to be the same all year. Most firms do some seasonal advertising. Some do *only* seasonal advertising: For example, Hallmark advertises its greeting cards only before major holidays.

Finally, the advertiser has to choose the pattern of the ads. *Continuity* means scheduling ads evenly within a given period. *Pulsing* means scheduling ads unevenly over a given time period. Thus, 52 ads could either be scheduled at one per week during the year or pulsed in several bursts. The idea is to advertise heavily for a short period to build awareness that carries over to the next advertising period. Those who favor pulsing feel that it can be used to achieve the same impact as a steady schedule but at a much lower cost. However, some media planners believe that although pulsing achieves minimal awareness, it sacrifices depth of advertising communications.

Recent advances in technology have had a substantial impact on the media planning and buying functions. Today, for example, new computer software applications called *optimizers* allow media planners to evaluate vast combinations of television programs and prices. Such programs help advertisers to make better decisions about which mix of networks, programs, and day parts will yield the highest reach per ad dollar.[13]

EVALUATING ADVERTISING

The advertising program should evaluate both the communication effects and the sales effects of advertising regularly. Measuring the *communication effects* of an ad—*copy testing*—tells whether the ad is communicating well. Copy testing can be done before or after an ad is printed or broadcast. Before the ad is placed, the advertiser can show it to consumers, ask how they like it, and measure recall or attitude changes resulting from it. After the ad is run, the advertiser can measure how the ad affected consumer recall or product awareness, knowledge, and preference.

But what *sales* are caused by an ad that increases brand awareness by 20 percent and brand preference by 10 percent? The *sales effects* of advertising are often harder to measure than the communication effects. Sales are affected by many factors besides advertising—such as product features, price, and availability.

One way to measure the sales effect of advertising is to compare past sales with past advertising expenditures. Another way is through experiments. For example, to test the effects of different advertising spending levels, Coca-Cola could vary the amount it spends on advertising in different market areas and measure the differences in the resulting sales levels. It could spend the normal amount in one market area, half the normal amount in another area, and twice the normal amount in a third area. If the three market areas are similar, and if all other marketing efforts in the area are the same, then differences in sales in the three areas could be related to advertising level. More complex experiments could be designed to include other variables, such as difference in the ads or media used.

OTHER ADVERTISING CONSIDERATIONS

In developing advertising strategies and programs, the company must address two additional questions. First, how the company will organize its advertising function—who will perform which advertising tasks? Second, how will the company adapt its advertising strategies and programs to the complexities of international markets?

Organizing for Advertising

Different companies organize in different ways to handle advertising. In small companies, advertising might be handled by someone in the sales department. Large companies set up advertising departments whose job it is to set the advertising budget, work with the ad agency, and handle other advertising not done by the agency. Most large companies use outside advertising agencies because they offer several advantages.

---

[13]See Gary Schroeder, "Behavioral Optimization," *American Demographics,* August 1998, pp. 34–36; and Erwin Ephron, "Ad World Was Ripe for Its Conversion to Optimizers," *Advertising Age,* February 22, 1999, p. S16.

How does an **advertising agency** work? Advertising agencies were started in the mid-to-late 1800s by salespeople and brokers who worked for the media and received a commission for selling advertising space to companies. As time passed, the salespeople began to help customers prepare their ads. Eventually, they formed agencies and grew closer to the advertisers than to the media. Today's agencies employ specialists who can often perform advertising tasks better than the company's own staff. Agencies also bring an outside point of view to solving the company's problems, along with lots of experience from working with different clients and situations. Thus, today, even companies with strong advertising departments of their own use advertising agencies.

Some ad agencies are huge—the largest U.S. agency, Grey Advertising, has an annual income of $422 million on billings (the dollar amount of advertising placed for clients) of more than $2.8 billion. In recent years, many agencies have grown by gobbling up other agencies, thus creating huge agency holding companies. The largest of these agency "megagroups," Omnicom Group, includes several large advertising, public relations, and promotion agencies—DDB Needham, BBDO, TBWA, and several others—with combined worldwide gross income of $4.8 billion on billings exceeding $37 billion.[14]

Most large advertising agencies have the staff and resources to handle all phases of an advertising campaign for their clients, from creating a marketing plan to developing ad campaigns and preparing, placing, and evaluating ads. Agencies usually have four departments: *creative,* which develops and produces ads; *media,* which selects media and places ads; *research,* which studies audience characteristics and wants; and *business,* which handles the agency's business activities. Each account is supervised by an account executive, and people in each department are usually assigned to work on one or more accounts.

Ad agencies traditionally have been paid through commissions and fees. In the past, the agency typically received 15 percent of the media cost as a rebate. For example, suppose the agency bought $60,000 of magazine space for a client. The magazine would bill the advertising agency for $51,000 ($60,000 less 15 percent), and the agency would then bill the client for $60,000, keeping the $9,000 commission. If the client bought space directly from the magazine, it would have paid $60,000 because commissions are paid only to recognized advertising agencies.

However, both advertisers and agencies have become more and more unhappy with the commission system. Larger advertisers complain that they pay more for the same services received by smaller ones simply because they place more advertising. Advertisers also believe that the commission system drives agencies away from low-cost media and short advertising campaigns. Another factor is vast changes in how ad agencies reach consumers that go way beyond network TV or magazine advertising. "The commission formula tends to encourage costly media buys and has been criticized for overlooking important emerging mediums such as the Internet," say one advertising analyst. Therefore, she continues, "The 15 percent commission on media spending that .. . was once standard in the advertising business . . . is about as dead as the three-martini lunch." New agency payment methods may include anything from fixed retainers or straight hourly fees for labor to incentives keyed to performance of the agencies' ad campaigns, or some combination of these.[15]

> **active exercise**

Take a moment to read how one prominent company is setting new ground rules for paying ad agencies.

Another trend is affecting the advertising agency business: Many agencies have sought growth by diversifying into related marketing services. These new diversified agencies offer a complete list of integrated marketing and promotion services under one roof, including advertising, sales promotion, marketing research, public relations, and direct and online marketing. Some have even added marketing consulting, television production, and sales training units in an effort to become full "marketing partners" to their clients.

However, agencies are finding that most advertisers don't want much more from them than traditional media advertising services plus direct marketing, sales promotion, and sometimes public relations. Thus, many agencies have recently limited their diversification efforts in order to focus more on traditional services. Some have even started their own "creative boutiques," smaller and more independent agencies that can develop creative campaigns for clients free of large-agency bureaucracy.

[14]Information on advertising agency income and billings obtained online at http://adage/dataplace, December 1999.

[15]Patricia Winters Lauro, "New Method of Agency Payments Drive a Stake Through the Heart of the Old 15% Commission," *New York Times,* April 2, 1999, p. 2.

International Advertising Decisions

International advertisers face many complexities not encountered by domestic advertisers. The most basic issue concerns the degree to which global advertising should be adapted to the unique characteristics of various country's markets. Some large advertisers have attempted to support their global brands with highly standardized worldwide advertising, with campaigns that work as well in Bangkok as they do in Baltimore. For example, Jeep has created a worldwide brand image of ruggedness and reliability; Coca-Cola's Sprite brand uses standardized appeals to target the world's youth. Gillette's ads for its Sensor Excel for Women are almost identical worldwide, with only minor adjustments to suit the local culture. Ericsson, the Swedish telecommunications giant, spent $100 million on a standardized global television campaign with the tag line "make yourself heard," which features Agent 007, James Bond.

Standardization produces many benefits—lower advertising costs, greater global advertising coordination, and a more consistent worldwide image. But it also has drawbacks. Most importantly, it ignores the fact that country markets differ greatly in their cultures, demographics, and economic conditions. Thus, most international advertisers "think globally but act locally." They develop global advertising *strategies* that make their worldwide advertising efforts more efficient and consistent. Then they adapt their advertising *programs* to make them more responsive to consumer needs and expectations within local markets.

For example, Coca-Cola has a pool of different commercials that can be used in or adapted to several different international markets. Some can be used with only minor changes—such as language—in several different countries. Local and regional managers decide which commercials work best for which markets. Recently, in a reverse of the usual order, a series of Coca-Cola commercials developed for the Russian market, using a talking bear and a man who transforms into a wolf, was shown in the United States. "This approach fits perfectly with the global nature of Coca-Cola," says the president of Coca-Cola's Nordic division. "[It] offers people a special look into a culture that is different from their own."[16]

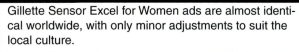

Gillette Sensor Excel for Women ads are almost identical worldwide, with only minor adjustments to suit the local culture.

Offrez à vos jambes une mise en beauté en quelques minutes.

Let your legs feel the beauty of a two-minute makeover.

---

[16]Patti Bond, "Today's Topic: From Russia with Fizz, Coke Imports Ads," *Atlanta Journal and Constitution,* April 4, 1998, pp. E2. Also see Jack Neff, "P&G Hammers Last Nail into Commission Coffin," *Advertising Age,* September 20, 1999, p. 4.

Global advertisers face several special problems. For instance, advertising media costs and availability differ vastly from country to country. Countries also differ in the extent to which they regulate advertising practices. Many countries have extensive systems of laws restricting how much a company can spend on advertising, the media used, the nature of advertising claims, and other aspects of the advertising program. Such restrictions often require advertisers to adapt their campaigns from country to country.

For example, alcoholic products cannot be advertised or sold in Muslim countries. Tobacco products are subjected to strict regulation in many countriesthe United Kingdom now wants not only to ban tobacco advertising but also to outlaw sports sponsorship by tobacco companies. In many countries, Norway and Sweden, for example, no TV ads may be directed at children under 12. Moreover, Sweden is lobbying to extend that ban to all EU member countries. To play it safe, McDonald's advertises itself as a family restaurant in Sweden.

Comparative ads, while acceptable and even common in the United States and Canada, are less commonly used in the United Kingdom, unacceptable in Japan, and illegal in India and Brazil. PepsiCo found that its comparative taste test ad in Japan was refused by many television stations and actually led to a lawsuit. China has restrictive censorship rules for TV and radio advertising; for example, the words *the best* are banned, as are ads that "violate social customs" or present women in "improper ways." Coca-Cola's Indian subsidiary was forced to end a promotion that offered prizes, such as a trip to Hollywood, because it violated India's established trade practices by encouraging customers to buy in order to "gamble."[17]

Thus, although advertisers may develop global strategies to guide their overall advertising efforts, specific advertising programs must usually be adapted to meet local cultures and customs, media characteristics, and advertising regulations.

> active concept check

Now let's take a moment to test your knowledge of what you've just read.

> Sales Promotion

Advertising and personal selling often work closely with another promotion tool, sales promotion. **Sales promotion** consists of short-term incentives to encourage the purchase or sale of a product or service. Whereas advertising and personal selling offer reasons to buy a product or service, sales promotion offers reasons to buy *now*.

Examples of sales promotions are found everywhere. A freestanding insert in the Sunday newspaper contains a coupon offering 50 cents off Folgers coffee. An e-mail from CDnow offers $5.00 off your next CD purchase over $9.99. The end-of-the-aisle display in the local supermarket tempts impulse buyers with a wall of Coke cartons. An executive who buys a new Compaq laptop computer gets a free carrying case, or a family buys a new Taurus and receives a rebate check for $500. A hardware store chain receives a 10 percent discount on selected Black & Decker portable power tools if it agrees to advertise them in local newspapers. Sales promotion includes a wide variety of promotion tools designed to stimulate earlier or stronger market response.

RAPID GROWTH OF SALES PROMOTION

Sales promotion tools are used by most organizations, including manufacturers, distributors, retailers, trade associations, and nonprofit institutions. They are targeted toward final buyers (*consumer promotions*), business customers (*business promotions*), retailers and wholesalers (*trade promotions*), and members of the sales force (*sales force promotions*). Today, in the average consumer packaged-goods company, sales promotion accounts for 74 percent of all marketing expenditures.[18]

---

[17]See "U.K. Tobacco Ad Ban Will Include Sports Sponsorship," *AdAgeInternational.com,* May 1997; "Coca-Cola Rapped for Running Competition in India," *AdAgeInternational.com,* February 1997; Naveen Donthu, "A Cross Country Investigation of Recall of and Attitude Toward Comparative Advertising," *Journal of Advertising,* 27, June 22, 1998, pp. 111; John Shannon, "Comparative Ads Call for Prudence," *Marketing Week,* May 6, 1999, p. 32 and "A Trojan Horse for Advertisers," *Business Week,* April 3, 2000, p. 10.

[18]"Promotion Practices Condensed," *Potentials,* November 1998, p. 6.

Several factors have contributed to the rapid growth of sales promotion, particularly in consumer markets. First, inside the company, product managers face greater pressures to increase their current sales, and promotion is viewed as an effective short-run sales tool. Second, externally, the company faces more competition and competing brands are less differentiated. Increasingly, competitors are using sales promotion to help differentiate their offers. Third, advertising efficiency has declined because of rising costs, media clutter, and legal restraints. Finally, consumers have become more deal oriented and ever-larger retailers are demanding more deals from manufacturers.

The growing use of sales promotion has resulted in *promotion clutter,* similar to advertising clutter. Consumers are increasingly tuning out promotions, weakening their ability to trigger immediate purchase. Manufacturers are now searching for ways to rise above the clutter, such as offering larger coupon values or creating more dramatic point-of-purchase displays.

In developing a sales promotion program, a company must first set sales promotion objectives and then select the best tools for accomplishing these objectives.

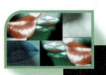

active poll   <

Give your opinion on a question regarding trade promotions.

SALES PROMOTION OBJECTIVES

Sales promotion objectives vary widely. Sellers may use consumer promotions to increase short-term sales or to help build long-term market share. Objectives for trade promotions include getting retailers to carry new items and more inventory, getting them to advertise the product and give it more shelf space, and getting them to buy ahead. For the sales force, objectives include getting more sales force support for current or new products or getting salespeople to sign up new accounts. Sales promotions are usually used together with advertising or personal selling. Consumer promotions must usually be advertised and can add excitement and pulling power to ads. Trade and sales force promotions support the firm's personal selling process.

In general, sales promotions should be *consumer relationship building.* Rather than creating only short-term sales or temporary brand switching, they should help to reinforce the product's position and build long-term relationships with consumers. Increasingly, marketers are avoiding "quick fix," price-only promotions in favor of promotions designed to build brand equity. Even price promotions can be designed to help build customer relationships. Examples include all of the "frequency marketing programs" and clubs that have mushroomed in recent years. For example, Waldenbooks sponsors a Preferred Reader Program, which has attracted more than 4 million members, each paying $5 to receive mailings about new books, a 10 percent discount on book purchases, toll-free ordering, and many other services. American Express's Custom Extras program automatically awards customers deals and discounts based on frequency of purchases at participating retailers. Norwegian Cruise Lines sponsors a loyalty program called Latitudes, a co-branding effort with Visa. The program includes a two-for-one cruise offer and a Latitudes Visa card that rewards users with points redeemable for discounts on NCL cruises.

If properly designed, every sales promotion tool has the potential to build consumer relationships. Here's another example of a loyalty-building promotion:[19]

The Valley View Center Mall in Dallas sponsors the Smart Shoppers Club, a program that rewards customers who tap onto its computerized interactive touch-screen kiosks. To obtain a membership and personal identification number, mallgoers fill out a short application that asks simple demographic and psychographic questions. Then, each time members visit the mall, they input their ID number into one of the mall's three touch-screen kiosks and receive daily discount retail coupons, prizes awarded randomly each week, and

[19]For these and other examples, see Cyndee Miller, "Rewards for the Best Customers," *Marketing News,* July 5, 1993, pp. 1, 6; Louise O'Brien and Charles Jones, "Do Rewards Really Create Loyalty?" *Harvard Business Review,* May–June 1995, pp. 75–82; Grahame R. Dowling and Mark Uncles, "Do Customer Loyalty Programs Really Work?" *Sloan Management Review,* Summer 1997, pp. 71–82; and "Building Brand Loyalty," *Advertising Age's Business Marketing,* May 1998, pp. S1–S3; and Richard G. Barlow, "Future Looks Bright for Frequency Marketing," *Marketing News,* July 5, 1999, p. 14.

a calendar of events. While customers reap discounts and prizes, Valley View retailers get valuable marketing information about their customers. The shopping center is one of only about 10 of the nation's 35,000 malls to use this high-tech consumer loyalty program.

MAJOR SALES PROMOTION TOOLS

Many tools can be used to accomplish sales promotion objectives. Descriptions of the main consumer, trade, and business promotion tools follow.

Consumer Promotion Tools

The main consumer promotion tools include samples, coupons, cash refunds, price packs, premiums, advertising specialties, patronage rewards, point-of-purchase displays and demonstrations, and contests, sweepstakes, and games.

Samples are offers of a trial amount of a product. Sampling is the most effective—but most expensive—way to introduce a new product. Some samples are free; for others, the company charges a small amount to offset its cost. The sample might be delivered door-to-door, sent by mail, handed out in a store, attached to another product, or featured in an ad. Sometimes, samples are combined into sample packs, which can then be used to promote other products and services. Procter & Gamble has even distributed samples via the Internet:[20]

> When Procter & Gamble decided to relaunch Pert Plus shampoo, it extended its $20 million ad campaign by constructing a new Web site (www.pertplus.com). P&G had three objectives for the Web site: to create awareness for reformulated Pert Plus, get consumers to try the product, and gather data about Web users. The site's first page invites visitors to place their heads against the computer screen in a mock attempt to measure the cleanliness of their hair. After "tabulating the results," the site tells visitors that they "need immediate help." The solution: "How about a free sample of new Pert Plus?" Visitors obtain the sample by filling out a short demographic form. The site offers other interesting features as well. For example, clicking "get a friend in a lather" produces a template that will send an e-mail to a friend with an invitation to visit the site and receive a free sample. How did the

Internet sampling: Within just two months, this Pert Plus site generated 170,000 visits and 83,000 sample requests.

[20]Debra Aho Williamson, "P&G's Reformulated Pert Plus Builds Consumer Relationships," *Advertising Age*, June 28, 1999, p. 52.

sampling promotion work out? Even P&G was shocked by the turnout. Within just two months of launching the site, 170,000 people visited and 83,000 requested samples. More surprising, given that the site is only 10 pages deep, the average person visited the site 1.9 times and spent a total of 7.5 minutes each visit.

Coupons are certificates that give buyers a saving when they purchase specified products. Most consumers love coupons: They clipped 4.8 billion of them last year with an average face value of 70 cents, for a total savings of $3.4 billion.[21] Coupons can stimulate sales of a mature brand or promote early trial of a new brand. However, as a result of coupon clutter, redemption rates have been declining in recent years. Thus, most major consumer goods companies are issuing fewer coupons and targeting them more carefully.

In the past, marketers have relied almost solely on mass-distributed coupons delivered through the mail or on freestanding inserts or ads in newspapers and magazines. Today, however, although Sunday newspapers still account for 80 percent of all coupons, marketers are cultivating new outlets. They are increasingly distributing coupons through shelf dispensers at the point of sale, by electronic point-of-sale coupon printers, or through "paperless coupon systems." An example is Catalina Marketing Network's Checkout Direct system, which dispenses personalized discounts to targeted buyers at the checkout counter in stores. Some companies are now offering coupons on their Web sites or through online coupon services such as coolsavings.com, valupage.com, hotcoupons.com, and directcoupons.com. For example, participants in CoolSavings include JCPenney, Toys "R" Us, Boston Market, Domino's Pizza, and H&R Block.[22]

active example   <

Take a moment to read more about recent advances in online consumer promotions.

Cash refund offers (or **rebates**) are like coupons except that the price reduction occurs after the purchase rather than at the retail outlet. The consumer sends a "proof of purchase" to the manufacturer, who then refunds part of the purchase price by mail. For example, Toro ran a clever preseason promotion on some of its snowblower models, offering a rebate if the snowfall in the buyer's market area turned out to be below average. Competitors were not able to match this offer on such short notice, and the promotion was very successful.

Price packs (also called **cents-off deals**) offer consumers savings off the regular price of a product. The reduced prices are marked by the producer directly on the label or package. Price packs can be single packages sold at a reduced price (such as two for the price of one), or two related products banded together (such as a toothbrush and toothpaste). Price packs are very effective—even more so than coupons—in stimulating short-term sales.

Premiums are goods offered either free or at low cost as an incentive to buy a product, ranging from toys included with kids' products to phone cards, compact disks, and computer CD-ROMs. A premium may come inside the package (in-pack), outside the package (on-pack), or through the mail. In its "Treasure Hunt" promotion, for example, Quaker Oats inserted $5 million worth of gold and silver coins in Ken-L Ration dog food packages. In another premium promotion, Cutty Sark offered a brass tray with the purchase of one bottle of its scotch and a desk lamp with the purchase of two. Last year, United Airlines rewarded Chicago-area 75,000 Mileage Plus frequent flier club members with a custom compact disk. The 10-song, Chicago-themed compilation disk, entitled "Chicago—Our Kind of Town," was widely played on local radio stations. It became so popular that United ended up selling it at record stores. The airline plans similar custom-designed premiums for four other major cities it serves.[23]

Advertising specialties are useful articles imprinted with an advertiser's name given as gifts to consumers. Typical items include pens, calendars, key rings, matches, shopping bags, T-shirts, caps,

[21]"DSN Charts: Coupons," *Discount Store News,* May 3, 1999, p. 4.

[22]See "Loyal Shoppers Can Score by Using In-Store Kiosks," *Advertising Age,* May 1998, p. S4; "1998 Gallery of Excellence: Catalina Marketing Corp.," *Supermarket Business,* November 1998, p. 19; Gregg Cebrzyski, "Domino's to Join Other Chains in Testing Internet Coupons," *Nation's Restaurant News,* May 25, 1998, p. 12; and "Electronic Coupon Clipping," *USA Today,* May 11, 1999, p. 1B.

[23]See Kate Bertrand, "Premiums Prime the Market," *Advertising Age's Business Marketing,* May 1998, p. S6; and Paul Nolan, "Promotions Come Alive with the Sound of Music," *Potentials,* April 1999, p. 10.

nail files, and coffee mugs. Such items can be very effective. In a recent study, 63 percent of all consumers surveyed were either carrying or wearing an ad specialty item. More than three-quarters of those who had an item could recall the advertiser's name or message before showing the item to the interviewer.[24]

Patronage rewards are cash or other awards offered for the regular use of a certain company's products or services. For example, airlines offer frequent flier plans, awarding points for miles traveled that can be turned in for free airline trips. Marriott Hotels has adopted an honored-guest plan that awards points to users of their hotels. Baskin-Robbins offers frequent-purchase awards—for every 10 purchases, customers receive a free quart of ice cream.

Point-of-purchase (POP) promotions include displays and demonstrations that take place at the point of purchase or sale. An example is a five-foot-high cardboard display of Cap'n Crunch next to Cap'n Crunch cereal boxes. Unfortunately, many retailers do not like to handle the hundreds of displays, signs, and posters they receive from manufacturers each year. Manufacturers have responded by offering better POP materials, tying them in with television or print messages, and offering to set them up.

Contests, sweepstakes, and **games** give consumers the chance to win something, such as cash, trips, or goods, by luck or through extra effort. A *contest* calls for consumers to submit an entry—a jingle, guess, suggestion—to be judged by a panel that will select the best entries. A *sweepstakes* calls for consumers to submit their names for a drawing. A *game* presents consumers with something—bingo numbers, missing letters—every time they buy, which may or may not help them win a prize. A sales contest urges dealers or the sales force to increase their efforts, with prizes going to the top performers.

> **active example**

Consider how the Internet affecting coupon promotion.

Trade Promotion Tools

More sales promotion dollars are directed to retailers and wholesalers (68 percent) than to consumers (32 percent). Trade promotion can persuade resellers to carry a brand, give it shelf space, promote it in advertising, and push it to consumers. Shelf space is so scarce these days that manufacturers often have to offer price-offs, allowances, buy-back guarantees, or free goods to retailers and wholesalers to get products on the shelf and, once there, to stay on it.

Manufacturers use several trade promotion tools. Many of the tools used for consumer promotions—contests, premiums, displays—can also be used as trade promotions. Or the manufacturer may offer a straight **discount** off the list price on each case purchased during a stated period of time (also called a *price-off, off-invoice,* or *off-list*). The offer encourages dealers to buy in quantity or to carry a new item. Dealers can use the discount for immediate profit, for advertising, or for price reductions to their customers.

Manufacturers also may offer an **allowance** (usually so much off per case) in return for the retailer's agreement to feature the manufacturer's products in some way. An *advertising allowance* compensates retailers for advertising the product. A *display allowance* compensates them for using special displays.

Manufacturers may offer *free goods,* which are extra cases of merchandise, to resellers who buy a certain quantity or who feature a certain flavor or size. They may offer *push money*—cash or gifts to dealers or their sales forces to "push" the manufacturer's goods. Manufacturers may give retailers free *specialty advertising items* that carry the company's name, such as pens, pencils, calendars, paperweights, matchbooks, memo pads, and yardsticks.

Business Promotion Tools

Companies spend billions of dollars each year on promotion to industrial customers. These business promotions are used to generate business leads, stimulate purchases, reward customers, and motivate salespeople. Business promotion includes many of the same tools used for consumer or trade promotions. Here, we focus on two additional major business promotion tools—conventions and trade shows, and sales contests.

[24]See "Power to the Key Ring and T-Shirt," *Sales & Marketing Management,* December 1989, p. 14; and Chad Kaydo, "Your Logo Here," *Sales & Marketing Management,* April 1998, pp. 65–70.

Many companies and trade associations organize *conventions and trade shows* to promote their products. Firms selling to the industry show their products at the trade show. More than 4,300 trade shows take place every year, drawing as many as 85 million people. Vendors receive many benefits, such as opportunities to find new sales leads, contact customers, introduce new products, meet new customers, sell more to present customers, and educate customers with publications and audiovisual materials. Trade shows also help companies reach many prospects not reached through their sales forces. About 90 percent of a trade show's visitors see a company's salespeople for the first time at the show. Business marketers may spend as much as 35 percent of their annual promotion budgets on trade shows.[25]

A *sales contest* is a contest for salespeople or dealers to motivate them to increase their sales performance over a given period. Sales contests motivate and recognize good company performers, who may receive trips, cash prizes, or other gifts. Some companies award points for performance, which the receiver can turn in for any of a variety of prizes. Sales contests work best when they are tied to measurable and achievable sales objectives (such as finding new accounts, reviving old accounts, or increasing account profitability).

video example <

Consider a fictional case in which a company confronts some trade promotion issues.

DEVELOPING THE SALES PROMOTION PROGRAM

The marketer must make several other decisions in order to define the full sales promotion program. First, the marketer must decide on the *size of the incentive.* A certain minimum incentive is necessary if the promotion is to succeed; a larger incentive will produce more sales response. The marketer also must set *conditions for participation.* Incentives might be offered to everyone or only to select groups.

The marketer must decide how to *promote and distribute the promotion* program itself. A 50-cents-off coupon could be given out in a package, at the store, by mail, or in an advertisement. Each distribution method involves a different level of reach and cost. Increasingly, marketers are blending several media into a total campaign concept. The *length of the promotion* is also important. If the sales promotion period is too short, many prospects (who may not be buying during that time) will miss it. If the promotion runs too long, the deal will lose some of its "act now" force.

Evaluation is also very important. Yet many companies fail to evaluate their sales promotion programs, and others evaluate them only superficially. Manufacturers can use one of many evaluation methods. The most common method is to compare sales before, during, and after a promotion. Suppose a company has a 6 percent market share before the promotion, which jumps to 10 percent during the promotion, falls to 5 percent right after, and rises to 7 percent later on. The promotion seems to have attracted new triers and more buying from current customers. After the promotion, sales fell as consumers used up their inventories. The long-run rise to 7 percent means that the company gained some new users. If the brand's share had returned to the old level, then the promotion would have changed only the *timing* of demand rather than the *total* demand.

Consumer research would also show the kinds of people who responded to the promotion and what they did after it ended. *Surveys* can provide information on how many consumers recall the promotion, what they thought of it, how many took advantage of it, and how it affected their buying. Sales promotions also can be evaluated through *experiments* that vary factors such as incentive value, length, and distribution method.

Clearly, sales promotion plays an important role in the total promotion mix. To use it well, the marketer must define the sales promotion objectives, select the best tools, design the sales promotion program, implement the program, and evaluate the results. Moreover, sales promotion must be coordinated carefully with other promotion mix elements within the integrated marketing communications program.

[25]See Richard Szathmary, "Trade Shows," *Sales & Marketing Management,* May 1992, pp. 83–84; Srinath Gopalakrishna, Gary L. Lilien, Jerome D. Williams, and Ian Sequeira, "Do Trade Shows Pay Off?" *Journal of Marketing,* July 1995, pp. 75–83; Barbara Axelson, "Trade Shows Gain Larger Share of Marketing Budgets: Computers Help Make Manufacturing Top Category," *Advertising Age's Business Marketing,"* May 1999, p. S14; and Peter Jenkins, "Making the Most of Trade Shows," *Nation's Business,* June 1999, p. 8.

> video example

Take a moment to watch how two companies in the financial industry use various kinds of promotions.

> active concept check

Now let's take a moment to test your knowledge of what you've just read.

> Public Relations

Another major mass-promotion tool is *public relations*—building good relations with the company's various publics by obtaining favorable publicity, building up a good corporate image, and handling or heading off unfavorable rumors, stories, and events. Public relations departments may perform any or all of the following functions:[26]

- *Press relations or press agentry:* Creating and placing newsworthy information in the news media to attract attention to a person, product, or service.
- *Product publicity:* Publicizing specific products.
- *Public affairs:* Building and maintaining national or local community relations.
- *Lobbying:* Building and maintaining relations with legislators and government officials to influence legislation and regulation.
- *Investor relations:* Maintaining relationships with shareholders and others in the financial community.
- *Development:* Public relations with donors or members of nonprofit organizations to gain financial or volunteer support.

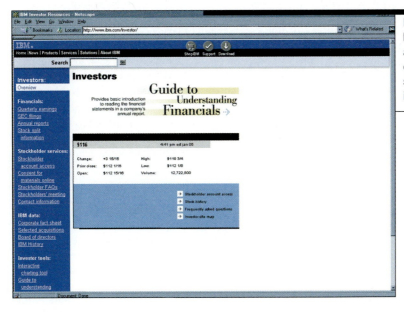

Public relations involves many functions beyond product publicity, including public affairs, lobbying, and investor relations. For example, most company Web sites feature special sections for current and potential investors like this one for IBM.

[26]Adapted from Scott Cutlip, Allen Center, and Glen Broom, *Effective Public Relations,* 8th ed. (Upper Saddle River, NJ: Prentice Hall, 1999), chap. 1.

Public relations is used to promote products, people, places, ideas, activities, organizations, and even nations. Trade associations have used public relations to rebuild interest in declining commodities such as eggs, apples, milk, and potatoes. New York City turned its image around when its "I Love New York!" campaign took root, bringing millions more tourists to the city. Johnson & Johnson's masterly use of public relations played a major role in saving Tylenol from extinction after its product-tampering scare. Nations have used public relations to attract more tourists, foreign investment, and international support.

active example   <

Take a moment to read how small companies can benefit from PR.

Public relations can have a strong impact on public awareness at a much lower cost than advertising. The company does not pay for the space or time in the media. Rather, it pays for a staff to develop and circulate information and to manage events. If the company develops an interesting story, it could be picked up by several different media, having the same effect as advertising that would cost millions of dollars. It would have more credibility than advertising. Public relations results can sometimes be spectacular.

Despite its potential strengths, public relations is often described as a marketing stepchild because of its limited and scattered use. The public relations department is usually located at corporate headquarters. Its staff is so busy dealing with various publics—stockholders, employees, legislators, city officials—that public relations programs to support product marketing objectives may be ignored. Marketing managers and public relations practitioners do not always talk the same language. Many public relations practitioners see their job as simply communicating. In contrast, marketing managers tend to be much more interested in how advertising and public relations affect sales and profits.

This situation is changing, however. Many companies now want their public relations departments to manage all of their activities with a view toward marketing the company and improving the bottom line. They know that good public relations can be a powerful brand-building tool. Two well-known marketing consultants provide the following advice, which points to the potential power of public relations as a first step in building brands:

Just because a heavy dose of advertising is associated with most major brands doesn't necessarily mean that advertising built the brands in the first place. The birth of a brand is usually accomplished with [public relations], not advertising. Our general rule is [PR] first, advertising second. [Public relations] is the nail, advertising the hammer. [PR] creates the credentials that provide the credibility for advertising. . . . Anita Roddick built the Body Shop into a major brand with no advertising at all. Instead, she traveled the world on a relentless quest for publicity. . . . Until recently Starbucks Coffee Co. didn't spend a hill of beans on advertising, either. In 10 years, the company spent less than $10 million on advertising, a trivial amount for a brand that delivers annual sales of $1.3 billion. Wal-Mart Stores became the world's largest retailer . . . with very little advertising. . . . In the toy field, Furby, Beanie Babies, and Tickle Me Elmo became highly successful . . . and on the Internet, Yahoo!, Amazon.com, and Excite became powerhouse brands, [all] with virtually no advertising.[27]

Thus, some companies are setting up special units called *marketing public relations* to support corporate and product promotion and image making directly. Many companies hire marketing public relations firms to handle their PR programs or to assist the company public relations team.

MAJOR PUBLIC RELATIONS TOOLS

Public relations professionals use several tools. One of the major tools is *news*. PR professionals find or create favorable news about the company and its products or people. Sometimes news stories occur naturally, and sometimes the PR person can suggest events or activities that would create news. *Speeches* can also create product and company publicity. Increasingly, company executives must field questions from the media or give talks at trade associations or sales meetings, and these events can either build or hurt the company's image.

Another common PR tool is *special events,* ranging from news conferences, press tours, grand openings, and fireworks displays to laser shows, hot air balloon releases, multimedia presentations

---

[27]Al Ries and Laura Ries, "First Do Some Publicity," *Advertising Age,* February 8, 1999, p. 42.

and star-studded spectaculars, or educational programs designed to reach and interest target publics. Here's an example of an interesting public relations program launched by Levi-Strauss & Company:

> In the increasingly more casual business world, as companies relax their dress codes, they are often dismayed to find employees showing up at the office in anything from sweatsuits to torn jeans. Where can they turn for a little fashion advice? Levi-Strauss & Company to the rescue! The world's largest apparel maker has put together an elaborate and stealthy program to help companies advise their people on how to dress casually without being sloppy. To promote the program initially, Levi mailed a newsletter to 65,000 human resource managers and sent videos to some 7,000 companies. Since 1992, the company has provided information and advice to more than 30,000 companies, including Charles Schwab & Company, IBM, Nynex, and Aetna Life & Casualty. Through the program, Levi offers snazzy brochures and videos showing how to dress casually. Other activities range from putting on fashion shows and manning a toll-free number for employees who have questions about casual wear to holding seminars for human resource directors. Levi also created a Web page from which human resources managers can obtain advice and Levi's Casual Businesswear Kit, a detailed guide for starting and maintaining company dress policies. Levi's avoids outright product pitches. Instead, the company explains, it's simply "trying to create a dress code for dress-down wear." Of course, it wouldn't hurt if that wear had the Levi label attached.[28]

Public relations people also prepare *written materials* to reach and influence their target markets. These materials include annual reports, brochures, articles, and company newsletters and magazines. *Audiovisual materials,* such as films, slide-and-sound programs, and video- and audiocassettes, are being used increasingly as communication tools. *Corporate identity materials* can also help create a corporate identity that the public immediately recognizes. Logos, stationery, brochures, signs, business forms, business cards, buildings, uniforms, and company cars and trucks—all become marketing tools when they are attractive, distinctive, and memorable. Finally, companies can improve public goodwill by contributing money and time to *public service activities.*

A company's Web site can be a good public relations vehicle. Consumers and members of other publics can visit the site for information and entertainment. Such sites can be extremely popular. For example, Butterball's site (**www.butterball.com**), which features cooking and carving tips, received 550,000 visitors in one day during Thanksgiving week last year. Web sites can also be ideal for handling crisis situations. For example, when several bottles of Odwalla apple juice sold on the West Coast were found to contain *E. coli* bacteria, Odwalla initiated a massive product recall. Within only three hours, it set up a Web site laden with information about the crisis and Odwalla's response. Company staffers also combed the Internet looking for newsgroups discussing Odwalla and posted links to the site. In another example, American Home Products quickly set up a Web site to distribute accurate information and advice after a model died reportedly after inhaling its Primatene Mist. The Primatene site, up less than 12 hours after the crisis broke, remains in place today (**www.primatene.com**). In all, notes one analyst, "Today, public relations is reshaping the Internet and the Internet, in turn, is redefining the practice of public relations." Says another, "People look to the Net for information, not salesmanship, and that's the real opportunity for public relations."[29]

As with the other promotion tools, in considering when and how to use product public relations, management should set PR objectives, choose the PR messages and vehicles, implement the PR plan, and evaluate the results. The firm's publics relations should be blended smoothly with other promotion activities within the company's overall integrated marketing communications effort.

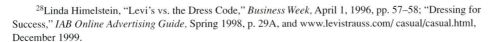

> **active concept check**

Now let's take a moment to test your knowledge of what you've just read.

[28]Linda Himelstein, "Levi's vs. the Dress Code," *Business Week,* April 1, 1996, pp. 57–58; "Dressing for Success," *IAB Online Advertising Guide,* Spring 1998, p. 29A, and www.levistrauss.com/ casual/casual.html, December 1999.

[29]Mark Gleason, "Edelman Sees Niche in Web Public Relations," *Advertising Age,* January 20, 1997, p. 30; and Michael Krauss, "Good PR Critical to Growth on the Net," *Marketing News,* January 18, 1999, p. 8.

Now that you've reached the end of the chapter, you may wish to explore the concepts you've been reading about in greater detail, or test yourself to see how well you've comprehended the material. In the box below you'll find a number of links. Click on any one of these links to find additional chapter resources.

> **end-of-chapter resources**

- **Review of Concept Connections**
- **Practice Quiz**
- **Issues for Discussion**
- **Key Terms**
- **Marketing Applications**
- **Internet Connections**
- **Company Case**

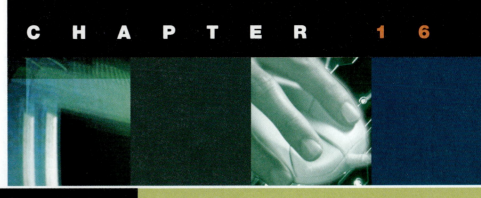

Personal Selling and Sales Management

> What's Ahead

When someone says "salesperson," what image comes to mind? Perhaps it's the stereotypical "traveling salesman"—the fast-talking, ever-smiling peddler who travels his territory foisting his wares on reluctant customers. Such stereotypes, however, are sadly out of date. Today, most professional salespeople are well-educated, well-trained men and women who work to build long-term, value-producing relationships with their customers. They succeed not by taking customers in but by helping them out—by assessing customer needs and solving customer problems.

Consider Lear Corporation, one of the largest, fastest-growing, and most successful automotive suppliers in the world. Each year, Lear produces more than $12 billion worth of automotive interiors—seat systems, instrument panels, door panels, floor and acoustic systems, overhead systems, and electronic and electrical distribution systems. Its customers include most of the world's leading automotive companies, from Ford, General Motors, Fiat, and Volvo to Mercedes-Benz, Ferrari, Rolls-Royce, Toyota, and more than a dozen others. Lear now operates more than 300 facilities in 33 countries around the globe. During the past few years, Lear has achieved record-breaking sales and earnings growth. Lear's sales during the past five years have more than tripled, and its "average content per car" in North America has increased more than fourfold since 1990. It currently owns about a 30 percent share of the North American interior components market.

Lear Corporation owes its success to many factors, including a strong customer orientation and a commitment to continuous improvement, teamwork, and customer value. But perhaps more than any other part of the organization, it's Lear's outstanding sales force that makes the company's credo, "Consumer driven. Customer focused," ring true. In fact, Lear's sales force was recently rated by *Sales & Marketing Management* magazine as one of "America's Best Sales Forces." What makes this an outstanding sales force? Lear knows that good selling these days takes much more than just a sales rep covering a territory and convincing customers to buy the product. It takes teamwork, relationship building, and doing what's best for the customer. Lear's sales force excels at these tasks.

Lear's sales depend completely on the success of its customers. If the automakers don't sell cars, Lear doesn't sell interiors. So the Lear sales force strives to create not just sales, but customer success. In fact, Lear salespeople aren't "sales reps," they're "account managers" who function more as consultants than as order getters. "Our salespeople don't really close deals," notes a senior marketing executive. "They consult and work with customers to learn exactly what's needed and when."

To more fully match up with customers' needs, Lear has diversified its product line to become a kind of "one-stop shopping" source. Until a few years ago, Lear supplied only seats; now it sells almost everything for a car's interior. Providing complete interior solutions for customers also benefits Lear. "It used to be that we'd build a partnership and then get only a limited amount of revenue from it," the executive says. "Now we can get as much as possible out of our customer relationships."

Lear is heavily customer focused, so much so that it's broken up into separate divisions dedicated to specific customers. For example, there's a Ford division and a General Motors division, and each operates as its own profit center. Within each division, high-level "platform teams"—made up of salespeople, engineers, and program managers—work closely with their customer counterparts. These platform teams are closely supported by divisional manufacturing, finance, quality, and advanced technology groups. Lear's limited customer base, consisting of only a few dozen customers in all, allows Lear's sales teams to get very close to their customers. "Our teams don't call on purchasers; they're linked to customer operations at all levels," the marketer notes. "We try to put a system in place that creates continuous contact with customers." In fact, Lear often locates its sales offices in customers' plants. For example, the team that handles GM's light truck division works at GM's truck operation campus. "We can't just be there to give quotes and ask for orders," the marketing executive says. "We need to be involved with customers every step of the way—from vehicle concept through launch."

Lear's largest customers are worth billions of dollars in annual sales to the company. Maintaining profitable relationships with such large customers takes much more than a nice smile and a firm handshake. Certainly there's no place for the "smoke and mirrors" or "flimflam" sometimes mistakenly associated with personal selling. Success in such a selling environment requires careful teamwork among well-trained, dedicated sales professionals who are bent on profitably taking care of their customers.[1]

[1]Quotes from Andy Cohen, "Top of the Charts: Lear Corporation," *Sales & Marketing Management,* July 1998, p. 40. Also see Sarah Lorge, "Better Off Branded," *Sales & Marketing Management,* March 1998, pp. 39–42; Terril Yue Jones, "The Forbes Platinum: Consumer Durables: Low-Cost Supplier," *Forbes,* January 11, 1999, pp. 156–58; "Lear Corporation," *Sales & Marketing Management,* July 1999, p. 62; and "This Is Lear," accessed online at www.lear.com/d.htm, March 2000.

> **objectives**

Before you begin, take a moment to familiarize yourself with the key objectives of this chapter.

> **gearing up**

Before we begin our exploration this chapter, take a short warm-up test to see what you know about this topic.

> **video example**

Take a moment to watch a salesperson at work.

Robert Louis Stevenson once noted that "everyone lives by selling something." We are all familiar with the sales forces used by business organizations to sell products and services to customers around the world. But sales forces are also found in many other kinds of organizations. For example, colleges use recruiters to attract new students, and churches use membership committees to attract new members. Hospitals and museums use fund-raisers to contact donors and raise money. Even governments use sales forces. The U.S. Postal Service, for instance, uses a sales force to sell Express Mail and other services to corporate customers, and the Agricultural Extension Service sends agricultural specialists to sell farmers on new farming methods. In this chapter, we examine the role of personal selling in the organization, sales force management decisions, and basic principles of personal selling.

 The Role of Personal Selling

There are many types of personal selling jobs, and the role of personal selling can vary greatly from one company to another. Here, we look at the nature of personal selling positions and at the role the sales force plays in modern marketing organizations.

THE NATURE OF PERSONAL SELLING

Selling is one of the oldest professions in the world. The people who do the selling go by many names: *salespeople, sales representatives, account executives, sales consultants, sales engineers, agents, district managers, marketing representatives,* and *account development reps,* to name just a few.

People hold many stereotypes of salespeople—including some unfavorable ones. "Salesman" may bring to mind the image of Arthur Miller's pitiable Willy Loman in *Death of a Salesman.* Or you might think of Meredith Willson's cigar-smoking, back-slapping, joke-telling Harold Hill in *The Music Man.* Both examples depict salespeople as loners, traveling their territories, trying to foist their wares on unsuspecting or unwilling buyers.

However, modern salespeople are a far cry from these unfortunate stereotypes. Today, most salespeople are well-educated, well-trained professionals who work to build and maintain long-term customer relationships by listening to their customers, assessing customer needs, and organizing the company's efforts to solve customer problems. Consider Boeing, the aerospace giant that dominates the worldwide commercial aircraft market with a 55 percent market share. It takes more than a friendly smile and a firm handshake to sell expensive airplanes:

Selling high-tech aircraft at $70 million or more a copy is complex and challenging. A single big sale can easily run into billions of dollars. Boeing salespeople head up an extensive team of company specialists—sales and service technicians, financial analysts, planners, engineers—all dedicated to finding ways to satisfy airline customer needs. The salespeople begin by becoming experts on the airlines, much like Wall Street analysts would. They find out where each airline wants to grow, when it wants to replace planes, and details of its financial situation. The team runs Boeing and competing planes through computer systems, simulating the airline's routes, cost per seat, and other factors to show that their planes are most efficient. Then the high-level negotiations begin. The selling process is nerve-rackingly slow—it can take two or three years from the first sales presentation to the day the sale is announced. Sometimes top executives from both the airline and Boeing are brought in to close the deal. After getting the order, salespeople then must stay in almost constant touch to keep track of the account's equipment needs and to make certain the customer stays satisfied. Success depends on building solid, long-term relationships with customers, Is based on performance and trust. According to one analyst, Boeing's salespeople "are the vehicle by which information is collected and contacts are made so all other things can take place."[2]

The term **salesperson** covers a wide range of positions. At one extreme, a salesperson might be largely an *order taker,* such as the department store salesperson standing behind the counter. At the other extreme are *order getters,* whose positions demand the *creative selling* of products and services ranging from appliances, industrial equipment, or airplanes to insurance, advertising, or consulting services. Other salespeople engage in *missionary selling:* These salespeople are not expected or permitted to take an order but only build goodwill or educate buyers. An example is a salesperson for a pharmaceutical company who calls on doctors to educate them about the company's drug products and to urge them to prescribe these products to their patients. Here, we focus on the more creative types of selling and on the process of building and managing an effective sales force.

THE ROLE OF THE SALES FORCE

Personal selling is the interpersonal arm of the promotion mix. Advertising consists of one-way, nonpersonal communication with target consumer groups. In contrast, personal selling involves two-way, personal communication between salespeople and individual customers—whether face-to-face, by telephone, through video conferences, or by other means. Personal selling can be more effective than advertising in more complex selling situations. Salespeople can probe customers to learn more about their problems. They can adjust the marketing offer to fit the special needs of each customer and can negotiate terms of sale. They can build long-term personal relationships with key decision makers.

The role of personal selling varies from company to company. Some firms have no salespeople at all—for example, companies that sell only through mail-order catalogs or companies that sell through manufacturer's reps, sales agents, or brokers. In most firms, however, the sales force plays a major role. In companies that sell business products, such as Xerox or DuPont, the company's salespeople work directly with customers. In fact, to many customers, salespeople may be the only contact. To these customers, the sales force *is* the company. In consumer product companies such as Procter & Gamble or Nike that sell through intermediaries, final consumers rarely meet salespeople or even know about them. Still, the sales force plays an important behind-the-scenes role. It works with wholesalers and retailers to gain their support and to help them be more effective in selling the company's products.

The sales force serves as a critical link between a company and its customers. In many cases, salespeople serve both masters—the seller and the buyer. First, they *represent the company to customers.* They find and develop new customers and communicate information about the company's products and services. They sell products by approaching customers, presenting their products, answering objections, negotiating prices and terms, and closing sales. In addition, salespeople provide services to customers, carry out market research and intelligence work, and fill out sales call reports.

At the same time, salespeople *represent customers to the company,* acting inside the firm as "champions" of customers' interests. Salespeople relay customer concerns about company products and actions back to those who can handle them. They learn about customer needs and work with others in the company to develop greater customer value. The salesperson often acts as an "account manager" who manages the relationship between the seller and buyer. Thus, salespeople must work closely with other marketing and nonmarketing people within the firm.

As companies move toward a stronger market orientation, their sales forces are becoming more market focused and customer oriented. The old view was that salespeople should worry about sales

---

[2]See Bill Kelley, "How to Sell Airplanes, Boeing-Style," *Sales & Marketing Management,* December 9, 1985, pp. 32–34; Andy Cohen, "Boeing," *Sales & Marketing Management,* October 1997, p. 68; and Laurence Zukerman, "On Center Runway, Boeing's Little 717," *New York Times,* June 15, 1999, p. 6.

and the company should worry about profit. However, the current view holds that salespeople should be concerned with more than just producing *sales*—they also must know how to produce *customer satisfaction* and *company profit*. Beyond winning new customers and making sales, they must be able to help the company to create long-term, profitable relationships with customers.

> ## active example

Take a moment to consider one perspective on personal selling.

> ## active concept check

Now let's take a moment to test your knowledge of what you've just read.

> ## Managing the Sales Force

We define **sales force management** as the analysis, planning, implementation, and control of sales force activities. It includes designing sales force strategy and structure and recruiting, selecting, training, compensating, supervising, and evaluating the firm's salespeople. These major sales force management decisions are shown in Figure 16.1 and are discussed in the following sections.

DESIGNING SALES FORCE STRATEGY AND STRUCTURE

Marketing managers face several sales force strategy and design questions. How should salespeople and their tasks be structured? How big should the sales force be? Should salespeople sell alone or work in teams with other people in the company? Should they sell in the field or by telephone? We address these issues below.

Sales Force Structure

A company can divide up sales responsibilities along any of several lines. The decision is simple if the company sells only one product line to one industry with customers in many locations. In that case the company would use a *territorial sales force structure*. However, if the company sells many products to many types of customers, it might need either a *product sales force structure,* a *customer sales force structure,* or a combination of the two.

Territorial Sales Force Structure.   In the **territorial sales force structure,** each salesperson is assigned to an exclusive geographic area and sells the company's full line of products or services to all customers in that territory. This organization has many advantages. It clearly defines the salesperson's job, and because only one salesperson works the territory, he or she gets all the credit or blame for territory sales. The territorial structure also increases the salesperson's desire to build local business relationships that, in turn, improve selling effectiveness. Finally, because each salesperson travels within a limited geographic area, travel expenses are relatively small.

A territorial sales organization is often supported by many levels of sales management positions. For example, Campbell Soup uses a territorial structure in which each salesperson is responsible for selling all Campbell Soup products. Starting at the bottom of the organization, *sales merchandisers*

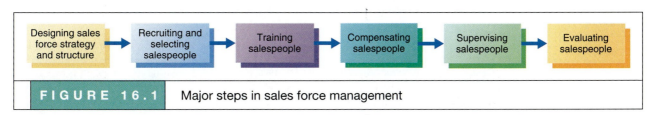

FIGURE 16.1   Major steps in sales force management

report to *sales representatives,* who report to *retail supervisors,* who report to *directors of retail sales operations,* who report to 1 of 22 *regional sales managers.* Regional sales managers, in turn, report to 1 of 4 *general sales managers* (West, Central, South, and East), who report to a *vice president* and *general sales manager.*

Product Sales Force Structure.   Salespeople must know their products—especially when the products are numerous and complex. This need, together with the growth of product management, has led many companies to adopt a **product sales force structure,** in which the sales force sells along product lines. For example, Kodak uses different sales forces for its film products than for its industrial products. The film products sales force deals with simple products that are distributed intensively, whereas the industrial products sales force deals with complex products that require technical understanding.

The product structure can lead to problems, however, if a single large customer buys many different company products. For example, Baxter International, a hospital supply company, has several product divisions, each with a separate sales force. Several Baxter salespeople might end up calling on the same hospital on the same day. This means that they travel over the same routes and wait to see the same customer's purchasing agents. These extra costs must be compared with the benefits of better product knowledge and attention to individual products.

Customer Sales Force Structure.   More and more companies are now using a **customer sales force structure,** in which they organize the sales force along customer or industry lines. Separate sales forces may be set up for different industries, for serving current customers versus finding new ones, and for major accounts versus regular accounts.

Organizing the sales force around customers can help a company to become more customer focused and build closer relationships with important customers. For example, giant ABB, the $30-billion-a-year Swiss-based industrial equipment maker, changed from a product-based to a customer-based sales force. The new structure resulted in a stronger customer orientation and improved service to clients:

Until four months ago, David Donaldson sold boilers for ABB. . . . After 30 years, Donaldson sure knew boilers, but he didn't know much about the broad range of other products offered by ABB's U.S. Power Plant division. Customers were frustrated because as many as a dozen ABB salespeople called on them at different times to peddle their products. ABB's bosses decided that this was a poor way to run a sales force. So [recently], David Donaldson and 27 other power plant salespeople began new jobs. [Donaldson] now also sells turbines, generators, and three other product lines. He handles six major accounts . . . instead of a [mixed batch] of 35. His charge: Know the customer intimately and sell him the products that help him operate productively. Says Donaldson: "My job is to make it easy for my customers to do business with us. . . . I show them where to go in ABB whenever they have a problem." The president of ABB's power plant businesses [adds]: "If you want to be a customer-driven company, you have to design the sales organization around individual buyers rather than around your products."[3]

IBM made a similar shift from a product-based structure to a customer-based one. Before the shift, droves of salespeople representing different IBM software, hardware, and services divisions might call on a single large client, creating confusion and frustration. Such large customers wanted a "single face," one point of contact for all of IBM's vast array of products and services. Following the restructuring, a single IBM "client executive" works with each large customer and manages a team of IBMers—product reps, systems engineers, consultants, and others—who work with the customer. The client executive becomes an expert in the customer's industry. Greg Buseman, a client executive in the distribution industry who spends most of his time working with a major consumer packaged-goods customer, describes his role this way: "I am the owner of the business relationship with the client. If the client has a problem, I'm the one who pulls together software or hardware specialists or consultants. At the customer I work most closely with, we usually have 15 to 20 projects going at once, and I have to manage them."[4] Such an intense focus on customers is widely credited for IBM's dramatic turnaround in recent years.

[3]Patricia Sellers, "How to Remake Your Sales Force," *Fortune,* May 4, 1992, p. 96. Also see Charles Fleming and Leslie Lopez, "The Corporate Challenge—No Boundaries: ABB's Dramatic Plan Is to Recast Its Business Structure Along Global Lines," *Wall Street Journal,* September 28, 1998, p. R16; and "Employing 200,000 People in over 100 Countries," accessed online at www.abb.com, September 1999.

[4]Geoffrey Brewer, "Love the Ones You're With," *Sales & Marketing Management,* February 1997, pp. 38–45.

This Procter & Gamble "customer business development team" serves a major southeastern grocery retailer. It consists of a customer business development manager and five account executives (shown here), along with specialists from other functional areas.

Procter & Gamble has also moved to a customer sales force structure in recent years. P&G sales reps are now organized into "customer business development teams." Each CBD team is assigned to a major P&G customer. Each team consists of a customer business development manager, several account executives (each responsible for a specific category of P&G products), and specialists in marketing strategy, operations, information systems, logistics, and finance. This organization places the focus on serving the complete needs of each important customer.

Complex Sales Force Structures. When a company sells a wide variety of products to many types of customers over a broad geographic area, it often combines several types of sales force structures. Salespeople can be specialized by customer and territory, by product and territory, by product and customer, or by territory, product, and customer. No single structure is best for all companies and situations. Each company should select a sales force structure that best serves the needs of its customers and fits its overall marketing strategy.

Sales Force Size

Once the company has set its structure, it is ready to consider *sales force size*. Salespeople constitute one of the company's most productive—and most expensive—assets. Therefore, increasing their number will increase both sales and costs.

In recent years, sales forces have been shrinking in size. One study revealed that, in just the two years from 1996 to 1998, the average company's sales force decreased by a whopping 26 percent.[5] One cause is advances in selling technology, such as selling on the Internet or the use of account management software, which make salespeople more efficient in handling customers or replace the salespeople altogether. Another cause is recent merger mania, on both the seller and customer sides. When two sellers merge, they rarely need a doubled sales force. "When you merge two sales forces, you'll have about one and a half sales forces when you're done," says a sales consultant.[6] Similarly, the merging of two customer firms means fewer customers, and fewer customers means that fewer salespeople are needed to call on them.

Many companies use some form of *workload approach* to set sales force size. Using this approach, a company first groups accounts into different classes according to size, account status, or other factors related to the amount of effort required to maintain them. It then determines the number of salespeople needed to call on each class of accounts the desired number of times. The company might think as follows: Suppose we have 1,000 Type-A accounts and 2,000 Type-B accounts. Type-A accounts require 36 calls a year and Type-B accounts require 12 calls a year. In this case, the sales force's *workload*—the number of calls it must make per year—is 60,000 calls [(1,000 × 36) + (2,000 × 12) = 36,000 + 24,000 = 60,000]. Suppose our average salesperson can make 1,000 calls a year. Thus, the company needs 60 salespeople (60,000 ÷ 1,000).

Other Sales Force Strategy and Structure Issues

Sales management must also decide who will be involved in the selling effort and how various sales and sales support people will work together.

Outside and Inside Sales Forces. The company may have an **outside sales force** (or *field sales force*), an **inside sales force,** or both. Outside salespeople travel to call on customers. Inside salespeople conduct business from their offices via telephone or visits from prospective buyers.

[5]Melinda Ligos, "The Incredible Shrinking Sales Force," *Sales & Marketing Management,* December 1998, p. 15.

[6]Ibid., p. 15.

To reduce time demands on their outside sales forces, many companies have increased the size of their inside sales forces. Inside salespeople include technical support people, sales assistants, and telemarketers. *Technical support people* provide technical information and answers to customers' questions. *Sales assistants* provide clerical backup for outside salespeople. They call ahead and confirm appointments, conduct credit checks, follow up on deliveries, and answer customers' questions when outside salespeople cannot be reached. *Telemarketers* use the phone to find new leads and qualify prospects for the field sales force, or to sell and service accounts directly.

The inside sales force frees outside salespeople to spend more time selling to major accounts and finding major new prospects. Depending on the complexity of the product and customer, a telemarketer can make from 20 to 33 decision-maker contacts a day, compared to the average of 4 that an outside salesperson can make. For many types of products and selling situations, **telemarketing** can be as effective as a personal call but much less expensive. Whereas the average personal sale costs about $165, a routine industrial telemarketing call costs only about $5 and a complex call about $20.[7] Notes a DuPont telemarketer: "I'm more effective on the phone. [When you're in the field], if some guy's not in his office, you lose an hour. On the phone, you lose 15 seconds. . . . Through my phone calls, I'm in the field as much as the rep is." There are other advantages. "Customers can't throw things at you," quips the rep, "and you don't have to outrun dogs."[8]

Telemarketing can be used successfully by both large and small companies:

IBM's traditional image has long been symbolized by the salesman in the blue suit, crisp white shirt, and red tie—an imposing fellow far more comfortable in Corporate America's plush executive suites than in the cramped quarters of some fledgling entrepreneur. Small businesses were often ignored. Typical is the Fess Parker Winery & Vineyard, a $4.5 million company in Los Olivos, California, that employs 25 people. "I never would've thought of IBM as someone to call for a business our size" says general manager Charlie Kears. To sell its electronic-business solutions to such small businesses, IBM is now boosting emphasis on its telemarketing effort. Stroll through the IBM call center in suburban Atlanta, with its sea of cubicles, and a new image of the IBM salesperson emerges: Men and women, many recent college grads, sporting golf shirts and khakis or—gasp!—blue jeans. They wear headsets and talk on the phone with customers they'll likely never meet in person. Phone selling, once deemed a poor stepchild at IBM, is now in vogue. IBM's roughly 1,200 phone reps now generate 30 percent of IBM's revenues from small and midsize businesses. The reps focus on specific industries and each calls on as many as 300 accounts. They nurture client relationships, pitch IBM solutions, and, when needed, refer customers to product and service specialists within the call center or to resellers in their region. How do customers like dealing with telesales reps? According to Kears, it's been "terrific"—he's never on hold for long, and the reps are very helpful, he says. "Plus, I get a lot of e-mails from my rep in Atlanta, and I usually hear from someone there every other week."[9]

Climax Portable Machine Tools has proven that a small company can use telemarketing to save money and still lavish attention on buyers. Under the old system, Climax sales engineers spent one-third of their time on the road, training distributor salespeople and accompanying them on calls. They could make about 4 contacts a day. Now, each of 5 sales engineers on Climax's telemarketing team calls about 30 prospects a day, following up on leads generated by ads and direct mail. Because it takes about 5 calls to close a sale, the sales engineers update a prospect's computer file after each contact, noting the degree of commitment, requirements, next call date, and personal comments. "If anyone mentions he's going on a fishing trip, our sales engineer enters that in the computer and uses it to personalize the next phone call," says Climax's president, noting that's just one way to build good relations. Another is that the first mailing to a prospect includes the sales engineer's business card with his picture on it. Of course, it takes more than friendli-

[7]See Michele Marchetti, "The Costs of Doing Business," *Sales & Marketing Management,* September 1999, p. 56.

[8]See Martin Everett, "Selling by Telephone," *Sales & Marketing Management,* December 1993, pp. 75–79.

[9]Geoffrey Brewer, "Lou Gerstner Has His Hands Full," *Sales & Marketing Management,* May 8, 1998, pp. 36–41.

ness to sell $15,000 machine tools over the phone (special orders may run $200,000), but the telemarketing approach is working well. When Climax customers were asked, "Do you see the sales engineer often enough?" the response was overwhelmingly positive. Obviously, many people didn't realize that the only contact they'd had with Climax had been on the phone.[10]

Just as telemarketing is changing the way that many companies go to market, the Internet offers explosive potential for restructuring sales forces and conducting sales operations. More and more companies are now using the Internet to support their personal selling efforts—not just for selling, but for everything from training salespeople to conducting sales meetings and servicing accounts.

Team Selling.   For years, the customer has been solely in the hands of the salesperson. The salesperson identified the prospect, arranged the call, explored the customer's needs, created and proposed a solution, closed the deal, and turned cheerleader as others delivered what he or she promised. For selling relatively simple products, this approach can work well. But if the products are more complex and the service requirements greater, the salesperson simply can't go it alone. Instead, most companies now are using **team selling** to service large, complex accounts.

More and more, companies are finding that sales teams can unearth problems, solutions, and sales opportunities that no individual salesperson could. Such teams might include experts from any area or level of the selling firm—sales, marketing, technical and support services, R&D, engineering, operations, finance, and others. In team selling situations, the salesperson shifts from "soloist" to "orchestrator."[11]

In many cases, the move to team selling mirrors similar changes in customers' buying organizations. According to the director of sales education at Dow Chemical, over 80 percent of purchasing decisions are now being made by multifunctional buying teams, including purchasing, engineering, and financial management staff. To sell effectively to such selling teams, he states, "Our sellers . . . have to captain selling teams. There are no more lone wolves."[12]

Some companies, like IBM, Xerox, and Procter & Gamble have used teams for a long time. Others have only recently reorganized to adopt the team concept. For example, Cutler-Hammer, which supplies circuit breakers, motor starters, and other electrical equipment to heavy industrial manufacturers such as Ford Motor, recently developed "pods" of salespeople that focus on a specific geographical region, industry, or market. Each pod member contributes unique expertise and knowledge about a product or service that salespeople can leverage when selling to increasingly sophisticated buying teams.[13]

Team selling does have some pitfalls. For example, selling teams can confuse or overwhelm customers who are used to working with only one salesperson. Salespeople who are used to having customers all to themselves may have trouble learning to work with and trust others on a team. Finally, difficulties in evaluating individual contributions to the team selling effort can create some sticky compensation issues.

Still, team selling can produce dramatic results. For example, Dun & Bradstreet, the world's largest marketer of business information and related services, recently established sales teams made up of representatives from its credit, collection, and marketing business units, which up to then had worked separately. Their mission was to work as a team to call on higher-ups in customer organizations, learn about customer needs, and offer solutions. The teams concentrated on D&B's top 50 customers.

When one of the D&B sales teams asked to meet with the chief financial officer of a major telecommunications company, the executive responded, "I'm delighted you asked, but why talk?" He

[10]See "A Phone Is Better Than a Face," *Sales & Marketing Management,* October 1987, p. 29. Also see Brett A. Boyle, "The Importance of the Industrial Inside Sales Force: A Case Study," *Industrial Marketing Management,* September 1996, pp. 339–48; Victoria Fraza, "Upgrading Inside Sales," *Industrial Distribution,* December 1997, pp. 44–49; and Michele Marchetti, "Look Who's Calling," *Sales & Marketing Management,* May 1998, pp. 43–46.

[11]Richard C. Whiteley, "Orchestrating Service," *Sales & Marketing Management,* April 1994, pp. 29–30.

[12]Rick Mullin, "From Lone Wolves to Team Players," *Chemical Week,* January 14, 1998, pp. 33–34.

[13]Robert Hiebeler, Thomas B. Kelly, and Charles Ketteman, *Best Practices: Building Your Business with Customer-focused Solutions* (New York: Arthur Andersen/Simon & Schuster, 1998), pp. 122–24. Also see Richard C. Whiteley, "Orchestrating Service," *Sales & Marketing Management,* April 1994, pp. 29–30; Mark A. Moon and Susan Forquer Gupta, "Examining the Formation of Selling Centers: A Conceptual Framework," *Journal of Personal Selling and Sales Management,* Spring 1997, pp. 31–41; and Donald W. Jackson Jr., Scott M. Widmier, Ralph Giacobbe, and Janet E. Keith, "Examining the Use of Team Selling by Manufacturers' Representatives: A Situational Approach," *Industrial Marketing Management,* March 1999, pp. 155–64.

found out after a one-hour meeting. The D&B team listened as he discussed problems facing his organization, and by the end of the information-seeking session, the team had come up with several solutions for the executive and had identified $1.5 million in D&B sales opportunities from what had been a $700,000 customer. More teams met with more clients, creating more opportunities. About a year after the program started, D&B's marketing department had targeted $200 million in sales opportunities, about half of which would not have been found under the old system. Now these teams are getting together with D&B's top 200 customers.[14]

active exercise

Take a moment to study the sales force design of one of the most successful personal-selling organizations in the world.

RECRUITING AND SELECTING SALESPEOPLE

At the heart of any successful sales force operation is the recruitment and selection of good salespeople. The performance difference between an average salesperson and a top salesperson can be substantial. In a typical sales force, the top 30 percent of the salespeople might bring in 60 percent of the sales. Thus, careful salesperson selection can greatly increase overall sales force performance. Beyond the differences in sales performance, poor selection results in costly turnover. When a salesperson quits, the costs of finding and training a new salesperson—plus the costs of lost sales—can run as high as $50,000 to $75,000. Also, a sales force with many new people is less productive.[15]

What Makes a Good Salesperson?

Selecting salespeople would not be a problem if the company knew what traits to look for. If it knew that good salespeople were outgoing, aggressive, and energetic, for example, it could simply check applicants for these characteristics. But many successful salespeople are bashful, soft-spoken, and laid back.

Still, the search continues for the magic list of traits that spells sure-fire sales success. One survey suggests that good salespeople have a lot of enthusiasm, persistence, initiative, self-confidence, and job commitment. They are committed to sales as a way of life and have a strong customer orientation. Another study suggests that good salespeople are independent and self-motivated and are excellent listeners. Still another study advises that salespeople should be a friend to the customer as well as persistent, enthusiastic, attentive, and—above all—honest. They must be internally motivated, disciplined, hardworking, and able to build strong relationships with customers. Finally, studies show that good salespeople are team players rather than loners.[16]

How can a company find out what traits salespeople in its industry should have? Job *duties* suggest some of the traits a company should look for. Does the job require a lot of planning and paperwork? Does it call for much travel? Will the salesperson face a lot of rejections? Will the salesperson be working with high-level buyers? The successful salesperson should be suited to these duties. The company also should look at the characteristics of its most successful salespeople for clues to needed traits.

[14]See Christopher Meyer, "How the Right Measures Help Teams Excel," *Harvard Business Review,* May–June 1994, pp. 95–103; Michele Marchetti, "Why Teams Fail," *Sales & Marketing Management,* June 1997, p. 91; Melinda Ligos, "On with the Show," *Sales & Marketing Management,* November 1998, pp. 70–76; and Jackson, Widmier, Giacobbe, and Keith, "Examining the Use of Team Selling by Manufacturers' Representatives: A Situational Approach," pp. 155–64.

[15]See George H. Lucas Jr., A. Parasuraman, Robert A. Davis, and Ben M. Enis, "An Empirical Study of Sales Force Turnover," *Journal of Marketing,* July 1987, pp. 34–59; Lynn G. Coleman, "Sales Force Turnover Has Managers Wondering Why," *Marketing News,* December 4, 1989, p. 6; Thomas R. Wotruba and Pradeep K. Tyagi, "Met Expectations and Turnover in Direct Selling," *Journal of Marketing,* July 1991, pp. 24–35; and Chad Kaydo, "Overturning Turnover," *Sales & Marketing Management,* November 1997, pp. 50–60.

[16]See Geoffrey Brewer, "Mind Reading: What Drives Top Salespeople to Greatness?" *Sales & Marketing Management,* May 1994, pp. 82–88; Barry J. Farber, "Success Stories for Salespeople," *Sales & Marketing Management,* May 1995, pp. 30–31; Roberta Maynard, "Finding the Essence of Good Salespeople," *Nation's Business,* February 1998, p. 10; and Jeanie Casison, "Closest Thing to Cloning," *Incentive,* June 1999, p. 7.

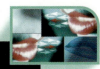

Recruiting Procedures

After management has decided on needed traits, it must *recruit* salespeople. The human resources department looks for applicants by getting names from current salespeople, using employment agencies, placing classified ads, and contacting college students. Another source is to attract top salespeople from other companies. Proven salespeople need less training and can be immediately productive.

Until recently, companies sometimes found it hard to sell college students on selling. Many thought that selling was a job and not a profession, that salespeople had to be deceitful to be effective, and that selling involved too much insecurity and travel. In addition, some women believed that selling was a man's career. To counter such objections, recruiters now offer high starting salaries and income growth and note that more than one-fourth of the presidents of large U.S. corporations started out in marketing and sales. They point out that over 23 percent of all professional salespeople in the United States are women. Women account for a much higher percentage of the sales force in some industries, such as lodging (63 percent), banking and financial services (53 percent), and health services (52 percent).[17]

Selecting Salespeople

Recruiting will attract many applicants from whom the company must select the best. The selection procedure can vary from a single informal interview to lengthy testing and interviewing. Many companies give formal tests to sales applicants. Tests typically measure sales aptitude, analytical and organizational skills, personality traits, and other characteristics. Test results count heavily in companies such as IBM, Prudential, Procter & Gamble, and Gillette. Gillette claims that tests have reduced turnover by 42 percent and that test scores have correlated well with the later performance of new salespeople. But test scores provide only one piece of information in a set that includes personal characteristics, references, past employment history, and interviewer reactions.[18]

TRAINING SALESPEOPLE

Many companies used to send their new salespeople into the field almost immediately after hiring them. They would be given samples, order books, and general instructions ("sell west of the Mississippi"). To many companies, a training program translated into high expense for instructors, materials, space, and salary for a person who was not yet selling, and a loss of sales opportunities because the person was not in the field.

Today's new salespeople, however, may spend anywhere from a few weeks or months to a year or more in training. The average training period is four months. In all, U.S. companies spend more than $7 billion annually on training salespeople and devote more than 33 hours per year to the average salesperson.[19] Although training can be expensive, it can also yield dramatic returns on the training investment. For example, Nabisco did an extensive analysis of the return on investment of its two-day Professional Selling Program, which teaches sales reps how to plan for and make professional presentations to their retail customers. Although it cost about $1,000 to put each sales rep through the program, the training resulted in additional sales of more than $122,000 per rep and yielded almost $21,000 of additional profit per rep.[20]

Training programs have several goals. Salespeople need to know and identify with the company, so most training programs begin by describing the company's history and objectives, its organization,

[17]"23 Percent of U.S. Salespeople Are Women," *American Salesman,* April 1995, p. 8. Also see Nancy Arnott, "It's a Woman's World," *Sales & Marketing Management,* March 1995, pp. 55–59; "Selling Sales to Students," *Sales & Marketing Management,* January 1998, p. 15; and Ray Holley, "Corporate Pirates Wage Battles for Top Salespeople," *Computer Reseller News,* June 21, 1999, p. 107.

[18]See "To Test or Not to Test," *Sales & Marketing Management,* May 1994, p. 86.

[19]Sarah Lorge, "Getting into Their Heads," *Sales & Marketing Management,* February 1998, pp. 58–67.

[20]Robert Klein, "Nabisco Sales Soar After Sales Training," *Marketing News,* January 6, 1997, p. 23.

Sales training: U.S. companies spend more than $7 billion annually on training salespeople and devote more than 33 hours per year to the average salesperson.

its financial structure and facilities, and its chief products and markets. Salespeople also need to know the company's products, so sales trainees are shown how products are produced and how they work. They also need to know customers' and competitors' characteristics, so the training program teaches them about competitors' strategies and about different types of customers and their needs, buying motives, and buying habits. Because salespeople must know how to make effective presentations, they are trained in the principles of selling. Finally, salespeople need to understand field procedures and responsibilities. They learn how to divide time between active and potential accounts and how to use an expense account, prepare reports, and route communications effectively.

COMPENSATING SALESPEOPLE

To attract salespeople, a company must have an appealing compensation plan. These plans vary greatly both by industry and by companies within the same industry. The level of compensation must be close to the "going rate" for the type of sales job and needed skills. To pay less than the going rate would attract too few quality salespeople; to pay more would be unnecessary.

Compensation is made up of several elements—a fixed amount, a variable amount, expenses, and fringe benefits. The fixed amount, usually a salary, gives the salesperson some stable income. The variable amount, which might be commissions or bonuses based on sales performance, rewards the salesperson for greater effort. Expense allowances, which repay salespeople for job-related expenses, let salespeople undertake needed and desirable selling efforts. Fringe benefits, such as paid vacations, sickness or accident benefits, pensions, and life insurance, provide job security and satisfaction.

Management must decide what *mix* of these compensation elements makes the most sense for each sales job. Different combinations of fixed and variable compensation give rise to four basic types of compensation plans—straight salary, straight commission, salary plus bonus, and salary plus commission. A study of sales force compensation plans showed that 70 percent of all companies surveyed use a combination of base salary and incentives. The average plan consisted of about 60 percent salary and 40 percent incentive pay.[21]

[21]Christen P. Heide, "All Levels of Sales Reps Post Impressive Earnings," press release, www.dartnell.com, May 5, 1997; and *Dartnell's 30th Sales Force Compensation Survey,* Dartnell Corporation, August 1998.

The sales force compensation plan can both motivate salespeople and direct their activities. For example, if sales management wants salespeople to emphasize new account development, it might pay a bonus for opening new accounts. Thus, the compensation plan should direct the sales force toward activities that are consistent with overall marketing objectives.

Table 16.1 illustrates how a company's compensation plan should reflect its overall marketing strategy. For example, if the overall strategy is to grow rapidly and gain market share, the compensation plan should reward high sales performance and encourage salespeople to capture new accounts. This might suggest a larger commission component coupled with new-account bonuses. In contrast, if the marketing goal is to maximize profitability of current accounts, the compensation plan might contain a larger base-salary component, with additional incentives based on current account sales or customer satisfaction. In fact, more and more companies are moving away from high commission plans that may drive salespeople to make short-term grabs for business. Notes one sales force expert, "The last thing you want is to have someone ruin a customer relationship because they're pushing too hard to close a deal." Instead, companies are designing compensation plans that reward salespeople for building customer relationships and growing the long-run value of each customer.[22]

> active poll

Give your opinion on a question regarding the compensation of salespeople.

SUPERVISING SALESPEOPLE

New salespeople need more than a territory, compensation, and training—they need *supervision*. Through supervision, the company *directs* and *motivates* the sales force to do a better job.

Directing Salespeople

How much should sales management be involved in helping salespeople manage their territories? It depends on everything from the company's size to the experience of its sales force. Thus, companies vary widely in how closely they supervise their salespeople.

TABLE 16.1	The Relationship Between Overall Marketing Strategy and Sales Force Compensation		
	STRATEGIC GOAL		
	To Gain Market Share Rapidly	**To Solidify Market Leadership**	**To Maximize Profitability**
Ideal salesperson	◆ An independent self-starter	◆ A competitive problem solver	◆ A team player ◆ A relationship manager
Sales focus	◆ Deal making ◆ Sustained high effort	◆ Consultative selling	◆ Account penetration
Compensation role	◆ To capture accounts ◆ To reward high performance	◆ To reward new and existing account sales	◆ To manage the product mix ◆ To encourage team selling ◆ To reward account management

Source: Adapted from Sam T. Johnson, "Sales Compensation: In Search of a Better Solution," *Compensation & Benefits Review,* November–December 1993, pp. 53–60. Copyright © 1998 American Management Association, NY, http://www.amanet.org. All Rights reserved, used with permission.

[22]Geoffrey Brewer, "Brain Power," *Sales & Marketing Management,* May 1997, pp. 39–48; Don Peppers and Martha Rogers, "The Money Trap," *Sales & Marketing Management,* May 1997, pp. 58–60; Michele Marchetti, "No Commissions? Are You Crazy?" *Sales & Marketing Management,* May 1998, p. 83; and Don Peppers and Martha Rogers, "The Price of Customer Service," *Sales & Marketing Management,* April 1999, pp. 20–21.

Many companies help their salespeople in identifying customer targets and setting call norms. In addition, companies may specify how much time their sales forces should spend prospecting for new accounts. Companies may also direct salespeople in how to use their time efficiently. One tool is the *annual call plan* that shows which customers and prospects to call on in which months and which activities to carry out. Activities include taking part in trade shows, attending sales meetings, and carrying out marketing research. Another tool is *time-and-duty analysis.* In addition to time spent selling, the salesperson spends time traveling, waiting, eating, taking breaks, and doing administrative chores.

Figure 16.2 shows how salespeople spend their time. On average, actual face-to-face selling time accounts for less than 30 percent of total working time! If selling time could be raised from 30 percent to 40 percent, this would be a 33 percent increase in the time spent selling. Companies always are looking for ways to save time—using phones instead of traveling, simplifying record-keeping forms, finding better call and routing plans, and supplying more and better customer information.

Many firms have adopted *sales force automation systems,* computerized sales force operations for more efficient order-entry transactions, improved customer service, and better salesperson decision-making support. Salespeople use computers to profile customers and prospects, analyze and forecast sales, manage account relationships, schedule sales calls, make presentations, enter orders, check inventories and order status, prepare sales and expense reports, process correspondence, and carry out many other activities. Sales force automation not only lowers sales force costs and improves productivity, it also improves the quality of sales management decisions. Here is an example of successful sales force automation:[23]

Owens-Corning recently put its sales force online with FAST—its newly developed Field Automation Sales Team system. FAST gives Owens-Corning salespeople a constant supply of information about their company and the people they're dealing with. Using laptop computers, each salesperson can access three types of programs. First, FAST gives them a set of *generic tools,* everything from word processing to fax and e-mail transmission to creating presentations online. Second, it provides *product information*—tech bulletins, customer specifications, pricing information, and other data that can help close a sale. Finally, it offers up a wealth of *customer information*—buying history, types of products ordered, and preferred payment terms. Reps previously stored such information in loose-leaf books, calendars, and account cards. FAST makes working directly with customers easier than ever. Salespeople can prime themselves on backgrounds of clients; call up prewritten sales letters; transmit orders and resolve customer-service issues on the spot during customer calls; and have samples, pamphlets, brochures, and other materials sent to clients with a few keystrokes.

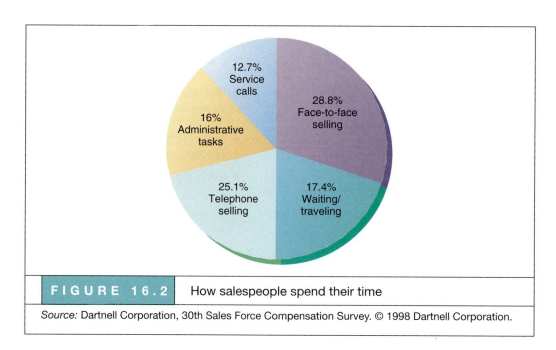

| FIGURE 16.2 | How salespeople spend their time |

Source: Dartnell Corporation, 30th Sales Force Compensation Survey. © 1998 Dartnell Corporation.

[23]Tony Seideman, "Who Needs Managers?" *Sales & Marketing Management,* part 2, June 1994, pp. 15–17. Also see Tim McCollum, "High-Tech Marketing Hits the Target," *Nation's Business,* June 1997, pp. 39–42; Ginger Conlon, "Plug and Play," *Sales & Marketing Management,* December 1998, pp. 64–67; and Erika Rasmusson, "The 5 Steps to Successful Sales Force Automation," *Sales & Marketing Management,* March 1999, pp. 34–40.

Perhaps the fastest-growing sales force technology tool is the Internet. In a survey by Dartnell Corporation of 1,000 salespeople, 61 percent reported using the Internet regularly in their daily selling activities. The most common uses include gathering competitive information, monitoring customer Web sites, and researching industries and specific customers. As more and more companies provide their salespeople with Web access, experts expect continued growth in sales force Internet usage.[24]

Motivating Salespeople

Some salespeople will do their best without any special urging from management. To them, selling may be the most fascinating job in the world. But selling can also be frustrating. Salespeople often work alone, and they must sometimes travel away from home. They may face aggressive competing salespeople and difficult customers. They sometimes lack the authority to do what is needed to win a sale and may thus lose large orders they have worked hard to obtain. Therefore, salespeople often need special encouragement to do their best.

Management can boost sales force morale and performance through its organizational climate, sales quotas, and positive incentives. *Organizational climate* describes the feeling that salespeople have about their opportunities, value, and rewards for a good performance within the company. Some companies treat salespeople as if they are not very important. Other companies treat their salespeople as their prime movers and allow virtually unlimited opportunity for income and promotion. Not surprisingly, in companies that hold their salespeople in low esteem, there is high turnover and poor performance. Where salespeople are held in high esteem, there is less turnover and higher performance.

Many companies motivate their salespeople by setting **sales quotas**—standards stating the amount they should sell and how sales should be divided among the company's products. Compensation is often related to how well salespeople meet their quotas. Companies also use various *positive incentives* to increase sales force effort. *Sales meetings* provide social occasions, breaks from routine, chances to meet and talk with "company brass," and opportunities to air feelings and to identify with

THE EVOLUTION OF MORE EFFECTIVE INCENTIVES FOR BUSINESS.

For rewards that drive business results, American Express Incentive Services has some of the most innovative ideas you'll find anywhere. Cash and retail gift certificates only go so far compared with high-tech rewards like Persona℠ Select – an electronically prepaid reward card that frees recipients to purchase what they want most. Do more for your associates. Do more for your business. Persona℠ Select. Only from American Express.

1.800.700.7610, ext. 900 | www.aeis.com do more AMERICAN EXPRESS Incentive Services

Sales force incentives: Many companies offer cash, trips, or merchandise as incentives. American Express suggests that companies reward outstanding sales performers with high-tech Persona Select cards—electronically prepaid reward cards that allow recipients to purchase whatever they want most.

[24]Christen Heide, "Rep Use of the Internet Up 226 Percent in 2 Years," *Sales & Marketing Management Executive Report,* August 19, 1998, pp. 8–9; and Melinda Ligos, "Point, Click, and Sell," *Sales & Marketing Management,* May 1999, pp. 51–56.

a larger group. Companies also sponsor *sales contests* to spur the sales force to make a selling effort above what would normally be expected. Other incentives include honors, merchandise and cash awards, trips, and profit-sharing plans.[25]

active exercise <

Consider how one firm recruits, compensates, and motivates its salespeople.

EVALUATING SALESPEOPLE

We have thus far described how management communicates what salespeople should be doing and how it motivates them to do it. This process requires good feedback. Good feedback means getting regular information about salespeople to evaluate their performance. Management gets information about its salespeople in several ways. The most important source is *sales reports,* including weekly or monthly work plans and longer-term territory marketing plans. Salespeople also write up their completed activities on *call reports* and turn in *expense reports* for which they are partly or wholly repaid. Additional information comes from personal observation, customer surveys, and talks with other salespeople.

The sales manager might begin with a *qualitative evaluation,* looking at a salesperson's knowledge of the company, products, customers, competitors, territory, and tasks. Personal traits—manner, appearance, speech, and temperament—can be rated. The sales manager can also review any problems in motivation or compliance. Each company must decide what would be most useful to know. It should communicate these criteria to salespeople so that they understand how their performance is evaluated and can make an effort to improve it.

Using sales force reports and other information, sales management can also conduct a more *formal evaluation* of members of the sales force. Formal evaluation produces several benefits. It forces management to develop and communicate clear standards for judging performance and to gather well-balanced information about each salesperson. Formal evaluation gives salespeople constructive feedback that helps them to improve future performance. Finally, salespeople are motivated to perform well because they know they will have to sit down with the sales manager and explain their performance.

One type of formal evaluation compares and ranks the sales performance of one salesperson against others. Such comparisons can be misleading, however. Salespeople may perform differently because of differences in territory potential, workload, level of competition, company promotion effort, and other factors. Furthermore, sales are not usually the best indicator of achievement. Management should be more interested in how much each salesperson contributes to net profits, a concern that requires looking at each salesperson's sales mix and expenses.

A second type of formal evaluation compares a salesperson's current performance with past performance. Such a comparison should directly indicate the person's progress. Table 16.2 provides an example. The sales manager can learn many things about Chris Bennett from this table. Bennett's total sales increased every year (line 3). This does not necessarily mean that Bennett is doing a better job. The product breakdown shows that Bennett has been able to push the sales of product B further than those of product A (lines 1 and 2). According to the quotas for the two products (lines 4 and 5), the success in increasing product B sales may be at the expense of product A sales. According to gross profits (lines 6 and 7), the company earns twice as much gross profit (as a ratio to sales) on A as it does on B. Bennett may be pushing the higher-volume, lower-margin product at the expense of the more profitable product. Although Bennett increased total sales by $1,100 between 1998 and 1999 (line 3), the gross profits on these total sales actually decreased by $580 (line 8).

Sales expense (line 9) shows a steady increase, although total expense as a percentage of total sales seems to be under control (line 10). The upward trend in Bennett's total dollar expenses does not seem to be explained by any increase in the number of calls (line 11), although it may be related to his success in acquiring new customers (line 14). However, there is a possibility that in prospecting for new customers, Bennett is neglecting present customers, as indicated by an upward trend in the annual number of lost customers (line 15).

The last two lines in the table show the level and trend in Bennett's sales and gross profits per customer. These figures become more meaningful when they are compared with overall company aver-

---

[25]For more on sales incentives, see Vincent Alonzo, "Money Isn't Everything," *Sales & Marketing Management,* January 1999, pp. 28–29; and James Champy, "Are Your Sellers Devoted to the Cause?" *Sales & Marketing Management,* May 1999, p. 22.

TABLE 16.2

Territory: Midland	Salesperson: Chris Bennett			
	1996	1997	1998	1999
1. Net sales product A	$251,300	$253,200	$270,000	$263,100
2. Net sales product B	$423,200	$439,200	553,900	561,900
3. Net sales total	$674,500	$692,400	$823,900	$825,000
4. Percent of quota product A	95.6	92.0	88.0	84.7
5. Percent of quota product B	120.4	122.3	134.9	130.8
6. Gross profits product A	$ 50,260	$ 50,640	$ 54,000	$ 52,620
7. Gross profits product B	$ 42,320	$ 43,920	$ 53,390	$ 56,190
8. Gross profits total	$ 92,580	$ 94,560	$109,390	$108,810
9. Sales expense	$ 10,200	$ 11,100	$ 11,600	$ 13,200
10. Sales expense to total sales (%)	1.5	1.6	1.4	1.6
11. Number of calls	1,675	1,700	1,680	1,660
12. Cost per call	$ 6.09	$ 6.53	$ 6.90	$ 7.95
13. Average number of customers	320	324	328	334
14. Number of new customers	13	14	15	20
15. Number of lost customers	8	10	11	14
16. Average sales per customer	$ 2,108	$ 2,137	$ 2,512	$ 2,470
17. Average gross profit per customer	$ 289	$ 292	$ 334	$ 326

Evaluating Salespeople's Performance

ages. If Chris Bennett's average gross profit per customer is lower than the company's average, Chris may be concentrating on the wrong customers or may not be spending enough time with each customer. Looking back at the annual number of calls (line 11), Bennett may be making fewer calls than the average salesperson. If distances in the territory are not much different, this may mean Chris is not putting in a full workday, is poor at planning routing or minimizing waiting time, or spends too much time with certain accounts.

> **active concept check**

Now let's take a moment to test your knowledge of what you've just read.

> **Principles of Personal Selling**

We now turn from designing and managing a sales force to the actual personal selling process. Personal selling is an ancient art that has spawned a large body of literature and many principles. Effective salespeople operate on more than just instinct—they are highly trained in methods of territory analysis and customer management.

THE PERSONAL SELLING PROCESS

Most companies take a *customer-oriented approach* to personal selling. They train salespeople to identify customer needs and to find solutions. This approach assumes that customer needs provide sales opportunities, that customers appreciate good suggestions, and that customers will be loyal to salepeople who have their long-term interests at heart. The problem-solver salesperson fits better with the marketing concept than does a hard-sell salesperson or the glad-handing extrovert. Buyers today want solutions, not smiles; results, not razzle-dazzle. They want salespeople who listen to their concerns, understand their needs, and respond with the right products and services.

STEPS IN THE SELLING PROCESS

Most training programs view the **selling process** as consisting of several steps that the salesperson must master (see Figure 16.3). These steps focus on the goal of getting new customers and obtaining orders from them. However, most salespeople spend much of their time maintaining existing accounts and building long-term customer *relationships*. We discuss the relationship aspect of the personal selling process in a later section.

Prospecting and Qualifying

The first step in the selling process is **prospecting**—identifying qualified potential customers. Approaching the right potential customers is crucial to selling success. As one expert puts it: "If the sales force starts chasing anyone who is breathing and seems to have a budget, you risk accumulating a roster of expensive-to-serve, hard-to-satisfy customers who never respond to whatever value proposition you have." He continues, "The solution to this isn't rocket science. [You must] train salespeople to actively scout the right prospects. If necessary, create an incentive program to reward proper scouting."[26]

The salesperson must often approach many prospects to get just a few sales. Although the company supplies some leads, salespeople need skill in finding their own. They can ask current customers for referrals. They can build referral sources, such as suppliers, dealers, noncompeting salespeople, and bankers. They can join organizations to which prospects belong or can engage in speaking and writing activities that will draw attention. They can search for names in newspapers or directories and use the telephone and mail to track down leads. Or they can drop in unannounced on various offices (a practice known as "cold calling").

Salespeople also need to know how to *qualify* leads—that is, how to identify the good ones and screen out the poor ones. Prospects can be qualified by looking at their financial ability, volume of business, special needs, location, and possibilities for growth.

Preapproach

Before calling on a prospect, the salesperson should learn as much as possible about the organization (what it needs, who is involved in the buying) and its buyers (their characteristics and buying styles). This step is known as the **preapproach.** The salesperson can consult standard industry and online sources, acquaintances, and others to learn about the company. The salesperson should set *call objectives,* which may be to qualify the prospect, to gather information, or to make an immediate sale. Another task is to decide on the best approach, which might be a personal visit, a phone call, or a letter. The best timing should be considered carefully because many prospects are busiest at certain times. Finally, the salesperson should give thought to an overall sales strategy for the account.

Approach

During the **approach** step, the salesperson should know how to meet and greet the buyer and get the relationship off to a good start. This step involves the salesperson's appearance, opening lines, and the

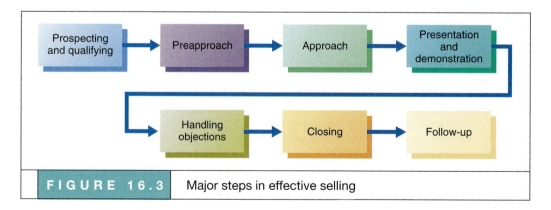

FIGURE 16.3 Major steps in effective selling

[26]Bob Donath, "Delivering Value Starts with Proper Prospecting," *Marketing News,* November 10, 1997, p. 5. Also see Sarah Lorge, "The Best Way to Prospect," *Sales & Marketing Management,* January 1998, p. 80.

follow-up remarks. The opening lines should be positive, such as "Mr. Johnson, I am Chris Bennett from the Alltech Company. My company and I appreciate your willingness to see me. I will do my best to make this visit profitable and worthwhile for you and your company." This opening might be followed by some key questions to learn more about the customer's needs or by showing a display or sample to attract the buyer's attention and curiosity.

Presentation and Demonstration

During the **presentation** step of the selling process, the salesperson tells the product "story" to the buyer, showing how the product will make or save money. The salesperson describes the product features but concentrates on presenting customer benefits. Using a *need-satisfaction approach,* the salesperson starts with a search for the customer's needs by getting the customer to do most of the talking.

This approach calls for good listening and problem-solving skills. "I think of myself more as a . . . well, psychologist," notes one experienced salesperson. "I listen to customers. I listen to their wishes and needs and problems, and I try to figure out a solution. If you're not a good listener, you're not going to get the order." Another salesperson suggests, "It's no longer enough to have a good relationship with a client. You have to understand their problems. You have to feel their pain."[27]

The qualities that purchasing agents *dislike most* in salespeople include being pushy, late, and unprepared or disorganized. The qualities they *value most* include empathy, honesty, dependability, thoroughness, and follow-through.[28] Sales presentations can be improved with demonstration aids, such as booklets, flip charts, slides, videotapes or videodiscs, and product samples. If buyers can see or handle the product, they will better remember its features and benefits.

Sales presentations can be improved with product samples or demonstrations. Visual aids can show how a product performs and provide other information about it. Booklets and brochures remain useful as "leave behinds" for customer reference. Today, advanced presentation technologies allow for full multimedia presentations to only one or a few people. Audio and videocassettes, laptop computers with presentation software, and online presentation technologies have replaced the flip chart. Advanced Sterilization Products, a Johnson & Johnson company, even provides its sales force with a virtual reality presentation, called the STERRAD Experience. Originally designed for use at conferences, the presentation equipment has been redesigned for sales calls and consists of a small video player with five headsets, all easily transported in an ordinary-size briefcase. Prospects don a helmet for a virtual reality tour of the inner workings of the STERRAD Sterilization System for medical devices and surgical instruments. The presentation provides more information in a more engaging way than could be done by displaying the actual machinery.[29]

Handling Objections

Customers almost always have objections during the presentation or when asked to place an order. The problem can be either logical or psychological, and objections are often unspoken. In **handling objections,** the salesperson should use a positive approach, seek out hidden objections, ask the buyer to clarify any objections, take objections as opportunities to provide more information, and turn the objections into reasons for buying. Every salesperson needs training in the skills of handling objections.

Closing

After handling the prospect's objections, the salesperson now tries to close the sale. Some salespeople do not get around to **closing** or do not handle it well. They may lack confidence, feel guilty about asking for the order, or fail to recognize the right moment to close the sale. Salespeople should know how to recognize closing signals from the buyer, including physical actions, comments, and questions. For example, the customer might sit forward and nod approvingly or ask about prices and credit terms. Salespeople can use one of several closing techniques. They can ask for the order, review points of agreement, offer to help write up the order, ask whether the buyer wants this model or that one, or note that the buyer will lose out if the order is not placed now. The salesperson may offer the buyer special reasons to close, such as a lower price or an extra quantity at no charge.

[27]David Stamps, "Training for a New Sales Game," *Training,* July 1997, pp. 46–52.

[28]Brewer, "Brain Power," p.42; and Rosemay P. Ramsey and Ravipreet S. Sohi, "Listening to Your Customers: The Impact of Perceived Salesperson Listening Behavior on Relationship Outcomes," *Journal of the Academy of Marketing Science,* Spring 1997, pp. 127–37.

[29]"Briefcase Full of Views: Johnson & Johnson Uses Virtual Reality to Give Prospects an Inside Look at Its Products," *American Demographics,* April 1997.

New sales presentation technologies: Advanced Sterilization Products, a Johnson & Johnson Company, provides its sales force with a presentation in which prospects don a helmet for a virtual reality tour of the inner workings of the STERRAD Sterilization System for medical devices and surgical instruments.

Follow-up

The last step in the selling process—**follow-up**—is necessary if the salesperson wants to ensure customer satisfaction and repeat business. Right after closing, the salesperson should complete any details on delivery time, purchase terms, and other matters. The salesperson then should schedule a follow-up call when the initial order is received to make sure there is proper installation, instruction, and servicing. This visit would reveal any problems, assure the buyer of the salesperson's interest, and reduce any buyer concerns that might have arisen since the sale.

active example <

Consider how one company adapts the steps of the personal-selling process to build its business.

RELATIONSHIP MARKETING

The principles of personal selling as just described are *transaction oriented*—their aim is to help salespeople close a specific sale with a customer. But in many cases, the company is not seeking simply a sale: It has targeted a major customer that it would like to win and keep. The company would like to show that it has the capabilities to serve the customer over the long haul in a mutually profitable *relationship*.

Most companies today are moving away from transaction marketing, with its emphasis on making a sale. Instead, they are practicing **relationship marketing,** which emphasizes maintaining profitable long-term relationships with customers by creating superior customer value and satisfaction. They are realizing that when operating in maturing markets and facing stiffer competition, it costs a lot more to wrest new customers from competitors than to keep current customers.

Today's customers are large and often global. They prefer suppliers who can sell and deliver a coordinated set of products and services to many locations. They favor suppliers who can quickly solve problems that arise in their different parts of the nation or world, and who can work closely with customer teams to improve products and processes. For these customers, the sale is only the beginning of the relationship.

Unfortunately, some companies are not set up for these developments. They often sell their products through separate sales forces, each working independently to close sales. Their technical people may not be willing to lend time to educate a customer. Their engineering, design, and manufacturing people may have the attitude that "it's our job to make good products and the salesperson's to sell them to customers." However, other companies are recognizing that winning and keeping accounts requires more than making good products and directing the sales force to close lots of sales. It requires a carefully coordinated whole-company effort to create value-laden, satisfying relationships with important customers.

Relationship marketing is based on the premise that important accounts need focused and ongoing attention. Studies have shown that the best salespeople are those who are highly motivated and good closers, but more than this, they are customer problem solvers and relationship builders. Good salespeople working with key customers do more than call when they think a customer might be ready to place an order. They also study the account and understand its problems. They call or visit frequently, work with the customer to help solve the customer's problems and improve its business, and take an interest in customers as people.

> active concept check

Now let's take a moment to test your knowledge of what you've just read.

> video exercise

Apply what you've learned about personal selling to a specific case.

> Chapter Wrap-Up

Now that you've reached the end of the chapter, you may wish to explore the concepts you've been reading about in greater detail, or test yourself to see how well you've comprehended the material. In the box below you'll find a number of links. Click on any one of these links to find additional chapter resources.

> end-of-chapter resources

- **Review of Concept Connections**
- **Practice Quiz**
- **Issues for Discussion**
- **Key Terms**
- **Marketing Applications**
- **Internet Connections**
- **Company Case**

C H A P T E R   1 7

Direct and Online Marketing: The New Marketing Model

> What's Ahead

When 19-year-old Michael Dell began selling personal computers out of his college dorm room in 1984, few would have bet on his chances for success. In those days, most computer makers sold their PCs through an extensive network of all-powerful distributors and resellers. Even as the fledgling Dell Computer Corporation began to grow, competitors and industry insiders scoffed at the concept of mail-order computer marketing. PC buyers, they contended, needed the kind of advice and hand-holding that only full-service channels could provide.

Yet young Michael Dell has proved the skeptics wrong—way wrong. In little more than a decade and a half, he has turned his dorm-room mail-order business into a burgeoning, $22 billion computer empire. Dell Computer is now the world's largest direct marketer of computer systems, the number-two PC maker, and the world's fastest-growing computer manufacturer. Over the past three years, Dell's sales have increased at an average of 53 percent per year, twice as fast as any competitor and five times the industry average. Profits have skyrocketed 89 percent per year. Since 1990, Dell's stock has risen an incredible 29,600 percent! Direct buyers now account for nearly a third of all PC sales, and Dell's once-skeptical competitors are now scrambling to build their own direct-marketing systems.

What's the secret to Dell's stunning success? Anyone at Dell can tell you without hesitation: It's the company's radically different business model—the *direct model*. "We have a tremendously clear business model," says Michael Dell, the 34-year-old founder. "There's no confusion about what the value proposition is, what the company offers, and why it's great for customers. That's a very simple thing, but it has tremendous power and appeal." It also garners tremendous success for the company.

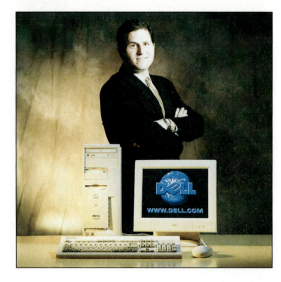

Dell's direct-marketing approach delivers greater customer value through an unbeatable combination of product customization, low prices, fast delivery, and award-winning customer service. A customer can talk by phone with a Dell representative on Monday morning; order a fully customized, state-of-the-art PC to suit his or her special needs; and have the machine delivered to his or her doorstep by Wednesday—all at a price that's 10 to 15 percent below competitors' prices for a comparably performing PC. Dell backs its products with high-quality service and support. As a result, Dell consistently ranks among the industry leaders in product reliability and service, and its customers are routinely among the industry's most satisfied.

Dell customers get exactly the machines they need. Michael Dell's initial idea was to serve individual buyers by letting them customize machines with the special features they wanted at low prices. However, this one-to-one approach also appeals strongly to corporate buyers, because Dell can so easily preconfigure each computer to precise requirements. Dell routinely preloads machines with a company's own software and even undertakes tedious tasks such as pasting inventory tags onto each machine so that computers can be delivered directly to a given employee's desk. As a result, nearly two-thirds of Dell's sales now come from large corporate, government, and educational buyers.

Direct selling results in more efficient selling and lower costs, which translate into lower prices for customers. Because Dell builds machines to order, it carries barely any inventory. Dealing one-to-one with customers helps the company react immediately to shifts in demand, so Dell doesn't get stuck with PCs no one wants. Finally, by selling directly, Dell has no dealers to pay. As a result, on average, Dell's costs are 12 percent lower than those of Compaq, its leading PC competitor.

Dell knows that time is money, and the company is obsessed with "speed." For example, Dell has long been a model of just-in-time manufacturing and efficient supply chain management. It has also mastered the intricacies of today's lightning-fast electronic commerce. The combination makes Dell a lean and very fast operator. According to one account, "Dell calls it 'velocity'—squeezing time out of every step in the process—from the moment an order is taken to collecting the cash. [By selling direct, manufacturing to order, and] tapping credit cards and electronic payment, Dell converts the average sale to cash in less than 24 hours. By contrast, Compaq Computer Corp., which sells primarily through dealers, takes 35 days, and even mail-order rival Gateway 2000 takes 16.4 days." Such blazing speed results in more satisfied customers and still lower costs. For example, customers are often delighted to find their new computers arriving within as few as 36 hours of placing an order. And because Dell doesn't order parts until an order is booked, it can take advantage of ever-falling component costs. On average, its parts are 60 days newer than those in competing machines, and, hence, 60 days farther down the price curve. This gives Dell a 6 percent profit advantage from parts costs alone.

Flush with success, Dell has taken its direct-marketing formula a step further. It's selling PCs on the Internet—lots of PCs. Now, by simply clicking the "Buy a Dell" icon at Dell's Web site (www.dell.com), customers can design and price customized computer systems electronically. Then, with a click on the "purchase" button, they can submit an order, choosing from online payment options that include a credit card, company purchase order, or corporate lease. Dell dashes out a digital confirmation to customers within five minutes of receiving the order. After receiving confirmation, customers can check the status of the order online at any time.

The Internet is a perfect extension of Dell's direct-marketing model. Customers who are already comfortable buying direct from Dell now have an even more powerful way to do so. "The Internet," says Michael Dell, "is the ultimate direct model. . . . [Customers] like the immediacy, convenience, savings, and personal touches that the [Internet] experience provides. Not only are some sales done completely online, but people who call on the phone after having visited Dell.com are twice as likely to buy."

The direct-marketing pioneer now sells more than $30 million worth of computers daily from its Web site, accounting for over 40 percent of revenues. In just a single quarter last year, Dell.com received some 25 million visits at more than 50 country-specific sites. Buyers range from individuals purchasing home computers to large business users buying high-end $30,000 servers. Michael Dell sees online marketing as the next great conquest in the company's direct-marketing crusade. "The Internet is like a booster rocket on our sales and growth," he proclaims. "Our vision is to have *all* customers conduct *all* transactions on the Internet, globally."

As you might imagine, competitors are no longer scoffing at Michael Dell's vision of the future. It's hard to argue with success, and Michael Dell has been very successful. By following his hunches, at the tender age of 34 he has built one of the world's hottest computer companies. In the process, he's amassed a personal fortune exceeding $16.5 billion.[1]

> ## o b j e c t i v e s

Before you begin, take a moment to familiarize yourself with the key objectives of this chapter.

> ## g e a r i n g   u p

Before we begin our exploration this chapter, take a short warm-up test to see what you know about this topic.

Many of the marketing tools that we've examined in previous chapters were developed in the context of *mass marketing:* targeting broad markets with standardized messages and offers distributed through intermediaries. Today, however, with the trend toward more narrowly targeted or one-to-one marketing, more and more companies are adopting *direct marketing,* either as a primary marketing

[1]Quotes and Dell performance statistics from Gary McWilliams, "Whirlwind on the Web," *Business Week,* April 7, 1997, pp. 132–36; Bill Robbins and Cathie Hargett, "Dell Internet Sales Top $1 Million a Day," press release, Dell Computer Corporation, March 4, 1997; "The InternetWeek Interview—Michael Dell," *InternetWeek,* April 13, 1999, p. 8; and information accessed online at www.dell.com/corporate/access/ factpak/index.htm, January 2000. Also see "Nerdy Like a Fox," *Business Week,* January 1999, p. 74; James Cox, "Technology, Stock Market Click for World's Richest," *USA Today,* June 21, 1999, p. 2A; Melanie Warner, "The Young and the Loaded," *Fortune,* September 27, 1999, p. S12 and David Rynecki, "Has Dell Become Just Another Growth Stock?" *Fortune,* February 21, 2000, pp. 317–318.

approach or as a supplement to other approaches. Increasingly, companies are turning to direct marketing in an effort to reach carefully targeted customers more efficiently and to build stronger, more personal, one-to-one relationships with them.

In this chapter, we explore the exploding world of direct marketing. We look at the nature, role, and growing applications of direct marketing and its newest form, Internet marketing and e-commerce. We address the following questions: What is direct marketing? What are its benefits to companies and their customers? How do customer databases support direct marketing? What channels do direct marketers use to reach individual prospects and customers? What marketing opportunities do online and Internet channels provide? How can companies use integrated direct marketing for competitive advantage? What public and ethical issues are raised by direct and online marketing?

> What Is Direct Marketing?

Mass marketers have typically sought to reach masses of buyers with a single product and a standard message delivered through the mass media. Thus, Procter & Gamble originally launched Crest toothpaste in one version with a single message ("Crest fights cavities"), hoping that hundreds of millions of Americans would get the message and buy the brand from their local retailer. P&G did not need to know its customers' names or anything else about them, only that they wanted to take good care of their teeth. Under this mass-marketing model, most marketing involved one-way connections aimed *at* consumers, not two-way interactions *with* them.

In contrast, **direct marketing** consists of direct connections with carefully targeted individual consumers to both obtain an immediate response and cultivate lasting customer relationships. Direct marketers communicate directly with customers, often on a one-to-one, interactive basis. Using detailed databases, they tailor their marketing offers and communications to the needs of narrowly defined segments or even individual buyers. Beyond brand and image building, they usually seek a direct, immediate, and measurable consumer response. For example, Dell Computer interacts directly with customers, by telephone or through its Web site, to design built-to-order systems that meet customers' individual needs. Buyers order directly from Dell, and Dell quickly and efficiently delivers the new computers to their homes or offices.

THE NEW DIRECT-MARKETING MODEL

Early direct marketers—catalog companies, direct mailers, and telemarketers—gathered customer names and sold goods mainly through the mail and by telephone. Today, however, fired by rapid advances in database technologies and new marketing media—especially the Internet and other electronic channels—direct marketing has undergone a dramatic transformation.

In previous chapters, we've discussed direct marketing as direct distribution, as marketing channels that contain no intermediaries. We've also included direct marketing as one element of the marketing communications mix—as an approach for communicating directly with consumers. In fact, direct marketing is both these things. Most companies still use direct marketing as a supplementary channel or medium for marketing their goods. Thus, Lexus markets mostly through mass-media advertising and its high-quality dealer network but also supplements these channels with direct marketing. Its direct marketing includes promotional videos and other materials mailed directly to prospective buyers and a Web page (www.lexus.com) that provides consumers with information about various models, competitive comparisons, financing, and dealer locations. Similarly, Barnes & Noble conducts most of its business through brick-and-mortar bookstores but also markets directly through its Web site. Compaq Computer advertises heavily and makes most of its sales through retailers but also sells directly to consumers via telemarketing and the Internet. Most department stores sell the majority of their merchandise off their store shelves but also mail out catalogs.

However, for many companies today, direct marketing is much more than just a supplementary channel or medium. For these companies, direct marketing—especially in its newest transformation, Internet marketing and e-commerce—constitutes a new and complete model for doing business. "The Internet is not just another marketing channel; it's not just another advertising medium; it's not just a way to speed up transactions," says one strategist. "The Internet is the foundation for a new industrial order. [It] will change the relationship between consumers and producers in ways more profound than you can yet imagine."[2] This new *direct model*, suggests another analyst, is "revolutionizing the way we think about . . . how to construct relationships with suppliers and customers, how to create value for them, and how to make money in the process; in other words, [it's] revolutionizing marketing."[3]

[2]Gary Hamel and Jeff Sampler, "The E-Corporation: More Than Just Web-Based, It's Building a New Industrial Order," *Fortune,* December 7, 1998, pp. 80–92.

[3]Alan Mitchell, "Internet Zoo Spawns New Business Models," *Marketing Week,* January 21, 1999, pp. 24–25.

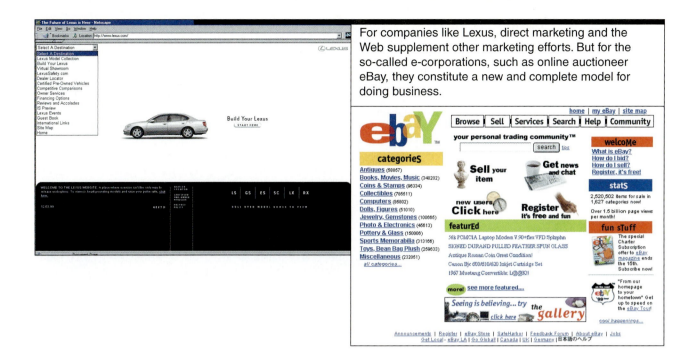

For companies like Lexus, direct marketing and the Web supplement other marketing efforts. But for the so-called e-corporations, such as online auctioneer eBay, they constitute a new and complete model for doing business.

> ## active example

Consider an unlikely but successful example of direct Internet marketing.

Whereas most companies use direct marketing and the Internet as supplemental approaches, firms employing the direct model use it as the *only* approach. Some of these companies, such as Dell Computer, Amazon.com, and the so-called e-corporations (eBay, eToys, E*Trade, and others), began as only direct marketers. Other companies—such as Cisco Systems, Charles Schwab, IBM, and many others—are rapidly transforming themselves into direct-marketing superstars.

As our chapter-opening story suggests, perhaps the company that best exemplifies this new direct marketing model is Dell Computer. On its Web page, Dell explains its direct model this way:

Dell's award-winning customer service, industry-leading growth, and financial performance continue to differentiate the company from competitors. At the heart of that performance is Dell's unique *direct-to-customer business model.* "Direct" refers to the company's relationships with its customers, from home-PC users to the world's largest corporations. There are no retailers or other resellers adding unnecessary time and cost, or diminishing Dell's understanding of customer expectations. Why are computer-systems customers and investors increasingly turning to Dell and its unique direct model? There are several reasons: (1) *Price for Performance:* By eliminating resellers, retailers, and other costly intermediary steps, together with the industry's most efficient procurement, manufacturing, and distribution process, Dell offers its customers more powerful, more richly configured systems for the money than competitors. (2) *Customization:* Every Dell system is built to order—customers get exactly, and only, what they want. (3) *Service and Support:* Dell uses knowledge gained from direct contact before and after the sale to provide award-winning, tailored customer service. (4) *Latest Technology:* Dell's efficient model means the latest relevant technology is introduced in its product lines much more quickly than through slow-moving indirect distribution channels. Inventory is turned over every 10 or fewer days, on average, keeping related costs low. (5) *Superior Shareholder Value:* During the past fiscal year, the value of Dell common stock more than doubled. In [the previous two years], Dell was the top-performing stock among the Standard & Poor's 500 and Nasdaq 100, and represented the top-performing U.S. stock on the Dow Jones World Stock Index.

Thus, Dell has built its entire approach to the marketplace around direct marketing. This direct model has proven highly successful, not just for Dell, but for the fast-growing number of other companies that employ it.

Many strategists have hailed direct marketing as the marketing model of the new millennium. They envision a day when all buying and selling will involve direct connections between companies and their customers. According to one account, the new model "will fundamentally change customers' expectations about convenience, speed, comparability, price, and service. Those new expectations will reverberate throughout the economy, affecting every business." Comparing the adoption of the Internet and other new direct-marketing technologies to the early days of the airplane, Amazon.com CEO Jeff Bezos says, "It's the Kitty Hawk era of electronic commerce." Even those offering more cautious predictions agree that the Internet and e-commerce will have a tremendous impact on future business strategies.

active concept check   <

Now let's take a moment to test your knowledge of what you've just read.

> ## Benefits and Growth of Direct Marketing

Whether employed as a complete business model or as a supplement to a broader integrated marketing mix, direct marketing brings many benefits to both buyers and sellers. As a result, direct marketing is growing very rapidly.

BENEFITS TO BUYERS

Direct marketing benefits buyers in many ways. It is *convenient:* Customers don't have to battle traffic, find parking spaces, and trek through stores and aisles to find and examine products. They can do comparative shopping by browsing through mail catalogs or surfing Web sites. Direct marketers never close their doors. Buying is *easy* and *private:* Customers encounter fewer buying hassles and don't have to face salespeople or open themselves up to persuasion and emotional pitches. Business buyers can learn about available products and services without waiting for and tying up time with salespeople.

Direct marketing often provides shoppers with greater *product access and selection.* For example, the world's the limit for the Web. Unrestrained by physical boundaries, cyberstores can offer an almost unlimited selection. Try comparing the incredible selections offered by Web merchants such as Amazon.com, CDnow, or Virtual Vineyards to the more meager assortments of their counterparts in the brick-and-mortar world.

Beyond a broader selection of sellers and products, online and Internet channels also give consumers access to a wealth of comparative *information,* information about companies, products, and competitors. Good sites often provide more information in more useful forms than even the most solicitous salesclerk can. eToys, for example, offers parents toy recommendations from consumer and educational groups. CDnow offers best-seller lists and record reviews.

Finally, online buying is *interactive* and *immediate.* Consumers often can interact with the seller's site to create exactly the configuration of information, products, or services they desire, then order or download them on the spot. Moreover, the Internet and other forms of direct marketing give consumers a greater measure of control. "The Internet will empower consumers like nothing else ever has," notes one analyst. "Think about this: Already 16 percent of car buyers shop online before showing up at a dealership, and they aren't comparing paint jobs—they're arming themselves with information on dealer costs. . . . The new reality is consumer control."[4]

[4]Hamel and Sampler, "The E-Corporation: More Than Just Web-Based, It's Building a New Industrial Order," p. 82.

> active exercise

Explore one way the online direct marketers try to use their technology to benefit consumers.

BENEFITS TO SELLERS

Direct marketing also yields many benefits to sellers. First, direct marketing is a powerful tool for *customer relationship building.* Direct marketers build or buy databases containing detailed information about potentially profitable customers. Using these databases, they build strong, ongoing customer relationships. With today's technology, a direct marketer can select small groups or even individual consumers, personalize offers to their special needs and wants, and promote these offers through individualized communications.

For example, Mead Johnson's "Enfamil Family Beginnings" direct-mail program builds relationships with expectant and new mothers. It begins with a note of congratulations to expectant mothers, followed by a series of mailings rich with information about infant nutrition and health. Samples of Enfamil are timed to the mother's expected due date. "Now we're number one [in sales]," says Mead Johnson's director of consumer relationship marketing. "This program has had a huge impact on that."[5] Similarly, P&G's Pampers Parenting Institute Web site (www.pampers.com) builds relationships by offering parents of young children more than just product information. It gives ongoing advice on baby development, health, and safety; a newsletter; a resource library; and an "ask our experts" feature where they can get answers to personal parenting questions.

Direct marketing can also be timed to reach prospects at just the right moment. Because they reach more interested consumers at the best times, direct-marketing materials receive higher readership and response. Direct marketing also permits easy testing of alternative media and messages.

Because of its one-to-one, interactive nature, the Internet is an especially potent direct-marketing tool. Companies can interact online with customers to learn more about specific needs and wants. In turn, online customers can ask questions and volunteer feedback. Based on this ongoing interaction, companies can increase customer value and satisfaction through product and service refinements.

Building direct relationships: Mead Johnson's "Enfamil Family Beginnings" direct mail program builds relationships with expectant and new mothers.

[5]Carol Krol, "Mead Johnson Finds Winning Formula for Reaching Moms," *Advertising Age,* April 26, 1999, p. 25.

Direct marketing via the Internet and other electronic channels yields additional advantages, such as *reducing costs* and *increasing speed and efficiency.* Online marketers avoid the expense of maintaining a store and the accompanying costs of rent, insurance, and utilities. Online retailers such as Amazon.com reap the advantage of a negative operating cycle: Amazon receives cash from credit card companies just a day after customers place an order. Then it can hold on to the money for 46 days until it pays suppliers, the book distributors and publishers.

By using the Internet to link directly to suppliers, factories, distributors, and customers, businesses like Dell Computer and General Electric are wringing waste out of the system and passing on savings to customers. Because customers deal directly with sellers, online marketing often results in lower costs and improved efficiencies for channel and logistics functions such as order processing, inventory handling, delivery, and trade promotion. Finally, communicating electronically often costs less than communicating on paper through the mail. For instance, a company can produce digital catalogs for much less than the cost of printing and mailing paper ones.

Online marketing also offers greater *flexibility,* allowing the marketer to make ongoing adjustments to its offers and programs. For example, once a paper catalog is mailed, the products, prices, and other catalog features are fixed until the next catalog is sent. However, an online catalog can be adjusted daily or even hourly, adapting product assortments, prices, and promotions to match changing market conditions.

Finally, the Internet is a truly *global* medium that allows buyers and sellers to click from one country to another in seconds. A Web surfer from Paris or Istanbul can access a Lands' End catalog as easily as someone living on 1 Lands' End Lane in Dodgeville, Wisconsin, the direct retailer's hometown. Thus, even small online marketers find that they have ready access to global markets.

active example <

Consider how businesses in the traditional retail industry have tried to harness the benefits of online direct marketing.

THE GROWTH OF DIRECT MARKETING

Sales through traditional direct-marketing channels (telephone marketing, direct mail, catalogs, direct-response television, and others) have been growing rapidly. Whereas U.S. retail sales over the past five years have grown at about 6 percent annually, direct-marketing sales grew at about 8 percent annually. These sales include sales to the consumer market (55 percent) and business-to-business sales (45 percent).[6]

While direct marketing through traditional channels is growing rapidly, online marketing is growing explosively. The number of U.S. households with access to the Internet has grown from only about 6 million in 1994 to more than 40 million today, to a projected 60 million by 2003. Sales via the Internet are expected to grow at an incredible 60 percent per year over the next five years.[7] We will examine online and Internet marketing more closely later in this chapter.

In the consumer market, the extraordinary growth of direct marketing is a response to rapid advances in technology and to the new marketing realities discussed in previous chapters. Market "demassification" has resulted in an ever-increasing number of market niches with distinct preferences. Direct marketing allows sellers to focus efficiently on these minimarkets with offers that better match specific consumer needs.

Other trends have also fueled the rapid growth of direct marketing in the consumer market. Higher costs of driving, traffic congestion, parking headaches, lack of time, a shortage of retail sales help, and lines at checkout counters all encourage at-home shopping. Consumers are responding favorably to direct marketers' toll-free phone numbers, their willingness to accept telephone orders 24 hours a day, 7 days a week, and their growing commitment to customer service. The growth of 24-hour and 48-hour delivery via Federal Express, Airborne, UPS, DHL, and other express carriers has made direct shopping fast as well as easy. Finally, the growth of affordable computer power and customer databases has enabled direct marketers to single out the best prospects for any product they wish to sell.

[6]See *Economic Impact: U.S. Direct Marketing Today,* Direct Marketing Association, 1999, accessed online at www.the-dma.org/ser vices/libres-ecoimpact1b1a.shtml.

[7]Facts on Internet usage and sales found in *Economic Impact: U.S. Direct Marketing Today,* 1999; and furnished by Forrester Research, August 1999.

Direct marketing has also grown rapidly in business-to-business marketing, partly in response to the ever-increasing costs of reaching business markets through the sales force. When personal sales calls cost $165 per contact, they should be made only when necessary and to high-potential customers and prospects. Lower cost-per-contact mediasuch as telemarketing, direct mail, and the newer electronic media—often prove more cost effective in reaching and selling to more prospects and customers.

> active concept check

Now let's take a moment to test your knowledge of what you've just read.

> Customer Databases and Direct Marketing

Table 17.1 lists the main differences between mass marketing and so-called *one-to-one marketing*.[8] Companies that know about individual customer needs and characteristics can customize their offers, messages, delivery modes, and payment methods to maximize customer value and satisfaction. Today's companies also have a very powerful tool for accessing pertinent information about individual customers and prospects: the customer database.

A **customer database** is an organized collection of comprehensive data about individual customers or prospects, including geographic, demographic, psychographic, and behavioral data. The database can be used to locate good potential customers, tailor products and services to the special needs of targeted consumers, and maintain long-term customer relationships. *Database marketing* is the process of building, maintaining, and using customer databases and other databases (products, suppliers, resellers) for the purpose of contacting and transacting with customers.

Many companies confuse a customer mailing list with a customer database. A customer mailing list is simply a set of names, addresses, and telephone numbers. A customer database contains much

TABLE 17.1	Mass Marketing versus One-to-One Marketing
Mass Marketing	**One-to-One Marketing**
Average customer	Individual customer
Customer anonymity	Customer profile
Standard product	Customized market offering
Mass production	Customized production
Mass distribution	Individualized distribution
Mass advertising	Individualized message
Mass promotion	Individualized incentives
One-way message	Two-way messages
Economies of scale	Economies of scope
Share of market	Share of customer
All customers	Profitable customers
Customer attraction	Customer retention

Source: Adapted from Don Peppers and Martha Rogers, *The One-to-One Future* (New York: Doubleday/Currency, 1993).

[8]See Don Peppers and Martha Rogers, *The One-to-One Future* (New York: Doubleday/Currency, 1993).

more information. In business-to-business marketing, the salesperson's customer profile might contain the products and services the customer has bought; past volumes and prices; key contacts (and their ages, birthdays, hobbies, and favorite foods); competitive suppliers; status of current contracts; estimated customer spending for the next few years; and assessments of competitive strengths and weaknesses in selling and servicing the account. In consumer marketing, the customer database might contain a customer's demographics (age, income, family members, birthdays), psychographics (activities, interests, and opinions), buying behavior (past purchases, buying preferences), and other relevant information. For example, the catalog company Fingerhut maintains a database containing some 1,300 pieces of information about each of 30 million households. Ritz-Carlton's database holds more than 500,000 individual customer preferences. And Pizza Hut's database lets it track the purchases of more than 50 million customers.[9]

Database marketing is most frequently used by business-to-business marketers and service retailers (hotels, banks, and airlines). Increasingly, however, other kinds of companies are also employing database marketing. Armed with the information in their databases, these companies can identify small groups of customers to receive fine-tuned marketing offers and communications. Kraft Foods has amassed a list of more than 30 million users of its products who have responded to coupons or other Kraft promotions. Based on their interests, the company sends these customers tips on issues such as nutrition and exercise, as well as recipes and coupons for specific Kraft brands. Blockbuster, the massive entertainment company, uses its database of 36 million households and 2 million daily transactions to help its video-rental customers select movies and to steer them to other Blockbuster subsidiaries. American Express uses its database to tailor offers to cardholders. In Belgium, it is testing a system that links cardholder spending patterns with postal-zone data. If a new restaurant opens, for example, the company might offer a special discount to cardholders who live within walking distance and who eat out a lot. And FedEx uses its sophisticated database to create 100 highly targeted, customized direct-mail and telemarketing campaigns each year to its nearly 5 million customers shipping to 212 countries. By analyzing customers carefully and reaching the right customers at the right time with the right promotions, FedEx achieves response rates of 20 to 25 percent and earns an 8-to-1 return on its direct-marketing dollars.[10]

Smaller companies can also make good use of database marketing. Here are two examples:[11]

Over the last few years, nearly 9,000 grocery chains have introduced frequent-shopper programs. Now they're rifling through household shopping histories as fast as they can to tell cardholders what's running low in the pantry. Dick's Supermarkets, an eight-store chain in Wisconsin, uses transaction data from its loyalty-card program to personalize shopping lists that it mails every two weeks to nearly 30,000 members. The shopping lists . . . contain timed offers based on past purchases. A consumer who bought Tide several weeks ago, for example, may be offered a $1.50 coupon to restock. If that customer buys laundry detergent every week, he or she may be offered twice as much to purchase a larger size of Tide, or two packages of the size normally purchased.

Some grocers are going a step further, tweaking promotions based on past responses as well as purchase data. Nature's NorthWest health food chain [uses its database] to distribute custom-printed newsletters at its checkouts. When the cashier scans a frequent shopper card, the card's transaction history triggers a newsletter reflecting that consumer's purchase history and areas of interest (individuals can check off interests on their application for the card). Bought herbal supplements and organic meat on your last visit? Interested in exercise? Your newsletter might have a schedule of local exercise classes, a recipe for meat, and a coupon for more herbs. The newsletter prints at the checkout counter in seven seconds, faster than a cashier can make change and bag the groceries. Nature's NorthWest tracks which bar coded coupons are redeemed from the newsletter, and then adjusts the newsletter each time to better suit that shopper.

[9]Carol Krol, "Pizza Hut's Database Makes Its Couponing More Efficient," *Advertising Age,* November 30, 1998, p. 27.

[10]For these and other examples, see Jonathan Berry, "A Potent New Tool for Selling: Database Marketing," *Business Week,* September 4, 1994, pp. 56–62; Weld F. Royal, "Do Databases Really Work?" *Sales & Marketing Management,* October 1995, pp. 66–74; Daniel Hill, "Love My Brand," *Brandweek,* January 19, 1998, pp. 26–29; and "FedEx Taps into Data Warehousing," *Advertising Age's Business Marketing,* January 1999, p. 25.

[11]Betsy Spethmann, "Can We Talk?" *American Demographics,* March 1999, pp. 42–44. Also see Tricia Campbell, "Database Marketing for the Little Guys," *Sales & Marketing Management,* June 1999, p. 69.

Companies use their databases in four ways:[12]

1. *Identifying prospects:* Many companies generate sales leads by advertising their products or offers. Ads generally have some sort of response feature, such as a business reply card or toll-free phone number. The database is built from these responses. The company sorts through the database to identify the best prospects, then reaches them by mail, phone, or personal calls in an attempt to convert them into customers.

2. *Deciding which customers should receive a particular offer:* Companies identify the profile of an ideal customer for an offer. Then they search their databases for individuals most closely resembling the ideal type. By tracking individual responses, the company can improve its targeting precision over time. Following a sale, it can set up an automatic sequence of activities: One week later, send a thank-you note; five weeks later, send a new offer; ten weeks later (if the customer has not responded), phone the customer and offer a special discount.

3. *Deepening customer loyalty:* Companies can build customers' interest and enthusiasm by remembering their preferences and by sending appropriate information, gifts, or other materials. For example, Mars, a market leader in pet food as well as candy, maintains an exhaustive pet database. In Germany, the company has compiled the names of virtually every German family that owns a cat. It has obtained these names by contacting veterinarians, via its Katzen-Online.de Web site, and by offering the public a free booklet titled "How to Take Care of Your Cat." People who request the booklet fill out a questionnaire, providing their cat's name, age, birthday, and other information. Mars then sends a birthday card to each cat in Germany each year, along with a new cat food sample and money-saving coupons for Mars brands. The result is a lasting relationship with the cat's owner.

4. *Reactivating customer purchases:* The database can help a company make attractive offers of product replacements, upgrades, or complementary products just when customers might be ready to act. For example, a General Electric customer database contains each customer's demographic and psychographic characteristics along with an appliance purchasing history. Using this database, GE marketers assess how long specific customers have owned their current appliances and which past customers might be ready to purchase again. They can determine which customers need a new GE videorecorder, compact disc player, stereo receiver, or something else to go with other recently purchased electronics products. Or they can identify the best past GE purchasers and send them gift certificates or other promotions to apply against their next GE purchases. A rich customer database allows GE to build profitable new business by locating good prospects, anticipating customer needs, cross-selling products and services, and rewarding loyal customers.

[12]See Joe Schwartz, "Databases Deliver the Goods," *American Demographics,* September 1989, pp. 23–25; Gary Levin, "Database Draws Fevered Interest," *Advertising Age,* June 8, 1992, p. 31; Jonathan Berry, "A Potent New Tool for Selling: Database Marketing," *Business Week,* September 5, 1994, pp. 56–62; Richard Cross and Janet Smith, "Customer Bonding and the Information Core," *Direct Marketing Magazine,* February, 1995, p. 28; Frederick Newell, *The New Rules of Marketing* (New York: McGraw-Hill, 1997); R. M. Gordon, "Consumer Guidance," *Marketing Management,* Spring 1998, pp. 59–60; and Sara Sellar, "Dust Off That Data," *Sales & Marketing Management,* May 1999, p. 69.

Like many other marketing tools, database marketing requires a special investment. Companies must invest in computer hardware, database software, analytical programs, communication links, and skilled personnel. The database system must be user friendly and available to various marketing groups, including those in product and brand management, new-product development, advertising and promotion, direct mail, telemarketing, field sales, order fulfillment, and customer service. A well-managed database should lead to sales gains that will more than cover its costs.

active concept check <

Now let's take a moment to test your knowledge of what you've just read.

> Forms of Direct Marketing

The major forms of direct marketing—as shown in Figure 17.1—include *face-to-face selling, telemarketing, direct-mail marketing, catalog marketing, direct-response television marketing, kiosk marketing,* and *online marketing.*

FACE-TO-FACE SELLING

The original and oldest form of direct marketing is the sales call, which we examined in the previous chapter. Today most business-to-business marketers rely heavily on a professional sales force to locate prospects, develop them into customers, build lasting relationships, and grow the business. Or they hire manufacturers' representatives and agents to carry out the direct-selling task. In addition, many consumer companies use a direct-selling force to reach final consumers: insurance agents, stockbrokers, and salespeople working part- or full-time for direct-sales organizations such as Avon, Amway, Mary Kay, and Tupperware.

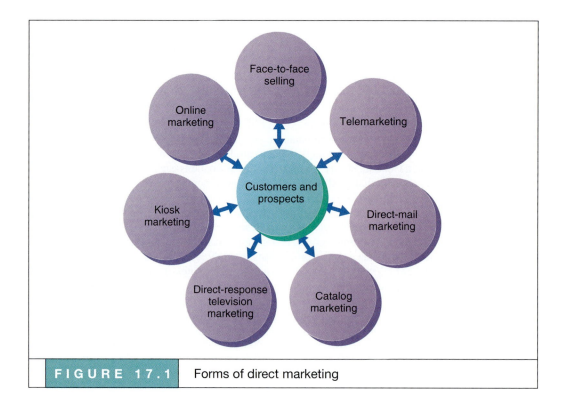

FIGURE 17.1 Forms of direct marketing

TELEMARKETING

Telemarketing—using the telephone to sell directly to consumers—has become the major direct-marketing communication tool. Telephone marketing now accounts for over 38 percent of all direct-marketing media expenditures.[13] We're all familiar with telemarketing directed toward consumers, but business-to-business marketers also use telemarketing extensively.

Marketers use *outbound* telephone marketing to sell directly to consumers and businesses. *Inbound* toll-free 800 numbers are used to receive orders from television and radio ads, direct mail, or catalogs. The use of 800 numbers has taken off in recent years as more and more companies have begun using them, and as current users have added new features such as toll-free fax numbers. Residential use has also grown. To accommodate this rapid growth, new toll-free area codes (888, 877, 866) have been added. After the 800 area code was established in 1967, it took almost 30 years before its 8 million numbers were used up. In contrast, 888 area code numbers, established in 1996, were used up in only 2 years.[14]

Other marketers use 900 numbers to sell consumers information, entertainment, or the opportunity to voice an opinion on a pay-per-call basis. For example, for a charge, consumers can obtain weather forecasts from American Express (900-WEATHER—$.75 a minute), pet care information from Quaker Oats (900-990-PETS—$.95 a minute), advice on snoring and other sleep disorders from Somnus (900-USA-SLEEP—$2.00 for the first minute, then $1.00 a minute), golf lessons from *Golf Digest* (900-454-3288—$.95 a minute), or individual answers to nutrition questions from a registered dietician sponsored by the American Dietetic Association (900-CALL-AN-RD—$1.95 for the first minute, then $.95 a minute). In addition to its 800 number and Internet site, Nintendo offers a 900 number, for $1.50 per minute, for game players wanting assistance with the company's video games. Ronald McDonald House Charities uses a 900 number to raise funds. Each call to 900-CALL-RMHC results in a $15.00 contribution, which is simply charged to the caller's local phone bill. Overall, the use of 900 numbers has grown by more than 10 percent a year over the past five years.[15]

Many consumers appreciate many of the offers they receive by telephone. Properly designed and targeted telemarketing provides many benefits, including purchasing convenience and increased product and service information. However, the recent explosion in unsolicited telephone marketing has annoyed many consumers who object to the almost daily "junk phone calls" that pull them away from the dinner table or fill their answering machines. Lawmakers around the country are responding

Telemarketing: Each call to 900-CALL-RMHC results in a $15 contribution charged to the caller's phone bill.

---

[13]*Economic Impact: U.S. Direct Marketing Today.*

[14]Matthew L. Wald, "Third Area Code Is Added in the Land of the Toll-Free," *New York Times,* April 4, 1998, p. 10.

[15]Kevin R. Hopkins, "Dialing in to the Future," *Business Week,* July 28, 1997, p. 90; and Holly McCord, "1-900-CALL-AN-RD," *Prevention,* August 1997, p. 54.

with legislation ranging from banning unsolicited telemarketing calls during certain hours to letting households sign up for "Do not call" lists. Most telemarketers support some action against random and poorly targeted telemarketing. As a Direct Marketing Association executive notes, "We want to target people who want to be targeted."[16]

active example <

Examine the services offered by one telemarketing organization.

DIRECT-MAIL MARKETING

Direct-mail marketing involves sending an offer, announcement, reminder, or other item to a person at a particular address. Using highly selective mailing lists, direct marketers send out millions of mail pieces each year—letters, ads, samples, foldouts, and other "salespeople with wings." Direct mail accounts for over 24 percent of all direct-marketing media expenditures. Together, telemarketing and direct-mail marketing account for over 60 percent of direct-marketing expenditures and 66 percent of direct-marketing sales.[17]

Direct mail is well suited to direct, one-to-one communication. It permits high target-market selectivity, can be personalized, is flexible, and allows easy measurement of results. Whereas the cost per thousand people reached is higher than with mass media such as television or magazines, the people who are reached are much better prospects. Direct mail has proved successful in promoting all kinds of products, from books, magazine subscriptions, and insurance to gift items, clothing, gourmet foods, and industrial products. Direct mail is also used heavily by charities to raise billions of dollars each year. The following example shows the power of direct mail in obtaining contributions, in this case for an ailing public TV–radio station:

> When planning its capital improvement campaign, public TV–radio station WFYI set what it thought was an ambitious five-year, $5 million fund-raising goal. The results, however, far outstripped projections. Instead of sending out the usual glossy, full-color brochures, WFYI used a brutally frank approach centering on its dire financial straits. It used cardboard, rubber stamps, and duct tape to create an introductory mailer. A silvery, die-cut TV set illustrated the message, "In 1969, Indianapolis was the largest city in the nation without a public television station." Turning the page, the copy continued "It could be again," with the TV now held together with duct tape. An inexpensively printed follow-up brochure showed a time line of the station's 18-year history. Above the line in black were milestones and accomplishments. Below, in red, equipment failures. When the time line hit 1996, expenses had become an angry, unreadable blotch of red ink. The direct approach worked: Despite sending out only 500 mailers, the campaign raised some $3.5 million in only the first nine months. That's an astounding return of $7,000 per piece.[18]

The direct-mail industry constantly seeks new methods and approaches. For example, videocassettes and CDs are now among the fastest-growing direct-mail media. With VCRs now in most American homes, marketers mailed out tens of millions of cassettes each year. For instance, to introduce its Donkey Kong Country video game, Nintendo of America created a 13-minute MTV-style video and sent 2 million copies to avid video game players. This direct-mail video helped Nintendo sell 6.1 million units of the game in only 45 days, making it the fastest-selling game in industry history.[19] Some direct marketers even mail out computer diskettes. For example, Ford sends a computer

[16]See James Heckman, "How Telemarketers Are Coping with the Rising Tide of State Regs," *Marketing News,* April 12, 1999, p. 4; and Catherine Siskos, "Pulling the Plug on Telemarketers," *Kiplinger's Personal Finance Magazine,* July 1999, pp. 18–20.

[17]*Economic Impact: U.S. Direct Marketing Today.*

[18]Debra Ray, "'Poor Mouth' Direct Mail Brochure Nets $3.5 Million in Contributions," *Direct Marketing,* February 1998, pp. 38–39.

[19]Junu Bryan Kim, "Marketing with Video: The Cassette Is in the Mail," *Advertising Age,* May 22, 1995, p. S1. Also see Albert Fried-Cassorla, "The Bright Future of Direct Mail: (Yes, Even in the Online Era!)," *Direct Marketing,* March 1998, pp. 40–42.

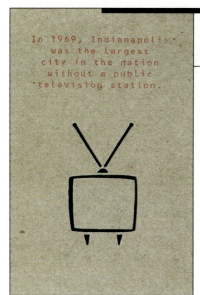

Direct mail's fundraising power: Using a brutally frank approach centering on its dire financial straits, public TV–radio station WFYI far outstripped what it thought was an ambitious five-year fundraising goal.

diskette called "Disk Drive Test Drive" to consumers responding to its ads in computer publications. The diskette's menu provides technical specifications and attractive graphics about Ford cars and answers frequently asked questions.

Until recently, all mail was paper based and handled by the U.S. Post Office, telegraphic services, or for-profit mail carriers such as Federal Express, DHL, or Airborne Express. Recently, however, three new forms of mail delivery have become popular:

- *Fax mail:* Fax machines allow delivery of paper-based messages over telephone lines. Fax mail has one major advantage over regular mail: The message can be sent and received almost instantaneously. Marketers now routinely send fax mail announcing offers, sales, and other events to prospects and customers with fax machines. Fax numbers of companies and individuals are now available through published directories. However, some prospects and customers resent receiving unsolicited fax mail, which ties up their machines and consumes their paper.

- *E-mail:* E-mail (short for *electronic mail*) allows users to send messages or files directly from one computer to another. Messages arrive almost instantly and are stored until the receiving person retrieves them. Many marketers now send sales announcements, offers, product information, and other messages to e-mail addresses—sometimes to a few individuals, sometimes to large groups. As people begin to receive more e-mail messages, including unimportant ones, they may look for an "agent" software program to sort out the more important messages from those that can be ignored or discarded.

- *Voice mail:* Voice mail is a system for receiving and storing oral messages at a telephone address. Telephone companies sell this service as a substitute for answering machines. The person with a voice mail account can check messages by dialing into the voice mail system and entering a personal code. Some marketers have set up automated programs that exclusively target voice mail boxes and answering machines with prerecorded messages. These systems target homes between 10 A.M. and 4 P.M. and businesses between 7 P.M. and 9 P.M. when people are least likely to answer. If the automated dialer hears a live voice, it disconnects. Such systems thwart hang-ups by annoyed potential customers. However, they can also create substantial ill will.[20]

These new forms deliver direct mail at incredible speeds compared to the post office's "snail mail" pace. Yet, much like mail delivered through traditional channels, they may be resented as "junk mail" if sent to people who have no interest in them. For this reason, marketers must carefully identify appropriate targets so as not to waste their money and recipients' time.

[20]Kruti Trivedi, "Telemarketers Don't Want You, Just Your Answering Machine," *Wall Street Journal,* August 6, 1999, p. B1.

active example   ◄

Consider the challenges and potential benefits of taking direct-mail marketing abroad.

CATALOG MARKETING

Rapid advances in technology, along with the move toward personalized, one-to-one marketing, have resulted in dramatic changes in **catalog marketing.** *Catalog Age* magazine used to define a *catalog* as "a printed, bound piece of at least eight pages, selling multiple products, and offering a direct ordering mechanism." Today, only a few years later, this definition is sadly out of date. With the stampede to the Internet, although printed catalogs remain the primary medium, more and more catalogs are going electronic. Many traditional print catalogers have added Web-based catalogs to their marketing mixes and a variety of new Web-only catalogers have emerged.

Catalog marketing has grown explosively during the past 25 years. Annual catalog sales (both print and electronic) are expected to grow from a current $80 billion to more than $107 billion by 2002.[21] Some huge general-merchandise retailers—such as JCPenney and Spiegel—sell a full line of merchandise through catalogs. More recently, the giants have been challenged by thousands of specialty catalogs that serve highly specialized market niches. Consumers can buy just about anything from a catalog. Sharper Image sells $2,400 jet-propelled surfboards. The Banana Republic Travel and Safari Clothing Company features everything you would need to go hiking in the Sahara or the rain forest. And each year Lillian Vernon sends out 33 editions of its catalogs with total circulation of 178 million copies to its 20-million person database, selling everything from shoes to decorative lawn birds and monogrammed oven mitts.[22]

Specialty department stores, such as Neiman Marcus, Bloomingdale's, and Saks Fifth Avenue, use catalogs to cultivate upper-middle-class markets for high-priced, often exotic, merchandise. Several major corporations have also developed or acquired catalog divisions. For example, Avon now issues 10 women's fashion catalogs along with catalogs for children's and men's clothes. Walt Disney Company mails out over 6 million catalogs each year featuring videos, stuffed animals, and other Disney items.

The Internet has had a tremendous impact on catalog selling. In the face of increasing competition from Internet retailing, one expert even predicts "catalogs are doomed .. . mail-order catalogs as we know them today won't even survive."[23] Thus, even traditional catalogers are adding Wed-based catalogs. In fact, more than three-quarters of all catalog companies now present merchandise and take orders over the Internet. For example, the Lands' End Web site, which debuted in 1995, now gets 180,000 e-mail queries a year, surpassing its print mail response.[24] Here's another example that illustrates this dramatic shift in catalog marketing:

> When novelty gifts marketer Archie McPhee launched its Web site in September 1995, response was "underwhelming," says Mark Pahlow, president of the catalog company. "But when we added the shopping basket ordering feature in summer 1997, it came alive." You might say it roared to life. According to Pahlow, the site now has 35,000 unique visitors each month, generating 55 percent of the cataloger's total sales. In fact, the Web numbers are so positive that Archie McPhee has slashed circulation of its print catalog from 1 million to less than 300,000, and reduced the frequency from five issues a year to three. Archie McPhee's Web-based catalog makes good sense for many reasons. "We did the math," Pahlow says. The Web site has saved the company more than 50 percent in the costs of producing, printing, and mailing its color catalog, which had been as high as $700,000 annually. Using the Web site, Archie McPhee can also offer interactive features, such as "The Nerd Test" and a fortune-telling ball, as well as much more merchandise. "A

[21]*Economic Impact: U.S. Direct Marketing Today.*

[22]"Lillian Vernon Announces New Catalog Title," *Direct Marketing,* April 1998, pp. 15–16.

[23]Irwin Helford, "Your Catalogs Are Doomed!" *Catalog Age,* August 1999, pp. 101, 106.

[24]Bruce Horovitz, "Catalog Craze Delivers Holiday Deals," *USA Today,* December 1, 1998, p. 3B.

Web-based catalogs: Most catalog companies now present merchandise and take orders over the Internet. Novelty gifts marketer Archie McPhee's site attracts 35,000 unique visitors each month and generates 55 percent of the cataloger's total sales.

48-page catalog would show fewer than 200 items, whereas the Web site offers more than 500," Pahlow notes. Another benefit of the site is its real-time inventory feature. "The day a new product arrives, it is shown on the site. The moment we run out of an item, we pull it off. We are also able to show items we have small quantities of as Web-only specials."[25]

Along with the benefits, however, Web-based catalogs also present challenges. Whereas a print catalog is intrusive and creates its own attention, Web catalogs are passive and must be marketed. "Attracting new customers is much more difficult to do with a Web catalog," says an industry consultant. "You have to use advertising, linkage, and other means to drive traffic to it." Thus, even catalogers who are sold on the Web are not likely to abandon their print catalogs completely. For example, Archie McPhee relies on its print catalogs to promote its site. "I think we will always produce at least one catalog a year," Pahlow says.

> active exercise

Explore further the developing relationship between catalog marketing and the Internet.

DIRECT-RESPONSE TELEVISION MARKETING

Direct-response television marketing takes one of two major forms. The first is *direct-response advertising.* Direct marketers air television spots, often 60 or 120 seconds long, that persuasively describe a product and give customers a toll-free number for ordering. Television viewers often encounter 30-minute advertising programs, or *infomercials,* for a single product.

Some successful direct-response ads run for years and become classics. For example, Dial Media's ads for Ginsu knives ran for seven years and sold almost 3 million sets of knives worth more than $40 million in sales; its Armourcote cookware ads generated more than twice that much. The current infomercial champ?

It's three o'clock in the morning. Plagued with insomnia, you grab the remote and flip around until a grinning blonde in an apron catches your attention: "I'm going to show you something you won't believe! Juicy meals in minutes! Something else you won't believe . . .

[25]Example adapted in part from Moira Pascale, "Archie's Online Boom Cuts Circulation," accessed online at www.catalogagemag. com, August 1999.

For years, infomercials have been associated with somewhat questionable pitches for juicers and other kitchen gadgets, get-rich-quick schemes, and nifty ways to stay in shape without working very hard at it. Recently, however, a number of large companies—GTE, Johnson & Johnson, MCA Universal, Sears, Procter & Gamble, Revlon, Apple Computer, Cadillac, Volvo, Anheuser-Busch, even the U.S. Navy—have begun using infomercials to sell their wares over the phone, refer customers to retailers, or send out coupons and product information.[27]

Home shopping channels, another form of direct-response television marketing, are television programs or entire channels dedicated to selling goods and services. Some home shopping channels, such as the Quality Value Channel (QVC) and the Home Shopping Network (HSN), broadcast 24 hours a day. On HSN, the program's hosts offer bargain prices on products ranging from jewelry, lamps, collectible dolls, and clothing to power tools and consumer electronics—usually obtained by the home shopping channel at closeout prices. The show is upbeat, with the hosts honking horns, blowing whistles, and praising viewers for their good taste. Viewers call a toll-free number to order goods. At the other end of the operation, 400 operators handle more than 1,200 incoming lines, entering orders directly into computer terminals. Orders are shipped within 48 hours. QVC sells more than $1.6 billion worth of merchandise each year and averages 113,000 orders per day. Sears, Kmart, JCPenney, Spiegel, and other major retailers are now looking into the home shopping industry.[28]

Beyond infomercials, home shopping channels, and other direct-response television marketing approaches, many experts think that advances in two-way, interactive television and linkages with Internet technology will one day make television shopping one of the major forms of direct marketing.[29]

video example <

Take a look an one company's contributions to direct-response television marketing.

KIOSK MARKETING

Some companies place information and ordering machines—called *kiosks* (in contrast to vending machines, which dispense actual products)—in stores, airports, and other locations. Hallmark and American Greetings use kiosks to help customers create and purchase personalized greeting cards. Tower Records has listening kiosks that let customers listen to the music before purchase. Kiosks in the do-it-yourself ceramics stores of California-based Color Me Mine Inc. contain clip-art images that customers can use to decorate the ceramics pieces they purchase in the store. At Car Max, the used car superstore, customers use a kiosk with a touch-screen computer to get information about its vast

[26]Erika Brown, "Ooh! Aah!" *Forbes,* March 8, 1999, p. 56.

[27]See Timothy R. Hawthorne, "Opening Doors to Retail Sales," *Direct Marketing,* January 1998, pp. 48–51; Jacqueline M. Graves, "The Fortune 500 Opt for Infomercials," *Fortune,* March 6, 1995, p. 20; "Infomercials," *Advertising Age,* September 8, 1997, pp. A1–A2; Carol Krol, "Navy Infomercial Aims at Prospective Recruits," *Advertising Age,* May 31, 1999, p. 12; Dave Guilford, "Cadillac Takes New Route for Sevill STS: Infomercial," *Advertising Age,* August 23, 1999, p. 8; and Jean Halliday, "Volvo Ready to Act on Leads After Infomercial Success," *Advertising Age,* January 25, 1999, p. 61.

[28]See Dale D. Buss, "Capturing Customers with TV Retailing," *Nation's Business,* February 1997, pp. 29–32; "Shopping from the Sofa," *American Demographics,* April 1997, pp. 31–32; Doreen Carvajal, "Publishers Find New Market Through Television Shopping Network," *New York Times,* February 14, 1998, p. D1; and John Lippman, "Home Shopping's Held Steps Down as CEO, Chairman," *Wall Street Journal,* March 8, 1999.

[29]See Frank Rose, "The End of TV as We Know It," *Fortune,* December 23, 1996, pp. 58–68; Elizabeth Lesly and Robert D. Hof, "Is Digital Convergence for Real?" *Business Week,* June 23, 1997, pp. 42–43; Amy Cortese, "Not @Home Alone: Bill Comes Knocking," *Business Week,* July 14, 1997, p. 24; B. G. Yovovich, "Webbed Feet: Marketing Opportunities Emerge from Interactive Television Applications and Services," *Marketing News,* January 19, 1998, pp. 1, 18; and Horst Stipp, "Should TV Marry PC?" *American Demographics,* July 1998, pp. 16–18.

inventory of as many as 1,000 cars and trucks. Customers can choose a handful and print out photos, prices, features, and locations on the store's lot. The use of such kiosks is expected to increase fivefold during the next three years.[30]

Business marketers also use kiosks. For example, Dow Plastics places kiosks at trade shows to collect sales leads and to provide information on its 700 products. The kiosk system reads customer data from encoded registration badges and produces technical data sheets that can be printed at the kiosk or faxed or mailed to the customer. The system has resulted in a 400 percent increase in qualified sales leads.[31]

Like about everything else these days, kiosks are also going online, as many companies merge the powers of the real and virtual worlds. For example, in some Levi-Strauss stores, you can plug your measurements into a Web kiosk and have custom-made jeans delivered to your home within two weeks. Gap has installed interactive kiosks, called Web lounges, in some of its stores that provide gift ideas or let customers match up outfits without trying them on in dressing rooms. Outdoor equipment retailer REI recently outfitted its stores with kiosks that provide customers with product information and let them place orders online.[32]

> active poll

Take a moment to give your opinion on a question concerning direct marketing.

> active concept check

Now let's take a moment to test your knowledge of what you've just read.

> Online Marketing and Electronic Commerce

Online marketing is conducted through interactive online computer systems, which link consumers with sellers electronically. There are two types of online marketing channels: commercial online services and the Internet.

Commercial online services offer online information and marketing services to subscribers who pay a monthly fee. The best known online service provider is giant America Online, which has more than 21 million subscribers. Microsoft Network (MSN) and Prodigy trail far behind AOL with 2.45 million and 1 million subscribers, respectively.[33] These online services provide subscribers with information (news, libraries, education, travel, sports, reference), entertainment (fun and games), shopping services, dialogue opportunities (bulletin boards, forums, chat boxes), and e-mail.

After growing rapidly through the mid-1990s, the commercial online services have now been overtaken by the **Internet** as the primary online marketing channel. In fact, all of the online service firms now offer Internet access as a primary service. The Internet is a vast and burgeoning global web of computer networks. It evolved from a network created by the Defense Department during the 1960s, initially to link government labs, contractors, and military installations. Today, this huge, public computer network links computer users of all types all around the world. Anyone with a PC, a

---

[30]DeAnn Weimer, "Can You Keep 'Em Down on the Mall?" *Business Week,* December 15, 1997, pp. 66–70; "Lining Up for Interactive Kiosks," *Nation's Business,* February 1998, p. 46; Warren S. Hersch, "Kiosks Poised to Be a Huge Growth Market," *Computer Reseller News,* May 18, 1998, p. 163; and Catherine Yang, "No Web Site Is an Island, *Business Week,* March 22, 1999, p. EB38.

[31]"Interactive: Ad Age Names Finalists," *Advertising Age,* February 27, 1995, pp. 12–14.

[32]Yang, "No Web Site Is an Island," p. EB38.

[33]See Matt Richtel, "Small Internet Providers Survive Among Giants," *New York Times,* August 16, 1999, p. 1; Dean Foust and David Ricks, "In a Squeeze at Mindspring," *Business Week,* September 20, 1999, pp. 139–42; and Timothy J. Mullaney, "AOL Rules!" *Business Week,* April 3, 2000, pp. EB134–EB136.

Commercial online services: Leader America Online has more than 19 million subscribers who pay a monthly fee for its information and marketing services.

modem, and the right software can browse the Internet to obtain or share information on almost any subject and to interact with other users.[34]

Internet usage surged with the development of the user-friendly **World Wide Web** (the **Web**) and Web browser software such as Netscape Navigator and Microsoft Internet Explorer. Today, even novices can surf the Internet and experience fully integrated text, graphics, images, and sound. Users can send e-mail, exchange views, shop for products, and access news, food recipes, art, and business information. The Internet itself is free, although individual users usually must pay a commercial access provider to be hooked up to it.

RAPID GROWTH OF ONLINE MARKETING

Although still in their infancy, Internet usage and online marketing are growing explosively. Today, some 40 million U.S. households are dialing into the Internet, up from just 6 million in 1994. The U.S. Internet population is expected to swell to some 60 million households by the year 2002. Total U.S. purchasing on the Web is expected to skyrocket from zero in 1994 and about $130 billion in 1999 to $1.4 trillion by 2003.[35]

This explosion of Internet usage heralds the dawning of a new world of *electronic commerce.* **Electronic commerce** is the general term for a buying and selling process that is supported by electronic means. *Electronic markets* are "market*spaces,*" rather than physical "market*places,*" in which sellers offer their products and services electronically, and buyers search for information, identify what they want, and place orders using a credit card or other means of electronic payment.

The electronic commerce explosion is all around us. Here are just a few examples:

■ A reporter wants to buy a 35mm camera. She turns on her computer, logs onto the Shopper's Advantage Web site, clicks on cameras, then clicks on 35mm cameras. A list of all the major brands appears, along with information about each brand. She can retrieve a photo of each camera and reviews by experts. Finding the camera she wants, she places an order by typing in her credit card number, address, and preferred shipping mode.

■ An affluent investor decides to do his own banking and investing. He signs onto discount brokerage Charles Schwab Company's SchwabNOW Web site (**www.schwab. com**), checks the current status of his investment account, and obtains reports on several stocks he is considering buying. After completing his research, he reviews current stock prices and places his buy and sell orders.

■ An executive is planning a trip to London and wants to locate a hotel that meets her needs. She signs onto the Travelocity Web site (**www.travelocity.com**) and inputs her criteria (rate, location, amenities, safety). The computer produces a list of appropriate hotels, and she can book a room once she has made her choice. Eventually, videos giving a "guided tour" of each hotel will be included in the program.

[34]For more on the basics of using the Internet, see Raymond D. Frost and Judy Strauss, *The Internet: A New Marketing Tool—2000* (Upper Saddle River, NJ: Prentice Hall, 2000).

[35]Internet usage statistics provided by Forrester Research, August 1999.

E-commerce is exploding: The Charles Schwab Web site allows clients to check the status of their accounts, research stocks, receive investment advice, place buy and sell orders, and create their own customized home pages.

According to one study, nearly 60 percent of all Internet users have used the Web to shop, a 15 percent increase over just a year ago.[36] Whereas business-to-consumer e-commerce is growing rapidly, business-to-business Internet commerce is exploding. Business buyers are far and away the largest Web users, accounting for more than 90 percent of all e-commerce.[37]

THE ONLINE CONSUMER

When people envision the typical Internet user, some mistakenly envision a pasty-faced computer nerd or "cyberhead." Others envision a young, techy, upscale male professional. Such stereotypes are sadly outdated.

The Internet population does differ demographically from the general population. As a whole, the Internet population is still younger, more affluent, better educated, and more male than the general population. However, as more and more people find their way onto the Internet, the cyberspace population is becoming more mainstream and diverse. For example, one recent study of Internet "newbies"—those who started using the Internet in the past year—found that 71 percent had no college degree, 65 percent earn less than $50,000 a year, and only 25 percent were younger than 30.[38] An industry analyst summarizes:

> The Internet isn't just a geek's playground anymore. These days, everybody's logging on. . . . Doral Main, a 51-year-old mother of two and office manager of a low-income property company in Oakland, CA, saves precious time by shopping the Internet for greeting cards and getaways. Her Net-newbie father, Charles, 73, goes online to buy supplies for his wood-carving hobby. Even niece Katrina, 11, finds excitement on the Web, picking gifts she wants from the Disney.com site. "It's addictive," Main says of the Net. [Indeed,] the Web isn't mostly a hangout for techno-nerds anymore.[39]

Thus, increasingly, the Internet provides online marketers with access to a broad range of demographic segments. For example, 46 percent of Internet users are women, up from only 37 percent three years ago. And although more than half of all users are professionals or managers, this percentage is decreasing.[40]

Internet users come from all age groups. For example, the populations of almost 9 million "Net kids" and more than 8 million teens (predicted to reach almost 22 million and 17 million, respectively, by the year 2002) have attracted a host of online marketers. America Online offers a Kids Only area

[36]"Females Lead Online Growth Spurt," CommerceNet and Nielsen Media Research, June 17, 1999, accessed online at www.cyberatlas.com.

[37]Information provided by Forrester Research, August 1999. Also see Laura Cohn, "B2B: The Hottest Net Bet Yet?" *Business Week,* January 17, 2000, pp. 36–37.

[38]Sharon Machlis, "Web Retailers Retool for Mainstream Users," *Computerworld,* March 22, 1999, p. 40.

[39]Roger O. Crockett, "A Web That Looks Like the World," *Business Week,* March 22, 1999, pp. EB46–EB47.

[40]See "Females Lead Online Growth Spurt," CommerceNet and Nielsen Media Research, June 17, 1999, accessed online at www.cyberatlas.com.

featuring homework help and online magazines along with the usual games, software, and chat rooms. The Microsoft Network site carries Disney's Daily Blast, which offers kids games, stories, comic strips with old and new Disney characters, and current events tailored to preteens. Nickelodeon (**www.nick.com**) offers Natalie's Backseat Traveling Web Show, which includes games based on a Nickelodeon character named Natalie. "Similar to the offline market," observes one expert, "kids and teens have a profound impact on online purchasing decisions. . . . Instead of grabbing parents' coat sleeves, today's kids ask parents for credit card numbers in place of an allowance and buy products online."[41]

Although Internet users are younger on average than the population as a whole, seniors age 55 to 64 make up some 22 percent of today's online households and that number will grow to 40 percent by 2003. Whereas younger groups are more likely to use the Internet for entertainment and socializing, older Internet surfers go online for more serious matters. For example, 24 percent of people in this age group use the Internet for investment purposes, compared with only 3 percent of those 25 to 29. Thus, older Netizens make an attractive market for Web businesses, ranging from florists and automotive retailers to financial services providers.[42]

Internet users also differ psychographically from the general consumer population. Forrester Research and SRI Consulting have developed approaches for measuring attitudes, preferences, and behavior of online service and Internet users. SRI Consulting's Web site (**www.future.sri.com/VALS/survey/html**) allows visitors to take the VALS 2 questionnaire and get immediate feedback on their VALS 2 type. The firm has identified 10 different psychographic segments ranging from Wizards, skilled users who identify strongly with the Internet, to Socialites, who are strongly oriented toward social aspects of the Internet.[43]

Finally, Internet consumers differ in their approaches to buying and in their responses to marketing. They are empowered consumers who have greater control over the marketing process. People who use the Internet place greater value on information and tend to respond negatively to messages aimed only at selling. Whereas traditional marketing targets a somewhat passive audience, online marketing targets people who actively select which Web sites they will visit and which ad banners they will click on. They decide what marketing information they will receive about which products and services and under what conditions. Thus, in online marketing, the consumer controls more of the interaction.

Internet search engines such as Yahoo! Go Network, and Excite give consumers access to varied information sources, making them better informed and more discerning shoppers. In fact, online buyers are increasingly creators of product information, not just consumers of it. As greater numbers of consumers join Internet interest groups that share product-related information, "word of Web" is joining "word of mouth" as an important buying influence. Thus, the new world of e-commerce will require new marketing approaches.

CONDUCTING ONLINE MARKETING

Marketers can conduct online marketing in four ways: by creating an electronic presence online; placing ads online; participating in Internet forums, newsgroups, or "Web communities"; or using online e-mail or Webcasting.

Creating an Electronic Online Presence

A company can establish an electronic online presence in two ways: It can buy space on a commercial online service or it can open its own Web site. Buying a location on a commercial online service involves either renting storage space on the online service's computer or establishing a link from the company's own computer to the online service's shopping mall. JCPenney, for example, has links to America Online, Microsoft Network, and Prodigy, gaining access to the millions of consumers who subscribe to these services. The online services typically design the storefront for the company and introduce it to their subscribers. For these services, the company pays the online service an annual fee plus a small percentage of the company's online sales.

---

[41]"Kids and Teens to Spend More Online," June 7, 1999, accessed online at www.cyberatlas.com. Also see Roger O. Crockett, "Forget the Mall. Kids Shop the Net," *Business Week,* July 26, 1999, p. EB14; Eryn Brown, "The Future of Net Shopping? Your Teens," *Fortune,* April 12, 1999, p. 152: and "Just Surfin' Through" *American Demographic,* January 2000, p.12.

[42]See Crockett, "A Web That Looks Like the World," p. EB47; and Joanne Cleaver, "Surfing for Seniors," *Marketing News,* July 19, 1999, pp. 1, 7.

[43]See Rebecca Piirto Heath, "The Frontiers of Psychographics," *American Demographics,* July 1996, pp. 38–43; Paul C. Judge, "Are Tech Buyers Different?" *Business Week,* January 26, 1998, pp. 64–65, 68; and the SRI Consulting Web site (future.sri.com), June 1999.

Corporate Web site: The highly entertaining Candystand Web site doesn't sell LifeSavers products. However, it does offer a rich variety of features that create an entertaining online experience for children and teenagers. It also gathers useful customer feedback.

In addition to buying a location on an online service, or as an alternative, most companies have now created their own Web sites. These sites vary greatly in purpose and content. The most basic type is a **corporate Web site.** These sites are designed to build customer goodwill and to supplement other sales channels rather than to sell the company's products directly. For example, you can't buy ice cream at **www.benjerrys.com**, but you can learn all about Ben & Jerry's company philosophy, products, and locations; send a free E-card to a friend or subscribe to the Chunk Mail newsletter; and while away time in the Fun Stuff area, playing "Ask Habeeni" or "The Phish Game." Similarly, Nabisco's LifeSavers Candystand Web site doesn't sell candy but does generate consumer excitement and goodwill, as well as valuable feedback to LifeSavers brand managers:

Nabisco's highly entertaining LifeSavers Candystand Web site (www.candystand.com) features a rich variety of more than 27 interactive games, along with a variety of informational features and promotions, primarily designed to interest children and teenagers. Candystand contains 11 themed sections, each dedicated to a particular LifeSavers brand. "Our philosophy is to create an exciting online experience that reflects the fun and quality associated with the LifeSavers brands," says Silvio Bonvini, senior manager of new media at LifeSavers Company. "For the production cost of about two television spots we have a marketing vehicle that lives 24 hours a day, 7 days a week, 365 days a year." Candystand attracts more than 300,000 unique visitors a month. The site also offers LifeSavers an efficient channel for gathering customer feedback. Its "What Do You Think?" feature has generated 180,000 responses since the site launched in March 1997. "It's instant communication that we pass along directly to our brand people," Bonvini says. "It's not filtered by an agency or edited in any way." Comments collected from the Web site have resulted in improved packaging of one LifeSavers product and the resurrection of the abandoned Wintergreen flavor in the Carefree sugarless gum line.[44]

Corporate Web sites typically offer a rich variety of information and other features in an effort to answer customer questions, build closer customer relationships, and generate excitement about the company. They generally provide information about the company's history, its mission and philosophy, and the products and services that it offers. They might also tell about current events, company personnel, financial performance, and employment opportunities. Most corporate Web sites also provide entertainment features to attract and hold visitors. Finally, the site might also provide opportunities for customers to ask questions or make comments through e-mail before leaving the site.

Other companies create a **marketing Web site.** These sites are designed to engage consumers in an interaction that will move them closer to a purchase or other marketing outcome. Such a site might include a catalog, shopping tips, and promotional features such as coupons, sales events, or contests. Companies aggressively promote their marketing Web sites in print and broadcast advertising and

[44]Don Peppers and Martha Rogers, "Opening the Door to Consumers," *Sales & Marketing Management*, October 1998, pp. 22–29.

through "banner-to-site" ads that pop up on other Web sites. Consumers can find a Web site for buying almost anything—clothing from Lands' End or JCPenney, books from Barnes & Noble, or flowers from Grant's Flowers to be sent anywhere in the world.

Toyota operates a marketing Web site at www.toyota.com. Once a potential customer clicks in, the car maker wastes no time trying to turn the inquiry into a sale. The site offers plenty of entertainment and useful information, from cross-country trip guides and tips for driving with kids to events such as a Golf Skills Challenge and a Bike Express. But the site is also loaded with more serious selling features, such as detailed descriptions of current Toyota models and information on dealer locations and services, complete with maps and dealer Web links. Visitors who want to go further can use the ShopToyota feature to choose a Toyota, select equipment, and price it, then contact a dealer and even apply for credit. Or they fill out an online order form (supplying name, address, phone number, and e-mail address) for brochures and a free, interactive CD-ROM that shows off the features of Toyota models. The chances are good that before the CD-ROM arrives, a local dealer will call to invite the prospect in for a test drive. Toyota's Web site has now replaced its 800 number as the number-one source of customer leads.

Business-to-business marketers also make good use of marketing Web sites. For example, corporate buyers can visit Sun Microsystems' Web site (www.sun.com), select detailed descriptions of Sun's products and solutions, request sales and service information, and interact with staff members. Customers visiting GE Plastics' Web site (www.ge.com/plastics) can draw on more than 1,500 pages of information to get answers about the company's products anytime and from anywhere in the world. FedEx's Web site (www.fedex.com) allows customers to schedule their own shipments, request a courier, and track their packages in transit.[45]

Creating a Web site is one thing; getting people to *visit* the site is another. The key is to create enough value and excitement to get consumers to come to the site, stick around, and come back again. This means that companies must constantly update their sites to keep them fresh and exciting. Doing so involves time and expense, but the expense is necessary if the online marketer wishes to cut through the increasing online clutter. In addition, many online marketers spend heavily on good old-fashioned advertising and other offline marketing avenues to attract visitors to their sites. Says one analyst, "The reality today is you can't build a brand simply on the Internet. You have to go offline."[46]

For some types of products, attracting visitors is easy. Consumers buying new cars, computers, or financial services will be open to information and marketing initiatives from sellers. Marketers of lower-involvement products, however, may face a difficult challenge in attracting Web site visitors. As one veteran notes, "If you're shopping for a computer and you see a banner that says, 'We've ranked the top 12 computers to purchase,' you're going to click on the banner. [But] what kind of banner could encourage any consumer to visit dentalfloss.com?"[47] For such low-interest products, the company should create a corporate Web site to answer customer questions and build goodwill, using it only to supplement selling efforts through other channels.

Placing Advertisements Online

Companies can use online advertising to build their Internet brands or to attract visitors to their Web sites. **Online ads** pop up while Internet users are surfing online services or Web sites. Such ads include banner ads, pop-up windows, "tickers" (banners that move across the screen), and "roadblocks" (full-screen ads that users must pass through to get to other screens they wish to view). For example, a Web user or America Online subscriber who is looking up airline schedules or fares might find a flashing banner on the screen exclaiming, "Rent a car from Alamo and get up to 2 days free!" To attract visitors to its own Web site, Toyota sponsors Web banner ads on other sites, ranging from ESPN SportZone (www.espn.com) to Parent Soup (www.parentsoup.com), a kind of online coffee klatch through which moms and dads exchange views. Another form of Web advertising is *content sponsorships*. For example, Advil sponsors ESPN SportZone's Injury Report and Oldsmobile sponsors AOL's Celebrity Circle.

Companies spent almost $2 billion on Web advertising in 1998, and spending is expected to increase to almost $8.9 billion by 2002.[48] Still, this represents only a tiny fraction of overall advertising media expenditures when compared with the more than $40 billion each spent for advertising in newspapers and on broadcast television. Many marketers still question the value of Internet advertising as an effective tool. Costs are reasonable compared with those of other advertising media. For

[45]Melanie Berger. "It's Your Move," *Sales & Marketing Management,* March 1998, pp. 45–53.

[46]Laurie Freeman, "Why Internet Brands Take Offline Avenues," *Marketing News,* July 1999, p. 4; and Paul C. Judge, "The Name's the Thing," *Business Week,* November 15, 1999, pp. 35–39.

[47]John Deighton, "The Future of Interactive Marketing," *Harvard Business Review,* November–December 1996, p. 154.

[48]Online advertising expenditure figures were obtained online at www.emarketer.com/stats, September 1999.

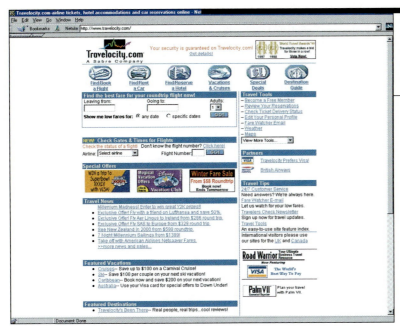

example, Web advertising on ESPNet SportZone, which attracts more than 500,000 Web surfers and 20 million "hits"—the number of times the site is accessed—per week, costs about $300,000 per year. However, Web surfers can easily ignore these banner ads and often do. Moreover, the industry has yet to come up with good measures of Web advertising impact—of who clicks on Web ads and how the ads affect them. Thus, although many firms are experimenting with Web advertising, it still plays only a minor role in their promotion mixes.

> ## active exercise

Consider how some firms are practicing online advertising.

Participating in Forums, Newsgroups, and Web Communities

Companies may decide to participate in or sponsor Internet forums, newsgroups, and bulletin boards that appeal to specific special-interest groups. Such activities may be organized for commercial or noncommercial purposes. *Forums* are discussion groups located on commercial online services. A forum may operate a library, a "chat room" for real-time message exchanges, and even a classified ad directory. For example, America Online boasts some 14,000 chat rooms, which account for a third of its members' online time. It also provides "buddy lists," which alert members when friends are online, allowing them to exchange instant messages. Most forums are sponsored by special-interest groups. Thus, as a major musical instruments manufacturer, Yamaha might start a forum on classical music.

Newsgroups are the Internet version of forums. However, such groups are limited to people posting and reading messages on a specified topic, rather than managing libraries or conferencing. Internet users can participate in newsgroups without subscribing. There are thousands of newsgroups dealing with every imaginable topic, from healthful eating and caring for your Bonsai tree to collecting antique cars or exchanging views on the latest soap opera happenings.

Bulletin board systems (BBSs) are specialized online services that center on a specific topic or group. There are over 60,000 BBSs originating in the United States, dealing with topics such as vacations, health, computer games, and real estate. Marketers might want to identify and participate in newsgroups and BBSs that attract subscribers who fit their target markets. However, newsgroups and BBS users often resent commercial intrusions on their Net space, so the marketer must tread carefully, participating in subtle ways that provide real value to participants.

The popularity of forums and newsgroups has resulted in a rash of commercially sponsored Web sites called *Web communities*. Such sites allow members to congregate online and exchange views on issues of common interest. They are the cyberspace equivalent to a Starbucks coffee-house, a place where everybody knows your e-mail address. For example, iVillage is a Web community in which "smart, compassionate, real women" can obtain information and exchange views on families, fitness, relationships, travel, finances, or just about any other topic. The site reaches 7.3 million unique visitors per month, greater than the combined monthly average paid circulation of *Cosmopolitan, Glamour, Vogue,* and *Marie Claire* magazines. Tripod is an online hangout for twentysomethings, offering chat rooms and free home pages for posting job resumés. Parent Soup is an online community of more than 200,000 parents who spend time online gathering parenting information, chatting with other parents about kid-related issues, and linking with other related sites.

Visitors to these Internet neighborhoods develop a strong sense of community. Such communities are attractive to advertisers because they draw consumers with common interests and well-defined demographics. For example, Parent Soup provides an ideal environment for the Web ads of Johnson & Johnson, Gerber's, Wal-Mart, and other companies targeting family audiences. Moreover, cyberhood consumers visit frequently and stay online longer, increasing the chance of meaningful exposure to the advertiser's message.

Web communities can be either social or work related. One successful work-related community is Agriculture Online (or griculture Online). This site offers commodity prices, recent farm news, and chat rooms of all types. Rural surfers can visit the Electronic Coffee Shop and pick up the latest down-on-the-farm joke or join a hot discussion on controlling soybean cyst nematodes. @griculture Online has been highly successful, attracting as many as 5 million hits per month.[49]

Using E-mail and Webcasting

A company can encourage prospects and customers to send questions, suggestions, and even complaints to the company via e-mail. Customer service representatives can quickly respond to such messages. The company may also develop Internet-based electronic mailing lists of customers or prospects. Such lists provide an excellent opportunity to introduce the company and its offerings to new customers and to build ongoing relationships with current ones. Using the lists, online marketers can send out customer newsletters, special product or promotion offers based on customer purchasing histories, reminders of service requirements or warranty renewals, or announcements of special events.

3Com Corporation, a manufacturer of high-tech computer hardware, made good use of e-mail to generate and qualify customer leads for its Network Interface Cards. The company used targeted e-mail and banner ads on 18 different computer-related Web sites to attract potential buyers to its own Web site featuring a "3Com Classic" sweepstakes, where by filling out the entry form, visitors could register to win a 1959 Corvette. The campaign generated 22,000 leads, which were further qualified using e-mail and telemarketing. "Hot" leads were passed along to 3Com's inside sales force. "[Sales reps] were very skeptical," says a 3Com marketing manager, "but they were blown away by how well the contest did." Of the 482 leads given to reps, 71 turned into actual sales that totaled $2.5 million. What's more, states the manager, "Now I've got 22,000 names in my e-mail database that I can go back and market to."[50]

Companies can also sign on with any of a number of **"Webcasting"** services, such as PointCast and Ifusion, which automatically download customized information to recipients' PCs. For a monthly fee, subscribers to these services can specify the channels they want—news, company information, entertainment, and others—and the topics they're interested in. Then, rather than spending hours scouring the Internet, they can sit back while the Webcaster automatically delivers information of interest to their desktops.[51]

Webcasting, also known as "push" programming, affords an attractive channel through which online marketers can deliver their Internet advertising or other information content. The major commercial online services are also beginning to offer Webcasting to their members. For example, America Online offers a feature called Driveway that will fetch information, Web pages, and e-mail based on members' preferences and automatically deliver it to their PCs.

As with other types of online marketing, companies must be careful that they don't cause resentment among Internet users who are already overloaded with "junk e-mail." Warns one analyst,

[49]See Ian P. Murphy, "Web 'Communities' a Target Marketer's Dream," *Advertising Age,* July 7, 1997, p. 2; Patricia Riedman, "Web Communities Offer Shopping Options for Users," *Advertising Age,* October 26, 1998, p. S10; Neil Cross, "Building Global Communities," *Business Week,* March 22, 1999, pp. EB42–EB43; and Richard Siklos, "Weaving Yet Another Web for Women," *Business Week,* January 17, 2000, p. 101.

[50]Erika Rasmusson, "Tracking Down Sales," *Sales & Marketing Management,* June 1998, p. 19.

[51]See Mary J. Cronin, "Using the Web to Push Key Data to Decision Makers," *Fortune,* September 19, 1997, p. 254; and Tim McCollum, "All the News That's Fit to Print," *Nation's Business,* June 1998, pp. 59–61.

"There's a fine line between adding value and the consumer feeling that you're being intrusive."[52] Companies must beware of irritating consumers by sending unwanted e-mail to promote their products. Netiquette, the unwritten rules that guide Internet etiquette, suggests that marketers should ask customers for permission to e-mail marketing pitches—and tell recipients how to stop the flow of e-mail promotions at any time. This approach, known as permission-based marketing, is emerging as a new model for e-mail marketing.

THE PROMISE AND CHALLENGES OF ONLINE MARKETING

Online marketing offers great promise for the future. Its most ardent apostles envision a time when the Internet and e-commerce will replace magazines, newspapers, and even stores as sources of information and buying. Yet despite all the hype and promise, online marketing may be years away from realizing its full potential. Even then, it is unlikely to fulfill such sweeping predictions. To be sure, online marketing will become a full and complete business model for some companies; Internet firms such as Amazon.com, eBay, Yahoo!, and Netscape; and direct-marketing companies such as Dell Computer. Michael Dell's goal is one day "to have *all* customers conduct *all* transactions on the Internet, globally." But for most companies, online marketing will remain just one important approach to the marketplace that works alongside other approaches in a fully integrated marketing mix.

For many marketers, including fast-growing Internet superstars such as Amazon.com, the Web is still not a money-making proposition. According to one report, less than half of today's Web sites are profitable.[53] Here are just some of the challenges that online marketers face:

■ *Limited consumer exposure and buying:* Although expanding rapidly, online marketing still reaches only a limited marketspace. Moreover, many Web users do more window browsing than actual buying. One source estimates that although 65 percent of current Internet users have used the Web to check out products and compare prices prior to a purchase decision, only 14 percent of Internet users have actually purchased anything online. Still fewer have used their credit card.[54]

■ *Skewed user demographics and psychographics:* Although the Web audience is becoming more mainstream, online users still tend to be more upscale and technically oriented than the general population. This makes online marketing ideal for marketing computer hardware and software, consumer electronics, financial services, and certain other classes of products. However, it makes online marketing less effective for selling mainstream products.

■ *Chaos and clutter:* The Internet offers millions of Web sites and a staggering volume of information. Thus, navigating the Internet can be frustrating, confusing, and time-consuming for consumers. In this chaotic and cluttered environment, many Web ads and sites go unnoticed or unopened. Even when noticed, marketers will find it difficult to hold consumer attention. One study found that a site must capture Web surfers' attention within eight seconds or lose them to another site. That leaves very little time for marketers to promote and sell their goods.

■ *Security:* Consumers still worry that unscrupulous snoopers will eavesdrop on their online transactions or intercept their credit card numbers and make unauthorized purchases. In turn, companies doing business online fear that others will use the Internet to invade their computer systems for the purposes of commercial espionage or even sabotage. Online marketers are developing solutions to such security problems. However, there appears to be an ongoing competition between the technology of Internet security systems and the sophistication of those seeking to break them.

■ *Ethical concerns:* Privacy is a primary concern. Marketers can easily track Web site visitors, and many consumers who participate in Web site activities provide extensive personal information.

[52]Amy Cortese, "It's Called Webcasting, and It Promises to Deliver the Info You Want, Straight to Your PC," *Business Week,* Feb-ruary 24, 1997, pp. 95–104. Also see Kenneth Leung, "Marketing with Electronic Mail Without Spam," *Marketing News,* January 19, 1998, p. 11; Philip M. Perry, "E-mail Hell: The Dark Side of the Internet Age," *Folio: The Magazine for Magazine Management,* June 1998, pp. 74–75; and Chad Kaydo, "As Good As It Gets," *Sales & Marketing Management,* March 2000, pp. 55–60.

[53]Heather Green, "Cyberspace Winners: How They Did It," *Business Week,* June 22, 1998, pp. 154–60; and "Believe It or Not, Web Stores Can Make Money," *Computerworld,* December 7, 1998, p. 4. Also see Michael D. Donahue, "Adapting the Internet to the Needs of Business," *Advertising Age,* February 2, 1998, p. 26; Shikhar Ghosh, "Making Business Sense of the Internet," *Harvard Business Review,* March–April 1998, pp. 126–35; and Lisa Bransten, "E-Commerce (A Special Report)—A New Model—The Bottom Line: If They Built It, Will Profits Come?" *Wall Street Journal,* July 12, 1999, p. R8.

[54]"eCommerce: Consumers and Shopping Online," accessed online at www.emarketer.com/estats/ec_shop.html, September 1999.

This may leave consumers open to information abuse if companies make unauthorized use of the information in marketing their products or exchanging electronic lists with other companies. There are also concerns about segmentation and discrimination. The Internet currently serves upscale consumers well. However, poorer consumers have less access to the Internet, leaving them increasingly less informed about products, services, and prices.[55]

Despite these challenges, companies large and small are quickly integrating online marketing into their marketing mixes. As it continues to grow, online marketing will prove to be a powerful tool for building customer relationships, improving sales, communicating company and product information, and delivering products and services more efficiently and effectively.

active concept check <

Now let's take a moment to test your knowledge of what you've just read.

> Integrated Direct Marketing

Too often, a company's individual direct-marketing efforts are not well integrated with one another or with other elements of its marketing and promotion mixes. For example, a firm's media advertising may be handled by the advertising department working with a traditional advertising agency. Meanwhile, its direct-mail and catalog business efforts may be handled by direct-marketing specialists while its Web site is developed and operated by an outside Internet firm.

Within a given direct-marketing campaign, too many companies use only a "one-shot" effort to reach and sell a prospect or a single vehicle in multiple stages to trigger purchases. For example, a magazine publisher might send a series of four direct-mail notices to a household to get a subscriber to renew before giving up. A more powerful approach is **integrated direct marketing,** which involves using carefully coordinated multiple-media, multiple-stage campaigns. Such campaigns can greatly improve response. Whereas a direct-mail piece alone might generate a 2 percent response, adding a Web site and toll-free phone number might raise the response rate by 50 percent. Then, a well-designed outbound telemarketing effort might lift response by an additional 500 percent. Suddenly, a 2 percent response has grown to 15 percent or more by adding interactive marketing channels to a regular mailing.

More elaborate integrated direct-marketing campaigns can be used. Consider the multimedia, multistage campaign shown in Figure 17.2. Here, the paid ad creates product awareness and stimulates inquiries. The company immediately sends direct mail to those who inquire. Within a few days, the company follows up with a phone call seeking an order. Some prospects will order by phone; others might request a face-to-face sales call. In such a campaign, the marketer seeks to improve response rates and profits by adding media and stages that contribute more to additional sales than to additional costs.

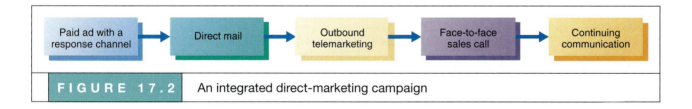

| Paid ad with a response channel | → | Direct mail | → | Outbound telemarketing | → | Face-to-face sales call | → | Continuing communication |

FIGURE 17.2   An integrated direct-marketing campaign

[55]See "Digital Divide Persists in the U.S.," obtained online at www.cyberatlas.com, July 8, 1999; "Privacy: On-Line Groups Are Offering Up Privacy Plans," *Wall Street Journal,* June 22, 1998, p. B1; Edward C. Baig, Marcia Stepanek, and Neil Gross, "Privacy: The Internet Wants Your Personal Information. What's in It for You?" *Business Week,* April 5, 1999, pp. 84–90; and Marcia Stepanek, "A Small Town Reveals America's Digital Divide," *Business Week,* October 4, 1999, pp. 188–98.

> # video exercise

Consider an example of online marketing and integrated direct marketing.

> # active concept check

Now let's take a moment to test your knowledge of what you've just read.

> ## Public Policy and Ethical Issues in Direct Marketing

Direct marketers and their customers usually enjoy mutually rewarding relationships. Occasionally, however, a darker side emerges. The aggressive and sometimes shady tactics of a few direct marketers can bother or harm consumers, giving the entire industry a black eye. Abuses range from simple excesses that irritate consumers to instances of unfair practices or even outright deception and fraud. During the past few years, the direct-marketing industry has also faced growing concerns about invasion-of-privacy issues.[56]

IRRITATION, UNFAIRNESS, DECEPTION, AND FRAUD

Direct-marketing excesses sometimes annoy or offend consumers. Most of us dislike direct-response TV commercials that are too loud, too long, and too insistent. Especially bothersome are dinnertime or late-night phone calls. Beyond irritating consumers, some direct marketers have been accused of taking unfair advantage of impulsive or less sophisticated buyers. TV shopping shows and program-long "infomercials" seem to be the worst culprits. They feature smooth-talking hosts, elaborately staged demonstrations, claims of drastic price reductions, "while they last" time limitations, and unequaled ease of purchase to inflame buyers who have low sales resistance.

Worse yet, so-called heat merchants design mailers and write copy intended to mislead buyers. Political fund-raisers, among the worst offenders, sometimes use gimmicks such as "look-alike" envelopes that resemble official documents, simulated newspaper clippings, and fake honors and awards. Other direct marketers pretend to be conducting research surveys when they are actually asking leading questions to screen or persuade consumers. Fraudulent schemes, such as investment scams or phony collections for charity, have also multiplied in recent years. Crooked direct marketers can be hard to catch: Direct-marketing customers often respond quickly, do not interact personally with the seller, and usually expect to wait for delivery. By the time buyers realize that they have been bilked, the thieves are usually somewhere else plotting new schemes.

> # active example

Consider the work of one organization dedicated to stamping out direct-marketing fraud.

[56]Portions of this section are based on Terrence H. Witkowski, "Self-Regulation Will Suppress Direct Marketing's Downside," *Marketing News,* April 24, 1989, p. 4. Also see Katie Muldoon, "The Industry Must Rebuild Its Image," *Direct,* April 1995, p. 106; Jim Castelli, "How to Handle Personal Information," *American Demographics,* March 1996, pp. 50–57; and Elyssa Yoon-Jung Lee, "How Do You Say 'Leave Me Alone?'" *Money,* June 1998, p. 140.

INVASION OF PRIVACY

Invasion of privacy is perhaps the toughest public policy issue now confronting the direct-marketing industry. These days, it seems that almost every time consumers enter a sweepstakes, apply for a credit card, take out a magazine subscription, or order products by mail, telephone, or the Internet, their names are entered into some company's already bulging database. Using sophisticated computer technologies, direct marketers can use these databases to "microtarget" their selling efforts.

Consumers often benefit from such database marketing—they receive more offers that are closely matched to their interests. However, many critics worry that marketers may know *too* much about consumers' lives and that they may use this knowledge to take unfair advantage of consumers. At some point, they claim, the extensive use of databases intrudes on consumer privacy.

For example, they ask, should AT&T be allowed to sell marketers the names of customers who frequently call the 800 numbers of catalog companies? Should a company like American Express be allowed to make data on its 175 million American cardholders available to merchants who accept AmEx cards? Is it right for credit bureaus to compile and sell lists of people who have recently applied for credit cards—people who are considered prime direct-marketing targets because of their spending behavior? Or is it right for states to sell the names and addresses of driver's license holders, along with height, weight, and gender information, allowing apparel retailers to target tall or overweight people with special clothing offers?

In their drives to build databases, companies sometimes get carried away. For example, when first introduced, Intel's new Pentium III chip contained an imbedded serial number that allowed the company to trace users' equipment. When privacy advocates screamed, Intel disabled the feature. Similarly, Microsoft caused substantial privacy concerns when it introduced its Windows 95 software. It used a "Registration Wizard," which allowed users to register their new software online. However, when users went online to register, without their knowledge, Microsoft took the opportunity to "read" the configurations of their PCs. Thus, the company gained instant knowledge of the major software products running on each customer's system. When users learned of this invasion, they protested loudly and Microsoft abandoned the practice. Such actions have spawned a quiet but determined "privacy revolt" among consumers and public policy makers.[57]

In one survey of consumers, 79 percent of respondents said that they were concerned about threats to their personal privacy. In a survey of Internet users, 71 percent of respondents said there should be laws to protect Web privacy and a full 84 percent objected to firms selling information about users to other companies. In yet another survey, *Advertising Age* asked advertising industry executives how they felt about database marketing and the privacy issue. The responses of two executives show that even industry insiders have mixed feelings:[58]

> There are profound ethical issues relating to the marketing of specific household data—financial information, for instance. . . . For every household in the United States, the computer can guess with amazing accuracy . . . things like credit use, net worth, and investments, the kind of information most people would never want disclosed, let alone sold to any marketer.

> It doesn't bother me that people know I live in a suburb of Columbus, Ohio, and have X number of kids. It [does] bother me that these people know the names of my wife and kids and where my kids go to school. They . . . act like they know me when the bottom line is they're attempting to sell me something. I do feel that database marketing has allowed companies to cross the fine line of privacy. . . . [And] in a lot of cases, I think they know they have crossed it.

The direct-marketing industry is addressing issues of ethics and public policy. For example, the Direct Marketing Association (DMA)—the largest association for businesses interested in interactive and database marketing with more than 4,600 member companies—recently developed its "Privacy Promise to American Consumers." This initiative, an effort to build consumer confidence in shopping direct, requires that all DMA members adhere to a carefully developed set of consumer privacy rules. The Privacy Promise requires that members notify customers when any personal information is rented, sold, or exchanged with others. Members must also honor consumer requests not to receive mail, telephone, or other solicitations again.

---

[57]John Hagel III and Jeffrey F. Rayport, "The Coming Battle for Customer Information," *Harvard Business Review,* January–February 1997, pp. 53–65; Bruce Horovitz, "AmEx Kills Database Deal After Privacy Outrage," *USA Today,* July 15, 1998, p. B1; Carol Krol, "Consumers Reach the Boiling Point," *Advertising Age,* March 29, 1999, p. 22; and Heather Green, Mike France, and Marcia Stepanek, "It's Time for Rules in Wonderland," *Business Week,* March 20, 2000, pp. 83–96.

[58]Melanie Rigney, "Too Close for Comfort, Execs Warn," *Advertising Age,* January 13, 1992, p. 31. Also see "Summary of '1992 Harris-Equifax Consumer Privacy Survey,'" *Marketing News,* August 16, 1993, p. A18; and Jennifer Lach, "The New Gatekeepers," *American Demographics,* June 1999, pp. 41–42.

The DMA recently developed its "Privacy Promise to American Consumers," which attempts to build consumer confidence by requiring that all DMA members adhere to certain carefully developed consumer privacy rules.

Direct marketers know that, left untended, such problems will lead to increasingly negative consumer attitudes, lower response rates, and calls for more restrictive state and federal legislation. More importantly, most direct marketers want the same things that consumers want: honest and well-designed marketing offers targeted only toward consumers who will appreciate and respond to them. Direct marketing is just too expensive to waste on consumers who don't want it.

> active concept check

Now let's take a moment to test your knowledge of what you've just read.

> Chapter Wrap-Up

Now that you've reached the end of the chapter, you may wish to explore the concepts you've been reading about in greater detail, or test yourself to see how well you've comprehended the material. In the box below you'll find a number of links. Click on any one of these links to find additional chapter resources.

> end-of-chapter resources

- Review of Concept Connections
- Practice Quiz
- Tying it All Together (Audio)
- Key Terms
- Critical Thinking Exercises
- Experimential Exercises
- MyPHLIP Companion Web Site
- Case 1
- Case 2
- You Be the Consultant

Competitive Strategies: Attracting, Retaining, and Growing Customers

CHAPTER 18

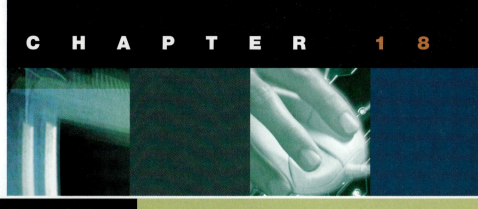

> What's Ahead

Entering the new millennium, PC maker Gateway, Inc. faces some daunting challenges—plummeting PC prices that put the squeeze on profit margins; the exploding and often baffling Internet; and deep-pockets competitors like IBM, Compaq, and Dell, all vying for shares of the consumer's computer budget. To survive and thrive, Gateway will need a strong, customer-focused marketing strategy—and it appears to have found one. Call it an "own the customer" strategy, one that focuses not just on gaining share of the market but also on growing "share of customer" and capturing customer lifetime value.

"At the core of [Gateway's] strategy is a simple idea," writes *Business Week* analyst Steven Brull. "Grab customers early on and keep them generating incremental revenue through a variety of services. The relationship starts with the purchase of a PC. . . . Then Gateway [locks] in those customers through financing, Internet access, and a personalized portal that will steer them to Gateway's e-commerce sites."

Thus, Gateway has devised a three-phase strategy for attracting, retaining, and growing customers. Phase one centers on PC sales. Gateway attracts new buyers through media advertising, telemarketing, online selling, and its national network of almost 200 Gateway Country retail stores. It targets primarily first-time buyers and small businesses, customers who have not yet formed strong brand loyalties. Gateway's low prices, financing, and training classes make it easy for these new buyers to get started on a Gateway machine. Gateway was the first computer company to introduce consumer-PC leases—it lets buyers pay for their computers in monthly installments as low as $28 over a two-year period. When the two years are up, buyers can keep the machine or receive trade-in value toward a new model. To help novice buyers figure out how to use their new computers, Gateway offers training courses that start at $75 for three hours. This extended financing and training relationship serves buyers well. It also benefits Gateway: Higher margins on credit and training revenues help offset the razor-thin margins Gateway gets on its low-priced PCs.

The PC purchase is just the first stop on what Gateway hopes will be a lifelong journey with the customer. In phase two, the connection lengthens. To entice buyers online, and to develop a more permanent relationship, Gateway offers a free one-year subscription to Gateway.net, the company's Internet access service. About 400,000 customers already subscribe to Gateway.net and the company is mounting a direct-marketing campaign to woo its 5 million customers who are not yet subscribers. It is also courting non-Gateway customers with sales pitches at its Gateway Country stores. After the free year ends, customers pay $17.95 a month to continue, creating additional sales and a longer-term customer connection for Gateway. The company expects to have as many as 3 million subscribers by the end of 2000, making it the number-two Internet service provider behind America Online.

In phase three, the relationship deepens. Beyond selling computers and linking customers to the Internet through Gateway.net, Gateway goes all out to earn a big share of customers' e-commerce business. "The big dollars can be earned after the PC is plugged into the Net," says analyst Brull. "To keep customers coming back, Gateway offers each customer a customized home page created in partnership with portal Yahoo!" When completing a PC sale, Gateway reps collect information for tailoring home pages to individual preferences. "When we deliver a PC," adds Jeffrey Weitzen, Gateway's president and chief operating officer, "we want you to be registered on the Net, with software loaded and a personalized portal for news, weather, and stocks."

Of course, the personalized Web page also puts customers within a mouse click of the company's SpotShop.com site. Once there, they can buy any of more than 30,000 items, including computer hardware, software, and accessories but also office and personal technology products, ranging from digital cameras and projectors to personal digital assistants. Moreover, it looks as though Gateway might have plans for garnering an even greater share of customers' online dollars in other categories. For example, the company has registered such Web addresses as spotgames.com, travelinfospot.com, and spotedu.com.

Thus, Gateway isn't just a PC company anymoreits interests in the customer go far beyond the initial sale. In fact, Gateway anticipates that within the next two years or so services such as training, consulting, and Internet access will account for more than a third of its sales and half its profits. "Smart marketers build lifetime customer relationships, rather than trying to drive a [specific] purchase event," says another analyst. "In the past (or for those still living there), the goal . . . was to make the phone ring, or cause the prospect to buy a product in the shortest possible time. The reality today is that as growth slows, the requirement changes from finding sales to growing customers . . . from 'selling' to 'managing lifetime value.' [More than any other PC company,] Gateway has been focused on the ongoing relationship."

Says Gateway's president, "Gateway works harder than anyone to build lifelong relationships with consumers based on trust and complete personalization. Our clients have responded to that relationship with repeat purchases and by recommending us to friends, family members, and business associates. We're going to continue working harder than ever to remain worthy of our client's loyalty." Gateway's "own the customer" strategy appears to be working well. The company's sales have grown by more than 20 percent in each of the last two years, and over the past five years its stock price has jumped eightfold. Perhaps more importantly, the relationship between Gateway and its customers appears to go both ways. In a recent study by AC Nielsen's Tech*Watch, Gateway ranked number one in customer loyalty among major PC makers.[1]

> objectives

Before you begin, take a moment to familiarize yourself with the key objectives of this chapter.

> gearing up

Before we begin our exploration this chapter, take a short warm-up test to see what you know about this topic.

Today's companies face their toughest competition ever. In previous chapters, we argued that to succeed in today's fiercely competitive marketplace, companies will have to move from a *product and selling philosophy* to a *customer and marketing philosophy*. This chapter spells out in more detail how companies can go about outperforming competitors in order to win and keep customers. To win in today's marketplace, companies must become adept not just in *building products,* but in *building customers.* The answer lies in doing a better job than competitors do of delivering customer value and satisfaction.

We first address several important questions relating *customer relationship marketing.* What are the key building blocks for attracting, retaining, and growing profitable customers? What are customer value and satisfaction? How is customer satisfaction related to customer loyalty and retention? How can a company grow its "share of customer"? Who in the organization is responsible for building and maintaining customer relationships? What is the role of total quality marketing? Next, we examine *competitive marketing strategies*—how companies analyze their competitors and develop successful, value-based strategies for attracting, retaining, and growing customers.

> Customer Relationship Marketing

Traditional marketing theory and practice have focused on attracting new customers rather than retaining existing ones. Today, however, although attracting new customers remains an important marketing task, the emphasis has shifted toward **relationship marketing**—creating, maintaining, and enhancing strong relationships with customers and other stakeholders. Beyond designing strategies to *attract* new customers and create *transactions* with them, companies are going all out to *retain* current customers and build profitable, long-term *relationships* with them. The new view is that marketing is the science and art of finding, retaining, *and* growing profitable customers.

Why the new emphasis on retaining and growing customers? In the past, many companies took their customers for granted. Facing an expanding economy and rapidly growing markets, companies

[1]Quotes and other information from "Gateway Ranks #1 in Both Client Loyalty and U.S. Consumer Desktop Shipments," press release accessed online at www.gateway.com, June 15, 1999; Steven V. Brull, "A Net Gain for Gateway," *Business Week,* July 19, 1999, pp. 77–78; Aaron Goldberg, "Going Long," *MC Technology Marketing Intelligence,* May 1999, p. 14; and Gary McWilliams, "Gateway Managers to Smooth Out Earnings and Bull Ahead in Internet-Service Business," *Wall Street Journal,* July 12, 1999, p. C2.

could practice a "leaky bucket" approach to marketing. Growing markets meant a plentiful supply of new customers. Companies could keep filling the marketing bucket with new customers without worrying about losing old customers through holes in the bottom of the bucket.

However, companies today are facing some new marketing realities. Changing demographics, more sophisticated competitors, and overcapacity in many industriesall of these factors mean that there are fewer customers to go around. Many companies are now fighting for shares of flat or fading markets. Thus, the costs of attracting new consumers are rising. In fact, it costs five times as much to attract a new customer as it does to keep a current customer satisfied.[2]

Companies are also realizing that losing a customer means losing more than a single sale: It means losing the entire stream of purchases that the customer would make over a lifetime of patronage. For example, here is a dramatic illustration of **customer lifetime value:**

> Stew Leonard, who operates a highly profitable single-store supermarket, says that he sees $50,000 flying out of his store every time he sees a sulking customer. Why? Because his average customer spends about $100 a week, shops 50 weeks a year, and remains in the area for about 10 years. If this customer has an unhappy experience and switches to another supermarket, Stew Leonard has lost $50,000 in revenue. The loss can be much greater if the disappointed customer shares the bad experience with other customers and causes them to defect.

Similarly, the customer lifetime value of a Taco Bell customer exceeds $12,000. Lexus estimates that a single satisfied and loyal customer is worth $600,000 in lifetime sales.[3] Thus, working to retain and grow customers makes good economic sense. A company can lose money on a specific transaction but still benefit greatly from a long-term relationship.

ATTRACTING, RETAINING, AND GROWING CUSTOMERS

The key to building lasting relationships is the creation of superior customer value and satisfaction. Satisfied customers are more likely to be loyal customers, and loyal customers are more likely to give the company a larger share of their business. We now look more closely at the concepts of customer value and satisfaction, loyalty and retention, and share of customer.

Customer lifetime value: Stew Leonard's does all it can to keep customers satisfied.

[2]See Kevin J. Clancy and Robert S. Shulman, "Breaking the Mold," *Sales & Marketing Management,* January 1994, pp. 82–84; Thomas O. Jones and W. Earl Sasser Jr., "Why Satisfied Customers Defect," *Harvard Business Review,* November–December 1995, pp. 88–99; Susan Fournier, Susan Dobscha, and David Glen Mick, "Preventing the Premature Death of Relationship Marketing," *Harvard Business Review,* January–February 1998, pp. 42–50; and Erika Rasmusson, "Complaints Can Build Relationships," *Sales & Marketing Management,* September 1999, p. 89.

[3]Libby Estell, "This Call Center Accelerates Sales," *Sales & Marketing Management,* February 1999, p. 72.

Relationship Building Blocks: Customer Value and Satisfaction

Attracting and retaining customers can be a difficult task. Today's customers face a vast array of product and brand choices, prices, and suppliers. The company must answer a key question: How do customers make their choices? The answer is that customers choose the marketing offer that they believe will give them the most value. They are satisfied with and continue to buy offers that consistently meet or exceed their value expectations. Let's look more closely at customer value and satisfaction.

Customer Value. Consumers buy from the firm that they believe offers the highest **customer delivered value**—the difference between total customer value and total customer cost (see Figure 18.1).[4] For example, suppose that a large construction firm wants to buy a bulldozer. It will buy the bulldozer from either Caterpillar or Komatsu. The salespeople for the two companies carefully describe their respective offers to the buyer. The construction firm evaluates the two competing bulldozer offers to assess which one delivers the greatest value. It adds all the values from four sources—product, services, personnel, and image. First, it judges that Caterpillar's bulldozer provides higher reliability, durability, and performance. It also decides that Caterpillar has better accompanying services—delivery, training, and maintenance. The customer views Caterpillar personnel as more knowledgeable and responsive. Finally, it places higher value on Caterpillar's reputation. Thus, the customer decides that Caterpillar offers more *total customer value* than does Komatsu.

Does the construction firm buy the Caterpillar bulldozer? Not necessarily. The firm also will examine the **total customer cost** of buying Caterpillar's bulldozer versus Komatsu's. The total customer cost consists of more than just monetary costs. As Adam Smith observed more than two centuries ago, "The real price of anything is the toil and trouble of acquiring it." Total customer cost also includes the buyer's anticipated time, energy, and psychic costs. The construction firm evaluates these costs along with monetary costs to form a complete estimate of its costs.

The buying firm now compares total customer value to total customer cost and determines the total delivered value associated with Caterpillar's bulldozer. In the same way, it assesses the total delivered value for the Komatsu bulldozer. The firm then buys from the company that offers the highest delivered value.

Some marketers might rightly argue that this concept of how buyers choose among product alternatives is too rational. They might cite examples in which buyers did not choose the offer with the

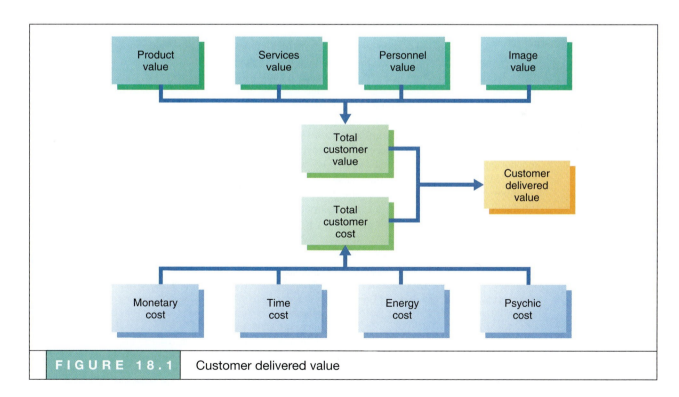

FIGURE 18.1 Customer delivered value

[4]For a thorough discussion on defining value, see Howard E. Butz Jr. and Leonard D. Goodstein, "Measuring Customer Value: Gaining Strategic Advantage," *Organizational Dynamics,* Winter 1996, pp. 63–77; and Robert B. Woodruff, "Customer Value: The Next Source of Competitive Advantage," *Journal of the Academy of Marketing Science,* Spring 1997, pp. 139–53.

highest delivered value. For example, suppose that the Caterpillar salesperson convinces the construction firm that Caterpillar's bulldozer offers a higher delivered value. Nonetheless, the customer decides to buy the Komatsu bulldozer. Why would the buyer make such a decision? There are many possible explanations. Perhaps the construction firm's buyers enjoy a long-term friendship with the Komatsu salesperson. Or the firm's buyers might be under strict orders to buy at the lowest price. Or perhaps the construction firm rewards its buyers for short-term performance, causing them to choose the less expensive Komatsu bulldozer, even though the Caterpillar machine will perform better and be less expensive to operate in the long run.

Clearly, buyers operate under various constraints and sometimes make choices that give more weight to their personal benefit than to company benefit. However, the customer delivered value framework applies to many situations and yields rich insights. It suggests that sellers must first assess the total customer delivered value associated with their own and competing marketing offers to determine how their own offers stack up. If competitors deliver greater value, the firm must act.

How might Caterpillar use this concept of buyer decision making to help it succeed in selling its bulldozer to this buyer? It can improve its offer in either of two ways. First, it can increase total customer value by strengthening or augmenting the product, services, personnel, or image benefits of its offer. Second, it can reduce total customer cost by lowering its price or by lessening the buyer's time, energy, and psychic costs. In fact, although Caterpillar products cost more than competing brands, the company claims that its higher quality, superior service, and strong reputation make its products a better value in the long run. Its goal is to provide customers with the lowest total cost per cubic yard of earth moved, ton of coal uncovered, or mile of road graded over the life of the product.[5]

Customer Satisfaction.   Thus, consumers form expectations about the value of marketing offers and make buying decisions based on these expectations. **Customer satisfaction** with a purchase depends on the product's actual performance relative to a buyer's expectations. A customer might experience various degrees of satisfaction. If the product's performance falls short of expectations, the customer is dissatisfied. If performance matches expectations, the customer is satisfied. If performance exceeds expectations, the customer is highly satisfied or delighted.[6]

But how do buyers form their expectations? Expectations are based on the customer's past buying experiences, the opinions of friends and associates, and marketer and competitor information and promises. Marketers must be careful to set the right level of expectations. If they set expectations too low, they may satisfy those who buy but fail to attract enough buyers. In contrast, if they raise expectations too high, buyers are likely to be disappointed. For example, Holiday Inn ran a campaign a few years ago called "No Surprises," which promised consistently trouble-free accommodations and service. However, Holiday Inn guests still encountered a host of problems, and the expectations created by the campaign only made customers more dissatisfied. Holiday Inn had to withdraw the campaign.

The American Customer Satisfaction Index, which tracks customer satisfaction in more than two dozen U.S. manufacturing and service industries, shows that overall customer satisfaction has been declining slightly in recent years.[7] It is unclear whether this has resulted from a decrease in product and service quality or from an increase in customer expectations. In either case, it presents an opportunity for companies that can consistently deliver superior customer value and satisfaction.

Today's most successful companies are raising expectations—and delivering performance to match. These companies embrace *total customer satisfaction.* For example, Honda claims "One reason our customers are so satisfied is that we aren't." Cigna vows "100% Satisfaction. 100% of the Time." Such companies track their customers' expectations, perceived company performance, and customer satisfaction. However, although the customer-centered firm seeks to deliver high customer satisfaction relative to competitors, it does not attempt to *maximize* customer satisfaction. A company can always increase customer satisfaction by lowering its price or increasing its services, but this may result in lower profits. Thus, the purpose of marketing is to generate customer value profitably. This

[5]See Donald V. Fites, "Make Your Dealers Your Partners," *Harvard Business Review,* March–April 1996, pp. 84–95; De Ann Weimer, "A New Cat on the Hot Seat," *Business Week,* March 1998, pp. 56–62; Woodruff, "Customer Value: The Next Source of Competitive Advantage," pp. 139–53; and James C. Anderson and James A. Narus, "Business Marketing: Understand What Customers Value," *Harvard Business Review,* November–December 1998, pp. 53–61.

[6]For an excellent discussion of the determinants of customer satisfaction, see Richard A. Spreng, Scott B. MacKenzie, and Richard W. Olshavsky, "A Reexamination of the Determinants of Customer Satisfaction," *Journal of Marketing,* July 1996, pp. 15–32; and Ruth N. Bolton and Katherine N. Lemon, "A Dynamic Model of Customers' Usage of Services: Usage as an Antecedent and Consequence of Satisfaction," *Journal of Marketing,* May 1999, pp. 171–86.

[7]See Claes Fornell, Michael D. Johnson, Eugene W. Anderson, Jaesung Cha, and Barbara Everitt Bryant, "The American Customer Satisfaction Index: Nature, Purpose, and Findings," *Journal of Marketing,* October 1996, pp. 7–18; Kevin Heubusch, ". . . But Quality Is Down," *American Demographics,* May 1998, p. 42; and Mike Campbell, "Happy Bank Customers? Think Again," *Bank Marketing,* April 1999, p. 10.

requires a very delicate balance: The marketer must continue to generate more customer value and satisfaction but not "give away the house."

> active example

Take a moment to read how customers are finding new venues to vent their grievances against companies.

Customer Loyalty and Retention

Highly satisfied customers produce several benefits for the company. Satisfied customers are less price sensitive, talk favorably to others about the company and its products, and remain loyal for a longer period. However, the relationship between customer satisfaction and loyalty varies greatly across industries and competitive situations. Figure 18.2 shows the relationship between customer satisfaction and loyalty in five different markets.[8] In all cases, as satisfaction increases, so does loyalty. In highly competitive markets, such as those for automobiles and personal computers, there is surprisingly little difference between the loyalty of less satisfied customers and those who are merely satisfied. However, there is a tremendous difference between the loyalty of *satisfied* customers and *completely satisfied* customers.

Even a slight drop from complete satisfaction can create an enormous drop in loyalty. For example, one study showed that completely satisfied customers are nearly 42 percent more likely to be loyal than merely satisfied customers. Another study by AT&T showed that 70 percent of customers who say they are satisfied with a product or service are still willing to switch to a competitor; customers who are *highly* satisfied are much more loyal. Xerox found that its totally satisfied customers are six times more likely to repurchase Xerox products over the next 18 months than its satisfied customers.[9] This means that com-

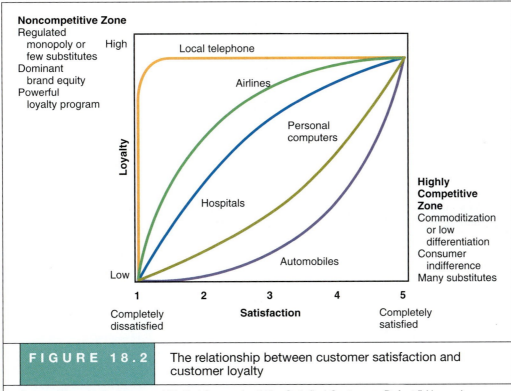

FIGURE 18.2   The relationship between customer satisfaction and customer loyalty

Source: Thomas O. Jones and W. Earl Sasser Jr., "Why Satisfied Customers Defect," *Harvard Business Review*, November–December 1995, p. 91. Copyright © 1997 by the President and Fellows of Harvard College; all rights reserved. Reprinted by permission of *Harvard Business Review*.

[8]Jones and Sasser, Jr. "Why Satisfied Customers Defect," pp. 88–99. Also see Thomas A. Stewart, "A Satisfied Customer Isn't Enough," *Fortune*, July 21, 1997, pp. 112–13.

panies must aim high if they want to hold on to their customers. Customer *delight* creates an emotional affinity for a product or service, not just a rational preference, and this creates high customer loyalty.

Figure 18.2 also shows that in noncompetitive markets, such as those served by regulated monopolies or those dominated by powerful or patent-protected brands, customers tend to remain loyal no matter how dissatisfied they are. This might seem like an ideal situation for the protected or dominant firm. However, such firms may pay a high price for customer dissatisfaction in the long run.

For example, during the 1960s and 1970s, Xerox flourished under the protection of patents on its revolutionary photocopy process. Customers had no choice but to remain loyal to Xerox, and sales and profits soared despite customer dissatisfaction over machine malfunctions and rising prices. In fact, customer dissatisfaction led to even *greater* short-run profits for Xerox: Disgruntled customers were forced to pay for service when machines broke down, and some even leased extra machines as backups. But as the 1980s dawned, Xerox paid dearly for its failure to keep its customers satisfied. Japanese competitors skirted patents and entered the market with higher quality copiers sold at lower prices. Dissatisfied customers gleefully defected to the new competitors. Xerox's share of the world copier market plunged from over 80 percent to less than 35 percent in just five years.[10] Thus, even highly successful companies must pay close attention to customer satisfaction and its relationship to customer loyalty. Xerox has now developed industry-leading, customer-driven quality, customer satisfaction, and customer retention programs. As a result, although it has lost its dominance, it is once again a profitable industry leader.

At the same time, a high customer satisfaction rating doesn't guarantee customer loyalty. A major insurance firm learned this when comparing its performance to competitor State Farm:

> A study comparing the competitor to State Farm showed only a 6.5 point spread between the percentage of respondents who were totally satisfied with the competitor and the percent totally satisfied with State Farm. So, how can we explain State Farm's consistently higher profitability over the years? The answer lies in customer loyalty. By using discounts and guarantees for long-term loyal customers and an agent compensation plan that encourages customer retention, State Farm has created strong customer loyalty. Although the study showed fairly minor differences in those totally satisfied, loyalty measures widened the gap between the companies. When customers were asked how strongly they preferred their life insurance company over others, there was an 11 percent spread between the competitor and State Farm. The gulf widened to a 15 percentage point State Farm lead on the statement, "I am very loyal to my company, it would take a lot to get me to switch." Twice as many respondents strongly agreed with the statement, "I would go out of my way to stay with my life insurance company," for State Farm than for the competitor.[11]

Thus, customer satisfaction remains an extremely important component in customer loyalty—a company will find it difficult to earn customer loyalty without first earning high levels of customer satisfaction. However, companies should also carefully examine customer loyalty itself, which often is a better indicator of customer attitudes and behavior.

active exercise <

Explore some ways in which the Internet is affecting customer loyalty.

Growing "Share of Customer"

Beyond simple attracting and retaining good customers, marketers want to constantly increase their *share of customer.* They want to capture a greater share of the customer's purchasing in their product categories, either by becoming the sole supplier of products the customer is currently buying or by

---

[9]Jones and Sasser, "Why Satisfied Customers Defect," p. 91. For other examples, see Roger Sant, "Did He Jump or Was He Pushed?" *Marketing News,* May 12, 1997, pp. 2, 21.

[10]See Joseph Juran, "Made in the U.S.A.: A Renaissance in Quality," *Harvard Business Review,* July–August 1993, pp. 42–50.

[11]Harry Seymour and Laura Rifkin, "Study Shows Satisfaction Not the Same as Loyalty," *Marketing News,* October 26, 1998, pp. 40, 42.

Growing "share of customer": American Airline's Airpass program benefits both the company and its customers. The customer gets better rates and more services; American gets most of the customer's business.

persuading the customer to purchase additional company products. Thus, banks want a greater "share of wallet," supermarkets want to increase their "share of stomach," car companies want a greater "share of garage," and airlines want a greater "share of travel."

Today, the goal isn't to win some business from a lot of customers—it's to win all the business of current customers. Feverishly chasing market share is out; trying to maximize share of customers is in. For example, seeking maximum share of Perot System's travel dollars, American Airlines sold the company a program called Airpass. Now, unless a travel schedule demands otherwise, all Perot employees fly American. It works like this: When Perot employees book flights, they don't have to bother waiting for tickets; they simply present a card at the ticket counter or gate. Miles are automatically credited to their American frequent flier accounts. Upgrades are readily available and, to complete the package, American allows all Perot employees to use its Ambassadors Clubs for business and leisure travel. For all of this, Perot gets charged at a discounted travel rate against a corporate commitment for a specified number of travel miles. In return, American gets most of Perot's business. It's a winning proposition for everyone—except American's competitors. They just got excluded from a lot of Perot's travel business.[12]

One of the best ways to increase share of customer is through cross-selling. Cross-selling means getting more business from current customers of one product or service by selling them additional offerings. For example, the recent merger between Citibank and Travelers is helping both units of the

[12]Example based on James Champy, "Taking Sales to New Heights," *Sales & Marketing Management,* July 1998, p. 26.

Citibank Group to cross-sell the company's services.[13] A new Travelers Financial Edge program allows independent Travelers agents to introduce a number of Citibank products to their insurance clients, such as credit cards and student loans, as well as an equipment leasing program for commercial customers. Similarly, under a new Citibank Partners program, Citibank representatives can offer a fuller slate of financial services to their customers, such as insurance from Travelers and mutual funds from Salomon Smith Barney (another Citibank Group unit). To support the effort to cross-sell a broader range of services for customers, Citibank's personal bankers will be dubbed "client financial analysts" and its branches will be called "Citibank Financial Centers." As a result, Citibank Group will obtain a larger share of each customer's financial services dollars.

video example <

One way of growing the "share of customer" is by collaborating with another organization or industry. Consider how one firm did so successfully.

BUILDING LASTING CUSTOMER RELATIONSHIPS

We can now see the importance of not just finding customers, but of keeping and growing them as well. Relationship marketing is oriented toward the long term. Today's smart companies not only want to create customers, they want to "own" them for life.

In this section, we discuss several questions about how companies actually build lasting customer relationships. What levels of relationships can companies build with their customers and what relationship-building tools do they use? Who is responsible for delivering customer value and satisfaction? What is the role of total marketing quality?

Customer Relationship Levels and Tools

Companies can build customer relationships at many levels—economic, social, technical, and legal—depending on the nature of the target market. At one extreme, a company with many low-margin customers may seek to develop *basic relationships* with them. For example, Procter & Gamble does not phone all of its Tide customers to get to know them personally and express its appreciation for their business. Instead, P&G creates relationships through brand-building advertising, sales promotions, a 1-800 customer response number, and its Tide ClothesLine Web site (**www.tide.com**). At the other

Basic relationships: Procter & Gamble doesn't get to know Tide customers personally, but it does create close relationships through brand-building advertising, sales promotions, a 1-800 customer response number, and its Tide ClothesLine Web site.

[13]See Philip Kotler, *Kotler on Marketing* (New York: Free Press, 1999), pp. 129–39; Don Peppers and Martha Rogers, "Growing Revenues with Cross-Selling," *Sales & Marketing Management,* February 1999, p. 24; Phil Zinkewicz, "Travelers Agents Begin Getting Access to Citicorp Products," *Rough Notes,* February 1999, pp. 22, 26; and Tara Siegel, "Citigroup Is Ready to Realize Benefits of Cross Selling," *Wall Street Journal,* March 15, 1999, p. B11.

extreme, in markets with few customers and high margins, sellers want to create *full partnerships* with key customers. For example, P&G customer teams work closely with Wal-Mart, Safeway, and other large retailers. Boeing works closely with American Airlines, Delta, and other airlines in designing its airplanes and ensuring that Boeing airplanes fully satisfy their requirements. In between these two extreme situations, other levels of relationship marketing are appropriate.

Today, more and more companies are developing customer loyalty and retention programs. Beyond offering consistently high value and satisfaction, marketers can use a number of specific marketing tools to develop stronger bonds with consumers.[14] First, a company might build value and satisfaction by adding *financial benefits* to the customer relationship. For example, many companies now offer *frequency marketing programs* that reward customers who buy frequently or in large amounts. Airlines offer frequent flier programs, hotels give room upgrades to their frequent guests, and supermarkets give patronage refunds.

Other companies sponsor *club marketing programs* that offer members special discounts and other benefits. For example:[15]

Swiss watchmaker, Swatch, uses its club to cater to collectors, who on average buy nine of the company's quirky watches every year. Club members can buy exclusives, such as the "Garden Turf" watch, a clear watch with an Astroturf band. They also receive the *World Journal,* a magazine filled with Swatch-centric news from the four corners of the globe. Swatch counts on enthusiastic word of mouth from club members as a boost to business. "Our members are like walking billboards," says the manager of Swatch's club, Trish O'Callaghan. "They love, live, and breathe our product. They are ambassadors for Swatch."

Upon submitting a $25 fee to the Volkswagen Club, members receive the first issue of a club magazine, *Volkswagen World,* a T-shirt, a road atlas and decal, a phone card, and discount offers on travel and recreation. Members can also take advantage of discounts on parts and service from local dealers, and, as a particularly nifty touch, members can apply for a club Visa card with a picture of their own VW on the front.

Thanks in part to its magic club aimed at children, Spain's Telepizza now claims a 65 percent share of the Spanish pizza market compared to less than 20 percent for Pizza Hut. As the largest membership club in Spain, with 3 million children enrolled, the magic club offers children small prizes, usually simple magic tricks, with every order.

Harley-Davidson sponsors the Harley Owners Group (HOG), which now numbers 330,000 members, about a third of all Harley owners. The first-time buyer of a Harley-Davidson motorcycle gets a free one-year membership with annual renewal costing $40. HOG benefits include a magazine (*Hog Tales*), a copy of the *H.O.G. Touring Handbook,* a complete *H.O.G. World Atlas,* an emergency pickup service, a specially designed insurance program, theft reward service, discount hotel rates, and a *Fly & Ride* program enabling members to rent Harleys while on vacation.

A second approach is to add *social benefits* as well as financial benefits. Here the company increases its social bonds with customers by learning individual customers' needs and wants and then personalizing its products and services. For example, to build better relationships with its customers, in the summer of 1994 and again in 1999 Saturn invited all of its owners to a "Saturn Homecoming" at its manufacturing facility in Spring Hill, Tennessee. The two-day affair included family events, plant tours, entertainment, and physical challenge activities designed to build trust and a team spirit. Says Saturn's manager of corporate communications, "The Homecoming party is another way of building . . . relationships, and it shows that we treat our customers differently than any other car company." More than 60,000 people attended the most recent homecoming, traveling from as far as

[14]Leonard L. Berry and A. Parasuraman, *Marketing Services: Competing Through Quality* (New York: Free Press, 1991), pp. 136–42.

[15]See Louise O'Brien and Charles Jones, "Do Rewards Really Create Loyalty?" *Harvard Business Review,* May–June 1995, pp. 75–82; "Harley Owners Journey to Meet Their Maker . . . Again and Again," *Colloquy,* 5, no. 4, 1997, pp. 13–14; Constance L. Hays, "What Companies Need to Know Is in the Pizza Dough," *New York Times,* July 26, 1998, p. 3, and Richard G. Barlow, "Future Looks Bright for Frequency Marketing," *Marketing News,* July 5, 1999, p. 14.

Alaska and Taiwan, with another 150,000 celebrating the occasion at the dealerships where they bought their cars.[16]

A third approach to building customer relationships is to add *structural ties* as well as financial and social benefits. For example, a business marketer might supply customers with special equipment or computer linkages that help them manage their orders, payroll, or inventory. McKesson Corporation, a leading pharmaceutical wholesaler, has invested millions of dollars in its electronic data interchange (EDI) system to help small pharmacies manage their inventory, their order entry, and their shelf space. FedEx offers Web links to its customers to keep them from defecting to competitors such as UPS. Customers can use the Web site to link with FedEx's computers, arrange shipments, and check the status of their FedEx packages.

Relationship marketing means that marketers must focus on managing their customers as well as their products. At the same time, they don't want relationships with every customer. In fact, there are undesirable customers for every company. Ultimately, marketing involves attracting, keeping, and growing *profitable* customers. Thus, in addition to assessing the value that it delivers *to* customers, a firm should actively measure the value *of* individual customers to the firm. Once it has identified profitable customers, it can create attractive offers and special handling to bind these customers to the company for a lifetime. But what should the company do with unprofitable customers? If it can't turn them into profitable ones, it may even want to "fire" customers that are too unreasonable or that cost more to serve than they are worth.

Figure 18.3 shows a useful type of analysis for assessing the value of a customer to a firm.[17] Customers make up the columns of the figure and products or services make up the rows. Each cell contains a symbol for the profitability of selling a given product or service to a given customer. Customer C_1 is very profitable—he or she buys three profit-making products, products P_1, P_2, and P_3. Customer C_2 yields mixed profitability, buying one profitable product and one unprofitable product. Customer C_3 generates losses by purchasing one profitable product and two unprofitable ones ("loss leaders"). What can the company do about consumers like C_3? First, the company should consider raising the prices of its less profitable products or eliminating them. Second, the company also can try to cross-sell its profit-making products to its unprofitable customers. If these actions cause customers like C_3 to defect, it may be for the good. In fact, the company might benefit by *encouraging* its unprofitable customers to switch to competitors.[18]

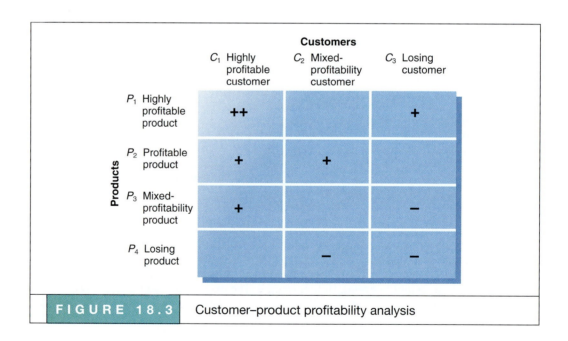

FIGURE 18.3   Customer–product profitability analysis

[16]Andy Cohen, "It's Party Time for Saturn," *Sales & Marketing Management,* June 1994, p. 19; T. L. Stanley, Betsy Spethman, Terry Lefton, and Karen Benezra, "Brand Builders," *Brandweek,* March 20, 1995, p. 20; Michelle Krebs, "Another Hoedown at Saturn Ranch," *New York Times,* March 14, 1999; and information accessed online at www.saturn.com/homecoming, January 2000.

[17]See Thomas M. Petro, "Profitability: The Fifth 'P' of Marketing," *Bank Marketing,* September 1990, pp. 48–52.

[18]See Rick Brooks, "Unequal Treatment: Alienating Customers Isn't Always a Bad Idea, Many Firms Discover," *Wall Street Journal,* January 7, 1999, p. A1; and Erika Rasmusson, "Wanted: Profitable Customers," *Sales & Marketing Management,* May 1999, pp. 28–34.

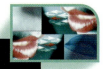

Delivering Customer Value and Satisfaction

Marketers alone cannot deliver superior customer value and satisfaction. Although it plays a leading role, marketing can be only a partner in attracting, keeping, and growing customers. Relationship marketing requires that marketers must work closely with other company departments to form an effective *value chain* that serves the customer. Moreover, the company can be effective only to the extent that it works effectively with its marketing system partners to form a competitively superior *value-delivery network*. We now take a closer look at the concepts of a company value chain and value-delivery network.

Company Value Chain.   Each company department can be thought of as a link in the company's **value chain**.[19] That is, each department carries out value-creating activities to design, produce, market, deliver, and support the firm's products. The firm's success depends not only on how well each department performs its work, but also on how well the activities of various departments are coordinated.

For example, we learned previously that the goal of Ritz-Carlton Hotels is to deliver "a truly memorable experience." Marketers make up an important link in the Ritz-Carlton value chain that creates this experience. They conduct research to learn about customer needs, design services to meet these needs, advertise to inform guests about services and locations, and perform other value-creating activities.

However, other departments must also perform well in order to make the Ritz-Carlton experience a reality. For example, the Ritz-Carlton housekeeping and maintenance staffs make certain that everything at the Ritz-Carlton looks and works just right, meeting customers' exacting standards for room cleanliness and functioning. The human resources department hires people-oriented employees, trains them carefully, and motivates them to ferret out and attend to even the slightest customer want. Ritz-Carlton employees treat customers as individuals, not as nameless, faceless members of a mass market. Whenever possible, they refer to guests by name and give each guest a warm welcome every day. Finally, the information systems department maintains an extensive customer database, which holds more than 500,000 individual customer preferences, accessible by all hotels in the worldwide Ritz chain. A frequent guest who requests a specific type of room at the Ritz in San Francisco will be delighted to find a similar room assigned when he or she checks into the Atlanta Ritz months later, arranged just the way that he or she likes it.[20]

A company's value chain is only as strong as its weakest link. Success depends on how well each department performs its work of adding value for customers and on how well the activities of different departments are coordinated. At Ritz-Carlton, if customer-contact people are poorly selected or trained, or if rooms are anything less than spotless, marketers cannot fulfill their promise of a truly memorable experience.

Customer Value-Delivery Network.   In its search for competitive advantage, the firm needs to look beyond its own value chain and into the value chains of its suppliers, distributors, and ultimately customers. Consider McDonald's. People do not swarm to the world's 24,500 McDonald's restaurants only because they love the chain's hamburgers. In fact, according to one national survey, consumers rank McDonald's behind Burger King and Wendy's in taste preference.[21] Still, McDonald's commands over a 16 percent share of the nation's fast-food business and over 40 percent of the burger segment. Consumers flock to the McDonald's *system,* not just to its food products. Throughout the

[19]Michael E. Porter, *Competitive Advantage: Creating and Sustaining Superior Performance* (New York: Free Press, 1985); and Michael E. Porter, "What Is Strategy?" *Harvard Business Review,* November–December 1996, pp. 61–78.

[20]Edwin McDowell, "Ritz-Carlton's Keys to Good Service," *New York Times,* March 31, 1993, p. 1; Don Peppers, "Digitizing Desire," *Forbes,* April 10, 1995, p. 76; Ginger Conlon, "True Romance," *Sales & Marketing Management,* May 1996, pp. 85–89; and "Ritz-Carlton Hotels Reign in Three Categories of *Travel & Leisure*'s 'World Best Awards' List," accessed online at www.ritz.carlton.com/corporate/ worldbest.htm, September 1999.

[21]Jennifer Waters, "High-Tech Test Restaurant Offers Customer Orders, More Efficiency," *Advertising Age,* April 14, 1997, p. 49.

world, McDonald's finely tuned system delivers a high standard of what the company calls QSCV—quality, service, cleanliness, and value. McDonald's is effective only to the extent that it successfully partners with its franchisees, suppliers, and others to jointly deliver exceptionally high customer value.

More companies today are "partnering" with the other members of the supply chain to improve the performance of the customer **value-delivery network.** For example, Honda has designed a program for working closely with its suppliers to help them reduce their costs and improve quality. When Honda chose Donnelly Corporation to supply all of the mirrors for its U.S.-made cars, it sent engineers swarming over Donnelly's plants, looking for ways to improve its products and operations. This helped Donnelly reduce its costs by 2 percent in the first year. As a result of its improved performance, Donnelly's sales to Honda have grown from $5 million annually to more than $60 million in less than 10 years. In turn, Honda has gained an efficient, low-cost supplier of quality components. As a result of Honda's partnerships with Donnelly and other suppliers, Honda customers receive greater value in the form of lower-cost, higher-quality cars.[22]

Increasingly in today's marketplace, competition no longer takes place between individual competitors. Rather, it takes place between the entire value-delivery networks created by these competitors. Thus, Honda's performance against another automaker—say Toyota—depends on the quality of Honda's overall value-delivery network versus Toyota's. Companies no longer compete—their entire marketing networks do.

active exercise   <

Take a moment to read how the Internet can be used to enhance a company's customer value-delivery network.

Total Quality Marketing

Customer relationships and company profitability are linked closely to product and service quality. Higher levels of quality result in greater customer satisfaction, while at the same time supporting higher prices and often lower costs. Therefore, *quality improvement programs* normally increase profitability. Today's executives view the task of improving product and service quality as a top priority.

Japan was the first country to award a national quality prize, the Deming prize, named after the American statistician who taught the importance of quality to postwar Japan. The quest for quality paid off handsomely. Consumers around the world flocked to buy high-quality Japanese products, leaving many American and European firms playing catch-up. In recent years, however, Western firms have closed the quality gap. Many have started their own quality programs in an effort to compete both globally and at home with the Japanese.

In the mid-1980s, the United States established the Malcolm Baldrige National Quality Award, which encourages U.S. firms to implement quality practices. Not wanting to be left out of the quality race, Europe developed the European Quality Award in 1993. It also initiated an exacting set of quality standards called ISO 9000. Whereas the Baldrige and other quality awards measure less tangible aspects of quality, such as customer satisfaction and continuous improvement, ISO 9000 is a set of specific international standards on quality management and quality assurance. More than 74 countries have officially recognized ISO 9000 as an international standard for quality systems. Many companies in these countries are now demanding ISO certification as a prerequisite for doing business with a seller. To earn ISO 9000 certification, sellers must undergo a quality audit every six months by a registered ISO (International Standards Organization) assessor. Thus, total quality has become a truly global concern.[23]

Most customers will no longer accept or tolerate average quality. If companies want to stay in the race, let alone be profitable, they have no choice but to adopt quality concepts. But what exactly is quality? Various experts have defined *quality* as "fitness for use," "conformance to requirements," and "freedom from variation." The American Society for Quality defines **quality** as the totality of features

---

[22]Myron Magnet, "The New Golden Rule of Business," *Fortune,* February 21, 1994, pp. 60–63. For more on supply chain management and strategic alliances, see also Rosabeth Moss Kanter, "Why Collaborate?" *Executive Excellence,* April 1999, p. 8; and Gabor Gari, "Leveraging the Rewards of Strategic Alliances," *The Journal of Business Strategy,* April 1999, pp. 40–43.

[23]See Otis Port, "Baldrige's Other Reward," *Business Week,* March 10, 1997, p. 75; "ISO 9000 and Quality: A World Class Advantage," special section, *Industrial Distribution,* January 1998, p. 61; Zhiwei Zhu and Larry Scheuermann, "A Comparison of Quality Programmes: Total Quality Management and ISO 9000," *Total Quality Management,* March 1999, pp. 291–97; and "Standards and Certification: ISO 9000," American Society for Quality, accessed online at www.asq.com, January 2000.

and characteristics of a product or service that bear on its ability to satisfy stated or implied needs.[24] This is clearly a customer-centered definition of quality. It suggests that a company has delivered quality whenever its product and service meet or exceed customers' needs, requirements, and expectations.

It is important to distinguish between performance quality and conformance quality. *Performance quality* refers to the *level* at which a product performs its functions. For example, a Mercedes provides higher performance quality than a Honda Civic: It has a smoother ride, handles better, and lasts longer. It is more expensive and sells to a market with higher means and requirements. *Conformance quality* refers to freedom from defects and the *consistency* with which a product delivers a specified level of performance. Thus, a Mercedes and a Honda Civic can be said to offer equivalent conformance quality to their respective markets to the extent that each consistently delivers what its market expects. A $50,000 car that meets all of its requirements is a quality car; so is an $18,000 car that meets all of its requirements. But if the Mercedes handles badly, or if the Honda gives poor fuel efficiency, then both cars have failed to deliver quality, and customer satisfaction suffers accordingly.

Total quality management (TQM) swept the corporate boardrooms of the 1980s. Many companies adopted the language of TQM but not the substance. Others viewed TQM as a cure-all for all the company's problems. Still others became obsessed with narrowly defined TQM principles and lost sight of broader concerns for customer value and satisfaction. As a result, many TQM programs begun in the 1980s failed, causing a backlash against TQM. Still, when applied in the context of creating customer satisfaction, total quality principles remain a requirement for success. Although many firms don't use the TQM label anymore, for most top companies customer-driven quality has become a way of doing business. They apply the notion of *return on quality (ROQ),* and they make certain that the quality they offer is the quality that customers want. This quality, in turn, results in improved sales and profits.[25]

Total quality is the key to creating customer value, satisfaction, and retention. Just as marketing is everyone's job, total quality is everyone's job:

> Marketers who don't learn the language of quality improvement, manufacturing, and operations will become as obsolete as buggy whips. The days of functional marketing are gone. We can no longer afford to think of ourselves as market researchers, advertising people, direct marketers, marketing strategists—we have to think of ourselves as customer satisfiers—customer advocates focused on whole processes.[26]

Marketers play a major role in helping their companies define and deliver high-quality products and services to target customers. First, marketers bear the major responsibility for correctly identifying the customers' needs and requirements and for communicating customer expectations correctly to product designers. They must take part in designing strategies and programs that help the company win through total quality excellence. Marketers must be the customer's watchdog or guardian, complaining loudly for the customer when the product or the service is not right. Second, marketing must deliver marketing quality as well as production quality. It must perform each marketing activity—marketing research, sales training, advertising, customer service, and others—to high-quality standards.

> ## video example

Consider how one prominent firm in the leisure industry works to deliver quality to its customers.

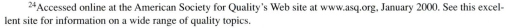

> ## active concept check

Now let's take a moment to test your knowledge of what you've just read.

---

[24]Accessed online at the American Society for Quality's Web site at www.asq.org, January 2000. See this excellent site for information on a wide range of quality topics.

[25]See Melissa Larson, "Whatever Happened to TQM?" *Quality,* June 1999, pp. 32–35; "TQM Is Alive," *Quality,* February 1999, p. 12; Roland T. Rust, Anthony J. Zahorik, and Timothy L. Keiningham, "Return on Quality (ROQ): Making Service Quality Financially Accountable," *Journal of Marketing,* April 1995, pp. 58–70; and Roland T. Rust, Timothy Keiningham, Stephen Clemens, and Anthony Zahorik, "Return on Quality at Chase Manhattan Bank," *Interfaces,* March–April 1999, pp. 62–72.

[26]J. Daniel Beckham, "Expect the Unexpected in Health Care Marketing Future," *The Academy Bulletin,* July 1992, p. 3.

Today, understanding customers is crucial, but it's not enough. Under the marketing concept, companies gain competitive advantage by satisfying target consumer needs *better than competitors do*. Thus, marketing strategies must consider not only the needs of target consumers but also the strategies of competitors. The first step is **competitor analysis,** the process of identifying, assessing, and selecting key competitors. The second step is developing **competitive marketing strategies** that strongly position the company against competitors and give it the greatest possible competitive advantage.

COMPETITOR ANALYSIS

To plan effective competitive marketing strategies, the company needs to find out all it can about its competitors. It must constantly compare its products, prices, channels, and promotion with those of close competitors. In this way the company can find areas of potential competitive advantage and disadvantage. As shown in Figure 18.4, competitor analysis involves first identifying and assessing competitors and then selecting which competitors to attack or avoid.

Identifying Competitors

Normally, it would seem a simple task for a company to identify its competitors. At the narrowest level, a company can define its competitors as other companies offering similar products and services to the same customers at similar prices. Thus, Coca-Cola might view Pepsi as a major competitor, but not Budweiser or Kool-Aid. Buick might see Ford as a major competitor, but not Mercedes or Hyundai.

But companies actually face a much wider range of competitors. The company might define competitors as all firms making the same product or class of products. Thus, Buick would see itself as competing against all other automobile makers. Even more broadly, competitors might include all companies making products that supply the same service. Here Buick would see itself competing not only against other automobile makers but also against companies that make trucks, motorcycles, or even bicycles. Finally, and still more broadly, competitors might include all companies that compete for the same consumer dollars. Here Buick would see itself competing with companies that sell major consumer durables, new homes, or vacations abroad.

Companies must avoid "competitor myopia." A company is more likely to be "buried" by its latent competitors than its current ones. For example, in its detergent business, Unilever has worried most about growing competition from Procter & Gamble and other detergent manufacturers. But Unilever may face a much greater threat from research being done on an ultrasonic washing machine. If perfected, this machine would wash clothes in water with little or no detergent. What greater threat is there to the detergent business than detergentless washing?

Similarly, Encyclopedia Britannica viewed itself as competing with other publishers of printed encyclopedia sets selling for as much as $2,200 per set. However, it learned a hard lesson when Microsoft Encarta, an encyclopedia on CD-ROM, was introduced and sold for only $50. It seems that parents bought the *Britannica* less for its intellectual content than out of a desire to do what's right for their children. Although less comprehensive than the *Britannica,* Encarta and other CD-ROM encyclopedias served this "do what's right" purpose well. By the time *Britannica* introduced its own CD-ROM and online versions, its sales plunged by more than 50 percent. Thus, Encyclopedia Britannica's real competitor was the computer.[27]

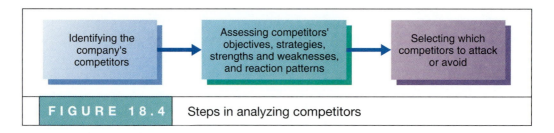

| Identifying the company's competitors | → | Assessing competitors' objectives, strategies, strengths and weaknesses, and reaction patterns | → | Selecting which competitors to attack or avoid |

FIGURE 18.4   Steps in analyzing competitors

[27]Philip B. Evans and Thomas S. Wurster, "Strategy and the New Economics of Information," *Harvard Business Review,* September– October 1997, pp. 70–83; Michael Krantz, "Click Till You Drop," *Time,* July 20, 1998, pp. 34–39; Ed Tallent, "Encyclopedia Britannica Online," *Library Journal,* May 15, 1999, pp. 138–39; and "Withering Britannica Bets It All on the Web," *Fortune,* November 22, 1999, p. 344. For more on identifying competitors, see "Bruce H. Clark and David Montgomery, "Managerial Identification of Competitors," *Journal of Marketing,* July 1999, pp. 67–83.

Assessing Competitors

Having identified the main competitors, marketing management now asks: What does each competitor seek in the marketplace? What is each competitor's strategy? What are various competitor's strengths and weaknesses, and how will each react to actions the company might take?

Each competitor has a mix of objectives. The company wants to know the relative importance that a competitor places on current profitability, market share growth, cash flow, technological leadership, service leadership, and other goals. Knowing a competitor's mix of objectives reveals whether the competitor is satisfied with its current situation and how it might react to different competitive actions. A company also must monitor its competitors' objectives for various segments. If the company finds that a competitor has discovered a new segment, this might be an opportunity. If it finds that competitors plan new moves into segments now served by the company, it will be forewarned and, hopefully, forearmed.

The more that one firm's strategy resembles another firm's strategy, the more the two firms compete. In most industries, the competitors can be sorted into groups that pursue different strategies. For example, in the major appliance industry, General Electric, Whirlpool, and Maytag all belong to the same strategic group. Each produces a full line of medium-price appliances supported by good service. Sub Zero and KitchenAid, on the other hand, belong to a different strategic group. They produce a narrower line of higher-quality appliances, offer a higher level of service, and charge a premium price.

Some important insights emerge from identifying strategic groups. For example, if a company enters one of the groups, the members of that group become its key competitors. Thus, the company needs to look at all of the dimensions that identify strategic groups within the industry. It needs to know each competitor's product quality, features, and mix; customer services; pricing policy; distribution coverage; sales force strategy; and advertising and sales promotion programs. It also must study the details of each competitor's R&D, manufacturing, purchasing, financial, and other strategies.

Marketers need to assess each competitor's strengths and weaknesses carefully in order to answer the critical question: What *can* our competitors do? Companies normally learn about their competitors' strengths and weaknesses through secondary data, personal experience, and hearsay. They also can conduct primary marketing research with customers, suppliers, and dealers. Or they can **benchmark** themselves against other firms, comparing the company's products and processes to those of competitors or leading firms in other industries to find ways to improve quality and performance. Benchmarking has become a powerful tool for increasing a company's competitiveness.

Finally, the company wants to know: What *will* our competitors do? A competitor's objectives, strategies, and strengths and weaknesses go a long way toward explaining its likely actions, as well as its likely reactions to company moves such as price cuts, promotion increases, or new-product introductions. In addition, each competitor has a certain philosophy of doing business, a certain internal culture and guiding beliefs. Marketing managers need a deep understanding of a given competitor's mentality if they want to anticipate how the competitor will act or react.

Each competitor reacts differently. Some do not react quickly or strongly to a competitor's move. They may feel their customers are loyal; they may be slow in noticing the move; they may lack the funds to react. Some competitors react only to certain types of moves and not to others. Other competitors react swiftly and strongly to any action. Thus, Procter & Gamble does not let a new detergent come easily into the market. Many firms avoid direct competition with P&G and look for easier prey, knowing that P&G will react fiercely if challenged.

In some industries, competitors live in relative harmony; in others, they fight constantly. Knowing how major competitors react gives the company clues on how best to attack competitors or how best to defend the company's current positions.

Selecting Competitors to Attack and Avoid

A company has already largely selected its major competitors through prior decisions on customer targets, distribution channels, and marketing mix strategy. These decisions define the strategic group to which the company belongs. Management now must decide which competitors to compete against most vigorously.

The company can focus on one of several classes of competitors. Most companies prefer to aim their shots at their *weak competitors*. This requires fewer resources and less time. But in the process, the firm may gain little. The argument could be made that the firm also should compete with *strong competitors* in order to sharpen its abilities. Furthermore, even strong competitors have some weaknesses, and succeeding against them often provides greater returns.

Most companies will compete with *close competitors*—those that resemble them most—rather than *distant competitors*. Thus, Chevrolet competes more against Ford than against Lexus. At the same time, the company may want to avoid trying to "destroy" a close competitor. For example, in the late 1970s, Bausch & Lomb moved aggressively against other soft lens manufacturers with great success. However, this forced weak competitors to sell out to larger firms such as Schering-Plough and Johnson & Johnson. As a result, Bausch & Lomb faced much larger competitors—and it suffered the consequences. Johnson & Johnson acquired Vistakon, a small nicher with only $20 million in annual sales. Backed by Johnson & Johnson's deep pockets, however, the small but nimble Vistakon developed and introduced its innovative Acuvue disposable lenses. According to one analyst, "The speed of the [Acuvue] rollout and the novelty of [Johnson & Johnson's] big-budget ads left giant Bausch & Lomb . . . seeing stars." By 1992, Vistakon was number one in the fast-growing disposable segment and had captured about 25 percent of the entire U.S. contact lens market.[28] In this case, success in hurting a close rival brought in tougher competitors.

A company really needs and benefits from competitors. The existence of competitors results in several strategic benefits. Competitors may help increase total demand. They may share the costs of market and product development and help to legitimize new technologies. They may serve less attractive segments or lead to more product differentiation. Finally, they lower the antitrust risk and improve bargaining power versus labor or regulators. For example, Intel's recent aggressive pricing on low-end computer chips has sent smaller rivals like MD and 3Com reeling. However, Intel may want to be careful not to knock these competitors completely out. "If for no other reason than to keep the feds at bay," notes one analyst, "Intel needs AMD, 3Com, and other rivals to stick around." Says another: "Intel may have put the squeeze on a little too hard. If AMD collapsed, the FTC would surely react."[29]

However, a company may not view all of its competitors as beneficial. An industry often contains *"well-behaved"* competitors and *"disruptive"* competitors.[30] Well-behaved competitors play by the rules of the industry. Disruptive competitors, in contrast, break the rules. They try to buy share rather than earn it, take large risks, and in general shake up the industry. For example, American Airlines finds Delta and United to be well-behaved competitors because they play by the rules and attempt to set their fares sensibly. But American finds Continental and America West disruptive competitors because they destabilize the airline industry through continual heavy price discounting and wild promotional schemes. The implication is that "well-behaved" companies would like to shape an industry that consists of only well-behaved competitors. A company might be smart to support well-behaved competitors, aiming its attacks at disruptive competitors. Thus, some analysts claim that American used huge fare discounts from time to time intentionally designed to teach disruptive airlines a lesson or to drive them out of business altogether.

active example <

Consider some additional ways that competitors may benefit a firm.

COMPETITIVE STRATEGIES

Having identified and evaluated its major competitors, the company now must design broad competitive marketing strategies by which it can gain competitive advantage by offering superior customer value. But what broad marketing strategies might the company use? Which ones are best for a particular company, or for the company's different divisions and products?

No one strategy is best for all companies. Each company must determine what makes the most sense given its position in the industry and its objectives, opportunities, and resources. Even within a company, different strategies may be required for different businesses or products. Johnson & Johnson uses one marketing strategy for its leading brands in stable consumer markets and a different marketing strategy for its new high-tech health care businesses and products. We now look at broad competitive marketing strategies companies can use.

[28]See Porter, *Competitive Advantage,* pp. 226–27; and Joseph Weber, "How J&J's Foresight Made Contact Lenses Pay," *Business Week,* May 4, 1992, p. 132.

[29]Andy Reinhardt, "Intel Is Taking No Prisoners," *Business Week,* July 12, 1999, p. 38.

[30]See Porter, *Competitive Advantage,* chap. 6.

Basic Competitive Strategies

More than a decade ago, Michael Porter suggested four basic competitive positioning strategies that companies can follow—three winning strategies and one losing one.[31] The three winning strategies include:

Overall cost leadership: Here the company works hard to achieve the lowest costs of production and distribution so that it can price lower than its competitors and win a large market share. Texas Instruments, Dell Computer, and Wal-Mart are leading practitioners of this strategy.

Differentiation: Here the company concentrates on creating a highly differentiated product line and marketing program so that it comes across as the class leader in the industry. Most customers would prefer to own this brand if its price is not too high. IBM and Caterpillar follow this strategy in information technology products and services and heavy construction equipment, respectively.

Focus: Here the company focuses its effort on serving a few market segments well rather than going after the whole market. For example, Ritz-Carlton focuses on the top 5 percent of corporate and leisure travelers. Glassmaker AFG Industries focuses on users of tempered and colored glass—it makes 70 percent of the glass for microwave oven doors and 75 percent of the glass for shower doors and patio tabletops.

Companies that pursue a clear strategy—one of the above—are likely to perform well. The firm that carries out that strategy best will make the most profits. But firms that do not pursue a clear strategy—*middle-of-the-roaders*—do the worst. Sears, Holiday Inn, and International Harvester encountered difficult times because they did not stand out as the lowest in cost, highest in perceived value, or best in serving some market segment. Middle-of-the-roaders try to be good on all strategic counts, but end up being not very good at anything.

More recently, two marketing consultants, Michael Treacy and Fred Wiersema, offered a new classification of competitive marketing strategies.[32] They suggest that companies gain leadership positions by delivering superior value to their customers. Companies can pursue any of three strategies—called *value disciplines*—for delivering superior customer value. These are:

Operational excellence: The company provides superior value by leading its industry in price and convenience. It works to reduce costs and to create a lean and efficient value-delivery system. It serves customers who want reliable, good-quality products or services, but who want them cheaply and easily. Examples include Wal-Mart and Dell Computer.

Customer intimacy: The company provides superior value by precisely segmenting its markets and then tailoring its products or services to match exactly the needs of targeted customers. It specializes in satisfying unique customer needs through a close relationship with and intimate knowledge of the customer. It builds detailed customer databases for segmenting and targeting, and empowers its marketing people to respond quickly to customer needs. It serves customers who are willing to pay a premium to get precisely what they want, and it will do almost anything to build long-term customer loyalty and to capture customer lifetime value. Examples include Nordstrom department stores, Lands' End outfitters, and Kraft General Foods.

Product leadership: The company provides superior value by offering a continuous stream of leading-edge products or services that make their own and competing products obsolete. It is open to new ideas, relentlessly pursues new solutions, and works to reduce cycle times so that it can get new products to market quickly. It serves customers who want state-of-the-art products and services, regardless of the costs in terms of price or inconvenience. Examples include Intel, Motorola, and Nike.

Some companies successfully pursue more than one value discipline at the same time. For example, Federal Express excels at both operational excellence and customer intimacy. However, such companies are rare—few firms can be the best at more than one of these disciplines. By trying to be *good at all* of the value disciplines, a company usually ends up being *best at none.*

---

[31]Michael E. Porter, *Competitive Strategy: Techniques for Analyzing Industries and Competitors* (New York: Free Press, 1980), chap. 2; and Porter, "What Is Strategy?" Also see James Surowiecki, "The Return of Michael Porter," *Fortune,* February 1, 1999, pp. 135–38.

[32]Michael Treacy and Fred Wiersema, "Customer Intimacy and Other Value Disciplines," *Harvard Business Review,* January–February 1993, pp. 84–93; Michael Treacy and Fred Wiersema, "How Market Leaders Keep Their Edge," *Fortune,* February 6, 1995, pp. 88–98; Michael Treacy and Fred Wiersema, *The Discipline of Market Leaders: Choose Your Customers, Narrow Your Focus, Dominate Your Market* (Perseus Press, 1997); and Fred Wiersema, *Customer Intimacy: Pick Your Partners, Shape Your Culture, Win Together* (Knowledge Exchange, 1998).

Treacy and Wiersema have found that leading companies focus on and excel at a single value discipline, while meeting industry standards on the other two. Such companies design their entire value-delivery network to single-mindedly support the chosen discipline. For example, Wal-Mart knows that customer intimacy and product leadership are important. Compared with other discounters, it offers very good customer service and an excellent product assortment. Still, it offers less customer service and less depth in its product assortment than do Lands' End or Nordstrom, which pursue customer intimacy. Instead, Wal-Mart focuses obsessively on operational excellence—on reducing costs and streamlining its order-to-delivery process in order to make it convenient for customers to buy just the right products at the lowest prices.

Classifying competitive strategies as value disciplines is appealing. It defines marketing strategy in terms of the single-minded pursuit of delivering superior value to customers. It recognizes that management must align every aspect of the company with the chosen value discipline—from its culture, to its organizational structure, to its operating and management systems and processes.

Competitive Positions

Firms competing in a given target market, at any point in time, differ in their objectives and resources. Some firms are large, others small. Some have many resources, others are strapped for funds. Some are old and established, others new and fresh. Some strive for rapid market share growth, others for long-term profits. The firms occupy different competitive positions in the target market.

We now examine competitive strategies based on the roles firms play in the target market—that of leading, challenging, following, or niching. Every industry contains a **market leader,** the firm with the largest market share. Most also contain one or more **market challengers,** runner-up firms that are fighting hard to increase their market share. **Market followers** are runner-up firms that want to hold their share without rocking the boat. Finally, **market nichers** serve small segments not being pursued by other firms.

We now look at specific marketing strategies that are available to market leaders, challengers, followers, and nichers (see Table 18.1).[33] Remember, however, that these classifications often do not apply to a whole company, but only to its position in a specific industry. Large and diversified companies such as IBM, Microsoft, Procter & Gamble, or Disney might be leaders in some markets and nichers in others. For example, Procter & Gamble leads in many segments, such as dishwashing and laundry detergents, disposable diapers, and shampoo, but it challenges Lever in the hand soaps and Kimberly-Clark in facial tissues. Such companies often use different strategies for different business units or products, depending on the competitive situations of each.

active example   <

Consider how one well-established company is working to maintain its competitive position.

Market Leader Strategies

Most industries contain an acknowledged market leader. The leader has the largest market share and usually leads the other firms in price changes, new-product introductions, distribution coverage, and promotion spending. The leader may or may not be admired or respected, but other firms concede its

TABLE 18.1	Strategies for Market Leaders, Challengers, Followers, and Nichers		
Market Leader Strategies	**Market Challenger Strategies**	**Market Follower Strategies**	**Market Nicher Strategies**
Expand total market	Full frontal attack	Follow closely	By customer, market,
Protect market share	Indirect attack	Follow at a distance	quality–price, service
Expand market share			Multiple niching

[33]For more discussion on defense and attack strategies, see Philip Kotler, *Marketing Management: Analysis, Planning, Implementation, and Control,* 10th ed. (Upper Saddle River, NJ: Prentice Hall, 2000), chap. 8.

dominance. Competitors focus on the leader as a company to challenge, imitate, or avoid. Some of the best-known market leaders are General Motors (autos), Kodak (photography), IBM (computers and information technology services), Caterpillar (earth-moving equipment), Coca-Cola (soft drinks), Wal-Mart (retailing), McDonald's (fast food), and Gillette (razors and blades).

A leader's life is not easy. It must maintain a constant watch. Other firms keep challenging its strengths or trying to take advantage of its weaknesses. The market leader can easily miss a turn in the market and plunge into second or third place. A product innovation may come along and hurt the leader (as when Nokia's and Ericsson's digital phones took the lead from Motorola's analog models). The leader might grow arrogant or complacent and misjudge the competition (as when Sears lost its lead to Wal-Mart and other emerging retailers). Or the leader might look old-fashioned against new and peppier rivals (as when Levi's lost serious ground to more current or stylish brands like Gap, Lees, Tommy Hilfiger, DKNY, or Guess).

To remain number one, leading firms can take any of three actions. First, they can find ways to expand total demand. Second, they can protect their current market share through good defensive and offensive actions. Third, they can try to expand their market share further, even if market size remains constant.

Expanding the Total Market.   The leading firm normally gains the most when the total market expands. If Americans take more pictures, Kodak stands to gain the most because it sells over 80 percent of this country's film. If Kodak can convince more Americans to take pictures, or to take pictures on more occasions, or to take more pictures on each occasion, it will benefit greatly.

Market leaders can expand the market by developing new users, new uses, and more usage of its products. They usually can find *new users* in many places. For example, Revlon might find new perfume users in its current markets by convincing women who do not use perfume to try it. It might find users in new demographic segments, such as by producing cologne for men. Or it might expand into new geographic segments, perhaps by selling its perfume in other countries.

Marketers can expand markets by discovering and promoting *new uses* for the product. For example, Intel invests heavily to develop new PC applications, which in turn increases the demand for microprocessors. It knows that it will get a 90 percent share of the new computer chip business. Another example of new-use expansion is Arm & Hammer baking soda. Its sales had flattened after 125 years; then the company discovered that consumers were using baking soda as a refrigerator deodorizer. It launched a heavy advertising and publicity campaign focusing on this use and persuaded consumers in half of America's homes to place an open box of baking soda in their refrigerators and to replace it every few months. Today, its Web site (www.armandhammer.com) regularly features new uses, from removing residue left behind by hairstyling products and sweetening garbage disposals, laundry hampers, refrigerators, and trash cans to creating a home spa in your bathroom.

Finally, marketer leaders can encourage *more usage* by convincing people to use the product more often or to use more per occasion. For example, Campbell urges people to eat soup more often by running ads containing new recipes and by offering a toll-free hot line (1-888-MMM-GOOD), staffed by live "recipe representatives" who offer recipes to last-minute cooks at a loss for meal ideas. Gillette's new Mach3 shaving system encourages more usage by actually "telling" consumers when a cartridge

Expanding the market: Campbell's Web site encourages more usage by offering home-made dinner ideas, a free Campbell's Cookbook, and Meal-mail (a recipe a day via e-mail).

is worn out. Each Mach3 Cartridge features a blue stripe that slowly fades with repeated use. After about a dozen shaves, it fades away completely, signaling the user to move on to the next cartridge in order to continue getting "the optimal Mach3 shaving experience." The more users change the cartridge, the more cartridges Gillette sells.

Protecting Market Share.   While trying to expand total market size, the leading firm also must constantly protect its current business against competitors' attacks. Coca-Cola must also constantly guard against PepsiCo; Gillette against Bic; Kodak against Fuji; McDonald's against Burger King; General Motors against Ford.

What can the market leader do to protect its position? First, it must prevent or fix weaknesses that provide opportunities for competitors. It needs to keep its costs down and its prices in line with the value the customers see in the brand. The leader should "plug holes" so that competitors do not jump in. But the best defense is a good offense, and the best response is *continuous innovation*. The leader refuses to be content with the way things are and leads the industry in new products, customer services, distribution effectiveness, and cost cutting. It keeps increasing its competitive effectiveness and value to customers.

For example, International Gaming Technology (IGT) is a company that manufactures slot machines and video poker machines for casinos around the world. It has achieved the daunting 75 percent market share in its mature market. Unlike the people who use its products, IGT doesn't rely on luck. Instead, it has formed partnerships with both casino operators and competitive gaming manufacturers to develop innovative new equipment to replace the old. IGT spends aggressively on R&D, allocating $31 million annually to create new games. "We know months, years, in advance what our customers want," says Robert Shay, a sales director for IGT. In this way, IGT takes the offensive, sets the pace, and exploits competitors' weaknesses.[34]

Expanding Market Share.   Market leaders also can grow by increasing their market shares further. In many markets, small market share increases mean very large sales increases. For example, in the coffee market, a 1 percent increase in market share is worth $48 million; in soft drinks, $500 million!

Studies have shown that, on average, profitability rises with increasing market share. Because of these findings, many companies have sought expanded market shares to improve profitability. General Electric, for example, declared that it wants to be at least number one or two in each of its markets or else get out. GE shed its computer, air-conditioning, small appliances, and television businesses because it could not achieve top-dog position in these industries.

Companies must not think, however, that gaining increased market share will improve profitability automatically. Much depends on their strategy for gaining increased share. There are many high-share companies with low profitability and many low-share companies with high profitability. The cost of buying higher market share may far exceed the returns. Higher shares tend to produce higher profits only when unit costs fall with increased market share, or when the company offers a superior-quality product and charges a premium price that more than covers the cost of offering higher quality.

Market Challenger Strategies

Firms that are second, third, or lower in an industry are sometimes quite large, such as Colgate, Ford, Kmart, Avis, Dell, and PepsiCo. These runner-up firms can adopt one of two competitive strategies: They can challenge the leader and other competitors in an aggressive bid for more market share (market challengers). Or they can play along with competitors and not rock the boat (market followers). We now look at competitive strategies for market challengers.

A market challenger must first define which competitors to challenge and its strategic objective. The challenger can attack the market leader, a high-risk but potentially high-gain strategy that makes good sense if the leader is not serving the market well. To succeed with such an attack, a company must have some sustainable competitive advantage over the leader—a cost advantage leading to lower prices or the ability to provide better value at a premium price. If the company goes after the market leader, its objective may be to wrest a certain market share. Bic knows that it can't topple Gillette in the razor market—it simply wants a larger share. Or the challenger's goal might be to take over market leadership. Wal-Mart began as a nicher in small towns in the Southwest, grew rapidly to challenge market leader Sears, and finally assumed market leadership, all within a span of less than 25 years.

Alternatively, the challenger can avoid the leader and instead challenge firms its own size, or smaller local and regional firms. These smaller firms may be underfinanced and not serving their customers well. Several of the major beer companies grew to their present size not by challenging large competitors, but by gobbling up small local or regional competitors. If the company goes after a small local company, its objective may be to put that company out of business. The important point remains: The challenger must choose its opponents carefully and have a clearly defined and attainable objective.

[34]Erika Rasmusson, "The Jackpot," *Sales & Marketing Management,* June 1998, pp. 35–41.

How can the market challenger best attack the chosen competitor and achieve its strategic objectives? It may launch a full *frontal attack*, matching the competitor's product, advertising, price, and distribution efforts. It attacks the competitor's strengths rather than its weaknesses. The outcome depends on who has the greater strength and endurance. If the market challenger has fewer resources than the competitor, a frontal attack makes little sense. For example, the runner-up razor-blade manufacturer in Brazil attacked Gillette, the market leader. The attacker was asked if it offered the consumer a better razor blade. "No," was the reply. "A lower price?" "No." "A better package?" "No." "A clever advertising campaign?" "No." "Better allowances to the trade?" "No." "Then how do you expect to take share away from Gillette?" "Sheer determination" was the reply. Needless to say, the offensive failed. Even great size and strength may not be enough to challenge a firmly entrenched, resourceful competitor successfully.

Rather than challenging head on, the challenger can make an *indirect attack* on the competitor's weaknesses or on gaps in the competitor's market coverage. For example, PepsiCo often finds it difficult to go head-to-head against market leader Coca-Cola. So in 1998 it tried the indirect approach by acquiring juice giant Tropicana. As the world's largest juice company, Tropicana arms PepsiCo with a powerful new weapon in the war against Coca-Cola. In the $3 billion market for orange juice, Tropicana's 42 percent share blows away Coke-owned Minute-Maid, which has only 24 percent share. The purchase gave PepsiCo at least one way to beat Coca-Cola.[35]

Similarly, rather than copying the competitor's product and mounting a costly frontal attack, the challenger might diversify into unrelated products or leapfrog into new technologies to replace existing products. Thus, Minolta toppled Canon from the lead in the 35mm SLR camera market when it introduced its technologically advanced autofocusing Maxxum camera. Canon's market share dropped toward 20 percent while Minolta's zoomed past 30 percent. It took Canon three years to introduce a matching technology. Such indirect challenges make good sense when the company has fewer resources than the competitor.

Market Follower Strategies

Not all runner-up companies want to challenge the market leader. Challenges are never taken lightly by the leader. If the challenger's lure is lower prices, improved service, or additional product features, the leader can quickly match these to diffuse the attack. The leader probably has more staying power in an all-out battle for customers. A hard fight might leave both firms worse off. Thus, many firms prefer to follow rather than challenge the leader.

A follower can gain many advantages. The market leader often bears the huge expenses of developing new products and markets, expanding distribution, and educating the market. The market follower, on the other hand, can learn from the leader's experience and copy or improve on the leader's products and programs, usually with much less investment. Although the follower will probably not overtake the leader, it often can be as profitable. A good example of a follower is Dial Corporation, maker of such well-known brands as Dial, Tone, and Pure & Natural hand soaps, Armour Star canned meats, Purex laundry products, and Renuzit air freshener:

> Flashy it isn't. "We want to be the dullest story in America," declares Dial's CEO. Dial doesn't try to come up with innovative new products. . . . It doesn't spend zillions to make its offerings household names across the nation. Instead, Dial prefers to coast in the slipstream of giant rivals, such as Procter & Gamble. [Its] lineup consists largely of me-too products and second-tier regional brands. . . . Instead of spending big on research and development or marketing, Dial leaves it to others. . . . And Dial lets other companies educate consumers about new products. P&G, for instance, introduced concentrated powder detergents in 1990. Dial followed over a year later with its own concentrated version, Purex—priced as much as one-third lower than P&G's Tide. Despite this low profile, the company does well in its markets. For example, Dial soap is America's number-one antibacterial soap and Purex has staked out a leadership position in the value segment of the laundry detergent market. Renuzit is the nation's number-two air freshener brand and Amour Star is number two in canned meats.[36]

Following is not the same as being passive or a carbon copy of the leader. The follower has to define a growth path, but one that does not create competitive retaliation. A market follower must know how to hold current customers and win a fair share of new ones. It must find the right balance

---

[35]Holman W. Jenkins Jr., "Business World: On a Happier Note, Orange Juice," *Wall Street Journal*, September 23, 1998, p. A23.

[36]Amy Barrett, "Dial Succeeds by Stepping in Bigger Footsteps," *Business Week*, June 13, 1994, pp. 82–83; Seth Lubove, "Cleaning Up," *Forbes*, December 28, 1998, p. 110; and "The Dial Corporation: Company Profile," accessed online at www.dialcorp.com, January 2000.

between following closely enough to win customers from the market leader but following at enough of a distance to avoid retaliation. Each follower tries to bring distinctive advantages to its target market—location, services, financing. The follower is often a major target of attack by challengers. Therefore, the market follower must keep its manufacturing costs low and its product quality and services high. It must also enter new markets as they open up.

Market Nicher Strategies

Almost every industry includes firms that specialize in serving market niches. Instead of pursuing the whole market, or even large segments, these firms target subsegments. Nichers are often smaller firms with limited resources. But smaller divisions of larger firms also may pursue niching strategies. Firms with low shares of the total market can be highly profitable through smart niching.

Why is niching profitable? The main reason is that the market nicher ends up knowing the target customer group so well that it meets their needs better than other firms that casually sell to this niche. As a result, the nicher can charge a substantial markup over costs because of the added value. Whereas the mass marketer achieves *high volume,* the nicher achieves *high margins.*

Nichers try to find one or more market niches that are safe and profitable. An ideal market niche is big enough to be profitable and has growth potential. It is one that the firm can serve effectively. Perhaps most importantly, the niche is of little interest to major competitors. The firm can build the skills and customer goodwill to defend itself against a major competitor as the niche grows and becomes more attractive. Here are just a few examples of profitable nichers:[37]

> Logitech has become a $450 million global success story by focusing on human interface devices—computer mice, game controllers, keyboards, and others. It makes every variation of computer mouse imaginable. Logitech turns out mice for left- and right-handed people, cordless mice that use radio waves, mice shaped like real mice for children, and 3-D mice that let the user appear to move behind screen objects. This year, the company's 200 millionth mouse will roll off the production line. Breeding computer mice has been so successful that Logitech dominates the world market, with Microsoft as its runner-up.

- By focusing on hospital face masks, Tecnol Medical Products competes against two giants: Johnson & Johnson and 3M. Tecnol has transformed an ordinary face mask into a lucrative line of specialty masks that shield health care workers from infection. Now the little-known company has surpassed Johnson & Johnson and 3M to become the top mask supplier to U.S. hospitals.

- In his book *Hidden Champions,* Herman Simon documents the surprising number of German companies that are barely known but have strong profits and global market shares exceeding 50 percent in their respective niches. Tetra has 80 percent of the world tropical fish market; Hohner owns a stunning 85 percent of the harmonica market; Bechner makes 50 percent of the world's umbrellas; and Steiner Optical make 80 percent of the world's military field glasses.

The key idea in niching is specialization. A market nicher can specialize along any of several market, customer, product, or marketing mix lines. For example, it can specialize in serving one type of *end user,* as when a law firm specializes in the criminal, civil, or business law markets. The nicher can specialize in serving a given *customer-size* group—many nichers specialize in serving small customers who are neglected by the majors. Some nichers focus on one or a few *specific customers,* selling their entire output to a single company, such as Wal-Mart or General Motors. Still other nichers specialize by *geographic market,* selling only in a certain locality, region, or area of the world. *Quality–price* nichers operate at the low or high end of the market. For example, Hewlett-Packard specializes in the high-quality, high-price end of the hand-calculator market. Finally, *service nichers* offer services not available from other firms. An example is a bank that takes loan requests over the phone and hand delivers the money to the customer.

Niching carries some major risks. For example, the market niche may dry up, or it might grow to the point that it attracts larger competitors. That is why many companies practice *multiple niching.* By developing two or more niches, a company increases its chances for survival. Even some large firms prefer a multiple niche strategy to serving the total market. For example, Alberto Culver is a midsize company that has used a multiple niching strategy to grow profitably without incurring the wrath of the market leader. CEO Howard Bernick explains the Alberto Culver philosophy this way: "We know who we are and, perhaps more importantly, we know who we are not. We know that if we try to out-Procter Procter, we will fall flat on our face." Instead, the company known mainly for its Alberto VO5

---

[37]Stephanie Anderson, "Who's Afraid of J&J and 3M?" *Business Week,* December 5, 1994, pp. 66–68; Hermann Simon, *Hidden Champions* (Boston: Harvard Business School Press, 1996); and information accessed online from "Financial Highlights" and "Company Fact Sheet" on the Logitech Web site at www.logitech. com, January 2000.

Great Blues Artists Play Hohner Harmonicas.

Phil Wiggins Plays
Hohner's Marine Band Harmonica.

Available in music stores
everywhere.

http://hohnerusa.com

HOHNER

Profitable nichers: Small but profitable Hohner owns a stunning 85 percent of the harmonica market.

hair products has focused its marketing muscle on acquiring a stable of small niche brands. Its other items include flavor enhancers Molly McButter and Mrs. Dash, static-cling fighter Static Guard, and Consort men's hairspray. Each of these brands is number one in its niche.[38]

> ## active concept check

Now let's take a moment to test your knowledge of what you've just read.

> ## Balancing Customer and Competitor Orientations

Whether a company is a market leader, challenger, follower, or nicher, it must watch its competitors closely and find the competitive marketing strategy that positions it most effectively. It must continu-

---

[38]Jim Kirk, "Company Finds Itself, Finds Success: Alberto-Culver Adopts Strategy of Knowing Its Strengths and Promoting Small Brands, Rather Than Tackling Giants," *Chicago Tribune,* January 22, 1998, Business Section, p. 1; and information obtained from the Alberto Culver Web site at www.alberto-culver.com, January 2000.

ally adapt its strategies to the fast-changing competitive environment. This question now arises: Can the company spend too much time and energy tracking competitors, damaging its customer orientation? The answer is yes! A company can become so competitor centered that it loses its even more important customer focus.

A **competitor-centered company** is one that spends most of its time tracking competitors' moves and market shares and trying to find strategies to counter them. This approach has some pluses and minuses. On the positive side, the company develops a fighter orientation. It trains its marketers to be on a constant alert, watching for weaknesses in their own position, and searching out competitors' weaknesses. On the negative side, the company becomes too reactive. Rather than carrying out its own customer-oriented strategy, it bases its own moves on competitors' moves. As a result, because so much depends on what the competitors do, the company does not move in a planned direction toward a goal. It may end up simply matching or extending industry practices rather than seeking innovative new ways to bring more value to customers.

A **customer-centered company,** by contrast, focuses more on customer developments in designing its strategies. Clearly, the customer-centered company is in a better position to identify new opportunities and set long-run strategies that make sense. By watching customer needs evolve, it can decide what customer groups and what emerging needs are the most important to serve, then concentrate its resources on delivering superior value to target customers. In practice, today's companies must be **market-centered companies,** watching both their customers and their competitors. They must not let competitor watching blind them to customer focusing.

Figure 18.5 shows that companies have moved through four orientations over the years. In the first stage, they were product oriented, paying little attention to either customers or competitors. In the second stage, they became customer oriented and started to pay attention to customers. In the third stage, when they started to pay attention to competitors, they became competitor oriented. Today, companies need to be market oriented, paying balanced attention to both customer and competitors. Rather than simply watching competitors and trying to beat them on current ways of doing business, they need to watch customers and find innovative ways to deliver more value than competitors do.[39]

active example <

Take a moment to read about a business that many consider to be a true market-centered company.

active concept check <

Now let's take a moment to test your knowledge of what you've just read.

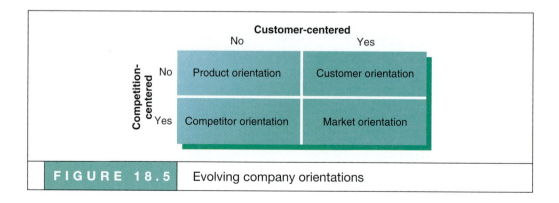

	Customer-centered	
	No	Yes
Competition-centered No	Product orientation	Customer orientation
Competition-centered Yes	Competitor orientation	Market orientation

FIGURE 18.5 Evolving company orientations

[39]For interesting discussions, see W. Cahn Kim and Renée Mauborgne, "Value Innovation: The Strategic Logic of High Growth," *Harvard Business Review,* January–February 1997, pp. 103–12; and W. Chan Kim and Renee Mauborgne, "Creating New Market Space," *Harvard Business Review,* January–February 1999, pp. 83–93.

Chapter Wrap-Up

Now that you've reached the end of the chapter, you may wish to explore the concepts you've been reading about in greater detail, or test yourself to see how well you've comprehended the material. In the box below you'll find a number of links. Click on any one of these links to find additional chapter resources.

> end-of-chapter resources

- **Review of Concept Connections**
- **Practice Quiz**
- **Tying it All Together (Audio)**
- **Key Terms**
- **Critical Thinking Exercises**
- **Experimential Exercises**
- **MyPHLIP Companion Web Site**
- **Case 1**
- **Case 2**
- **You Be the Consultant**

The Global Marketplace

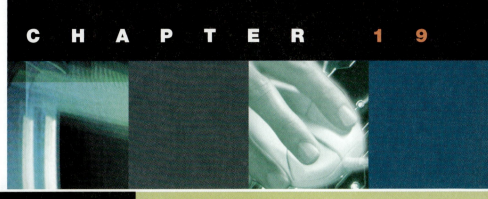

> What's Ahead

What could be more American than basketball? The sport was invented in the United States, and each year tens of millions of excited fans crowd their local gyms or huddle around their television sets to cheer on their favorite rec league, high school, college, or pro teams. But basketball is rapidly becoming a worldwide craze. For example, a recent *New York Times* survey of more than 45,000 teenagers on five continents asked, "What are your favorite entertainment pursuits?" The answers: (1) watching television, (2) basketball.

No organization is doing more to promote worldwide basketball than the National Basketball Association (NBA). During the past decade, the NBA has become a truly global marketing enterprise. The 1999 NBA finals reached more than 600 million television viewers in 195 countries throughout the world, and worldwide sales of NBA-licensed basketballs, backboards, T-shirts, and other merchandise top $3 billion a year. The NBA is now a powerful worldwide brand. A *Fortune* article summarizes:

Deployed by global sponsors Coca-Cola, Reebok, and McDonald's, well-paid [NBA superstars] hawk soda, sneakers, burgers, and basketball to legions of mostly young fans [worldwide]. That they are recognized from Santiago to Seoul says a lot about the soaring worldwide appeal of hoops—and about the marketing juggernaut known as the NBA. After watching their favorite stars swoop in and slam-dunk on their local TV stations, fans of the league now cheer the *mate* in Latin America, the *trofsla* in Iceland, and the *smash* in France. Care to guess the most popular basketball team in China? Why, it's the "Red Oxen" from Chicago, of course.

Basketball has even become a diplomatic tool. A few seasons back, the U.S. secretary of state, in an effort to preserve a fragile peace in Bosnia, requested that the NBA allow the broadcast of basketball games in the war-torn country. As a result, the NBA finals were aired in Bosnia for the first time ever. According to a State Department official, NBA broadcasts are "the most popular program there. The Bosnians are very big basketball buffs."

Like many other businesses, the NBA's primary motive for going global is growth. The league now sells out most of its games, and domestic licensing revenues have flattened in recent years. According to NBA Commissioner David Sterns, "There are just so many seats in an arena and so many hours of television programming, period. The domestic business is becoming mature. That's why we're moving internationally." Compared with the NBA's overall yearly revenues of $2 billion, current international revenues are modest—estimated at a little more than $60 million from TV rights fees, sponsorships, and the league's share of licensing sales. But worldwide potential is huge, and the league is investing heavily to build its popularity and business abroad. For example, its international staff of 105 is nearly double the number of people who ran the entire league back in the early 1980s.

Thanks to skillful marketing, and to the growing worldwide popularity of basketball itself, the NBA's investment appears to be paying off. According to *Fortune,* the NBA enjoys huge natural advantages over football, baseball, and other rivals:

It's selling a sport, basketball, that's played nearly everywhere and easily understood. (Try explaining a nickel defense to a Swede.) Pro and amateur leagues have been thriving for years in Europe and Asia, and basketball has been an Olympic sport since 1936. The U.S. "Dream Team" in 1992 was a worldwide sensation, sparking even greater interest in pro basketball in the U.S. . . . By then the groundwork had been laid for the NBA's global growth. Two men deserve much of the credit: David Stern and Michael Jordan, with a big assist from Nike. [The NBA and Nike] turned Jordan into a worldwide celebrity, known not just for his gravity-defying skills but also for his winning personality and competitive zeal. . . . In China, which has its own professional basketball leagues, boys on the streets of Beijing and Shanghai [wore] Bulls gear because they wanted to be like Mike. . . . A 1997 survey of 28,000 teenagers in 45 countries by [a global ad agency] found that Jordan was the world's favorite athlete by far.

Broader forces also helped to promote the league's efforts to go global: the collapse of communism and the growth of market economies, the globalization of American consumer companies, and a revolution in worldwide television. Most recent is the explosion of the global Internet. The NBA's site (*www.NBA.com*) offers programming in several languages and draws 35 percent of its visitors from outside the United States.

However, beyond these natural forces, the NBA's success abroad results in large part from the league's strong marketing efforts. To exploit international opportunities

The NBA rolled out a marketing machine that's been fine-tuned for a decade in the United States. Television programming leads the way—not just broadcasts of games but an array of NBA-produced programs, mostly targeted at kids and teenagers, that promote the league and its players. Two weekly programs, a highlights show called *NBA Action* and a teen show called *NBA Jam* that features music, fashion, and player profiles, are produced solely for the international marketplace. . . . Once television has pried open a market, the NBA and its partners move in with an array of live events, attractions, and grassroots activities. [For example,] McDonald's and the NBA sponsor a program called 2Ball that teaches basic basketball skills to thousands of kids outside the U.S. Coca-Cola, meanwhile, targets basketball-crazed teenagers by putting NBA and team logos on Sprite soft drink cans sold in 30 countries. "We're using the NBA and their players to help sell Sprite, but at the same time it does a lot for the NBA," says [Coca-Cola's] director for worldwide sports.

The NBA has encountered a rash of recent problems—Michael Jordan's retirement and the end of the Chicago Bulls dynasty, negative publicity surrounding several high-profile players, and a prolonged player's strike that cut the 1998–1999 season in half. These and other events are presenting fresh challenges to the league's marketing prowess. In the post-Jordan era, the NBA faces the task of trying to extend one of pro sport's greatest growth spurts without the person most responsible for its past success. Still, the future looks bright. For example, the NBA emerged from the potentially disastrous player's strike nearly unscathed—overall attendance slipped only 2 percent and several teams actually saw large jumps in attendance. Although TV ratings for the NBA finals dipped in the year following Jordan's departure, the games still topped the Nielsen ratings.

Thus, most experts expect more slam dunks for the NBA as it continues to extend its international reach. One sustaining factor in the NBA's global appeal is the continuing presence of foreign-born players. Almost every team roster includes one: Toni Kukoc from Croatia, Luc Longley from Australia, Georghe Muresan from Romania, Arvydas Sabonis from Lithuania, or Detlef Shrempf from Germany. Such players attract large followings in their home countries. As *Fortune* concludes:

Imagine, then, the impact in China if a promising 18-year-old, 7-foot-1 center named Wong Zhizhi, who played for that country's . . . Olympic team, develops into an NBA star. Basketball's popularity is already exploding in China, one of the very few nations where the NBA gives away its TV programming because [it] is determined to make inroads there. Nearly all of China's 250 million TV households get the *NBA Action* highlights show and a game of the week on Saturday mornings; this year China Central TV broadcast the NBA All-Star game live for the first time. Winning the loyalty of two billion Chinese won't be a *kou qui*—a slam-dunk—but Stern is, well, bullish. "The upside is tremendous," he says. Can Ping-Pong survive an NBA invasion? Stay tuned.[1]

---

[1]Extracts and quotes from Marc Gunther, "They All Want to Be Like Mike," *Fortune,* July 21, 1997, pp. 51–53: © 1997 Time, Inc., all rights reserved; and Warren Cohen, "Slam-Dunk Diplomacy," *U.S. News & World Report,* June 8, 1998, p. 7. Also see Stefan Fatsis, "NBA Bravely Plans for Post-Jordan Era," *Wall Street Journal,* February 6, 1998, p. B1; "NBA Will Face Difficult Recovery from Lockout," *Greensboro News Record,* December 24, 1998, p. C2; Mark Hyman, "Another Ruined Season That Wasn't," *Business Week,* June 7, 1999, p. 40; David Bauder, "Mike Takes the Air out of NBA Ratings," *Raleigh News & Observer,* June 24, 1999, p. E7; "Worldwide TV Coverage of the 1999 NBA Finals," accessed online at www.nba.com, September 1999; and Daniel Roth, "The NBA's Next Shot," *Fortune,* February 21, 2000, pp. 207–215.

objectives <

Before you begin, take a moment to familiarize yourself with the key objectives of this chapter.

gearing up <

Before we begin our exploration this chapter, take a short warm-up test to see what you know about this topic.

In the past, U.S. companies paid little attention to international trade. If they could pick up some extra sales through exporting, that was fine. But the big market was at home, and it teemed with opportunities. The home market was also much safer. Managers did not need to learn other languages, deal with strange and changing currencies, face political and legal uncertainties, or adapt their products to different customer needs and expectations. Today, however, the situation is much different.

> Global Marketing In the Twenty-First Century

The world is shrinking rapidly with the advent of faster communication, transportation, and financial flows. Products developed in one country—Gucci purses, Mont Blanc pens, McDonald's hamburgers, Japanese sushi, German BMWs—are finding enthusiastic acceptance in other countries. We would not be surprised to hear about a German businessperson wearing an Italian suit meeting an English friend at a Japanese restaurant who later returns home to drink Russian vodka and watch *Frazier* on TV.

International trade is booming. Since 1969, the number of multinational corporations in the world's 14 richest countries has more than tripled, from 7,000 to 24,000. Experts predict that by 2005, world exports of goods and services will reach 28 percent of world gross domestic product, up from only 9 percent 20 years ago. International trade now accounts for a quarter of the United States' GDP, and between 1996 and 2006, U.S. exports are expected to increase 51 percent.[2]

True, many companies have been carrying on international activities for decades. Coca-Cola, IBM, Kodak, Nestlé, Bayer, Sony, and other companies are familiar to most consumers around the world. But today global competition is intensifying. Foreign firms are expanding aggressively into new international markets, and home markets are no longer as rich in opportunity. Domestic companies that never thought about foreign competitors suddenly find these competitors in their own backyards. The firm that stays at home to play it safe not only might lose its chance to enter other markets but also risks losing its home market.

In the United States, names such as Sony, Toyota, Nestlé, Norelco, Mercedes, and Panasonic have become household words. Other products and services that appear to be American are in fact produced or owned by foreign companies: Bantam books, Baskin-Robbins ice cream, GE and RCA televisions, Firestone tires, Carnation milk, Pillsbury food products, Universal Studios, and Motel 6, to name just a few. Few U.S. industries are now safe from foreign competition.

Although some companies would like to stem the tide of foreign imports through protectionism, in the long run this would only raise the cost of living and protect inefficient domestic firms. The better way for companies to compete is to continuously improve their products at home and expand into foreign markets. Many U.S. companies have been successful at international marketing: IBM, Xerox, Corning, Coca-Cola, McDonald's, Gillette, Colgate, General Electric, Caterpillar, Ford, Kodak, 3M, Boeing, Motorola, and dozens of other American firms have made the world their market. But there are too few such firms. In fact, just 5 U.S. companies account for 12 percent of all exports; 1,000 manufacturers (out of 300,000) account for 60 percent.[3]

---

[2]John Alden, "What in the World Drives UPS?" *International Business,* April 1998, pp. 6–7; Karen Pennar, "Two Steps Forward, One Step Back," *Business Week,* August 31, 1998, p. 116; and Michelle Wirth Fellman, "A New World for Marketers," *Marketing News,* May 10, 1999, p. 13.

[3]See "Top 50 U.S. Industrial Exporters," *Fortune,* August 22, 1994, p. 132; Edmund Faltermayer, "Competitiveness: How U.S. Companies Stack Up Now," *Fortune,* April 18, 1994, pp. 52–64; and "The Fortune Global 5 Hundred," *Fortune,* August 2, 1999, p. F1.

The longer companies delay taking steps toward internationalizing, the more they risk being shut out of growing markets in Western Europe, Eastern Europe, the Pacific Rim, and elsewhere. Domestic businesses that thought they were safe now find companies from neighboring countries invading their home markets. All companies will have to answer some basic questions: What market position should we try to establish in our country, in our economic region, and globally? Who will our global competitors be, and what are their strategies and resources? Where should we produce or source our products? What strategic alliances should we form with other firms around the world?

Ironically, although the need for companies to go abroad is greater today than in the past, so are the risks. Companies that go global confront several major problems. High debt, inflation, and unemployment in many countries have resulted in highly unstable governments and currencies, which limits trade and exposes U.S. firms to many risks. For example, in 1998 Russia created a global economic crisis when it devalued the ruble, effectively defaulting on its global debts. A more widespread Asian economic downturn had a far-reaching impact on Western firms with significant markets or investments there.

Governments are placing more regulations on foreign firms, such as requiring joint ownership with domestic partners, mandating the hiring of nationals, and limiting profits that can be taken from the country. Moreover, foreign governments often impose high tariffs or trade barriers in order to protect their own industries. Finally, corruption is an increasing problem—officials in several countries often award business not to the best bidder but to the highest briber.

Still, companies selling in global industries have no choice but to internationalize their operations. A *global industry* is one in which the competitive positions of firms in given local or national markets are affected by their global positions. A **global firm** is one that, by operating in more than one country, gains marketing, production, R&D, and financial advantages that are not available to purely domestic competitors. The global company sees the world as one market. It minimizes the importance of national boundaries and raises capital, obtains materials and components, and manufactures and markets its goods wherever it can do the best job. For example, Ford's "world truck" sports a cab made in Europe and a chassis built in North America. It is assembled in Brazil and imported to the United States for sale. Otis Elevator gets its elevators' door systems from France, small geared parts from Spain, electronics from Germany, and special motor drives from Japan. It uses the United States only for systems integration. Thus, global firms gain advantages by planning, operating, and coordinating their activities on a worldwide basis.

Because firms around the world are globalizing at a rapid rate, domestic firms in global industries must act quickly before the window closes. This does not mean that small and medium-size firms must operate in a dozen countries to succeed. These firms can practice global niching. In fact, companies marketing on the Internet may find themselves going global whether they intend it or not. But the world is becoming smaller, and every company operating in a global industry—whether large or small—must assess and establish its place in world markets.

As shown in Figure 19.1, a company faces six major decisions in international marketing. Each decision will be discussed in detail in this chapter.

> ## active example

Consider how American e-tailers have fared as they've expanded abroad.

> ## active concept check

Now let's take a moment to test your knowledge of what you've just read.

| Looking at the global marketing environment | Deciding whether to go international | Deciding which markets to enter | Deciding how to enter the market | Deciding on the global marketing program | Deciding on the global marketing organization |

FIGURE 19.1   Major decisions in international marketing

Before deciding whether to operate internationally, a company must thoroughly understand the international marketing environment. That environment has changed a great deal in the past two decades, creating both new opportunities and new problems. The world economy has globalized. World trade and investment have grown rapidly, with many attractive markets opening up in Western and Eastern Europe, China and the Pacific Rim, Russia, and elsewhere. There has been a growth of global brands in automobiles, food, clothing, electronics, and many other categories. The number of global companies has grown dramatically. The international financial system has become more complex and volatile, and U.S. companies face increasing trade barriers erected to protect domestic markets from outside competition.

THE INTERNATIONAL TRADE SYSTEM

The U.S. company looking abroad must start by understanding the international *trade system.* When selling to another country, the U.S. firm faces various trade restrictions. The most common is the **tariff,** which is a tax levied by a foreign government against certain imported products. The tariff may be designed either to raise revenue or to protect domestic firms. The exporter also may face a **quota,** which sets limits on the amount of goods the importing country will accept in certain product categories. The purpose of the quota is to conserve on foreign exchange and to protect local industry and employment. An **embargo,** or boycott, which totally bans some kinds of imports, is the strongest form of quota.

American firms may face **exchange controls** that limit the amount of foreign exchange and the exchange rate against other currencies. The company also may face **nontariff trade barriers,** such as biases against U.S. company bids or restrictive product standards or other rules that go against American product features:

> One of the cleverest ways the Japanese have found to keep foreign manufacturers out of their domestic market is to plead "uniqueness." Japanese skin is different, the government argues, so foreign cosmetics companies must test their products in Japan before selling there. The Japanese say their stomachs are small and have room for only the *mikan,* the local tangerine, so imports of U.S. oranges are limited. Now the Japanese have come up with what may be the flakiest argument yet: Their snow is different, so ski equipment should be too.[4]

At the same time, certain forces *help* trade between nations. Examples include the General Agreement on Tariffs and Trade and various regional free trade agreements.

The World Trade Organization and GATT

The General Agreement on Tariffs and Trade (GATT) is a 50-year-old treaty designed to promote world trade by reducing tariffs and other international trade barriers. Since the treaty's inception in 1948, member nations (currently numbering more than 120) have met in eight rounds of GATT negotiations to reassess trade barriers and set new rules for international trade. The first seven rounds of negotiations reduced the average worldwide tariffs on manufactured goods from 45 percent to just 5 percent.

The most recently completed GATT negotiations, dubbed the Uruguay Round, dragged on for seven long years before concluding in 1993. The benefits of the Uruguay Round will be felt for many years as the accord promotes long-term global trade growth. It reduced the world's remaining merchandise tariffs by 30 percent, which could boost global merchandise trade by up to 10 percent, or $270 billion in current dollars, by the year 2002. The new agreement also extended GATT to cover trade in agriculture and a wide range of services, and it toughened international protection of copyrights, patents, trademarks, and other intellectual property.[5]

Beyond reducing trade barriers and setting international standards for trade, the Uruguay Round established the World Trade Organization (WTO) to enforce GATT rules. One of the WTO's first

[4]"The Unique Japanese," *Fortune,* November 24, 1986, p. 8. For more on nontariff and other barriers, see Warren J. Keegan and Mark C. Green, *Principles of Global Marketing* (Upper Saddle River, NJ: Prentice Hall, 1997), pp. 200–203.

[5]Douglas Harbrecht and Owen Ullmann, "Finally GATT May Fly," *Business Week,* December 29, 1993, pp. 36–37; and Ping Deng, "Impact of GATT Uruguay Round on Various Industries," *American Business Review,* June 1998, pp. 22–29. Also see Charles W. L. Hill, *International Business* (Chicago: Richard A. Irwin, 1997), pp. 165–68; "Special Article: World Trade: Fifty Years On," *The Economist,* May 16, 1998, pp. 21–23; and Helene Cooper, "The Millennium—Trade & Commerce: Trading Blocks," *Wall Street Journal,* January 11, 1999, p. R50.

major tasks was to host negotiations on the General Agreement on Trade in Services, which deals with worldwide trade in banking, securities, and insurance services. In general, the WTO acts as an umbrella organization, overseeing GATT, the General Agreement on Trade in Services, and a similar agreement governing intellectual property. In addition, the WTO mediates global disputes and imposes trade sanctions, authorities that the previous GATT organization never possessed. A fresh round of WTO negotiations began in Seattle in late 1999.

Regional Free Trade Zones

Certain countries have formed *free trade zones* or **economic communities**—groups of nations organized to work toward common goals in the regulation of international trade. One such community is the *European Union (EU)*. Formed in 1957, the European Union—then called the Common Market—set out to create a single European market by reducing barriers to the free flow of products, services, finances, and labor among member countries and developing policies on trade with nonmember nations. Today, the European Union represents one of the world's single largest markets. Its 15 member countries contain more than 370 million consumers and account for 20 percent of the world's exports. During the next decade, as more European nations seek admission, the EU could contain as many as 450 million people in 28 countries.

European unification offers tremendous trade opportunities for U.S. and other non-European firms. However, it also poses threats. As a result of increased unification, European companies will grow bigger and more competitive. Perhaps an even bigger concern, however, is that lower barriers *inside* Europe will only create thicker *outside* walls. Some observers envision a "Fortress Europe" that heaps favors on firms from EU countries but hinders outsiders by imposing obstacles such as stiffer import quotas, local content requirements, and other nontariff barriers.

Progress toward European unification has been slow—many doubt that complete unification will ever be achieved. However, on January 1, 1999, 11 of the 15 member nations took a significant step toward unification by adopting the Euro as a common currency. These 11 nations represent 290 million people and a $6.5 trillion market. Currencies of the individual countries will be phased out gradually until January 1, 2002, when the Euro will become the only currency. Adoption of the Euro will decrease much of the currency risk associated with doing business in Europe, making member countries with previously weak currencies more attractive markets. In addition, by removing currency conversion hurdles, the switch will likely increase cross-border trade and highlight differences in pricing and marketing from country to country.[6]

Even with the adoption of the Euro as a standard currency, from a marketing viewpoint, creating an economic community will not create a homogenous market. As one international analyst suggests, "Even though you have fiscal harmonization, you can't go against 2,000 years of tradition."[7] With 14 different languages and distinctive national customs, it is unlikely that the EU will ever become the "United States of Europe." Although economic and political boundaries may fall, social and cultural differences will remain, and companies marketing in Europe will face a daunting mass of local rules. Still, even if only partly successful, European unification will make a more efficient and competitive Europe a global force with which to reckon.[8]

In North America, the United States and Canada phased out trade barriers in 1989. In January 1994, the *North American Free Trade Agreement (NAFTA)* established a free trade zone among the United States, Mexico, and Canada. The agreement created a single market of 360 million people who produce and consume $6.7 trillion worth of goods and services. As it is implemented over a 15-year period, NAFTA will eliminate all trade barriers and investment restrictions among the three countries. Prior to NAFTA, tariffs on American products entering Mexico averaged 13 percent, whereas U.S. tariffs on Mexican goods averaged 6 percent.

Thus far, the agreement has allowed trade between the countries to flourish. Each day the United States exchanges more than $1 billion in goods and services with Canada, its largest trading partner. Over the past four years, exports from the United States to Mexico have increased 116 percent. In 1998, Mexico passed Japan to become America's second largest trading partner.[9]

---

[6]Stanley Reed, "We Have Liftoff! The Strong Launch of the Euro Is Hailed Around the World," *Business Week,* January 18, 1999, pp. 34–37.

[7]James Welsh, "Enter the Euro," *World Trade,* January 1999, pp. 34–38.

[8]For more on the European Union, see "Around Europe in 40 Years," *The Economist,* May 31, 1997, p. S4; "European Union to Begin Expansion," *New York Times,* March 30, 1998, p. A5; Joan Warner, "Mix Us Culturally? It's Impossible," *Business Week,* April 27, 1998, p. 108; and Paul J. Deveney, "World Watch," *Wall Street Journal,* May 20, 1999, p. A12.

[9]Aaron Robertson, "North America: Trade Brisk Despite Bumps in the Road," *World Trade,* May 1999, pp. 28–32; and Tom Foster, "The NAFTA Gateway," *Logistics Management and Distribution Report,* May 1999, pp. S10–S11.

Other free trade areas have formed in Latin America and South America. For example, MERCO-SUR now links six members, including full members Argentina, Brazil, Paraguay, and Uruguay and associate members Bolivia and Chile. With a population of more than 200 million and a combined economy of more than $1 trillion a year, these countries make up the largest trading bloc after NAFTA and the European Union. There is talk of a free trade agreement between the EU and MERCOSUR.[10]

Although the recent trend toward free trade zones has caused great excitement and new market opportunities, this trend also raises some concerns. For example, in the United States, unions fear that NAFTA will lead to the further exodus of manufacturing jobs to Mexico where wage rates are much lower. Environmentalists worry that companies that are unwilling to play by the strict rules of the U.S. Environmental Protection Agency will relocate in Mexico where pollution regulation has been lax.[11]

Each nation has unique features that must be understood. A nation's readiness for different products and services and its attractiveness as a market to foreign firms depend on its economic, political–legal, and cultural environments.

ECONOMIC ENVIRONMENT

The international marketer must study each country's economy. Two economic factors reflect the country's attractiveness as a market: the country's industrial structure and its income distribution.

The country's *industrial structure* shapes its product and service needs, income levels, and employment levels. The four types of industrial structures are as follows:

■ *Subsistence economies:* In a subsistence economy, the vast majority of people engage in simple agriculture. They consume most of their output and barter the rest for simple goods and services. They offer few market opportunities.

■ *Raw material exporting economies:* These economies are rich in one or more natural resources but poor in other ways. Much of their revenue comes from exporting these resources. Examples are Chile (tin and copper), Zaire (copper, cobalt, and coffee), and Saudi Arabia (oil). These countries are good markets for large equipment, tools and supplies, and trucks. If there are many foreign residents and a wealthy upper class, they are also a market for luxury goods.

■ *Industrializing economies:* In an industrializing economy, manufacturing accounts for 10 to 20 percent of the country's economy. Examples include Egypt, the Philippines, India, and Brazil. As manufacturing increases, the country needs more imports of raw textile materials, steel, and heavy machinery, and fewer imports of finished textiles, paper products, and automobiles. Industrialization typically creates a new rich class and a small but growing middle class, both demanding new types of imported goods.

■ *Industrial economies:* Industrial economies are major exporters of manufactured goods and investment funds. They trade goods among themselves and also export them to other types of economies for raw materials and semifinished goods. The varied manufacturing activities of these industrial nations and their large middle class make them rich markets for all sorts of goods.

The second economic factor is the country's *income distribution.* Countries with subsistence economies may consist mostly of households with very low family incomes. In contrast, industrialized nations may have low-, medium-, and high-income households. Still other countries may have households with only either very low or very high incomes. However, in many cases, poorer countries may have small but wealthy segments of upper-income consumers. Also, even in low-income and developing economies, people may find ways to buy products that are important to them:

Philosophy professor Nina Gladziuk thinks carefully before shelling out her hard-earned zlotys for Poland's dazzling array of consumer goods. But spend she certainly does. Although she earns just $550 a month from two academic jobs, Gladziuk, 41, enjoys making purchases: They are changing her lifestyle after years of deprivation under communism. In the past year, she has furnished a new apartment in a popular neighborhood near Warsaw's Kabaty Forest, splurged on foreign-made beauty products, and spent a weekend in Paris before attending a seminar financed by her university. . . . Meet Central Europe's fast-rising consumer class. From white-collar workers like Gladziuk to factory workers in Budapest to hip young professionals in Prague, incomes are rising and confidence surging as a result of four years of economic growth. In the region's leading economies—the Czech Republic, Hungary, and Poland—the new class

[10]Larry Rohter, "Latin America and Europe to Talk Trade," *New York Times,* June 26, 1999, p. 2.

[11]For more reading, see Paul Magnusson, "NAFTA: Where's That Giant Sucking Sound?" *Business Week,* July 7, 1997, p. 45; David M. Gould, "Has NAFTA Changed North American Trade?" *Economic Review—Federal Reserve Bank of Dallas,* first quarter, 1998, pp. 12–23; Lori Wallach and Michelle Sforza, "NAFTA at 5," *The Nation,* January 25, 1999, p. 7.

of buyers is growing not only in numbers but also in sophistication. . . . In Hungary, ad agency Young & Rubicam labels 11 percent of the country as "aspirers," with dreams of the good life and buying habits to match. Nearly one-third of all Czechs, Hungarians, and Poles—some 17 million people—are under 30 years old, eager to snap up everything from the latest fashions to compact disks.[12]

Thus, international marketers face many challenges in understanding how the economic environment will affect decisions about which global markets to enter and how.

POLITICAL–LEGAL ENVIRONMENT

Nations differ greatly in their political–legal environments. At least four political–legal factors should be considered in deciding whether to do business in a given country: attitudes toward international buying, government bureaucracy, political stability, and monetary regulations.

In their *attitudes toward international buying,* some nations are quite receptive to foreign firms and others are quite hostile. For example, India has bothered foreign businesses with import quotas, currency restrictions, and limits on the percentage of the management team that can be nonnationals. As a result, many U.S. companies left India. In contrast, neighboring Asian countries such as Singapore, Thailand, Malaysia, and the Philippines court foreign investors and shower them with incentives and favorable operating conditions.[13]

A second factor is *government bureaucracy*—the extent to which the host government runs an efficient system for helping foreign companies: efficient customs handling, good market information, and other factors that aid in doing business. A common shock to Americans is how quickly barriers to trade disappear in some countries if a suitable payment (bribe) is made to some official.

Political stability is another issue. Governments change hands, sometimes violently. Even without a change, a government may decide to respond to new popular feelings. The foreign company's property may be taken, its currency holdings may be blocked, or import quotas or new duties may be set. International marketers may find it profitable to do business in an unstable country, but the unstable situation will affect how they handle business and financial matters.

Finally, companies must also consider a country's *monetary regulations.* Sellers want to take their profits in a currency of value to them. Ideally, the buyer can pay in the seller's currency or in other world currencies. Short of this, sellers might accept a blocked currency—one whose removal from the country is restricted by the buyer's government—if they can buy other goods in that country that they need themselves or can sell elsewhere for a needed currency. Besides currency limits, a changing exchange rate also creates high risks for the seller.

Most international trade involves cash transactions. Yet many nations have too little hard currency to pay for their purchases from other countries. They may want to pay with other items instead of cash, which has led to a growing practice called **countertrade.** Countertrade may now account for more than one-half of all international trade. It takes several forms: *Barter* involves the direct

---

[12]David Woodruff, "Ready to Shop Until They Drop," *Business Week;* June 22, 1998, pp. 104–8.

[13]Manjeet Kripalani, "As the Politicians Squabble, India Stagnates," *Business Week,* May 5, 1997, p. 58; and Amy Louise Kazmin, "Why New Delhi Is Picking on Pepsi," *Business Week,* May 18, 1998, p. 54.

exchange of goods or services, as when Australian ranchers swapped beef on the hoof for Indonesian goods including beer, palm oil, and cement. Another form is *compensation* (or *buyback*), whereby the seller sells a plant, equipment, or technology to another country and agrees to take payment in the resulting products. Thus, Goodyear provided China with materials and training for a printing plant in exchange for finished labels. Another form is *counterpurchase,* in which the seller receives full payment in cash but agrees to spend some portion of the money in the other country within a stated time period. For example, Pepsi sells its cola syrup to Russia for rubles and agrees to buy Russian-made Stolichnaya vodka for sale in the United States.

Countertrade deals can be very complex. For example, a few years back, DaimlerChrysler agreed to sell 30 trucks to Romania in exchange for 150 Romanian jeeps, which it then sold to Ecuador for bananas, which were in turn sold to a German supermarket chain for German currency. Through this roundabout process, DaimlerChrysler finally obtained payment in German money. In another case, when Occidental Petroleum Company wanted to sell oil to Yugoslavia, it hired a trading firm, SGD International, to arrange a countertrade. SGD arranged for a New York City automobile dealer-distributor, Global Motors Inc., to import more than $400 million worth of Yugoslavian Yugo automobiles, paid for by Occidental oil. Global then paid Occidental in cash. SGD, however, was paid in Yugos, which it peddled piecemeal by trading them for everything from cash to Caribbean resort hotel rooms, which it in turn sold to tour packagers and travel agencies for cash.[14]

CULTURAL ENVIRONMENT

Each country has its own folkways, norms, and taboos. The seller must examine the ways consumers in different countries think about and use certain products before planning a marketing program. There are often surprises. For example, the average French man uses almost twice as many cosmetics and beauty aids as his wife. The Germans and the French eat more packaged, branded spaghetti than do Italians. Italian children like to eat chocolate bars between slices of bread as a snack. Women in Tanzania will not give their children eggs for fear of making them bald or impotent.

Companies that ignore such differences can make some very expensive and embarrassing mistakes. Here's an example:

> McDonald's and Coca-Cola managed to offend the entire Muslim world by putting the Saudi Arabian flag on their packaging. The flag's design includes a passage from the Koran (the sacred text of Islam), and Muslims feel very strongly that their Holy Writ should never be wadded up and tossed in the garbage. Nike faced a similar situation in Arab countries when Muslims objected to a stylized "Air" logo on its shoes that resembled "Allah" in Arabic script. Nike apologized for the mistake and pulled the shoes from distribution.[15]

Business norms and behavior also vary from country to country. American business executives need to be briefed on these factors before conducting business in another country. Here are some examples of different global business behavior:[16]

■ South Americans like to sit or stand very close to each other when they talk business—in fact, almost nose-to-nose. The American business executive tends to keep backing away as the South American moves closer. Both may end up being offended.

■ Fast and tough bargaining, which works well in other parts of the world, is often inappropriate in Japan and other Asian countries. Moreover, in face-to-face communications, Japanese business executives rarely say no. Thus, Americans tend to become impatient with having to spend time in polite conversation about the weather or other such topics before getting down to business. They also become frustrated when they don't know where they stand. However, when Americans come to the point quickly, Japanese business executives may find this behavior offensive.

---

[14]For these and other examples, see Louis Kraar, "How to Sell to Cashless Buyers," *Fortune,* November 7, 1988, pp. 147–54; Nathaniel Gilbert, "The Case for Countertrade," *Across the Board,* May 1992, pp. 43–45; Kwanena Anyane-Ntow and Santhi C. Harvey, "A Countertrade Primer," *Management Accounting (USA),* April 1995, p. 47; Darren McDermott and S. Karen Witcher, "Bartering Gains Currency," *Wall Street Journal,* April 6, 1998, p. A10; and Anne Millen Porter, "Global Economic Meltdown Boosts Barter Business," *Purchasing,* February 11, 1999, pp. 21–25.

[15]Rebecca Piirto Heath, "Think Globally," *Marketing Tools,* October 1996, pp. 49–54; and "The Power of Writing," *National Geographic,* August 1999, p. 128–29.

[16]For other examples, see Sak Onkvisit and John J. Shaw, *International Marketing: Analysis and Strategy* (Upper Saddle River, NJ: Prentice Hall, 1997), chap. 6, "Tips, Tricks and Pitfalls to Avoid When Doing Business in the Tough but Lucrative Korean Market," *Business America,* June 1997, p. 7; Dana May Casperson, "Minding Your Manners in Latin America," *Sales & Marketing Management,* March 1998, p. 96; Valerie Frazee, "Getting Started in Mexico," *Workforce,* January 1997, pp. 16–17; Teresa C. Morrison, Wayne A. Conaway, and Joseph J. Douress, *Dun & Bradstreet's Guide to Doing Business Around the World* (New York: Prentice Hall, 1997); and Philip Kotler, *Marketing Management: Analysis, Planning, Implementation, and Control,* 10th ed. (Upper Saddle River, NJ: Prentice Hall, 2000), chap. 7.

Overlooking cultural differences can result in embarrassing mistakes. When it learned that this stylized "Air" logo resembled "Allah" in Arabic script, Nike apologized and pulled the shoes from distribution.

- In France, wholesalers don't want to promote a product. They ask their retailers what they want and deliver it. If an American company builds its strategy around the French wholesaler's cooperation in promotions, it is likely to fail.

- When American executives exchange business cards, each usually gives the other's card a cursory glance and stuffs it in a pocket for later reference. In Japan, however, executives dutifully study each other's cards during a greeting, carefully noting company affiliation and rank. They hand their card to the most important person first.

By the same token, companies that understand cultural nuances can use them to advantage when positioning products internationally. For example, consider French cosmetics giant L'Oréal:

It's a sunny afternoon outside Parkson's department store in Shanghai, and a marketing battle is raging for the attention of Chinese women. Tall, pouty models in beige skirts and sheer tops pass out flyers promoting Revlon's new spring colors. But their effort is drowned out by L'Oréal's eye-catching show for its Maybelline brand. To a pulsing rhythm, two gangly models in shimmering lycra tops dance on a podium before a large backdrop depicting the New York City skyline. The music stops, and a makeup artist transforms a model's face while a Chinese saleswoman delivers the punch line. "This brand comes from America. It's very trendy," she shouts into her microphone. "If you want to be fashionable, just choose Maybelline." Few of the women in the crowd realize that the trendy "New York" Maybelline brand belongs to French cosmetics giant L'Oréal. . . . Blink an eye and L'Oréal has just sold 85 products around the world, from Redken hair care and Ralph Lauren perfumes to Helena Rubinstein cosmetics. In the battle for global beauty markets, L'Oréal has developed a winning formula: . . . conveying the allure of different cultures through its many products. Whether it's selling Italian elegance, New York street smarts, or French beauty through its brands, L'Oréal is reaching out to a vast range of people across incomes and cultures.[17]

Thus, understanding cultural traditions, preferences, and behaviors can help companies to avoid embarrassing mistakes and to take advantage of cross-cultural opportunities.

[17]Gail Edmondson, "The Beauty of Global Branding," *Business Week,* June 28, 1999, pp. 70–75.

Companies that understand cultural nuances can use them to advantage. L'Oréal's winning formula is to convey the allure of different cultures through its many products.

active example   <

Consider some examples of cultural differences in business customs.

active concept check   <

Now let's take a moment to test your knowledge of what you've just read.

> **Deciding Whether to Go International**

Not all companies need to venture into international markets to survive. For example, many companies are local businesses that need to market well only in the local marketplace. Operating domestically is easier and safer. Managers need not learn another country's language and laws, deal with volatile currencies, face political and legal uncertainties, or redesign their products to suit different customer needs and expectations. However, companies that operate in global industries, where their strategic positions in specific markets are affected strongly by their overall global positions, must compete on a worldwide basis if they are to succeed.

Any of several factors might draw a company into the international arena. Global competitors might attack the company's domestic market by offering better products or lower prices. The company might want to counterattack these competitors in their home markets to tie up their resources. Or the company might discover foreign markets that present higher profit opportunities than the domestic market does. The company's domestic market might be stagnant or shrinking, or the company might need an enlarged customer base in order to achieve economies of scale. The company might want to reduce its dependence on any one market so as to reduce its risk. Finally, the company's customers might be expanding abroad and require international servicing.

Before going abroad, the company must weigh several risks and answer many questions about its ability to operate globally. Can the company learn to understand the preferences and buyer behavior of consumers in other countries? Can it offer competitively attractive products? Will it be able to adapt to other countries' business cultures and deal effectively with foreign nationals? Do the company's managers have the necessary international experience? Has management considered the impact of regulations and the political environments of other countries?

Because of the risks and difficulties of entering international markets, most companies do not act until some situation or event thrusts them into the global arena. Someone—a domestic exporter, a foreign importer, a foreign government—may ask the company to sell abroad. Or the company may be saddled with overcapacity and must find additional markets for its goods.

> active exercise

Consider a valuable resource of information on international trade and business.

> active concept check

Now let's take a moment to test your knowledge of what you've just read.

> Deciding Which Markets to Enter

Before going abroad, the company should try to define its international *marketing objectives and policies*. It should decide what *volume* of foreign sales it wants. Most companies start small when they go abroad. Some plan to stay small, seeing international sales as a small part of their business. Other companies have bigger plans, seeing international business as equal to or even more important than their domestic business.

The company must also choose *how many* countries it wants to market in. Generally, it makes sense to operate in fewer countries with deeper commitment and penetration in each. The Bulova Watch Company decided to operate in many international markets and expanded into more than 100 countries. As a result, it spread itself too thin, made profits in only two countries, and lost around $40 million. In contrast, although consumer product company Amway is now breaking into markets at a furious pace, it is doing so only after decades of gradually building up its overseas presence. Known for its neighbor-to-neighbor direct-selling networks, Amway expanded into Australia in 1971, a country far away but similar to the U.S. market. Then, in the 1980s, Amway expanded into 10 more countries, and the pace increased rapidly from then on. By 1994 Amway was firmly established in 60 countries, including Hungary, Poland, and the Czech Republic. Following its substantial success in Japan, China, and other Asian countries, the company entered India in 1998. Entering the new millennium, international proceeds account for over 70 percent of the company's overall sales.[18]

Next, the company needs to decide on the *types* of countries to enter. A country's attractiveness depends on the product, geographical factors, income and population, political climate, and other factors. The seller may prefer certain country groups or parts of the world. In recent years, many major new markets have emerged, offering both substantial opportunities and daunting challenges.

After listing possible international markets, the company must screen and rank each one. Consider the following example:

Many mass marketers dream of selling to China's more than 1.2 billion people. For example, Colgate is waging a pitched battle in China, seeking control of the world's largest toothpaste market. Yet, this country of infrequent brushers offers great potential. Only 20 percent of

[18]Charles A. Coulombe, "Global Expansion: The Unstoppable Crusade," *Success,* September 1994, pp. 18–20; "Amway Hopes to Set Up Sales Network in India," *Wall Street Journal,* February 17, 1998, p. B8; and Gerald S. Couzens, "Dick Devos," *Success,* November 1998, pp. 52–57.

China's rural dwellers brush daily, so Colgate and its competitors are aggressively pursuing promotional and educational programs, from massive ad campaigns to visits to local schools to sponsoring oral care research. Through such efforts, in this $350 million market dominated by local brands, Colgate has expanded its market share from 7 percent in 1995 to 24 percent today.[19]

Colgate's decision to enter the Chinese market seems fairly simple and straightforward: China is a huge market without established competition. Given the low rate of brushing, this already huge market can grow even larger. Yet we still can question whether market size *alone* is reason enough for selecting China. Colgate also must consider other factors: Will the Chinese government remain stable and supportive? Does China provide for the production and distribution technologies needed to produce and market Colgate's products profitably? Will Colgate be able to overcome cultural barriers and convince Chinese consumers to brush their teeth regularly? Can Colgate compete effectively with dozens of local competitors? Colgate's current success in China suggests that it could answer yes to all of these questions. Still, the company's future in China is filled with uncertainties.

Possible global markets should be ranked on several factors, including market size, market growth, cost of doing business, competitive advantage, and risk level. The goal is to determine the potential of each market, using indicators such as those shown in Table 19.1. Then the marketer must decide which markets offer the greatest long-run return on investment.

TABLE 19.1	Indicators of Market Potential
1. Demographic Characteristics	**4. Technological Factors**
Size of population	Level of technological skills
Rate of population growth	Existing production technology
Degree of urbanization	Existing consumption technology
Population density	Education levels
Age structure and composition of the population	
2. Geographic Characteristics	**5. Sociocultural Factors**
Physical size of a country	Dominant values
Topographical characteristics	Lifestyle patterns
Climate conditions	Ethnic groups
	Linguistic fragmentation
3. Economic Factors	**6. National Goals and Plans**
GDP per capita	Industry priorities
Income distribution	Infrastructure investment plans
Rate of growth of GNP	
Ratio of investment to GNP	

Source: Susan P. Douglas, C. Samuel Craig, and Warren Keegan, "Approaches to Assessing International Marketing Opportunities for Small and Medium-Sized Businesses," *Columbia Journal of World Business,* Fall 1982, pp. 26–32. Copyright 1982, 1999. *Columbia Journal of World Business.* Reprint with permission. Also see Tamer S. Cavusil, "Measuring the Potential of Emerging Markets: An Indexing Approach," *Business Horizons,* January–February 1997, pp. 87–91.

[19]See "Crest, Colgate Bare Teeth in Competition for China," *Advertising Age International,* November 1996, p. I3; Mark L. Clifford, "How You Can Win in China," *Business Week,* May 26, 1997, pp. 66–68; and Ben Davies, "The Biggest Market Retains Its Luster," *Asia Money,* January 1998, pp. 47–49.

General Electric's appliance division sells more than 150 million appliances each year in 150 world markets under the Monogram, GE Profile, GE, Hotpoint, and RCA brand names. This experienced global marketer uses what it calls a "smart bomb" strategy for selecting global markets to enter. GE Appliances executives examine each potential country microscopically, measuring factors such as strength of local competitors, market growth potential, and availability of skilled labor. Then they target only markets in which they can earn more than 20 percent on their investment. The goal: "To generate the best returns possible on the smallest investment possible." Once targets are selected, GE Appliances zeros in with marketing smart bombs—products and programs tailored to yield the best performance in each market. As a result of this strategy, GE is trouncing competitors Whirlpool and Maytag in Asian markets.[20]

> ## Deciding How to Enter the Market

Once a company has decided to sell in a foreign country, it must determine the best mode of entry. Its choices are *exporting, joint venturing,* and *direct investment.* Figure 19.2 shows three market entry strategies, along with the options each one offers. As the figure shows, each succeeding strategy involves more commitment and risk, but also more control and potential profits.

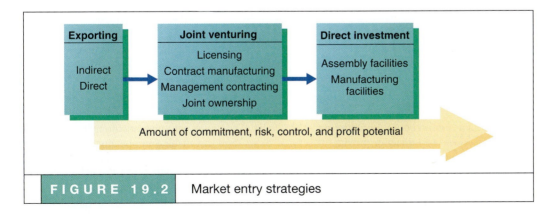

Exporting	**Joint venturing**	**Direct investment**
Indirect Direct	Licensing Contract manufacturing Management contracting Joint ownership	Assembly facilities Manufacturing facilities

Amount of commitment, risk, control, and profit potential

FIGURE 19.2   Market entry strategies

[20]Linda Grant, "GE's 'Smart Bomb' Strategy," *Fortune,* July 21, 1997, pp. 109–10; Richard J. Babyak, "GE Appliances: The Polar Approach," *Appliance Manufacturer,* February 1997, p. G22; and Joe Jancsurak, "Asia to Drive World Appliance Growth," *Appliance Manufacturer,* February 1999, pp. G3–G6.

EXPORTING

The simplest way to enter a foreign market is through **exporting.** The company may passively export its surpluses from time to time, or it may make an active commitment to expand exports to a particular market. In either case, the company produces all its goods in its home country. It may or may not modify them for the export market. Exporting involves the least change in the company's product lines, organization, investments, or mission.

Companies typically start with *indirect exporting,* working through independent international marketing intermediaries. Indirect exporting involves less investment because the firm does not require an overseas sales force or set of contacts. It also involves less risk. International marketing intermediaries—domestic-based export merchants or agents, cooperative organizations, and export-management companies—bring know-how and services to the relationship, so the seller normally makes fewer mistakes.

Sellers may eventually move into *direct exporting,* whereby they handle their own exports. The investment and risk are somewhat greater in this strategy, but so is the potential return. A company can conduct direct exporting in several ways: It can set up a domestic export department that carries out export activities. It can set up an overseas sales branch that handles sales, distribution, and perhaps promotion. The sales branch gives the seller more presence and program control in the foreign market and often serves as a display center and customer service center. The company can also send home-based salespeople abroad at certain times in order to find business. Finally, the company can do its exporting either through foreign-based distributors who buy and own the goods or through foreign-based agents who sell the goods on behalf of the company.

JOINT VENTURING

A second method of entering a foreign market is **joint venturing**—joining with foreign companies to produce or market products or services. Joint venturing differs from exporting in that the company joins with a host country partner to sell or market abroad. It differs from direct investment in that an association is formed with someone in the foreign country. There are four types of joint ventures: licensing, contract manufacturing, management contracting, and joint ownership.

Licensing

Licensing is a simple way for a manufacturer to enter international marketing. The company enters into an agreement with a licensee in the foreign market. For a fee or royalty, the licensee buys the right to use the company's manufacturing process, trademark, patent, trade secret, or other item of value. The company thus gains entry into the market at little risk; the licensee gains production expertise or a well-known product or name without having to start from scratch.

Coca-Cola markets internationally by licensing bottlers around the world and supplying them with the syrup needed to produce the product. In Japan, Budweiser beer flows from Kirin breweries, Lady Borden ice cream is churned out at Meiji Milk Products dairies, and Marlboro cigarettes roll off production lines at Japan Tobacco, Inc. Tokyo Disneyland is owned and operated by Oriental Land Company under license from the Walt Disney Company. The 45-year license gives Disney licensing fees plus 10 percent of admissions and 5 percent of food and merchandise sales. And in an effort to bring online retail investing to people abroad, online brokerage E*Trade has to date launched E*Trade-branded Web sites in six countries outside the United States, initially forming licensing agreements and launching sites in Canada, Australia–New Zealand, France, and the Nordic region, whose Swedish site also serves residents of Denmark, Norway, Finland, and Iceland. In addition, E*Trade established joint ventures and launched Web sites in both the United Kingdom and Japan. The Nordic licensee later became a wholly owned subsidiary of E*Trade.[21]

Licensing has potential disadvantages, however. The firm has less control over the licensee than it would over its own production facilities. Furthermore, if the licensee is very successful, the firm has given up these profits, and if and when the contract ends, it may find it has created a competitor.

Contract Manufacturing

Another option is **contract manufacturing**—the company contracts with manufacturers in the foreign market to produce its product or provide its service. Sears used this method in opening up department stores in Mexico and Spain, where it found qualified local manufacturers to produce many of the products it sells. The drawbacks of contract manufacturing are decreased control over the manufacturing process and loss of potential profits on manufacturing. The benefits are the chance to start faster, with less risk, and the later opportunity either to form a partnership with or to buy out the local manufacturer.

---

[21]Robert Neff, "In Japan, They're Goofy About Disney," *Business Week,* March 12, 1990, p. 64; and "In Brief: e-Trade Licensing Deal Gives It an Israeli Link," *American Banker,* May 11, 1998.

Licensing: Online brokerage E*Trade used licensing agreements to launch sites in Canada, Australia–New Zealand, France, and the Nordic region, whose Swedish site also serves residents of Denmark, Norway, Finland, and Iceland.

Management Contracting

Under **management contracting,** the domestic firm supplies management know-how to a foreign company that supplies the capital. The domestic firm exports management services rather than products. Hilton uses this arrangement in managing hotels around the world.

Management contracting is a low-risk method of getting into a foreign market, and it yields income from the beginning. The arrangement is even more attractive if the contracting firm has an option to buy some share in the managed company later on. The arrangement is not sensible, however, if the company can put its scarce management talent to better uses or if it can make greater profits by undertaking the whole venture. Management contracting also prevents the company from setting up its own operations for a period of time.

Joint Ownership

Joint ownership ventures consist of one company joining forces with foreign investors to create a local business in which they share joint ownership and control. A company may buy an interest in a local firm, or the two parties may form a new business venture. Joint ownership may be needed for economic or political reasons. The firm may lack the financial, physical, or managerial resources to undertake the venture alone. Or a foreign government may require joint ownership as a condition for entry.

KFC entered Japan through a joint ownership venture with Japanese conglomerate Mitsubishi. KFC sought a good way to enter the large but difficult Japanese fast-food market. In turn, Mitsubishi, one of Japan's largest poultry producers, understood the Japanese culture and had money to invest. Together, they helped KFC succeed in the semiclosed Japanese market. Surprisingly, with Mitsubishi's guidance, KFC developed decidedly un-Japanese positioning for its Japanese restaurants:

> While its initial reception in Japan was great, KFC still had a number of obstacles to overcome. The Japanese were uncomfortable with the idea of fast food and franchising. They saw fast food as artificial, made by mechanical means, and unhealthy. KFC Japan knew that it had to build trust in the KFC brand and flew to Kentucky to do it. There it filmed the most authentic version of Colonel Sanders's beginnings possible. To show the philosophy of KFC—the southern hospitality, old American tradition, and authentic home cooking—the agency first created the quintessential southern mother. With "My Old Kentucky Home" by Stephen Foster playing in the background, the commercial showed Colonel Sanders's mother making and feeding her grandchildren KFC chicken made with 11 secret spices. It conjured up scenes of good home cookin' from the deep American South, positioning KFC as wholesome, aristocratic food. In the end, the Japanese people could not get enough of this special American chicken made with 11 spices. The campaign was hugely successful, and in less than 8 years KFC expanded its presence from 400 locations to more than 1,000. Most Japanese now know "My Old Kentucky Home" by heart.[22]

[22]See Cynthia Kemper, "KFC Tradition Sold Japan on Chicken," *Denver Post,* June 7, 1998, p. J4.

Joint ownership has certain drawbacks. The partners may disagree over investment, marketing, or other policies. Whereas many U.S. firms like to reinvest earnings for growth, local firms often prefer to take out these earnings; and whereas U.S. firms emphasize the role of marketing, local investors may rely on selling.

DIRECT INVESTMENT

The biggest involvement in a foreign market comes through **direct investment**—the development of foreign-based assembly or manufacturing facilities. If a company has gained experience in exporting and if the foreign market is large enough, foreign production facilities offer many advantages. The firm may have lower costs in the form of cheaper labor or raw materials, foreign government investment incentives, and freight savings. The firm may improve its image in the host country because it creates jobs. Generally, a firm develops a deeper relationship with government, customers, local suppliers, and distributors, allowing it to adapt its products to the local market better. Finally, the firm keeps full control over the investment and therefore can develop manufacturing and marketing policies that serve its long-term international objectives.

The main disadvantage of direct investment is that the firm faces many risks, such as restricted or devalued currencies, falling markets, or government changes. In some cases, a firm has no choice but to accept these risks if it wants to operate in the host country.

active example <

Consider how some important U.S. firms have turned to the global market.

active concept check <

Now let's take a moment to test your knowledge of what you've just read.

> ### Deciding on the Global Marketing Program

Companies that operate in one or more foreign markets must decide how much, if at all, to adapt their marketing mixes to local conditions. At one extreme are global companies that use a **standardized marketing mix,** selling largely the same products and using the same marketing approaches worldwide. At the other extreme is an **adapted marketing mix.** In this case, the producer adjusts the marketing mix elements to each target market, bearing more costs but hoping for a larger market share and return.

The question of whether to adapt or standardize the marketing mix has been much debated in recent years. The marketing concept holds that marketing programs will be more effective if tailored to the unique needs of each targeted customer group. If this concept applies within a country, it should apply even more in international markets. Consumers in different countries have widely varied cultural backgrounds, needs and wants, spending power, product preferences, and shopping patterns. Because these differences are hard to change, most marketers adapt their products, prices, channels, and promotions to fit consumer desires in each country.

However, some global marketers are bothered by what they see as too much adaptation, which raises costs and dilutes global brand power. As a result, many companies have created so-called world brands—more or less the same product sold the same way to all consumers worldwide. Marketers at these companies believe that advances in communication, transportation, and travel are turning the world into a common marketplace. These marketers claim that people around the world want basically the same products and lifestyles. Despite what consumers say they want, all consumers want good products at lower prices.

Such arguments ring true. The development of the Internet, the rapid spread of cable and satellite TV around the world, and the creation of telecommunications networks linking previously remote places have all made the world a smaller place. For instance, the disproportionately American programming beamed into homes in the developing world has sparked a convergence of consumer appetites, particularly among youth. One economist calls these emerging consumers the "global MTV generation." "They prefer Coke to tea, Nikes to sandals, Chicken McNuggets to rice, and credit cards to cash," he says.[23] Fashion trends spread almost instantly, propelled by TV and Internet chat groups. Around the world, news and comment on almost any topic or product is available at the click of a mouse or twist of a dial. The resulting convergence of needs and wants has created global markets for standardized products, particularly among the young middle class.

Proponents of global standardization claim that international marketers should adapt products and marketing programs only when local wants cannot be changed or avoided. Standardization results in lower production, distribution, marketing, and management costs, and thus lets the company offer consumers higher quality and more reliable products at lower prices. In fact, some companies have successfully marketed global products—for example, Coca-Cola soft drinks, McDonald's hamburgers, Black & Decker tools, and Sony Walkmans.

However, even for these "global" brands, companies make some adaptations. Moreover, the assertion that global standardization will lead to lower costs and prices, causing more goods to be snapped up by price-sensitive consumers, is debatable. Consider these examples:[24]

> Mattel Toys had sold its Barbie doll successfully in dozens of countries without modification. But in Japan, it did not sell well. Takara, Mattel's Japanese licensee, surveyed eighth-grade Japanese girls and their parents and found that they thought the doll's breasts were too big and that its legs were too long. Mattel, however, was reluctant to modify the doll because this would require additional production, packaging, and advertising costs. Finally, Takara won out and Mattel made a special Japanese Barbie. Within two years, Takara had sold over 2 million of the modified dolls.
>
> - Frito-Lay had successfully sold its Cheetos cheese snacks in dozens of countries with little modification, but the company was stymied when it came to China. How do you sell a cheese-based product in a country where cheese is not a dietary staple? Brand managers at Guangzhou Frito-Lay would not be deterred. After consumer tests of 600 different flavors, the company launched a cheeseless version of Cheetos in "Savory American Cream" flavor and teriyaki-tasting "Zesty Japanese Steak." The flexibility paid off; after six months the brand was selling out across China.
>
> - Even MTV, with its largely global programming, has retrenched along more local lines. Pummeled by dozens of local music channels in Europe, such as Germany's *Viva*, Holland's *The Music Factory*, and Scandinavia's *ZTV*, MTV Europe has had to drop its pan-European programming, which featured a large amount of American and British pop along with local European favorites. In its place, the division created regional channels broadcast by four separate MTV stations—MTV: U.K. & Ireland, MTV: Northern Europe, MTV: Central Europe, and MTV: Southern Europe. Each of the four channels shows programs tailored to music tastes of its local market, along with more traditional pan-European pop selections. Within each region, MTV further subdivides its programming. For example, within the United Kingdom, MTV offers sister stations M2 and VH-1, along with three new digital channels: MTV Extra, MTV Base, and VH-1 Classic. Says the head of MTV Europe, "We hope to offer every MTV fan something he or she will like to watch any time of the day."

In these cases, incremental revenues from adapting products far exceeded the incremental costs.

So which approach is best—global standardization or adaptation? Clearly, global standardization is not an all-or-nothing proposition but rather a matter of degree. Companies should look for more standardization to help keep down costs and prices and to build greater global brand power. But they must not replace long-run marketing thinking with short-run financial thinking. Although standardi-

[23]Lawrence Donegan, "Heavy Job Rotation MTV Europe Sacks 80 Employees in the Name of 'Regionalisation,' " *The Guardian,* November 21, 1997, p. 19.

[24]Karen Benezra, "Fritos 'Round the World," *Brandweek,* March 27, 1995, pp. 32, 35; Cyndee Miller, "Chasing Global Dream," *Marketing News,* December 2, 1996, pp. 1, 2; and Christian Lorenz, "MTV Europe Launches Channels," *Billboard,* February 27, 1999, p. 48.

zation saves money, marketers must make certain that they offer what consumers in each country want.[25]

Many possibilities exist between the extremes of standardization and complete adaptation. For example, although Whirlpool ovens, refrigerators, clothes washers, and other major appliances share the same interiors worldwide, their outer styling and features are designed to meet the preferences of consumers in different countries. Coca-Cola sells virtually the same Coke beverage worldwide, and it pulls advertisements for specific markets from a common pool of ads designed to have cross-cultural appeal. However, Coca-Cola is less sweet or less carbonated in certain countries. The company also sells a variety of other beverages created specifically for the tastebuds of local markets and modifies its distribution channels according to local conditions.

Similarly, McDonald's uses the same basic operating formula in its restaurants around the world but adapts its menu to local tastes. For example, it uses chili sauce instead of ketchup on its hamburgers in Mexico. In India, where cows are considered sacred, McDonald's serves chicken, fish, vegetable burgers, and the Maharaja Mac—two all-mutton patties, special sauce, lettuce, cheese, pickles, onions on a sesame-seed bun. In Vienna, its restaurants include "McCafes," which offer coffee blended to local tastes, and in Korea, it sells roast pork on a bun with a garlicky soy sauce.[26]

Some international marketers suggest that companies should "think globally but act locally." They advocate a "glocal" strategy in which the firm standardizes certain core marketing elements and localizes others.[27] The corporate level gives strategic direction; local units focus on the individual consumer differences. They conclude: global marketing, yes; global standardization, not necessarily.

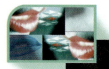

active poll <

Give your opinion on a question concerning the impact of global companies on developing countries.

PRODUCT

Five strategies allow for adapting product and promotion to a foreign market (see Figure 19.3).[28] We first discuss the three product strategies and then turn to the two promotion strategies.

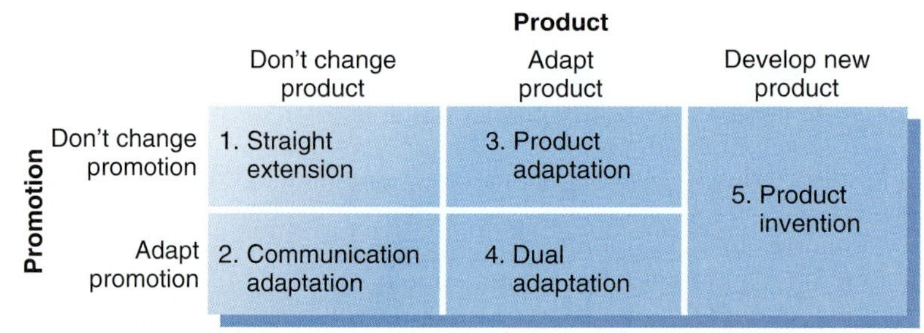

	Product		
	Don't change product	Adapt product	Develop new product
Don't change promotion	1. Straight extension	3. Product adaptation	
			5. Product invention
Adapt promotion	2. Communication adaptation	4. Dual adaptation	

(Promotion — row labels on vertical axis)

FIGURE 19.3 Five international product and promotion strategies

[25]See Theodore Levitt, "The Globalization of Markets," *Harvard Business Review,* May-June 1983, pp. 92–102; David M. Szymanski, Sundar G. Bharadwaj, and Rajan Varadarajan, "Standardization versus Adaptation of International Marketing Strategy: An Empirical Investigation," *Journal of Marketing,* October 1993, pp. 1–17; Ashish Banerjee, "Global Campaigns Don't Work; Multinationals Do," *Advertising Age,* April 18, 1994, p. 23; Miller, "Chasing Global Dream," pp. 1, 2; Jeryl Whitelock and Carole Pimblett, "The Standardization Debate in International Marketing," *Journal of Global Marketing,* 1997, p. 22; and David A. Aaker and Ericj Joachimsthaler, "The Lure of Global Branding," *Harvard Business Review,* November–December 1999, pp. 137–44.

[26]See "In India, Beef-Free Mickie D," *Business Week,* April 7, 1995, p. 52; Jeff Walters, "Have Brand Will Travel," *Brandweek,* October 6, 1997, pp. 22–26; and David Barboza, "From Abroad, McDonald's Finds Value in Local Control," *New York Times,* February 12, 1999, p. 1.

[27]See Martha M. Hamilton, "Going Global: A World of Difference," *Washington Post,* May 10, 1998, p. H1.

[28]See Warren J. Keegan, *Global Marketing Management,* 4th ed. (Upper Saddle River, NJ: Prentice Hall, 1989), pp. 378–81; and Warren J. Keegan and Mark C. Green, *Principles of Global Marketing* (Upper Saddle River, NJ: Prentice Hall, 1997), pp. 294–98.

Straight product extension means marketing a product in a foreign market without any change. Top management tells its marketing people: "Take the product as is and find customers for it." The first step, however, should be to find out whether foreign consumers use that product and what form they prefer.

Straight extension has been successful in some cases and disastrous in others. Kellogg cereals, Gillette razors, IBM computer services, Heineken beer, and Black & Decker tools are all sold successfully in about the same form around the world. But General Foods introduced its standard powdered Jell-O in the British market only to find that British consumers prefer a solid wafer or cake form. Likewise, Philips began to make a profit in Japan only after it reduced the size of its coffeemakers to fit into smaller Japanese kitchens and its shavers to fit smaller Japanese hands. Straight extension is tempting because it involves no additional product development costs, manufacturing changes, or new promotion. But it can be costly in the long run if products fail to satisfy foreign consumers.

Product adaptation involves changing the product to meet local conditions or wants. For example, Procter & Gamble's Vidal Sassoon shampoos contain a single fragrance worldwide but the amount of scent varies by country: less in Japan, where subtle scents are preferred, and more in Europe. General Foods blends different coffees for the British (who drink their coffee with milk), the French (who drink their coffee black), and Latin Americans (who prefer a chicory taste). In Japan, Mister Donut serves coffee in smaller and lighter cups that better fit the fingers of the average Japanese consumer; even the doughnuts are a little smaller. Gerber serves the Japanese baby food fare that might turn the stomachs of many Western consumers—local favorites include flounder and spinach stew, cod roe spaghetti, mugwort casserole, and sardines ground up in white radish sauce. In Brazil, Levi's developed its Femina jeans featuring curvaceous cuts that provide the ultratight fit traditionally favored by Brazilian women. Finnish cellular phone superstar Nokia customized its 6100 series phone for every major market. Developers built in rudimentary voice recognition for Asia where keyboards are a problem and raised the ring volume so the phone could be heard on crowded Asian streets.[29]

In some instances, products must also be adapted to local superstitions or spiritual beliefs. In Asia, the supernatural world often relates directly to sales. Hyatt Hotels' experience with the concept of *feng shui* is a good example:

A practice widely followed in China, Hong Kong, and Singapore (and which has spread to Japan, Vietnam, and Korea), *feng shui* means "wind and water." Practitioners of *feng shui,* or geomancers, will recommend the most favorable conditions for any venture, particularly the placement of office buildings and the arrangement of desks, doors, and other items within. To have good *feng shui,* a building should face the water and be flanked by mountains. However, it should not block the view of the mountain spirits. The Hyatt Hotel in Singapore was designed without *feng shui* in mind, and as a result had to be redesigned to boost business. Originally the front desk was parallel to the doors and road, and this was thought to lead to wealth flowing out. Furthermore, the doors were facing northwest, which easily let undesirable spirits in. The geomancer recommended design alterations so that wealth could be retained and undesirable spirits kept out.[30]

Product invention consists of creating something new for the foreign market. This strategy can take two forms. It might mean reintroducing earlier product forms that happen to be well adapted to the needs of a given country. For example, the National Cash Register Company reintroduced its crank-operated cash register at half the price of a modern cash register and sold large numbers in Asia, Latin America, and Spain. Or a company might create a new product to meet a need in another country. For example, an enormous need exists for low-cost, high-protein foods in less developed countries. Companies such as Quaker Oats, Swift, Monsanto, and Archer Daniels Midland are researching the nutrition needs of these countries, creating new foods, and developing advertising campaigns to gain product trial and acceptance. Product invention can be costly but the payoffs are worthwhile.

[29]For these and other examples, see Andrew Kupfer, "How to Be a Global Manager," *Fortune,* March 14, 1988, pp. 52–58; Maria Shao, "For Levi's: A Flattering Fit Overseas," *Business Week,* November 5, 1990, 76–77; Joseph Weber, "Campbell: Now It's M-M-Global," *Business Week,* March 15, 1993, pp. 52–53; Zachary Schiller, "Make It Simple," *Business Week,* September 9, 1996, p. 102; Chester Dawson, "Gerber Feeding Booming Japanese Baby Food Market," *Durham Herald-Sun,* February 21, 1998, p. C10; and Jack Neff, "Test It in Paris, France, Launch It in Paris, Texas," *Advertising Age,* May 31, 1999, p. 28.

[30]J. S. Perry Hobson, *"Feng Shui:* Its Impacts on the Asian Hospitality Industry," *International Journal of Contemporary Hospitality Management,* 6, no. 6, 1994, pp. 21–26; Bernd H. Schmitt and Yigang Pan, "In Asia, the Supernatural Means Sales," *New York Times,* February 19, 1995, pp. 3, 11; and Sally Taylor, "Tackling the Curse of Bad Feng Shui," *Publishers Weekly,* April 27, 1998, p. 24.

PROMOTION

Companies can either adopt the same promotion strategy they used in the home market or change it for each local market. Consider advertising messages. Some global companies use a standardized advertising theme around the world. For example, to help communicate its global reach, IBM Global Services runs virtually identical "People Who Think. People Who Do. People Who Get It." ads in dozens of countries around the world. Of course, even in highly standardized promotion campaigns, some small changes might be required to adjust for language and minor cultural differences. For instance, when Heinz Pet Food introduced its 9 Lives cat food in Russia, it used its standardized advertising featuring Morris the Cat. It turns out, however, that Morris needed a makeover. Russian consumers prefer a fatter-looking spokeskitty (it's considered healthier), so Heinz put a beefier Morris on the package.[31]

Colors also are changed sometimes to avoid taboos in other countries. Purple is associated with death in most of Latin America; white is a mourning color in Japan; and green is associated with jungle sickness in Malaysia. Even names must be changed. In Sweden, Helene Curtis changed the name of its Every Night Shampoo to Every Day because Swedes usually wash their hair in the morning. Kellogg also had to rename Bran Buds cereal in Sweden, where the name roughly translates as "burned farmer."

Other companies follow a strategy of **communication adaptation,** fully adapting their advertising messages to local markets. The Schwinn Bicycle Company might use a pleasure theme in the United States and a safety theme in Scandinavia. Kellogg ads in the United States promote the taste and nutrition of Kellogg's cereals versus competitors' brands. In France, where consumers drink little milk and eat little for breakfast, Kellogg's ads must convince consumers that cereals are a tasty and healthful breakfast. In India, where many consumers eat heavy, fried breakfasts, Kellogg's advertising convinces buyers to switch to a lighter, more nutritious breakfast diet.

Standardized advertising: To help communicate its global reach, IBM Global Services uses a standardized advertising theme in dozens of countries around the world: "People Who Think. People Who Do. People Who Get It." These ads are from Canada and the United Kingdom.

[31]Erika Rasmusson, "Global Warning," *Sales & Marketing Management,* November 1998, p. 17; and Bradley Johnson, "IBM Talks Global Clout, in Foreign Languages," *Advertising Age,* June 7, 1999, p. 10.

Media also need to be adapted internationally because media availability varies from country to country. TV advertising time is very limited in Europe, for instance, ranging from four hours a day in France to none in Scandinavian countries. Advertisers must buy time months in advance, and they have little control over airtimes. Magazines also vary in effectiveness. For example, magazines are a major medium in Italy and a minor one in Austria. Newspapers are national in the United Kingdom but are only local in Spain.

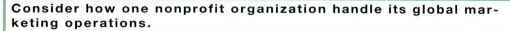

> video example

Consider how one nonprofit organization handle its global marketing operations.

PRICE

Companies also face many problems in setting their international prices. For example, how might Black & Decker price its power tools globally? It could set a uniform price all around the world, but this amount would be too high a price in poor countries and not high enough in rich ones. It could charge what consumers in each country would bear, but this strategy ignores differences in the actual costs from country to country. Finally, the company could use a standard markup of its costs everywhere, but this approach might price Black & Decker out of the market in some countries where costs are high.

Regardless of how companies go about pricing their products, their foreign prices probably will be higher than their domestic prices. A Gucci handbag may sell for $60 in Italy and $240 in the United States. Why? Gucci faces a *price escalation* problem. It must add the cost of transportation, tariffs, importer margin, wholesaler margin, and retailer margin to its factory price. Depending on these added costs, the product may have to sell for two to five times as much in another country to make the same profit. For example, a pair of Levi's jeans that sells for $30 in the United States typically fetches $63 in Tokyo and $88 in Paris. A computer that sells for $1,000 in New York may cost £1,000 in the United Kingdom. A Chrysler automobile priced at $10,000 in the United States sells for more than $47,000 in South Korea.

Another problem involves setting a price for goods that a company ships to its foreign subsidiaries. If the company charges a foreign subsidiary too much, it may end up paying higher tariff duties even while paying lower income taxes in that country. If the company charges its subsidiary too little, it can be charged with *dumping*. Dumping occurs when a company either charges less than its costs or less than it charges in its home market. Thus, Harley-Davidson accused Honda and Kawasaki of dumping motorcycles on the U.S. market. The U.S. International Trade Commission agreed and responded with a special five-year tariff on Japanese heavy motorcycles, starting at 45 percent in 1983 and gradually dropping to 10 percent by 1988. Various governments are always watching for dumping abuses, and they often force companies to set the price charged by other competitors for the same or similar products.[32]

Recent economic and technological forces have had an impact on global pricing. For example, in the European Union, the transition by 11 countries to a single currency will certainly reduce the amount of price differentiation. In 1998, for instance, a bottle of Gatorade cost 3.5 European Currency Units (ECU) in Germany but only about 0.9 in Spain. Once consumers recognize price differentiation by country, companies will be forced to harmonize prices throughout the countries that have adopted the single currency. Companies and marketers that offer the most unique or necessary products or services will be least affected by such "price transparency." For instance, Mail Boxes, Etc., which has 350 stores in Europe, believes that customers who need to send faxes won't refuse to do so because it costs more in Paris than in Italy.[33]

The Internet will also make global price differences more obvious. When firms sell their wares over the Internet, customers can see how much products sell for in different countries. They might even be able to order a given product directly from the company location or dealer offering the lowest price. This will force companies toward more standardized international pricing.[34]

[32]See Michael Oneal, "Harley-Davidson: Ready to Hit the Road Again," *Business Week,* July 21, 1986, p. 70; and "EU Proposes Dumping Change," *East European Markets,* February 14, 1997, pp. 2–3.

[33]Maricris G. Briones, "The Euro Starts Here," *Marketing News,* July 20, 1998, pp. 1, 39.

[34]Ram Charan, "The Rules Have Changed," *Fortune,* March 16, 1998, pp. 159–62.

DISTRIBUTION CHANNELS

The international company must take a **whole-channel view** of the problem of distributing products to final consumers. Figure 19.4 shows the three major links between the seller and the final buyer. The first link, the *seller's headquarters organization,* supervises the channels and is part of the channel itself. The second link, *channels between nations,* moves the products to the borders of the foreign nations. The third link, *channels within nations,* moves the products from their foreign entry point to the final consumers. Some U.S. manufacturers may think their job is done once the product leaves their hands, but they would do well to pay more attention to its handling within foreign countries.

Channels of distribution within countries vary greatly from nation to nation. First, there are the large differences in the *numbers and types of intermediaries* serving each foreign market. For example, a U.S. company marketing in China must operate through a frustrating maze of state-controlled wholesalers and retailers. Chinese distributors often carry competitors' products and frequently refuse to share even basic sales and marketing information with their suppliers. Hustling for sales is an alien concept to Chinese distributors, who are used to selling all they can obtain. Working with or getting around this system sometimes requires substantial time and investment.

When Coke first entered China, for example, customers bicycled up to bottling plants to get their soft drinks. Many shopkeepers still don't have enough electricity to run soft drink coolers. Now, Coca-Cola is setting up direct-distribution channels, investing heavily in refrigerators and trucks, and upgrading wiring so that more retailers can install coolers.[35] Moreover, it's always on the lookout for innovative distribution approaches:

> Stroll through any residential area in a Chinese city and sooner or later you'll encounter a senior citizen with a red arm band eyeing strangers suspiciously. These are the pensioners who staff the neighborhood committees, which act as street-level watchdogs for the ruling Communist Party. In Shanghai, however, some of these socialist guardians have been signed up by the ultimate symbol of American capitalism, Coca-Cola. As part of its strategy to get the product to the customer, Coke approached 14 neighborhood committees . . . with a proposal. The head of Coke's Shanghai division outlines the deal: "We told them, 'You have some old people who aren't doing much. Why don't we stock our product in your office? Then you can sell it, earn some commission, and raise a bit of cash.'" Done. So . . . how are the party snoops adapting to the market? Not badly, reports the manager. "We use the neighborhood committees as a sales force," he says. Sales aren't spectacular, but because the committees supervise housing projects with up to 200 families, they have proved to be useful vehicles for building brand awareness.[36]

Another difference lies in the *size and character of retail units* abroad. Whereas large-scale retail chains dominate the U.S. scene, much retailing in other countries is done by many small, independent retailers. In India, millions of retailers operate tiny shops or sell in open markets. Their markups are high, but the actual price is lowered through haggling. Supermarkets could offer lower prices, but supermarkets are difficult to build and open because of many economic and cultural barriers. Incomes are low, and people prefer to shop daily for small amounts rather than weekly for large amounts. They also lack storage and refrigeration to keep food for several days. Packaging is not well developed because it would add too much to the cost. These factors have kept large-scale retailing from spreading rapidly in developing countries.

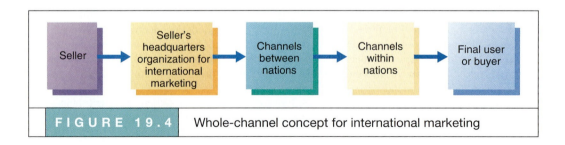

| Seller | → | Seller's headquarters organization for international marketing | → | Channels between nations | → | Channels within nations | → | Final user or buyer |

FIGURE 19.4   Whole-channel concept for international marketing

[35]See Maria Shao, "Laying the Foundation for the Great Mall of China," *Business Week,* January 25, 1988, pp. 68–69; and Mark L. Clifford and Nicole Harris, "Coke Pours into China," *Business Week,* October 28, 1996, p. 73.

[36]Richard Tomlinson, "The China Card," *Fortune,* May 25, 1998, p. 82; and Paul Mooney, "Deals on Wheels," *Far East Economic Review,* May 20, 1999, p. 53.

> ## video exercise

Consider a fictional case of one company confronting some challenges of global marketing.

> ## active concept check

Now let's take a moment to test your knowledge of what you've just read.

> ## Deciding on the Global Marketing Organization

Companies manage their international marketing activities in at least three different ways: Most companies first organize an export department, then create an international division, and finally become a global organization.

A firm normally gets into international marketing by simply shipping out its goods. If its international sales expand, the company organizes an *export department* with a sales manager and a few assistants. As sales increase, the export department can expand to include various marketing services so that it can actively go after business. If the firm moves into joint ventures or direct investment, the export department will no longer be adequate.

Many companies get involved in several international markets and ventures. A company may export to one country, license to another, have a joint ownership venture in a third, and own a subsidiary in a fourth. Sooner or later it will create an *international division* or subsidiary to handle all its international activity.

International divisions are organized in a variety of ways. The international division's corporate staff consists of marketing, manufacturing, research, finance, planning, and personnel specialists. They plan for and provide services to various operating units, which can be organized in one of three ways. They can be *geographical organizations,* with country managers who are responsible for salespeople, sales branches, distributors, and licensees in their respective countries. Or the operating units can be *world product groups,* each responsible for worldwide sales of different product groups. Finally, operating units can be *international subsidiaries,* each responsible for its own sales and profits.

Several firms have passed beyond the international division stage and become truly *global organizations.* They stop thinking of themselves as national marketers who sell abroad and start thinking of themselves as global marketers. The top corporate management and staff plan worldwide manufacturing facilities, marketing policies, financial flows, and logistical systems. The global operating units report directly to the chief executive or executive committee of the organization, not to the head of an international division. Executives are trained in worldwide operations, not just domestic *or* international. The company recruits management from many countries, buys components and supplies where they cost the least, and invests where the expected returns are greatest.

Proctor & Gamble recently took a big step in this direction by undertaking a global reorganization called Organization 2005. P&G is replacing its old geography-based organization with seven global business units organized by categories like baby care, beauty care, and fabric-and-home care. Each unit is located in a different country. The reorganization is intended to streamline product development processes and quickly bring innovative products to the global market. These units will develop and sell their products on a worldwide basis.[37]

[37]Peter Galuszka and Ellen Neuborne, "P&G's Hottest New Product: P&G," *Business Week,* October 5, 1998, p. 96.

Moving into the twenty-first century, major companies must become more global if they hope to compete. As foreign companies successfully invade their domestic markets, companies must move more aggressively into foreign markets. They will have to change from companies that treat their international operations as secondary, to companies that view the entire world as a single borderless market.[38]

active concept check   <

Now let's take a moment to test your knowledge of what you've just read.

> **Chapter Wrap-Up**

Now that you've reached the end of the chapter, you may wish to explore the concepts you've been reading about in greater detail, or test yourself to see how well you've comprehended the material. In the box below you'll find a number of links. Click on any one of these links to find additional chapter resources.

> end-of-chapter resources

- Review of Concept Connections
- Practice Quiz
- Tying it All Together (Audio)
- Key Terms
- Critical Thinking Exercises
- Experimental Exercises
- MyPHLIP Companion Web Site
- Case 1
- Case 2
- You Be the Consultant

[38]See Kenichi Ohmae, "Managing in a Borderless World," *Harvard Business Review,* May–June 1989, pp. 152–61; William J. Holstein, "The Stateless Corporation," *Business Week,* May 14, 1990, pp. 98–105; and John A. Byrne and Kathleen Kerwin, "Borderless Management," *Business Week,* May 23, 1994, pp. 24–26.

Marketing and Society: Social Responsibility and Marketing Ethics

Chapter Outline

> What's Ahead

When Ben Cohen and Jerry Greenfield first met in the seventh grade, they were, by their own admission, the "two slowest kids round the track." However, in 1978, after staring a life of mediocrity full in the face, the two friends decided to try something different. They took a $5 correspondence course on making ice cream, borrowed $12,000, and started their own scoop shop—Ben & Jerry's Handmade—in an abandoned gas station in Burlington, Vermont. The rest, as they say, is history. Two decades later, despite many growing pains, Ben & Jerry's has become the nation's number-two superpremium ice cream brand, with a 39 percent market share that trails only Häagen-Dazs's 43 percent share. Last year, Ben & Jerry's sold more than $209 million worth of ice cream and frozen yogurt products through supermarkets, convenience stores, and 150 Ben & Jerry's scoop shops around the country.

Why the strong appeal? For one thing, Ben & Jerry's is a master at creating innovative flavors such as Rainforest Crunch, Cherry Garcia, Chocolate Chip Cookie Dough, Phish Food, Chunky Monkey, and Chubby Hubby. Moreover, the company has taken on the appealing, laid-back personality of its founders. "If you passed [Ben and Jerry] in the street," notes one industry observer, "with their sloppy T-shirts and portly figures. . . , you'd probably think they were a couple of Grateful Dead roadies. [Under their leadership, Ben & Jerry's] markets its products with a combination of down-home hippie folksiness and 'right-on' credibility."

But behind the creative flavors and folksy image, Ben & Jerry's is a company that cares deeply about its social responsibilities. The company's mission statement challenges all employees, from top management to ice cream scoopers in each store, to include concern for individual and community welfare in their day-to-day decisions. It reads as follows:

Ben & Jerry's is dedicated to the creation and demonstration of a new corporate concept of *linked prosperity.* Our mission consists of three interrelated parts: *Product:* To make, distribute and sell the finest quality all natural ice cream and related products in a variety of innovative flavors made from Vermont dairy products. *Economic:*

To operate the company on a sound financial basis of profitable growth, increasing value for shareholders, and creating career opportunities and financial rewards for our employees. *Social:* To operate the company in a way that actively recognizes the central role that business plays in the structure of society by initiating innovative ways to improve the quality of life of the broad community—local, national, and international. Underlying the mission of Ben & Jerry's is the determination to seek new and creative ways of addressing all three parts, while holding a deep respect for the individuals, inside and outside the company, and for the communities of which they are a part.

The notion of linked prosperity—also called values-led business or caring capitalism—forms the heart and soul of the company. Ben & Jerry's aims to do well *while also* doing good.

Ben & Jerry's does more than just pay lip service to social and environmental concerns—the mission also translates into specific company policies and actions. For example, whereas the average U.S. corporation earmarks less than 2 percent of pretax profits to philanthropy, Ben & Jerry's has a set policy to donate a whopping 7.5 percent to a variety of social and environmental causes (last year that amounted to about $792,600). The funds are dispensed through the Ben & Jerry's Foundation, employee Community Action Teams, and corporate grants made by the company's Director of Social Mission Development. Each supports projects that exhibit "creative problem solving and hopefulness . . . relating to children and families, disadvantaged groups, and the environment."

The company routinely assesses the environmental and social impact of almost everything it does. For example, it buys only hormone-free milk and cream and uses only organic fruits and nuts. After two years of research, Ben & Jerry's last year switched to a new, environmentally friendly pint container they call the Eco-Pint. Its Rainforest Crunch ice cream contains Brazil nuts harvested by cooperative farms benefiting tribal peoples in the Amazon rain forests. Closer to home, Ben & Jerry's recently sponsored a concert in Burlington, Vermont, by rock band Phish to raise money to clean up Lake Champlain.

Ben & Jerry's also goes to great lengths to buy from minority and disadvantaged suppliers. For example, even though it raises ingredient prices a few cents a pint, Ben & Jerry's buys the brownies for its Chocolate Fudge Brownie ice cream from a nonprofit New York bakery that trains and employs disadvantaged workers. To use the brownies, it had to devise a new ice cream recipe and change its production process. Similarly, to support Vermont farmers and their causes, Ben & Jerry's buys its hormone-free milk and cream exclusively from Vermont dairies, an action which cost the company an extra $375,000 last year.

Ben & Jerry's obeys its social conscience in other ways as well. For example, it used to make a popular ice cream called Oreo Mint but discontinued the flavor because it didn't like doing business with tobacco merchant RJR, whose Nabisco unit at the time supplied the Oreos. The company changed recipes and started making a new flavor called Mint Chocolate Cookie. For their social responsibility and their involvement in community action programs, Ben and Jerry were awarded with the National Retail Federation's American Spirit Award for 1999.

Such caring capitalism has earned Ben & Jerry's a measure of respect and the loyal patronage of many consumers. However, there is a downside—having a double bottom line of values and profits is not easy. Such policies cost money, which some critics claim is "wasted on righteousness." In the words of one especially harsh critic, "Ben and Jerry want to use ice cream to solve the world's problems. They call it running a values-led business; I call it a mess. What makes it a mess are its conflicting objectives. Operating a business is tough enough. Once you add social goals to the demands of serving customers, making a profit, and returning value to shareholders, you tie yourself up in knots. [Ben and Jerry's] ideas are simplistic, and partly as a result their company has been hurt."

For sure, it's sometimes difficult to take good intentions to the bank. Over the years, the company has at times found it difficult to live up to the title of the founders' recent book *Ben & Jerry's Double Dip: Lead with Your Values and Make Money Too.* It's done fine with the values part but has produced less than stellar financial returns. Over the past several years, its once-meteoric sales growth has slowed, its profits have wavered, and its stock price has languished. Notes the critic: "As for dividends, to date they have been entirely spiritual."

However, such spiritual returns appear to satisfy Ben & Jerry's owners, still mostly small shareholders from Vermont rather than large institutions. Shareholder's meetings—which include a cabaret style production, a state-of-the-ice-cream address by the CEO, and plenty of free ice cream—are well attended. The general consensus among shareholders is that they're just happy to be a part of the company, regardless of the stock's performance. "According to Jerry, [shareholder meetings] are incredibly well attended by the locals in a carnival-type atmosphere," states an industry analyst. "The shareholders who do ask questions . . . ask the board why it isn't being more progressive and radical." They appear to agree with Alan Parker, Ben & Jerry's director of investor relations and social accounting, who says, "We . . . desire to be the kind of company that measures its success as much by its social contribution as by its financial success."[1]

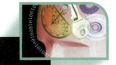

> **objectives**

Before you begin, take a moment to familiarize yourself with the key objectives of this chapter.

[1]Quotes and excerpts from Rhymer Rigby, "Tutti-Frutti Management," *Management Today,* February 1998, pp. 54–56; Alex Taylor III, "Yo, Ben! Yo, Jerry! It's Just Ice Cream," *Fortune,* April 28, 1997, p. 374; Frank Byrt, "Investors Get a Craving for Ben & Jerry's," *Wall Street Journal,* May 4, 1999; and "Ben & Jerry's Mission Statement," accessed online at www.benjerry.com/mission.html, January 2000. Also see Tom McInerney, "Double Trouble: Combining Business and Ethics," *Business Ethics Quarterly,* January 1998, pp. 187–89; Jennifer Karas, "Ben & Jerry's Co-Founders Honored for Commitment to Community Action," *Stores,* June 1999, p. 83; "Environmentally Conscious Carton," *Dairy Foods,* May 1999, p. 48; Andrew Serwer, "Ben & Jerry's Is Back: Ice Cream and a Hot Stock," *Fortune,* August 2, 1999, p. 267; and "Everything You Ever Wanted to Know About Ben & Jerry's," accessed online at www.benjerry.com/aboutbj.html, January 2000.

Responsible marketers discover what consumers want and respond with the right products, priced to give good value to buyers and profit to the producer. The *marketing concept* is a philosophy of customer satisfaction and mutual gain. Its practice leads the economy by an invisible hand to satisfy the many and changing needs of millions of consumers.

Not all marketers follow the marketing concept, however. In fact, some companies use questionable marketing practices, and some marketing actions that seem innocent in themselves strongly affect the larger society. Consider the sale of cigarettes. On the face of it, companies should be free to sell cigarettes, and smokers should be free to buy them. But this transaction affects the public interest. First, the smoker is harming his or her health and may be shortening his or her own life. Second, smoking places a financial burden on the smoker's family and on society at large. Third, other people around the smoker may suffer discomfort and harm from secondhand smoke. Finally, marketing cigarettes to adults might also influence young people to begin smoking. Thus, the marketing of tobacco products has sparked substantial debate and negotiation in recent years.[2] This example shows that private transactions may involve larger questions of public policy.

This chapter examines the social effects of private marketing practices. We examine several questions: What are the most frequent social criticisms of marketing? What steps have private citizens taken to curb marketing ills? What steps have legislators and government agencies taken to curb marketing ills? What steps have enlightened companies taken to carry out socially responsible and ethical marketing? We examine how marketing affects and is affected by each of these issues.

> Social Criticisms of Marketing

Marketing receives much criticism. Some of this criticism is justified; much is not. Social critics claim that certain marketing practices hurt individual consumers, society as a whole, and other business firms.

MARKETING'S IMPACT ON INDIVIDUAL CONSUMERS

Consumers have many concerns about how well the American marketing system serves their interests. Surveys usually show that consumers hold mixed or even slightly unfavorable attitudes toward marketing practices. Consumers, consumer advocates, government agencies, and other critics have accused marketing of harming consumers through high prices, deceptive practices, high-pressure selling, shoddy or unsafe products, planned obsolescence, and poor service to disadvantaged consumers.

High Prices

Many critics charge that the American marketing system causes prices to be higher than they would be under more "sensible" systems. They point to three factors—*high costs of distribution, high advertising and promotion costs,* and *excessive markups.*

High Costs of Distribution.   A long-standing charge is that greedy intermediaries mark up prices beyond the value of their services. Critics charge that there are too many intermediaries, that intermediaries are inefficient and poorly run, or that they provide unnecessary or duplicate services. As a result, distribution costs too much, and consumers pay for these excessive costs in the form of higher prices.

How do resellers answer these charges? They argue that intermediaries do work that would otherwise have to be done by manufacturers or consumers. Markups reflect services that consumers themselves want—more convenience, larger stores and assortment, longer store hours, return privileges, and others. Moreover, the costs of operating stores keep rising, forcing retailers to raise their prices. In fact, they argue, retail competition is so intense that margins are actually quite low. For example, after

---

[2]See John McCain and Robert Pitofsky, "Sorting Through Tobacco Dilemma," *Advertising Age,* March 16, 1998, p. 24; Kirk Davidson, "Up in Smoke: For Tobacco, There's No Turning Back," *Marketing News,* May 25, 1998, pp. 6, 21; and "A Victory for Tobacco's Victims," *New York Times,* July 1999, p. 14.

taxes, supermarket chains are typically left with barely 1 percent profit on their sales. If some resellers try to charge too much relative to the value they add, other resellers will step in with lower prices. Low-price stores such as Wal-Mart, Best Buy, and other discounters pressure their competitors to operate efficiently and keep their prices down.

High Advertising and Promotion Costs.   Modern marketing is also accused of pushing up prices to finance heavy advertising and sales promotion. For example, a dozen tablets of a heavily promoted brand of aspirin sell for the same price as 100 tablets of less promoted brands. Differentiated products—cosmetics, detergents, toiletries—include promotion and packaging costs that can amount to 40 percent or more of the manufacturer's price to the retailer. Critics charge that much of the packaging and promotion adds only psychological value to the product rather than functional value. Retailers use additional promotion—advertising, displays, and sweepstakes—that add several cents more to retail prices.

Marketers respond that consumers can usually buy functional versions of products at lower prices. However, they *want* and are willing to pay more for products that also provide psychological bene-fits—that make them feel wealthy, attractive, or special. Brand-name products may cost more, but branding gives buyers confidence. Heavy advertising adds to product costs but is needed to inform millions of potential buyers of the merits of a brand. If consumers want to know what is available on the market, they must expect manufacturers to spend large sums of money on advertising. Also, heavy advertising and promotion may be necessary for a firm to match competitors' efforts—the business would lose "share of mind" if it did not match competitive spending. At the same time, companies are cost-conscious about promotion and try to spend their money wisely.

Excessive Markups.   Critics also charge that some companies mark up goods excessively. They point to the drug industry, where a pill costing 5 cents to make may cost the consumer $2 to buy. They point to the pricing tactics of funeral homes that prey on the confused emotions of bereaved relatives and to the high charges for television repair and auto repair.

Marketers respond that most businesses try to deal fairly with consumers because they want repeat business. Most consumer abuses are unintentional. When shady marketers do take advantage of con-sumers, they should be reported to Better Business Bureaus and to state and federal agencies. Marketers also respond that consumers often don't understand the reason for high markups. For exam-ple, pharmaceutical markups must cover the costs of purchasing, promoting, and distributing existing medicines plus the high research and development costs of formulating and testing new medicines.

Deceptive Practices

Marketers are sometimes accused of deceptive practices that lead consumers to believe they will get more value than they actually do. Deceptive practices fall into three groups: deceptive pricing, pro-motion, and packaging. *Deceptive pricing* includes practices such as falsely advertising "factory" or "wholesale" prices or a large price reduction from a phony high retail list price. *Deceptive promotion* includes practices such as overstating the product's features or performance, luring the customer to the store for a bargain that is out of stock, or running rigged contests. *Deceptive packaging* includes

A heavily promoted brand of antacid sells for much more than a virtu-ally identical nonbranded or store-branded product. Critics charge that pro-motion adds only psy-chological value to the product rather than func-tional value.

exaggerating package contents through subtle design, not filling the package to the top, using misleading labeling, or describing size in misleading terms.

To be sure, questionable marketing practices do occur. For example, at one time or another, we've all gotten an envelope in the mail screaming something like "You have won $10,000,000!" In recent years, sweepstakes companies have come under the gun for their deceptive communication practices. In fact, many states have brought lawsuits against companies like American Family Publishers and Publishers Clearing House. The suits allege that the companies' promotional strategies entice people to buy thousands of dollars' worth of products hoping to better their odds of winning. The Wisconsin Attorney General asserts that "there are older consumers who send [sweepstakes companies] checks and money orders on a weekly basis with a note that says they were very upset that the prize patrol did not come."[3]

Deceptive practices have led to legislation and other consumer protection actions. For example, in 1938 Congress reacted to such blatant deceptions as Fleischmann's Yeast's claim to straighten crooked teeth by enacting the Wheeler-Lea Act giving the Federal Trade Commission (FTC) power to regulate "unfair or deceptive acts or practices." The FTC has published several guidelines listing deceptive practices. The toughest problem is defining what is "deceptive." For example, some years ago, Shell Oil advertised that Super Shell gasoline with platformate gave more mileage than did the same gasoline without platformate. Now this was true, but what Shell did not say is that almost *all* gasoline includes platformate. Its defense was that it had never claimed that platformate was found only in Shell gasoline. But even though the message was literally true, the FTC felt that the ad's *intent* was to deceive.

Marketers argue that most companies avoid deceptive practices because such practices harm their business in the long run. If consumers do not get what they expect, they will switch to more reliable products. In addition, consumers usually protect themselves from deception. Most consumers recognize a marketer's selling intent and are careful when they buy, sometimes to the point of not believing completely true product claims. One noted marketing thinker, Theodore Levitt, claims that some advertising puffery is bound to occur—and that it may even be desirable: "There is hardly a company that would not go down in ruin if it refused to provide fluff, because nobody will buy pure functionality. . . . Worse, it denies . . . man's honest needs and values. Without distortion, embellishment, and elaboration, life would be drab, dull, anguished, and at its existential worst."[4]

High-Pressure Selling

Salespeople are sometimes accused of high-pressure selling that persuades people to buy goods they had no thought of buying. It is often said that encyclopedias, insurance, real estate, cars, and jewelry are *sold,* not *bought.* Salespeople are trained to deliver smooth, canned talks to entice purchase. They sell hard because sales contests promise big prizes to those who sell the most.

Marketers know that buyers often can be talked into buying unwanted or unneeded things. Laws require door-to-door and telephone salespeople to announce that they are selling a product. Buyers also have a "three-day cooling-off period" in which they can cancel a contract after rethinking it. In addition, consumers can complain to Better Business Bureaus or to state consumer protection agencies when they feel that undue selling pressure has been applied. But in most cases, marketers have little to gain from high-pressure selling. Such tactics may work in the short run but will damage the marketer's long-run relationships with customers.

Shoddy or Unsafe Products

Another criticism is that products lack the quality they should have. One complaint is that many products are not made well and services not performed well. A second complaint is that many products deliver little benefit. For example, some consumers are surprised to learn that many of the "healthy" foods being marketed today, such as cholesterol-free salad dressings, low-fat frozen dinners, and high-fiber bran cereals, may have little nutritional value. In fact, they may even be harmful.

[Despite] sincere efforts on the part of most marketers to provide healthier products, . . . many promises emblazoned on packages and used as ad slogans continue to confuse nutritionally uninformed consumers and . . . may actually be harmful to that group. . . . [Many consumers] incorrectly assume the product is "safe" and eat greater amounts than are good for them. . . . For example, General Foods USA's new Entenmann's "low-cholesterol, low-calorie" cherry coffee cake . . . may confuse some consumers who shouldn't eat much of it. While each serv-

---

[3]James Heckman, "Don't Shoot the Messenger: More and More Often, Marketing Is the Regulators' Target," *Marketing News,* May 24, 1999, pp. 1, 9.

[4]Theodore Levitt, "The Morality (?) of Advertising," *Harvard Business Review,* July–August 1970, pp. 84–92. For counterpoints, see Heckman, "Don't Shoot the Messenger, 1999, pp. 1, 9.

ing is only 90 calories, not everyone realizes that the suggested serving is tiny [one-thirteenth of the small cake]. Although eating half an Entenmann's cake may be better than eating half a dozen Dunkin' Donuts, . . . neither should be eaten in great amounts by people on restrictive diets.[5]

A third complaint concerns product safety. Product safety has been a problem for several reasons, including manufacturer indifference, increased production complexity, poorly trained labor, and poor quality control. For years, Consumers Union—the nonprofit testing and information organization that publishes *Consumer Reports*—has reported various hazards in tested products: electrical dangers in appliances, carbon monoxide poisoning from room heaters, injury risks from lawn mowers, and faulty automobile design, among many others. The organization's testing and other activities have helped consumers make better buying decisions and encouraged businesses to eliminate product flaws.

However, most manufacturers *want* to produce quality goods. The way a company deals with product quality and safety problems can damage or help its reputation. Companies selling poor-quality or unsafe products risk damaging conflicts with consumer groups and regulators. Moreover, unsafe products can result in product liability suits and large awards for damages. More fundamentally, consumers who are unhappy with a firm's products may avoid future purchases and talk other consumers into doing the same. Today's marketers know that customer-driven quality results in customer satisfaction, which in turn creates profitable customer relationships.

Planned Obsolescence

Critics also have charged that some producers follow a program of planned obsolescence, causing their products to become obsolete before they actually should need replacement. For example, critics charge that some producers continually change consumer concepts of acceptable styles to encourage more and earlier buying. An obvious example is constantly changing clothing fashions. Other producers are accused of holding back attractive functional features, then introducing them later to make older models obsolete. Critics claim that this occurs in the consumer electronics and computer industries. For example, Intel and Microsoft have been accused in recent years of holding back their next-generation computer chips or software until demand is exhausted for the current generation. Still other producers are accused of using materials and components that will break, wear, rust, or rot sooner than they should. One writer put it this way: "The marvels of modern technology include the development of a soda can which, when discarded, will last forever—and a . . . car, which, when properly cared for, will rust out in two or three years."[6]

Marketers respond that consumers *like* style changes; they get tired of the old goods and want a new look in fashion or a new design in cars. No one has to buy the new look, and if too few people like it, it will simply fail. Companies frequently withhold new features when they are not fully tested, when they add more cost to the product than consumers are willing to pay, and for other good reasons. But they do so at the risk that a competitor will introduce the new feature and steal the market. Moreover, companies often put in new materials to lower their costs and prices. They do not design their products to break down earlier, because they do not want to lose customers to other brands. Instead, they implement total quality programs to ensure that products will consistently meet or exceed customer expectations. Thus, much of so-called planned obsolescence is the working of the competitive and technological forces in a free society—forces that lead to ever-improving goods and services.[7]

Poor Service to Disadvantaged Consumers

Finally, the American marketing system has been accused of poorly serving disadvantaged consumers. For example, critics claim that the urban poor often have to shop in smaller stores that carry inferior goods and charge higher prices. A Consumers Union study compared the food-shopping habits of low-income consumers and the prices they pay relative to middle-income consumers in the same city. The study found that the poor do pay more for inferior goods. The results suggested that the presence of large national chain stores in low-income neighborhoods made a big difference in keeping prices down. However, the study also found evidence of "redlining," a type of economic discrimination in which major chain retailers avoid placing stores in disadvantaged neighborhoods.

---

[5]Sandra Pesmen, "How Low Is Low? How Free Is Free?" *Advertising Age,* May 7, 1990, p. S10; and Karolyn Schuster, "The Dark Side of Nutrition," *Food Management,* June 1999, pp. 34–39.

[6]Cliff Edwards, "Where Have All the Edsels Gone?" *Greensboro News Record,* May 24, 1999, p. B6.

[7]For a thought-provoking short case involving planned obsolescence, see James A. Heely and Roy L. Nersesian, "The Case of Planned Obsolescence," *Management Accounting,* February 1994, p. 67. Also see Joel Dryfuss, "Planned Obsolescence Is Alive and Well," *Fortune,* February 15, 1999, p. 192.

Similar redlining charges have been leveled at the home insurance, consumer lending, and banking industries.[8]

Clearly, better marketing systems must be built in low-income areas—one hope is to get large retailers to open outlets in low-income areas. Moreover, low-income people clearly need consumer protection. The FTC has taken action against merchants who advertise false values, sell old merchandise as new, or charge too much for credit. The commission is also trying to make it harder for merchants to win court judgments against low-income people who were wheedled into buying something.

active example <

Consider how redlining in the new technology area is causing a "digital divide."

MARKETING'S IMPACT ON SOCIETY AS A WHOLE

The American marketing system has been accused of adding to several "evils" in American society at large. Advertising has been a special target—so much so that the American Association of Advertising Agencies launched a campaign to defend advertising against what it felt to be common but untrue criticisms.

False Wants and Too Much Materialism

Critics have charged that the marketing system urges too much interest in material possessions. People are judged by what they *own* rather than by who they *are*. To be considered successful, people must own a large home, two cars, and the latest consumer electronics. This drive for wealth and possessions hit new highs in the 1980s, when phrases such as "greed is good" and "shop 'til you drop" seemed to characterize the times.

In the new millennium, even though many social scientists have noted a reaction against the opulence and waste of the previous decades and a return to more basic values and social commitment, our infatuation with material things continues.

> It's hard to escape the notion that what Americans really value is stuff. Since 1987, we've had more shopping malls than high schools. We average six hours a week shopping and only forty minutes playing with our children. Our rate of saving is 2 percent—only a quarter of what it was in the 1950s, when we earned less than half as much in real dollars. In each of the past three years, more U.S citizens have declared personal bankruptcy than have graduated from college. All this acquisition isn't making us happier; the number of Americans calling themselves "very happy" peaked in 1957.[9]

The critics do not view this interest in material things as a natural state of mind but rather as a matter of false wants created by marketing. Businesses hire Madison Avenue to stimulate people's desires for goods, and Madison Avenue uses the mass media to create materialistic models of the good life. People work harder to earn the necessary money. Their purchases increase the output of American industry, and industry in turn uses Madison Avenue to stimulate more desire for the industrial output. Thus, marketing is seen as creating false wants that benefit industry more than they benefit consumers.

These criticisms overstate the power of business to create needs, however. People have strong defenses against advertising and other marketing tools. Marketers are most effective when they appeal to existing wants rather than when they attempt to create new ones. Furthermore, people seek information when making important purchases and often do not rely on single sources. Even minor purchases that may be affected by advertising messages lead to repeat purchases only if the product performs as promised. Finally, the high failure rate of new products shows that companies are not able to control demand.

[8]See Judith Bell and Bonnie Maria Burlin, "In Urban Areas: Many More Still Pay More for Food," *Journal of Public Policy and Marketing,* Fall 1993, pp. 268–70; Alan R. Andreasen, "Revisiting the Disadvantages: Old Lesson and New Problems," *Journal of Public Policy and Marketing,* Fall 1993, pp. 270–75; Tony Attrino, "Nationwide Settles Redlining Suit in Ohio," *National Underwriter,* April 27, 1998, p. 4; Angelo B. Henderson, "First Chicago Unit Agrees to Lend $3 Billion in Detroit," *Wall Street Journal,* June 26, 1998; and Kathryn Graddy and Diana C. Robertson, "Fairness of Pricing Decisions," *Business Ethics Quarterly,* April 1999, pp. 225–43.

[9]John De Graaf, "The Overspent American/Luxury Fever," *The Amicus Journal,* Summer 1999, pp. 41–43.

The American Marketing Association runs ads to counter common advertising criticisms.

On a deeper level, our wants and values are influenced not only by marketers but also by family, peer groups, religion, ethnic background, and education. If Americans are highly materialistic, these values arose out of basic socialization processes that go much deeper than business and mass media could produce alone. Moreover, some social critics see materialism as a positive and rewarding force:

> When we purchase an object, what we really buy is meaning. Commercialism is the water we swim in, the air we breathe, our sunlight and our shade. . . . Materialism is a vital source of meaning and happiness in the modern world. . . . We have not just asked to go this way, we have demanded. Now most of the world is lining up, pushing and shoving, eager to elbow into the mall. Getting and spending has become the most passionate, and often the most imaginative, endeavor of modern life. While this is dreary and depressing to some, as doubtless it should be, it is liberating and democratic to many more.[10]

> ### active exercise

Consider the plight of an industry that may actually suffer because of its target audience's materialistic habits.

Too Few Social Goods

Business has been accused of overselling private goods at the expense of public goods. As private goods increase, they require more public services that are usually not forthcoming. For example, an

---

[10]James Twitchell, "Two Cheers for Materialism," *The Wilson Quarterly,* Spring 1999, pp. 16–26; and Twitchell, *Lead Us into Temptation: The Triumph of American Materialism* (New York: Columbia University Press, 1999).

increase in automobile ownership (private good) requires more highways, traffic control, parking spaces, and police services (public goods). The overselling of private goods results in "social costs." For cars, the social costs include traffic congestion, air pollution, and deaths and injuries from car accidents.

A way must be found to restore a balance between private and public goods. One option is to make producers bear the full social costs of their operations. For example, the government could require automobile manufacturers to build cars with even more safety features and better pollution control systems. Automakers would then raise their prices to cover extra costs. If buyers found the price of some cars too high, however, the producers of these cars would disappear, and demand would move to those producers that could support the sum of the private and social costs.

A second option is to make consumers pay the social costs. For example, a number of highway authorities around the world are starting to charge "congestion tolls" in an effort to reduce traffic congestion:

> Already, in Southern California, drivers are being charged premiums to travel in underused car pool lanes; Singapore, Norway, and France are managing traffic with varying tolls; peak surcharges are being studied for roads around New York, San Francisco, Los Angeles, and other cities. [Economists] point out that traffic jams are caused when drivers are not charged the costs they impose on others, such as delays. The solution: Make 'em pay.[11]

Interestingly, in San Diego, regular drivers can use the HOV (high-occupancy vehicle) lanes, but they must pay a price based on traffic usage at the time. The toll ranges from 50 cents off-peak to $4.00 during rush hour.[12] More generally, if the costs of driving rise high enough, consumers will travel at nonpeak times or find alternative transportation modes.

Cultural Pollution

Critics charge the marketing system with creating *cultural pollution*. Our senses are being constantly assaulted by advertising. Commercials interrupt serious programs; pages of ads obscure printed matter; billboards mar beautiful scenery. These interruptions continually pollute people's minds with messages of materialism, sex, power, or status. Although most people do not find advertising overly annoying (some even think it is the best part of television programming), some critics call for sweeping changes.

Marketers answer the charges of "commercial noise" with these arguments: First, they hope that their ads reach primarily the target audience. But because of mass-communication channels, some ads are bound to reach people who have no interest in the product and are therefore bored or annoyed. People who buy magazines addressed to their interests—such as *Vogue* or *Fortune*—rarely complain about the ads because the magazines advertise products of interest. Second, ads make much of television and radio free to users and keep down the costs of magazines and newspapers. Many people think commercials are a small price to pay for these benefits. Finally, today's consumers have alternatives. For example, they can zip and zap TV commercials or avoid them altogether on many cable or satellite channels. Thus, advertisers are making their ads more entertaining and informative.

Making consumers pay the social costs: On this private highway in California, consumers pay "congestion tolls" to drive in the unclogged fast lane.

[11]Kim Clark, "Real-World-O-Nomics: How to Make Traffic Jams a Thing of the Past," *Fortune*, March 31, 1997, p. 34.

[12]Lee Hultgreen and Kim Kawada, "San Diego's Interstate 15 High-Occupancy/Toll Lane Facility Using Value Pricing," *ITE Journal*, June 1999, pp. 22–27.

Too Much Political Power

Another criticism is that business wields too much political power. "Oil," "tobacco," "auto," and "pharmaceuticals" senators support an industry's interests against the public interest. Advertisers are accused of holding too much power over the mass media, limiting their freedom to report independently and objectively. One critic has asked: "How can [most magazines] afford to tell the truth about the scandalously low nutritional value of most packaged foods . . . when these magazines are being subsidized by such advertisers as General Foods, Kellogg's, Nabisco, and General Mills? . . . The answer is *they cannot and do not*."[13]

American industries do promote and protect their own interests. They have a right to representation in Congress and the mass media, although their influence can become too great. Fortunately, many powerful business interests once thought to be untouchable have been tamed in the public interest. For example, Standard Oil was broken up in 1911, and the meatpacking industry was disciplined in the early 1900s after exposures by Upton Sinclair. Ralph Nader caused legislation that forced the automobile industry to build more safety into its cars, and the Surgeon General's Report resulted in cigarette companies putting health warnings on their packages. More recently, giants such as AT&T, Microsoft, Intel, and R.J. Reynolds have felt the impact of regulators seeking to balance the interests of big business against those of the public. Moreover, because the media receive advertising revenues from many different advertisers, it is easier to resist the influence of one or a few of them. Too much business power tends to result in counterforces that check and offset these powerful interests.

MARKETING'S IMPACT ON OTHER BUSINESSES

Critics also charge that a company's marketing practices can harm other companies and reduce competition. Three problems are involved: acquisitions of competitors, marketing practices that create barriers to entry, and unfair competitive marketing practices.

Critics claim that firms are harmed and competition reduced when companies expand by acquiring competitors rather than by developing their own new products. The large number of acquisitions and rapid pace of industry consolidation over the past two decades have caused concern that vigorous young competitors will be absorbed and that competition will be reduced. In virtually every major industry—financial services, utilities, transportation, automobiles, telecommunications, health care, entertainment—the number of major competitors is shrinking.[14]

Acquisition is a complex subject. Acquisitions can sometimes be good for society. The acquiring company may gain economies of scale that lead to lower costs and lower prices. A well-managed company may take over a poorly managed company and improve its efficiency. An industry that was not very competitive might become more competitive after the acquisition. But acquisitions can also be harmful and, therefore, are closely regulated by the government.

Critics have also charged that marketing practices bar new companies from entering an industry. Large marketing companies can use patents and heavy promotion spending, and can tie up suppliers or dealers to keep out or drive out competitors. Those concerned with antitrust regulation recognize that some barriers are the natural result of the economic advantages of doing business on a large scale. Other barriers could be challenged by existing and new laws. For example, some critics have proposed a progressive tax on advertising spending to reduce the role of selling costs as a major barrier to entry.

Finally, some firms have in fact used unfair competitive marketing practices with the intention of hurting or destroying other firms. They may set their prices below costs, threaten to cut off business with suppliers, or discourage the buying of a competitor's products. Various laws work to prevent such predatory competition. It is difficult, however, to prove that the intent or action was really preda-

---

[13]From an advertisement for *Fact* magazine, which does not carry advertisements.

[14]See Shawn Tully, "It's Time for Merger Mania II," *Fortune,* June 7, 1999, pp. 231–32.

tory. In recent years, Wal-Mart, American Airlines, Intel, and Microsoft have all been accused of various predatory practices. Take Microsoft, for example:

> [Last year,] Microsoft's $3.4 billion in net income accounted for 41 percent of the profits of the 10 largest publicly traded software companies. Its reach extends beyond the PC into everything from computerized toys and TV set-top boxes to selling cars and airline tickets over the Internet. In its zeal to become a leader not just in operating systems but on the Internet, the company bundled its Internet Explorer browser into its Windows software. This move sparked an antitrust suit by the government, much to the delight of Microsoft's rivals. After all, Web-browsing innovator Netscape has seen its market share plummet as it tries to sell what Microsoft gives away for free.[15]

Although competitors and the government charge that Microsoft's actions are predatory, the question is whether this is unfair competition or the healthy competition of a more efficient company against the less efficient.

active concept check <

Now let's take a moment to test your knowledge of what you've just read.

> ## Citizen and Public Actions to Regulate Marketing

Because some people view business as the cause of many economic and social ills, grassroots movements have arisen from time to time to keep business in line. The two major movements have been *consumerism* and *environmentalism*.

CONSUMERISM

American business firms have been the target of organized consumer movements on three occasions. The first consumer movement took place in the early 1900s. It was fueled by rising prices, Upton Sinclair's writings on conditions in the meat industry, and scandals in the drug industry. The second consumer movement, in the mid-1930s, was sparked by an upturn in consumer prices during the Great Depression and another drug scandal.

The third movement began in the 1960s. Consumers had become better educated, products had become more complex and potentially hazardous, and people were unhappy with American institutions. Ralph Nader appeared on the scene to force many issues, and other well-known writers accused big business of wasteful and unethical practices. President John F. Kennedy declared that consumers had the right to safety, to be informed, to choose, and to be heard. Congress investigated certain industries and proposed consumer-protection legislation. Since then, many consumer groups have been organized, and several consumer laws have been passed. The consumer movement has spread internationally and has become very strong in Europe.[16]

But what is the consumer movement? **Consumerism** is an organized movement of citizens and government agencies to improve the rights and power of buyers in relation to sellers. Traditional *sellers' rights* include:

 The right to introduce any product in any size and style, provided it is not hazardous to personal health or safety; or, if it is, to include proper warnings and controls.

 The right to charge any price for the product, provided no discrimination exists among similar kinds of buyers.

---

[15]Steve Hamm, "Microsoft's Future," *Business Week,* January 19, 1998, pp. 58–68; and Ronald. A. Cass, "Microsoft, Running Scared," *New York Times,* June 28, 1999, p. 17.

[16]For more details, see Paul N. Bloom and Stephen A. Greyser, "The Maturing of Consumerism," *Harvard Business Review,* November–December 1981, pp. 130–39, Robert J. Samualson, "The Aging of Ralph Nader," *Newsweek,* December 16, 1985, p. 57; Douglas A. Harbrecht, "The Second Coming of Ralph Nader," *Business Week,* March 6, 1989, p. 28; George S. Day and David A. Aaker, "A Guide to Consumerism," *Marketing Management,* Spring 1997, pp. 44–48; and Benet Middleton, "Consumerism: A Pragmatic Ideology," *Consumer Policy Review,* November–December, 1998, pp. 213–17.

- The right to spend any amount to promote the product, provided it is not defined as unfair competition.

- The right to use any product message, provided it is not misleading or dishonest in content or execution.

- The right to use any buying incentive schemes, provided they are not unfair or misleading.

Traditional *buyers' rights* include:

- The right not to buy a product that is offered for sale.

- The right to expect the product to be safe.

- The right to expect the product to perform as claimed.

Comparing these rights, many believe that the balance of power lies on the sellers' side. True, the buyer can refuse to buy. But critics feel that the buyer has too little information, education, and protection to make wise decisions when facing sophisticated sellers. Consumer advocates call for the following additional consumer rights:

- The right to be well informed about important aspects of the product.

- The right to be protected against questionable products and marketing practices.

- The right to influence products and marketing practices in ways that will improve the "quality of life."

Each proposed right has led to more specific proposals by consumerists. The right to be informed includes the right to know the true interest on a loan (truth in lending), the true cost per unit of a brand (unit pricing), the ingredients in a product (ingredient labeling), the nutritional value of foods (nutritional labeling), product freshness (open dating), and the true benefits of a product (truth in advertising). Proposals related to consumer protection include strengthening consumer rights in cases of business fraud, requiring greater product safety, and giving more power to government agencies. Proposals relating to quality of life include controlling the ingredients that go into certain products (detergents) and packaging (soft drink containers), reducing the level of advertising "noise," and putting consumer representatives on company boards to protect consumer interests.

Consumers have not only the *right* but also the *responsibility* to protect themselves instead of leaving this function to someone else. Consumers who believe they got a bad deal have several remedies available, including contacting the company or the media; contacting federal, state, or local agencies; and going to small-claims courts.

ENVIRONMENTALISM

Whereas consumerists consider whether the marketing system is efficiently serving consumer wants, environmentalists are concerned with marketing's effects on the environment and with the costs of serving consumer needs and wants. **Environmentalism** is an organized movement of concerned citizens, businesses, and government agencies to protect and improve people's living environment. Environmentalists are not against marketing and consumption; they simply want people and organizations to operate with more care for the environment. The marketing system's goal, they assert, should not be to maximize consumption, consumer choice, or consumer satisfaction, but rather to maximize life quality. "Life quality" means not only the quantity and quality of consumer goods and services but also the quality of the environment. Environmentalists want environmental costs included in both producer and consumer decision making.

Consumer desire for more information led to putting ingredients, nutrition, and dating information on product labels.

The first wave of modern environmentalism in the United States was driven by environmental groups and concerned consumers in the 1960s and 1970s. They were concerned with damage to the ecosystem caused by strip mining, forest depletion, acid rain, loss of the atmosphere's ozone layer, toxic wastes, and litter. They also were concerned with the loss of recreational areas and with the increase in health problems caused by bad air, polluted water, and chemically treated food.

The second environmentalism wave was driven by government, which passed laws and regulations during the 1970s and 1980s governing industrial practices impacting the environment. This wave hit some industries hard. Steel companies and utilities had to invest billions of dollars in pollution control equipment and costlier fuels. The auto industry had to introduce expensive emission controls in cars. The packaging industry had to find ways to reduce litter. These industries and others have often resented and resisted environmental regulations, especially when they have been imposed too rapidly to allow companies to make proper adjustments. Many of these companies claim they have had to absorb large costs that have made them less competitive.

As we move into the twenty-first century, the first two environmentalism waves are merging into a third and stronger wave in which companies are accepting responsibility for doing no harm to the environment. They are shifting from protest to prevention, and from regulation to responsibility. More and more companies are adopting policies of **environmental sustainability**—developing strategies that both sustain the environment and produce profits for the company. According to one strategist, "The challenge is to develop a *sustainable global economy:* an economy that the planet is capable of supporting indefinitely. . . . [It's] an enormous challenge—and an enormous opportunity."[17]

video example

> **Watch how one prominent company balances its need to grow with environmentally sustainable policies.**

Figure 20.1 shows a grid that companies can use to gauge their progress toward environmental sustainability. At the most basic level, a company can practice *pollution prevention.* This involves more than pollution control—cleaning up waste after it has been created. Pollution prevention means eliminating or minimizing waste before it is created. Companies emphasizing prevention have responded with "green marketing" programs—developing ecologically safer products, recyclable and biodegradable packaging, better pollution controls, and more energy-efficient operations. They are finding that they can be both green *and* competitive. Consider how the Dutch flower industry has responded to its environmental problems:

> Intense cultivation of flowers in small areas was contaminating the soil and groundwater with pesticides, herbicides, and fertilizers. Facing increasingly strict regulation, . . . the Dutch understood that the only effective way to address the problem would be to develop a closed-loop system. In advanced Dutch greenhouses, flowers now grow in water and rock wool, not in soil. This lowers the risk of infestation, reducing the need for fertilizers and pesticides, which are delivered in water that circulates and is reused. The . . . closed-loop system also reduces variation in growing conditions, thus improving product quality. Handling costs have gone down because the flowers are cultivated on specially designed platforms. . . .The net result is not only dramatically lower environmental impact but also lower costs, better product quality, and enhanced global competitiveness.[18]

At the next level, companies can practice *product stewardship*—minimizing not just pollution from production but all environmental impacts throughout the full product life cycle. Many companies are adopting *design for environment (DFE)* practices, which involve thinking ahead in the design stage to create products that are easier to recover, reuse, or recycle. DFE not only helps to sustain the environment, it can be highly profitable:

[17]Stuart L. Hart, "Beyond Greening: Strategies for a Sustainable World," *Harvard Business Review,* January–February 1997, pp. 66–76. Also see Jacquelyn Ottman, "What Sustainability Means to Marketers," *Marketing News,* July 21, 1997, p. 4; and James L. Kolar, "Environmental Sustainability: Balancing Pollution Control with Economic Growth," *Environmental Quality Management,* Spring 1999, pp. 1–10.

[18]Michael E. Porter and Claas van der Linde, "Green *and* Competitive: Ending the Stalemate," *Harvard Business Review,* September–October 1995, pp. 120–34.

	Internal	External
Tomorrow	**New environmental technology** Is the environmental performance of our products limited by our existing technology base? Is there potential to realize major improvements through new technology?	**Sustainability vision** Does our corporate vision direct us toward the solution of social and environmental problems? Does our vision guide the development of new technologies, markets, products, and processes?
Today	**Pollution prevention** Where are the most significant waste and emission streams from our current operations? Can we lower costs and risks by eliminating waste at the source or by using it as useful input?	**Product stewardship** What are the implications for product design and development if we assume responsibility for a product's entire life cycle? Can we add value or lower costs while simultaneously reducing the impact of our products?

FIGURE 20.1	The environmental sustainability grid

Source: Stuart L. Hart, "Beyond Greening: Strategies for a Sustainable World," *Harvard Business Review,* January–February 1997, p. 74. Copyright © 1997 by the President and Fellows of Harvard College; all rights reserved. Reprinted by permission of *Harvard Business Review.*

Consider Xerox Corporation's Asset Recycle Management (ARM) program, which uses leased Xerox copiers as sources of high-quality, low-cost parts and components for new machines. A well-developed [process] for taking back leased copiers combined with a sophisticated remanufacturing process allows . . . components to be reconditioned, tested, and then reassembled into "new" machines. Xerox estimates that ARM savings in raw materials, labor, and waste disposal in 1995 alone were in the $300-million to $400-million range. . . . By redefining product-in-use as part of the company's asset base, Xerox has discovered a way to add value and lower costs. It can continually provide lease customers with the latest product upgrades, giving them state-of-the-art functionality with minimum environmental impact.[19]

At the third level of environmental sustainability, companies look to the future and plan for *new environmental technologies.* Many organizations that have made good headway in pollution prevention and product stewardship are still limited by existing technologies. To develop fully sustainable strategies, they will need to develop new technologies. Monsanto is doing this by shifting its agricultural technology base from bulk chemicals to biotechnology. By controlling plant growth and pest resistance through bioengineering rather than through the application of pesticides or fertilizers, Monsanto hopes to find an environmentally sustainable path to increased agricultural yields.[20]

Finally, companies can develop a *sustainability vision,* which serves as a guide to the future. It shows how the company's products and services, processes, and policies must evolve and what new technologies must be developed to get there. This vision of sustainability provides a framework for pollution control, product stewardship, and environmental technology.

---

[19]Hart, "Beyond Greening," p. 72. For other examples, see Jacquelyn Ottman, "Environmental Winners Show Sustainable Strategies," *Marketing News,* April 27, 1998, p. 6.

[20]Hart, "Beyond Greening," p. 73; Linda Grant, "Monsanto's Bet: There's Gold in Going Green," *Fortune,* April 14, 1997, pp. 116–18; and Carl Pope, "Billboards of the Garden Wall," *Sierra,* January–February 1999, pp. 12–13.

active example <

Take a moment to read how a public service organization keeps track of businesses' environmental record.

Most companies today focus on the lower-left quadrant of the grid in Figure 20.1, investing most heavily in pollution prevention. Some forward-looking companies practice product stewardship and are developing new environmental technologies. Few companies have well-defined sustainability visions. However, emphasizing only one or a few cells in the environmental sustainability grid in Figure 20.1 can be shortsighted. For example, investing only in the bottom half of the grid puts a company in a good position today but leaves it vulnerable in the future. In contrast, a heavy emphasis on the top half suggests that a company has good environmental vision but lacks the skills needed to implement it. Thus, companies should work at developing all four dimensions of environmental sustainability.

Environmentalism creates some special challenges for global marketers. As international trade barriers come down and global markets expand, environmental issues are having an ever-greater impact on international trade. Countries in North America, Western Europe, and other developed regions are developing stringent environmental standards. In the United States, for example, more than two dozen major pieces of environmental legislation have been enacted since 1970, and recent events suggest that more regulation is on the way. A side accord to the North American Free Trade Agreement (NAFTA) set up a commission for resolving environmental matters. The European Union's Eco-Management and Audit Regulation provides guidelines for environmental self-regulation.[21]

However, environmental policies still vary widely from country to country, and uniform worldwide standards are not expected for many years. Although countries such as Denmark, Germany, Japan, and the United States have fully developed environmental policies and high public expectations, major countries such as China, India, Brazil, and Russia are in only the early stages of developing such policies. Moreover, environmental factors that motivate consumers in one country may have no impact on consumers in another. For example, PVC soft drink bottles cannot be used in Switzerland or Germany. However, they are preferred in France, which has an extensive recycling process for them. Thus, international companies are finding it difficult to develop standard environmental practices that work around the world. Instead, they are creating general policies and then translating these policies into tailored programs that meet local regulations and expectations.

PUBLIC ACTIONS TO REGULATE MARKETING

Citizen concerns about marketing practices will usually lead to public attention and legislative proposals. New bills will be debated—many will be defeated, others will be modified, and a few will become workable laws.

Many of the laws that affect marketing are listed in chapter 3. The task is to translate these laws into the language that marketing executives understand as they make decisions about competitive relations, products, price, promotion, and channels of distribution. Figure 20.2 illustrates the major legal issues facing marketing management.

active example <

Consider how one company initiates public action to influence the practices of other businesses.

[21]See John Audley, *Green Politics and Global Trade: NAFTA and the Future of Environmental Politics* (Georgetown University Press, 1997); Lars K. Hallstrom, "Industry Versus Ecology: Environment in the New Europe," *Futures,* February 1999, pp. 25–38; Joe McKinney, "NAFTA: Four Years down the Road," *Baylor Business Review,* Spring 1999, pp. 22–23; Andreas Diekmann and Axel Franzen, "The Wealth of Nations and Environmental Concern," *Environment and Behavior,* July 1999, pp. 540–49.

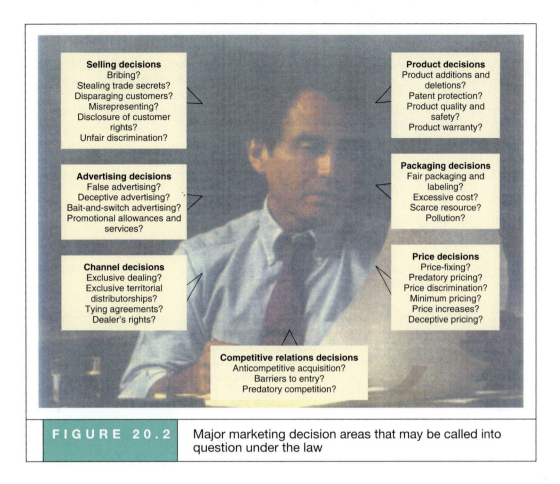

| FIGURE 20.2 | Major marketing decision areas that may be called into question under the law |

> active concept check

Now let's take a moment to test your knowledge of what you've just read.

> Business Actions Toward Socially Responsible Marketing

At first, many companies opposed consumerism and environmentalism. They thought the criticisms were either unfair or unimportant. But by now, most companies have grown to accept the new consumer rights, at least in principle. They might oppose certain pieces of legislation as inappropriate ways to solve specific consumer problems, but they recognize the consumer's right to information and protection. Many of these companies have responded positively to consumerism and environmentalism in order to serve consumer needs better.

ENLIGHTENED MARKETING

The philosophy of **enlightened marketing** holds that a company's marketing should support the best long-run performance of the marketing system. Enlightened marketing consists of five principles: *consumer-oriented marketing, innovative marketing, value marketing, sense-of-mission marketing,* and *societal marketing.*

Consumer-Oriented Marketing

Consumer-oriented marketing means that the company should view and organize its marketing activities from the consumer's point of view. It should work hard to sense, serve, and satisfy the needs of a defined group of customers. Consider the following example:

> Barat College, a women's college in Lake Forest, Illinois, published a college catalog that openly spelled out Barat College's strong and weak points. Among the weak points it shared with applicants were the following: "An exceptionally talented student musician or mathematician . . . might be advised to look further for a college with top faculty and facilities in that field. . . . The full range of advanced specialized courses offered in a university will be absent. . . . The library collection is average for a small college, but low in comparison with other high-quality institutions."

"Telling it like it is" is intended to build confidence so that applicants really know what they will find at Barat College and to emphasize that Barat College will strive to improve its consumer value as rapidly as time and funds permit.

Innovative Marketing

The principle of **innovative marketing** requires that the company continuously seek real product and marketing improvements. The company that overlooks new and better ways to do things will eventually lose customers to another company that has found a better way. An excellent example of an innovative marketer is Colgate-Palmolive:

> The American Marketing Association (AMA) recently named Colgate-Palmolive its new-product marketer of the year. Colgate took the honors by launching an abundance of innovative and highly successful new consumer products, including three AMA Edison "Best New Product" Award winners—Colgate Total toothpaste, the Colgate Wave toothbrush, and Softsoap Aquarium Series Liquid Soap. In all, more than a third of Colgate-Palmolive's current sales comes from products launched during the past five years. Perhaps the best example of the company's passion for continuous improvement is its recently introduced Total toothpaste. Marketing research showed shifts in consumer demographics and concerns—a growing population of aging, health-conscious, and better educated consumers. For these consumers, Colgate-Palmolive came up with Total, a breakout brand that provides a combination of benefits, including cavity prevention, tartar control, fresh breath, and long-lasting effects. The company also launched an innovative marketing program for the new product, which included advertising in health magazines targeting educated consumers who have high involvement in the health of their mouth and teeth. The new brand helped revitalize the mature toothpaste category. Consumers responded by making Colgate-Palmolive the toothpaste market leader for the first time since 1962, with a 32 percent share versus Procter & Gamble's 25 percent.[22]

Value Marketing

According to the principle of **value marketing,** the company should put most of its resources into value-building marketing investments. Many things marketers do—one-shot sales promotions, minor packaging changes, advertising puffery—may raise sales in the short run but add less *value* than would actual improvements in the product's quality, features, or convenience. Enlightened marketing calls for building long-run consumer loyalty by continually improving the value consumers receive from the firm's marketing offer.

Sense-of-Mission Marketing

Sense-of-mission marketing means that the company should define its mission in broad *social* terms rather than narrow *product* terms. When a company defines a social mission, employees feel better about their work and have a clearer sense of direction. For example, defined in narrow product terms, Ben & Jerry's mission might be "to sell ice cream and frozen yogurt." However, as discussed at the beginning of the chapter, the company states its mission more broadly as one of "linked prosperity," including product, economic, and social missions. Reshaping the basic task of selling consumer products into the larger mission of serving the interests of consumers, employees, and others in the company's various "communities" gives Ben & Jerry's a vital sense of purpose. Like Ben & Jerry's, many companies today are undertaking socially responsible actions or even building social responsibility into their underlying missions.

---

[22]Michelle Wirth Fellman, "New Product Marketer of 1997," *Marketing News,* March 30, 1998, pp. E2, E12; and "Tooth Truths," *Discount Merchandiser,* June 1999, p. 52.

> ## active example

Take a moment to read about one of the most famous instances of sense-of-mission marketing.

Societal Marketing

Following the principle of **societal marketing,** an enlightened company makes marketing decisions by considering consumers' wants and interests, the company's requirements, and society's long-run interests. The company is aware that neglecting consumer and societal long-run interests is a disservice to consumers and society. Alert companies view societal problems as opportunities.

> ## active example

Take a moment to read how a huge sports-wear corporation is becoming more socially responsible.

A societally oriented marketer wants to design products that are not only pleasing but also beneficial. The difference is shown in Figure 20.3. Products can be classified according to their degree of immediate consumer satisfaction and long-run consumer benefit. **Deficient products,** such as bad-tasting and ineffective medicine, have neither immediate appeal nor long-run benefits. **Pleasing products** give high immediate satisfaction but may hurt consumers in the long run. An example is cigarettes. **Salutary products** have low appeal but benefit consumers in the long run; for instance, seat belts and air bags. **Desirable products** give both high immediate satisfaction and high long-run benefits—a tasty *and* nutritious breakfast food.

An example of a desirable product is Herman Miller's Avian office chair, which is not just attractive and functional but also environmentally responsible:

> Herman Miller, one of the world's largest office furniture makers, has received numerous awards for environmentally responsible products and business practices. In 1994 the company formed an Earth Friendly Design Task Force responsible for infusing the company's design process with its environmental values. The task force carries out life cycle analyses on the company's products, including everything from how much of a product can be made from recycled materials to how much of the product itself can be recycled at the end of its useful life. For example, the company's Avian chair is designed for the lowest possible ecological impact and 100 percent recyclability. Herman Miller reduced material used in the chair by using gas-assist injection molding for the frame, which resulted in hollow frame members (like the bones of birds, hence the chair's name). The frame needs no paint nor other finish. All materials are recyclable. No ozone-depleting materials are used. The chair is shipped partially assembled, thus reducing the packaging and energy needed

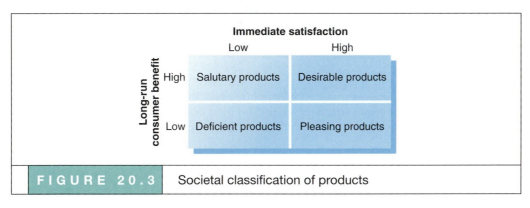

		Immediate satisfaction	
		Low	High
Long-run consumer benefit	High	Salutary products	Desirable products
	Low	Deficient products	Pleasing products

FIGURE 20.3   Societal classification of products

Herman Miller's Earth Friendly Design Task Force infuses the company's design process with its environmental values. For example, the Avian chair is designed for the lowest possible ecological impact and 100 percent recyclability.

to ship it. Finally, a materials schematic is imbedded in the bottom of the seat to help recycle the chair at the end of its life. This is truly a desirable product—it's won awards for design and function *and* for environmental responsibility.[23]

Companies should try to turn all of their products into desirable products. The challenge posed by pleasing products is that they sell very well but may end up hurting the consumer. The product opportunity, therefore, is to add long-run benefits without reducing the product's pleasing qualities. For example, Sears developed a phosphate-free laundry detergent that was also very effective. The challenge posed by salutary products is to add some pleasing qualities so that they will become more desirable in the consumers' minds. For example, synthetic fats and fat substitutes, such as NutraSweet's Simplesse and Procter & Gamble's Olestra, have improved the appeal of more healthful low-calorie and low-fat foods.

video example <

Listen to a member of one company comment on how it supports social causes through charitable donations.

MARKETING ETHICS

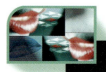

active poll <

Give your opinion on question of marketing and ethical conduct.

Conscientious marketers face many moral dilemmas. The best thing to do is often unclear. Because not all managers have fine moral sensitivity, companies need to develop *corporate marketing ethics policies*—broad guidelines that everyone in the organization must follow. These policies should cover

[23]Information accessed online at www.HermanMiller.com/ company/environment/conservation.html, January 2000.

distributor relations, advertising standards, customer service, pricing, product development, and general ethical standards.

The finest guidelines cannot resolve all the difficult ethical situations the marketer faces. Table 20.1 lists some difficult ethical situations marketers could face during their careers. If marketers choose immediate sales-producing actions in all these cases, their marketing behavior might well be described as immoral or even amoral. If they refuse to go along with *any* of the actions, they might be ineffective as marketing managers and unhappy because of the constant moral tension. Managers need a set of principles that will help them figure out the moral importance of each situation and decide how far they can go in good conscience.

But *what* principle should guide companies and marketing managers on issues of ethics and social responsibility? One philosophy is that such issues are decided by the free market and legal system. Under this principle, companies and their managers are not responsible for making moral judgments. Companies can in good conscience do whatever the system allows.

A second philosophy puts responsibility not in the system but in the hands of individual companies and managers. This more enlightened philosophy suggests that a company should have a "social conscience." Companies and managers should apply high standards of ethics and morality when making corporate decisions, regardless of "what the system allows." History provides an endless list of exam-

TABLE 20.1	Some Morally Difficult Situations in Marketing

1. You work for a cigarette company and up to now have not been convinced that cigarettes cause cancer. However, recent public policy debates now leave no doubt in your mind about the link between smoking and cancer. What would you do?

2. Your R&D department has changed one of your products slightly. It is not really "new and improved," but you know that putting this statement on the package and in advertising will increase sales. What would you do?

3. You have been asked to add a stripped-down model to your line that could be advertised to pull customers into the store. The product won't be very good, but salespeople will be able to switch buyers up to higher priced units. You are asked to give the green light for this stripped-down version. What would you do?

4. You are thinking of hiring a product manager who just left a competitor's company. She would be more than happy to tell you all the competitor's plans for the coming year. What would you do?

5. One of your top dealers in an important territory recently has had family troubles, and his sales have slipped. It looks like it will take him a while to straighten out his family trouble. Meanwhile you are losing many sales. Legally, you can terminate the dealer's franchise and replace him. What would you do?

6. You have a chance to win a big account that will mean a lot to you and your company. The purchasing agent hints that a "gift" would influence the decision. Your assistant recommends sending a fine color television set to the buyer's home. What would you do?

7. You have heard that a competitor has a new product feature that will make a big difference in sales. The competitor will demonstrate the feature in a private dealer meeting at the annual trade show. You can easily send a snooper to this meeting to learn about the new feature. What would you do?

8. You have to choose between three ad campaigns outlined by your agency. The first (a) is a soft-sell, honest information campaign. The second (b) uses sex-loaded emotional appeals and exaggerates the product's benefits. The third (c) involves a noisy, irritating commercial that is sure to gain audience attention. Pretests show that the campaigns are effective in the following order: c, b, and a. What would you do?

9. You are interviewing a capable female applicant for a job as salesperson. She is better qualified than the men just interviewed. Nevertheless, you know that some of your important customers prefer dealing with men, and you will lose some sales if you hire her. What would you do?

ples of company actions that were legal and allowed but were highly irresponsible. Consider the following example:

> Prior to the Pure Food and Drug Act, the advertising for a diet pill promised that a person taking this pill could eat virtually anything at any time and still lose weight. Too good to be true? Actually the claim was quite true; the product lived up to its billing with frightening efficiency. It seems that the primary active ingredient in this "diet supplement" was tapeworm larvae. These larvae would develop in the intestinal tract and, of course, be well fed; the pill taker would in time, quite literally, starve to death.[24]

Each company and marketing manager must work out a philosophy of socially responsible and ethical behavior. Under the societal marketing concept, each manager must look beyond what is legal and allowed and develop standards based on personal integrity, corporate conscience, and long-run consumer welfare. A clear and responsible philosophy will help the marketing manager deal with the many knotty questions posed by marketing and other human activities.

As with environmentalism, the issue of ethics provides special challenges for international marketers. Business standards and practices vary a great deal from one country to the next. For example, whereas bribes and kickbacks are illegal for U.S. firms, they are standard business practice in many South American countries. The question arises as to whether a company must lower its ethical standards to compete effectively in countries with lower standards. In a recent study, two researchers posed this question to chief executives of large international companies and got a unanimous response: No.[25] For the sake of all of the company's stakeholders—customers, suppliers, employees, shareholders, and the public—it is important to make a commitment to a common set of shared standards worldwide.

For example, John Hancock Mutual Life Insurance Company operates successfully in Southeast Asia, an area that by Western standards has widespread questionable business and government practices. Despite warnings from locals that Hancock would have to bend its rules to succeed, Hancock Chairman Stephen Brown notes:

> We faced up to this issue early on when we started to deal with Southeast Asia. We told our people that we had the same ethical standards, same procedures, same policies in these countries that we have in the United States, and we do. . . . We just felt that things like payoffs were wrong—and if we had to do business that way, we'd rather not do business. Our employees would not feel good about having different levels of ethics. There may be countries where you have to do that kind of thing. We haven't found that country yet, and if we do, we won't do business there.[26]

Many industrial and professional associations have suggested codes of ethics, and many companies are now adopting their own codes. For example, the American Marketing Association, an international association of marketing managers and scholars, developed the code of ethics shown in Table 20.2. Companies are also developing programs to teach managers about important ethics issues and help them find the proper responses. They hold ethics workshops and seminars and set up ethics committees.

Further, more than 200 major U.S. companies have appointed high-level ethics officers to champion ethics issues and to help resolve ethics problems and concerns facing employees. For example, in 1991 Nynex created a new position of vice president of ethics, supported by a dozen full-time staff and a million-dollar budget. Since then, the new department has trained some 95,000 Nynex employees. Such training includes sending 22,000 managers to full-day workshops that include case studies on ethical actions in marketing, finance, and other business functions. One workshop deals with the use of improperly obtained competitive data, which managers are instructed is not permitted.[27]

[24]Dan R. Dalton and Richard A. Cosier, "The Four Faces of Social Responsibility," *Business Horizons,* May–June 1982, pp. 19–27.

[25]John F. Magee and P. Ranganath Nayak, "Leaders' Perspectives on Business Ethics," *Prizm,* Arthur D. Little, Inc., Cambridge, MA, first quarter, 1994, pp. 65–77. Also see Kumar C. Rallapalli, "A Paradigm for Development and Promulgation of a Global Code of Marketing Ethics," *Journal of Business Ethics,* January 1999, pp. 125–37.

[26]Ibid., pp. 71–72. Also see Thomas Donaldson, "Values in Tension: Ethics away from Home," *Harvard Business Review,* September–October 1996, pp. 48–62; and Patrick E. Murphy, "Character and Virtue Ethics in International Marketing: An Agenda for Managers, Researchers, and Educators," *Journal of Business Ethics,* January 1999, pp. 107–24.

[27]Mark Hendricks, "Ethics in Action," *Management Review,* January 1995, pp. 53–55.

TABLE 20.2	American Marketing Association Code of Ethics

Members of the American Marketing Association are committed to ethical, professional conduct. They have joined together in subscribing to this Code of Ethics embracing the following topics:

Responsibilities of the Marketer

Marketers must accept responsibility for the consequences of their activities and make every effort to ensure that their decisions, recommendations, and actions function to identify, serve, and satisfy all relevant publics: customers, organizations and society.

Marketers' Professional Conduct Must Be Guided By

1. The basic rule of professional ethics: not knowingly to do harm;

2. The adherence to all applicable laws and regulations;

3. The accurate representation of their education, training and experience; and

4. The active support, practice, and promotion of this Code of Ethics.

Honesty and Fairness

Marketers shall uphold and advance the integrity, honor, and dignity of the marketing profession by:

1. Being honest in serving consumers, clients, employees, suppliers, distributors, and the public;

2. Not knowingly participating in conflict of interest without prior notice to all parties involved; and

3. Establishing equitable fee schedules including the payment or receipt of usual, customary, and/or legal compensation for marketing exchanges.

Rights and Duties of Parties in the Marketing Exchange Process

Participants in the marketing exchange process should be able to expect that:

1. Products and services offered are safe and fit for their intended uses;

2. Communications about offered products and services are not deceptive;

3. All parties intend to discharge their obligations, financial and otherwise, in good faith; and

4. Appropriate internal methods exist for equitable adjustment and/or redress of grievances concerning purchases.

It Is Understood That the Above Would Include, but Is Not Limited to the Following Responsibilities of the Marketer: In the Area of Product Development and Management

♦ disclosure of all substantial risks associated with product or service usage;

♦ identification of any product component substitution that might materially change the product or impact on the buyer's purchase decision;

♦ identification of extra cost-added features.

In the Area of Promotions

♦ avoidance of false and misleading advertising;

♦ rejection of high-pressure manipulations, or misleading sales tactics;

♦ avoidance of sales promotions that use deception or manipulation.

T A B L E 2 0 . 2	*(Continued)*

In the Area of Distribution

♦ not manipulating the availability of a product for purpose of exploitation;

♦ not using coercion in the marketing channel;

♦ not exerting undue influence over the reseller's choice to handle a product.

In the Area of Pricing

♦ not engaging in price fixing;

♦ not practicing predatory pricing;

♦ disclosing the full price associated with any purchase.

In the Area of Marketing Research

♦ prohibiting selling or fundraising under the guise of conducting research;

♦ maintaining research integrity by avoiding misrepresentation and omission of pertinent research data;

♦ treating outside clients and suppliers fairly.

Organizational Relationships

Marketers should be aware of how their behavior may influence or impact on the behavior of others in organizational relationships. They should not demand, encourage, or apply coercion to obtain unethical behavior in their relationships with others, such as employees, suppliers, or customers.

1. Apply confidentiality and anonymity in professional relationships with regard to privileged information;

2. Meet their obligations and responsibilities in contracts and mutual agreements in a timely manner;

3. Avoid taking the work of others, in whole, or in part, and representing this work as their own or directly benefiting from it without compensation or consent of the originator or owner;

4. Avoid manipulation to take advantage of situations to maximize personal welfare in a way that unfairly deprives or damages the organization of others.

Any AMA member found to be in violation of any provision of this Code of Ethics may have his or her Association membership suspended or revoked.

Source: Reprinted with permission from American Marketing Association Code of Ethics, published by the American Marketing Association.

Many companies have developed innovative ways to educate employees about ethics:

Citicorp has developed an ethics board game, which teams of employees use to solve hypothetical quandaries. General Electric employees can tap into specially designed software on their personal computers to get answers to ethical questions. At Texas Instruments, employees are treated to a weekly column on ethics over an electronic news service. One popular feature: a kind of Dear Abby mailbag, answers provided by the company's ethics officer, . . . that deals with the troublesome issues employees face most often.[28]

Still, written codes and ethics programs do not ensure ethical behavior. Ethics and social responsibility require a total corporate commitment. They must be a component of the overall corporate culture. According to David R. Whitman, chairman of the board of Whirlpool Corporation, "In the final

---

[28]Kenneth Labich, "The New Crisis in Business Management," *Fortune,* April 20, 1992, pp. 167–76, p. 176.

analysis, 'ethical behavior' must be an integral part of the organization, a way of life that is deeply ingrained in the collective corporate body. . . . In any business enterprise, ethical behavior must be a tradition, a way of conducting one's affairs that is passed from generation to generation of employees at all levels of the organization. It is the responsibility of management, starting at the very top, to both set the example by personal conduct and create an environment that not only encourages and rewards ethical behavior, but which also makes anything less totally unacceptable."[29]

The future holds many challenges and opportunities for marketing managers as they move into the new millennium. Technological advances in every area, from telecommunications, information technology, and the Internet to health care and entertainment, provide abundant marketing opportunities. However, forces in the socioeconomic, cultural, and natural environments increase the limits under which marketing can be carried out. Companies that are able to create new customer value in a socially responsible way will have a world to conquer.

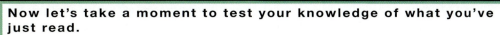

> ## active concept check

Now let's take a moment to test your knowledge of what you've just read.

> ## Chapter Wrap-Up

Now that you've reached the end of the chapter, you may wish to explore the concepts you've been reading about in greater detail, or test yourself to see how well you've comprehended the material. In the box below you'll find a number of links. Click on any one of these links to find additional chapter resources.

> ## end-of-chapter resources

- **Review of Concept Connections**
- **Practice Quiz**
- **Tying it All Together (Audio)**
- **Key Terms**
- **Critical Thinking Exercises**
- **Experimential Exercises**
- **MyPHLIP Companion Web Site**
- **Case 1**
- **Case 2**
- **You Be the Consultant**

---

[29]From "Ethics as a Practical Matter," a message from David R. Whitman, chairman of the board of Whirlpool Corporation, as reprinted in Ricky E. Griffin and Ronald J. Ebert, *Business* (Upper Saddle River, NJ: Prentice Hall, 1989), pp. 578–79. For more on marketing ethics, see Lynn Sharp Paine, "Managing for Organizational Integrity," *Harvard Business Review,* March–April 1994, pp. 106–17; Tom McInerney, "Double Trouble: Combining Business and Ethics," *Business Ethics Quarterly,* January 1998, pp. 187–89; John F. Gaski, "Does Marketing Ethics Really Have Anything to Say?" *Journal of Business Ethics,* February 1999, pp. 315–34; and Thomas W. Dunfee, N. Craig Smith, and William T. Ross, "Social Contracts and Marketing Ethics," *Journal of Marketing,* July 1999, pp. 14–32.

WP-Studio, 98
Wright, Gary, 60
WTO (World Trade Organization),
    462–463

X

Xerox, 36, 88, 139, 149, 378, 383, 435,
    436, 497

Y

Yahoo!, 89, 372, 418, 423
Yamaha, 109, 110, 249, 421
Yankelovich and Partners, 93
Yankelovich Monitor, 78
Yaohan, 215, 320
YMCA, 27

Z

Zeien, Alfred M., 217
Zenith, 15
Zip City Brewing, 321
Zone pricing, 267–268
Zoo-Doo Compost Company, 262, 263